American Casebook Series
Hornbook Series and Basic Legal Texts
Black Letter Series and Nutshell Series

of

WEST PUBLISHING COMPANY
P.O. Box 64526
St. Paul, Minnesota 55164–0526

Accounting

FARIS' ACCOUNTING AND LAW IN A NUT-SHELL, 377 pages, 1984. Softcover. (Text)

FIFLIS' ACCOUNTING ISSUES FOR LAWYERS, TEACHING MATERIALS, Fourth Edition, 706 pages, 1991. Teacher's Manual available. (Casebook)

SIEGEL AND SIEGEL'S ACCOUNTING AND FINANCIAL DISCLOSURE: A GUIDE TO BASIC CONCEPTS, 259 pages, 1983. Softcover. (Text)

Administrative Law

AMAN AND MAYTON'S HORNBOOK ON ADMINISTRATIVE LAW, Approximately 750 pages, 1993. (Text)

BONFIELD AND ASIMOW'S STATE AND FEDERAL ADMINISTRATIVE LAW, 826 pages, 1989. Teacher's Manual available. (Casebook)

GELLHORN AND LEVIN'S ADMINISTRATIVE LAW AND PROCESS IN A NUTSHELL, Third Edition, 479 pages, 1990. Softcover. (Text)

MASHAW, MERRILL, AND SHANE'S CASES AND MATERIALS ON ADMINISTRATIVE LAW—THE AMERICAN PUBLIC LAW SYSTEM, Third Edition, 1187 pages, 1992. (Casebook)

ROBINSON, GELLHORN AND BRUFF'S THE ADMINISTRATIVE PROCESS, Third Edition, 978 pages, 1986. (Casebook)

Admiralty

HEALY AND SHARPE'S CASES AND MATERIALS ON ADMIRALTY, Second Edition, 876 pages, 1986. (Casebook)

MARAIST'S ADMIRALTY IN A NUTSHELL, Second Edition, 379 pages, 1988. Softcover. (Text)

SCHOENBAUM'S HORNBOOK ON ADMIRALTY AND MARITIME LAW, Student Edition, 692 pages, 1987 with 1992 pocket part. (Text)

Agency—Partnership

DEMOTT'S FIDUCIARY OBLIGATION, AGENCY AND PARTNERSHIP: DUTIES IN ONGOING BUSINESS RELATIONSHIPS, 740 pages, 1991. Teacher's Manual available. (Casebook)

FESSLER'S ALTERNATIVES TO INCORPORATION FOR PERSONS IN QUEST OF PROFIT, Third Edition, 339 pages, 1991. Softcover. (Casebook)

HENN'S CASES AND MATERIALS ON AGENCY, PARTNERSHIP AND OTHER UNINCORPORATED BUSINESS ENTERPRISES, Second Edition, 733 pages, 1985. Teacher's Manual available. (Casebook)

REUSCHLEIN AND GREGORY'S HORNBOOK ON THE LAW OF AGENCY AND PARTNERSHIP, Second Edition, 683 pages, 1990. (Text)

SELECTED CORPORATION AND PARTNERSHIP STATUTES, RULES AND FORMS. Softcover. Revised 1991 Edition, 953 pages.

STEFFEN AND KERR'S CASES ON AGENCY-PARTNERSHIP, Fourth Edition, 859 pages, 1980. (Casebook)

STEFFEN'S AGENCY-PARTNERSHIP IN A NUTSHELL, 364 pages, 1977. Softcover. (Text)

Agricultural Law

MEYER, PEDERSEN, THORSON AND DAVIDSON'S AGRICULTURAL LAW: CASES AND MATERIALS, 931 pages, 1985. Teacher's Manual avail-

Agricultural Law—Cont'd
able. (Casebook)

Alternative Dispute Resolution
KANOWITZ' CASES AND MATERIALS ON ALTERNATIVE DISPUTE RESOLUTION, 1024 pages, 1986. Teacher's Manual available. (Casebook) 1990 Supplement.

NOLAN–HALEY'S ALTERNATIVE DISPUTE RESOLUTION IN A NUTSHELL, 298 pages, 1992. Softcover. (Text)

RISKIN AND WESTBROOK'S DISPUTE RESOLUTION AND LAWYERS, 468 pages, 1987. Teacher's Manual available. (Casebook)

RISKIN AND WESTBROOK'S DISPUTE RESOLUTION AND LAWYERS, Abridged Edition, 223 pages, 1987. Softcover. Teacher's Manual available. (Casebook)

RISKIN'S DISPUTE RESOLUTION FOR LAWYERS VIDEO TAPES, 1992. (Available for purchase by schools and libraries.)

American Indian Law
CANBY'S AMERICAN INDIAN LAW IN A NUTSHELL, Second Edition, 336 pages, 1988. Softcover. (Text)

GETCHES AND WILKINSON'S CASES AND MATERIALS ON FEDERAL INDIAN LAW, Second Edition, 880 pages, 1986. (Casebook)

Antitrust—see also Regulated Industries, Trade Regulation
BARNES AND STOUT'S ECONOMIC FOUNDATIONS OF REGULATION AND ANTITRUST LAW, 102 pages, 1992. Softcover. Teacher's Manual available. (Casebook)

FOX AND SULLIVAN'S CASES AND MATERIALS ON ANTITRUST, 935 pages, 1989. Teacher's Manual available. (Casebook) 1993 Supplement.

GELLHORN'S ANTITRUST LAW AND ECONOMICS IN A NUTSHELL, Third Edition, 472 pages, 1986. Softcover. (Text)

HOVENKAMP'S BLACK LETTER ON ANTITRUST, Second Edition approximately 325 pages, April 1993 Pub. Softcover. (Review)

HOVENKAMP'S HORNBOOK ON ECONOMICS AND FEDERAL ANTITRUST LAW, Student Edition, 414 pages, 1985. (Text)

POSNER AND EASTERBROOK'S CASES AND ECONOMIC NOTES ON ANTITRUST, Second Edi

tion, 1077 pages, 1981. (Casebook) 1984–85 Supplement.

SULLIVAN'S HORNBOOK OF THE LAW OF ANTITRUST, 886 pages, 1977. (Text)

Appellate Advocacy—see Trial and Appellate Advocacy

Architecture and Engineering Law
SWEET'S LEGAL ASPECTS OF ARCHITECTURE, ENGINEERING AND THE CONSTRUCTION PROCESS, Fourth Edition, 889 pages, 1989. Teacher's Manual available. (Casebook)

Art Law
DUBOFF'S ART LAW IN A NUTSHELL, Second Edition, approximately 325 pages, 1993. Softcover. (Text)

Banking Law
BANKING LAW: SELECTED STATUTES AND REGULATIONS. Softcover. 263 pages, 1991.

LOVETT'S BANKING AND FINANCIAL INSTITUTIONS LAW IN A NUTSHELL, Third Edition, 470 pages, 1992. Softcover. (Text)

SYMONS AND WHITE'S BANKING LAW: TEACHING MATERIALS, Third Edition, 818 pages, 1991. Teacher's Manual available. (Casebook)

Statutory Supplement. *See Banking Law: Selected Statutes*

Bankruptcy—see Creditors' Rights

Business Planning—see also Corporate Finance
PAINTER'S PROBLEMS AND MATERIALS IN BUSINESS PLANNING, Second Edition, 1008 pages, 1984. (Casebook) 1990 Supplement.

Statutory Supplement. *See Selected Corporation and Partnership*

Civil Procedure—see also Federal Jurisdiction and Procedure
AMERICAN BAR ASSOCIATION SECTION OF LITIGATION—READINGS ON ADVERSARIAL JUSTICE: THE AMERICAN APPROACH TO ADJUDICATION, 217 pages, 1988. Softcover. (Coursebook)

CLERMONT'S BLACK LETTER ON CIVIL PROCEDURE, Third Edition, approximately 350 pages, May, 1993 Pub. Softcover. (Review)

COUND, FRIEDENTHAL, MILLER AND SEXTON'S

Civil Procedure—Cont'd

CASES AND MATERIALS ON CIVIL PROCEDURE, Fifth Edition, 1284 pages, 1989. Teacher's Manual available. (Casebook)

COUND, FRIEDENTHAL, MILLER AND SEXTON'S CIVIL PROCEDURE SUPPLEMENT. 476 pages, 1991. Softcover. (Casebook Supplement)

FEDERAL RULES OF CIVIL PROCEDURE—EDUCATIONAL EDITION. Softcover. 761 pages, 1992.

FRIEDENTHAL, KANE AND MILLER'S HORNBOOK ON CIVIL PROCEDURE, Second Edition, approximately 1000 pages, May 1993 Pub. (Text)

KANE AND LEVINE'S CIVIL PROCEDURE IN CALIFORNIA: STATE AND FEDERAL 1992 Edition, 551 pages. Softcover. (Casebook Supplement)

KANE'S CIVIL PROCEDURE IN A NUTSHELL, Third Edition, 303 pages, 1991. Softcover. (Text)

KOFFLER AND REPPY'S HORNBOOK ON COMMON LAW PLEADING, 663 pages, 1969. (Text)

LEVINE, SLOMANSON AND WINGATE'S CALIFORNIA CIVIL PROCEDURE, CASES AND MATERIALS, 546 pages, 1991. Teacher's Manual available. (Casebook)

MARCUS, REDISH AND SHERMAN'S CIVIL PROCEDURE: A MODERN APPROACH, 1027 pages, 1989. Teacher's Manual available. (Casebook) 1991 Supplement.

MARCUS AND SHERMAN'S COMPLEX LITIGATION—CASES AND MATERIALS ON ADVANCED CIVIL PROCEDURE, Second Edition, 1035 pages, 1992. Teacher's Manual available. (Casebook)

PARK AND McFARLAND'S COMPUTER-AIDED EXERCISES ON CIVIL PROCEDURE, Third Edition, 210 pages, 1991. Softcover. (Coursebook)

SIEGEL'S HORNBOOK ON NEW YORK PRACTICE, Second Edition, Student Edition, 1068 pages, 1991. Softcover. (Text) 1992 Supplemental Pamphlet.

SLOMANSON AND WINGATE'S CALIFORNIA CIVIL PROCEDURE IN A NUTSHELL, 230 pages, 1992. Softcover. (Text)

Commercial Law

BAILEY AND HAGEDORN'S SECURED TRANSACTIONS IN A NUTSHELL, Third Edition, 390 pages, 1988. Softcover. (Text)

EPSTEIN, MARTIN, HENNING AND NICKLES' BASIC UNIFORM COMMERCIAL CODE TEACHING MATERIALS, Third Edition, 704 pages, 1988. Teacher's Manual available. (Casebook)

HENSON'S HORNBOOK ON SECURED TRANSACTIONS UNDER THE U.C.C., Second Edition, 504 pages, 1979, with 1979 pocket part. (Text)

MEYER AND SPEIDEL'S BLACK LETTER ON SALES AND LEASES OF GOODS, Approximately 300 pages, 1993. Softcover. (Review)

NICKLES' BLACK LETTER ON COMMERCIAL PAPER, 450 pages, 1988. Softcover. (Review)

NICKLES, MATHESON AND DOLAN'S MATERIALS FOR UNDERSTANDING CREDIT AND PAYMENT SYSTEMS, 923 pages, 1987. Teacher's Manual available. (Casebook)

NORDSTROM, MURRAY AND CLOVIS' PROBLEMS AND MATERIALS ON SALES, 515 pages, 1982. (Casebook)

NORDSTROM, MURRAY AND CLOVIS' PROBLEMS AND MATERIALS ON SECURED TRANSACTIONS, 594 pages, 1987. (Casebook)

RUBIN AND COOTER'S THE PAYMENT SYSTEM: CASES, MATERIALS AND ISSUES, 885 pages, 1989. Teacher's Manual Available. (Casebook)

SELECTED COMMERCIAL STATUTES. Softcover. 1897 pages, 1992.

SPEIDEL, SUMMERS AND WHITE'S COMMERCIAL LAW: TEACHING MATERIALS, Fourth Edition, 1448 pages, 1987. Teacher's Manual available. (Casebook)

SPEIDEL, SUMMERS AND WHITE'S COMMERCIAL PAPER: TEACHING MATERIALS, Fourth Edition, 578 pages, 1987. Reprint from Speidel et al., Commercial Law, Fourth Edition. Teacher's Manual available. (Casebook)

SPEIDEL, SUMMERS AND WHITE'S SALES: TEACHING MATERIALS, Fourth Edition, 804 pages, 1987. Reprint from Speidel et al., Commercial Law, Fourth Edition. Teacher's Manual available. (Casebook)

SPEIDEL, SUMMERS AND WHITE'S SECURED

Commercial Law—Cont'd

TRANSACTIONS: TEACHING MATERIALS, Fourth Edition, 485 pages, 1987. Reprint from Speidel et al., Commercial Law, Fourth Edition. Teacher's Manual available. (Casebook)

STOCKTON AND MILLER'S SALES AND LEASES OF GOODS IN A NUTSHELL, Third Edition, 441 pages, 1992. Softcover. (Text)

STONE'S UNIFORM COMMERCIAL CODE IN A NUTSHELL, Third Edition, 580 pages, 1989. Softcover. (Text)

WEBER AND SPEIDEL'S COMMERCIAL PAPER IN A NUTSHELL, Third Edition, 404 pages, 1982. Softcover. (Text)

WHITE AND SUMMERS' HORNBOOK ON THE UNIFORM COMMERCIAL CODE, Third Edition, Student Edition, 1386 pages, 1988. (Text)

Community Property

MENNELL AND BOYKOFF'S COMMUNITY PROPERTY IN A NUTSHELL, Second Edition, 432 pages, 1988. Softcover. (Text)

VERRALL AND BIRD'S CASES AND MATERIALS ON CALIFORNIA COMMUNITY PROPERTY, Fifth Edition, 604 pages, 1988. (Casebook)

Comparative Law

BARTON, GIBBS, LI AND MERRYMAN'S LAW IN RADICALLY DIFFERENT CULTURES, 960 pages, 1983. (Casebook)

FOLSOM, MINAN AND OTTO'S LAW AND POLITICS IN THE PEOPLE'S REPUBLIC OF CHINA IN A NUTSHELL, 451 pages, 1992. Softcover. (Text)

GLENDON, GORDON AND OSAKWE'S COMPARATIVE LEGAL TRADITIONS: TEXT, MATERIALS AND CASES ON THE CIVIL LAW, COMMON LAW AND SOCIALIST LAW TRADITIONS, 1091 pages, 1985. (Casebook)

GLENDON, GORDON AND OSAKWE'S COMPARATIVE LEGAL TRADITIONS IN A NUTSHELL. 402 pages, 1982. Softcover. (Text)

Computers and Law

MAGGS, SOMA AND SPROWL'S COMPUTER LAW—CASES, COMMENTS, AND QUESTIONS, 731 pages, 1992. Teacher's Manual available. (Casebook)

MAGGS AND SPROWL'S COMPUTER APPLICATIONS IN THE LAW, 316 pages, 1987. (Coursebook)

MASON'S USING COMPUTERS IN THE LAW: AN INTRODUCTION AND PRACTICAL GUIDE, Second Edition, 288 pages, 1988. Softcover. (Coursebook)

Conflict of Laws

CRAMTON, CURRIE AND KAY'S CASES–COMMENTS–QUESTIONS ON CONFLICT OF LAWS, Fourth Edition, 876 pages, 1987. (Casebook)

HAY'S BLACK LETTER ON CONFLICT OF LAWS, 330 pages, 1989. Softcover. (Review)

SCOLES AND HAY'S HORNBOOK ON CONFLICT OF LAWS, Student Edition, 1160 pages, 1992. (Text)

SIEGEL'S CONFLICTS IN A NUTSHELL, 470 pages, 1982. Softcover. (Text)

Constitutional Law—Civil Rights—see also First Amendment and Foreign Relations and National Security Law

ABERNATHY'S CIVIL RIGHTS AND CONSTITUTIONAL LITIGATION, CASES AND MATERIALS, Second Edition, 753 pages, 1992. (Casebook)

BARNES AND STOUT'S THE ECONOMICS OF CONSTITUTIONAL LAW AND PUBLIC CHOICE, 127 pages, 1992. Softcover. Teacher's Manual available. (Casebook)

BARRON AND DIENES' BLACK LETTER ON CONSTITUTIONAL LAW, Third Edition, 440 pages, 1991. Softcover. (Review)

BARRON AND DIENES' CONSTITUTIONAL LAW IN A NUTSHELL, Second Edition, 483 pages, 1991. Softcover. (Text)

ENGDAHL'S CONSTITUTIONAL FEDERALISM IN A NUTSHELL, Second Edition, 411 pages, 1987. Softcover. (Text)

FARBER AND SHERRY'S HISTORY OF THE AMERICAN CONSTITUTION, 458 pages, 1990. Softcover. Teacher's Manual available. (Text)

FISHER AND DEVINS' POLITICAL DYNAMICS OF CONSTITUTIONAL LAW, 333 pages, 1992. Softcover. (Casebook Supplement)

GARVEY AND ALEINIKOFF'S MODERN CONSTITUTIONAL THEORY: A READER, Second Edition, 559 pages, 1991. Softcover. (Reader)

LOCKHART, KAMISAR, CHOPER AND SHIFFRIN'S CONSTITUTIONAL LAW: CASES–COMMENTS–QUESTIONS, Seventh Edition, 1643 pages,

Constitutional Law—Civil Rights—Cont'd

1991. (Casebook) 1992 Supplement.

LOCKHART, KAMISAR, CHOPER AND SHIFFRIN'S THE AMERICAN CONSTITUTION: CASES AND MATERIALS, Seventh Edition, 1255 pages, 1991. Abridged version of Lockhart, et al., Constitutional Law: Cases–Comments–Questions, Seventh Edition. (Casebook) 1992 Supplement.

LOCKHART, KAMISAR, CHOPER AND SHIFFRIN'S CONSTITUTIONAL RIGHTS AND LIBERTIES: CASES AND MATERIALS, Seventh Edition, 1333 pages, 1991. Reprint from Lockhart, et al., Constitutional Law: Cases–Comments–Questions, Seventh Edition. (Casebook) 1992 Supplement.

MARKS AND COOPER'S STATE CONSTITUTIONAL LAW IN A NUTSHELL, 329 pages, 1988. Softcover. (Text)

NOWAK AND ROTUNDA'S HORNBOOK ON CONSTITUTIONAL LAW, Fourth Edition, 1357 pages, 1991. (Text)

ROTUNDA'S MODERN CONSTITUTIONAL LAW: CASES AND NOTES, Fourth Edition, approximately 1100 pages, April, 1993 Pub. (Casebook)

VIEIRA'S CONSTITUTIONAL CIVIL RIGHTS IN A NUTSHELL, Second Edition, 322 pages, 1990. Softcover. (Text)

WILLIAMS' CONSTITUTIONAL ANALYSIS IN A NUTSHELL, 388 pages, 1979. Softcover. (Text)

Consumer Law—see also Commercial Law

EPSTEIN AND NICKLES' CONSUMER LAW IN A NUTSHELL, Second Edition, 418 pages, 1981. Softcover. (Text)

SELECTED COMMERCIAL STATUTES. Softcover. 1897 pages, 1992.

SPANOGLE, ROHNER, PRIDGEN AND RASOR'S CASES AND MATERIALS ON CONSUMER LAW, Second Edition, 916 pages, 1991. Teacher's Manual available. (Casebook)

Contracts

BARNES AND STOUT'S THE ECONOMICS OF CONTRACT LAW, 127 pages, 1992. Softcover. Teacher's Manual available. (Casebook)

CALAMARI AND PERILLO'S BLACK LETTER ON CONTRACTS, Second Edition, 462 pages, 1990. Softcover. (Review)

CALAMARI AND PERILLO'S HORNBOOK ON CONTRACTS, Third Edition, 1049 pages, 1987. (Text)

CALAMARI, PERILLO AND BENDER'S CASES AND PROBLEMS ON CONTRACTS, Second Edition, 905 pages, 1989. Teacher's Manual Available. (Casebook)

CORBIN'S TEXT ON CONTRACTS, One Volume Student Edition, 1224 pages, 1952. (Text)

FESSLER AND LOISEAUX'S CASES AND MATERIALS ON CONTRACTS—MORALITY, ECONOMICS AND THE MARKET PLACE, 837 pages, 1982. Teacher's Manual available. (Casebook)

FRIEDMAN'S CONTRACT REMEDIES IN A NUTSHELL, 323 pages, 1981. Softcover. (Text)

FULLER AND EISENBERG'S CASES ON BASIC CONTRACT LAW, Fifth Edition, 1037 pages, 1990. (Casebook)

HAMILTON, RAU AND WEINTRAUB'S CASES AND MATERIALS ON CONTRACTS, Second Edition, 916 pages, 1992. Teacher's Manual available. (Casebook)

KEYES' GOVERNMENT CONTRACTS IN A NUTSHELL, Second Edition, 557 pages, 1990. Softcover. (Text)

SCHABER AND ROHWER'S CONTRACTS IN A NUTSHELL, Third Edition, 457 pages, 1990. Softcover. (Text)

SUMMERS AND HILLMAN'S CONTRACT AND RELATED OBLIGATION: THEORY, DOCTRINE AND PRACTICE, Second Edition, 1037 pages, 1992. Teacher's Manual available. (Casebook)

Copyright—see Patent and Copyright Law

Corporate Finance—see also Business Planning

HAMILTON'S CASES AND MATERIALS ON CORPORATION FINANCE, Second Edition, 1221 pages, 1989. (Casebook)

OESTERLE'S THE LAW OF MERGERS, ACQUISITIONS AND REORGANIZATIONS, 1096 pages, 1991. (Casebook) 1992 Supplement.

Corporations

HAMILTON'S BLACK LETTER ON CORPORATIONS, Third Edition, 732 pages, 1992. Softcover. (Review)

HAMILTON'S CASES AND MATERIALS ON CORPORATIONS—INCLUDING PARTNERSHIPS AND

Corporations—Cont'd

LIMITED PARTNERSHIPS, Fourth Edition, 1248 pages, 1990. Teacher's Manual available. (Casebook) 1990 Statutory Supplement.

HAMILTON'S THE LAW OF CORPORATIONS IN A NUTSHELL, Third Edition, 518 pages, 1991. Softcover. (Text)

HENN'S TEACHING MATERIALS ON THE LAW OF CORPORATIONS, Second Edition, 1204 pages, 1986. Teacher's Manual available. (Casebook)

> Statutory Supplement. *See Selected Corporation and Partnership*

HENN AND ALEXANDER'S HORNBOOK ON LAWS OF CORPORATIONS, Third Edition, Student Edition, 1371 pages, 1983, with 1986 pocket part. (Text)

SELECTED CORPORATION AND PARTNERSHIP STATUTES, RULES AND FORMS. Revised 1991 Edition, 953 pages. Softcover.

SOLOMON, SCHWARTZ AND BAUMAN'S MATERIALS AND PROBLEMS ON CORPORATIONS: LAW AND POLICY, Second Edition, 1391 pages, 1988. Teacher's Manual available. (Casebook) 1992 Supplement.

> Statutory Supplement. *See Selected Corporation and Partnership*

Corrections

KRANTZ' THE LAW OF CORRECTIONS AND PRISONERS' RIGHTS IN A NUTSHELL, Third Edition, 407 pages, 1988. Softcover. (Text)

KRANTZ AND BRANHAM'S CASES AND MATERIALS ON THE LAW OF SENTENCING, CORRECTIONS AND PRISONERS' RIGHTS, Fourth Edition, 619 pages, 1991. Teacher's Manual available. (Casebook)

Creditors' Rights

BANKRUPTCY CODE, RULES AND OFFICIAL FORMS, LAW SCHOOL EDITION. 910 pages, 1992. Softcover.

EPSTEIN'S DEBTOR-CREDITOR LAW IN A NUTSHELL, Fourth Edition, 401 pages, 1991. Softcover. (Text)

EPSTEIN, LANDERS AND NICKLES' CASES AND MATERIALS ON DEBTORS AND CREDITORS, Third Edition, 1059 pages, 1987. Teacher's Manual available. (Casebook)

EPSTEIN, NICKLES AND WHITE'S HORNBOOK

ON BANKRUPTCY, Approximately 1000 pages, January, 1992 Pub. (Text)

LOPUCKI'S PLAYER'S MANUAL FOR THE DEBTOR-CREDITOR GAME, 123 pages, 1985. Softcover. (Coursebook)

NICKLES AND EPSTEIN'S BLACK LETTER ON CREDITORS' RIGHTS AND BANKRUPTCY, 576 pages, 1989. (Review)

RIESENFELD'S CASES AND MATERIALS ON CREDITORS' REMEDIES AND DEBTORS' PROTECTION, Fourth Edition, 914 pages, 1987. (Casebook) 1990 Supplement.

WHITE AND NIMMER'S CASES AND MATERIALS ON BANKRUPTCY, Second Edition, 764 pages, 1992. Teacher's Manual available. (Casebook)

Criminal Law and Criminal Procedure—see also Corrections, Juvenile Justice

ABRAMS' FEDERAL CRIMINAL LAW AND ITS ENFORCEMENT, 866 pages, 1986. (Casebook) 1988 Supplement.

BUCY'S WHITE COLLAR CRIME, CASES AND MATERIALS, 688 pages, 1992. Teacher's Manual available. (Casebook)

DIX AND SHARLOT'S CASES AND MATERIALS ON CRIMINAL LAW, Third Edition, 846 pages, 1987. (Casebook)

GRANO'S PROBLEMS IN CRIMINAL PROCEDURE, Second Edition, 176 pages, 1981. Teacher's Manual available. Softcover. (Coursebook)

HEYMANN AND KENETY'S THE MURDER TRIAL OF WILBUR JACKSON: A HOMICIDE IN THE FAMILY, Second Edition, 347 pages, 1985. (Coursebook)

ISRAEL, KAMISAR AND LaFAVE'S CRIMINAL PROCEDURE AND THE CONSTITUTION: LEADING SUPREME COURT CASES AND INTRODUCTORY TEXT. 802 pages, 1992 Edition. Softcover. (Casebook)

ISRAEL AND LaFAVE'S CRIMINAL PROCEDURE—CONSTITUTIONAL LIMITATIONS IN A NUTSHELL, Fourth Edition, 461 pages, 1988. Softcover. (Text)

JOHNSON'S CASES, MATERIALS AND TEXT ON CRIMINAL LAW, Fourth Edition, 759 pages, 1990. Teacher's Manual available. (Casebook)

JOHNSON'S CASES AND MATERIALS ON CRIMI-

Criminal Law and Criminal Procedure— Cont'd

NAL PROCEDURE, 859 pages, 1988. (Casebook) 1992 Supplement.

KAMISAR, LAFAVE AND ISRAEL'S MODERN CRIMINAL PROCEDURE: CASES, COMMENTS AND QUESTIONS, Seventh Edition, 1593 pages, 1990. (Casebook) 1992 Supplement.

KAMISAR, LAFAVE AND ISRAEL'S BASIC CRIMINAL PROCEDURE: CASES, COMMENTS AND QUESTIONS, Seventh Edition, 792 pages, 1990. Softcover reprint from Kamisar, et al., Modern Criminal Procedure: Cases, Comments and Questions, Seventh Edition. (Casebook) 1992 Supplement.

LAFAVE'S MODERN CRIMINAL LAW: CASES, COMMENTS AND QUESTIONS, Second Edition, 903 pages, 1988. (Casebook)

LAFAVE AND ISRAEL'S HORNBOOK ON CRIMINAL PROCEDURE, Second Edition, 1309 pages, 1992 with 1992 pocket part. (Text)

LAFAVE AND SCOTT'S HORNBOOK ON CRIMINAL LAW, Second Edition, 918 pages, 1986. (Text)

LOEWY'S CRIMINAL LAW IN A NUTSHELL, Second Edition, 321 pages, 1987. Softcover. (Text)

LOW'S BLACK LETTER ON CRIMINAL LAW, Revised First Edition, 443 pages, 1990. Softcover. (Review)

SALTZBURG AND CAPRA'S CASES AND COMMENTARY ON AMERICAN CRIMINAL PROCEDURE, Fourth Edition, 1341 pages, 1992. Teacher's Manual available. (Casebook) 1992 Supplement.

SUBIN, MIRSKY AND WEINSTEIN'S THE CRIMINAL PROCESS: PROSECUTION AND DEFENSE FUNCTIONS, Approximately 450 pages, February, 1993 Pub. Softcover. Teacher's Manual available. (Text)

VORENBERG'S CASES ON CRIMINAL LAW AND PROCEDURE, Second Edition, 1088 pages, 1981. Teacher's Manual available. (Casebook) 1990 Supplement.

Domestic Relations

CLARK'S HORNBOOK ON DOMESTIC RELATIONS, Second Edition, Student Edition, 1050 pages, 1988. (Text)

CLARK AND GLOWINSKY'S CASES AND PROB-

LEMS ON DOMESTIC RELATIONS, Fourth Edition. 1150 pages, 1990. Teacher's Manual available. (Casebook) 1992 Supplement.

KRAUSE'S BLACK LETTER ON FAMILY LAW, 314 pages, 1988. Softcover. (Review)

KRAUSE'S CASES, COMMENTS AND QUESTIONS ON FAMILY LAW, Third Edition, 1433 pages, 1990. (Casebook)

KRAUSE'S FAMILY LAW IN A NUTSHELL, Second Edition, 444 pages, 1986. Softcover. (Text)

KRAUSKOPF'S CASES ON PROPERTY DIVISION AT MARRIAGE DISSOLUTION, 250 pages, 1984. Softcover. (Casebook)

Economics, Law and—see also Antitrust, Regulated Industries

BARNES AND STOUT'S CASES AND MATERIALS ON LAW AND ECONOMICS, 538 pages, 1992. Teacher's Manual available. (Casebook)

GOETZ' CASES AND MATERIALS ON LAW AND ECONOMICS, 547 pages, 1984. (Casebook)

MALLOY'S LAW AND ECONOMICS: A COMPARATIVE APPROACH TO THEORY AND PRACTICE, 166 pages, 1990. Softcover. (Text)

Education Law

ALEXANDER AND ALEXANDER'S PUBLIC SCHOOL LAW, Third Edition, 880 pages, 1992. Teacher's Manual available. (Coursebook)

ALEXANDER AND ALEXANDER'S THE LAW OF SCHOOLS, STUDENTS AND TEACHERS IN A NUTSHELL, 409 pages, 1984. Softcover. (Text)

YUDOF, KIRP AND LEVIN'S EDUCATIONAL POLICY AND THE LAW, Third Edition, 860 pages, 1992. (Casebook)

Employment Discrimination—see also Gender Discrimination

ESTREICHER AND HARPER'S CASES AND MATERIALS ON THE LAW GOVERNING THE EMPLOYMENT RELATIONSHIP, Second Edition, 966 pages, 1992. (Casebook) Statutory Supplement.

JONES, MURPHY AND BELTON'S CASES AND MATERIALS ON DISCRIMINATION IN EMPLOYMENT, (The Labor Law Group). Fifth Edition, 1116 pages, 1987. (Casebook) 1990 Supplement.

PLAYER'S FEDERAL LAW OF EMPLOYMENT DIS-

Employment Discrimination—Cont'd

CRIMINATION IN A NUTSHELL, Third Edition, 338 pages, 1992. Softcover. (Text)

PLAYER'S HORNBOOK ON EMPLOYMENT DISCRIMINATION LAW, Student Edition, 708 pages, 1988. (Text)

PLAYER, SHOBEN AND LIEBERWITZ' CASES AND MATERIALS ON EMPLOYMENT DISCRIMINATION LAW, 827 pages, 1990. Teacher's Manual available. (Casebook) 1992 Supplement.

Energy and Natural Resources Law—see also Oil and Gas

LAITOS' CASES AND MATERIALS ON NATURAL RESOURCES LAW, 938 pages, 1985. Teacher's Manual available. (Casebook)

LAITOS AND TOMAIN'S ENERGY AND NATURAL RESOURCES LAW IN A NUTSHELL, 554 pages, 1992. Softcover. (Text)

SELECTED ENVIRONMENTAL LAW STATUTES—EDUCATIONAL EDITION. Softcover. 1296 pages, 1992.

Environmental Law—see also Energy and Natural Resources Law; Sea, Law of

BONINE AND MCGARITY'S THE LAW OF ENVIRONMENTAL PROTECTION: CASES—LEGISLATION—POLICIES, Second Edition, 1042 pages, 1992. (Casebook)

FINDLEY AND FARBER'S CASES AND MATERIALS ON ENVIRONMENTAL LAW, Third Edition, 763 pages, 1991. Teacher's Manual available. (Casebook)

FINDLEY AND FARBER'S ENVIRONMENTAL LAW IN A NUTSHELL, Third Edition, 355 pages, 1992. Softcover. (Text)

PLATER, ABRAMS AND GOLDFARB'S ENVIRONMENTAL LAW AND POLICY: NATURE, LAW AND SOCIETY, 1039 pages, 1992. Teacher's Manual available. (Casebook)

RODGERS' HORNBOOK ON ENVIRONMENTAL LAW, 956 pages, 1977, with 1984 pocket part. (Text)

SELECTED ENVIRONMENTAL LAW STATUTES—EDUCATIONAL EDITION. Softcover. 1296 pages, 1992.

Equity—see Remedies

Estate Planning—see also Trusts and Estates; Taxation—Estate and Gift

LYNN'S INTRODUCTION TO ESTATE PLANNING

IN A NUTSHELL, Fourth Edition, 352 pages, 1992. Softcover. (Text)

Evidence

BERGMAN'S TRANSCRIPT EXERCISES FOR LEARNING EVIDENCE, 273 pages, 1992. Teacher's Manual available. (Coursebook)

BROUN AND BLAKEY'S BLACK LETTER ON EVIDENCE, 269 pages, 1984. Softcover. (Review)

BROUN, MEISENHOLDER, STRONG AND MOSTELLER'S PROBLEMS IN EVIDENCE, Third Edition, 238 pages, 1988. Teacher's Manual available. Softcover. (Coursebook)

CLEARY, STRONG, BROUN AND MOSTELLER'S CASES AND MATERIALS ON EVIDENCE, Fourth Edition, 1060 pages, 1988. (Casebook)

FEDERAL RULES OF EVIDENCE FOR UNITED STATES COURTS AND MAGISTRATES. Softcover. 549 pages, 1992.

FRIEDMAN'S THE ELEMENTS OF EVIDENCE, 315 pages, 1991. Teacher's Manual available. (Coursebook)

GRAHAM'S FEDERAL RULES OF EVIDENCE IN A NUTSHELL, Third Edition, 486 pages, 1992. Softcover. (Text)

LEMPERT AND SALTZBURG'S A MODERN APPROACH TO EVIDENCE: TEXT, PROBLEMS, TRANSCRIPTS AND CASES, Second Edition, 1232 pages, 1983. Teacher's Manual available. (Casebook)

LILLY'S AN INTRODUCTION TO THE LAW OF EVIDENCE, Second Edition, 585 pages, 1987. (Text)

MCCORMICK, SUTTON AND WELLBORN'S CASES AND MATERIALS ON EVIDENCE, Seventh Edition, 932 pages, 1992. Teacher's Manual available. (Casebook)

MCCORMICK'S HORNBOOK ON EVIDENCE, Fourth Edition, Student Edition, 672 pages, 1992. (Text)

ROTHSTEIN'S EVIDENCE IN A NUTSHELL: STATE AND FEDERAL RULES, Second Edition, 514 pages, 1981. Softcover. (Text)

Federal Jurisdiction and Procedure

CURRIE'S CASES AND MATERIALS ON FEDERAL COURTS, Fourth Edition, 783 pages, 1990. (Casebook)

CURRIE'S FEDERAL JURISDICTION IN A NUTSHELL, Third Edition, 242 pages, 1990.

Federal Jurisdiction and Procedure—Cont'd

Softcover. (Text)

FEDERAL RULES OF CIVIL PROCEDURE—EDU-CATIONAL EDITION. Softcover. 761 pages, 1992.

REDISH'S BLACK LETTER ON FEDERAL JURIS-DICTION, Second Edition, 234 pages, 1991. Softcover. (Review)

REDISH'S CASES, COMMENTS AND QUESTIONS ON FEDERAL COURTS, Second Edition, 1122 pages, 1989. (Casebook) 1992 Supplement.

VETRI AND MERRILL'S FEDERAL COURTS PROBLEMS AND MATERIALS, Second Edition, 232 pages, 1984. Softcover. (Coursebook)

WRIGHT'S HORNBOOK ON FEDERAL COURTS, Fourth Edition, Student Edition, 870 pages, 1983. (Text)

First Amendment

GARVEY AND SCHAUER'S THE FIRST AMEND-MENT: A READER, 527 pages, 1992. Softcover. (Reader)

SHIFFRIN AND CHOPER'S FIRST AMENDMENT, CASES—COMMENTS—QUESTIONS, 759 pages, 1991. Softcover. (Casebook) 1992 Supplement.

Foreign Relations and National Security Law

FRANCK AND GLENNON'S FOREIGN RELATIONS AND NATIONAL SECURITY LAW, 941 pages, 1987. (Casebook)

Future Interests—see Trusts and Estates

Gender Discrimination—see also Employment Discrimination

KAY'S TEXT, CASES AND MATERIALS ON SEX-BASED DISCRIMINATION, Third Edition, 1001 pages, 1988. (Casebook) 1992 Supplement.

THOMAS' SEX DISCRIMINATION IN A NUT-SHELL, Second Edition, 395 pages, 1991. Softcover. (Text)

Health Law—see Medicine, Law and

Human Rights—see International Law

Immigration Law

ALEINIKOFF AND MARTIN'S IMMIGRATION: PROCESS AND POLICY, Second Edition, 1056 pages, 1991. (Casebook)

Statutory Supplement. *See Immigra-*

tion and Nationality Laws

IMMIGRATION AND NATIONALITY LAWS OF THE UNITED STATES: SELECTED STATUTES, REGU-LATIONS AND FORMS. Softcover. 519 pages, 1992.

WEISSBRODT'S IMMIGRATION LAW AND PROCE-DURE IN A NUTSHELL, Third Edition, 497 pages, 1992. Softcover. (Text)

Indian Law—see American Indian Law

Insurance Law

DEVINE AND TERRY'S PROBLEMS IN INSUR-ANCE LAW, 240 pages, 1989. Softcover. Teacher's Manual available. (Coursebook)

DOBBYN'S INSURANCE LAW IN A NUTSHELL, Second Edition, 316 pages, 1989. Soft-cover. (Text)

KEETON'S COMPUTER-AIDED AND WORKBOOK EXERCISES ON INSURANCE LAW, 255 pages, 1990. Softcover. (Coursebook)

KEETON AND WIDISS' INSURANCE LAW, Stu-dent Edition, 1359 pages, 1988. (Text)

WIDISS AND KEETON'S COURSE SUPPLEMENT TO KEETON AND WIDISS' INSURANCE LAW, 502 pages, 1988. Softcover. Teacher's Manual available. (Casebook)

WIDISS' INSURANCE: MATERIALS ON FUNDA-MENTAL PRINCIPLES, LEGAL DOCTRINES AND REGULATORY ACTS, 1186 pages, 1989. Teacher's Manual available. (Casebook)

YORK AND WHELAN'S CASES, MATERIALS AND PROBLEMS ON GENERAL PRACTICE INSURANCE LAW, Second Edition, 787 pages, 1988. Teacher's Manual available. (Casebook)

International Law—see also Sea, Law of

BERMANN, DAVEY, FOX AND GOEBEL'S CASES AND MATERIALS ON EUROPEAN COMMUNITY LAW, Approximately 1200 pages, 1993. (Casebook) Statutory Supplement. *See European Economic Community: Selected Documents*

BUERGENTHAL'S INTERNATIONAL HUMAN RIGHTS IN A NUTSHELL, 283 pages, 1988. Softcover. (Text)

BUERGENTHAL AND MAIER'S PUBLIC INTERNA-TIONAL LAW IN A NUTSHELL, Second Edition, 275 pages, 1990. Softcover. (Text)

EUROPEAN ECONOMIC COMMUNITY: SELECTED DOCUMENTS. Approximately 550 pages,

International Law—Cont'd

1993. Softcover

FOLSOM'S EUROPEAN COMMUNITY LAW IN A NUTSHELL, 423 pages, 1992. Softcover. (Text)

FOLSOM, GORDON AND SPANOGLE'S INTERNATIONAL BUSINESS TRANSACTIONS—A PROBLEM-ORIENTED COURSEBOOK, Second Edition, 1237 pages, 1991. Teacher's Manual available. (Casebook) 1991 Documents Supplement.

FOLSOM, GORDON AND SPANOGLE'S INTERNATIONAL BUSINESS TRANSACTIONS IN A NUTSHELL, Fourth Edition, 548 pages, 1992. Softcover. (Text)

HENKIN, PUGH, SCHACHTER AND SMIT'S CASES AND MATERIALS ON INTERNATIONAL LAW, Second Edition, 1517 pages, 1987. (Casebook) Documents Supplement.

INTERNATIONAL LITIGATION AND ARBITRATION: SELECTED TREATIES, STATUTES AND RULES. Approximately 275 pages, 1993. Softcover

INTERNATIONAL ORGANIZATIONS IN THEIR LEGAL SETTING: SELECTED DOCUMENTS. Approximately 500 pages, March, 1993 Pub. Softcover

JACKSON AND DAVEY'S CASES, MATERIALS AND TEXT ON LEGAL PROBLEMS OF INTERNATIONAL ECONOMIC RELATIONS, Second Edition, 1269 pages, 1986. (Casebook) 1989 Documents Supplement.

KIRGIS' INTERNATIONAL ORGANIZATIONS IN THEIR LEGAL SETTING, Second Edition, approximately 1150 pages, March, 1993 Pub. Teacher's Manual available. (Casebook) Statutory Supplement.

LOWENFELD'S INTERNATIONAL LITIGATION AND ARBITRATION, Approximately 875 pages, 1993. (Casebook) Statutory Supplement. *See International Litigation: Selected Documents*

WESTON, FALK AND D'AMATO'S INTERNATIONAL LAW AND WORLD ORDER—A PROBLEM-ORIENTED COURSEBOOK, Second Edition, 1335 pages, 1990. Teacher's Manual available. (Casebook) Documents Supplement.

Interviewing and Counseling

BINDER AND PRICE'S LEGAL INTERVIEWING

AND COUNSELING, 232 pages, 1977. Softcover. Teacher's Manual available. (Coursebook)

BINDER, BERGMAN AND PRICE'S LAWYERS AS COUNSELORS: A CLIENT-CENTERED APPROACH, 427 pages, 1991. Softcover. (Coursebook)

SHAFFER AND ELKINS' LEGAL INTERVIEWING AND COUNSELING IN A NUTSHELL, Second Edition, 487 pages, 1987. Softcover. (Text)

Introduction to Law—see Legal Method and Legal System

Introduction to Law Study

HEGLAND'S INTRODUCTION TO THE STUDY AND PRACTICE OF LAW IN A NUTSHELL, 418 pages, 1983. Softcover. (Text)

KINYON'S INTRODUCTION TO LAW STUDY AND LAW EXAMINATIONS IN A NUTSHELL, 389 pages, 1971. Softcover. (Text)

Judicial Process—see Legal Method and Legal System

Jurisprudence

CHRISTIE'S JURISPRUDENCE—TEXT AND READINGS ON THE PHILOSOPHY OF LAW, 1056 pages, 1973. (Casebook)

SINHA'S JURISPRUDENCE (LEGAL PHILOSOPHY) IN A NUTSHELL. Approximately 350 pages, 1993. Softcover. (Text)

Juvenile Justice

FOX'S JUVENILE COURTS IN A NUTSHELL, Third Edition, 291 pages, 1984. Softcover. (Text)

Labor and Employment Law—see also Employment Discrimination, Workers' Compensation

FINKIN, GOLDMAN AND SUMMERS' LEGAL PROTECTION OF INDIVIDUAL EMPLOYEES, (The Labor Law Group). 1164 pages, 1989. (Casebook)

GORMAN'S BASIC TEXT ON LABOR LAW— UNIONIZATION AND COLLECTIVE BARGAINING, 914 pages, 1976. (Text)

LESLIE'S LABOR LAW IN A NUTSHELL, Third Edition, 388 pages, 1992. Softcover. (Text)

NOLAN'S LABOR ARBITRATION LAW AND PRAC-

Labor and Employment Law—Cont'd

TICE IN A NUTSHELL, 358 pages, 1979. Softcover. (Text)

OBERER, HANSLOWE, ANDERSEN AND HEINSZ' CASES AND MATERIALS ON LABOR LAW—COLLECTIVE BARGAINING IN A FREE SOCIETY, Third Edition, 1163 pages, 1986. Teacher's Manual available. (Casebook) Statutory Supplement. 1991 Case Supplement.

RABIN, SILVERSTEIN AND SCHATZKI'S LABOR AND EMPLOYMENT LAW: PROBLEMS, CASES AND MATERIALS IN THE LAW OF WORK, (The Labor Law Group). 1014 pages, 1988. Teacher's Manual available. (Casebook) 1988 Statutory Supplement.

WOLLETT, GRODIN AND WEISBERGER'S COLLECTIVE BARGAINING IN PUBLIC EMPLOYMENT, (The Labor Law Group). Fourth Edition, approximately 600 pages, April, 1993 Pub. (Casebook)

Land Finance—Property Security—see Real Estate Transactions

Land Use

CALLIES AND FREILICH'S CASES AND MATERIALS ON LAND USE, 1233 pages, 1986. (Casebook) 1991 Supplement.

HAGMAN AND JUERGENSMEYER'S HORNBOOK ON URBAN PLANNING AND LAND DEVELOPMENT CONTROL LAW, Second Edition, Student Edition, 680 pages, 1986. (Text)

WRIGHT AND GITELMAN'S CASES AND MATERIALS ON LAND USE, Fourth Edition, 1255 pages, 1991. Teacher's Manual available. (Casebook)

WRIGHT AND WRIGHT'S LAND USE IN A NUTSHELL, Second Edition, 356 pages, 1985. Softcover. (Text)

Legal History—see also Legal Method and Legal System

PRESSER AND ZAINALDIN'S CASES AND MATERIALS ON LAW AND JURISPRUDENCE IN AMERICAN HISTORY, Second Edition, 1092 pages, 1989. Teacher's Manual available. (Casebook)

Legal Method and Legal System—see also Legal Research, Legal Writing

ALDISERT'S READINGS, MATERIALS AND CASES IN THE JUDICIAL PROCESS, 948 pages, 1976. (Casebook)

BERCH, BERCH AND SPRITZER'S INTRODUCTION TO LEGAL METHOD AND PROCESS, Second Edition, 585 pages, 1992. Teacher's Manual available. (Casebook)

BODENHEIMER, OAKLEY AND LOVE'S READINGS AND CASES ON AN INTRODUCTION TO THE ANGLO-AMERICAN LEGAL SYSTEM, Second Edition, 166 pages, 1988. Softcover. (Casebook)

DAVIES AND LAWRY'S INSTITUTIONS AND METHODS OF THE LAW—INTRODUCTORY TEACHING MATERIALS, 547 pages, 1982. Teacher's Manual available. (Casebook)

DVORKIN, HIMMELSTEIN AND LESNICK'S BECOMING A LAWYER: A HUMANISTIC PERSPECTIVE ON LEGAL EDUCATION AND PROFESSIONALISM, 211 pages, 1981. Softcover. (Text)

KEETON'S JUDGING, 842 pages, 1990. Softcover. (Coursebook)

KELSO AND KELSO'S STUDYING LAW: AN INTRODUCTION, 587 pages, 1984. (Coursebook)

KEMPIN'S HISTORICAL INTRODUCTION TO ANGLO-AMERICAN LAW IN A NUTSHELL, Third Edition, 323 pages, 1990. Softcover. (Text)

MEADOR'S AMERICAN COURTS, 113 pages, 1991. Softcover. (Text)

REYNOLDS' JUDICIAL PROCESS IN A NUTSHELL, Second Edition, 308 pages, 1991. Softcover. (Text)

Legal Research

COHEN AND OLSON'S LEGAL RESEARCH IN A NUTSHELL, Fifth Edition, 370 pages, 1992. Softcover. (Text)

COHEN, BERRING AND OLSON'S HOW TO FIND THE LAW, Ninth Edition, 716 pages, 1989. (Text)

COHEN, BERRING AND OLSON'S FINDING THE LAW, 570 pages, 1989. Softcover reprint from Cohen, Berring and Olson's How to Find the Law, Ninth Edition. (Coursebook)

Legal Research Exercises, 4th Ed., for use with Cohen, Berring and Olson, 253 pages, 1992. Teacher's Manual available.

ROMBAUER'S LEGAL PROBLEM SOLVING—ANALYSIS, RESEARCH AND WRITING, Fifth Edition, 524 pages, 1991. Softcover. Teacher's Manual with problems availa-

Legal Research—Cont'd

ble. (Coursebook)

STATSKY'S LEGAL RESEARCH AND WRITING: SOME STARTING POINTS, Fourth Edition, approximately 270 pages, 1993. Softcover. Teacher's Manual available. (Coursebook) Student Workbook.

TEPLY'S LEGAL RESEARCH AND CITATION, Fourth Edition, 436 pages, 1992. Softcover. (Coursebook)

Student Library Exercises, Fourth Edition, 276 pages, 1992. Answer Key available.

Legal Writing and Drafting

CHILD'S DRAFTING LEGAL DOCUMENTS: PRINCIPLES AND PRACTICES, Second Edition, 425 pages, 1992. Softcover. Teacher's Manual available. (Coursebook)

DICKERSON'S MATERIALS ON LEGAL DRAFTING, 425 pages, 1981. Teacher's Manual available. (Coursebook)

FELSENFELD AND SIEGEL'S WRITING CONTRACTS IN PLAIN ENGLISH, 290 pages, 1981. Softcover. (Text)

GOPEN'S WRITING FROM A LEGAL PERSPECTIVE, 225 pages, 1981. (Text)

MARTINEAU'S DRAFTING LEGISLATION AND RULES IN PLAIN ENGLISH, 155 pages, 1991. Softcover. Teacher's Manual available. (Text)

MELLINKOFF'S DICTIONARY OF AMERICAN LEGAL USAGE, 703 pages, 1992. Softcover. (Text)

MELLINKOFF'S LEGAL WRITING—SENSE AND NONSENSE, 242 pages, 1982. Softcover. Teacher's Manual available. (Text)

PRATT'S LEGAL WRITING: A SYSTEMATIC APPROACH, Second Edition, approximately 550 pages, April, 1993 Pub. Teacher's Manual available. (Coursebook)

RAY AND COX'S BEYOND THE BASICS: A TEXT FOR ADVANCED LEGAL WRITING, 427 pages, 1991. Softcover. Teacher's Manual available. (Text)

RAY AND RAMSFIELD'S LEGAL WRITING: GETTING IT RIGHT AND GETTING IT WRITTEN, 250 pages, 1987. Softcover. (Text)

SQUIRES AND ROMBAUER'S LEGAL WRITING IN A NUTSHELL, 294 pages, 1982. Softcover.

(Text)

STATSKY AND WERNET'S CASE ANALYSIS AND FUNDAMENTALS OF LEGAL WRITING, Third Edition, 424 pages, 1989. Teacher's Manual available. (Text)

TEPLY'S LEGAL WRITING, ANALYSIS AND ORAL ARGUMENT, 576 pages, 1990. Softcover. Teacher's Manual available. (Coursebook)

WEIHOFEN'S LEGAL WRITING STYLE, Second Edition, 332 pages, 1980. (Text)

Legislation—see also Legal Writing and Drafting

DAVIES' LEGISLATIVE LAW AND PROCESS IN A NUTSHELL, Second Edition, 346 pages, 1986. Softcover. (Text)

ESKRIDGE AND FRICKEY'S CASES AND MATERIALS ON LEGISLATION: STATUTES AND THE CREATION OF PUBLIC POLICY, 937 pages, 1988. Teacher's Manual available. (Casebook) 1992 Supplement.

NUTTING AND DICKERSON'S CASES AND MATERIALS ON LEGISLATION, Fifth Edition, 744 pages, 1978. (Casebook)

STATSKY'S LEGISLATIVE ANALYSIS AND DRAFTING, Second Edition, 217 pages, 1984. Teacher's Manual available. (Text)

Local Government

FRUG'S CASES AND MATERIALS ON LOCAL GOVERNMENT LAW, 1005 pages, 1988. (Casebook) 1991 Supplement.

McCARTHY'S LOCAL GOVERNMENT LAW IN A NUTSHELL, Third Edition, 435 pages, 1990. Softcover. (Text)

REYNOLDS' HORNBOOK ON LOCAL GOVERNMENT LAW, 860 pages, 1982 with 1990 pocket part. (Text)

VALENTE AND McCARTHY'S CASES AND MATERIALS ON LOCAL GOVERNMENT LAW, Fourth Edition, 1158 pages, 1992. Teacher's Manual available. (Casebook)

Mass Communication Law

GILLMOR, BARRON, SIMON AND TERRY'S CASES AND COMMENT ON MASS COMMUNICATION LAW, Fifth Edition, 947 pages, 1990. (Casebook)

GINSBURG, BOTEIN AND DIRECTOR'S REGULATION OF THE ELECTRONIC MASS MEDIA: LAW

Mass Communication Law—Cont'd

AND POLICY FOR RADIO, TELEVISION, CABLE AND THE NEW VIDEO TECHNOLOGIES, Second Edition, 657 pages, 1991. (Casebook) Statutory Supplement.

ZUCKMAN, GAYNES, CARTER AND DEE'S MASS COMMUNICATIONS LAW IN A NUTSHELL, Third Edition, 538 pages, 1988. Softcover. (Text)

Medicine, Law and

FISCINA, BOUMIL, SHARPE AND HEAD'S MEDICAL LIABILITY, 487 pages, 1991. Teacher's Manual available. (Casebook)

FURROW, JOHNSON, JOST AND SCHWARTZ' HEALTH LAW: CASES, MATERIALS AND PROBLEMS, Second Edition, 1236 pages, 1991. Teacher's Manual available. (Casebook)

FURROW, JOHNSON, JOST AND SCHWARTZ' BIOETHICS: HEALTH CARE LAW AND ETHICS, Reprint from Furrow et al., Health Law, Second Edition. Softcover. Teacher's Manual available. (Casebook)

FURROW, JOHNSON, JOST AND SCHWARTZ' THE LAW OF HEALTH CARE ORGANIZATION AND FINANCE, Reprint from Furrow et al., Health Law, Second Edition. Softcover. Teacher's Manual available.

FURROW, JOHNSON, JOST AND SCHWARTZ' LIABILITY AND QUALITY ISSUES IN HEALTH CARE, Reprint from Furrow et al., Health Law, Second Edition. Softcover. Teacher's Manual available. (Casebook)

HALL AND ELLMAN'S HEALTH CARE LAW AND ETHICS IN A NUTSHELL, 401 pages, 1990. Softcover (Text)

JARVIS, CLOSEN, HERMANN AND LEONARD'S AIDS LAW IN A NUTSHELL, 349 pages, 1991. Softcover. (Text)

KING'S THE LAW OF MEDICAL MALPRACTICE IN A NUTSHELL, Second Edition, 342 pages, 1986. Softcover. (Text)

SHAPIRO AND SPECE'S CASES, MATERIALS AND PROBLEMS ON BIOETHICS AND LAW, 892 pages, 1981. (Casebook) 1991 Supplement.

Military Law

SHANOR AND TERRELL'S MILITARY LAW IN A NUTSHELL, 378 pages, 1980. Softcover. (Text)

Mining Law—see Energy and Natural Resources Law

Mortgages—see Real Estate Transactions

Natural Resources Law—see Energy and Natural Resources Law, Environmental Law

Negotiation

GIFFORD'S LEGAL NEGOTIATION: THEORY AND APPLICATIONS, 225 pages, 1989. Softcover. (Text)

TEPLY'S LEGAL NEGOTIATION IN A NUTSHELL, 282 pages, 1992. Softcover. (Text)

WILLIAMS' LEGAL NEGOTIATION AND SETTLEMENT, 207 pages, 1983. Softcover. Teacher's Manual available. (Coursebook)

Office Practice—see also Computers and Law, Interviewing and Counseling, Negotiation

HEGLAND'S TRIAL AND PRACTICE SKILLS IN A NUTSHELL, 346 pages, 1978. Softcover (Text)

MUNNEKE'S LAW PRACTICE MANAGEMENT: MATERIALS AND CASES, 634 pages, 1991. Teacher's Manual available. (Casebook)

Oil and Gas—see also Energy and Natural Resources Law

HEMINGWAY'S HORNBOOK ON THE LAW OF OIL AND GAS, Third Edition, Student Edition, 711 pages, 1992. (Text)

KUNTZ, LOWE, ANDERSON AND SMITH'S CASES AND MATERIALS ON OIL AND GAS LAW, Second Edition, approximately 1000 pages, 1993. Teacher's Manual available. (Casebook) Forms Manual. Revised.

LOWE'S OIL AND GAS LAW IN A NUTSHELL, Second Edition, 465 pages, 1988. Softcover. (Text)

Partnership—see Agency—Partnership

Patent and Copyright Law

CHOATE, FRANCIS AND COLLINS' CASES AND MATERIALS ON PATENT LAW, INCLUDING TRADE SECRETS, COPYRIGHTS, TRADEMARKS, Third Edition, 1009 pages, 1987. (Casebook)

HALPERN, SHIPLEY AND ABRAMS' CASES AND MATERIALS ON COPYRIGHT, 663 pages, 1992. (Casebook)

Patent and Copyright Law—Cont'd

MILLER AND DAVIS' INTELLECTUAL PROPERTY—PATENTS, TRADEMARKS AND COPYRIGHT IN A NUTSHELL, Second Edition, 437 pages, 1990. Softcover. (Text)

NIMMER, MARCUS, MYERS AND NIMMER'S CASES AND MATERIALS ON COPYRIGHT AND OTHER ASPECTS OF ENTERTAINMENT LITIGATION—INCLUDING UNFAIR COMPETITION, DEFAMATION, PRIVACY, ILLUSTRATED, Fourth Edition, 1177 pages, 1991. (Casebook) Statutory Supplement. See *Selected Intellectual Property Statutes*

SELECTED INTELLECTUAL PROPERTY AND UNFAIR COMPETITION STATUTES, REGULATIONS AND TREATIES. Softcover.

Products Liability

FISCHER AND POWERS' CASES AND MATERIALS ON PRODUCTS LIABILITY, 685 pages, 1988. Teacher's Manual available. (Casebook)

PHILLIPS' PRODUCTS LIABILITY IN A NUTSHELL, Third Edition, 307 pages, 1988. Softcover. (Text)

Professional Responsibility

ARONSON, DEVINE AND FISCH'S PROBLEMS, CASES AND MATERIALS IN PROFESSIONAL RESPONSIBILITY, 745 pages, 1985. Teacher's Manual available. (Casebook)

ARONSON AND WECKSTEIN'S PROFESSIONAL RESPONSIBILITY IN A NUTSHELL, Second Edition, 514 pages, 1991. Softcover. (Text)

LESNICK'S BEING A LAWYER: INDIVIDUAL CHOICE AND RESPONSIBILITY IN THE PRACTICE OF LAW, 422 pages, 1992. Softcover. Teacher's Manual available. (Coursebook)

MELLINKOFF'S THE CONSCIENCE OF A LAWYER, 304 pages, 1973. (Text)

PIRSIG AND KIRWIN'S CASES AND MATERIALS ON PROFESSIONAL RESPONSIBILITY, Fourth Edition, 603 pages, 1984. Teacher's Manual available. (Casebook)

ROTUNDA'S BLACK LETTER ON PROFESSIONAL RESPONSIBILITY, Third Edition, 492 pages, 1992. Softcover. (Review)

SCHWARTZ, WYDICK AND PERSCHBACHER'S PROBLEMS IN LEGAL ETHICS, Third Edition, approximately 400 pages, 1993. (Coursebook)

SELECTED STATUTES, RULES AND STANDARDS ON THE LEGAL PROFESSION. Softcover. 940 pages, 1992.

SMITH AND MALLEN'S PREVENTING LEGAL MALPRACTICE, 264 pages, 1989. Reprint from Mallen and Smith's Legal Malpractice, Third Edition. (Text)

SUTTON AND DZIENKOWSKI'S CASES AND MATERIALS ON PROFESSIONAL RESPONSIBILITY FOR LAWYERS, 839 pages, 1989. Teacher's Manual available. (Casebook)

WOLFRAM'S HORNBOOK ON MODERN LEGAL ETHICS, Student Edition, 1120 pages, 1986. (Text)

WYDICK AND PERSCHBACHER'S CALIFORNIA LEGAL ETHICS, 439 pages, 1992. Softcover. (Coursebook)

Property—see also Real Estate Transactions, Land Use, Trusts and Estates

BARNES AND STOUT'S THE ECONOMICS OF PROPERTY RIGHTS AND NUISANCE LAW, 87 pages, 1992. Softcover. Teacher's Manual available. (Casebook)

BERNHARDT'S BLACK LETTER ON PROPERTY, Second Edition, 388 pages, 1991. Softcover. (Review)

BERNHARDT'S REAL PROPERTY IN A NUTSHELL, Second Edition, 448 pages, 1981. Softcover. (Text)

BOYER, HOVENKAMP AND KURTZ' THE LAW OF PROPERTY, AN INTRODUCTORY SURVEY, Fourth Edition, 696 pages, 1991. (Text)

BROWDER, CUNNINGHAM, NELSON, STOEBUCK AND WHITMAN'S CASES ON BASIC PROPERTY LAW, Fifth Edition, 1386 pages, 1989. Teacher's Manual available. (Casebook)

BRUCE, ELY AND BOSTICK'S CASES AND MATERIALS ON MODERN PROPERTY LAW, Second Edition, 953 pages, 1989. Teacher's Manual available. (Casebook)

BURKE'S PERSONAL PROPERTY IN A NUTSHELL, Second Edition, approximately 400 pages, May, 1993 Pub. Softcover. (Text)

CUNNINGHAM, STOEBUCK AND WHITMAN'S HORNBOOK ON THE LAW OF PROPERTY, Second Edition, approximately 900 pages, May, 1993 Pub. (Text)

DONAHUE, KAUPER AND MARTIN'S CASES AND MATERIALS ON PROPERTY, AN INTRODUCTION TO THE CONCEPT AND THE INSTITUTION, Third

Property—Cont'd

Edition, approximately 1000 pages, 1993. Teacher's Manual available. (Casebook)

HILL'S LANDLORD AND TENANT LAW IN A NUTSHELL, Second Edition, 311 pages, 1986. Softcover. (Text)

JOHNSON, JOST, SALSICH AND SHAFFER'S PROPERTY LAW, CASES, MATERIALS AND PROBLEMS, 908 pages, 1992. Teacher's Manual available. (Casebook)

KURTZ AND HOVENKAMP'S CASES AND MATERIALS ON AMERICAN PROPERTY LAW, Second Edition, approximately 1350 pages, March, 1993 Pub. Teacher's Manual available. (Casebook)

MOYNIHAN'S INTRODUCTION TO REAL PROPERTY, Second Edition, 239 pages, 1988. (Text)

Psychiatry, Law and

REISNER AND SLOBOGIN'S LAW AND THE MENTAL HEALTH SYSTEM, CIVIL AND CRIMINAL ASPECTS, Second Edition, 1117 pages, 1990. Teacher's Manual available. (Casebook) 1992 Supplement.

Real Estate Transactions

BRUCE'S REAL ESTATE FINANCE IN A NUTSHELL, Third Edition, 287 pages, 1991. Softcover. (Text)

MAXWELL, RIESENFELD, HETLAND AND WARREN'S CASES ON CALIFORNIA SECURITY TRANSACTIONS IN LAND, Fourth Edition, 778 pages, 1992. Teacher's Manual available. (Casebook)

NELSON AND WHITMAN'S BLACK LETTER ON LAND TRANSACTIONS AND FINANCE, Second Edition, 466 pages, 1988. Softcover. (Review)

NELSON AND WHITMAN'S CASES AND MATERIALS ON REAL ESTATE TRANSFER, FINANCE AND DEVELOPMENT, Fourth Edition, 1346 pages, 1992. (Casebook)

NELSON AND WHITMAN'S HORNBOOK ON REAL ESTATE FINANCE LAW, Second Edition, 941 pages, 1985 with 1989 pocket part. (Text)

Regulated Industries—see also Mass Communication Law, Banking Law

GELLHORN AND PIERCE'S REGULATED INDUSTRIES IN A NUTSHELL, Second Edition, 389 pages, 1987. Softcover. (Text)

MORGAN, HARRISON AND VERKUIL'S CASES AND MATERIALS ON ECONOMIC REGULATION OF BUSINESS, Second Edition, 666 pages, 1985. (Casebook)

Remedies

DOBBS' HORNBOOK ON REMEDIES, Second Edition, approximately 1000 pages, April, 1993 Pub. (Text)

DOBBS' PROBLEMS IN REMEDIES. 137 pages, 1974. Teacher's Manual available. Softcover. (Coursebook)

DOBBYN'S INJUNCTIONS IN A NUTSHELL, 264 pages, 1974. Softcover. (Text)

FRIEDMAN'S CONTRACT REMEDIES IN A NUTSHELL, 323 pages, 1981. Softcover. (Text)

LEAVELL, LOVE AND NELSON'S CASES AND MATERIALS ON EQUITABLE REMEDIES, RESTITUTION AND DAMAGES, Fourth Edition, 1111 pages, 1986. Teacher's Manual available. (Casebook)

O'CONNELL'S REMEDIES IN A NUTSHELL, Second Edition, 320 pages, 1985. Softcover. (Text)

SCHOENBROD, MACBETH, LEVINE AND JUNG'S CASES AND MATERIALS ON REMEDIES: PUBLIC AND PRIVATE, 848 pages, 1990. Teacher's Manual available. (Casebook) 1992 Supplement.

YORK, BAUMAN AND RENDLEMAN'S CASES AND MATERIALS ON REMEDIES, Fifth Edition, 1270 pages, 1992. Teacher's Manual available. (Casebook)

Sea, Law of

SOHN AND GUSTAFSON'S THE LAW OF THE SEA IN A NUTSHELL, 264 pages, 1984. Softcover. (Text)

Securities Regulation

HAZEN'S HORNBOOK ON THE LAW OF SECURITIES REGULATION, Second Edition, Student Edition, 1082 pages, 1990. (Text)

RATNER'S SECURITIES REGULATION IN A NUTSHELL, Fourth Edition, 320 pages, 1992. Softcover. (Text)

RATNER AND HAZEN'S SECURITIES REGULATION: CASES AND MATERIALS, Fourth Edition, 1062 pages, 1991. Teacher's Manual available. (Casebook) Problems and Sample Documents Supplement.

Statutory Supplement. *See Securities*

Securities Regulation—Cont'd

Regulation, Selected Statutes

SECURITIES REGULATION, SELECTED STATUTES, RULES, AND FORMS. Softcover. Approximately 1375 pages, 1993.

Sports Law

CHAMPION'S SPORTS LAW IN A NUTSHELL,. Approximately 300 pages, January, 1993 Pub. Softcover. (Text)

SCHUBERT, SMITH AND TRENTADUE'S SPORTS LAW, 395 pages, 1986. (Text)

Tax Practice and Procedure

GARBIS, RUBIN AND MORGAN'S CASES AND MATERIALS ON TAX PROCEDURE AND TAX FRAUD, Third Edition, 921 pages, 1992. Teacher's Manual available. (Casebook)

MORGAN'S TAX PROCEDURE AND TAX FRAUD IN A NUTSHELL, 400 pages, 1990. Softcover. (Text)

Taxation—Corporate

KAHN AND GANN'S CORPORATE TAXATION, Third Edition, 980 pages, 1989. Teacher's Manual available. (Casebook) 1991 Supplement.

SCHWARZ AND LATHROPE'S BLACK LETTER ON CORPORATE AND PARTNERSHIP TAXATION, 537 pages, 1991. Softcover. (Review)

WEIDENBRUCH AND BURKE'S FEDERAL INCOME TAXATION OF CORPORATIONS AND STOCKHOLDERS IN A NUTSHELL, Third Edition, 309 pages, 1989. Softcover. (Text)

Taxation—Estate & Gift—see also Estate Planning, Trusts and Estates

MCNULTY'S FEDERAL ESTATE AND GIFT TAXATION IN A NUTSHELL, Fourth Edition, 496 pages, 1989. Softcover. (Text)

PEAT AND WILLBANKS' FEDERAL ESTATE AND GIFT TAXATION: AN ANALYSIS AND CRITIQUE, 265 pages, 1991. Softcover. (Text)

PENNELL'S CASES AND MATERIALS ON INCOME TAXATION OF TRUSTS, ESTATES, GRANTORS AND BENEFICIARIES, 460 pages, 1987. Teacher's Manual available. (Casebook)

Taxation—Individual

DODGE'S THE LOGIC OF TAX, 343 pages, 1989. Softcover. (Text)

GUNN AND WARD'S CASES, TEXT AND PROB-

LEMS ON FEDERAL INCOME TAXATION, Third Edition, 817 pages, 1992. Teacher's Manual available. (Casebook)

HUDSON AND LIND'S BLACK LETTER ON FEDERAL INCOME TAXATION, Fourth Edition, 410 pages, 1992. Softcover. (Review)

MCNULTY'S FEDERAL INCOME TAXATION OF INDIVIDUALS IN A NUTSHELL, Fourth Edition, 503 pages, 1988. Softcover. (Text)

POSIN'S FEDERAL INCOME TAXATION, Second Edition, approximately 650 pages, May, 1993 Pub. Softcover. (Text)

ROSE AND CHOMMIE'S HORNBOOK ON FEDERAL INCOME TAXATION, Third Edition, 923 pages, 1988, with 1991 pocket part. (Text)

SELECTED FEDERAL TAXATION STATUTES AND REGULATIONS. Softcover. 1686 pages, 1993.

Taxation—International

DOERNBERG'S INTERNATIONAL TAXATION IN A NUTSHELL, 325 pages, 1989. Softcover. (Text)

KAPLAN'S FEDERAL TAXATION OF INTERNATIONAL TRANSACTIONS: PRINCIPLES, PLANNING AND POLICY, 635 pages, 1988. (Casebook)

Taxation—Partnership

BERGER AND WIEDENBECK'S CASES AND MATERIALS ON PARTNERSHIP TAXATION, 788 pages, 1989. Teacher's Manual available. (Casebook) 1991 Supplement.

BISHOP AND BROOKS' FEDERAL PARTNERSHIP TAXATION: A GUIDE TO THE LEADING CASES, STATUTES, AND REGULATIONS, 545 pages, 1990. Softcover. (Text)

BURKE'S FEDERAL INCOME TAXATION OF PARTNERSHIPS IN A NUTSHELL, 356 pages, 1992. Softcover. (Text)

SCHWARZ AND LATHROPE'S BLACK LETTER ON CORPORATE AND PARTNERSHIP TAXATION, 537 pages, 1991. Softcover. (Review)

Taxation—State & Local

GELFAND AND SALSICH'S STATE AND LOCAL TAXATION AND FINANCE IN A NUTSHELL, 309 pages, 1986. Softcover. (Text)

HELLERSTEIN AND HELLERSTEIN'S CASES AND MATERIALS ON STATE AND LOCAL TAXATION, Fifth Edition, 1071 pages, 1988. (Case-

Taxation—State & Local—Cont'd
book)

Torts—see also Products Liability

BARNES AND STOUT'S THE ECONOMIC ANALY-
SIS OF TORT LAW, 161 pages, 1992.
Softcover. Teacher's Manual available.
(Casebook)

CHRISTIE AND MEEKS' CASES AND MATERIALS
ON THE LAW OF TORTS, Second Edition, 1264
pages, 1990. (Casebook)

DOBBS' TORTS AND COMPENSATION—PERSON-
AL ACCOUNTABILITY AND SOCIAL RESPONSIBIL-
ITY FOR INJURY, 955 pages, 1985. Teacher's
Manual available. (Casebook) 1990 Sup-
plement.

KEETON, KEETON, SARGENTICH AND STEIN-
ER'S CASES AND MATERIALS ON TORT AND
ACCIDENT LAW, Second Edition, 1318 pages,
1989. (Casebook)

KIONKA'S BLACK LETTER ON TORTS, 339
pages, 1988. Softcover. (Review)

KIONKA'S TORTS IN A NUTSHELL, Second Edition, 449 pages, 1992. Softcover. (Text)

PROSSER AND KEETON'S HORNBOOK ON
TORTS, Fifth Edition, Student Edition, 1286
pages, 1984 with 1988 pocket part. (Text)

ROBERTSON, POWERS AND ANDERSON'S CASES
AND MATERIALS ON TORTS, 932 pages, 1989.
Teacher's Manual available. (Casebook)

Trade Regulation—see also Antitrust, Regulated Industries

McMANIS' UNFAIR TRADE PRACTICES IN A
NUTSHELL, Third Edition, approximately
450 pages, 1993. Softcover. (Text)

SCHECHTER'S BLACK LETTER ON UNFAIR
TRADE PRACTICES, 272 pages, 1986. Softcover. (Review)

WESTON, MAGGS AND SCHECHTER'S UNFAIR
TRADE PRACTICES AND CONSUMER PROTEC-
TION, CASES AND COMMENTS, Fifth Edition,
957 pages, 1992. Teacher's Manual available. (Casebook)

Trial and Appellate Advocacy—see also Civil Procedure

APPELLATE ADVOCACY, HANDBOOK OF, Second Edition, 182 pages, 1986. Softcover.
(Text)

BERGMAN'S TRIAL ADVOCACY IN A NUTSHELL,

Second Edition, 354 pages, 1989. Softcover. (Text)

BINDER AND BERGMAN'S FACT INVESTIGATION:
FROM HYPOTHESIS TO PROOF, 354 pages,
1984. Teacher's Manual available.
(Coursebook)

CARLSON'S ADJUDICATION OF CRIMINAL JUS-
TICE: PROBLEMS AND REFERENCES, 130
pages, 1986. Softcover. (Casebook)

CARLSON AND IMWINKELRIED'S DYNAMICS OF
TRIAL PRACTICE: PROBLEMS AND MATERIALS,
414 pages, 1989. Teacher's Manual available. (Coursebook) 1990 Supplement.

CLARY'S PRIMER ON THE ANALYSIS AND PRE-
SENTATION OF LEGAL ARGUMENT, 106 pages,
1992. Softcover. (Text)

DESSEM'S PRETRIAL LITIGATION IN A NUT-
SHELL, 382 pages, 1992. Softcover. (Text)

DESSEM'S PRETRIAL LITIGATION: LAW, POLICY
AND PRACTICE, 608 pages, 1991. Softcover.
Teacher's Manual available. (Coursebook)

DEVINE'S NON-JURY CASE FILES FOR TRIAL
ADVOCACY, 258 pages, 1991. (Coursebook)

GOLDBERG'S THE FIRST TRIAL (WHERE DO I
SIT? WHAT DO I SAY?) IN A NUTSHELL, 396
pages, 1982. Softcover. (Text)

HAYDOCK, HERR, AND STEMPEL'S FUNDAMEN-
TALS OF PRE-TRIAL LITIGATION, Second Edition, 786 pages, 1992. Softcover. Teacher's Manual available. (Coursebook)

HAYDOCK AND SONSTENG'S TRIAL: THEORIES,
TACTICS, TECHNIQUES, 711 pages, 1991.
Softcover. (Text)

HEGLAND'S TRIAL AND PRACTICE SKILLS IN A
NUTSHELL, 346 pages, 1978. Softcover.
(Text)

HORNSTEIN'S APPELLATE ADVOCACY IN A
NUTSHELL, 325 pages, 1984. Softcover.
(Text)

JEANS' HANDBOOK ON TRIAL ADVOCACY, Student Edition, 473 pages, 1975. Softcover.
(Text)

LISNEK AND KAUFMAN'S DEPOSITIONS: PRO-
CEDURE, STRATEGY AND TECHNIQUE, Law
School and CLE Edition. 250 pages, 1990.
Softcover. (Text)

MARTINEAU'S CASES AND MATERIALS ON AP-
PELLATE PRACTICE AND PROCEDURE, 565
pages, 1987. (Casebook)

Trial and Appellate Advocacy—Cont'd

SONSTENG, HAYDOCK AND BOYD'S THE TRIALBOOK: A TOTAL SYSTEM FOR PREPARATION AND PRESENTATION OF A CASE, 404 pages, 1984. Softcover. (Coursebook)

WHARTON, HAYDOCK AND SONSTENG'S CALIFORNIA CIVIL TRIALBOOK, Law School and CLE Edition. 148 pages, 1990. Softcover. (Text)

Trusts and Estates

ATKINSON'S HORNBOOK ON WILLS, Second Edition, 975 pages, 1953. (Text)

AVERILL'S UNIFORM PROBATE CODE IN A NUTSHELL, Second Edition, 454 pages, 1987. Softcover. (Text)

BOGERT'S HORNBOOK ON TRUSTS, Sixth Edition, Student Edition, 794 pages, 1987. (Text)

CLARK, LUSKY AND MURPHY'S CASES AND MATERIALS ON GRATUITOUS TRANSFERS, Third Edition, 970 pages, 1985. (Casebook)

DODGE'S WILLS, TRUSTS AND ESTATE PLANNING–LAW AND TAXATION, CASES AND MATERIALS, 665 pages, 1988. (Casebook)

McGOVERN, KURTZ AND REIN'S HORNBOOK ON WILLS, TRUSTS AND ESTATES–INCLUDING TAXATION AND FUTURE INTERESTS, 996 pages, 1988. (Text)

MENNELL'S WILLS AND TRUSTS IN A NUTSHELL, 392 pages, 1979. Softcover. (Text)

SIMES' HORNBOOK ON FUTURE INTERESTS, Second Edition, 355 pages, 1966. (Text)

TURANO AND RADIGAN'S HORNBOOK ON NEW YORK ESTATE ADMINISTRATION, 676 pages, 1986 with 1991 pocket part. (Text)

UNIFORM PROBATE CODE, OFFICIAL TEXT WITH COMMENTS. 863 pages, 1991. Softcover.

WAGGONER'S FUTURE INTERESTS IN A NUTSHELL, 361 pages, 1981. Softcover. (Text)

Water Law—see also Energy and Natural Resources Law, Environmental Law

GETCHES' WATER LAW IN A NUTSHELL, Second Edition, 459 pages, 1990. Softcover. (Text)

SAX, ABRAMS AND THOMPSON'S LEGAL CONTROL OF WATER RESOURCES: CASES AND MATERIALS, Second Edition, 987 pages, 1991. Teacher's Manual available. (Casebook)

TRELEASE AND GOULD'S CASES AND MATERIALS ON WATER LAW, Fourth Edition, 816 pages, 1986. (Casebook)

Wills—see Trusts and Estates

Workers' Compensation

HOOD, HARDY AND LEWIS' WORKERS' COMPENSATION AND EMPLOYEE PROTECTION LAWS IN A NUTSHELL, Second Edition, 361 pages, 1990. Softcover. (Text)

LITTLE, EATON AND SMITH'S CASES AND MATERIALS ON WORKERS' COMPENSATION, 537 pages, 1992. Teacher's Manual available. (Casebook)

WEST'S LAW SCHOOL
ADVISORY BOARD

*

[xix]

8/20/96   2-16, 37-53
8/22/96   181-87, 222-27
8/24/96   2-36
8/27/96   62-65, 86-96, 161-71
9/3/96   153-59
9/5/96   143-44

LEGAL WRITIN

A SYSTEMATIC

APPROACH

Second Edition

By

Diana V. Pratt

Director, Legal Research and Writing Program
Wayne State University Law School

AMERICAN CASEBOOK SERIES®

WEST PUBLISHING CO.

ST. PAUL, MINN., 1993

COPYRIGHT © 1989, 1990 WEST PUBLISHING CO.
COPYRIGHT © 1993 By WEST PUBLISHING CO.
          610 Opperman Drive
          P.O. Box 64526
          St. Paul, MN 55164–0526
          1–800–328–9352

Library of Congress Cataloging-in-Publication Data
Pratt, Diana Volkmann.
    Legal Writing : a systematic approach / by Diana V. Pratt. — 2nd ed.
        p.   cm. — (American casebook series)
    Includes index.
    ISBN **0–314–01843–3**
    1. Legal composition. I. Title. II. Series.
    KF250P73   1993
    808'.06634—dc20   93–9682
                                                                    CIP

ISBN 0–314–01843–3

    Pratt–Legal Writing 2d Ed. ACB

*À notre homme à Niger,
son père, sa grandmère, et les
volontaires du Corps de la Paix.*

*

Preface

The book is designed as a basic legal writing text for first year law students. It provides a systematic approach to learning legal analysis, organization and writing. Each step in the process is introduced separately so that students can concentrate on mastering each skill before attacking another one. Although the book was developed for a four credit course taught by full time lawyers, the process approach also works well in courses with a varying numbers of credits and styles of instruction.

The books begins with an introductory section that provides students with background information on the sources of the law, the structure of the court system, and a description of a typical civil case at the trial level. The purpose of this section is to give students a rudimentary understanding of the legal system and some basic vocabulary. It introduces statutory and case law, explains the relationship between trial and appellate courts, and provides enough information about trial court procedure so that students can understand the origins of the appellate cases they read. This section also introduces the fundamental parts of a case: issues, rules, holdings, reasoning, and policy, and provides several simple cases for practice. The section ends with the dissection of a statute. These chapters can be used as background for the legal research and writing course or as part of an orientation program.

The next section introduces legal analysis with an arson hypothetical. The analysis and the exercises in Chapter six are appropriate either for class discussion or as the basis for legal writing assignments.

The book launches into legal writing in earnest with a section devoted to writing simple office memoranda. The process provides methods for organizing the analysis and an approach to turning an outline into an office memo. The section also includes chapters on drafting questions presented, statements of facts, and on the writing process itself.

Writing a complicated office memorandum involves using the basic skills introduced in earlier sections and some additional ones. The next section explains how to integrate research into the process of creating a memo. It also provides strategies for organizing complex analysis. The final chapter in the section discusses writing in plain English by explaining some possible origins of legalese, and how to write like a lawyer while avoiding the pitfalls of legalese.

Persuasive writing is introduced in the next section at the trial court level. The first chapter introduces the trial judge as the audience. The following chapter explains the differences and similarities between objective and persuasive writing.

The section on appellate advocacy provides a discussion of the practical and theoretical aspects of writing an appellate brief with numerous examples. It introduces the appellate court and the standard of review the court will apply to appellate cases. It discusses formulating a theory of the case and incorporating that theory into the issues. The following chapter describes the basic components of an appellate brief and the function of each one. The section also includes a chapter on crafting a statement of facts and one on developing the argument.

The final section of the text is included for those legal writing programs that include oral argument as a finale.

DIANA PRATT

March, 1993

Acknowledgments

This book was only possible because of the help of my colleagues and students. I would like particularly to recognize the assistance of the legal writing faculty at Wayne Law School for their comments, suggestions, sample memos and their willingness to experiment with the book in the classroom: Marilyn Finkelman, Sandra Gross, Barbara Blumenfeld, Karen Scavone, Mary Margaret Bolda, and Cynthia Sherburn. Three former colleagues made important contributions to the effort. Melanie LaFave and Barbara Patek contributed advocacy materials. Seymour Nayer created the Dog Bite Problem. Brian Shannon and Melanie LaFave contributed the *Palmer v. Fuqua* Statements of Facts. Beverly Niemann made a major contribution to the preparation of the manuscript. Finally, Wayne students have used this book and made countless suggestions.

*

Summary of Contents

APPENDICES

Table of Contents

SECTION I. INTRODUCTION TO THE LAW

SECTION II. LEGAL ANALYSIS

SECTION III. THE BASIC OFFICE MEMORANDUM

SECTION VII. ORAL ADVOCACY

APPENDICES

LEGAL WRITING: A SYSTEMATIC APPROACH

Second Edition

*

Section I

INTRODUCTION TO THE LAW

The five chapters in this section form a brief introduction to the American legal system: the sources of the law, the structure of the court system, the time course of a typical civil case, and general information that will help you understand the cases and statutes you will be reading at the beginning of your law school career. While the discussion is by no means comprehensive, it is designed to provide context and some terminology for the legal analysis and legal writing that follow.

Chapter 1

SOURCES OF THE LAW

American Law comes from two primary sources, legislative law and judge made law. **Legislative law** is the collection of rules written explicitly to govern behavior within the society. These rules apply to society as a whole. The early colonial legislatures created the first American legislative law. A Massachusetts colonial ordinance from 1641–47, for example, divided up ownership of the Atlantic shoreline and shallow waters. The Massachusetts Supreme Judicial Court used this ordinance as the basis for a 1974 decision. *Opinion of the Justices,* 365 Mass. 681, 313 N.E.2d 561 (1974). Legislative law includes constitutions, statutes, and administrative regulations. These are arranged in a hierarchy of importance, specificity, and life span. All three categories of legislative law exist both at the federal and state levels.

The United States **Constitution** is the source of our federal system of government and the basic policy that prescribes the rights of individuals and the relationship between the states and the federal government. The Constitution has been in existence for about two hundred years. The system and much of the policy are as valid today as they were two hundred years ago. The document was designed to set the parameters of government, but not to deal with the daily operation of government. The Constitution is the most important of the three types of legislative law and the one with the longest life span. It has the least specificity and is the hardest to amend. Many of the framers were direct descendants of settlers who had emigrated from other countries to escape persecution for religious or political views. By requiring more than a simple majority for amendments to the Constitution, they intended to protect groups holding beliefs not shared by the majority. A three quarters majority of the state legislatures must approve an amendment to the U.S. Constitution. The Equal Rights Amendment, which would have given women rights equal with those of men, failed to muster the requisite majority. By making the Constitution so difficult to amend, the framers wanted to insure that the document would only be changed when necessary to reflect basic policy changes in the society. Because of its general nature, the Constitution is regularly subject to interpretation by the courts.

Statutes have more specificity than the Constitution. Congress enacts statutes to deal with particular large scale problems. A statute requires a simple majority of each house of Congress to become law with presidential approval and a two thirds majority of each house to become law after a presidential veto. Federal statutes identify major problems in society and structure the solutions to the problems. In the Civil Rights Act of 1964, 42 U.S.C. 1981 et seq., Congress attacked the problem of discrimination. Title VII of that statute deals specifically with discrimination in employment. While the Constitution requires that all men are to be treated equally under the law, Title VII prevents discrimination in the work place. The statute addresses the specific problem in order to insure the rights granted by the Constitution. A statute is much easier to amend than the Constitution; the same procedure used to enact a statute is used to amend it. Statutes more closely reflect policy changes in society. The life span of a statute is shorter than that of the Constitution.

The most specific type of legislative law is the administrative **regulation.** Regulations deal with the pragmatic details of implementing the policy adopted in a statute. While Title VII of the Civil Rights Act of 1964 prohibited discrimination in the terms or conditions of employment, the administrative regulations define, for example, sexual harassment and make it a condition of employment. 29 C.F.R. 1604.11 (1987). Regulations are **promulgated** by administrative agencies of the government. These agencies administer the statutes. They draft the regulations to help the public understand how the statute will work in practice. Usually the administrative agency has expertise in the particular field. While senators and congressmen need to be generalists able to deal with a myriad of problems, the agency personnel have the expertise to turn the general approach into a pragmatic solution. Regulations are even easier to change than statutes. This permits agency officials to amend rules to take advantage of developing technology and to address problems that were not anticipated in earlier versions of the regulations. Like constitutions, statutes, and regulations are subject to judicial interpretation.

The hierarchy of legislative law is readily apparent in the tax area. The Constitution authorizes Congress to raise revenue by taxation.[1] The government must have this power in order to finance its operations. This basic system of government finance has existed for two centuries. Congress, sensing public dissatisfaction with the existing taxation method, enacted the Tax Reform Act of 1986. The purpose of the statute was to simplify the law and spread the tax burden more equitably. This method of taxation will remain in existence until Congress amends or replaces the statute. While the statute set the corporate and personal income tax rates, the Internal Revenue Service promulgated regulations in order to put the tax reforms into practice. These IRS regulations will probably change several times over the life

1. U.S. Const. art. I, sec. 8.

of the statute as the administrative agency searches for the best way to implement the congressional intent.

States also have a hierarchy of legislative law that parallels that in the federal system. State constitutions are drafted to set the state policy. They, like the federal Constitution, are designed to have a long life span and are difficult to amend. State statutes address specific problems facing state legislators. State legislators, like their federal counterparts, do not have the expertise necessary to implement their policies at the pragmatic level. They rely on experts in state administrative agencies. These officials promulgate regulations at the state level to deal with specific applications of state statutes.

Legislative law explains what is required, permitted, or prohibited behavior in advance of action. This permits the public to predict the outcome of different types of behavior. This predictability allows society to run smoothly most of the time. Changes in legislative law occur as express acts by the appropriate legislative or administrative body. Legislative law is directed at the public at large and it is designed to be generally applicable. It does not anticipate or accommodate specific problems or individual situations.

The second source of our law is judge made law, called **common law or case law.** The common law system arrived in this country with the first settlers. They brought with them the legal system used in England. While the first cases relied on English precedent, very quickly a body of case law developed in the Colonies. The English common law provided the necessary stability to the colonial system. It was also flexible enough to adapt to different conditions in the New World. Although the American common law system has changed considerably since the seventeenth century, many of the basic legal rules and most of the legal vocabulary betray their English antecedents. The common law is composed of the decisions of individual cases. In each, the court must resolve the specific dispute with its individual facts. To decide a pending case, the court uses earlier cases involving the same or similar legal questions and facts as **precedent** (press-i-dent). The court takes the decision from a precedent case, and extracts a general rule. The court then uses this general rule to decide the pending case. The closer the precedent case is to the pending case in its questions and its facts, the better the precedent it becomes. The following example illustrates the way precedent works.

Pending Case

The purchasers of a house sued the sellers to recover the cost of exterminating termites and to repair the termite damage to the house. The sellers knew of the termites in the house, but did not disclose the problem to the purchasers. The purchasers did not ask if the house had termites. The question before the court was whether the sellers had a duty to disclose the presence of termites.

Precedent Case

The case involved the sale of a farmhouse infested with termites. In this case both the seller and his real estate agent knew there were termites in the house. The purchasers had no contact with the seller, but they did ask the real estate agent if the house had termites, and he replied that it did not and that the house was structurally sound. The court held that the vendor and his agent had an affirmative duty to disclose a termite infestation.[2]

The Court's Application of the Precedent to the Pending Case

Even though the purchasers did not ask if the house had termites, the court held that the sellers had a duty to disclose the termite problem.[3]

The common law provides the consistency necessary for ordinary functioning of society. Like legislative law, it permits the public to anticipate the outcome of different types of behavior. To the extent that a court has decided the same or a similar case, a lawyer can use this precedent to advise a client about the probable outcome of a case or the legality of proposed action. Based on the termite case, a lawyer can advise a client to disclose the presence of termites to a prospective purchaser and, by analogy, the presence of a rotten foundation.

The common law also accommodates change. As a case arises that is slightly different from the existing precedent, the court modifies the rule as necessary to decide the pending case. The termite example above demonstrates how the law might change. The facts of the two cases are different in two ways. The precedent case involved a real estate agent and not a seller who affirmatively misled the buyers. The pending case involved not an affirmative statement, but silence, and the buyers had direct contact with the sellers and not with an agent. Based on the differences, the sellers' lawyer probably argued that while his clients may have had an obligation to answer truthfully questions posed by the purchasers, there was no affirmative duty to volunteer the information. Opposing counsel probably argued that the presence of termites is material to the condition of the building, and that under the existing precedent, the sellers must disclose the information. While some courts might have accepted the argument raised by the sellers' attorney, the Pennsylvania court did not do so.

As you can see from this example, the development of the law is gradual. As the facts diverge from those in existing precedent, the court will either expand the rule to include the new facts or read the rule narrowly and reject its application. The lawyer's role is to argue the similarities and distinctions to the court and to propose analogies to other precedent. As an attorney, you will play a part in the development of the law.

---

2. *Glanski v. Ervine*, 269 Pa. Super. 182, 409 A.2d 425 (1979).

3. *Quashnock v. Frost*, 299 Pa. Super. 9, 445 A.2d 121 (1982).

Like legislative law, the common law system exists both at the federal and the state levels. While all common law decisions are precedent for later cases on the same or a similar issue, some decisions are better precedent than others. Decisions from the same state carry more weight than those from other states. Similarly, some decisions in the federal system are more persuasive than others. The relative weight given to different cases is discussed in Chapter 4. There is also a hierarchy of courts within each system; the higher the court the more weight that is given to its decisions. The next chapter explains this hierarchy of courts both in the federal system and in a sample state system.

The major difference between legislative law and case law lies in their focus. Legislative law is focused at the public in general. Although the representative or administrative body that drafted the rules may have had specific problems in mind while creating the solutions, the rules rarely apply to one individual or even one particular business. The general rules are then applied to a variety of specific situations. The common law, on the other hand, has its origins in the specific facts of the case. The court only decides the dispute between these parties. A later court will use that specific decision as the basis for a more general rule that can be applied to a later case. Where legislative law starts out with a potentially broad application, case law begins with a narrow application, is converted into a broader rule, then applied again to a specific fact situation.

The following exercises illustrate the development of legislative and common law.

Exercise 1A. Legislative Law

The town council in Pensacola Beach, Florida has asked for your help in drafting a local ordinance. Pensacola Beach is located in the western part of the State along the Gulf coast. It is a major tourist haven, particularly in the winter and spring. In addition to the northerners trying to find warmth and sunlight, bird lovers and fishermen are particularly attracted to the area. A number of species of ducks and other colorful birds winter along the Gulf coast. The fishing is excellent. Recently, the accumulation of plastic and styrofoam trash has become a problem. Not only is it unsightly, but it is not biodegradable. The fish and waterfowl are also adversely affected. The small pieces of styrofoam that are used in packaging get caught in their throats. They get tangled in the plastic rings that hold six packs together. The council would like to get rid of the problem for the benefit of the tourists, but not interfere with the tourist industry.

As you draft the local ordinance consider the following information:

a. The Pensacola solid waste department estimates that ninety percent of the trash found adjacent to the shoreline and the salt marshes is packaging for food, drink, and beach related activities, such as fishing, sunbathing, and picnicking.

b. One of the successful local businesses is a pottery shop. The potter works at his wheel in the front window of the shop and sells the pots. He packs the ceramics in styrofoam chips to protect them. Last month the potter purchased a three year supply of packing chips.

c. The local liquor stores sell ice in plastic bags to tourists who want to picnic in their boats or on the beach.

d. The fast food outlets all use plastic cutlery and styrofoam containers for the food and drinks they sell to tourists.

e. The hardware store sells styrofoam coolers.

f. The supermarket packages its meat, vegetables, and fruit on styrofoam trays covered in plastic wrap. The customers like to see what they are buying. Milk, orange juice, and soft drinks are sold in plastic containers.

Exercise 1B. Common Law

Mallory v. Harry's Bar

John Mallory was killed while he was driving home from a baseball game in August 1986. He was driving a silver gray 1985 Chrysler Imperial. Mallory was headed east on Longfield Drive through the intersection with Meadows Boulevard when a green Dodge pickup truck ran the red light on Meadows and hit the Chrysler on the driver's side. Mallory died instantly. Rory McAlpine was the driver of the pickup truck. An eyewitness estimated that McAlpine was driving 45 mph at the time of impact.

McAlpine had just left Harry's Bar when the collision occurred. He had been watching the Detroit Tigers play the Boston Red Sox on the big screen TV in the bar. According to other customers in the bar, Rory was already visibly inebriated when he entered Harry's that night. The bartender served him five boiler makers in the hour and a half he was in the bar.

The court decided that Harry's Bar was liable to Mallory's widow for his wrongful death. Harry's employee, the bartender, had a responsibility not to serve alcohol to a visibly intoxicated person. By serving five drinks over the course of one and a half hours to an intoxicated person, the bartender failed to meet his responsibility. While the bartender was not responsible for McAlpine's initial intoxication, he should not have served more alcohol to an intoxicated person. Harry's Bar is responsible under the doctrine of respondeat superior for the actions of its employee, the bartender. Consequently, Mrs. Mallory can collect damages from the bar. *employer must accept responsibility for agent*

Use this case as precedent to decide the following cases:

1. Art Melchior was driving home from Joe's Bar when he ran a stoplight and hit Emily Evans' car. Emily was seriously injured. Joe, who was tending bar that evening, remembered that Art was high after he had had a couple of drinks in an hour. Joe served him one more as

Art was a good customer. Is Joe's Bar liable to Emily Evans for the injuries caused by Art Melchior?

2. Milt Davis is a traveling salesman. He was staying at the Sleepytime Inn on a recent trip. He went to the bar at the Inn for a drink before dinner. He had two between 5 and 6 p.m. according to Evelyn Saunders, the waitress. He then left to drive down the road for dinner. On route he collided with a station wagon filled with children on the way home from a birthday party. All the passengers in the car suffered minor injuries; none was hurt seriously. Is Sleepytime Inn liable to the passengers of the car for the injuries caused by Milt Davis?

3. Mort Adams is the pitcher and captain of the Peppery Pizza softball team. The team plays every Monday and Thursday during the summer. After the games, the team goes to a local beer garden and shares a couple of pitchers of beer. One Monday evening, Mort went up to the counter and bought the first round, two pitchers of beer for 11 players. Al bought the next round and Joe the final round. Mort drank heavily from each round, while the rest of the team shared the remainder. After the second round, he showed signs of intoxication. Mort ran a stop sign on the way home from the beer garden and collided with a pick-up truck. The passenger was hospitalized with a broken hip. Cheryl, who was serving beer at the counter that night, remembers the team; they come in twice a week during the summer and occasionally during the off season. Mort was not intoxicated when he bought the first round. Neither Al nor Joe showed any signs of intoxication. Is the beer garden liable for the injuries Mort caused the passenger of the pick-up truck?

4. Janice Harmon gave a New Year's Eve party. There were about 50 guests at various points during the evening. She had a keg of beer and gallons of jug wine as well as cheese, pretzels, chips, and dip. One of the guests caused an accident while driving home. His car clipped the back left side of another vehicle. The passenger sitting on that side was injured. His blood alcohol level was 0.15%, which, according to a sheriff's deputy, indicated he was intoxicated. Is Janice liable for the injuries her guest caused the other motorist?

5. Martha and Harold Mitchell invited five couples for cocktails and dinner. Harold did the cooking and Martha served as bartender. Each of the guests had at least two drinks before dinner. Harold had prepared five courses for dinner, and Martha served a different wine with each course ending with dessert and champagne. Although everyone was inebriated by that time, Martha poured brandy for all to cap off the evening. One of the guests ran into a police car on the way home and injured an officer. Is Martha Mitchell liable for the injuries her guest caused the police officer?

Chapter 2

THE COURT SYSTEM

In both the federal and state court systems, there is a parallel pyramid of courts. A lawyer chooses the state or federal system according to the subject matter of the dispute. Federal and state courts have **jurisdiction** or authority over different types of cases. The trial courts form the base of the pyramid. Intermediate level appellate courts are in the middle with the highest level appellate court at the apex. The following brief introduction to the court systems is designed to show the hierarchy within which the case method operates.

THE FEDERAL COURT SYSTEM

The federal trial courts are called **district** courts. There are federal district courts in every state and the District of Columbia. Some states are large enough and have so much business that there are several districts. They are labelled with geographical terms, eastern, western, central, northern and/or southern districts. California, for example, is divided into northern, central, eastern, and southern districts. For geographical reasons, districts are sometimes further subdivided by **division.** Michigan, for example, has northern and southern divisions of its eastern and western districts.

The federal district courts have jurisdiction over two basic types of cases, cases involving **federal questions** and **diversity** cases. Federal questions arise primarily from federal statutes. Some federal statutes require that any dispute arising under its aegis be brought in the federal court system. These are cases where the federal courts have **exclusive jurisdiction** over the dispute. Other federal statutes allow the litigants to raise the issues in either the federal or the state system. Where there is a choice, attorneys choose a court for strategy reasons. The federal and state courts have **concurrent jurisdiction** over those cases.

Federal courts also have jurisdiction over diversity cases. These cases arise from disputes between residents of two different states. The notion behind diversity jurisdiction is that a neutral forum is a better place to decide the dispute than either of the two state court systems.

9

Diversity cases also require that the amount in controversy between the parties be more than $50,000; that is, at least $50,000.01.

Federal court procedure is governed by the Federal Rules of Civil Procedure. The admissibility of evidence in the federal courts is governed by the Federal Rules of Evidence. Although the federal procedural rules apply to cases in federal court, the judge will apply state substantive law in a diversity action or federal law in a case involving a federal question.

The trial court has two basic functions. First, this is the forum where the litigants present the facts involved in the dispute. The attorneys present the facts with live witnesses, records, and exhibits. The judge or jury listens to the evidence and **finds the facts;** that is, it determines what actually happened. You will learn about the difference between judge and jury trials in the next chapter. The fact finders not only hear the witnesses testify, but they also are able to watch the witnesses to see if they look and sound believable. Second, the fact finders apply the appropriate law to the facts to resolve the dispute.

As you will see in the next chapter, there are many places in the time course of a lawsuit where appeals may arise. Appeals from the federal District Courts are to the **United States Courts of Appeals** (28 U.S.C. sec. 1291). The nation is divided into eleven areas or circuits. The First Circuit has its headquarters in Boston, the Second Circuit is located in New York, the Ninth Circuit is in San Francisco and so forth. Two additional federal intermediate appellate courts are located in Washington, D.C., the United States Court of Appeals for the Federal Circuit and the United States Court of Appeals for the District of Columbia.

Any litigant dissatisfied by the outcome in the federal district court may appeal to the appropriate federal court of appeals. The first appeal is an **appeal of right.** Every litigant has the right to one appeal. The function of the intermediate level appellate court is to correct mistakes made in the trial court. Most disputes are resolved at the trial court level either because the litigants dismiss the case, they settle the case, or they do not wish to appeal the result from the trial court. Only a small percentage of all cases filed in the federal district courts are appealed.

Each federal circuit has a dozen or more judges. Unlike the district courts, where only one judge presides at each trial, the appellate court judges sit in panels of three to hear appeals. Only on rare occasions do all of the judges from one circuit meet to consider an appeal. When they do meet **"en banc"**, it is to resolve a potential conflict between decisions of different three judge panels. This will occur when the same issue is before two or more panels. The goal is to formulate one rule that can be applied in each of the cases. A consistent result fosters the predictability necessary to an efficient legal system.

The federal courts of appeals decide the appeal based on the **record below.** This record can include the pleadings filed in the trial court, a transcript of the trial or hearing, and exhibits used at the trial. Unlike the trial judge, the appellate judges do not listen to or see the witnesses. The paper record only contains the witness's words, not his tone of voice, his facial expression, or his nervous mannerisms. Because the fact finder was in a better position to assess the witness's credibility, the appellate court will usually defer to the judge or jury in deciding what the facts in the dispute actually were. There is, however, no such deference on matters of law; the appellate courts have as much access to the law as do the trial courts.

The intermediate level appellate courts review the decisions of trial level courts primarily to see if the trial court made a mistake and applied the wrong legal rule to the facts or misapplied the appropriate law. Only when the fact finder made an obvious mistake will the appellate court intervene to correct a factual error. Almost all legal errors that escaped the notice of the trial court will be corrected at the intermediate appellate court level. For litigants who are dissatisfied with the court of appeals' decision, there is normally no further appeal of right. These litigants may ask for **Certiorari** or leave to appeal from the United States Supreme Court.

The Supreme Court is the court of last resort. The Court has nine **justices.** Where the lower level courts are staffed by **judges,** the highest court in both the federal and state systems is composed of justices. A quorum of the Court is six justices. The justices vote on each application for Certiorari. At least four members of the Court must vote to grant Certiorari. Most of the 4000–5000 applications filed each year are denied. The Court has one major and two minor functions. Its major role is to oversee the gradual development of the law in important areas. This includes interpreting the United States Constitution.

The Court also has a minor error correction function. That is, if legal errors slip through the system from the district court and by the court of appeals or occasionally from the state systems, the Supreme Court is there to prevent a severe miscarriage of justice. These claims of error most often come from criminal defendants, who assert that states have deprived them of federally guaranteed rights. The state courts have jurisdiction of these cases because the defendant is charged with committing a crime under state law. In the course of the proceedings in the state court system, however, the defendants claim a violation of their individual federal rights. For this reason, these cases come from the highest level courts of the states to the United States Supreme Court. The most publicized of these cases are the death penalty cases.

The Supreme Court also has **original jurisdiction** over a few cases. Original jurisdiction means that the Supreme Court sits as a trial court in these cases. Original jurisdiction exists when the case is between two or more states. 28 U.S.C. sec. 1251. California and Arizona have been to the United States Supreme Court several times in their continuing dispute over the water in the Colorado River. When a dispute between states requires extensive fact finding, as the water law cases do, the Supreme Court appoints a master to sift through the facts and make a recommendation to the Court.

In addition to the regular federal courts, there are some specialty courts with jurisdiction over particular cases. The United States Claims Court has **exclusive jurisdiction** over cases involving claims against the United States government. There are also Bankruptcy Courts, an International Court of Trade, and a Tax Court.

All the decisions of the United States Supreme Court and most decisions from the courts of appeals are published. Some of the trial court opinions from the federal district courts are also published. These cases are all precedent for later cases.

A TYPICAL STATE COURT SYSTEM

All states have similar pyramid-shaped court systems, although there is some variation in the jurisdictional requirements and the naming system. In New York, for example, the court of last resort is called the Court of Appeals and the trial court of general jurisdiction is the supreme court. The Michigan Court structure has been chosen as an illustration of a state court system, because it is typical of many other jurisdictions. The state court systems usually have even more levels of court than the federal system, because they must deal with every case from the parking ticket to multi-million dollar cases between corporate giants. The federal system does not need to address the lower end of the scale.

Michigan has two levels of trial court. The lowest is the **district court.** Each county has one or more district courts with jurisdiction over minor criminal and civil cases. The district court even has a **small claims division** for cases involving less than $1750. Parties take their minor cases to the small claims division "in pro per"; that is, by themselves. These cases tend to involve landlord-tenant controversies over damage deposits, minor home repair contracts, and the like. If either party hires a lawyer to represent him, the case automatically leaves the small claims division and moves into district court. The small claims division provides an inexpensive way for parties to resolve minor disputes. Attorney fees would quickly consume the money recovered, so it makes sense to give the parties this alternative. The legal rules involved in small claims cases are straightforward and easily within the grasp of lay people.

There is a parallel division of the district court to handle minor traffic matters. Although these were once criminal cases, they are now called **civil infractions.** The defendant no longer pleads guilty or not guilty, but pleads responsible or not responsible. Those who plead responsible can mail in the ticket with the appropriate fine and not appear in court. Those who plead not responsible can appear and explain their side of the case to a hearing officer. As with the small claims division, a party appears in pro per in traffic court.

The district courts are courts of **limited jurisdiction.** They serve as the trial level courts for minor civil and criminal cases: civil cases with up to $10,000 in controversy, and criminal cases when the defendant is charged with a **misdemeanor.** Misdemeanors include shoplifting, impaired driving, accosting and soliciting, and similar offenses.

The district courts also have jurisdiction over the preliminary examinations in **felony** cases, those involving more serious criminal offenses. A **preliminary examination** is an initial hearing held within a few days or weeks of the time a defendant is arrested for a felony. The prosecutor must show that there is **probable cause** to believe that a crime was committed and that the defendant committed the crime. If the prosecutor fails to make this showing, the case is dismissed. If the prosecutor establishes that there is reason to believe a crime was committed and that the defendant was the perpetrator, the defendant is **bound over** to circuit court. The district court judge makes this preliminary decision in felony cases.

There is one other limit on the authority of the district court judge. The district courts can take civil cases where the plaintiff is asking for money. The district courts do not, however, have the power to award other kinds of relief except in unusual circumstances. The reason for this jurisdictional division is historical. Although most states have explicitly abolished the distinction between **law** and **equity,** remnants of the distinction persist and it is worth digressing briefly to explain the terms.

The American courts were based on the English court system. The first English courts were the law courts. In the law courts the parties asked for either the property or its financial equivalent to be returned. Each type of case or **"cause of action"** had specific requirements. For the plaintiff to recover, he had to meet all the technical requirements. If the plaintiff failed in even a minor way, the court would dismiss the case. This did not always produce a fair and just result. Sometimes the plaintiff wanted a different kind of **relief.** Perhaps, for example, he wanted **specific performance,** that the defendant carry out the conditions of a contract. He might also want **injunctive relief,** an order that the defendant either do something or refrain from doing something. The legal causes of action did not provide for either specific performance or injunctive relief. At first when a rich and powerful plaintiff could not get relief in a law court, he asked the king to do what was fair or equitable under the circumstances. Over time the king appointed a chancellor to handle these cases. By the late fourteenth century, a new system of courts had evolved, the **courts of chancery.** Charles Dickens' *Bleak House* is a nineteenth century criticism of these courts. Until quite recently in England, the law courts and the equity courts were distinct systems. At the time the system arrived on the American continent, law and equity were still separate.

Law and equity developed procedural differences and distinct vocabulary, some of which still persist. Parties have a right to a jury trial in a law case, but no such right in an equity case. There the judge fulfills both functions, finding the facts and applying the law. One of the most common types of equity cases is the divorce case. The vocabulary from the two systems is also different. In a **law** case, a **plaintiff** sues a **defendant** by filing a **complaint.** The parties may file **motions** at various times in the proceedings. The plaintiff is seeking money damages. On appeal, the appealing party is called an **appellant.** The opponent is the **appellee.** In **equity** cases, however, a **petitioner** files a **petition** to start the case. The opponent is called a **respondent.** The petitioner may be looking for **specific performance,** an **injunction,** or a **divorce.** He does not have the right to a jury trial. Under current American law, both sets of vocabulary exist, but the meanings no longer consistently conform to the law and equity distinction.

In Michigan, the distinction between law and equity has been abolished. Plaintiffs now sue defendants by filing complaints. They both file motions and on appeal, they are called appellants and appellees. But the parties only have a right to a jury trial in cases that would have been law cases and not in cases that would have been equity cases. If the plaintiff, for example, is seeking an injunction or a divorce, there is no right to a jury trial. The district courts do not have **equity jurisdiction.** The only time a district court judge can hear an equity case is when the case involves primarily law claims with a minor equity claim. Under those circumstances, the district court may hear the equity part of the case. The rule is quite recent and is designed to make the system more efficient. The parties are no longer required to go to district court for part of their case and another court for the rest of their case.

The basic equity jurisdiction, however, lies with the other level of trial court, the **circuit court.** This is the court that considers whether an injunction or temporary restraining order is proper, and the court that handles divorce cases. The circuit court also has jurisdiction over all civil cases with more than $10,000 in controversy and over all felony criminal cases. For this reason, the circuit courts are called courts of **general jurisdiction.** The circuit courts also have **appellate jurisdiction** of cases tried in the district court. As in the federal system, the parties have a right to one appeal. The circuit court corrects errors of law made by district court judges. The record on appeal includes the pleadings and a transcript of any trial or hearing. The transcript is typed from a tape recording made of all proceedings at the district court level. The circuit court also hears appeals from decisions of some administrative agencies. The trend is away from this process. The circuit court judges are good trial judges, but they hear appeals so rarely, they are not as proficient in this quite different role. For this reason, most appeals from administrative agency decisions are now to the intermediate level appellate court.

The **Michigan Court of Appeals** resembles the federal intermediate level appellate courts. In both systems, the courts' major role is to correct the legal errors made in the trial courts. Both courts sit in three judge panels to consider the appeal cases. The Michigan Court of Appeals judges, however, do not sit "en banc" as the federal circuit court of appeals judges sometimes do. This court, like its federal counterpart, does not hear testimony, but considers the evidence from the paper record. It gives deference on the facts to the trier of fact, who was present at the trial and saw all the indicia of credibility. The record of the trial or hearing in circuit court comes from the court reporter's stenographic notes. These notes yield a verbatim transcript that should not contain gaps where the witness's words were unintelligible or where the court clerk changed the tape. With the advent of videotaping, intermediate appellate courts may take a more active role in reviewing facts found in the lower courts. Some appellate courts are now reviewing videotapes of trial proceedings. Through this medium, appellate court judges are in the same position as trial court judges to evaluate the credibility of witnesses and to assess possible judicial misconduct.

The court of last resort in the Michigan system is the **Michigan Supreme Court.** There are seven justices on the supreme court bench. There are no appeals of right to this court, only appeals by leave. The court grants leave sparingly and only in cases of importance to the law of the state. When different panels of the court of appeals reach conflicting results on the same issue and the question is a significant one, the highest court will grant leave to consider the issue.

Michigan, like the federal system, has some specialty courts. There is a **Court of Claims,** where parties can sue the state for money. There are **probate courts** in all counties that handle civil commitments and the probate of decedents' estates. The **juvenile court** is a division of the probate court. The juvenile court has jurisdiction over both juvenile delinquents and cases involving child abuse and neglect. It both prosecutes and protects children.

The decisions of the Michigan Supreme Court and the significant decisions of the Michigan Court of Appeals are published. The decisions of the trial courts are not published. As a practical matter, only the published appellate decisions are available as precedent for later cases.

COMPARATIVE STRUCTURES OF FEDERAL AND STATE COURT SYSTEMS

<u>Federal Court System</u>

UNITED STATES SUPREME COURT
(most cases are appeals on a Writ of Certiorari)

|

UNITED STATES CIRCUIT COURTS OF APPEALS
(Eleven Regional, the D.C. and Federal Circuits)
(Appeal of right from the District Courts)

|

UNITED STATES DISTRICT COURTS
(Trial courts located in each state and divided by district and division.
They hear federal question and diversity cases.)

<u>Typical State System</u>

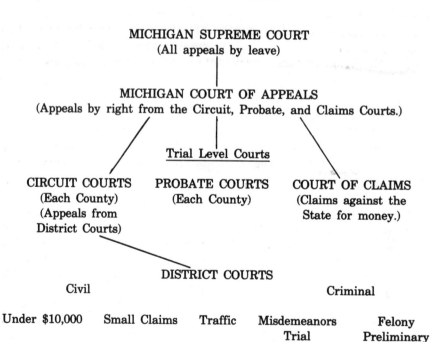

MICHIGAN SUPREME COURT
(All appeals by leave)

MICHIGAN COURT OF APPEALS
(Appeals by right from the Circuit, Probate, and Claims Courts.)

Trial Level Courts

CIRCUIT COURTS   PROBATE COURTS   COURT OF CLAIMS
(Each County)   (Each County)   (Claims against the
(Appeals from   State for money.)
District Courts)

DISTRICT COURTS
Civil   Criminal

Under $10,000   Small Claims   Traffic   Misdemeanors   Felony
                                              Trial   Preliminary
                                                               Examinations

[E7985]

Chapter 3

TIME COURSE OF A TYPICAL
CIVIL CASE

The purpose of this chapter is to introduce you to what happens in a typical civil case at the trial court level. Most of the cases you will read are appellate level decisions, but each of them started in a trial court. As you will discover there are many different points in the trial court proceeding where one or more parties can initiate an appeal. The reason for the appeal and the point at which it arose are often important to understanding the appellate court decision. As you read appellate cases, put them in their procedural context. Criminal cases follow a parallel procedure, which is governed by the Federal Rules of Criminal Procedure. The following discussion is only an overview of civil procedure and an introduction to some of the terminology. This discussion is based on the Federal Rules of Civil Procedure, the rules used in the federal courts. Each state also has a set of rules used in its courts. They are similar to the federal rules, but the terminology and the specific details may be different. As an attorney you will follow the court rules that are applicable to each case.

An attorney practicing at the trial court level works toward three goals at once: to settle the dispute, to prepare for the trial if there is no settlement, and to preserve the issues for an appeal in the event this becomes necessary. The rules of civil procedure are designed to aid all three goals.

A case begins with a transaction or occurrence that gives rise to a dispute. (Step 1) (The steps indicated in this discussion refer to the Civil Litigation Time Line located at the end of this chapter.) The client may contact the attorney immediately or wait until the last minute. (Step 2) The attorney's job is to gather the facts and research the law. (Step 3) The legal rules explain what the client must prove in order to prevail. The facts are the substance of the proof. A simple personal injury hypothetical will serve as an example. Jim Carter calls his attorney and reports that his mother, Susan Carter, fell on the ice on one of the walkways in his apartment complex. She is hospitalized with a broken hip.

17

The attorney finds from the legal research that in order for the potential plaintiff, Susan Carter, to recover she must show that (1) the apartment complex had a duty to maintain the premises in a safe condition, (2) it is foreseeable that if the complex failed to keep the premises safe that someone might be injured, (3) that the complex failed in its duty, (4) that the unsafe condition caused the injury, (5) and that as a result of that injury, she will have monetary and other damages.

The attorney will need to assemble the facts to prove each of these elements in the trial court. To prove the duty, the attorney will need to find out whose job it was to prevent the ice from building up on the sidewalk. This question involves knowing who owns the complex, whether the management is the same as the ownership, which employee or employees are responsible for keeping the walks clear of ice, and who supervises these employees. Each one of those responsible is a potential defendant in the case.

Next the attorney will need to prove there was ice on the walk at the time of the injury. If Jim Carter contacted his attorney immediately, the ice may still be on the walk. She may be able to get pictures of the scene. There may be eyewitnesses to the injury or there may be residents in the apartment complex who noticed the ice or perhaps even reported the unsafe condition to the management before the injury to Mrs. Carter occurred.

The plaintiff, Mrs. Carter, knows about the cause of the injury. Eyewitnesses, if there are any, can also provide information about this element. Finally, the attorney will need to prove the plaintiff's loss. How long will Mrs. Carter be hospitalized? What will be her hospital and medical bills? Does she work, and, if so, how much time will she be away from her employment as a result of the broken hip? How much money does she make for every day of lost work? Will there be any temporary or permanent physical impairment from the broken hip? How much pain has she suffered because of the broken hip? How long will the pain last? These are all factual questions related to proving the legal elements of the case. As you can see, the sooner the client approaches the attorney with the case, the easier it will be to collect the facts.

At the conclusion of the legal and factual research, the attorney is ready to advise the client. (Step 4) The advice may be that the client does not have a viable claim. If there is a cause of action, the attorney will advise the client about what is involved in a potential case. If the client elects to proceed, the attorney will begin the case by filing a **complaint.** (Step 5)

The complaint includes five basic elements. (Step 5A) First, the pleader must show that the court has **jurisdiction** or authority over the case. The jurisdiction of the federal district courts includes the authority to decide **federal questions** (28 U.S.C. sec. 1331), **diversity** cases (28 U.S.C. sec. 1332) and **civil rights** cases (28 U.S.C. sec. 1343).

A diversity case is one in which the parties, plaintiff and defendant, come from **different states.** In our hypothetical, if Mrs. Carter is a resident of New Jersey and is injured on the property of an apartment complex owned and operated by Michigan companies, the case would be a diversity case. When there is diversity jurisdiction, the pleader must also allege the amount in controversy, because the federal district courts only have jurisdiction of diversity cases where the amount is more than $50,000; that is, the case must involve at least $50,000.01. If in our hypothetical Susan Carter will be hospitalized for three weeks with hospital and medical bills of $41,964.83 and will be out of work for two months with lost salary of $14,240, she has more than the minimum required for diversity jurisdiction. The $50,000.01 is not required for federal question, civil rights cases, or the other types of federal cases listed under 28 U.S.C. secs. 1333–1367.

The pleader must also list the **parties** to the action. In our hypothetical, Mrs. Susan Carter is the plaintiff and the defendants may include the owner of the apartment complex, the management company, if different, the supervisor(s) in charge of keeping the walkways clear of ice and all the employees who failed to remove the ice.

Next, the complaint will give a brief summary of each of the elements of a slip and fall case and the basic facts that will be used to prove each element. The complaint must include brief allegations of fact for each required element of the cause of action. Finally, the pleader must state the relief the client is seeking. In our hypothetical, Mrs. Carter will be asking for money damages to compensate her for her hospital and medical bills, her lost salary, and an additional sum for the pain and suffering she endured and will endure as a result of the broken hip. The complaint in her case might read as follows:

UNITED STATES DISTRICT COURT FOR THE
EASTERN DISTRICT OF MICHIGAN

SUSAN B. CARTER,)	
Plaintiff)	
v.)	
HILLCREST APARTMENTS,)	File No. 88–13597–NI
INC. and MILESTONE MAN-)	
AGEMENT COMPANY,)	
Defendants)	

COMPLAINT

The plaintiff, Susan B. Carter, states:

Jurisdiction

     1. Plaintiff is a citizen of Ridgewood, New Jersey.

     2. Defendant, Hillcrest Apartments, Inc. is the owner of the Hillcrest Apartment complex, located in West Bloomfield, Michigan.

3. Defendant, Milestone Management Company, manages the Hillcrest Apartment complex.

4. Defendants, Hillcrest Apartments, Inc. and Milestone Management Company, are incorporated in Michigan and have their principal places of business in Detroit, Michigan.

5. On February 6, 1988, plaintiff was visiting her son, James D. Carter, who is a tenant at Hillcrest Apartments.

6. On February 6, 1988, plaintiff was seriously injured when she fell on the accumulated ice and snow on a sidewalk at Hillcrest Apartments.

7. The amount in controversy is in excess of $50,000.

Cause of Action

8. Defendant owner and manager of Hillcrest Apartments had a duty to exercise reasonable care to make the premises safe for the residents of the complex and their guests.

9. This duty included, but is not limited to, diminishing the hazards of ice and snow accumulation.

10. Defendants had the duty to keep the premises in good repair and the common areas, entry ways, corridors, stairs, yards, courts, walkways, and roads, free from accumulation of ice, snow, and other debris.

11. Defendant, Hillcrest Apartments, Inc., had a contractual duty under the lease agreement between itself and James D. Carter, to maintain the premises in a safe condition for the benefit of the tenants and their guests. Plaintiff is a third party beneficiary of that lease agreement.

12. It is foreseeable that if defendants failed to keep the premises in a safe condition, someone might be injured by accumulated ice and snow on the roads and walkways of the apartment complex.

13. Defendant, Milestone Management Company had actual notice of the accumulated ice and snow on the walks of the Hillcrest Apartment complex prior to February 6, 1988, as its employee, the resident manager, was on the premises every day of the week prior to that date.

14. Defendants had either actual or constructive notice prior to February 6, 1988 of the dangerous conditions that existed as a result of accumulated ice and snow on the walks and roads of Hillcrest Apartment complex.

15. Defendants breached their duties toward the plaintiff by not taking reasonable care to make the premises safe for the class, of which plaintiff is a member, and specifically, by not correcting the hazards of ice and snow.

16.   Defendants had the ability to carry out their duty of ice and snow removal as the ice and snow had been removed from the roads and walkways in the area surrounding the resident manager's quarters, the manager's office, and the club house.

17.   Defendants are responsible in respondeat superior for the breach of any duty by any of their employees.

18.   As a proximate result of the breach by defendants of their contractual and common law duties, plaintiff fell on the accumulated ice and snow on a walkway within the Hillcrest Apartment complex and broke her left hip.

19.   As a further proximate result of defendants' negligence, the plaintiff was taken by ambulance to Mercy Hospital, where she was hospitalized for 22 days. She was required to spend an additional seven weeks recuperating at home before she was able to return to her employment even on a part time basis.

20.   The plaintiff underwent surgery for the insertion of a pin in her left hip as treatment for the fractured hip.

21.   Plaintiff experienced excruciating pain at the time of the injury and surgery. The pain persisted throughout her hospitalization and recuperation.

22.   As a further proximate result of defendants' negligence, the plaintiff was required to spend thousands of dollars for her hospital and medical care.

23.   The plaintiff was unable to work during the period of her hospitalization and recuperation, and consequently, she lost her salary during that period.

Relief

24.   As a direct result of defendants' negligence, the plaintiff has been damaged well in excess of $50,000.00.

Plaintiff requests a judgment against defendants for an amount in excess of $50,000.00.

Dated: June 24, 1988.

_____

Susan B. Carter

Legal Writing Associates
Attorneys for the Plaintiff
by _____
      468 W. Markowsky Drive
      Detroit, Michigan 48202
      Telephone: (313) 764–8397

The Federal Rules of Civil Procedure also explain where the plaintiff should file the complaint, what must be included, how the defendant is to be served with the summons and complaint, who may serve the papers, and so forth. (Step 5B)

The defendant, who has been properly served with the summons and complaint, has several options. (Step 6) A defendant may do nothing. (Step 6A) In this case the plaintiff may get a **default judgment** from the court (Rule 55). The defendant may then move to set aside the default judgment. The court will normally grant this type of motion if the defendant had a good reason for failing to act and if not much time has elapsed. If the court does not set aside the default, the defendant may appeal.

The defendant's second option is to **answer** the complaint. (Step 6B) He will admit those allegations in the plaintiff's complaint that are true and deny those with which he disagrees. (Rule 8(b)). At the same time, the defendant will raise any **affirmative defenses** (Rule 8(c)) he has to the plaintiff's case. An affirmative defense basically explains that although everything in the plaintiff's complaint is true, the defendant is not responsible because of a legally recognized defense.

This is also the time when the defendant will raise any **counter-claim** or **cross-claim** he may have (Rule 13). A counterclaim is a claim the defendant may have against the plaintiff. If the claim arises out of the same transaction, the counterclaim must be raised at the same time as the responsive pleading. If it does not arise out of the same transaction or occurrence, the defendant may raise the counter-claim, but is not required to do so.

While a counterclaim is raised against an opposing party, a cross-claim is raised against a co-party; that is, someone on the same side of the case. The cross-claim must arise out of the same transaction or occurrence as the original claim or a counterclaim. Often in a cross-claim, one defendant is asserting that if he is responsible to the plaintiff, another defendant is liable to him for some or all of the relief, usually money.

The defendant's third option is to file a **motion.** (Step 6C) Often the defendant will answer the complaint and at the same time file one of the following motions. These motions fall into two categories. The first category includes motions that the defendant must file or he will lose them. They include **lack of jurisdiction over the person** (Rule 12(b)(2)), **improper venue** (Rule 12(b)(3) and 28 U.S.C. sec. 1404, **insufficiency of process** (Rule 12(b)(4)), and **insufficiency of service of process** (Rule 12(b)(5)). Lack of jurisdiction over the person means that the court has no authority over the defendant and cannot require him to come to court to defend this case. If the defendant chooses not to object, then he is voluntarily submitting to the authority of the court and has lost his chance to avoid the litigation. Improper venue means that the plaintiff filed the original complaint in the wrong court. Again if no objection is raised, the case continues in the wrong court. Insufficiency of process means that there is a defect in the papers served upon the defendant and insufficiency of service of process means there was a defect in the way that the papers were served. With each of these procedural defects, the defendant has one chance to object and if he fails to do so, the case proceeds as if there were no defect.

The second category of motions is more serious and the defendant does not waive his chance to object if he fails to do so in or with his responsive pleading. These motions include **lack of jurisdiction over the subject matter** (Rule 12(b)(1)), **failure to state a claim upon which relief can be granted** (Rule 12(b)(6)), **motion for a more definite statement** (Rule 12(e)), **motion to strike** (Rule 12(f)), and a **motion to disqualify the judge.** Lack of jurisdiction over the subject matter means that the court has no authority over this kind of case. If in our hypothetical Mrs. Carter had been injured in her home state of New Jersey and not while visiting her son in Michigan, there would be no diversity of citizenship between plaintiff and defendant. The case would belong in a New Jersey court. The federal district court would have no jurisdiction over the subject matter.

The most important motion a defendant can file at this stage of the process is a motion for failure to state a claim upon which relief can be granted. In some courts the motion is called a motion for dismissal, a motion for summary disposition, or a demurrer. In this motion the defendant is asserting that the plaintiff has omitted a legally necessary element of the cause of action. If, for example, Mrs. Carter fell on a sidewalk in an adjacent apartment complex owned and managed by a different company, this defendant would not be responsible for her injuries. Or, if Mrs. Carter fell because she broke the heel on her shoe and not because of the ice, this defendant would not be responsible as it has no duty to make sure that Mrs. Carter's heels are in good repair. Or, if Mrs. Carter fell on the ice, but did not hurt herself, there would also be one element missing from the cause of action and the defendant would not be liable. In considering a Rule 12(b)(6) motion, the court will treat everything the plaintiff has alleged in the complaint as true. If under those circumstances she has alleged enough to prevail, the court will deny the motion. If there is an element missing, the court will grant the Rule 12(b)(6) motion. The plaintiff may move to amend the complaint (Rule 15) and remedy the defect, or she may appeal if she believes that she has alleged everything that is necessary and an amendment will not help. Many of the cases you will read arose as an appeal from a Rule 12(b)(6) or similar state motion.

If the plaintiff's complaint is too general or too vague, the defendant may move for a more definite statement. He should not be required to defend a case he does not understand. If the plaintiff's attorney has researched the law and facts thoroughly and drafted the complaint with care, a motion for a more definite statement should not be necessary.

The other two motions are likewise uncommon. The defendant will file a motion to strike if the complaint contains redundant, immaterial, impertinent, or scandalous material. A carefully drafted complaint should contain none of these things. The defendant will file a motion to disqualify the judge when there is some reason why the judge may not be able to decide the case impartially. A judge can be disqualified if he is well acquainted with the attorneys or one of the parties or because he knows about the case. Frequently a judge will **recuse** himself from the case under these circumstances, not necessarily because he would discriminate against one side or the other, but to avoid even the appearance of impropriety. Occasionally something will happen during the course of the case to indicate that the judge has lost his impartiality and a motion to disqualify could be raised at this stage of the proceedings.

After the preliminary motions, the case moves into **discovery**. (Step 7) Discovery is a fairly recent phenomenon in our legal history. The theory behind discovery is that the more each side learns about the facts of the case, the more likely that the ultimate result will be fair, and that the parties will be able to settle the case. (Rules 26 and 29) Discovery is not limited to information that will be admissible at the trial; inadmissible information is discoverable if it is likely to lead to admissible information. While insurance policies, for example, are not admissible as evidence at a trial, the parties can still discover the policies. Knowledge of the policy limits may help the parties to reach an agreement.

The court may hold a **discovery conference** with the parties to set the scope of discovery and arrange the discovery schedule. In complex cases, a discovery conference or conferences will contribute to an orderly progress of the case. In simple cases like our slip and fall hypothetical, a discovery conference would not normally be necessary.

There are five basic types of discovery: **depositions** (Rules 27, 28, 30, 31, 32), **interrogatories to parties** (Rule 33), **production of documents** (Rule 34), **physical and mental examination of persons** (Rule 35), and **requests for admission** (Rule 36).

A deposition is an oral examination of a witness under oath. In our hypothetical, plaintiff's counsel will probably want to depose the resident manager to discover who was in charge of ice and snow removal in general, and who failed in this particular instance. The manager will have information about the chain of command and the personnel involved. In the course of the deposition, plaintiff's counsel will also find out what kind of a witness the manager would make. The personalities of the potential witnesses and the way a jury will react to them is part of both the trial and the settlement strategies. Defense counsel will want to depose the plaintiff for the same reason. If she would be a sympathetic witness in the eyes of the jury, it may be to the defendant's advantage to settle the case before the trial. A deposition of the plaintiff will also give defense counsel information about the extent and duration of the injury, whether Mrs. Carter has ever been injured before, whether this is her fourth slip and fall case, how long she was out of work, the amount of her salary, whether she is acutely aware of the pain or is a stoic patient, and so forth. The defense counsel may also want to depose Mrs. Carter's physician, particularly if he is anticipating that she will have permanent disability from the broken hip. Although depositions provide a great deal of useful information, they are time consuming and relatively expensive. A court reporter takes down a verbatim transcript of the deposition and then transcribes it. The party requesting the deposition must pay for the original, which is filed with the court, as well as a copy for that party's use. Attorneys for all the other parties will also order copies of the transcript. Even reasonably short transcripts can cost hundreds of dollars.

Interrogatories are a much less expensive form of discovery. They are written questions submitted to a party, either plaintiff or defendant. The party must answer the questions in writing and under oath. Interrogatories are used to get basic objective information. Plaintiff's counsel in our hypothetical will want to find out the names, addresses, and work schedules of employees in the apartment complex, how many claims have been filed against the complex in the last five years, and the like. Defense counsel will want to know all about Mrs. Carter: her age, medical and employment histories, if she drinks alcoholic beverages (maybe she was intoxicated on the night she fell), where she lives, if she has ever been involved in litigation before, etc.

Documents are important in most litigation and part of discovery is the **production of these documents.** In our hypothetical the plaintiff will want the defendant apartment complex to produce its insurance policy, while defendants will want to look at Mrs. Carter's hospital and medical records.

Because she has put her medical condition at issue, the defendants may request that Mrs. Carter be examined by a physician of their choice to get a second opinion on the extent and duration of the injury. **Requests for medical and psychological examinations** are common forms of discovery when the plaintiff or defendant has put his physical or mental condition at issue in the case.

Finally, discovery provides for **requests for admission.** There are some facts that the plaintiff is required to prove, but that the defendant readily admits are true. It would be a waste of time to require the plaintiff to prove these facts, and it will aid settlement to have agreement on some aspects of the case. The plaintiff can, therefore, ask the defendant to admit some facts necessary for the plaintiff's case, and the defendant can ask the plaintiff to admit facts necessary to an affirmative defense. Admissions are sometimes part of the strategy of the case. If the circumstances of the injury were horrendous, but the injury itself was mild and the plaintiff has completely recovered, the defendant may want to admit liability to keep the circumstances of the injury from the jury. The plaintiff would not want to request the defendant to admit liability in this case.

During the pre-trial stage (Step 8), either party may make pre-trial motions. The most common are discovery related motions and motions for **summary judgment** (Rule 56). The discovery motions include motions to compel discovery when the opposing party is recalcitrant and will not reveal discoverable material. If the opposing party still refuses to permit discovery after the court has issued an order to compel discovery, the initiating party may request the court to impose sanctions. A third type of discovery motion is a motion for a protective order to prevent discovery of information that is privileged and not discoverable.

A motion for summary judgment (Rule 56) alleges that the trial in whole or in part is not necessary because the plaintiff has failed to state a claim upon which relief can be granted. This is the basic (Rule 12(b)(6)) motion, but may now include information gleaned from the discovery process. The plaintiff may file a parallel motion alleging that the defendant has failed to state a valid defense to the plaintiff's claim. The third type of summary judgment motion alleges that there is no material fact at issue and that the court can decide the case as a matter of law on the facts as agreed upon by the parties. If summary judgment is granted to either party, the loser may appeal. You will encounter many cases where the appeal arose from a grant of summary judgment. Note that some jurisdictions use different terminology for what is in essence a Rule 56 summary judgment under the Federal Rules of Civil Procedure.

Most trial courts now hold a pre-trial conference (Rule 16). (Step 9) The purpose of the conference is fourfold: 1) to clarify the issues and defenses for trial by making sure that the pleadings—the complaint, answer, counterclaims, cross claims and their answers—conform to the issues and defenses that will be raised at the trial, 2) to make sure that discovery is complete, 3) to set the witnesses and exhibits for the trial, and 4) to explore settlement.

Some judges take an active role in trying to settle the case. Others will take a laissez-faire approach and merely ask if the parties can reach agreement. If the attorneys for all the parties have done their homework, they should know the strengths and weaknesses of their respective positions and be able to predict the likely outcome at trial. Many cases settle at or shortly before the pre-trial conference. A case like our hypothetical should be relatively easy to settle. Both sides know what Mrs. Carter's hospital and medical expenses are and the wages that she lost. A reasonable settlement would reimburse her for her out of pocket losses plus an additional sum for her pain, suffering, and inconvenience. This portion of a settlement commonly provides the attorney fees. Her attorney will in all likelihood have accepted her case under a contingent fee agreement. Under a contingent fee agreement, the attorney takes the case with the understanding that he will only get paid if the plaintiff wins. The agreement will provide the attorney with approximately one third of the total recovery after the costs, filing, motion and service fees, and discovery expenses have been deducted. Cases that do not have easily calculable damages, such as medical bills and lost wages, are not as easy to settle.

Another method of trying to resolve disputes short of actually trying the cases is mediation. Many courts now recommend or even require mediation, particularly in cases involving personal injury or monetary damages. The parties each prepare a mediation statement with the issues and facts they intend to present at the trial. The statements are presented to a panel of three mediators. The panel often includes a plaintiff's attorney, a defense attorney, and a neutral attorney. The attorneys for the parties make brief statements on behalf of their clients and the mediators vote on a settlement figure. A party who rejects a mediation award is liable for penalties if the ultimate result after the trial is close to the mediated amount. Mediation helps the judicial system handle the increasing volume of cases without excessive delay.

If the case does not settle, it proceeds to trial. (Step 10) Just before the trial begins, the parties have an opportunity to make more motions. They may renew their pre-trial motions or move for dismissal of part or all of the case (Rule 41). (Step 10B) They may also make motions in limine. (Step 10A) A motion in limine is designed to settle evidentiary questions before the trial in order to insure that the evidence presented is relevant and not unduly prejudicial. In our hypothetical, if the apartment complex salted the sidewalks within an hour of Mrs. Carter's fall and removed all the ice the next morning, Mrs. Carter's attorney might want to offer testimony of these subsequent remedial measures to prove that the icy walk was unsafe at the time she fell. Defense counsel would want to make a motion in limine to prevent this testimony. As you will discover in your Evidence course, evidence of subsequent remedial measures is not admissible to prove that the defendant was negligent (Federal Rule of Evidence 407). The trial judge would grant the defendant's motion to exclude evidence of the subsequent remedial measures.

There are two kinds of trials, bench trials and jury trials. In a bench trial, the judge finds the facts from the evidence presented, decides which legal rules to apply, and applies the legal rules to the facts to decide the case (Rule 52). In a jury trial, the responsibility is divided between the judge and the jury. The judge instructs the jury on the legal rules appropriate to the case, but the jury finds the facts and applies the rules to those facts to decide the case (Rule 38).

Jurors are chosen at random from the area served by the court. Their names may come from voter registration lists, drivers license lists, or similar non-discriminatory selection systems. Jurors serve varying lengths of time from one day or one trial to several months. Jury duty is one of our civic responsibilities and one of the things that makes the United States system of government different from that in most other countries. Ninety percent of all jury trials take place in the United States.

The actual jury is selected from the random pool of jurors by a process known as **voir dire.** (Step 10B) The object is to make certain that each juror selected has no bias which would make it impossible for him or her to weigh the evidence impartially. The clerk of the court administers an oath to the jury panel for that case. The jurors swear that they will answer the questions truthfully. From the pool of potential jurors, the clerk then draws enough names to fill the jury box. Normally six jurors will sit in civil cases and twelve will sit in criminal cases. The clerk will also draw one or two additional names for alternates. If, in the middle of the trial, a juror were to become ill or be unable to serve, the alternate would fill in, avoiding a complete retrial of the case.

The voir dire is conducted either by the judge or by the attorneys. It consists of a series of questions to those seated in the jury box to discover if there is some reason they could not decide the case impartially. The questions first probe to see if the jurors are acquainted with any of the parties to the case, their attorneys, or the witnesses. The judge or attorneys will then ask if the jurors or their immediate family members have any particular expertise on the subject of the case. The jurors must decide the case based on the evidence and law presented during the trial and not based on any outside expertise they bring to the case. In our hypothetical case, the voir dire might probe to see if any of the jurors had ever been involved in a slip and fall case or had ever broken a hip.

In order to insure impartiality, each party may excuse or **challenge** some jurors. There are two kinds of challenges, **challenges for cause** and **peremptory challenges.** A party can challenge a juror for cause if the juror has direct knowledge of the case and a pre-formed judgment as to how the case should be decided, or if the juror is related to or knows one of the parties or witnesses well and that relationship would interfere with the juror's ability to decide the case impartially.

In addition, each party has some peremptory challenges. The exact number of peremptory challenges depends on the type of case, the court, and the number of parties involved. The party need not explain why he is asking to have a particular juror excused under one of the peremptory challenges. The jury is set when all parties are satisfied with the jury or when they have exhausted their peremptory challenges. The clerk then swears in the jury. They swear they will listen to all the evidence impartially and will not decide the case until after all the evidence is in and the judge has instructed them on the law.

The standard they will use differs in criminal and civil cases. In a criminal case, the finder of fact must presume that the defendant is innocent until the prosecution has convinced the fact finder **beyond a reasonable doubt** that the defendant is guilty of the crime with which he is charged. In a civil case, the standard is not as strict. The plaintiff in the civil case must prove each element of the case **by a preponderance of the evidence;** that is, that each element is more likely than not. This is the **51% standard**. In our hypothetical case plaintiff's counsel must prove to the jury that it was more likely than not that there was ice on the walk, that it was foreseeable that someone might fall on the ice, that the defendant had a duty to remove the ice, that Mrs. Carter did fall on the ice, that her broken hip resulted from the fall, and that her medical expenses, lost wages and pain come from the broken hip.

The trial begins with the opening statements by the attorneys. (Step 10C) The opening statements are not part of the evidence, but an objective overview of what each side intends to prove during the trial. If it is less than objective or if counsel exaggerates the evidence, the jury will be disappointed and counsel and his client will lose credibility. Plaintiff's counsel begins. Counsel for the defendant may choose to make an opening statement before the presentation of any of the evidence or reserve the statement until after all of the plaintiff's evidence. This is a strategy decision. It depends on how sympathetic the witnesses for plaintiff and defendant are, how strong the case is for the defendant, and so forth.

The plaintiff has the burden of proving each element of her case, and the trial begins with her evidence. (Step 10D) The evidence consists of **testimony by witnesses** and **exhibits.** The questions her counsel poses on **direct examination** are not evidence, but the answers elicited from the witnesses are evidence. After the direct examination of each witness, defense counsel has an opportunity to **cross examine** the witness. Then, if necessary, plaintiff's counsel asks more questions on **redirect examination.** The defendant's attorney then has the option of **recross examination.** Plaintiff's counsel may introduce exhibits in the course of direct examination. In our hypothetical, hospital and medical bills, wage reports, and photographs are potential exhibits.

At any time during the trial, counsel may object to the **admission of evidence** based on the applicable **rules of evidence.** In the federal courts, these are the Federal Rules of Evidence. The judge will then rule on the admissibility of that evidence. This ruling may be the basis for a later appeal by the losing party.

At the close of the plaintiff's proofs, defense counsel may move for **judgment as a matter of law** stating that the plaintiff has failed to meet her burden of proof on all the elements necessary to the case (Rule 50(a)). (Step 10E) If the motion is granted, the plaintiff may appeal this decision. If the motion is denied, the defendant may use the denial as the basis for a later appeal.

In ruling on a motion for judgment as a matter of law, the judge will consider all of the evidence presented to that point in the trial and the elements that party was required to prove. If there was no evidence on one of the elements, the judge will grant the motion. In our hypothetical, for example, if Mrs. Carter presented no testimony or exhibit that there was ice on the sidewalk or other dangerous condition, the judge would grant the defendant's motion. If, on the other hand, the evidence was contradictory, Mrs. Carter and her son testified there was ice on the walk, but a neighbor and the manager testified that there was no ice, the judge would deny the motion. It is the province of the jury to decide which witnesses to believe; the judge cannot decide the credibility for the jury. Whenever there is evidence from which a reasonable juror could reach the opposite result, the judge must deny the motion. Although motions for judgment as a matter of law are common—attorneys do not want to lose the chance for a quick victory— they are rarely granted.

It is now the defendant's turn. (Step 10F) If defense counsel has reserved his opening statement, he will give it and then present evidence for the defendant. The testimony of witnesses and exhibits will call into question the plaintiff's evidence and will try to establish any appropriate affirmative defenses. The procedure for the defendant's case is like that for the plaintiff's evidence except that now defense counsel conducts direct examination and plaintiff's counsel cross examines the witnesses. If there is more than one defendant and each is represented by a different attorney, each will have an opportunity to present an opening statement and to present evidence for his client.

At the close of the defendant's proofs, defense counsel may renew his motion for judgment as a matter of law, alleging that in light of the defendant's evidence, plaintiff has failed to meet the burden of proof (Rule 50(a)). (Step 10G) If the defendant presented evidence on an affirmative defense, plaintiff's counsel may make a parallel motion for judgment as a matter of law. The judge's decision on the motion may be grounds for appeal by the losing party.

After the defendant's case, the plaintiff has a chance to present **rebuttal** evidence; that is, evidence that calls into question the evidence presented by the defendant. (Step 10H) The format is as before. After rebuttal there is a final opportunity for motions for judgment as a matter of law with the possibility of appeal from an adverse decision. (Step 10I)

The **closing arguments** follow and like the opening statements, they are not part of the evidence. (Step 10J) Because the plaintiff has the burden of proof on her case, plaintiff's attorney presents the first closing argument. As the name implies, the closing is not objective, but persuasive. The attorney will explain to the jury the different legal elements of the case and how the evidence establishes each of these elements. Counsel will try to persuade the jury that the plaintiff should prevail and may suggest an appropriate dollar figure. In his closing the defendant's attorney will explain to the jury how the evidence did not show all the necessary elements of the case or how, despite the plaintiff's position, the defendant has proved an affirmative defense. The plaintiff's attorney can have the final word in the rebuttal argument. Because the plaintiff has the burden of proof, she has two chances to convince the jury in closing argument.

Finally, the judge instructs the jury on the law to be applied in its deliberations. (Step 10K) Some federal district court judges and many state court systems have adopted standard **jury instructions** common to all civil or criminal cases and for some of the more common causes of action. The attorneys draft proposed instructions on those aspects of the case for which there are no standard instructions. The judge rules on these instructions, accepting those that comply with his understanding of the law and rejecting those that are not based on the law. The conference between the judge and the attorneys occurs out of the hearing of the jury. It takes place before closing argument so the attorneys know which instructions the judge will give. This gives the attorneys a chance to use the substance of the instructions in their closing arguments. After the judge instructs the jury, the attorneys have a chance to object to any instructions the judge gave or failed to give and to preserve these objections for appeal if that becomes necessary. (Step 10L) Objection to jury instructions is an important basis for appeal as it is a challenge based on law, not fact. An appellate court has greater leeway for overturning the trial court's decision if the judge did not properly instruct the jury on the law.

After deliberation (Step 10M), the jury will reach a verdict or decision in the case. (Step 10N) The verdict can be general or specific. A **general verdict** is an overall decision and it does not explain how the jury decided the different elements of the case. Possible general verdicts in the hypothetical case include no cause of action if the jury decided for the defendant and a sum of money if the jury decided for Mrs. Carter. In a complicated case a **special verdict** or a **general verdict accompanied by answers to interrogatories** (Rule 49) may be preferable, because it focuses the jury's attention on a series of factual decisions necessary to reach the verdict. After the jury announces its verdict, the judge enters a judgment based on that verdict. (Step 10O)

If the trial had been a bench rather than a jury trial, the procedure after closing arguments is simpler. The judge finds the facts in light of the applicable law and announces a verdict. The attorneys may present the judge with the appropriate law and show how they would apply that law to the facts presented at the trial. This occurs in written document called a **trial brief.** The judge enters a judgment based on the verdict after a bench trial as well.

The loser has several options at this point. He may decide that no major errors were committed during the trial and that it is neither worth the time nor money to proceed. He may **move for a new trial** based on the errors committed during the trial (Rule 59). If it appears that the jury reached a verdict which was contrary to the evidence and law, he may renew his motion for judgment as a matter of law (Rule 50(b)). Finally he may appeal either directly or, if the judge denied one or both motions, he may appeal the denial of the motion for a new trial or the motion for judgment as a matter of law. (Step 11) There is also the possibility of **cross appeals,** where neither side is content with the outcome, and **conditional rulings of grant of motion for judgment as a matter of law** (Rules 50(c), (d)).

As you can see, there are a number of points in the trial court civil procedure process where one or both parties may appeal. The way the appellate court views the case depends in some cases on the stage in the procedure. As you read appellate decisions, consider how the cases arose procedurally. The following Civil Litigation Time Line is included for easy reference.

CIVIL LITIGATION TIME LINE

1) Transaction or occurrence giving rise to litigation
2) Client contact with attorney
3) Legal research and factual investigation
4) Advise client

    no case

      OR

5) Complaint (Rules 3, 7a, 8, 9, 10, 11, 17)
   a) *Content*
   1) Jurisdiction (Rule 8(a)(1); e.g.

        28 U.S.C. sec. 1331—Federal question;

        28 U.S.C. sec. 1332—Diversity of citizenship

        28 U.S.C. sec. 1334—Civil Rights

        see also Substantive statutes with jurisdictional provisions)
   2) Amount in controversy (28 U.S.C. sec. 1332)
   3) Parties (Rules 17–25)

        (Joinder—Rules 18, 19, 20, 21;

        Interpleader—Rule 22;

        Class actions—Rule 23;

        Intervention—Rule 24)
   4) Facts to show pleader entitled to relief (Rule 8(a)(2))
   5) Demand for relief (Rule 8(a)(3))
   b) *Filing and Service*
   1) Where to file (Venue—28 U.S.C. 1391, generally)
   2) What must be filed (Rule 5(d))
   3) Service of Summons and Complaint on defendant (Rule 4)

        A) Requisites of good service

           i) Who may serve

             ii) How to serve

             iii) Constitutional requirements

       B) Jurisdiction

           i) In personam jurisdiction

              —Constitutional limitations

              —Statutory limitations

           ii) In rem jurisdiction

              —Seizure of property

              —Constitutional limitations

6) Defendant acts or fails to act:

  a) Defendant does nothing:

  1) Plaintiff gets Default Judgment (Rule 55)

    —Defendant may later move to set aside the Default Judgment

    —If not:

       i) May lead to **appeal**

       ii) May be subject to collateral attack

  OR

  b) Defendant answers:

  1) Admits or denies plaintiff's allegations (Rule 8(b))

  2) Affirmative defenses (Rule 8(c))

  3) Counterclaims and cross claims (Rule 13)

    AND/OR

  c) Defendant makes a motion:

The following motions are waived by defendant if not raised by motion or responsive pleading:

    (Rules 12(g), (h))

  1) Lack of jurisdiction over the person (Rule 12(b)(2))

  2) Improper venue (Rule 12(b)(3))

  3) Insufficiency of Process (Rule 12(b)(4))

  4) Insufficiency of Service of Process (Rule 12(b)(5))

The following motions are not waived if the defendant fails to make them at this point:

  1) Lack of jurisdiction over the subject matter (Rule 12(b)(1))

  2) Failure to state a claim upon which relief can be granted (Dismissal, Demurrer) (Rules 12(b)(6), 56)

    (May lead to amendment (Rule 15) or **appeal**)

  3) More definite statement (Rule 12(e))

  4) To strike (redundant, immaterial, impertinent, scandalous) (Rule 12(f))

5)   To disqualify the judge

7) Discovery with or without discovery conference (Rule 26 generally; see also Rule 29)

a)   Depositions (Rules 27, 28, 30, 31, 32)

b)   Interrogatories to Parties (Rule 33)

c)   Production of documents (Rule 34)

d)   Physical and mental examination of persons (Rule 35)

e)   Requests for admission (Rule 36)

8) Pre Trial Motions

a)   Discovery related motions

i) To compel discovery (Rule 37)

ii) For a protective order

iii) For sanctions (Rule 37)

b)   Summary Judgment (Rule 56)—alleging trial in whole or in part is unnecessary because:

i) Failure to state a claim upon which relief can be granted (Rule 12(b)(6))

ii) Failure to state a valid defense to claim

iii) No genuine issue of material fact

If Motion for Summary Judgment is granted to any party, may lead to an **appeal** by opponent.

9) Pre trial conference (Rule 16) in order to:

a)   Clarify the issues and defenses for trial

b)   Make sure the pleadings are in order

c)   Make sure discovery is complete

d)   Set witnesses and exhibits for trial

e)   Explore settlement

If settlement (no appeal)

OR

10) Trial

a)   Motions in limine—to settle evidentiary problems prior to trial—insure relevancy and avoid prejudice.

b)   Renewal of pre-trial motions and motion to dismiss (Rule 41) EITHER

Bench Trial where the judge decides the law and finds facts (Rule 52)

OR

Jury Trial where judge instructs on the law and jury finds facts (Rule 38)

Impanel Jury

Voir dire—by judge or attorneys to discover prejudice, to educate jurors (Rule 47)

---

c) Opening statements (Not part of the evidence—an objective overview of what each side hopes to prove)

Plaintiff's opening

Defendant's opening (may be reserved until beginning of defendant's case *)

d) Plaintiff's evidence (At steps d, f, h, there may be objections to the admission of evidence. The judge's ruling for or against admissibility may lead to an **appeal**.)

Witnesses

Direct examination—plaintiff's attorney

Cross examination—defendant's attorney

Redirect examination—plaintiff's attorney

Recross examination—defendant's attorney

Exhibits

e) Motion for judgment as a matter of law by the defendant alleging plaintiff failed to meet burden of proof (Rule 50(a))

If granted, may lead to **appeal.**

* (Defendant's opening may be here)

f) Defendant's evidence (witnesses, exhibits that contradict the plaintiff's case and presentation of defenses)

g) Motion for judgment as a matter of law by defendant alleging that in light of the defendant's evidence the plaintiff has failed to meet the burden of proof

OR motion by plaintiff on defenses (Rule 50(a))

If granted, may lead to appeal.

h) Rebuttal evidence by plaintiff

i) Motion for judgment as a matter of law by defendant (Rule 50(a))

If granted, may lead to appeal.

j) Closing arguments

Plaintiff

Defendant

Plaintiff's rebuttal

Jury Trial Only

k) Jury instructions drafted by attorneys, ruled on by judge, and given by judge

l) Objections to jury instructions (out of hearing of jury) (Rule 51) May be basis for **appeal**

m) Jury deliberation

---

n) Verdict—specific or general (Rule 49)

o) Judgment entered

Loser may move for a new trial (Rule 59)

   AND/OR

Loser may move for judgment as a matter law (Rule 50(b))

   AND/OR

Loser may **appeal**

   OR

Loser may accept the verdict and judgment

(Note also the possibility of cross appeals and conditional rulings on grant of motion for judgment as a matter of law.)

11) **Appeal** of final judgment 28 U.S.C. sec. 1291—**appeal** from trial court is of right; **appeals** from higher levels of appellate court (where there are two levels) is by leave or *Certiorari*

Note: In an appropriate case, you may wish to move for a temporary restraining order or a preliminary injunction. (Rule 65).

Chapter 4

UNDERSTANDING CASES

Most of the cases you will read in law school and use to analyze problems throughout your legal career are appellate decisions and selected decisions from the federal district courts. These cases are published in a series of books called **reporters.** This chapter is designed to help you understand the cases you read. Although the discussion relates specifically to appellate cases, it also applies in general to trial level opinions.

An appeal arises when the attorney for a dissatisfied party, called the **appellant** (or petitioner) brings the case to the appellate court alleging errors in the lower court that affected the outcome of the case. The attorney for the appellant must research all the applicable law and explain it to the court in a document called a **brief.** The brief will explain what the rule is or should be and how it should be applied in this case. His opponent, called the **appellee** (or respondent), will then write a brief in response explaining why the lower court was correct. While the judges assigned to the case must decide it, the attorneys have the responsibility for presenting the judges with the law, facts and arguments necessary to their decision. The appellate court does two things, one substantive and the other procedural. First, it considers appellant's contentions, and if they have merit, explains the substantive rules and how they should have been applied. Second, it explains what should happen to the case procedurally. If the appellate court agrees with the lower court, it will affirm the decision below. If the appellate court disagrees, it may reverse the decision and remand the case back to the lower court for action appropriate to the procedural posture of the case and the point at which the error(s) occurred.

THE ROLE OF CASES IN THE COMMON LAW SYSTEM

Precedent

As you learned in Chapter 1, judge made law, cases, are the backbone of the common law system. Cases also develop from legislative law as courts interpret the language of constitutions, statutes and regulations. Under the common law system, decisions in earlier cases are used to decide later cases. Every case, no matter what its ultimate origin, is potentially relevant to future decisions. Each earlier case is **precedent** for later cases. You saw the precedent system at work as you applied the decision in *Mallory v. Harry's Bar* to a variety of hypotheticals.

Precedent can come from any court in any jurisdiction. The closer the earlier case is factually to the pending case, the better the precedent it will be, and the easier it will be for the court to adopt the precedent.

Precedent is an earlier decision on the same, a similar or analogous issue with comparable facts that a court uses as the basis for deciding a pending case.

Stare Decisis

While all cases are potentially useful as precedent, courts are required to follow some earlier decisions under the doctrine of *stare decisis*. A court is bound by cases that it has decided previously and by all court decisions of higher courts in its system. A federal district court in the central district of California is bound by its own decisions and all decisions of the Court of Appeals for the Ninth Circuit and the United States Supreme Court. A supreme court in New York, a trial court, is bound by its own decisions, those of the Supreme Court Appellate Division, the intermediate level appellate court, and the New York Court of Appeals, the highest court in New York. The New York Court of Appeals has the last word on New York law, but it is bound by the United States Supreme Court decisions on matters of federal law and the U.S. Constitution, just as the U.S. Supreme Court must defer to the New York Court of Appeals decisions on matters of purely New York law.

As an attorney, you are required in your brief to present the court with the earlier decisions on the same issue that are binding on the court.[1] This does not mean, however, that you must present the case and give up; you are free to distinguish the case on factual or policy grounds. As you can see, *stare decisis* is an important doctrine for making our legal system predictable.

---

1. Rule 3.3, ABA Model Rules of Professional Conduct:

(a) A lawyer shall not knowingly:

(1) make a false statement of material fact or law to a tribunal;

(2) fail to disclose a material fact to a tribunal when disclosure is necessary to avoid assisting a criminal or fraudulent act by the client;

(3) fail to disclose to the tribunal legal authority in the controlling jurisdiction known to the lawyer to be directly adverse to the position of the client and not disclosed by opposing counsel; or

(4) offer evidence that the lawyer knows to be false. If a lawyer has offered material evidence and comes to know of its falsity, the lawyer shall take reasonable remedial measures.

From *ABA Model Rules of Professional Conduct*, Copyright © 1989 American Bar Association. Reprinted by permission.

Stare decisis is a legal doctrine that requires a court to apply existing precedent on the same issue that comes from that court or a higher level court in the same system.

WHAT TO LOOK FOR AS YOU READ CASES

As you read and prepare to use cases for legal analysis, find and articulate the following elements.

Issue

The appeal is framed in terms of legal questions, called **issues**, which the court must answer in order to decide the particular case. It will help you to understand cases if you can articulate the particular issues the court addressed. The following formula is useful as a starting point for issue formulation.

ISSUE = DOES THE LEGAL RULE APPLY TO THESE FACTS?

Incorporate the specific legal rule the court considered and the particular facts of the case into the formula. You can see that formula calls for a yes or no answer. Formulating issues in this way helps you to organize the court's analysis logically.

Rule

The rules used by the appellate courts come both from legislative law and case law. Often the rules come from both sources; a statute will provide the basic rule, which is then explained by a case. In either situation, once the court has a case involving the same or similar issue and similar facts, it must abstract a **general rule** from that case, and then apply the general rule to the pending case.

The following armed robbery hypothetical illustrates the process. A jury convicted the defendant of armed robbery. He has appealed the conviction and claims that although it may have been robbery, it was not armed robbery as he was not armed. The defendant robbed an old woman by threatening her with a switch blade knife. In trying to decide the issue, the court will look to earlier cases to see what constitutes being "armed". One obvious precedent involved a defendant, who was armed with a .45 caliber pistol. The defendant in the precedent case put the victim in fear for his life with the pistol and robbed him. The general rule that emerges is that the weapon must be sufficiently threatening so that the victim is in fear for his life. The court in the pending case will consider whether a victim could be put in fear for his life by a robber with a switch blade knife. The general rule is used to assess the specific facts of the case.

If it is a **case of first impression;** that is, the first case of its kind, the attorneys and the court may look for similar cases in a different factual context. In a retaliatory discharge case, for example, the court used the rule from a retaliatory eviction case, *Aweeka v. Bonds,* 20 Cal. App. 3d 278, 97 Cal. Rptr. 650 (1971), to provide a cause of action for the discharged employee against his former employer, *Frampton v. Central Indiana Gas Co.,* 260 Ind. 249, 297 N.E.2d 425 (1973). The creativity of the employee's counsel provided his client with the legal means for addressing a wrong that previously had not been recognized. The case of *Marvin v. Marvin,* 18 Cal. 3d 660, 557 P.2d 106, 134 Cal. Rptr. 815 (1976) is another example of this type of analogy. In that case, Michelle Triola Marvin was awarded "palimony" although she had not been legally married to Lee Marvin. You can see in these examples how the law develops under the common law system to accommodate changes in society. The changes occur by expanding predictable rules and applying them in new fact situations.

Rule is a general principle from legislative law or abstracted from a case that can then be applied to the specific facts of a similar pending case to decide the same issue.

Holding

In order to use precedent for later legal analysis, attorneys formulate the court's decision in a **holding.** A holding, like a statement of the issue, includes the rule and the facts. It is fact specific because the court only decided the issue between these parties under these facts. Not every fact in a case is important to the holding on a particular issue. In articulating holdings, include the necessary facts. Sometimes in the opinion, the court will state the holding for you. At other times, the holding will only be implied and you will need to formulate the holding for yourself. Often the court's language will be confusing; it will use the word "hold" but will not include the rule and/or the facts necessary to its decision. Consider the following three statements from the armed robbery hypothetical:

1. The defendant was armed when he committed the robbery.

2. The defendant, 5'11", 180 lbs., was armed when he pointed a switchblade knife with a seven inch blade at the victim, a seventy-three year old woman, 5'1", 105 lbs., and demanded that she give him her money, her watch, and her diamond ring.

3. The defendant was armed when he pointed a switchblade knife at the victim, because the weapon put the victim in fear for her life.

The best statement of the holding is example 3. Example 1 only states the result without providing any of the facts. Example 2 includes so many facts that it does not tell the reader what is essential to the holding. Example 3 includes the essentials: the weapon and the threat. The relative size of the perpetrator and the victim are unimportant.

During the first year in law school, you will become adept at stating holdings precisely, abstracting the essence from that holding, and applying that rule to a variety of hypothetical situations.

Often as in example 3, the holding fits neatly into one sentence. Sometimes, however, there are so many facts necessary to the holding that you must use two or more sentences to effectively communicate the court's holding with its legally relevant facts. Consider the following:

> In *Aschenbrenner,* the court held that the employee did not have good cause to voluntarily leave his job, because he had not attempted to resolve the problem with his employer. The claimant could have talked to his supervisor about the extensive overtime hours. He could have presented his grievance to his union grievance committee. Finally, he could have voluntarily cut back on his working hours to forty per week. When the claimant failed to use the three options available for working out the problem with his employer, the court ruled he was ineligible for unemployment benefits.

To state the court's holding including all the necessary facts, the writer needed a paragraph rather than a sentence. As you formulate fact specific holdings, use as many sentences as are necessary.

Holding = a statement of a court's decision on an issue that includes both the rule and the legally relevant facts.

Facts

There are two categories of facts: **substantive facts** and **procedural facts.** The substantive facts are the who, what, where, and when of the case. They are the legally significant facts that make the case unique. Remember the court decides this particular dispute between these particular parties. The **facts** are what limit the court's inquiry. The court will frame the issues using these **facts** and its **holding** will be limited to these facts.

The substantive facts are a critical part of a holding. Slight differences in fact can make the difference between a holding for one party or the other. If the robber in the hypothetical had threatened the old woman with a pocket knife, a butter knife, or a plastic knife, would the holding be the same?

The procedural facts explain what happened to the case procedurally in which courts. Procedural facts include, for example, that the trial court granted defendant's 12(b)(6) motion that plaintiff's complaint failed to state a claim upon which relief could be granted, and the appellate court's decision to affirm or reverse the decision below. **Substantive facts are the who, where, what and when the attorneys will use to frame the issues to the appellate court and that the court will use to frame its holding.**

Procedural facts explain the procedural basis for the appeal and the court's procedural decision.

Reasoning

The court's reasoning is the process it uses in choosing a rule and applying the rule to the facts. In the armed robbery hypothetical, for

example, a court might explain that from the victim's point of view, a
.45 caliber pistol causes the same fear as a switch blade knife. Sometimes the reasoning is implied. In reading the case, always try to
articulate for yourself the court's reasoning no matter how obvious it
may seem.

The reasoning is an important part of the case particularly if you
are asking the court to draw an analogy from another area of the law to
decide a case of first impression. At first glance a tenant evicted from
his apartment bears little relationship to an employee who has been
fired from his employment. But when you look at the reason for the
eviction, the reason for the discharge, and the way the court analyzed
the eviction case, the analogy is clearer. The court's reasoning in the
first case can be applied to the second case. The reasoning can help
you to understand why the court decided as it did, and it can be useful
in persuading a later court to decide an analogous case in your client's
favor.

**Reasoning = the process the court uses in choosing a rule and
applying it to the facts of a specific case to decide that case.**

Policy

Although not every opinion will contain policy, in many cases the
court will explain how its decision is consistent with public policy. This
is particularly true when the court is expanding a previous rule,
drawing an analogy from another area of the law, or deciding a case of
first impression. When the law is settled and this type of case is
common, the court will rarely explain the public policy behind its
decision.

Attorneys will often explain to the court in their briefs why the
position they advocate is consistent with the public policy, and why that
proposed by their opponent is contrary to public policy. While trial
level courts are more concerned with deciding cases, appellate courts
want to allow the law to develop in ways that are consistent with public
policy.

Public policy appears particularly in two kinds of cases. First,
courts will explain the public policy behind their decisions when they
want to discourage socially detrimental behavior. Second, courts will
often explain that their holdings are consistent with public policy when
they want to encourage socially desirable behavior. If armed robbery
in our hypothetical carries a mandatory sentence twice that for un-
armed robbery, the court might explain that it is expanding the
definition of an armed robber to include those with knives as well as
pistols to discourage the use of knives. In the *Marvin v. Marvin* case
on the other hand, the court was trying to encourage social responsibility. The court recognized that some relationships carry the same type
of promises and expectations as marriage and that society should
enforce these promises.

Policy = the public policy which will be furthered by the court's decision.

Dictum

Dictum, from the latin *obiter dictum* meaning clearly extraneous, is a part of the court's opinion that is unnecessary to deciding the case. Dictum does not carry the weight of a holding. A holding requires two steps. First, the issue must be fully argued by all sides to the dispute. Second, the court must consider the issue carefully in light of the arguments. Dictum is not the result of this adversary process. When it is unnecessary to the decision of the case, it may not have been either fully argued by opposing counsel or fully considered by the court. Even if one of the two steps is present, the result is still dictum. Sometimes dictum is easy to find. The court may say "if the facts had been x instead of y, we might have held b, but because the facts were y, we hold a." This type of dictum is useful for the attorney with a case with x facts, because it helps the attorney predict the outcome of his case. The more time that has passed between the opinion and his case, however, the less valuable the dictum becomes. The conditions may have changed and the judges who agreed with the dictum may have retired. When an attorney has no precedent, dictum is helpful in trying to argue the case for his client.

Sometimes dictum is not so easy to identify, and attorneys will not agree on whether a particular statement is holding or dictum. If there are two ways a court may approach a case to reach a particular result and the attorneys have argued both approaches, but only one approach is necessary to the decision, the court may discuss both approaches. Are they both holdings? Is one dictum? If both have been argued and the court has fully considered both, both are probably holdings. If one is discussed in detail and the other is treated in summary fashion, the second one is probably dictum.

Occasionally, the court makes a statement deciding the rights of someone who is not a party to the case. This statement is also dictum because the views of the absent party were not part of either the argument or the decision process.

Dictum = a statement by the court that is unnecessary to the court's decision. It does not carry the weight of a holding because it has not been fully argued by the parties and/or the court has not fully considered the issue.

OPINIONS

There are a number of different kinds of opinion the court may issue and the value of the opinion varies accordingly. Appellate courts are composed of more than one judge; there are nine justices of the United States Supreme Court, seven justices at the highest level of most state courts, and usually three judges at the intermediate appellate level. As a result there may be multiple opinions on a single case.

A majority opinion has the most weight and the greater the majority, the greater the weight of the opinion. A unanimous decision (9–0), (7–0), (3–0) carries more clout than a bare majority (5–4), (4–3), (2–1). While one justice or judge writes the opinion, the other members of the majority subscribe to that opinion. Sometimes one or more members will agree with the majority decision, but not the way the justice or judge reached that decision. This judge then writes a **concurring opinion,** explaining how he reached the same result. Sometimes the majority of the court will agree on the result, but there will be no majority on how to reach that result. This is called a **plurality decision.** In the United States Supreme Court, for example, three justices may agree on one analysis of the case and two more may agree on a separate approach to reach the same result, while four may disagree with the ultimate result. It is possible, albeit rare, to have nine different opinions in a single case. Justices or judges who disagree with the majority or plurality may write **dissenting** opinions, in which they explain why they would have reached a contrary result. When the issues in the case are controlled by existing precedent, the court may issue a *per curiam* opinion. This comes from the court as a whole and is not authored by any particular member of the court.

Finally you will sometimes read an opinion delivered by the court *en banc.* These cases come from the intermediate level appellate courts. These courts normally sit in three judge panels although there may be a dozen or more members of the court. The same issue may come to the court from different trial courts and two different three judge panels of the court might decide the case differently. To prevent contrary results and, as a consequence, uncertainty about the law, the court may sit *en banc.* In this case all judges on that court will decide the issue together. While not all intermediate appellate courts sit *en banc*, the federal courts of appeals do occasionally deliver *en banc* opinions.

As you read cases, be sure to consider the type of decision the court reached. All of these different types of opinions can be useful precedent, but you will need to remember and explain that the analysis came from a concurring or dissenting opinion, so you do not mislead your reader as to the weight given the analysis by the court.

ANATOMY OF A CASE

Reading cases is an active process. The following illustrates the dissection of a sample case. It includes not only the substantive and procedural elements, but it also explains the significance of the details you may find in reported cases.

Oregon v. Hancock illustrates the anatomy of a case. Read the case in conjunction with the explanations using the marginal numbers as a reference.

ardson, P.J., held that defendant, who was granted a temporary leave from penitentiary and who, during that leave and while living in a private residence, was found to be in possession of a sawed-off shotgun, was not guilty of possession of a weapon by a person committed to a penal institution.

Reversed and remanded. [12]

[13] Van Hoomissen, J., concurred and filed opinion.

[14] Thornton, J., dissented and filed opinion.

Convicts ⟺5 [15]

Inmate, who was granted a temporary leave from penitentiary to search for a job, and who, during that leave and while living in a private residence, was found to be in possession of a sawed-off shotgun, was not guilty of possession of a weapon by a person committed to a penal institution since he was not within the institution or under its direct custodial supervision when he possessed the shotgun. (Per Richardson, P.J., with one Judge concurring in result.) ORS 166.275.

[6A] 60 Or.App. 425

STATE of Oregon, Respondent, [3]

[1] v.

Gordon Charles HANCOCK, Appellant. [2]

No. 81 0842; CA A23448. [4]

Court of Appeals of Oregon.

Argued and Submitted June 18, 1982.

Decided Dec. 1, 1982. [5]

[7] Defendant was convicted in the Circuit [8] Court, Linn County, Wendell H. Tompkins, [9] J., of possession of a weapon by a person committed to a penal institution and being an ex-convict in possession of a firearm, and he appealed. The Court of Appeals, Rich-

[11]

Stephen J. Williams, Deputy Public Defender, Salem, argued the cause for appellant. With him on the brief was Gary D. Babcock, Public Defender, Salem. [16]

Daryl Dodson Wilson, Asst. Atty. Gen., Salem, argued the cause for respondent. With him on the brief was Dave Frohnmayer, Atty. Gen., and William F. Gary, Sol. Gen., Salem. [17]

Before RICHARDSON, P.J., and [10] THORNTON and VAN HOOMISSEN, JJ:

RICHARDSON, Presiding Judge. [11]

Defendant was convicted of possession of [18] a weapon by a person committed to a penal institution. ORS 166.275, and being an ex-convict in possession of a firearm. ORS

166.270. He appeals his conviction on the first charge. He contends that his motion for judgment of acquittal should have been granted because his conduct is not covered by ORS 166.275:

"Any person committed to any penal institution who, while under the jurisdiction of any penal institution or while being conveyed to or from any penal institution, possesses or carries upon his person, or has under his custody or control any dangerous instrument, or any weapon including but not limited to any blackjack, slingshot, billy, sand club, metal knuckles, explosive substance, dirk, dagger, sharp instrument, pistol, revolver or other firearm without lawful authority, is guilty of a felony and upon conviction thereof shall be punished by imprisonment in the penitentiary for a term not more than 20 years."

Defendant was an inmate of the Oregon State Penitentiary. Because he was due for parole in the near future, he was granted a temporary leave from the penitentiary to search for a job. During that leave and while living in a private residence, he was found to be in possession of a sawed-off shotgun.

He argues, citing *State v. Larsen,* 44 Or. App. 643, 606 P.2d 1159, *rev. den.* 289 Or. 373 (1980), that the statute is designed to protect institutional security and that he was not in the institution at the time he possessed the weapon. Essentially, he contends that the statute prohibits possession of weapons only in the institution or while being transported to or from it.

In *Larsen,* the defendant, an inmate of the penitentiary, was temporarily assigned to a work release center away from the penitentiary. He left the center without authorization, which was in essence an escape, ORS 162.155, and subsequently acquired a gun. He was convicted for violation of ORS 166.275. In vacating that conviction, we stated:

"* * * It is apparent that the intent of ORS 166.275 is to protect institutional security. The maximum penalty for violation of that statute is 20 years' imprisonment. Escape in the first degree, however, which may involve the use of a dangerous or deadly weapon to escape from custody or a correctional facility, ORS 162.165(1)(b), carries a maximum penalty of only 10 years' imprisonment. We decline to ascribe to the legislature the intent to punish a person more severely for the mere possession of any kind of weapon after escape than for the use of a dangerous or deadly weapon during an escape." 44 Or.App. at 651, 606 P.2d 1159.

The principal rationale of the decision in *Larsen* was that the defendant had effectively, albeit unlawfully, severed his ties with the penal institution and was no longer under direct custody supervision. Consequently there was no threat to institutional security by the defendant's possession of the weapon. In this case, too, defendant was no longer in the institution or under direct custody supervision. A threat to institutional security by possession of the weapon during his temporary leave simply did not exist.

The state presented evidence from a prison official that defendant was considered an inmate and would be an inmate until released on parole. The state argues that an inmate who is temporarily away from the institution and in possession of a weapon constitutes a threat to institutional security, because his status as an inmate may facilitate his smuggling the weapon into the prison on his return. Our conclusion in *Larsen* that the statute was designed to protect institutional security did not expand its reach to include all possession of weapons that potentially threaten institutional security. The statute does not penalize all possession of weapons by inmates, but only possession by inmates in a particular setting. That setting is within the institution or under its direct custodial supervision. Defendant's motion for judgment of acquittal on the charge of possession of a weapon by a person committed to a penal institution should have been allowed.

The court merged the two convictions and imposed sentence only on the charge of possession of a weapon by a person committed to a penal institution. The conviction on that charge is reversed, and the case is remanded for sentencing on the charge of ex-convict in possession of a firearm.

Reversed and remanded for resentencing.

25   VAN HOOMISSEN, Judge, concurring.

I concur in the result.

ORS 166.275 is a penal statute which cries for clarification. *See, e.g., State v. Larsen,* 44 Or.App. 643, 606 P.2d 1159, *rev. den.* 289 Or. 373 (1980). In the meantime, uncertainty as to legislative intent and the ambiguity in the statute must be resolved in favor of defendant. *Bell v. United States,* 349 U.S. 81, 83–4, 75 S.Ct. 620, 622, 99 L.Ed. 905 (1955); *State v. Perkins,* 45 Or.App. 91, 96, 607 P.2d 1202 (1980).

Felons sentenced to imprisonment may not be committed to a specific correctional facility by a sentencing judge. Rather, the law requires that a judge commit a convicted defendant to the legal and physical custody of the Corrections Division, ORS 137.-124(1), which thereafter may designate the particular corrections facility in which the felon is to be confined. ORS 137.124(2).

It is not clear to me what the phrase "any person committed to any penal institution" means. A sentencing judge is not authorized to commit anyone to a penal institution, and I doubt that the Corrections Division *commits* people to penal institutions. I also have difficulty with the phrase "while under the jurisdiction of any penal institution." I believe that technically a felon is always under the "jurisdiction" of the Corrections Division, not of the institution to which he or she may have been assigned. This case and *Larsen* should serve notice on
26 the legislature that this statute needs reexamination.

THORNTON, Judge, dissenting.

The majority holds, on the authority of
27 *State v. Larsen,* 44 Or.App. 643, 606 P.2d 1159, *rev. den.* 289 Or. 373 (1980), that defendant cannot be guilty of possession of a weapon because ORS 166.275 does not apply when the convicted person is outside the penal institution. I cannot agree.

In *Kneefe v. Sullivan,* 2 Or.App. 152, 465 P.2d 741, *rev. den.* (1970), we held that a work release enrollee who escaped while he was in physical custody in Multnomah County in connection with work release was still in the constructive custody of the Oregon State Correctional Institution in Marion County and therefore could be tried on the escape charge either in Multnomah County or Marion County.

Similarly, in *State v. Wolfe,* 10 Or.App. 118, 121, 497 P.2d 1222, *rev. den.* (1972), we held that a defendant who had been transferred from the correctional institution to work release for the purpose of attending the University of Oregon and who left the university without permission and was later apprehended in North Dakota was guilty of escape from the institution since he was technically an inmate of the institution at the time he escaped while on work release.

Here, defendant was committed to the Oregon State Prison and was under the jurisdiction of that institution at the time he was found in possession of a sawed-off shotgun. Defendant was both committed to a penal institution and under the jurisdiction of that penal institution when he unlawfully possessed the weapon. *State v. Wolfe, supra; Kneefe v. Sullivan, supra.* The conclusion is inescapable that the trial court did not err in denying defendant's motion for judgment of acquittal. Although *State v. Larsen, supra,* is distinguishable on the facts, I believe it was 28 incorrectly decided for the reasons outlined above. I would therefore overrule *Larsen* and affirm the trial court here.

For the foregoing reasons, I respectfully dissent.

1) The full name of the case is *State of Oregon v. Gordon Charles Hancock.* Names of cases are written either in italics or they are underlined. The name of the case can be shortened to *State v. Hancock,* as you see it written on the top of the next page, or as *Oregon v. Hancock.* If you were writing to an Oregon court and only using cases

from that jurisdiction, *State v. Hancock* would be sufficient. If, on the other hand, you were writing to a court in a different jurisdiction or using cases from several jurisdictions, "*State* " would be confusing and "*Oregon* " is clearer.

2) Hancock is the appealing party. He is called the **appellant.** Sometimes the appealing party is called the **petitioner.**

3) Oregon is the responding party in this appeal. It is called the **respondent.** Often the responding party is called the **appellee.**

4) No. 81 0842, CA A 23448 is the **docket number.** The first part of the number indicates that the appeal was the 842nd filed in 1981. It was filed in the Court of Appeals, CA, and is number A23448 overall in that court. Different jurisdictions use different numbering systems. If you wanted to find out more about this case, you could contact the court and use this number to identify the case.

5) The case was argued on June 18, 1982 and the court issued its opinion on December 1, 1982. The date a court decides a case is important for relating it to other decisions and for judging the weight to be given the case. An old case, from the 19th century or the 1920s, for example, may not reflect subsequent changes in technology or social values or it may still be good law. Be aware of these possibilities and check the date of every case you read.

6) 653 P.2d 1304 is part of the **citation** of the case. The full citation or cite includes the name of the case, the reporter volume and page, the jurisdiction and level of court, and the year of the decision. Court opinions are compiled in series of books called **reporters.** The first number refers to the volume of the reporter, volume 653. P.2d refers to the Pacific Regional Reporter, second series. Oregon cases are reported in the Pacific Reporter. The final number, 1304, refers to the page in that volume where the case begins.

6A) This case is also reported in the Oregon Reports, Court of Appeals. In this series, the case begins at page 425 of volume 60.

7) This **summary** of the case is not part of the opinion. It was written by an editor working for the reporter series. The summary is useful for quickly deciding if the case is useful to the issues you are researching. You must never rely on a summary or quote from it in your writing. It is the editor's view of what the case holds. You must always refer to the opinion itself for the issues, rules, holdings, reasoning, and policy.

8) This appeal came from a decision of the Circuit Court for Linn County. If you wish to see the complaint or another part of the record of this case, you would contact the trial court.

9) Judge Wendell H. Tompkins was the trial judge in this case.

10) Three judges sat on the panel that considered this case. Judge Richardson presided.

11) The presiding judge wrote the majority opinion.

12) Procedurally the judges reversed the decision of the trial court and remanded the case back to the trial court, so that Judge Tompkins could resentence the defendant, Hancock.

13) Judge Van Hoomissen wrote a concurring opinion.

14) Judge Thornton wrote a dissenting opinion.

15) This paragraph is called a **headnote.** It, too, was written by an editor. Headnotes give the holdings of a case on each issue discussed in the case. If you research the issue in this jurisdiction, you will be able to find this case and a digest of the issue, which is the language of the headnote. Headnotes are important research tools, but as with summaries, you must never rely on a headnote or quote from it; you must always go to the court's opinion as the primary source. The "Convicts key 5" is a **key number.** The key number includes both the word and the number. It is part of the West Publishing Company research system. It permits you to research the same issue in many different jurisdictions and in a variety of West publications.

16) Stephen J. Williams argued the case for the defendant. Gary D. Babcock helped him write the brief. If you had a similar case, you might wish to contact them for help with your case. You will find that attorneys are most helpful to each other.

17) Daryl Wilson, Dave Frohnmayer and William Gary represented the State of Oregon on the appeal.

18) *Procedural posture of the case.*

The defendant, Hancock, was convicted in the trial court of two charges: 1) "possession of a weapon by a person committed to a penal institution" in violation of Oregon Revised Statutes sec. 166.275, and 2) "being an ex-convict in possession of a firearm" in violation of Oregon Revised Statutes sec. 166.270. The opinion does not state whether he was tried in a bench trial or a jury trial. The trial court merged the counts and sentenced him on the first count, the more serious of the two. The defendant appealed his conviction on the first count. He did this by first making a motion for a judgment of acquittal on the first count in the trial court. The judge denied the motion. The defendant then appealed the denial of that motion. The appellate court reached a procedural holding in the case. It reversed the conviction on the first count and remanded the case back to the trial court for sentencing on the second count.

19) *Substantive facts.*

The defendant, Hancock, was an inmate at the Oregon State Penitentiary. Because he was due for parole, he was given a temporary leave to search for employment. While he was on leave and living in a private residence, he was discovered with a sawed-off shotgun.

20) *Issue on appeal.*

Was the defendant properly convicted of "possession of a weapon by a person committed to a penal institution" under Oregon Revised

Statutes sec. 166.725, when he was on "temporary leave from the penitentiary" and was in possession of a sawed-off shotgun while living in a private residence?

The issue statement contains both the rule in question and the specific facts of the defendant's case. Although the court explained the issue and the facts separately, you should put them together into a fact-specific issue statement.

21) *Rule.*

There are two parts to the rule. First, there is the statute, Oregon Revised Statutes sec. 166.275:

> "*Any person committed to any penal institution who, while under the jurisdiction of any penal institution, possesses* or carries upon his person, or has under his custody or control any dangerous instrument, or any *weapon* including but not limited to any blackjack, slingshot, billy, sand club, metal knuckles, explosive substance, dirk, dagger, sharp instrument, pistol, revolver or *other firearm* without lawful authority, *is guilty of a felony and upon conviction thereof shall be punished by imprisonment in the penitentiary for a term not more than 20 years.*"

The statute is not clear on its face. It does not explain what "under the jurisdiction of any penal institution" means. In order to find out what that language means, the court looks to the second part of the rule, the case of *State v. Larsen,* 44 Or. App. 643, 606 P.2d 1159, *review denied* 289 Or. 373 (1980). From the citation, you can see that the case was decided in the Oregon Court of Appeals and that the Oregon Supreme Court—"*review denied* 289 Or. 373"—did not grant review of the intermediate level decision. In essence, it acquiesced in the Court of Appeals decision. Under the doctrine of *stare decisis*, the Court of Appeals was required to use *State v. Larsen* to decide Hancock's appeal. You can see that the facts in *Larsen* were similar. The defendant there was not on leave from the penitentiary, but he was assigned to a work release center. He went AWOL and acquired a gun. The court took the essence of that decision to formulate the rule to be applied in Hancock's case. If a defendant "has severed his ties with the penal institution" and "is no longer under direct custody supervision", then he is no longer "under the jurisdiction of any penal institution" for purposes of the statute, Or. Rev. Stat. 166.275.

22) *Holding.*

In the opinion written by presiding Judge Richardson, the court held that defendant Hancock was not "in the jurisdiction of any penal institution" within the meaning of Or. Rev. Stat. 166.275. He was on "temporary leave from the penitentiary" and living in a private residence when he was discovered with a weapon.

You can see that the holding, like the issue, is fact specific. In this opinion, the Court of Appeals was only deciding this particular case with its specific facts.

23) *Policy.*

The public policy behind the statute was to protect the security of the state's penal institutions.

24) *Reasoning.*

The court reasoned that in light of the legislative intent to protect security in the state's penal institutions by imposing a stiffer sentence on those found with weapons while in those institutions, the more severe penalty should not be imposed if the security of the institution is not threatened. As defendant, Hancock, was on temporary leave from the penitentiary and living in a private residence, the sawed-off shotgun was not a threat to the security of the penitentiary.

You can see that all of the pieces of the case are interconnected: the facts, procedure, issue, rule, holding, policy and reasoning. You will understand cases best if you articulate each of the elements of a case as you read.

25) *Concurring opinion.*

Judge Van Hoomissen concurred in the result reached by Judge Richardson, but he used a different rule to reach that result. He would frame the issue in the same way as his colleague. He also found that the statute was ambiguous. In order to resolve the ambiguity, he used a different rule, a rule of statutory construction. When the legislative intent is uncertain and the statute is ambiguous, the ambiguity must be resolved in favor of the defendant. He cited two cases as his authority. One was a U.S. Supreme Court case, *Bell v. United States,* and the other was a later case from the Oregon Court of Appeals, *State v. Perkins.* His holding would be different from that of Judge Richardson. When the legislative intent is uncertain and the language of Or. Rev. Stat. 166.275—"person committed to a penal institution" and "under the jurisdiction of any penal institution" is ambiguous, the language should be read in favor of the defendant, such that an inmate on temporary leave, living in a private residence was neither "committed to" nor "under the jurisdiction of" "a penal institution."

26) Judge Van Hoomissen then requested that the legislature clarify the statute. In our tripartite system of government, it is the legislative responsibility to make law; it is not the province of the courts. This court was, in essence, making law by reading the statute narrowly. It is now up to the legislature to either accept the court's reading of legislative intent or to amend the statute. You will see this interplay between these two branches of government quite frequently.

27) Judge Thornton did not agree with the analysis of either of his colleagues and he wrote a dissenting opinion. He used two cases that interpret similar language but in a different context. Both *State v. Wolf* and *Kneefe v. Sullivan* involved inmates who were on work release from penal institutions when they escaped. Both were under the custody or jurisdiction of penal institutions and could be charged with escape. The rule Judge Thornton abstracts from these facts is

that an inmate temporarily released from a penal institution is under the jurisdiction of that penal institution. He would, therefore, hold that Hancock was under the jurisdiction of the Oregon State Penitentiary when he was on temporary leave, such that he was properly convicted of "possession of a weapon by a person committed to a penal institution" under Or. Rev. Stat. sec. 166.275 when he was discovered in possession of a sawed-off shotgun.

28) Note that Judge Thornton believed that *State v. Larsen* was incorrect and should be overruled. But as he did not have the votes to overrule that case, he concluded that it could be distinguished on its facts, but he did not explain how to distinguish the case. If you take a careful look at the facts of these cases, you can understand the judge's position. In *State v. Wolfe* and *Kneefe v. Sullivan,* the defendants were on work release and, therefore, in the custody of the correctional institution at the time they escaped. The defendant in *State v. Larsen* was also still in custody when he escaped, but he was no longer in custody after the escape and at the time he was discovered with a gun. Hancock was still on leave in a private residence, right where the Oregon State Penitentiary expected and permitted him to be, when he was found in possession of a shotgun. He was, in Judge Thornton's view, still in the custody of the correctional institution.

You can see from this example how the attorneys for the State and the defendant probably argued the case and how the judges used the precedent to reach different conclusions. Based on the law as presented in the case, how would you have decided it? Why?

CASE BRIEFING

As you read cases in law school and later for clients, you should dissect each case and write a summary of its essential components. Although not every case contains all the elements, begin by systematically searching for and articulating each piece.

Procedural posture—Note how the case arose with reference to the litigation time line and what the appellate court, if appropriate, decided procedurally.

Substantive facts—Pick out the substantive facts that were necessary to the court's holdings on the issues.

As you look at the issues, be sure to treat each issue separately, articulating the rule, holding, reasoning, and policy for each issue before moving on to subsequent issues.

Issue—State the issue in a fact specific way according to the basic formula—DOES THE RULE APPLY TO THE FACTS?

Rule—State the general rule the court used to resolve the case. The rule may include a statute and case law interpreting that statute. If the court considered several rules, chose one and rejected the rest, explain why the one rule was appropriate and the others were not.

Holding—State the fact specific holding of the case. Include the rule and all the facts that were essential to the court's decision. Generalize the facts only where the specific detail was not necessary to the court's decision. Remember a holding can be more than one sentence when there are many legally significant facts necessary to the court's decision on the issue.

Reasoning—Explain how the court chose the rule and applied it to the facts of the case.

Policy—State the public policy that supports the court's holding.

Concurring or Dissenting Opinions—Include the essential points from the concurring and dissenting opinions, if any.

Evaluate—This may be a two step process. First, think critically about the case. Do you agree with the court's decision, its reasoning, and the policy? If you disagree, how would you have decided the case? Second, if you are reading the case in the context of others on the same issue, put the case in its context. For law school courses, explain how it fits with the other cases on this topic in the assignment. Be sure to include the note cases. If you are briefing a case you are going to use in analyzing a legal problem, put the case in the context of the others you have found in your research on this issue.

While case briefing may seem to be inordinately time consuming, you will find your knowledge of the law and how the legal system works will increase dramatically if you actively grapple with the cases. Case briefing is a good method for doing just that. With time, you will develop short cuts and you will be much more adept at finding and articulating the components of a case. Conscientious case briefing at the beginning of your legal career will help this process.

Exercise 4A.

Read *Oregon v. Haley.* Find and articulate the elements of the case.

STATE v. HALEY
Court of Appeals, 1983.
64 Or. App. 209, 667 P.2d 560.

GILLETTE, PRESIDING JUDGE.

Defendant seeks reversal of his convictions for driving while suspended (Or. Rev. Stat. 487.560(1)) and driving under the influence of intoxicants (Or. Rev. Stat. 487.540), contending that the trial court erred by withdrawing his affirmative defense of necessity from the jury. Because defendant offered no evidence to support one of the two elements of that defense, the trial court's ruling was not reversible error. We therefore affirm.

Prior to trial, defendant stipulated that he was driving a motor vehicle on the night of his arrest, that his driver's license was suspended and that he was under the influence of intoxicants. Despite these stipulations, defendant pleaded not guilty to the charge of driving while suspended and raised a "necessity" defense under Or. Rev. Stat. 487.-560(2)(a). That statute states:

"(2) In a prosecution [for the crime of 'driving while suspended'] * * * it is an affirmative defense that:

"(a) An injury or immediate threat of injury to human or animal life and the urgency of the circumstances made it necessary for the defendant to drive a motor vehicle at the time and place in question; * * * "

In support of his defense, defendant introduced evidence that his father had fallen from a bar stool and broken his ankle and that he, defendant, was driving his father to the hospital when the police officer stopped their car. The state asked the court to withdraw the necessity defense from the jury; the court granted the motion. This appeal followed.

* * *

We hold that defendant, having raised a necessity defense, had the burden of proving by a preponderance of the evidence (1) that there was an injury or threat of injury to human or animal life and (2) that the urgency of the circumstances made it necessary for him to drive at the time and place in question. It follows from this holding that, if either element of the defense lacked evidentiary support, the trial judge had the authority to withdraw the defense from the jury's consideration. *State v. Peters,* 49 Or. App. 653, 619 P.2d 1360 (1980); *see also State v. Matthews,* 30 Or. App. 1133, 1135, 569 P.2d 662 (1977).[3]

Defendant next contends that the trial court erroneously interpreted Or. Rev. Stat. 487.560(2)(a) by requiring defendant to show that his father's injury was "life-threatening." The trial court's oral ruling on the state's withdrawal motion demonstrates that the court interpreted the statutory phrase "injury or threat of injury to human or animal life" to mean "life-threatening injury" and granted the motion in part because defendant had failed to produce evidence of a "life-threatening" injury.[4] The state agrees with the trial court's interpretation. Defen-

---

3. Our holding is consistent with other case law interpreting Or. Rev. Stat. 487.-560(2) and with the legislative history of that provision. *State v. Buttrey,* 293 Or. 575, 583, 651 P.2d 1075 (1982); *see State v. Peters, supra; State v. Lawrence,* 36 Or. App. 733, 736, 585 P.2d 727 (1978); Minutes, House Committee on Judiciary, May 5, 1975 at 2.

4. The state, arguing its motion for withdrawal, said:

"* * * [W]hat I am saying is [that defendant had] not shown that there was an *immediate life threatening situation.* * * * Neither [has defendant] shown

that it was necessary for [defendant] to drive rather than calling an ambulance; rather than seeking aid from other people in the bar; rather than calling the police; rather than having two people who were examined by another police officer who were found not to be under the influence of intoxicants. Have them drive. * * * "

The trial judge then made the following findings and statements in his oral ruling:

"* * * *

dant, on the other hand, contends that the statute does not require such evidence. We are thus called on to decide for the first time whether Or. Rev. Stat. 487.560(2)(a) requires proof of an injury of "life-threatening" severity.[5]

As noted, the statute requires a defendant to show "an injury or threat of injury to human or animal life." This phrase could mean either: (1) actual or threatened harm to a human being or an animal, as opposed to other, inanimate property, or (2) actual or threatened harm severe enough to cause the death of a human being or an animal. Neither the remainder of the statute nor its commentary resolves this ambiguity. We are convinced, however, that the legislature intended the statute to have the former meaning.

First, a comparison of the "necessity" defense at issue here and the more general "choice of evils" defense in Or. Rev. Stat. 161.200 suggests that the reference to "human or animal life" in Or. Rev. Stat. 487.-560(2)(a) is simply intended to make the "necessity" defense unavailable when the "injury or threat of injury" is to real or personal *property* rather than a living creature. By contrast, the "choice of evils" statute provides:

"(1) Unless inconsistent with * * * some other provision of law, conduct which would otherwise constitute an offense is justifiable and not criminal when:

"(a) That conduct is necessary as an emergency measure to avoid an imminent public or private injury; and

"Certainly there is no evidence at all that there was a *life threatening situation* here. * * *

" * * *

" * * * [T]here is no evidence in the case that there was a *threat of injury to life,* and so I will withdraw the emergency defense.

" * * *

" * * * I find that there was no *threat of injury to* the defendant's father's *life* and that there was no urgency or [of] circumstances that made it necessary for the defendant to drive a vehicle at the time and place in question * * *.

" * * *

" * * * There was no evidence in the case at all that it appeared to the defendant that there was a *life threatening* situation. * * *

" * * *

" * * * [The] injury had already taken place [and] there is nothing to indicate that the defendant's father's injury would have been worsened or that he could have been further injured had the defendant not driven him to the hospital. * * * " (Emphasis supplied.)

5. The state contends that we answered this question in the affirmative in *State v. Peters, supra.* The defendant in *Peters* alleged that his mother's illness required him to drive her to the hospital. The severity of the defendant's mother's illness was not in issue, but we noted in passing that "the jury could have found [from the evidence] that the situation appeared to defendant to be life-threatening." The state argues that this language establishes a requirement that defendants prove "life-threatening" injury in order to establish a necessity defense. The state is mistaken. As noted above, a defendant asserting a necessity defense must prove two elements: (1) actual or threatened injury and (2) urgent circumstances. The issue in *Peters* involved the second element. Our brief discussion of the "injury" element was therefore dictum rather than a considered interpretation of the pertinent statutory language.

"(b) The threatened injury is of such gravity that, according to ordinary standards of intelligence and morality, the desirability and urgency of avoiding the injury clearly outweigh the desirability of avoiding the injury sought to be prevented by the statute defining the offense in issue.

"* * * *"

This language and the Official Commentary to the 1971 Oregon Criminal Code, at 20, demonstrate that the choice of evils defense may be invoked by a defendant who has acted unlawfully in order to prevent the destruction of inanimate property. The necessity defense is similar in nature to the choice of evils defense but narrower: it will only shelter a defendant whose illegal action was intended to remedy or prevent injury to human or animal *life*. This difference in the scope of the two defenses was achieved by the legislature's use of the phrase "human or animal life" in Or. Rev. Stat. 487.560(2)(a). We think it is fair to assume that the creation of that distinction was the only purpose of the phrase "human or animal life."

Second, the imposition of a "life-threatening" standard could have unreasonably harsh effects in certain circumstances. For example, suppose that a suspended driver and another person travel 30 miles by motor vehicle to a remote area in order to camp and hike. In the course of a hike, the suspended driver's companion breaks his leg. It is clear to the suspended driver that his companion is not in danger of dying, although he is in pain. The driver is faced with a choice: he can violate Or. Rev. Stat. 487.560(1) and drive 30 miles for help, or he can *hike* that distance. The state's construction of subsection (2)(a) would compel the latter decision, but we think it unlikely that the legislature intended such a harsh result. We have often held that we "presume the legislature did not intend harsh results that literal application of statutory terms would cause." *State ex rel Juv. Dept. v. Gates,* 56 Or. App. 694, 699, 642 P.2d 1200 (1982); *Mallon v. Emp. Div.,* 41 Or. App. 479, 484, 599 P.2d 1164 (1979). *A fortiori,* we are not inclined to read into *ambiguous* language a meaning with the potential to produce such results.

Third, there is no harm in omitting a "life-threatening" requirement from the defense. If the state is concerned that, absent such a requirement, suspended drivers will use passengers' minor cuts and pulled muscles to establish the defense, the state's fear is unfounded. In addition to proving the existence or threat of an injury, a defendant must demonstrate that the "urgency of the circumstances" compelled him to drive. The circumstances attending most minor injuries will not be "urgent" enough to aid in the establishment of a necessity defense.

Finally, we note that, as a general rule of statutory construction, we are to resolve doubts about legislative intent in favor of criminal defendants. *State v. Linthwaite,* 52 Or. App. 511, 523 n. 12, 628 P.2d 1250 (1981), *rev'd and rem'd on other grounds,* 295 Or. 162, 665 P.2d 863

(1983); *see State v. Cloutier,* 286 Or. 579, 587–88, 596 P.2d 1278 (1979). In the absence of clear legislative intent or other reasons why we should read a requirement of "life-threatening" injury into the ambiguous language of Or. Rev. Stat. 487.560(2)(a), we decline to do so. To the extent that the trial court imposed such a requirement on defendant, the court erred.

Our refusal to apply a "life-threatening" standard does not, however, require reversal. As the findings quoted, *supra,* n. 4, demonstrate, the trial court found no evidence that "the urgency [of] the circumstances made it necessary" for defendant to drive his father to the hospital. This finding was based on evidence that defendant made no attempt to telephone an ambulance, the police or other emergency services, although he knew such services existed in the vicinity, and did not request the driving assistance of other individuals at the bar who were both sober[6] and licensed. Defendant offered no explanation for his failure to secure an alternative form of transportation for his father, and he points to no other evidence which could support an inference that the "urgency of the circumstances" compelled *him* to drive his injured parent to the hospital. The language of Or. Rev. Stat. 487.560(2)(a) makes it clear that a defendant seeking to establish a necessity defense must prove *both* injury and urgent circumstances. Defendant's failure to offer evidence to establish the latter element justified the trial court's decision to withdraw the necessity defense from the jury. *State v. Peters, supra.*

Affirmed.

Exercise 4B.

Read *Oregon v. Dugger.* Find and articulate the elements of the case.

STATE v. DUGGER
Court of Appeals, 1985.
73 Or. App. 109, 698 P.2d 491.

RICHARDSON, JUDGE.

Defendant publicly exposed his genitals while he was in the Frederick & Nelson department store, and he was charged with public indecency. Or. Rev. Stat. 163.465. He entered into a civil compromise with the store's management pursuant to Or. Rev. Stat. 135.703 *et seq.,* and the trial court dismissed the charge. The state appeals from the dismissal. We reverse.

Or. Rev. Stat. 135.703 provides:

"When a defendant is charged with a crime punishable as a misdemeanor for which the person injured by the act constituting

---

6. When a court or jury makes its assessment of the "urgency of the circumstances," it is appropriate to consider the fact that the defendant was intoxicated at the time.

the crime has a remedy by a civil action, the crime may be compromised, as provided in Or. Rev. Stat. 135.705, except when it was committed:

"(1) By or upon a peace officer while in the execution of the duties of his office;

"(2) Riotously; or

"(3) With an intent to commit a crime punishable only as a felony."

The state argues that public indecency is not the kind of offense to which Or. Rev. Stat. 135.703 applies, because the statute is limited to "cases in which the person injured by the act constituting the crime has a civil action remedy. Public indecency is not such a crime." The problem with the state's argument is that it does not go far enough. It is virtually unimaginable that *any* crime *cannot* produce *some* injury that is redressable through a civil action. Here, for example, the store *could* have lost business or suffered other compensable injury as a result of defendant's act. In our view, the issue is whether the statute applies to a criminal act that can produce a civilly redressable injury if that injury is not the sole consequence of the act and is incidental at most to the legislature's objective in criminalizing the act.

In *State v. Yos,* 71 Or. App. 57, 691 P.2d 508 (1984), decided while this appeal was pending, we held that a charge of reckless driving was properly dismissed by the trial court after the defendant had "entered into a civil compromise with the person whose auto he had struck" while driving recklessly. We explained:

"The civil compromise statute, Or. Rev. Stat. 135.703, applies to any 'crime punishable as a misdemeanor for which the person injured by the act constituting the crime has a remedy by a civil action.' The statute requires three elements to invoke the compromise procedure: (1) an act, (2) that is punishable as a misdemeanor and (3) for which *a person has a civil remedy.* All the elements are present here: defendant drove recklessly—a crime punishable as a misdemeanor—and *a person was injured* and would have a civil remedy in tort against the driver." 71 Or. App. at 59–60, 691 P.2d 508. (Emphasis added; footnote omitted.)

The problem with our reasoning in *Yos* begins with the emphasized language. *Yos* refers to *a* person injured by the defendant's act; the statute refers to *the* person injured by the act. The words "a person injured by the act" in the statutory context *might* indeed dictate the conclusion we reached in *Yos* that the civil compromise procedure is available to defendants charged with crimes of any kind, if the consequences of their conduct *happen to include* an injury for which a person has a remedy by civil action. However, the words "the person injured by the act" do not carry the same connotation of randomness; they indicate that there *must* be a *discrete* victim or victims in order for the act to constitute a crime.

We noted in *Yos:*

"While the statutory language compels this result, we wish to note our objection to it. Read together, this case and *State v. Duffy* [, 33 Or. App. 301, 576 P.2d 797 (1978),] now stand for the proposition that a reckless driver who misses people during his drive can be prosecuted, but one who hit someone can buy his way out. As a matter of public policy, that seems backwards. We commend the matter to the attention of the legislature." 71 Or. App. at 60, n. 4, 691 P.2d 508.

We now conclude that the language of the statute does not *compel* the result we reached in *Yos.* Even if the statutory language *supports* our interpretation in *Yos,* we now reject that interpretation, because it is not compelled and because, as the *Yos* footnote suggests, the interpretation produces an absurd and unreasonable result. *See Johnson v. Star Machinery Co.,* 270 Or. 694, 704, 530 P.2d 53 (1974). *Yos* was wrongly decided, and we overrule it.

The defendant in *Yos* was not entitled to a civil compromise of the reckless driving charge, because his offense endangered every person and vehicle on the road, as well as caused actual damage to one car and driver. The defendant in this case is not entitled to avail himself of the civil compromise procedure, because other members of the public who observed or could have observed his act were as entitled as the management of the store not to be subjected to it. Both reckless driving and public indecency are acts that the legislature has criminalized to protect the public at large. The coincidence that any given person is compensably injured by the commission of those acts has no cognizable relationship to the legislature's purpose in criminalizing them or to the legislature's purpose in establishing the civil compromise procedure as an alternative to the prosecution of misdemeanors that affect only persons who have a right to civil redress.[1]

Reversed and remanded for trial.

Exercise 4C.

Read *Jones v. City of Prairie City, Oregon.* Find and articulate the elements of the case.

JONES v. CITY OF PRAIRIE CITY
Court of Appeals, 1987.
86 Or. App. 701, 740 P.2d 236.

Van Hoomissen, Judge.

This is an action to recover damages for negligence. Defendant's motion to dismiss was allowed. ORCP 21 A(8). Plaintiff appeals. The

---

1. We do not suggest that the public's abstract interest in the prosecution of crime prevents the civil compromise of misdemeanors that can do nothing more than cause actual injury to a particular person or persons.

issue is whether plaintiff's complaint states a claim. We conclude that it does and reverse.

Plaintiff, a minor child, was bitten by a dog running at large in Prairie City (City). City's police department impounded the dog on the day that plaintiff was bitten. Two days later, City destroyed the dog. It had not been tested for rabies before it was destroyed and, because it could not thereafter be determined whether or not it was rabid, plaintiff had to undergo a series of rabies inoculations.

Plaintiff sued City, alleging that it was negligent in destroying the dog without waiting 10 days, in violation of Or. Rev. Stat. 609.090. City moved to dismiss the complaint for failure to state a claim for relief. The trial court held that plaintiff is not a member of the class of persons intended to be protected by Or. Rev. Stat. 609.090 and granted City's motion.

Or. Rev. Stat. 609.090 provides, in relevant part:

"(1) When any dog is found running at large in any county, precinct or city * * * or when a dog is a public nuisance * * *, every chief of police, constable, sheriff or deputy of either, or other police or dog control officer shall impound it * * *.

"(2) * * * If no owner appears to redeem a dog within the allotted time, or if the dog has been impounded as a public nuisance for killing or injuring a person, it shall be killed in a humane manner. * * *

"(3) Notwithstanding the provisions of subsection (2) of this section, any dog impounded for biting a person shall be held for not less than 10 days before redemption or destruction to determine if the dog is rabid."

Plaintiff argues that the statute is narrowly and clearly written, that there could be no intended beneficiary other than the person bitten by the dog and that there could be no harm to be prevented other than that which plaintiff sustained. City argues that the only purpose of the statute is to give public bodies authority to destroy dangerous dogs, that the 10-day requirement was enacted at the request of the Oregon Health Department and that the legislative history [1] suggests that its

---

1. The legislative history demonstrates that, before the 1975 amendment of Or. Rev. Stat. 609.090, cities had no express authority to destroy vicious dogs. They could destroy only stray dogs that were unclaimed after five days. Senator Heard, the bill's sponsor, stated that the purpose of the bill was to authorize cities to destroy a dog that had severely injured or killed a person. The bill was drafted in response to a specific incident in which a child was badly injured by a dog. Subsection 3, the 10-day hold provision, was added at the request of the Oregon Health Department.

Minutes, House Committee on Agriculture and Natural Resources (May 28, 1975).

Senator Heard's Administrative Assistant, Oleson, testified about the bill.

"They have worked with Mr. Dierdorff on a couple of amendments covering concerns about the bill which people brought to their attention in terms of shooting dogs on site. That should not be allowed and also in terms of the biting situation, the county health officer should have the dog quarantined for at least 10 days so they can detect rabies."

only purpose was to permit the destruction of dangerous dogs and not to create a basis for a private claim for dog bite victims.

The issues in a negligence case are "whether defendant's conduct caused a foreseeable kind of harm to an interest protected against that kind of negligent invasion, and whether the conduct creating the risk of that kind of harm was unreasonable under the circumstances." *Donaca v. Curry County*, 303 Or. 30, 38, 734 P.2d 1339 (1987). There are various methods of establishing what is foreseeable and what is reasonable. A plaintiff may rely on common law standards of care or on a statute which itself establishes a standard. *Shahtout v. Emco Garbage Co.*, 298 Or. 598, 695 P.2d 897 (1985). Further,

> "[w]hen a plaintiff (or a defendant seeking to prove negligence on plaintiff's part) invokes a governmental rule in support of that theory, the question is whether the rule, though not itself intended to create a civil claim, nevertheless so fixes the legal standard of conduct that there is no question of due care left for the fact finder to determine; in other words, that noncompliance with the rule is negligence as a matter of law." 298 Or. at 601, 695 P.2d 897.

Unless a court can justifiably say that no reasonable fact finder could find the risk foreseeable or that the defendant's conduct fell below acceptable standards, the questions of foreseeability and reasonableness are for the fact finder to decide. *Fazzolari v. Portland School Dist. No. 1J*, 303 Or. 1, 17, 734 P.2d 1326 (1987); *Donaca v. Curry Co. supra*, 303 Or. at 38, 734 P.2d 1339.

In this case, it is at least arguably foreseeable that, if a dog is destroyed before the time needed for testing for rabies expires, a person bitten by the dog would have to undergo treatment against rabies. The statute provides that City could have impounded the dog for the necessary 10 days, thus preventing it from running at large. In the absence of some explanation for a need to destroy the dog in less than 10 days, a reasonable fact finder could conclude that City's conduct was unreasonable. The fact that the legislative history of Or. Rev. Stat. 609.090 does not indicate an intent to create a new cause of action does not prevent the statute from being used to measure the standard of care of officials who impound dogs under the authority of that statute in determining whether City's conduct was reasonable under the circumstances. *Shahtout v. Emco Garbage Co., supra.*

Reversed and remanded.

Further discussion focused on the purpose of the amendment.

"Senator Roberts stated this allows for destruction of the dog *but does not do anything for the person who has been injured.*

"Dave Dierdorff stated *that is right,* but the person who is injured would still have possible action against the owner of the dog depending on the circumstances. This is primarily to allow a county to destroy a dog after holding it for the necessary 10 days quarantine period if that dog is dangerous to people." Minutes, Senate Committee on Agriculture and Natural Resources, (April 24, 1975, at 1.) (Emphasis supplied.)

Chapter 5

UNDERSTANDING STATUTES

Statutes play an increasingly important role in society and consequently, in a lawyer's job of representing his clients. Statutes are a form of legislative law and are enacted to address societal problems. Statutes exist at both the state and federal levels, and often there are statutes at both levels that are applicable to a particular legal issue. Unlike rules from cases, which resolve issues raised by specific facts, statutes are applicable to the public in general. The goal of this chapter is to introduce you to the legislative process, the component parts of a statute and how to use statutes to analyze legal issues. As a lawyer, you will be using statutes to advise clients about the consequences of prospective action and to predict the outcome of existing legal problems. Even though you may not be aware of any statute on a particular issue, you should always begin your research by looking for an applicable statute.

THE LEGISLATIVE PROCESS

The legislative process described here reflects the general process used by Congress and most state legislatures. It begins with a proposed piece of legislation, called a **bill.** A member of the legislature, the **sponsor,** presents the bill to the legislative house where he sits. With some limited exceptions [1], the idea may originate with either house of Congress or a state legislature. The bill is then referred for consideration to the **committee** (sometimes more than one committee) that has jurisdiction over the particular subject area. The committee has three basic options. It may reject the proposal, it may accept the proposal with or without amendments, and it may hold hearings on the proposal prior to voting on the bill. At a hearing, legislators consider testimony of governmental agencies with particular knowledge of the subject matter of the bill, major proponents and opponents of the bill, and interested members of the public. Depending on the vote of the

---

1. The United States Constitution, Art. I, Sec. 7 requires that revenue raising bills originate in the House of Representatives, although the Senate may concur or propose amendments.

committee, the bill will either die in the committee or be voted out to the full legislative house with a committee report on the bill.

Legislative bodies and their committees are political. The composition and chair of a committee are determined by the majority party in the legislature. In committee, the fate of a bill may well depend on whether it has either bipartisan or majority party support. Committee members will negotiate among themselves to gain support for legislation that is of particular interest to their constituents.

The full body then considers the bill and rejects or accepts it with or without amendments. A good deal of political negotiation may also occur at this stage of the process. The procedure varies with the legislative body. There may be considerable discussion of the bill or just a vote. In a bicameral legislature [2], the bill must also be approved by both legislative houses. When the two bodies approve the bill, but in different forms, a conference committee will meet to resolve the differences. The conference committee may also issue a report on the bill. When a bill dealing with the same subject was introduced in both legislative houses, there may be committee reports from both. The report from the house whose version ultimately becomes law will be more useful in determining the legislative intent behind the statute.

After both houses have approved the bill in its final form, it is sent to the **executive,** either the President or the governor [3], for approval. The executive can sign the bill or veto it. Normally, he will issue a veto message with an explanation of the reasons for his veto. It requires a super majority, usually two-thirds of the members of the legislative bodies, to override an executive veto. The executive has two other choices. If he does nothing, the time for executive action expires, and if the legislature is still in session, the bill becomes law without executive approval. If the legislative session ends before the time for executive approval or veto expires, the President or governor may do nothing, a pocket veto, and the bill dies with the legislative session.

Assuming the bill has survived the committee, both houses of the legislature, and is either approved by the executive or in spite of the executive, the bill becomes a **statute.**

ANATOMY OF A STATUTE

The following description of the component parts of a statute is a general one. Not every statute includes all of these parts, but in reading a statute, you must be aware of all the sections it may contain. Many statutes, particularly recent ones, begin with a section that gives the statute a **name.** Although in legal writing you must always begin with the full citation to the statute, the name is a useful short form to use later in a brief or memorandum when referring to the statute in

2. Congress and all state legislatures except Nebraska have bicameral systems.

3. North Carolina does not give its governor the power to approve or veto legislation.

general. The name may indicate the subject matter of the legislation or, as in the Gramm–Rudman–Hollings Act, 2 U.S.C. 901 et seq. (1988), it may reflect the names of the major sponsors of the legislation.

A second possible section is a **preamble** or purpose section. This will indicate in general or sometimes quite specific terms what the legislature intended to accomplish with the statute. This section is often useful in determining the legislative intent of statutory language that may be ambiguous in its application to a particular fact situation.

A common statutory section is a **definition** section. It defines the terms used in the statute. The definition section is useful in determining the parties and situations covered by the statute and, by the same token, those parties and situations that are not covered by the statute.

The most important section of a statute and the one that will always be present is the **operative** section. This is the section that explains what behavior is required, prohibited, or permitted. You must always read the operative section carefully as it is often drafted with conditions and exceptions and may appear as one sentence that continues for a page or more. The punctuation may also be important in deciphering the meaning of the operative section.

Failure to comply with the operative section of the statute may have criminal consequences. If this is the case, you will need to see what governmental agency has the authority to invoke the criminal sanctions. It may occur at either the local or a higher level. If a state statute is involved, for example, either a local prosecutor or the state attorney general or both may invoke the sanction. The statute may also provide defenses to the criminal charges. If your client has either been charged with a crime or may be subject to criminal prosecution under the statute, you will need to investigate whether any of the named or generally applicable defenses apply. If, on the other hand, your client has been hurt by the actions of a potential criminal defendant, you will need to know how to bring the matter to the attention of the appropriate prosecutorial agency.

The operative section of a statute may also involve your client in a civil action, either as a plaintiff or as a defendant. If your client is a plaintiff, the statute may provide a cause of action. If the client is a defendant, she may be liable to the plaintiff under the operative provision.

The statute may also provide **remedies.** In a civil case, a plaintiff may be entitled to damages or equitable relief, such as an injunction. In a criminal case, the statute may specify the maximum fine or term of imprisonment for violation of the statute.

A statute may also provide information on **procedure.** It may tell you which court has jurisdiction over cases invoking the statute, how to decide the proper venue, and how to calculate the statute of limitations. Although most parties must pay their own attorneys, a few statutes provide attorney fees for the prevailing party as a part of the judgment.

Governmental regulatory statutes often contain additional sections. If a commission or agency is necessary to administer the operative section of the statute, the legislation must create a body to implement the statute. When Congress enacted the National Environmental Policy Act of 1969, 42 U.S.C. § 4321 et seq. (1982 & Supp.1987), for example, it created the Environmental Protection Agency. To do its job, the agency may need the authority to issue regulations. The legislation must contain a provision authorizing the agency to promulgate the necessary rules. As the agency cannot exist without funding, the legislative body must authorize the necessary funding. Some agencies are funded annually as a part of the executive budget; others are financed by fees collected in the normal course of the agency's operations. The statute may contain a funding provision.

As you read statutes, look carefully at all of the sections with these possible provisions in mind, both for what the statute contains and for the information it does not provide and that you will need to find elsewhere.

As you read statutes, keep in mind the following usage conventions. While none of these is unique to legislative drafting, they are helpful in deciphering the lengthy sentences commonly used in legislation. The word **"shall"** makes the duty imposed by the following verb **mandatory**. In contrast, the auxiliary **"may"** leaves the duty imposed by the following verb **discretionary**. A person is permitted, but not required to act. These auxiliaries are marked in bold print in the illustrative statute that follows. The conjunctions **"and"** and **"or"** are also important. "And" requires that more than one thing be present and "or" provides alternatives. Statutory provisions often include both "and" and "or" in the same sentence. Terms of negation are critical to understanding statutes. Be particularly sensitive to a negative that appears in a general statement that is followed by a set of subsections. Finally, punctuation is useful in sorting out the relationships of different statutory provisions.

The Colorado Ski Safety and Liability Act, Colo.Rev.Stat. § 33–44–101 et seq. (1984), illustrates the anatomy of a statute. Read the statute in conjunction with the explanations that follow.

ARTICLE 44

SKI SAFETY AND LIABILITY

33–44–101. Short title.

33–44–102. Legislative declaration.

33–44–103. Definitions.

33–44–104. Negligence—civil actions.

33–44–105. Duties of passengers.

33–44–106. Duties of operators—signs.

33–44–107. Duties of ski area operators—signs required for skiers' information.

33–44–101. Short title

This article **shall** be known and **may** be cited as the "Ski Safety Act of 1979".

33–44–102. Legislative declaration

The general assembly hereby finds and declares that it is in the interest of the State of Colorado to establish reasonable safety standards for the operation of ski areas and for the skiers using them. Realizing the dangers that inhere in the sport of skiing, regardless of any and all reasonable safety measures which can be employed, the purpose of this article is to supplement the passenger tramway safety provisions of part 7 of article 5 of title 25, C.R.S.[4]; to further define the legal responsibilities of skiers using such ski areas; and to define the rights and liabilities existing between the skier and the ski area operator and between skiers.

33–44–103. Definitions

As used in this article, unless the context otherwise requires:

(1) "Base area lift" means any passenger tramway which skiers ordinarily use without first using some other passenger tramway.

(2) "Competitor" means a skier actually engaged in competition or in practice therefor with the permission of the ski area operator on any slope or trail or portion thereof designated by the ski area operator for the purpose of competition.

(3) "Conditions of ordinary visibility" means daylight and, where applicable, nighttime in nonprecipitating weather.

(4) "Passenger" means any person who is lawfully using any passenger tramway.

(5) "Passenger tramway" means a device as defined in section 25–5–702(4), C.R.S.

(6) "Ski area" means all ski slopes or trails and other places under the control of a ski area operator and administered as a single enterprise within this state.

(7) "Ski area operator" means "operator" as defined in section 25–5–702(3), C.R.S., and any person, partnership, corporation, or other commercial entity having operational responsibility for any

---

4. Colorado Revised Statutes.

ski areas, including an agency of this state or a political subdivision thereof.

(8) "Skier" means any person utilizing a ski area for the purpose of skiing or for the purpose of sliding downhill on snow or ice on skis, a toboggan, a sled, a tube, a ski-bob, or any other device.

(9) "Ski slopes or trails" means those areas designated by the ski area operator to be used by skiers for any of the purposes enumerated in subsection (8) of this section. Such designation **shall** be set forth on trail maps, if provided, and designated by signs indicating to the skiing public the intent that such areas be used by skiers for the purpose of skiing. Nothing in this subsection (9) or in subsection (8) of this section, however, **shall** imply that ski slopes or trails may not be restricted for use by persons using skis only or for use by persons using any other device described in subsection (8) of this section.

33–44–104. Negligence—civil actions

(1) A violation of any requirement of this article **shall,** to the extent such violation causes injury to any person or damage to property, constitute negligence on the part of the person violating such requirement.

(2) A violation by a ski area operator of any requirement of this article or any rule or regulation promulgated by the passenger tramway safety board pursuant to section 25–5–710(1)(a), C.R.S., **shall,** to the extent such violation causes injury to any person or damage to property, constitute negligence on the part of such operator.

(3) All rules adopted or amended by the passenger tramway safety board on or after July 1, 1979, **shall** be subject to sections 24–4–103(8)(c) and (8)(d) and 24–34–104(9)(b)(II), C.R.S.

33–44–105. Duties of passengers

(1) No passenger **shall** board a passenger tramway if he does not have sufficient physical dexterity, ability, and knowledge to negotiate or use such facility safely or until such passenger has asked for and received information sufficient to enable him to use the equipment safely. A passenger is required to follow any written or verbal instructions that are given to him regarding the use of the passenger tramway.

(2) No passenger **shall:**

(a) Embark upon or disembark from a passenger tramway except at a designated area except in the event of a stoppage of the passenger tramway (and then only under the supervision of the operator) or unless reasonably necessary in the event of an emergency to prevent injury to the passenger or others;

(b) Throw or expel any object from any passenger tramway while riding on such device, except as permitted by the operator;

(c) Act, while riding on a passenger tramway, in any manner that may interfere with proper or safe operation of such passenger tramway;

(d) Engage in any type of conduct that may contribute to or cause injury to any person;

(e) Place in an uphill track of a J–bar, T–bar, platter pull, rope tow, or any other surface lift any object that could cause another skier to fall;

(f) Embark upon a passenger tramway marked as closed;

(g) Disobey any instructions posted in accordance with this article or any verbal instructions by the ski area operator regarding the proper or safe use of a passenger tramway unless such verbal instructions are contrary to posted instructions.

33–44–106. Duties of operators—signs

(1) Each ski area operator **shall** maintain a sign system with concise, simple, and pertinent information for the protection and instruction of passengers. Signs **shall** be prominently placed on each passenger tramway readable in conditions of ordinary visibility and, where applicable, adequately lighted for nighttime passengers. Signs **shall** be posted as follows:

(a) At or near the loading point of each passenger tramway, regardless of the type, advising that any person not familiar with the operation of the device shall ask the operator of the device for assistance and instruction;

(b) At the interior of each two-car and multicar passenger tramway, showing:

(I) The maximum capacity in pounds of the car and the maximum number of passengers allowed;

(II) Instructions for procedures in emergencies.

(c) In a conspicuous place at each loading area of two-car and multicar passenger tramways, stating the maximum capacity in pounds of the car and the maximum number of passengers allowed;

(d) At all chair lifts, stating the following:

(I) "Prepare to Unload", which **shall** be not less than fifty feet ahead of the unloading area.

(II) "Keep Ski Tips Up", which **shall** be located ahead of any point where the skis may come in contact with a platform or the snow surface;

(III) "Unload Here", which **shall** be located at the point designated for unloading;

(IV) "Safety Gate", which **shall** be located where applicable;

(V) "Remove Pole Straps from Wrists", which **shall** be placed at or near the loading area;

(VI) "Check for Loose Clothing and Equipment", which **shall** be located before the "Prepare to Unload" sign.

(e) At all J-bars, T-bars, platter pulls, rope tows, and any other surface lift, stating the following:

(I) "Remove Pole Straps from Wrists", which **shall** be placed at or near the loading area;

(II) "Stay in Tracks", "Unload Here", and "Safety Gate", which **shall** be located where applicable;

(III) "Prepare to Unload", which **shall** be located not less than fifty feet ahead of each unloading area.

(f) Near the boarding area of all J-bars, T-bars, platter pulls, rope tows, and any other surface lift, advising passengers to check to be certain that clothing, scarves, and hair will not become entangled with the lift;

(g) At or near the boarding area of all lifts, regarding the requirements of section 33–44–109(6).

(2) Other signs not specified by subsection (1) of this section **may** be posted at the discretion of the ski area operator.

(3) The ski area operator, before opening the passenger tramway to the public each day, **shall** inspect such passenger tramway for the presence and visibility of the signs required by subsection (1) of this section.

(4) The extent of the responsibility of the ski area operator under this section **shall** be to post and maintain such signs as are required by subsection (1) of this section in such condition that they may be viewed during conditions of ordinary visibility. Evidence that signs required by subsection (1) of this section were present, visible, and readable where required at the beginning of the passenger tramway operation on any given day raises a presumption that all passengers using said devices have seen and understood said signs.

33–44–107. Duties of ski area operators—signs required for skiers' information

(1) Each ski area operator **shall** maintain a sign and marking system as set forth in this section in addition to that required by section 33–44–106. All signs required by this section **shall** be maintained so as to be readable and recognizable under conditions of ordinary visibility.

(2) A sign **shall** be placed in such a position as to be recognizable as a sign to skiers proceeding to the uphill loading point of

each base area lift depicting and explaining signs and symbols which the skier may encounter at the ski area as follows:

(a) The ski area's least difficult trails and slopes, designated by a green circle and the word "easiest";

(b) The ski area's most difficult trails and slopes, designated by a black diamond and the words "most difficult";

(c) The ski area's trails and slopes which have a degree of difficulty that falls between the green circle and the black diamond designation, designated by a blue square and the words "more difficult";

(d) Danger areas, designated by a red exclamation point inside a yellow triangle with a red band around the triangle and the word "Danger" printed beneath the emblem;

(e) Closed trails or slopes, designated by an octagonal-shaped sign with a red border around a white interior containing a black figure in the shape of a skier with a black band running diagonally across the sign from the upper right-hand side to the lower left-hand side and with the word "Closed" printed beneath the emblem.

(3) If applicable, a sign **shall** be placed at or near the loading point of each passenger tramway, as follows:

"**WARNING:** This lift services (most difficult) or (most difficult and more difficult) or (difficult) slopes only."

(4) If a particular trail or slope or portion of a trail or slope is closed to the public by a ski area operator, such operator **shall** place a sign notifying the public of that fact at each identified entrance of each portion of the trail or slope involved. Alternatively, such a trail or slope or portion thereof may be closed with ropes or fences.

(5) The ski area operator **shall** place a sign at or near the beginning of each trail or slope, which sign **shall** contain the appropriate symbol of the relative degree of difficulty of that particular trail or slope as set forth by subsection (2) of this section. This requirement **shall** not apply to a slope or trail designated "easiest" which to a skier is substantially visible in its entirety under conditions of ordinary visibility prior to his beginning to ski the same.

(6) The ski area operator **shall** mark its ski area boundaries in a fashion readily visible to skiers under conditions of ordinary visibility. Where the owner of land adjoining a ski area closes all or part of his land and so advises the ski area operator, such portions of the boundary **shall** be signed as required by paragraph (e) of subsection (2) of this section. This requirement **shall** not apply in heavily wooded areas or other nonskiable terrain.

(7) The ski area operator **shall** mark hydrants, water pipes, and all other man-made structures on slopes and trails which are

not readily visible to skiers under conditions of ordinary visibility from a distance of at least one hundred feet and **shall** cover such obstructions with a shock-absorbent material that will lessen injuries. Any type of marker **shall** be sufficient, including but not limited to wooden poles, flags, or signs, if the marker is visible from a distance of one hundred feet and if the marker itself does not constitute a serious hazard to skiers.

33-44-108. Ski area operators—additional duties

(1) Any motorized snow-grooming vehicle **shall** be equipped with a light visible at any time the vehicle is moving on or in the vicinity of a ski slope or trail.

(2) Whenever maintenance equipment is being employed to maintain or groom any ski slope or trail while such ski slope or trail is open to the public, the ski area operator **shall** place or cause to be placed a conspicuous notice to that effect at or near the top of that ski slope or trail.

(3) All snowmobiles operated on the ski slopes or trails of a ski area **shall** be equipped with at least the following: One lighted headlamp, one lighted red tail lamp, a brake system maintained in operable condition, and a fluorescent flag at least forty square inches mounted at least six feet above the bottom of the tracks.

(4) The ski area operator **shall** have no duty arising out of its status as a ski area operator to any skier skiing beyond the area boundaries marked as required by section 33-44-107(6).

(5) The ski area operator, upon finding a person skiing in a careless and reckless manner, **may** revoke that person's skiing privileges.

33-44-109. Duties of skiers—penalties

(1) Each skier solely has the responsibility for knowing the range of his own ability to negotiate any ski slope or trail and to ski within the limits of such ability.

(2) Each skier has the duty to maintain control of his speed and course at all times when skiing and to maintain a proper lookout so as to be able to avoid other skiers and objects. However, the primary duty **shall** be on the person skiing downhill to avoid collision with any person or objects below him. It is presumed, unless shown to the contrary by a preponderance of the evidence, that the responsibility for collisions by skiers with any person, natural object, or man-made structure marked in accordance with section 33-44-107(7) is solely that of the skier or skiers involved and not that of the ski area operator.

(3) No skier **shall** ski on a ski slope or trail that has been posted as "Closed" pursuant to section 33-44-107(2)(e) and (4).

(4) Each skier **shall** stay clear of snow-grooming equipment, all vehicles, lift towers, signs, and any other equipment on the ski slopes and trails.

(5) Each skier has the duty to heed all posted information and other warnings and to refrain from acting in a manner which may cause or contribute to the injury of the skier or others. Each skier **shall** be presumed to have seen and understood all information posted in accordance with this article near base area lifts, on the passenger tramways, and on such ski slopes or trails as he is skiing. Under conditions of decreased visibility, the duty is on the skier to locate and ascertain the meaning of all signs posted in accordance with section 33–44–107.

(6) Each ski used by a skier while skiing **shall** be equipped with strap or other device capable of stopping the ski should the ski become unattached from the skier. This requirement **shall** not apply to cross country skis.

(7) No skier **shall** cross the uphill track of a J-bar, T-bar, platter pull, or rope tow except at locations designated by the operator; nor shall a skier place any object in such an uphill track.

(8) Before beginning to ski from a stationary position or before entering a ski slope or trail from the side, the skier **shall** have the duty of avoiding moving skiers already on the ski slope or trail.

(9) No person **shall** move uphill on any passenger tramway or use any ski slope or trail while such person's ability to do so is impaired by the consumption of alcohol or by the use of any controlled substance, as defined in section 12–22–303(7), C.R.S., or other drug or while such person is under the influence of alcohol or any controlled substance, as defined in section 12–22–303(7), C.R.S., or other drug.

(10) No skier involved in a collision with another skier or person in which an injury results **shall** leave the vicinity of the collision before giving his name and current address to an employee of the ski area operator or a member of the voluntary ski patrol, except for the purpose of securing aid for a person injured in the collision; in which event the person so leaving the scene of the collision **shall** give his name and current address as required by this subsection (10) after securing such aid.

(11) No person **shall** knowingly enter upon public or private lands from an adjoining ski area when such land has been closed by its owner and so posted by the owner or by the ski area operator pursuant to section 33–44–107(6).

(12) Any person who violates any of the provisions of subsection (3), (9), (10), or (11) of this section is guilty of a class 2 petty offense and, upon conviction thereof, **shall** be punished by a fine of not more than three hundred dollars.

33–44–110.   Competition

(1) The ski area operator **shall,** prior to the beginning of a competition, allow each competitor a reasonable visual inspection of the course or area where the competition is to be held.

(2) The competitor **shall** be held to assume the risk of all course conditions including, but not limited to, weather and snow conditions, course construction or layout, and obstacles which a visual inspection should have revealed. No liability **shall** attach to a ski area operator for injury or death of any competitor proximately caused by such assumed risk.

33–44–111.   Statute of limitation

All actions against any ski area operator or its employees brought to recover damages for injury to person or property caused by the maintenance, supervision, or operation of a passenger tramway or a ski area **shall** be brought within three years after the claim for relief arises and not thereafter.

33–44–101. The statute begins with its short title. In this instance the title indicates the subject matter of the legislation.

33–44–102. The Colorado General Assembly begins by stating its purpose. The skiing industry is important to Colorado and the purpose is drafted carefully to recognize the interests of both ski area operators and the skiing public. The standard is a "reasonable" one. Note the caveat to skiers, "[r]ealizing the dangers that inhere in the sport of skiing, regardless of any and all **reasonable** safety measures which can be employed".

The legislation is designed to explain the rights, responsibilities, and liabilities of all parties. Remember that legislative bodies are political. From the purpose section, do you think that the statute favors the operator or the skier?

Note that there is also a reference to existing legislation, Colo. Rev. Stat. § 25–5–701 et seq. (1989). This is the Passenger Tramway Safety Act and you will need to read this act in conjunction with the Ski Safety Act of 1979. Among other things, it creates the passenger tramway safety board and authorizes it to promulgate rules and regulations.

33–44–103. The definition section should define the terms used in the statute in a way that eliminates any ambiguity. If you read these definitions carefully, however, you will see some ambiguity in numbers 3 and 8. In (3) "[c]onditions of ordinary visibility", it is not clear if the legislature intended the phrase "in nonprecipitating weather" to apply only to nighttime or if it should also apply to daylight. Grammatically, it refers only to nighttime. Is this what the legislature intended?

Subsection (8) defines a "skier" as someone who uses a variety of devices to slide "downhill on snow or ice". If your client was injured while on the snow equivalent of a surfboard, called a snow board, would he be considered to be a "skier" for purposes of the statute?

The second and third sentences of (9) "ski slopes or trails" seem to have little to do with defining the terms. The second sentence seems to impose a duty on the operator to designate the slopes or trails. This sentence belongs more logically in § 33–44–106 or 33–44–107. The third sentence permits the operator to limit access to slopes or trails.

The definition of a (6) "ski area" illustrates the use of "and" and "or". The area may include either slopes or trails. The drafters included both terms in order to cover ski areas that refer to "slopes" as well as those that use the term "trails". Ski areas also includes other places, so the term is not limited just to the slopes or trails. Note the "and" in "under the control of a ski operator **and** administered as a single enterprise within this state."

33–44–104. This section fulfills several of the functions described above. It defines a civil cause of action arising under the statute as a negligence cause of action. By implication it provides procedural information. If you have a client with a potential cause of action, you would research negligence for the elements of the cause of action and for the jurisdiction, venue, service and other procedural requirements. The applicable statute of limitation, for example, is given in Colo. Rev. Stat. § 13–80–102(1)(a) and (d) (1987) for negligence and wrongful death actions, respectively.

This section also refers you to the rules and regulations promulgated by the administrative agency, the passenger tramway safety board. An operator who violates these rules is negligent. Subsection (3) refers you to two additional statutory sections, Colo. Rev. Stat. § 24–4–103(8)(c) and (8)(d) (1988), and Colo. Rev. Stat. § 24–34–104(9)(b)(II) (1988). These sections deal with a general review of existing regulations. If your case dealt with a particular regulation, you would need to investigate further to see if the regulation was still in effect at the date the cause of action arose.

33–44–105. This section and sections 33–44–106 to 110 constitute the operative provisions of the statute. They explain the duties of passengers, operators, skiers, and competitors. Note that in section 105(1) the burden is on the passenger to assess his ability to ride a tramway and to ask for instruction if necessary. Does this change your view of which party, skier or ski operator had the greater influence with the legislature in drafting the statute? Subsection (2) begins with a negative that then applies to subsections (a)-(g). Note also the limitation in subsection 105(g). Passengers must follow verbal instructions unless they are contrary to the statute, the rules, or posted instructions.

33–44–106. This section specifies the signs a tramway, chair lift, or other type of lift operator must or may provide. Subsection (1) requires that the signs must be "readable in conditions of ordinary visibility". Subsection (4) contains the same condition. As noted above under 33–

44–103(3), the definition is ambiguous for daylight operation. Note also the presumption raised at the end of subsection (4). If you were representing a lift operator, you would advise your client to have a daily record showing that the necessary signs were "present, visible, and readable" at the start of business. The passenger is presumed to have seen and understood the signs. The test is not that the passenger actually saw and understood the signs, but that she should have seen and understood the signs. The statute does not tell you if the presumption is rebuttable; that is, that despite the presumption, your client can persuade the trier of fact that she did not see and/or did not understand the signs. To resolve the question, you could research similar negligence cases where courts had interpreted similar presumptions involving signs. You would also need to know what standard of proof to apply.

33–44–107. This section is the parallel provision enumerating the operator's duties with respect to ski slopes and trails. The definition of "conditions of ordinary visibility" appears in subsections (1), (5), (6), and (7). Subsection (7) includes a special requirement if the man-made structure is not visible "from a distance of at least one hundred feet". The markers required under this section are sufficient if they are "visible from a distance of one hundred feet and if the marker itself does not constitute a serious hazard to skiers". Does it matter that the language does not include a reference to "conditions of ordinary visibility"?

33–44–108. This section imposes additional duties and limitations of liability on operators. The first three subsections impose duties regarding maintenance equipment and snowmobiles used by the operator. Subsection (4) limits liability to the ski area if the operator has properly marked the boundaries. Subsection (5) permits the operator to revoke a "person's skiing privileges". Note that it does not require the operator to do so.

33–44–109. This section lists the duties of each skier both with reference to a cause of action against the operator and other skiers. Subsection (2) includes a presumption, but this presumption is a rebuttable presumption. A skier can show "by a preponderance of the evidence" that his collision with another person, a natural object or an appropriately marked man-made structure was caused by the negligence of the operator.

Another presumption appears in subsection (5). The skier is presumed "to have seen and understood" all the signs, even "under conditions of decreased visibility".

Under subsection (9), there is a reference to another statutory section, Colo. Rev. Stat. § 12–22–303(7) (1985). This section defines a controlled substance. If the injured or responsible party might have been under the influence of a controlled substance, you would want to check this definition. If the substance were alcohol, you would need to research further to see how "impaired by the consumption of alcohol" and "under the influence of alcohol" are defined.

This section also refers to possible criminal penalties for violation of subsections (3), (9), (10), and (11).

33–44–110. This section deals with the special circumstance of competitive skiing. Note in subsection (2) the reference to "assumption of risk". This is a defense to a negligence action. If it might be relevant to your case, you would need to research this common law defense further. Be sure also to see if there is a statute that adopts or modifies the common law doctrine.

33–44–111. This section provides for a three year statute of limitation in actions under the statute. This is a change from the two year statute of limitation that applies to negligence cases in general. As the statute does not expressly provide other procedural requirements for ski related causes of action, the general requirements for negligence cases apply.

You can see that even this relatively short and simple statute requires careful reading. It has much more complexity than was apparent at first blush. You are also left with some questions about the definitions and the presumptions.

ANNOTATIONS

Annotated versions of statutes contain references to cases where the courts have interpreted different statutory sections. The following are the annotations that appear with this statute.

33–44–101. Short title

Law reviews.

For article, "The Development of the Standard of Care in Colorado Ski Cases", see 15 Colo. Law 373 (1986).

33–44–103. Definitions

The term "ski area" does not include an area devoted to the parking of motor vehicles and the operation of shuttle busses. Therefore, none of the provisions of this act are applicable. *Mc-Lean v. Winter Park Recreational Ass'n*, 762 P.2d 751 (Colo. App. Ct. 1988).

33–44–107.

Applied in *Rimkus v. Northwest Colo. Ski Corp.*, 706 F.2d 1060 (10th Cir. 1983).

33–44–108.

Warning sign must be posted when maintenance equipment is present on slopes for purposes of "grooming and maintaining" a slope, but is not actively "grooming" in that particular location. *Phillips v. Monarch Recreation Corp.*, 668 P.2d 982 (Colo. Ct. App. 1983).

33–44–109. Duties of skiers—penalties

The term "responsibility" as used in subsection (2) encompasses the legal concept of "fault". In effect, the statute creates a rebuttable presumption that the skier is at fault whenever he collides with an object listed in subsection (2), and "fault" may be defined as the equivalent of negligence. *Pizza v. Wolf Creek Ski Development Corp.*, 711 P.2d 671 (Colo. 1985).

Given the connection between "responsibility" and "negligence" in the context of a skiing accident case, the term "responsibility" may be equated with the concept of "negligence" for purposes of applying the presumption contained within subsection (2) *Pizza v. Wolf Creek Ski Development Corp.*, 711 P.2d 671 (Colo. 1985).

The phrase "natural object" is not unconstitutionally vague. *Pizza v. Wolf Creek Ski Development Corp.*, 711 P.2d 671 (Colo. 1985).

Skiers as a group do not constitute a suspect class, and being free from a legislatively imposed rebuttable presumption of negligence is not a fundamental right. *Pizza v. Wolf Creek Ski Development Corp.*, 711 P.2d 671 (Colo. 1985).

Evidentiary presumption contained in subsection (2) places upon skier the burden of rebutting the presumption by presenting evidence of the ski area operator's negligence which outweighs the presumption of the skier's sole negligence. *Pizza v. Wolf Creek Ski Development Corp.*, 711 P.2d 671 (Colo. 1985).

Presumption is not unconstitutionally vague in describing rebuttal burden. *Pizza v. Wolf Creek Ski Development Corp.*, 711 P.2d 671 (Colo. 1985).

33–44–111. Statute of limitation

This section and not former § 13–80–110 is the applicable statute of limitations of actions to recover damages for an injury in a ski area. *Schafer v. Aspen Skiing Corp.*, 742 F.2d 580 (10th Cir. 1984).

Three year statute of limitations in this section does not violate equal protection or constitutional provisions governing special legislation, grant of special privileges or immunities, or access to courts. *Schafer v. Aspen Skiing Corp.*, 742 F.2d 580 (10th Cir. 1984).

Neither § 2–4–107 nor § 2–4–108 applicable in determining the computation of the statute of limitations in this section. *Schafer v. Aspen Skiing Corp.*, 742 F.2d 580 (10th Cir. 1984).

Statute not applicable to action resulting from injury occurring in a parking lot. Since the term "ski area" does not include an area devoted to the parking of motor vehicles and the operation of shuttle buses, none of the provisions of this act, including the statute of limitations in this section, are applicable. *McLean v. Winter Park Recreational Ass'n,* 762 P.2d 751 (Colo. App. Ct. 1988).

You can see under section 33–44–103 that the definition of "ski area" was interpreted in *McLean v. Winter Park Recreational Ass'n,* 762 P.2d 751 (Colo. App. Ct. 1988). Although by its express language, the definition appears to apply to the whole area, the court held that "ski area" does not include the parking lot. Can you figure out why the court may have reached this result?

There is one case interpreting section 33–44–109, *Pizza v. Wolf Creek Ski Development Corp.,* 711 P.2d 671 (Colo. 1985). From the annotations, you get a sense of what the case was about and what the court decided. The plaintiff was injured when he struck a natural object. The term "natural object" is not unconstitutionally vague. The presumption and what a plaintiff must prove in order to rebut this presumption are also not unconstitutionally vague. Under subsection (2), a skier is presumed to be responsible, and therefore, in negligence terms, to be at fault. A plaintiff must prove that the operator's negligence outweighs the plaintiff's presumed fault. Although these seem to be the court's holdings, you must never rely on the annotations; you must read the case to find out what the court actually held.

There are two cases interpreting the statute of limitation section, 33–44–111. The annotation to *Schafer v. Aspen Skiing Corp.,* 742 F.2d 580 (10th Cir. 1984), refers to former section 13–80–110. This provided for a six year statute of limitation in negligence cases. The court held that the applicable period was the three years provided by 33–44–111. The second case, *McLean v. Winter Park Recreation Ass'n,* 762 P.2d 751 (Colo. App. Ct. 1988), also arose as a dispute as to whether the former six year period or the three year period under 33–44–111 applied. As the cause of action arose in the parking lot and not in the "ski area", the court held that the six year period was applicable.

The annotations to the statute have answered some of the questions the express language of the statute left ambiguous. They have not, however, answered all of our questions. When a court is in doubt about the legislative intent behind a statute, it can look to two other sources to resolve the ambiguity: general rules of statutory construction and legislative history.

GENERAL CANONS OF STATUTORY CONSTRUCTION

A court will first look at the plain meaning of the statute and read the sections so they are internally consistent. It is only when there is some ambiguity in the meaning that the rules or canons of statutory construction come into play. While it would be helpful if legislatures used the canons consistently in drafting legislation, they do not. As a result, courts use these rules only as a guide and apply them where they are helpful.

There are two canons that apply to lists of items in a statute, *Expressio unius* and *Ejusdem generis.* *Expressio unius est exclusio alterius* means the specific expression of one thing excludes all others. If a statute contains a list of items, it only applies to the specific items mentioned to the exclusion of all others. Many lists, such as the one defining "skier" in the Ski Safety Act, include a list followed by a general term.

> (8) "Skier" means any person utilizing a ski area for the purpose of skiing or for the purpose of sliding downhill on snow or ice on skis, a toboggan, a sled, a tube, a ski-bob, **or any other device.**

Under the rule of *Ejusdem generis,* meaning of the same class, the other devices must be of the same class as the ski, sled, ski-bob, etc. A snow board, a surfboard modified for use on snow, would qualify as being in the same class as the items listed. Snow shoes, however, which are designed for walking on snow and not sliding downhill on snow would arguably not qualify.

The canon of **last antecedent** provides that a qualifying phrase modifies the immediately preceding word or phrase and not words or phrases that are more remote. This rule might be helpful in interpreting the definition of "conditions of ordinary visibility".

> (3) "Conditions of ordinary visibility" means daylight and, where applicable, nighttime **in nonprecipitating weather.**

Under the rule of last antecedent, the phrase "in nonprecipitating weather" refers to nighttime and not to daylight. Blind adherence to this canon of statutory construction would produce an illogical result. The legislature undoubtedly intended "in nonprecipitating weather" to refer to both daylight and nighttime. As you can see, the rules are not always helpful.

When the statute is still ambiguous and there are other statutes dealing with the same subject matter, courts will often read them *in pari materia;* that is, construe the statutes together as forming a larger rule on the same subject. The Ski Safety Act of 1979, for example, makes this construction express by reference in sections 33–44–103(7) and 33–44–104(2) to the Passenger Tramway Safety Act. Courts will look carefully at the two pieces of legislation, however, to make sure that the statutes relate to the same person or thing or that they have a common purpose.

As you have seen, courts have a certain amount of latitude in interpreting case law and applying it to the facts of the case under consideration. Courts have similar latitude in interpreting most statutes; they can interpret the statutes narrowly; that is, limit the application of the statute to its express provisions, or they can interpret the statute broadly. In some circumstances, the canons of statutory construction require courts to interpret statutes **strictly.** The most common of these instances is when courts are construing criminal statutes. When the statutory language is ambiguous, the court will interpret it strictly for the benefit of the criminal defendant. The reason for this is that defendants should not be required to answer for a crime that is described ambiguously.

Statutes in derogation of the common law are also construed strictly. Frequently, statutes codify common law rules. When the statutory rule, however, is contrary to existing common law, the courts will construe the statute strictly. The rationale behind this canon is less clear. A legislative body adopts a rule contrary to existing common law to reflect a change in social values or for public policy reasons. It is not the role of the courts to undo the legislative initiative.

LEGISLATIVE HISTORY

Finally, a court may look to the **legislative history** of a statute in order to discover the **legislative intent.** Legislative history is much more important at the federal than at either the state or local levels. Most states do not have the resources to compile or publish more than the most perfunctory record of the bill's transit through the legislative process. As you can see from the brief overview of the legislative process, not all legislative history is equally reliable. The term legislative history encompasses a wide variety of documents and transcripts of oral statements. It includes the statements made at a public hearing on a piece of legislation. The people who speak at hearings tend to be representatives of administrative agencies and the proponents and opponents of the proposed bill. Unless the legislature adopts wholesale the view of one of the speakers, her view of the bill will not state the legislative intent.

A committee report may be more reliable. If the bill as drafted and approved by that committee ultimately is enacted without change, the committee's view of what the statute means should be accurate. Statements made by members of the committee, even the bill's sponsors, may not be reliable when the subject matter was controversial and the committee members engaged in political give and take before reaching agreement. When a bill was introduced in both legislative houses in different forms, only the committee report of the house that produced the ultimate statute will be useful, and then, only if the form considered by that committee is substantially the same as the ultimate legislation. Under these circumstances, the better view of the legislative intent, if available, will be the conference committee report.

EXERCISE 5A.

The clients, Herb and Sue Martin, consulted our firm about the Wilson Farm Supply Company operation that is directly across from their property. The Martins and their four children enjoy living out in the country on their five acre farm. They have a horse and raise chickens, turkeys, and geese for their own use. Herb and Sue believe it teaches their children responsibility to care for the animals. Their house is set back from the road about one hundred feet and has a large front lawn with oak and maple trees.

When the Martins moved in eight years ago, the Wilson Farm Supply Co. was only a minor inconvenience during harvest season. The company sold farm machinery, fertilizer in bags, and miscellaneous farm equipment. The Wilson Co. is located on a forty acre parcel. The family homestead and the business occupy some of the land; the rest is devoted to raising corn. In the fall, the company dried grain, particularly corn, in its grain dryer. The dryer was noisy to a person standing next to it, and it generated some dust and "bees' wings". "Bees' wings" are the dried skins that cover kernels of corn. The Martins were not particularly inconvenienced and the grain drying only occurred in the end of September and the beginning of October.

Last spring, the company installed a new, state of the art, grain dryer. During harvest season, the new dryer ran almost continuously. It is noisier than the old model, and it generates substantially more dust and "bees' wings". The "bees' wings" were ½ an inch thick on the Martins' driveway on October 11th. The "bees' wings" stick to the windows and siding on their house, their car, and their animals.

The company also added liquid ammonia to its fertilizer line last spring. The ammonia is stored in a huge tank adjacent to the Wilson store. The tank is also state of the art. There is an automatic pressure release valve on the top of the tank. Whenever the pressure in the tank reaches the limit on the valve, it automatically releases ammonia gas into the surrounding atmosphere. As the prevailing wind is to the east, the fumes drift across the road to the Martins' property. The dozen or so releases that occurred over the course of the spring and summer poisoned the Martins' trees. The leaves withered and fell. A forestry expert will testify that the ammonia fumes killed the trees.

The Martins would like to bring a case against the Wilson Co. Our research indicates that there are two possible causes of action, a common law nuisance action for the dust and "bees wings" generated by the new grain dryer and a Michigan Environmental Protection Act, Mich. Comp. Laws § 691.1201 et seq. (1979), action for the dead trees. The Air Pollution Act, Mich. Comp. Laws § 336.11 et seq. (1979) does not apply. It does, however, refer in a recent amendment to the Michigan Right to Farm Act, Mich. Comp. Laws Ann. § 286.471 et seq. (West Supp.1989).

Please read the Michigan Right to Farm Act and its accompanying annotations to see if it potentially applies to this case. There is no applicable legislative history.

MICHIGAN RIGHT TO FARM ACT

AN ACT to provide for circumstances under which a farm shall not be found to be a public nuisance.

The People of the State of Michigan enact:

Short title. Sec. 1. This act shall be known and may be cited as the "Michigan right to farm act".

Definitions. Sec. 2. As used in this act:

(a) "Farm" means the land, buildings, and machinery used in the commercial production of farm products.

(b) "Farm operation" means a condition or activity which occurs on a farm in connection with the commercial production of farm products, and includes, but is not limited to, marketed produce at roadside stands or farm markets; noise; odors; fumes; operation of machinery and irrigation pumps; ground and aerial seeding and spraying; the application of chemical fertilizers, conditioners, insecticides, pesticides, and herbicides; and the employment and use of labor.

(c) "Farm product" means those plants and animals useful to [human beings] and includes, but is not limited to, forages and sod crops, grains and feed crops, dairy and dairy products, poultry and poultry products, livestock, including breeding and grazing, fruits, vegetables, flowers, seeds, grasses, trees, fish, apiaries, equine and other similar products, or any other product which incorporates the use of food, feed, fiber, or fur.

(d) "Generally accepted agricultural and management practices" means those practices as defined by the Commission of Agriculture. The commission shall give due consideration to available Michigan Department of Agriculture information and written recommendations from the Michigan State University College of Agriculture and Natural Resources Cooperative Extension Service and the Agricultural Experiment Station in cooperation with the United States Department of Agriculture Soil and Conservation Service and the Agricultural Stabilization and Conservation Service, the Department of Natural Resources and other professional and industry organizations.

(e) "Person" means an individual, corporation, partnership, association, or other legal entity.

Farm as nuisance. Sec. 3.(1) A farm or farm operation shall not be found to be a public or private nuisance if the farm or farm operation alleged to be a nuisance conforms to generally accepted agricultural and management practices according to policy as determined by the State Agricultural Commission. Generally accepted agricultural and management practices shall be reviewed annually by the State Agricultural Commission and revised as considered necessary.

Conditions. (2) A farm or farm operation shall not be found to be a public or private nuisance if the farm or farm operation existed before a change in the land use or occupancy of land within 1 mile of the boundaries of the farm land, and if before that change in land use or occupancy of land, the farm or farm operation would not have been a nuisance.

Applicability of act. Sec. 4. This act shall not affect the application of state and federal statutes.

Annotations

Roadside stands. A township ordinance which regulates roadside stands for the sale of agricultural products does not violate 1981 PA 93. Op. Atty Gen., May 1, 1984, No. 6222.

Construction, operation, and effect. The Right to Farm Act provides for circumstances under which a farm and its operation shall not be found to be a public or private nuisance and is a valid defense to a suit alleging that a farm building is a nuisance per se because it violates a zoning ordinance. *Northville Tp. v. Coyne,* 170 Mich. App. 446.

Construction and effect. The Michigan Right to Farm Act does not affect the application of state and federal statutes. *Village of Peck v. Hoist,* 153 Mich. App. 787.

*

Section II

LEGAL ANALYSIS

The most challenging, yet interesting, part of being a lawyer is analyzing legal issues. As a lawyer, you may be analyzing problems for clients who are contemplating future action. A corporate acquisition is an example of this purpose. You may also be analyzing problems for clients who are already embroiled in litigation; such as, a criminal defendant. Legal analysis is part of the lawyer's role in the public sector and in academics as well as in practice. If your analysis is thorough and creative, you may play a part in shaping the law. The chapter that follows is an introduction to the legal analysis of a basic problem.

Chapter 6

ANALYZING THE PROBLEM

Analyzing a legal problem involves four basic steps. First, you must isolate the issues posed by the problem. Second, you must find the rules appropriate to these legal questions. You will find the general rules in statutes and/or in court decisions of cases. Judicial opinions also provide important information about rules as they illustrate how the courts have applied the rules to specific fact situations. Much of your understanding of rules will come from these illustrations. Third, you must apply the rules to the facts of your legal problem. The process involves comparing and contrasting the facts of the reported cases with the facts in your problem. Finally, you must reach a conclusion and predict the probable outcome of each issue. While this four step process may seem straightforward, this is not necessarily the case. A legal problem does not come with the issues neatly labelled. Often you will begin your research with only a general idea of the issues involved and refine your view of the issues as you read cases or other resources on the subject.

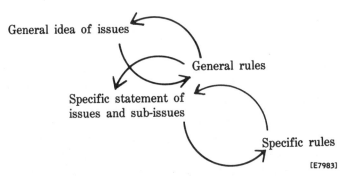

The second thing that makes analysis complicated is that issues often have sub-issues. In order to analyze an issue, you need to break it down into its smallest components, analyze each sub-issue, and then each issue. The third thing that makes analysis challenging is that the facts of the cases are rarely the same as the facts in your problem. In order to predict how a court would apply the rule to the problem facts, you will need to make a comparison of the two sets of facts. Some of the facts will be vital to the court's decision; others will be less so. To predict the probable outcome, you will need to figure out from the cases which facts were necessary to the decision. You can see the different analytical steps in the following arson example.

The county prosecutor's office received the following information from an investigation by the arson squad and the police department. The prosecutor wants to know if she should bring a criminal case against Mr. Mantle.

The fire department responded to a call at 5:41 pm on October 30, 1986. When the fire fighters tried to enter the building, they found that the front and back doors were locked. All of the fire fighters wore self contained breathing apparatus and were unable to smell any accelerant. The fire was brought under control at 7:15 pm and finally extinguished at 8:37 pm.

The next day, an investigator from the arson squad applied for and received a search warrant. He reported that the structure was wooden, the fire had originated in the basement, and there were two points of origin. Both points of origin were at the base of wooden support beams, located 15 and 20 feet respectively from the electrical circuit box, and at least 12 feet from the furnace. The depth of char in the support beams was nearly identical, which indicated that the fire started at or near the same time in both places. He found no trace of accelerant, gasoline or kerosene. From the burn pattern, he was able to tell that the fire then spread through the basement ceiling to the first floor.

The investigator also uncovered the following relevant information. The weather bureau reported that the weather on Friday, October 30, 1986, was clear with a temperature at 6 pm of 49 degrees Fahrenheit. The wind was from the northwest at 10 mph with gusts up to 25 mph. The house was listed for sale by Urban Realty and the owner was Marvin Mantle.

He inherited the house when his father passed away in November 1985. He and his wife cleaned out the house that winter and listed it with Urban Realty on March 24, 1986 for $45,000. Mantle continued the insurance coverage for that amount. When the six month listing expired on September 24, 1986, the agent, Rita Adams, suggested that the house might sell if they lowered the price. Mantle was not enthusiastic about a decrease, but he finally agreed to a relisting at $35,000. Rita explained that she and Mantle have keys to the house. She has showed the house to several potential buyers since the relisting, but no one has yet made an offer on the property. She had scheduled an appointment for the 31st with a young couple who wanted to take a second look at the house. The house is vacant and the utilities have been turned off. Mantle drained the pipes, so he would not have to pay to keep the furnace going.

Mantle lives with his family in Bloomfield Hills and works downtown. He normally leaves the office at 5 pm and arrives home for dinner well before Channel 2 News begins at 6 pm. On the night of the fire, he contacted both the fire and police departments. He explained that he had just arrived home from work when he turned on the television to see the 6 o'clock news. To his amazement, there was a live action report of a fire at his Dad's house. The investigator contacted Channel 2 News and discovered that the station had reported on the fire as a part of the "Devil's Night" coverage. The report on that fire aired at 6:22 pm.

Your research in the criminal statutes has uncovered two possibly applicable sections.

Sec. 750.72. BURNING DWELLING HOUSE—Any person who wilfully or maliciously burns any dwelling house, either occupied or unoccupied, or the contents thereof, whether owned by himself or another, or any building within the curtilage of such dwelling house, or the contents thereof, shall be guilty of a felony, punishable by imprisonment in the state prison not more than 20 years.

Sec. 750.73. BURNING OF OTHER REAL PROPERTY—Any person who wilfully or maliciously burns any building or other real property, or the contents thereof, other than those specified in the next preceding section of this chapter, the property of himself or another, shall be guilty of a felony, punishable by imprisonment in the state prison for not more than 10 years.

These two sections are helpful as they provide at least two issues to analyze. The prosecutor must prove (1) the wilful or malicious burning of a structure and that this structure was (2) either a dwelling or other real property. The statutory sections, however, do not define either what is necessary to show the wilful burning or what structures constitute dwellings. The cases listed in the annotations to the statutes provide the necessary information. The cases of *People v. Bailey*, 42 Mich. App. 359, 202 N.W.2d 557 (1972), and *People v. Horowitz*, 37 Mich. App. 151, 194 N.W.2d 375 (1971), are helpful in defining wilful and malicious burning of a structure. The elements or Corpus Delicti of the crime of arson are (1) a non-accidental cause for the fire, (2) motive, and (3) opportunity. *People v. Horowitz* provides additional information on the type of evidence the prosecution can use.

It is the nature of the offense of arson that it is usually committed surreptitiously. Rare is the occasion when eyewitnesses will be available. By necessity, proofs will normally be circumstantial.[1]

---

1. *People v. Horowitz*, 37 Mich. App. at 154, 194 N.W.2d at 376.

The cases also demonstrate two ways to prove a non-accidental cause for a fire, proof that either eliminates natural causes or that establishes a non-accidental cause.

You are now able to outline the issues and sub-issues you have to analyze as follows:

I. Is there sufficient evidence to charge Mantle with arson?

A. Was there a non-accidental cause of the fire either because there was no natural cause or because the facts show a non-accidental cause?

B. Did Mantle have the opportunity to set the fire?

C. Did Mantle have a motive for setting the fire?

II. Did the structure meet the definition of a dwelling as opposed to other real property?

The analysis should proceed one step at a time, but you are free to think about the issues and sub-issues in any order that you choose. Obviously, you will not be able to conclude the overall arson issue until you have reached a reasoned conclusion on each of the three elements. At this point the facts of the cases are critical. Only by knowing the kind of facts that courts have held are legally sufficient to meet each element will you be able to assess the prosecutor's potential case against Mantle. As the appellate courts upheld the arson convictions of both Bailey and Horowitz, you can use the facts of these cases in your analysis.

Both courts found that the defendants had the opportunity to start the fires. In *Bailey*, "defendant was in the house alone some ten to twenty minutes before the fire started"[2]. In *Horowitz*, the "defendants had catered two parties the night preceding the fire. Both defendants and their hired help returned to the business offices on Wyoming Avenue. Not long thereafter, at approximately 2:20 a.m., Horowitz and Kozin secured the premises and left in the company of their employees * * *. The fire was discovered at about 3:40 a.m."[3] "[T]here was no evidence of a breaking-in * * *."[4]

Then compare Mantle's situation to that in *Horowitz* and *Bailey*. In both cases, the defendants were at the scene shortly before the fires were discovered. Although there is no eye witness evidence to place Mantle at the house shortly before the fire broke out, there is circumstantial evidence. Mantle routinely drove by the house on his way home from work. On the night of the fire he arrived home 20 minutes later than usual. There was no evidence of a break in, and only Mantle and the real estate agent had keys to the house. Based on these facts, you can conclude that Mantle had the opportunity to set the fire.

2. *People v. Bailey*, 42 Mich. App. at 362, 202 N.W.2d at 559.

3. *Horowitz*, 37 Mich. App. at 155–156, 194 N.W.2d at 377.

4. *Horowitz* at 157, 194 N.W.2d at 378.

The prosecutor will also be able to show that Mantle had a motive similar to that possessed by the defendants in the cases. In *Bailey*, the court found sufficient motive from evidence "that defendant was in financial trouble; * * * defendant was aware that the home was covered against fire loss, but told officers on the scene that he didn't know whether he had insurance or not; * * * defendant attempted to get a woman to go to Florida with him when he received the insurance proceeds; defendant almost doubled the insurance coverage not long before the fire * * *." [5] The evidence in *Horowitz* demonstrated "that defendants owed three months rent; that they were indebted to the Michigan Department of Revenue for sales tax; that defendants owed $650 to the gas company; and that defendants carried $40,000 in fire insurance." [6]

Mantle had a similar financial motive for starting the fire. He had tried to sell his father's house for six months to no avail. It was insured for the initial $45,000 asking price. He stood to gain $10,000 more from the fire than from a sale at the reduced asking price of $35,000. The common motive in all three instances was to collect the insurance proceeds. The case against Mantle is not quite as strong as that in the two cases, however, because there is no evidence that Mantle was in financial difficulty. Despite this fact, a jury is likely to conclude that Mantle had a motive for setting the fire.

There are two ways to show the third element of arson, the non-accidental cause. In *Bailey*, the prosecutor chose to eliminate natural causes for the fire.

> Expert testimony at the trial revealed the following: (1) the fire was not caused by lightning because the day was clear and cold; (2) the greatest damage from the fire was in the living room; (3) on the day of the fire, the kitchen stove was functioning normally; (4) defendant's furnace was not the cause of the fire nor was the fuse box, any electrical source or outlet, the living room lamp or lamp cord, nor was any explosion the cause of the fire; (5) the dogs which died in the fire could not have caused the fire by biting on the electrical cords; (6) the lighting fixtures on the Christmas tree in defendant's living room did not cause the fire; (7) careless smoking or neglect was not the cause; (8) the northeast corner of the living room was the point of origin of the fire, and there was a considerable amount of white ash in the corner which would be the residue of the newspapers defendant generally stored there; (9) electrical equipment in that corner did not cause the fire; and (10) the living room couch and chair were not the source of the fire.[7]

The prosecutor in Mantle's situation could also rule out natural causes. The weather was clear and all the utilities had been turned off,

5. *Bailey*, 42 Mich. App. at 362, 202 N.W.2d at 559.

6. *Horowitz*, 37 Mich. App. at 157, 194 N.W.2d at 378.

7. *Bailey*, 42 Mich. App. at 362, 202 N.W.2d at 559.

precluding either weather or utility related causes. The house was unoccupied, so that human negligence did not cause the fire.

The prosecutor could also present evidence that the fire had been set as in *Horowitz*, where the court described the facts as follows:

> Mr. Roger LaCasse, a member of the Detroit Fire Department Arson Squad, testified that after the fire had been extinguished, he examined the south building. The interior was completely burned and the walls badly charred. He gathered two items from the ruins: a piece of what appeared to be molten plastic, removed from a table located in the south building, and a plastic container which apparently had melted from the top down with the base still intact. This, too, was discovered on a table in the same structure. The witness also related that he had detected the smell of flammable liquid in one of the exhibits.[8] He concluded by giving his opinion that the fire could have been caused by placing flammable liquids in plastic containers found in the ruins.[9]

> Another member of the arson squad, William O'Brien, testified that an arson detection device revealed the presence of a flammable substance in an area of the south building where he had smelled a suspicious odor. O'Brien further stated that he found a circular object (allegedly a plastic container) near the west end of the building. What appeared to be a cord or rope was embedded in or around this object. Adjacent to this container he discovered an unidentified liquid on the floor. He was later advised by the fire department chemist that both of these exhibits contained volatile varnish makers' and painters' naphtha.

> In the witness's opinion two devices containing flammable liquid were strategically placed in the south building with a triggering device to ignite them. He reasoned that the rope was wrapped around the outside of this container for the purpose of holding a lid in place.[10]

Although the investigation in Mantle's case did not uncover any evidence of inflammatory substances at the scene, the arson investigator believes that the fire was set. The char depth indicates that the fire had two points of origin. This is consistent with a non-accidental cause; fires of natural origin rarely have two simultaneous points of origin. The timing of the Mantle fire also supports an incendiary origin. It occurred on "Devil's Night", and one day before the real estate agent had scheduled a second visit with prospective buyers.

From a careful comparison of the facts in the cases and the problem, you are able to conclude that the prosecutor has a good case

8. When subjected to examination by the fire department chemist, this exhibit yielded highly flammable varnish makers' and painters' naphtha.

9. During cross-examination, the witness conceded that there were other possi-ble explanations for the fire. He admitted not having checked the gas lines or electrical wiring in the affected buildings.

10. *Horowitz*, 37 Mich. App. at 157–158, 194 N.W.2d at 377–378.

against Mantle for the wilful or malicious burning of the structure. This is the most direct type of legal analysis, where you need only compare your facts to those of a similar case. Often, however, the facts do not line up as neatly. Then you need to compare your facts to cases with facts that are both sufficient and insufficient to meet the legal standard. The remaining issue in this case, whether the structure was a dwelling or other real property, demonstrates the process.

There are two relevant cases. In *People v. Losinger*, 331 Mich. 490, 50 N.W.2d 137 (1951), the court held that the structure was a dwelling for purposes of the arson statute.

> The building is described as a cottage but more frequently as a cabin. Mr. Chase stated that he had built a foundation in the rear of the cabin on which he some day expected to build a house. It is true that it was a one-story building and was not partitioned off. The building itself appears, from the photograph, to have brick or composition walls and roof; however, it was described in the proceedings as having walls made of a brick roll. It had an air tight wooden floor build over a cement foundation. Mr. Chase testified that it contained three beds with inner spring mattresses and box springs, with bedding, curtains on the windows and between the beds. It contained some furniture, a kerosene cooking stove, cooking utensils, groceries and canned milk in the cupboards, some personal possessions, clothing, a heating stove and fuel and all equipment necessary so that occupants could move in and immediately have the facilities of a furnished dwelling house. Mr. Chase testified that he lived there during the hunting season the previous fall and had been there every month of the year, including the winter months, of each year, but was not certain that he was there after December 1, 1941, and before the fire. He, however, had never lived there for 90 days in succession because of his work in Lansing, but he planned to use the cottage when he retired. He had used the premises as a home, had slept in it, had lived in it steadily for periods of three weeks at a time and in addition had been there over night on many other occasions. He further testified that it was occupied during the fishing season and during the summer of 1942 he was there practically all the time and that his uncle had lived there a part of a previous winter. A one-car garage next to the building was completely destroyed by the fire in question.[11]

The court in *People v. Reed*, 13 Mich. App. 75, 163 N.W.2d 704 (1968), in contrast, held that the structure was not a dwelling.

> The evidence and exhibits reveal that the structure was in a dilapidated condition. There was running water in the kitchen but there was no bathroom or washing facilities and the interior was in a poor state of repair. During the period, prior to the fire, when the building was unoccupied a vandalism problem developed and by

11. *Losinger*, 331 Mich. at 501, 50 N.W.2d at 142.

order of the fire department the building had been boarded up. However, it had not been condemned, because as far as the fire marshal was concerned, although considered uninhabitable, the house could be restored to habitability by making improvements.

Although the owner testified that she was 'getting it ready' for her daughter, nothing had been done to restore the property for several months before the fire.

A consideration of all the evidence would lead to the conclusion that the structure in question was a former habitation that could be or was intended to be made habitable in the future, but that at the time of the burning was not habitable. This was a structure that had not been lived in for some months and there was no contemplation of living in it in the future in its present state of repair.[12]

Mantle's house has similarities to and differences from the structures in both cases. The house was unoccupied, unfurnished, and the utilities had been turned off. It was not equipped for a vacation visitor as was the cabin in *Horowitz*, but the house was ready for occupancy as soon as it was sold or leased. Unlike the building in *Reed*, the house was equipped with a bathroom and running water, and it was not boarded up. In analyzing issues where the facts are critical, it is often helpful to diagram the facts to highlight the similarities and differences. A diagram of this case shows that the Mantle house falls in the middle of a spectrum between the two cases.

Losinger	Mantle	*Reed*
Occupied occasionally for vacations and intended for retirement,	Unoccupied for 6 months,	Unoccupied and boarded up,
Good state of repair,	Good state of repair,	In poor repair,
Furnished with stove, cooking utensils, clothing and some food,	Unfurnished,	Unfurnished,
Kerosene heating stove.	Utilities turned off.	No bathroom or running water.

In order to figure out where to draw a line on a continuum, take a careful look at the court's language for what was crucial to the decision. The court in *People v. Reed* discussed the rationale behind the distinction in the following:

There is general agreement that arson at common law was an offense against the habitation rather than the safety of the property, and was considered a more serious crime than any other unlawful burning because it might result in the destruction of human life as well as property. This would appear to require that the crime of arson be founded on the burning of a structure that

12. *Reed*, 13 Mich. App. at 77, 163 N.W.2d at 705.

could reasonably be presumed to be a place of human habitation. The burning of any other structure, although unlawful, would be punished less severely.

The common law doctrine would appear to be reflected in our statutory law. C.L.1948, § 750.72 (Stat. Ann. 1962 Rev. § 28.267) relates to the burning of a dwelling house and carries a maximum penalty of 20 years while C.L. 1948, § 750.73 (Stat. Ann. 1962 Rev. § 28.268) relates to the burning of other real property and carries a maximum penalty of 10 years. The only substantial difference in the wording of the two statutes, other than penalty provisions, is that the first mentioned statute relates to a dwelling house occupied or unoccupied, rather than other real property.

Unless a structure is actually being dwelt in or lived in, it would seem that if it is unoccupied it would have to be a structure that could reasonably be presumed to be a place capable of being dwelt in or lived in to qualify as a dwelling house within the meaning of the statute.[13]

Based on this reasoning, you can conclude that Mantle's house qualifies as a dwelling, because it is suitable for habitation without renovation. Your overall analysis of the case will permit you to recommend to the prosecutor that she charge Marvin Mantle with the burning of a dwelling house under sec. 750.72.

Although this is an illustration of the most basic legal analysis, the same process applies to analyzing legal problems in general. The mix of issues and sub-issues will vary, as will the sources you will need to consult to understand the rules. Sometimes, a statute will provide all the information necessary to the analysis. If the defendant admits to owning the dog, you do not need to investigate the rule further for this sub-issue under the Illinois Dog Bite Statute. More often, you will need to consult a case or cases for a further general definition of a rule. In the arson illustration given above, the cases were necessary to provide the elements of proof necessary to establish arson: motive, opportunity, and a non-accidental cause for the fire. Even if you have formed an opinion as to the probable outcome of an issue based on the general definition, you cannot be confident of your conclusion until you have compared the facts of your legal problem with those in the cases that show what is sufficient or insufficient to meet the legal standard. Make sure that your comparison is based on the facts that are legally significant, not on extraneous facts.

Remember, too, that your legal analysis forms the basis for advising a client. As a result, you must be objective in your analysis. Your client's facts may not compare as neatly as you would like to those in a case. Mantle, in the arson example, had a financial motive for setting fire to the house; he stood to gain $45,000 from the insurance proceeds. The defendants in *Bailey* and *Horowitz* had the same goal of monetary

---

13. *Reed* at 78–79, 163 N.W.2d at 705–706.

gain, but these defendants had the added pressure of financial difficulties. As far as we know, Marvin Mantle has a good job and is not in debt. This makes the case against Mantle weaker than that in *Bailey* and *Horowitz*. If you gloss over this fact, your analysis is incomplete.

DEALING WITH COUNTER–ARGUMENTS

Often there is a counter-argument your opponent might make in response to your analysis of an issue or sub-issue. The attorney who will argue the case in court needs to be prepared to deal with the argument should it arise. As a result, you should anticipate and address possible counter-arguments in a memo. In the *Dobrin* dog bite case, for example, the defendant argued that a dog chained to a stake in the front yard was notice to members of the public that their presence was not permitted on the premises. As the dog was hiding in the bushes in that case, the court did not accept the defendant's argument. If you had a case, however, where there was a dog chained in plain view, you should anticipate that the defendant will argue that the dog provided notice that the public could not legally come on the premises.

ANALYZING PROBLEMS INVOLVING STATUTES

The process of analyzing legal problems involving statutes is similar. It involves identifying the issues, finding the applicable rules, applying the rules to the specific facts of the problem, and reaching a reasoned conclusion. The only difference is the nature of the rules you will employ.

The process begins by isolating the issues and sub-issues involved in the problem. As you have already discovered, you often need to know the rules before you can identify all the issues. In this respect, analyzing a problem involving a statute may be easier than dealing with a purely common law problem. The statute in its component parts may provide the elements of a cause of action and identify for you the specific vocabulary necessary to finding cases. The annotations to the different statutory provisions are normally arranged according to the required elements. If, for example, your client was injured while skiing in Colorado and wants to know if he has a cause of action, you would begin with the Ski Safety Act of 1979. In § 33–44–104, the statute tells you that a negligence action is possible if the injury was caused because someone, either another skier or the operator violated a provision of the act or a rule promulgated under this act or the Tramway Safety Act.

You are now ready to identify the issues in a general way. The cause of action is negligence, so you will need to research the elements of negligence. As with other legal analysis, the applicable rules provide the issues. Negligence requires (1) a duty owed to your client, (2) a breach of that duty, (3) that is a proximate cause of (4) the injury. The operative sections of the statute and possibly also the regulations define the duties.

Other sections of the statute may also give rise to issues. Section 33–44–109 raises the presumption that the ski area operator was not responsible unless "shown to the contrary by the preponderance of the evidence". The statute of limitation from section 33–44–111 may also be at issue. If the weather may have contributed to the injury, the "conditions of ordinary visibility" defined in section 33–44–103(3) may raise an issue.

The rules applicable to the problem also include the cases that define and interpret the statute and the elements of negligence. Remember that to illustrate the application of a rule to facts, you often need a spectrum of authority to show what is and is not sufficient to meet the test. The process of applying the rules to the facts of your client's case in order to reach a conclusion is the same analysis with which you are familiar.

Legal analysis is the essence of lawyering. The rest of this book is devoted to how to present your analysis in a variety of written and oral settings.

BASIC ANALYTICAL PROCEDURE

1) Identify the issues and sub-issues, breaking the problem into its smallest components.

2) Find the rules that govern these issues and sub-issues. The rules may include the general rules (from statutes and/or cases) as well as fact specific holdings from cases that illustrate what is sufficient and insufficient to meet the legal standard. To analyze the problem, you may need a spectrum of cases with facts both sufficient and insufficient to meet the rule.

3) Apply the rule to the facts in the problem, comparing and contrasting the facts with those in the cases. You may find it helpful to diagram the facts of the cases and the problem to help you visualize the comparison.

4) Reach well reasoned conclusions about the probable outcome of each issue and sub-issue.

Exercise 6A.

Read the dog bite statute and brief the four dog bite cases: *Messa, Dobrin, Siewerth,* and *Nelson.* Evaluate the cases to see how they fit together. When you finish, you should understand the elements of the statute and be able to articulate what facts are sufficient to meet each element. Consider the following problem in light of the statute and cases.

You are the only clerk in the Evanston office of the venerable firm of Austin, Martin, and Riddley. The following matter has been referred to you by Mark Porteus, a senior partner:

On February 1, our firm's client, Ralph Woodley, was visiting the privately owned "Randolph Zoo" in Elgin, Illinois, with his 5 year old son, Harvey. The zoo consists of several brick buildings containing exhibits of reptiles, fish, and other small animals.

After a few hours of wandering from one exhibit to another, Ralph decided that he and Harvey would visit one more and then leave for home. He spotted a brick building, somewhat set apart from the other buildings, and he set off for it on a pathway across the ice and snow with his son in tow.

Ralph and Harvey found a walk leading to the front door of the building. When they were about 10 yards away from the front door, a large German Shepherd suddenly appeared from behind a snow-covered hedge located five yards to the left. The dog was running loose. He ran up to Ralph and Harvey and nuzzled them playfully.

After a minute or two, Ralph and Harvey resumed their progress to the front door of the brick building. Harvey ran on ahead, picked up some snow, fashioned a snowball, and lobbed it at his father. Ralph ducked and turned and saw the snowball hit the German Shepherd on the back. Although the snowball did not have much velocity, and could not have caused any pain whatsoever, it sprayed the dog with snow and appeared to startle him.

The German Shepherd immediately set upon Harvey and bit him four times, with great force, on his right elbow.

Harvey's elbow was severely lacerated and required 117 stitches. I have had several phone calls from Ralph concerning this matter and he is, to put it mildly, distraught.

Mr. Woodley's friend, Seymour Spyer, went to the Randolph Zoo a week after these events and learned that the structure in front of which Harvey was mauled is not, in fact, an exhibition building. It is the private residence of the zoo's groundskeeper, Arthur Androcles. Mr. Androcles is provided the residence, and the yard in which these events took place, as part of his compensation.

Ralph says that there were no signs informing him that Androcles' building was a residence rather than another exhibition structure. He insists that there were no fences, borders or barriers setting Androcles' residence off from the rest of the zoo, and also insists that the residence looks like the exhibition buildings. He admits, however, as noted above, that Androcles' home is somewhat set apart from the other brick buildings in the zoo.

Ralph has told me there were no signs warning of dogs on the premises.

I have discussed this matter with Androcles' attorney over the telephone. He admitted that Androcles owns the dog. He stated, rather vehemently, that the dog had never bitten or harassed anyone before this episode. He said Androcles was away from the zoo that day and did not witness the events. He suggested that the dog would not have attacked if he had not been struck by the snowball, and he has refused all our demands for compensation. He admitted there were no signs warning of dogs.

Mr. Porteus filed a complaint incorporating the above information in the Kane County Courthouse in Elgin. The complaint named Harvey and his father as plaintiffs and Androcles as defendant. Androcles' attorney has filed a motion to dismiss on the grounds that the complaint fails to state a claim upon which relief can be granted. When the motion is heard next week, Judge Brouwer will assume, for purposes of the motion only, that all the facts alleged in the complaint are true.

§ 366   Liability of owner of dog attacking or injuring person

If a dog or other animal, without provocation, attacks or injures any person who is peaceably conducting himself in any place where he may lawfully be, the owner of such dog or other animal is liable in damages to such person for the full amount of the injury sustained.

P.A. 78–795, § 16, eff. Oct. 1, 1973.

MESSA v. SULLIVAN
Court of Appeals, 1965.
61 Ill. App. 2d 386, 209 N.E.2d 872.

BURMAN, PRESIDING JUSTICE.

Betty Messa brought this action against James Sullivan, Helen Sullivan and the Keyman's Club, an Illinois not for profit corporation, to recover damages for the bodily injuries which she sustained as the result of being bitten by the defendants' dog. The complaint was based on two theories: first, a common law action for the keeping of a vicious animal and, second, an action based on what is commonly known as the "Dog Bite Statute" (Ill. Rev. Stat. 1963, ch. 8, § 12d). The parties waived a jury and the case was tried by the court. On the common law count, the trial court held for the defendants because he found that the plaintiff was contributorily negligent. No appeal has been taken from the judgment entered on that issue. On the statutory count, however, the court concluded that the plaintiff should recover and therefore he entered judgment awarding the plaintiff damages only against James Sullivan and the Keyman's Club in the amount of $3,000. From this judgment these two defendants appeal. They contend that the plaintiff failed to prove, as she was required to prove in order to recover under the statute, that she was lawfully on the defendants' premises and that she did not provoke the dog to attack. Alternatively the defendants contend that the amount of the damage award is not supported by the evidence.

The plaintiff suffered her injuries in the Keyman's Club building, 4721 West Madison Street in the City of Chicago. Located on the lower level and on the first and second stories of this building were the following: a bowling alley, a barber shop, a cocktail lounge, banquet and meeting rooms, a ballroom and various other businesses and offices. A labor union office occupied the third floor and the fourth floor was vacant. James Sullivan, the president of the Club and the manager of its building for over twenty years, and his wife, Helen, occupied the fifth floor as their residence. No other use was made of the fifth floor. The Sullivans' apartment contained a safe in which the receipts from the operation of the building were kept. In addition, the apartment contained the defendants' furniture, personal property and their three year old German Shepherd dog, named "K.C.", which was kept there to protect the Club's property in the apartment. The various businesses located in the building were advertised by signs on the exterior of the structure and on a building directory which was located in the building lobby. There were, however, no notices anywhere that the fifth floor was used as a residence and not for commercial or business purposes.

All the floors of the building were served by an automatic elevator which could be reached on the ground floor by entering the building from Madison Street and by walking through the building lobby past the building office, which was located on the left of the lobby as one entered the building.

The plaintiff and the defendant, James Sullivan, testified concerning the events which occurred on the day in question. The plaintiff, who was a deaf mute, testified that at about two o'clock on the afternoon of June 12, 1961, she entered the defendants' building for the purpose of selling printed cards depicting the deaf and dumb alphabet. She said that this was the first time she had been in the building; that as she walked through the lobby she saw a woman at a telephone switchboard in the building office, that she entered the elevator and rode it to the fifth floor. When she got to that floor, the door on the elevator itself opened automatically. The plaintiff said that before she could step out of the elevator she had to manually open a second door which swung outward. She opened this door, which she said was heavy. She stepped out into the fifth floor hall and turned to the left where there was a door. At this point the defendants' dog ran out of the door and jumped on the plaintiff. She testified: " * * * the dog bit me on the leg, and he bit me on the body, and he bit me on the arm, and I tried to cover my face. And the dog was big, and the dog was bigger than I was, and he was on top of me, and three times he bit me." The plaintiff stated that she finally managed to get back to the elevator and to ride down to the lobby where she told the woman at the switchboard what had happened.

During her testimony, the plaintiff was shown plaintiff's exhibit number one, a picture of a sign reading in large letters:

WARNING

KEEP OUT

VICIOUS

POLICE DOGS

INSIDE

She identified the exhibit as a picture of a sign which was posted on the manually operated elevator door which swung outward into the fifth floor hall. However, she denied having seen the sign because, in her words, " * * * the door was so heavy. I was pushing the door, it was a sliding door, and I did not see the sign."

Concerning her injuries, the plaintiff identified two exhibits as accurate pictures of the large marks and wounds inflicted by the dog on her leg, on her right side and on her right arm. The plaintiff testified that the bites left "holes" in her arm, that she felt pain for about two months after the occurrence and that she could not sleep for two weeks after the events in question.

The defendant, James Sullivan, testified that on the day in question he and an office girl were in the building office; that he observed the plaintiff walk into the lobby and proceed directly to the elevator without looking at the directory; that he saw the plaintiff board the elevator; and that he noticed the elevator go to the fifth floor. He said that the door on the elevator itself opened automatically; that when this door opened on the fifth floor, there was a second door which must be opened outward by hand to gain entrance to the hall; and that a thirty inch high sign warning of the presence of vicious dogs was posted on this manually operated door so that the bottom of the sign was about three and one-half to four feet from the floor. He also stated that the door to his apartment on the fifth floor was to the right of the elevator door about fifteen feet down the hall. The defendant testified further that he saw the plaintiff after she came down from the fifth floor; that he tried to administer first-aid for the scratches on the plaintiff's arm; and that he observed a tear in her dress. In his discovery deposition, the defendant testified that there was no sign in the elevator itself regarding vicious dogs and that the manually operated elevator door on the fifth floor could be locked by a key, but that it was unlocked on the day of the occurrence.

The "Dog Bite Statute" with which this appeal is principally concerned provides:

If a dog, without provocation, attacks or injures any person who is peaceably conducting himself in any place where he may lawfully be, the owner of the dog is liable in damages to the person so attacked or injured to the full amount of the injury sustained. The term "owner" includes any person harboring or keeping a dog. The term "dog" includes both male and female of the canine species. (Ill. Rev. Stat. 1963, ch. 8, § 12d)

This court, in *Beckert v. Risberg*, 50 Ill. App. 2d 100, 199 N.E.2d 811, set forth the four elements of an action under this statute as follows:

(1) injury caused by a dog owned or harbored by the defendant;

(2) lack of provocation;

(3) peaceable conduct of the person injured, and

(4) the presence of the person injured in a place where he has a legal right to be.

There is no dispute that the plaintiff was bitten by a dog owned by the defendants and hence there is no question concerning the first element above. The defendants contend that the other elements are not satisfied, however, because the plaintiff's entry onto the fifth floor past a large sign warning her of the presence of the dog which bit her constituted an unlawful entry by the plaintiff and constituted provocative behavior on her part.

We do not agree that the plaintiff was not lawfully on the defendants' premises. From all indications on the exterior of the defendants' building, in its lobby and on the inside of the elevator cab itself, people like the plaintiff could only surmise that the entire building was devoted to business purposes and that it was intended that they should come there on business. No notices anywhere indicated that any part of the premises was used as a private residence. It is clear, therefore, that when she entered the building, crossed its lobby, entered the elevator and rode it to the fifth floor, the plaintiff was lawfully on the premises. In addition, we believe that she was also lawfully on the premises when she entered the fifth floor hall where she was attacked. Persons entering the building and riding its elevator would have no reason to believe that the fifth floor was used for residential purposes or that vicious dogs were kept there. The sole warning to this effect was posted in a place where it could be seen only split seconds before one would enter the danger area and only at a time when the elevator passenger would be concerned with pushing open the heavy door in order to step into the hall and continue on with his business there. We agree with the trial court that under these circumstances the warning sign was in the wrong location, that it did not give adequate warning of the danger and that hence the sign gives no grounds for holding that persons who enter the hall have no legal right to be there.

The cases primarily relied on by the defendants are distinguishable on their facts and are not applicable here. In *Fullerton v. Conan*, 87 Cal. App. 2d 354, 197 P.2d 59, the California District Court of Appeal affirmed a judgment for the defendant in a case brought by a five year old child to recover for injuries she received when bitten by the defendant's dog. She had sued under the California "Dog Bite Statute" which, like our own statute, required that the plaintiff lawfully be on the dog owner's premises. In that case, however, unlike the present case, it appears that the child had been given a direct, oral instruction not to go into the yard where the dog was. In another California dog bite case, *Gomes v. Byrne*, 51 Cal. 2d 418, 333 P.2d 754, the court affirmed a judgment for the defendant. That case is not like the case at bar because there the plaintiff saw and heard the dog before he entered the yard where the dog was kept. We do not believe that the other cases cited by the defendants are controlling and it would serve no useful purpose to extend this opinion by discussing them at length.

Next the defendants argue that the plaintiff was guilty of provocative behavior at the time she was attacked. They reason that the plaintiff approached the apartment and the dog without giving a warning as to the nature of her visit; that this act represented a threat to the security of the apartment; that the dog resented this threat and that the plaintiff should have known such conduct would be likely to provoke a dog to attack. We do not agree. Here the plaintiff had a legal right to be in the hallway. Her only actions at that point consisted of stepping off the elevator and walking a short distance toward the defendants' apartment door. We do not believe that the term "provocation" in the statute was intended to apply to a situation like this and thereby relieve from responsibility the owner of a vicious dog, which is specifically kept for protection, merely because the dog interprets the visitor's movements as hostile actions calling for attack.

Finally the defendants contend that the award of $3,000 is not supported by the evidence and that it is excessive. Our courts have consistently held that a damage award to a plaintiff in a personal injury case will not be set aside unless it is so palpably excessive as to indicate passion or prejudice on the part of the trier of fact (*Holsman v. Darling State Street Corp.*, 6 Ill. App. 2d 517, 128 N.E.2d 581, and cases there cited; *Eizerman v. Behn*, 9 Ill. App. 2d 263, 132 N.E.2d 788; *Lau v. West Towns Bus Co.*, 16 Ill. 2d 442, 158 N.E.2d 63) or unless it is so large as to shock the judicial conscience (*Barango v. E.L. Hedstrom Coal Co.*, 12 Ill. App. 2d 118, 138 N.E.2d 829; *Smelcer v. Sanders*, 39 Ill. App. 2d 164, 188 N.E.2d 391; *Myers v. Nelson*, 42 Ill. App. 2d 475, 192 N.E.2d 403). The record shows that the plaintiff sustained multiple wounds on her body, arms and legs and that she suffered great pain. We find nothing here to indicate passion or prejudice on the part of the trial judge and we do not believe that under the circumstances the award can be considered shocking to the judicial conscience. Hence we cannot substitute our judgment for that of the trial judge and set aside the award.

The judgment should be affirmed.

Affirmed.

MURPHY, J., and KLUCZYNSKI, J., concur.

DOBRIN v. STEBBINS

Court of Appeals, 1970.
122 Ill. App. 2d 387, 259 N.E.2d 405.

LEIGHTON, JUSTICE.

In a non-jury trial, plaintiff recovered a judgment against defendant for personal injuries he suffered when he was bitten by defendant's dog. Although plaintiff, who is the appellee in these proceedings has not filed a brief, we will review this appeal on the merits. *Daley v. Jack's Tivoli Liquor Lounge*, Inc., 118 Ill. App. 2d 264, 254 N.E.2d 814.

The facts are not in dispute. On July 16, 1964 defendant was the owner of a toy German Shepherd. He chained it to a pipe so that the dog was confined within defendant's property at 6225 West 79th Street in the City of Chicago. Plaintiff, then 17 years of age, was selling magazines. There was no sign or posted notice on defendant's property warning salesmen or others to keep off. Plaintiff went to defendant's home. He walked up a dirt path that led from the sidewalk. When plaintiff was within five or ten feet of the door, defendant's dog jumped on plaintiff, bit him in the abdomen and on the thigh. After getting away, plaintiff was taken to a nearby clinic where he received treatment for his injuries. Later in the day he visited his family doctor who replaced the bandages and gave him a tetanus shot. Pain from the dog bites lasted three or four days. Plaintiff's doctor submitted a bill which was paid.

Plaintiff filed suit against defendant and invoked what is colloquially the "Dog Bite Statute," Ill. Rev. Stat. 1963, ch. 8, sec. 12d which provides:

> Dogs attacking or injuring person—Liability of owner. If a dog, without provocation, attacks or injures any person who is peaceably conducting himself in any place where he may lawfully be, the owner of the dog is liable in damages to the person so attacked or injured to the full amount of the injury sustained. The term "owner" includes any person harboring or keeping a dog. The term "dog" includes both male and female of the canine species.

After hearing evidence, the trial judge awarded plaintiff damages in the sum of $750.00. Defendant appeals. He contends that plaintiff was a trespasser when he entered defendant's property; therefore no judgment could be recovered under the statute. In the alternative defendant contends that the damage award was excessive.

A trespasser is one who does an unlawful act or a lawful act in an unlawful manner to the injury of the person or property of another. 87 C.J.S. Trespass § 1; see *People v. Goduto*, 21 Ill. 2d 605, 174 N.E.2d 385. By this definition, plaintiff was not a trespasser on defendant's land when he went there during the ordinary hours of the day to solicit magazine subscriptions.

An owner of property who provides a path or walk from the public way to his door, without some indication (sign, posting of notice or words) warning away those who seek lawful business with him extends a license to use the path or walk during the ordinary hours of the day. Persons who thus make use of the path or walk are licensees. Restatement, Second, Torts, sec. 332, Comment b; *Stacy v. Shapiro*, 212 App. Div. 723, 209 N.Y.S. 305 (1925); *Reuter v. Kenmore Building Co.*, 153 Misc. 646, 276 N.Y.S. 545 (1934). Our decision in *Messa v. Sullivan*, 61 Ill. App. 2d 386, 209 N.E.2d 872 supports this view. Therefore, plaintiff was a licensee on defendant's land when he was bitten by defendant's dog. He was in a "[p]lace where he may lawfully be. * * *" within the meaning of Ill. Rev. Stat. 1963, ch. 8, sec. 12d.

This being so, proof that plaintiff while peaceably conducting himself and without provocation, was injured by defendant's dog justified entry of judgment in favor of plaintiff and against defendant. *Beckert v. Risberg*, 50 Ill. App. 2d 100, 199 N.E.2d 811; *Bailey v. Bly*, 87 Ill. App. 2d 259, 231 N.E.2d 8.

The damages the trial judge awarded plaintiff were within the limits of fair and reasonable compensation. *Johnson v. Eckberg*, 94 Ill. App. 634; *Sesterhenn v. Saxe*, 88 Ill. App. 2d 2, 232 N.E.2d 277. Judgment is affirmed.

Judgment affirmed.

STAMOS, P.J., and DRUCKER, J., concur.

SUPPLEMENTAL OPINION

LEIGHTON, JUSTICE.

Defendant petitions for rehearing on the ground that when plaintiff came upon defendant's property, he saw the dog that bit him. Defendant argues that the best warning a property owner can give to those who may come upon his land is his dog chained, in plain view and standing guard. Defendant contends that presence of his dog in this way was constructive notice to the plaintiff that he could enter defendant's property only at his peril.

We agree that a dog chained to guard its owner's property where it can be seen, is notice that entry on the land is forbidden. However, the record in this case does not support defendant's contention. Both plaintiff and the defendant testified that there were bushes on either side of the front door to defendant's home. Plaintiff testified that he never saw defendant's dog before it bit him because it "must have come out of the bushes * *." In other words, defendant's dog was not where plaintiff could see it. The petition for rehearing is denied.

Petition for rehearing denied.

STAMOS, P.J., and DRUCKER, J., concur.

SIEWERTH v. CHARLESTON

Court of Appeals, 1967.
89 Ill. App. 2d 64, 231 N.E.2d 644.

SULLIVAN, PRESIDING JUSTICE.

Plaintiff appeals from a judgment in his favor in the amount of $500.30, and asks that the judgment be reversed and remanded for a new trial on the question of damages only. Plaintiff contends that the damages allowed are totally inadequate and not supported by the record.

Defendant filed a cross-appeal and asks that the judgment in favor of the plaintiff be reversed.

Roy Siewerth, a minor, by Ralph Siewerth, his father and next friend, filed this action against Ruben Charleston for injuries sustained when the defendant's dog bit the plaintiff on or about the face.

Section 1 of "AN ACT to establish the liability of a person owning or harboring a dog which attacks or injures a person", (Ill. Rev. Stat. 1963, chap. 8, par. 12d) provides in part as follows:

> "If a dog, without provocation, attacks or injures any person who is peaceably conducting himself in any place where he may lawfully be, the owner of the dog is liable in damages to the person so attacked or injured to the full amount of the injury sustained.
> * * * "

The facts are these: on June 8, 1963, the plaintiff, Roy Siewerth, who was at that time seven years old, was playing with a playmate, Kevin Charleston, on the front porch or front stoop of the defendant's home. The boys were playing a game known as tic-tac-toe and were lying on the porch or stoop which was approximately 5 feet by 3 feet in area. A Rhodesian Ridgeback dog was also lying on the porch or stoop. The dog weighed approximately 100 pounds and when standing was about 27 inches high at the shoulders. Early in 1963, this female dog had given birth to a litter of nine puppies. About two or three weeks before June 8, 1963, the dog had been struck by an automobile and it was confined to a local animal hospital, where six stitches were placed upon its hind quarter. June 8, 1963, the day the occurrence took place, was extremely hot, nearing 100 degrees.

The evidence also showed that the plaintiff pushed or kicked the dog in the stomach twice prior to the occurrence. His playmate, Kevin Charleston, pushed or kicked the dog about two minutes after the plaintiff had pushed or kicked the dog the second time. The dog growled at plaintiff after each time he kicked or pushed the dog in the stomach, although the dog had never growled at him before, and the boys had played with the dog on many occasions. Plaintiff testified that when he pushed the dog with his feet the dog growled each time and he knew that he made the dog angry each time.

Kevin Charleston's mother, Barbara Charleston, was in the living room at the time of the occurrence and prior thereto. She had called to the boys to get off the porch when the dog first growled. Roy Siewerth, the plaintiff, testified that he heard Mrs. Charleston yell at him and Kevin to get off the porch only once. The boys remained on the porch. The evidence, however, showed that Mrs. Charleston told the boys to get off the porch twice just before the incident. After the dog growled the second time Mrs. Charleston told Roy Siewerth, the plaintiff, to go home. Roy Siewerth heard her but made no attempt to leave the porch. Prior to the date of the occurrence Mrs. Charleston told Roy Siewerth's mother that she did not want children on the porch. Mrs. Siewerth, the plaintiff's mother, also told her own children many times to stay off the Charleston porch. Shortly thereafter, Mrs. Charleston was prompted to go to the front door and noticed the plaintiff bleeding from the face and walking to his home. The evidence showed that the plaintiff, while lying on the porch, bent his head toward the dog and the dog's mouth came in contact with plaintiff's face. The dog's teeth had cut the plaintiff on the forehead partly back of the hairline, and also at the corner between the nose and right eye.

In addition to the foregoing, plaintiff testified that Kevin made the statement to one of two men who had taken statements from Kevin and the plaintiff, that "Lucy was right there and I was kicking him." When the man asked, "Who was kicking him?" Kevin said, "We both were." When the man asked the plaintiff whether he was kicking Lucy too, he said, "Me and him did." When the man asked Kevin how many times he kicked her, Kevin said, "About two or three times." When the man asked the plaintiff whether he kicked her more than once, the plaintiff nodded his head. He also stated that he remembered kicking the dog twice.

We will first discuss the cross-appeal of the defendant. The defendant raises only one point, namely, that the plaintiff failed to prove all of the necessary elements of the cause of action set forth in the complaint.

In *Beckert v. Risberg*, 50 Ill. App. 2d 100, 106, 199 N.E.2d 811, 814, the court said:

> "The elements of a cause of action under the statute are (1) injury caused by a dog owned or harbored by the defendant; (2) lack of provocation; (3) peaceable conduct of the person injured, and (4) the presence of the person injured in a place where he has a legal right to be."

The defendant argues that the plaintiff was guilty of provocation and that the attack by the dog was with provocation. The kicking or pushing of the dog by the plaintiff on two occasions, plus the kicking and pushing of the dog by Kevin Charleston, his playmate, sufficiently provoked the dog to constitute a complete bar to this statutory cause of action.

The plaintiff contends that he was bitten by a dog owned by the owner of the home without any provocation on the part of the plaintiff. He further argues that there was no provocation on the part of the plaintiff, as provocation needs intent and there was nothing in the record to show that the minor plaintiff intended to provoke the dog into the action of biting the plaintiff. This contention is without merit. The plaintiff testified that the dog growled after he was pushed or kicked by the plaintiff on each occasion, and that when the dog growled he knew that that made the dog angry. He further stated that the dog had never growled at him before. Even if, as the plaintiff argues, the provocation in the statute needs intent, the record shows intent on the part of the plaintiff. The plaintiff further argues that since he kicked or pushed the dog only twice, after each of which occasion the dog growled, and that subsequently the dog, before biting the plaintiff, was kicked by his playmate, Kevin Charleston, that the bite by the dog was not caused by the provocation of the plaintiff. With this contention we cannot agree. The kicking or pushing of the dog on two occasions by the plaintiff, and subsequently by Kevin Charleston, his playmate, constituted continuous provocation.

The conduct of the plaintiff, coupled with the conduct of Kevin Charleston, was completely sufficient to constitute provocation as contemplated by the statute.

Defendant also argues that the plaintiff failed to prove other necessary elements of the statutory cause of action. The other necessary elements argued by the defendant are that the person injured must be peaceably conducting himself and the person injured must be in a place where he may lawfully be. It is argued that the plaintiff was not peaceably conducting himself by his own admission, and that he was not in a place where he may lawfully be, because he was told to go home by Mrs. Charleston, the defendant's wife, before the dogbite occurred. We think it unnecessary to discuss these points further, in view of the fact that we are constrained to hold that the attack by the dog was not without provocation.

In view of our holding on the question of liability, it will be unnecessary for us to discuss the plaintiff's appeal on the grounds that the damages awarded were inadequate. The judgment in favor of the plaintiff is reversed.

Judgment reversed.

SCHWARTZ and DEMPSEY, JJ., concur.

NELSON v. LEWIS
Court of Appeals, 1976.
36 Ill. App. 3d 130, 344 N.E.2d 268.

KARNS, PRESIDING JUSTICE.

Plaintiff, by her father and next friend, brought an action under the Illinois "dog-bite" statute (Ill. Rev. Stat. 1973, ch. 8, par. 366) for injuries inflicted upon her by defendant's dog. From judgment entered on a jury verdict for the defendant, she appeals.

On the date of her injury, plaintiff Jo Ann Nelson, a two and a half year old, was playing "crack-the-whip" in defendant's backyard with his daughter and other children. Jo Ann was on the end of the "whip." The testimony shows that after she had been thrown off the whip, Jo Ann fell or stepped on the dog's tail while the dog was chewing a bone. The dog, a large Dalmatian, reacted by scratching the plaintiff in her left eye. There was no evidence that plaintiff or anyone else had teased or aggravated the dog before the incident, nor was there evidence that the dog had ever scratched, bitten, or attacked anyone else. According to its owner, the dog had not appeared agitated either before or after the incident. As a result of her injuries, Jo Ann incurred permanent damage to a tear duct in her left eye. It was established that Jo Ann's left eye will overflow with tears more frequently and as a result of less irritation than normal, but that her vision in the eye was not affected.

Our statute pertaining to liability of an owner of a dog attacking or injurying persons provides:

> If a dog or other animal without provocation, attacks or injures any person who is peacefully conducting himself in any place where he may lawfully be, the owner of such dog or other animal is liable in damages to such person for the full amount of the injury sustained. Ill. Rev. Stat. 1973, ch. 8, par. 366.

Under this statute there are four elements that must be proved: injury caused by a dog owned or harbored by the defendant; lack of provocation; peaceable conduct of the person injured; and the presence of the person injured in a place where he has a legal right to be. *Siewerth v. Charleston,* 89 Ill. App. 2d 64, 231 N.E.2d 644 (1967); *Messa v. Sullivan,* 61 Ill. App. 2d 386, 209 N.E.2d 872 (1965); *Beckert v. Risberg,* 50 Ill. App. 2d 100, 199 N.E.2d 811 (1964) *rev'd on other grounds* 33 Ill. 2d 44, 210 N.E.2d 207 (1965). There is no dispute but that the dog caused the plaintiff's injury; the defendant owned the dog; the plaintiff's conduct was peaceable; and she was injured in a place where she had a legal right to be. The issue presented is whether plaintiff's unintentional act constitutes "provocation" within the meaning of the statute.

It appears that this issue has not been passed upon by an Illinois court. The statute does not distinguish between intentional and unintentional acts of provocation and thus, defendant argues, an unintentional act, so long as it provokes an animal or dog, may constitute provocation. Defendant's position, that the mental state of the actor who provokes a dog is irrelevant is consistent with the commonly understood meaning of provocation. Provocation is defined as an act or process of provoking, stimulation or incitement. Webster's Third New International Dictionary. Thus it would appear that an unintentional act can constitute provocation within the plain meaning of the statute.

Only three reported decisions have considered the question of provocation within the meaning of this statute. In *Siewerth v. Charles-*

ton, supra, the court held there was provocation where the injured boy and his companion kicked a dog three times. The argument was there raised that provocation meant only an intentional act, but the court did not pass upon this contention as it found the injured boy's acts in kicking the dog clearly intentional and provoking. In *Messa v. Sullivan, supra,* the court found no provocation on the part of the plaintiff where she walked into a hallway patrolled by a watch dog that attacked her on sight. The court held the acts of the plaintiff did not constitute provocation within the intent of the statute and that plaintiff had a right to be on the defendant's premises. While plaintiff argues that in *Messa* the plaintiff did not intend to provoke the dog and there was no provocation found, it appears that the court's holding was based on a determination that plaintiff's actions and conduct were not of a provoking nature, not on any determination of the intent with which plaintiff's acts were done. The court stated that it did not believe "provocation" within the meaning of the statute was intended to apply to a situation where a vicious dog interpreted a visitor's non-threatening movements as hostile actions calling for attack. Similarly in *Steichman v. Hurst,* 2 Ill. App. 3d 415, 275 N.E.2d 679 (1971), it was held that the acts of a postal carrier in spraying the defendant's dog with a repellant was not provocation. Although language in the decision might be read to mean that absence of intent by the plaintiff to provoke is material, we do not believe that this is an accurate reading of the opinion. In *Steichman* the letter carrier had previous difficulties with defendant's dog and had made several efforts to avoid the dog on the day she was attacked. The court characterized her conduct as "reasonable measures for self protection evoked by the dog's actions and deterring him only momentarily." Thus, the plaintiff's acts, although intentional, did not amount to an incitement or provocation of the dog, triggering the attack.

In the present case, it was admitted that the plaintiff jumped or fell on the dog's tail; that the dog was of a peaceful and quiet temperament; and that the dog was gnawing on a bone when the incident occurred. Under these circumstances, we believe that the dalmatian was provoked, although the provocation was not intentional.

Plaintiff argues that since her act was unintentional, or that because she was of an age at which she could not be charged with scienter, she did not provoke the dog within the meaning of the act. Although her counsel presents a strong argument for interpreting the instant statute to impose essentially strict liability upon a dog owner for injuries caused to a child of tender years, we cannot agree that the public policy of this State compels the adoption of such a standard.

At common law in Illinois, one injured by a dog could recover from the owner only if he could prove that the dog had manifested a disposition "to bite mankind" and that the dog's keeper or owner had notice of this disposition. *Chicago and Alton Railroad Co. v. Kuckkuck,* 197 Ill. 304, 64 N.E. 358 (1902); *Domm v. Hollenbeck,* 259 Ill. 382, 102 N.E. 782 (1913); *Klatz v. Pfeffer,* 333 Ill. 90, 164 N.E. 224 (1928). He could not recover for an injury resulting from his own contributory negligence either by knowingly exposing himself to the dangerous dog (*Chicago and Alton Railroad Co. v. Kuckkuck, supra*) or by provoking the dog. *Keightlinger v. Egan,* 65 Ill. 235 (1872). A dog owner's liability rested upon negligence, and he could be liable only if he harbored a "vicious" dog. Thus, one injured by a dog bore a substantial burden of proof.

The instant statute, and its immediate predecessor, substantially eased this burden imposed by the common law. It eliminates the requisite proof that the dog was vicious towards humans and that the owner knew of this disposition, and made irrelevant questions of the injured person's contributory negligence (other than provocation). *Beckert v. Risberg,* 33 Ill. 2d 44, 210 N.E.2d 207 (1965). We do not believe, however, that it was meant to impose strict liability on dog owners for all injuries caused by dogs, except those intentionally provoked. Instead this act was apparently drawn to eliminate as much as possible any inquiry into subjective considerations. Whether the injured person was attacked or injured while conducting himself in a peaceful manner in a place where he could lawfully be are all matters which require no inquiry into a person's intent. We believe that the determination of "provocation" should also be made independently of such considerations. A determination of provocation does not require consideration of the degree of wilfulness, which motivates the provoking cause. Had the legislature intended only intentional provocation to be a bar to recovery we think it would have so specified. Its conclusion apparently was that an owner or keeper of a dog who would attack or injure someone without provocation should be liable. This implies that the intent of the plaintiff is immaterial. Nor do we think that the plaintiff's status as a child of tender years should relieve her of all responsibility for a provoking act. Our Supreme Court in *Beckert v. Risberg,* 33 Ill. 2d 44, 210 N.E.2d 207 (1965), sanctioned a jury instruction in the language of the statute where the plaintiff was a three year old boy. Although the court did not specifically address the issue, it appears by implication that a young child is not exempted from responsibility for his or her acts which provoke a dog under this statute.

We have been referred to decisions from other jurisdictions which permit an injured person to recover for unintentional acts which "provoke" a dog. Two of these cases, however, were decided on common law negligence theories, the courts concluding that these unintentional acts did not constitute contributory negligence. *Smith v. Pelah,* 2 Strange 1264, 93 Eng. Rep. 1171 (1795); *Fake v. Addicks,* 45 Minn. 37, 47 N.W. 450 (1890). Another case applied a statute which provided for strict liability for injuries inflicted by a dog unless the injury was voluntarily brought on by plaintiff with full knowledge of the probable consequences. *Wojewoda v. Rybarczyk,* 246 Mich. 641, 225 N.W. 555 (1929). These decisions are inapposite in that while they arise from similar factual situations they were decided upon legal theories which placed emphasis upon the injured person's scienter.

Although we believe that the instant statute does not impose liability upon a dog owner whose animal merely reacts to an unintentionally provocative act, the present appeal does not involve a vicious attack which was out of all proportion to the unintentional acts involved. *E.g. Messa v. Sullivan, supra.* The dalmatian here apparently only struck and scratched plaintiff with a forepaw in response to the plaintiff's stepping or falling on its tail while it was gnawing on a bone, an act which scarcely can be described as vicious. Therefore we hold that "provocation" within the meaning of the instant statute means either intentional or unintentional provocation; that the defendant's dog was provoked by the plaintiff's unintentional acts and did not viciously react to these acts; and that no reversible error was committed in the trial court.

For the foregoing reasons, the judgment of the Circuit Court of St. Clair County is affirmed.

AFFIRMED.

JONES and GEORGE J. MORAN, JJ., concur.

Exercise 6B.

Read and analyze the Susan Saxon problem in light of the statutes and cases provided. Be sure to follow the basic analytical procedure.

Susan Saxon came into our office yesterday to consult with us about a problem she is having at her job. She is employed by Umatilla Mining Company as a miner. The company mines for uranium and other trace metals used in the production of alloys. Although the company headquarters are in Pendleton, Oregon, the mining operation occurs in the hills five miles from Ukiah. She has been employed by the company since last February.

Ms. Saxon is a nice looking 21 year old woman. She graduated from high school four years ago and had worked for three years in an office doing secretarial work. In high school she had been on the varsity girls' swimming and track teams. Since graduation, she had kept in shape working out at a local health club. She explained that she found office work confining and preferred to work outside doing something physical.

In November that year, she saw an advertisement on television for vocational training. After discussing the various job opportunities with a counsellor, she enrolled in a program for training in mining skills and the heavy equipment used by the industry.

Hank Lawson, who taught the mining skills course, reports that three women entered the program, but of those three, only Susan completed the course. She finished second in a graduating class of 37. He recommended her highly to Umatilla and the company hired her on the basis of her performance in the vocational program and the skills test administered by the personnel manager, Harvey Borgren. He has talked to Borgren since then to see how his students are doing on the job. Borgren reported no complaints with Saxon's job performance. In fact, she was promoted to a permanent employee in May after the probationary period expired.

Lawson explained that Umatilla pays top wages in the industry and provides its employees with good health and retirement benefits. As a result, the employees have never found it necessary to form a union. The company has no formal grievance procedures; the few problems that arise are handled informally.

Ms. Saxon enjoys being a miner. Although she only weighs 135 lbs., she is 5'9" and strong enough to handle the drills and other heavy equipment.

When Ms. Saxon was hired, Harvey Borgren warned her about the job. "The men are tough" he said, "and they cuss constantly. If you take the job, don't come complaining to me about the way the men treat you." She had not expected the situation to be easy at first, but she anticipated that the men would start treating her like any other miner when they saw she could handle the job as well as any of them.

Despite Ms. Saxon's enthusiasm for the job itself, she has had problems with her fellow miners since the beginning. She is the only woman who has ever worked for the company in other than a secretarial capacity. She is part of a 12 person crew. Each of the men on the crew has propositioned her for sex at least once during the eight months of her employment. The men frequently make sexually explicit comments about her body parts either directly to her face or in loud voices she can overhear. In July when she complained to the foreman about the situation, he replied, "what do you expect with a body like that in a job like this?" He told her that the boys would get used to her after a while. The remarks have continued unabated, but not in the presence of the foreman.

Ms. Saxon has asked our advice. She wants to know if she has a cause of action for sexual harassment. She would like to quit, but she is worried that if she quits voluntarily, she may not be able to collect unemployment benefits. The job market in eastern Oregon is depressed and she will have great difficulty finding alternative employment. She must support herself.

There are two relevant statutes in Oregon.

The first one, Or. Rev. Stat. sec. 659.030(1)(b), from the Oregon Fair Employment Practices Act, makes discrimination in employment illegal. It provides:

> [I]t is an unlawful employment practice [f]or an employer, because of an individual's race, religion, color, sex, * * * to discriminate against such individual in compensation or in the terms, conditions or privileges of employment.

The second statute, Or. Rev. Stat. sec. 657.176(2) limits the receipt of unemployment benefits. It provides:

If the authorized representative designated by the assistant director finds that the individual:

(c) Voluntarily left work without good cause, the individual shall be disqualified from the receipt of benefits.

There are four relevant Oregon Court of Appeals decisions.

FRED MEYER, INC. v. BUREAU OF LABOR
Court of Appeals, 1979.
39 Or. App. 253, 592 P.2d 564.

* * *

We take the facts from the undisputed evidence and from the Commissioner's findings, and we accept those inferences of the Commissioner which can reasonably be drawn from the evidence. *Braidwood v. City of Portland,* 24 Or. App. 477, 480, 546 P.2d 777 *rev. den.* (1976). Hayes, who was 16 years old at the time, was employed as a stockboy by petitioner from May 25, 1972 to July 14, 1972, * * * As stockboy, Hayes unloaded freight, transported goods from stockroom to shelves, swept floors, mixed paints, bagged customer purchases and performed other tasks of a similar nature. His work was supervised by four individuals: Lester Bowman, manager of the department; Larry West, assistant manager; Terry Fetters, third-in-charge; and Tom Bonk, management trainee and fourth-in-charge.[2] These supervisory employes worked various shifts and each was present for only part of the time Hayes was working.

The charges of racial harassment involve Fetters and Bonk. On occasion when Hayes and two white stockboys were working together, Fetters would engage in social conversation with the other stockboys, who would cease work during the conversation. Fetters would then criticize Hayes because the task assigned to all three stockboys was not accomplished quickly enough. Fetters also asked Hayes if he belonged to the Black Panthers and repeated the inquiry on several occasions despite Hayes' negative answer and the absence of any behavior or statement from Hayes which might reasonably prompt such an inquiry. The Commissioner inferred that those inquiries and the differential treatment were intended to embarrass, offend and isolate Hayes because of his race and that they caused him to feel intimidated, isolated and inferior.

The incidents of racial harassment by Bonk were more serious and more numerous. Although it was difficult for the witnesses to be precise about events that transpired approximately five years before the contested case hearing, there is substantial evidence to support the

---

2. Only Bowman and West had authority to hire and fire employes; Fetters and Bonk were nonmanagement employes with some supervisory responsibilities and were included in the bargaining unit covered by a collective bargaining agreement.

Commissioner's findings about Bonk's racially-based remarks to Hayes. Most of Bonk's comments to Hayes may have been intended to be humorous, but they represented prejudicial stereotypes and interpersonal insensitivity, which were embarrassing and humiliating to Hayes. Bonk often asked Hayes if he liked Cadillac automobiles with white sidewall tires and fur upholstery. Affecting a black dialect, Bonk told a number of "Black Sambo" jokes in the presence of Hayes and others and asked Hayes whether he shared Sambo's laziness and food preferences. He called Hayes "Shaft," "Mohammed," and "Uncle Tom" on numerous occasions. Several times when he encountered Hayes in the storeroom or in the store, Bonk affected an exaggerated walk intended as a caricature of black persons' manner of walking. He commented on the texture and appearance of Hayes' hair at various times and, when Hayes was mixing paint, he compared the color of the paint to Hayes' skin color. Finally, on one occasion when a white female employe who was married to a black man entered the storeroom while Bonk was criticizing Hayes' performance of a particular job, he asked her, "How do you beat a nigger?" [3] At no time did Hayes respond to these incidents with joking or do anything to encourage Bonk to continue his racially-based remarks.[4]

* * * West, the assistant manager, overheard Bonk referring to Hayes as "Mohammed." Bonk also informed West that he had told Black Sambo jokes to Hayes and had teased him about Cadillacs. Bonk recited one of the jokes to West, who found it offensive and informed him that such joking was improper. West also admonished Bonk in a similar manner on another occasion, but did not advise his superiors of the problem because he thought his warnings to Bonk were sufficient to stop the abuse. They were not. Hayes testified, and the Commissioner found, that Bonk's harassment was more severe at the end of Hayes' initial period of employment than it had been at the beginning or the middle. Based upon Hayes' scant testimony and his own inferences, the Commissioner summarized Hayes' employment situation and its effect on him as follows:

> "I find that virtually every contact that the Complainant had with Mr. Bonk, one of his supervisors, amounted to an exposure to Mr. Bonk's pointless racial inquiries, or racial 'humor' and that the distress, eg. humiliation and embarrassment this exposure caused Complainant adversely affected his work performance. I further find that the treatment accorded Complainant by Mr. Fetters, and Mr. Fetters' participation in and knowledge of the treatment accorded to the Complainant by Mr. Bonk, further adversely affected Complainant's work performance."

3. The female employe remembered this phrasing. Hayes testified that Bonk asked, "How do you kill a nigger?"

4. Bonk also questioned Hayes about how he came to live in a suburban neighborhood, whether he was accepted and comfortable there and at a suburban high school, and talked frequently about Hayes' food preferences. Because of the abundance of other discriminatory incidents, we need not consider whether these inquiries were also motivated by racial prejudice.

Hayes' employment at the Division store was terminated by the variety department manager, Bowman, on July 14, 1972.

* * *

As set out above, there is substantial evidence that Hayes was subject to continual racial harassment during his first period of employment. The harassment and the failure of the assistant manager to rectify it constitute a violation of Or. Rev. Stat. § 659.030(1)(a), which provides that it is an unlawful employment practice for an employer to discriminate on the basis of race in "conditions or privileges of employment." Under Or. Rev. Stat. § 659.010(2), *Williams v. Joyce,* 4 Or. App. at 504, 479 P.2d 513 and *School District No. 1 v. Nilsen,* 271 Or. at 486, 534 P.2d 1135, the Commissioner is authorized to award compensatory damages if the evidence is sufficient to support his finding that Hayes suffered humiliation as a result of the harassment. We conclude that the internal reasoning is sufficient under *McCann* to support the award without a rule.

STEVENSON v. MORGAN
Court of Appeals, 1974.
17 Or. App. 428, 522 P.2d 1204.

THORNTON, JUDGE.

Claimant seeks judicial review of a decision of the Employment Appeals Board reversing the action of the referee and the administrator, both of whom had allowed claimant unemployment benefits. The Board ruled that claimant was disqualified under Or. Rev. Stat. § 657.-176(2)[1] because she had "left work voluntarily without good cause."

The issue before this court is whether the Board's order is (1) lawful in substance and procedure and (2) supported by "reliable, probative and substantial evidence in the whole record * * *." Or. Rev. Stat. § 183.480(7).

Claimant voluntarily terminated her employment at the Sunn Musical Equipment Company, claiming that she could no longer withstand alleged mistreatment by her supervisor. The administrator determined after investigation that claimant had established "good cause" for leaving her job and allowed the claim. The employer then requested a hearing before the referee. The referee found that the supervisor was harassing claimant and that such harassment constituted "good cause" for claimant to leave her employment. The Employment Appeals Board reversed, finding that the claimant did not have "good cause" because she had not attempted to discuss the problem

---

1. Or. Rev. Stat. § 657.176(2) provides:

"An individual whose unemployment is due to:

"* * *

"(2) Having left work voluntarily without good cause * * *

"* * *

shall * * * be disqualified * * *."

with the plant manager and was therefore disqualified under Or. Rev. Stat. § 657.176(2).

The referee found that claimant's supervisor was constantly finding fault with claimant's work; that the supervisor required claimant to use old animal glue on her job which was offensive to smell, more so than available new glue; that this caused claimant to become nauseated; that the supervisor was also treating claimant in an antagonistic and vindictive manner; that this treatment caused her to become anxious and nervous; and that all of this made claimant's working conditions intolerable and therefore constituted "good cause" to leave. Claimant testified that she once complained about her supervisor to a previous manager who told her that "you just have to live with it * * *." Claimant also offered evidence that whenever an employe attempted to see the plant manager the supervisor made it a practice to follow the employe into the manager's office and would remain throughout the entire conversation.

The employer did not present contradictory evidence concerning the supervisor.

We must first determine what is the scope of review by the Employment Appeals Board of a decision of the referee.

Or. Rev. Stat. 657.275 provides that the Board may review decisions of the referee but is silent as to the scope of that review. However Or. Rev. Stat. § 657.280 states that the conduct of hearings before the referee and an appeal to the Board shall be in accordance with the regulations prescribed by the Administrator of the Employment Division as authorized by Or. Rev. Stat. § 657.610.

The previous rules promulgated by the administrator provided that " * * * [i]n such review additional testimony will not be heard, nor the matter tried de novo." Oregon Administrative Rules, ch. 471, § 41–010 (July 23, 1962). However, on June 21, 1972, the administrator promulgated a new § 41–010 deleting the language just quoted. We conclude from the foregoing that under the accepted rules of statutory interpretation the scope of review by the Board of decisions of the referee is de novo on the record made before the referee. *See, Swift & Co. and Armour & Co. v. Peterson*, 192 Or. 97, 233 P.2d 216 (1951).

Having determined the scope of review by the Board, we turn to the principal issue, namely, whether the Board's decision that claimant did not have "good cause" for leaving her employment should be sustained. It would appear that the initial determination of "good cause" for leaving employment is a mixed question of law and fact for the administrative agency. This determination is, of course, subject to review by the referee, the Employment Appeals Board, and ultimately by the courts as authorized by the statutes.

This court had occasion to consider the meaning of the term "good cause" as used in Or. Rev. Stat. § 657.176(2) in *Fajardo v. Morgan*, Or. App., 98 Adv. Sh. 69, 516 P.2d 495 (1973). There we held that claimant had established that her employer arbitrarily discriminated against her because of her sex by paying her less for the same work done by men. Consequently, claimant had "good cause" and was justified in leaving her employment. In the course of that opinion we stated:

> " 'Good cause' is not defined in the Oregon Unemployment Insurance statute, but it has been defined elsewhere as

> " ' * * * such a cause as justifies an employee's voluntarily leaving the ranks of the employed and joining the ranks of the unemployed; the quitting must be for such a cause as would reasonably motivate in a similar situation the average able-bodied and qualified worker to give up his or her employment with its certain wage rewards in order to enter the ranks of the compensated unemployed. * * *

> " ' * * * In the final analysis, the question of what is good cause must be determined in the light of the facts of each particular case.' (Footnotes omitted.) 81 C.J.S. 253–54, Social Security and Public Welfare § 167." 98 Adv. Sh. at 72–73, 516 P.2d at 497.

"Good cause" may be said to be such cause as would similarly affect persons of reasonable and normal sensitivity, *Geckler v. Review Bd. of Ind. Emp. Sec. Div.*, 244 Ind. 473, 193 N.E.2d 357 (1963), and is limited to those instances where the unemployment is caused by external pressures so compelling that a reasonably prudent person, exercising ordinary common sense and prudence, would be justified in quitting work under similar circumstances. *Mikanowicz Unempl. Compensation Case*, 178 Pa. Super. 612, 115 A.2d 846 (1955); *Green Unempl. Compensation Case*, 174 Pa. Super. 286, 101 A.2d 119 (1953); *Citizens Bank of Shelbyville v. Industrial Com'n*, 428 S.W.2d 895 (Mo. App. 1968). Thus, the applicable standards to determine "good cause" are standards of reasonableness as applied to the average man or woman, not the supersensitive person. *Uniweld Products, Inc. v. Industrial Rel. Com'n*, etc., 277 So.2d 827 (Fla. App. 1973). The question of "good cause" is therefore to be determined from the particular circumstances of each case. *Fajardo v. Morgan*, supra; *Fleischmann v. Rochester General Hospital*, 43 A.D.2d 624, 349 N.Y.S.2d 185 (1973); *In re Tenenbaum*, 18 A.D.2d 742, 235 N.Y.S.2d 419 (1962).

Having examined the entire record it is our opinion that the evidence offered by claimant before the referee established a prima facie showing of "good cause" for leaving her employment. *Cameron et al. v. DeBoard* ; *MacInnes et al.*, 230 Or. 411, 370 P.2d 709 (1962); *von Poppenheim v. Morgan*, 9 Or. App. 495, 497 P.2d 866 (1972). The employer then was under a duty to rebut the employe's prima facie case. Here, however, the employer did not present any contradictory evidence at the hearing concerning conduct of the supervisor.

There is substantial evidence to support the referee's findings that claimant's supervisor was arbitrarily harassing claimant, that this harassment made claimant's working conditions such that a reasonably prudent workman would find them to be intolerable and that therefore claimant had "good cause" to quit her job.

It is our conclusion that the Board was in error in denying the claim because the claimant had not once again gone to the plant manager to complain about the treatment by the supervisor.

While we would agree that a reasonably prudent employe who is being unjustly harassed by a supervisor has a duty to take up his or her grievance with management before voluntarily terminating employment, here claimant had already done so once before without success. Further there was evidence that no employe could see the plant manager without the supervisor following the employe into the manager's office and being present during any conversation between the complaining employe and the manager.

We therefore reverse and remand with instructions to reinstate the order of the referee and allow the claim.

Reversed and remanded.

McCAIN v. EMPLOYMENT DIVISION
Court of Appeals, 1974.
17 Or. App. 442, 522 P.2d 1208.

THORNTON, JUDGE.

Claimant appeals from an adverse determination of the Employment Appeals Board. The Board affirmed the decision of both the referee and the Employment Division that claimant was disqualified from receiving unemployment benefits on the ground that she voluntarily left work without "good cause." Or. Rev. Stat. § 657.176(2).

Claimant was employed as a bookkeeper at the Beaver Heat Treating Corporation from September 5, 1972 through September 13, 1973. The corporation is an industrial plant employing approximately 20 men and 2 women (both office workers). Claimant voluntarily quit, after giving two weeks' notice of her resignation, for the expressed reason that she felt her employer's attitude toward women was demeaning to her, and that she could no longer work for such a "sexist" employer.

> "I felt that at that company there was a very, very demeaning attitude toward women in general; that women, in general, were held in contempt."

Claimant argues that this "sexist" attitude of her employer, holding women in contempt by treating them only as sex objects, constituted "good cause" for her to quit her job.

As evidence of such "sexist" attitudes at Beaver Heat Treating Corporation, claimant offered evidence that the plant manager displayed on his desk a postcard showing a woman with bare breasts. He dismissed claimant's objections stating that he liked to display this picture because the woman had big "jugs." There was also a large machinery advertisement poster on the office wall showing a woman in a bikini, which certain male employes liked because the model in the poster "was beautiful" and "had gorgeous tits [sic]."

Claimant objected that these displays were offensive to her. She especially objected to a cartoon posted on the wall in the lunchroom which was captioned "THE PERFECT WOMAN" and depicted a naked woman's legs, hips, buttocks and pubic area. No arms, head or upper torso appear in the cartoon. Large breasts were attached to the legs at hip level. While this cartoon would be deemed vulgar and offensive by many, we agree with the referee and the Board that the same would not constitute "good cause" for claimant to quit her job.

Since claimant voluntarily terminated suitable employment, she has the burden to show that she had "good cause" for doing so. *Stevenson v. Morgan*, Or. App., 99 Adv. Sh. 198, 522 P.2d 1204 (1974); *Toland v. Schneider*, 94 Idaho 556, 494 P.2d 154 (1972). In *Stevenson* we said that "good cause" to quit work must be such cause as would compel a reasonably prudent person to quit under similar circumstances, and that this determination is a factual evaluation based on the particular circumstances of each case. The Board's determination will be affirmed if there is reliable, probative and substantial evidence in the record to support that decision. Or. Rev. Stat. 183.480(7). *Balduyck v. Morgan*, 9 Or. App. 363, 497 P.2d 377 (1972).

In *Fajardo v. Morgan*, Or. App., 98 Adv. Sh. 69, 516 P.2d 495 (1973), we held that wage discrimination based on sex may constitute "good cause" to quit a job. Discrimination on the basis of sex is an unlawful employment practice. Or. Rev. Stat. § 659.030; 42 U.S.C.A. § 2000e–2 (1974); *Fajardo v. Morgan*, supra, 98 Adv. Sh. at 72, 516 P.2d 495. This does not mean, however, that an employer's "sexist" attitude, by itself, is an unlawful employment practice or such other cause as would constitute "good cause" for a female employe to quit. "Good cause" would exist only if this "sexist" attitude produced some actual discrimination, undue harassment, or other grievous cause of reasonable foundation, evidence of which must appear in the record. *James v. Unempl. Comp. Bd. of Review*, 6 Pa. Commw. 489, 296 A.2d 288 (1972); *accord*, *Fajardo v. Morgan*, supra.

Generally, offensive character habits of fellow workers, however distasteful they may be to claimant, will not constitute "good cause" for claimant to leave. *Green Unempl. Compensation Case*, 174 Pa. Super. 286, 101 A.2d 119 (1953). Claimant had the burden of producing evidence to establish at least a prima facie case. *von Poppenheim v. Morgan*, 9 Or. App. 495, 497 P.2d 866 (1972). Thus, claimant must at least establish that the prevailing sexual attitudes of her employer, or of her fellow employes, were such as amounted to sexual discrimination, harassment or some other cause of reasonable foundation sufficiently grievous to compel a reasonably prudent person to quit under similar circumstances. *Cf., Stevenson v. Morgan*, supra.

Claimant has not met that burden.

Affirmed.

LANGTRY, JUDGE (specially concurring).

I concur in the court's opinion, but think something additional needs to be said in this case.

The testimony as a whole leads to the inevitable inference that claimant began going out of her way to object to the cartoon and pictures soon after she became employed. She had no compelling need to go into the *men's* lunchroom where the cartoon was posted. The only things she went there for were use of a pencil sharpener and to get soft drinks and candy from a vending machine. Employer testified that there was another pencil sharpener available, and that he would have bought claimant one if she had asked for it. The evidence indicates claimant could have had someone bring her soft drinks and candy if she was offended when she went for them. Instead, she continued to go there, and finally took the cartoon down and placed it in the waste basket—causing herself more trouble.

I would hold that if the cartoon—a copy of it is in evidence, and it is hardly as horrendous as words have pictured it—were posted in such a way as to be forced on claimant, she may have had cause to quit because of undue harassment. But I think the facts here indicate she sought harassment and found it. This is not "good cause" for quitting employment in the sense in which we consider the term here.

ASCHENBRENNER v. EMPLOYMENT DIVISION

Court of Appeals, 1977.
29 Or. App. 345, 563 P.2d 757.

Before SCHWAB, C.J., and THORNTON and TANZER, JJ.

THORNTON, JUDGE.

The issue presented in this unemployment compensation appeal is whether the Employment Appeals Board (EAB) erred in ruling that claimant was disqualified from receiving benefits because of having voluntarily left his employment without good cause. Or. Rev. Stat. § 657.176(2)(c).[1]

The essential facts are set forth in EAB's findings of fact.

"(1) The claimant was employed by this employer and its predecessor in interest from May 1948 to July 30, 1976 at the last position of saw filer at the rate of $8.42 an hour. (2) Approximately two years prior to his separation from work a third shift was added. (3) The addition of this shift increased the work load of the claimant and he averaged approximately eleven hours a day, five days a week. (4) At one point he worked three weeks seven days a

---

1. Or. Rev. Stat. § 657.176(2)(c) provides:

"(2) If the authorized representative designated by the administrator finds:

"* * *

"(c) The individual voluntarily left work without good cause * * *."

week without a day off and worked a six day week on many occasions. (5) In May, 1976, the claimant underwent surgery and at approximately the same time his most experienced helper was transferred to another position. (6) When the claimant returned from his surgery he began working increased hours. (7) During the course of his employment claimant was a member of the lumber and sawmill worker's union Local 2798. (8) Sometime during the week ending July 10, 1976 the claimant told his supervisor he could not continue working the long hours and was considering resigning. (9) Approximately one week later he gave two weeks notice of resignation and left this work on July 30, 1976 in accordance with the resignation notice. (10) The grievance procedure under the labor agreement between claimant's union and the employer was not utilized in an attempt to have the hours reduced."

When a claimant voluntarily terminates suitable employment, he has the burden of showing good cause for leaving. *Wilton v. Employment Div.*, 26 Or. App. 549, 553 P.2d 1071 (1976). "Good cause to quit work" must be such cause as would impel a reasonably prudent person to quit under similar circumstances. *Hedrick v. Employment Div.*, 25 Or. App. 89, 548 P.2d 525 (1976). *See also, Koach v. Employment Division*, 25 Or. App. 585, 549 P.2d 1301, Sup. Ct. *review denied* (1976). This determination is a "factual evaluation based on the particular circumstances of each case." *McCain v. Employment Division*, 17 Or. App. 442, 445, 522 P.2d 1208, 1209 (1974).

In a factual determination of good cause for voluntarily leaving work, the order of the EAB is to be affirmed if based on reliable, probative and substantial evidence in the whole record, and not unlawful in substance and procedure. Or. Rev. Stat. § 183.482(8)(a) and (d); *Balduyck v. Morgan*, 9 Or. App. 363, 497 P.2d 377 (1972). This court cannot disturb a reasonable conclusion drawn from the facts by the factfinder, even if the court, were it sitting as a trier of fact, might reach a different conclusion. *Wilton v. Employment Div.*, supra; *Grigsby v. Employment Div.*, 24 Or. App. 499, 546 P.2d 788 (1976).

In the case at bar the appeals referee and a majority of the EAB found that claimant had voluntarily left his employment without good cause.

We have read the record and find that the conclusion of the majority of EAB is supported by substantial evidence. We are in accord with the referee and the majority of the EAB that under the facts at bar a reasonably prudent employe, before taking the drastic step of quitting his job, would have endeavored to resolve his work grievance with the plant manager, *Stevenson v. Morgan*, 17 Or. App. 428, 522 P.2d 1204 (1974), or to follow the union grievance procedures, or to voluntarily discontinue his overtime work (for which he was being paid extra) and return to a 40–hour week schedule. *See, Carson v. Employment Division*, 25 Or. App. 589, 550 P.2d 463 (1976). Further, although claimant testified that his health was being adversely affected by the overtime work, and that he had consulted his physician about nervousness and headaches he believed were caused by this, there was no showing by claimant that he was advised by his physician to quit work. *See, Wright v. Employment Division*, 24 Or. App. 323, 545 P.2d 613 (1976).

Failure of claimant to make sufficient efforts to present his work grievance to his superiors, and a lack of a showing that such actions would have been futile, justifies the conclusion that claimant's decision to leave work was without good cause under Or. Rev. Stat. § 657.-176(2)(c). *See, Glennen v. Employment Division*, 25 Or. App. 593, 549 P.2d 1288 (1976).

Affirmed.

Exercise 6C.

Ronald W. Griffin, a junior executive at Nissen Industries in Portland, Oregon, consulted us earlier this week about his missing house. He is understandably enraged and would like us to sue Mount Hood Development Corporation. Please read the attached materials carefully to see if Mr. Griffin has a cause of action against the development company and, if so, the extent of the damages he is likely to recover.

In December of last year, Ron Griffin received a Master of Science degree in Geology from the University of Montana. Just before graduation, he accepted an offer to work for Nissen Industries in Portland, Oregon. The position was in the professional/junior executive classification. Samuel Whitman, the personnel director explained to him that he would be based in the home office in Portland for the first year to eighteen months. He was also invited to take advantage of one of the company training courses during this introductory period. Griffin was eager to learn as much as he could about his new job. He applied for a special six week course in Scottsdale, Arizona, that was scheduled to begin on July 17.

Griffin drove to Portland in mid December to find a place to live before heading home to visit his parents over the holidays. As he preferred country to city living, he decide to look for something outside of Portland with a nice view of Mount Hood. An ad in the Classified Section of the Portland Tribune caught his eye.

> Small furnished house for rent on 50 acre parcel in Gresham. Terms to suit tenant. Contact Mount Hood Development Corporation at 226–9000 during business hours for information.

Griffin called the number the next morning and made an appointment with Harold Hudson to see the house at 1:30 that afternoon. Harold Hudson explained that he was a vice president of Mount Hood Development Corp. They agreed to meet in the McDonald's parking lot at the Gresham exit off route 26.

Ron Griffin had no difficulty finding the meeting place. Hudson arrived promptly at 1:30 and they set off to see the house. It was only two miles from the exit. Griffin was excited about the house. It was on a large undeveloped lot as promised in the classified ad. The commute would be an easy one as the Nissen headquarters was only 15 miles away on the same side of Portland. The view of Mount Hood was awe-inspiring.

The house itself was very small with a living-dining room, one bedroom, a kitchen and a bath. Hudson explained that the $350/month rent did not include utilities. The house had two electric wall heaters, but Hudson assured him that these would be adequate in the winter. The house was fully furnished. The furniture was not elegant, but it was sturdy and not unpleasant in appearance. The kitchen cupboards were full of pots and pans, dishes and glassware. Griffin could readily imagine living in the house.

He explained to Hudson that he wanted the house for at least a year and that he would probably be there for a full eighteen months; he did not want to rent a house for a shorter term. He asked Hudson if they could structure the lease to provide some flexibility after the initial twelve months. Hudson suggested that what Griffin really needed was a month to month rental. That would allow him to stay as long as he wanted. All he would need to do was give the development corporation a month's notice when he intended to depart. Griffin readily agreed. They headed back to the office in Portland to sign the agreement.

As they drove out to the highway, Hudson pointed out the boundaries of the property. On the corner was a large sign that proclaimed: "Future Home of Gresham Shopping Plaza—Mount Hood Development Corporation". Griffin asked Hudson if the corporation intended to build on the property in the near future. Hudson explained to him that there was a plan to build a shopping mall on the land at some time in the future. He assured Griffin, however, that the plan was years away from implementation. A shopping center of this magnitude needs at least two anchor department stores. He explained that it usually takes a year or more to negotiate with a department store for one of these positions. Griffin asked if the development corporation had signed an agreement with an anchor department store as yet. Hudson assured him that the corporation had not.

Ronald Griffin and Mount Hood Development Corporation signed a rental agreement on December 18th for the rental of the Gresham house on a month to month basis. The form seemed to be designed primarily for the rental of commercial space and not residential property. Hudson deftly crossed out the irrelevant portions of the lease agreement and typed in the necessary terms. He signed for the development corporation and Griffin signed for himself. He paid the first month's rent and a damage deposit of $500. Hudson wished him "Happy Holidays" and gave Griffin the key to his Gresham house.

Griffin enjoyed his job with Nissen Industries and the free time on his 50 acre country estate. The middle of every month he sent a check to Mount Hood Development Corporation. There was no other contact between them. On July 1st, Griffin dropped off his winter clothes at the cleaners, packed his summer things, and left for Scottsdale, Arizona for the special course. He mailed a check to the development corporation for the rent up to mid-August as he left town. He also paid his utility bills. Griffin arranged for the post office to hold his mail while he was gone. He did not have a forwarding address and could not imagine why he would want to have all the junk forwarded in any case.

When Griffin returned to Gresham on August 18th, he stopped by the post office and picked up his mail. It included two letters from Mount Hood Development Corporation, a phone bill, an electric bill, three editions of the biweekly "Gresham Sentinel", a couple of postcards from vacationing friends, and a lot of junk. Griffin decided to read it all when he got home. He picked up some groceries and headed out to the house.

THE HOUSE WAS GONE. In fact, a bulldozer had levelled all the land around where the house had stood. At that very moment a fleet of earth moving equipment was tackling the remainder of the 50 acre site. A trailer labelled "Office" had been set up on the edge of the site. Griffin parked his car and strode up to the office. He flung the door open and shouted at the surprised inhabitants, "what have you done with my house?" The two men explained to Griffin that they did not know anything about his house. They were building a shopping center and they would appreciate it if he would leave and let them get back to the business at hand.

Griffin walked back to his car. As he opened the door, a headline in the Gresham Sentinel caught his eye: "Shopping Plaza Construction to Begin August 14th". Griffin read the accompanying article.

> The Mount Hood Development Corporation announced today that construction on the Gresham Shopping Plaza would begin on August 14. Ron Chambers, the President of Mount Hood Development, was beaming with pride as he made the announcement. He said the project fulfilled the dream he and his fellow officers had had when they founded the corporation not quite five years ago. He thanked the community for its support, encouragement and investment in the dream.

> Mount Hood Development Corporation was founded in October 1984 by four local boys: Ronald Chambers, Harold Hudson, Scott Williams, and Douglas Cheever. They had five advanced degrees and nineteen years of experience between them. Their dream was to return to the mountains of Oregon and set up a successful business. As Scott Williams explained, they work very well together; with such a formidable team, they were bound to succeed.

> Their first venture was "Mountain Corners", a small neighborhood shopping center with grocery, drug, liquor, hardware and dry

cleaning stores. Mount Hood Development Corporation has its office in its first development. "Troutdale Corners" also a neighborhood shopping center, followed a year later. For the Troutdale project, the team was able to attract a Raceway Supermarket.

Gresham Shopping Plaza is a substantial undertaking. According to Harry Hudson, a successful shopping mall needs at least two anchor department stores. Mount Hood Development Corporation started negotiations with two potential anchors, BOOMING GALES and DEER'S ROE AND BUCK, late the previous summer. In the latter half of February, the development company signed agreements with both department stores. One of the terms included in both contracts at the insistence of the development company was that construction begin within six months. As Doug Cheever explained, "once we had the anchors, there was no reason not to put the investment money to work right away".

A picture of the beaming Mount Hood Development team was on the opposing page.

The first letter from Mount Hood Development Corporation was blunt:

July 10

Dear Mr. Griffin,

This is to notify you that your month to month lease will expire on August 13. Please remove your belongings before that date. A check for the damage deposit, less any deductions for damage to the premises, will be mailed to you at the termination of the lease.

Sincerely,

/s/_____

Harold Hudson

Vice President

Mount Hood Development Corporation

The second envelope from the development corporation contained a check for $500.

When I asked Griffin to itemize the belongings he had lost with the house, he replied, "I travel light. There were some papers and a few odds and ends. Fortunately, my clothes were at the cleaners. The worst of it is, I hate to move. I told the guy, I didn't want to move."

Please analyze the problem and decide if Griffin has a cause of action under the Oregon Unlawful Trade Practices Act against Mount Hood Development Corporation, and, if so, what measure of damages he will be able to collect. The applicable sections of the statute and four cases interpreting it appear below.

OREGON UNLAWFUL TRADE PRACTICES ACT

646.605 DEFINITIONS Or. Rev. Stat. § 646.605 et seq. (1989).

As used in §§ 646.605 to 646.652:

(1) "Trade" and "commerce" mean advertising, offering or distributing, whether by sale, rental or otherwise, any real estate, goods or services, and includes any trade or commerce directly or indirectly affecting the people of this state.

(2) "Documentary material" means the original or a copy of any book, record, report, memorandum, paper, communication, tabulation, map, chart, photograph, mechanical transcription, or other tangible document or recording, wherever situate.

(3) "Examination" of documentary material shall include inspection, study, or copying of any such material, and taking testimony under oath or acknowledgment in respect of any such documentary material or copy thereof.

(4) "Person" means natural persons, corporations, trusts, partnerships, incorporated or unincorporated associations, and any other legal entity except bodies or officers acting under statutory authority of this state or the United States.

(5) "Prosecuting attorney" means the Attorney General or the district attorney of any county in which a violation of Or. Rev. Stat.[5] § 646.605 to § 646.652 is alleged to have occurred.

(6) "Appropriate court" means the district or circuit court of a county:

(a) Where one or more of the defendants reside; or

(b) Where one or more of the defendants maintain a principal place of business; or

(c) Where one or more of the defendants are alleged to have committed an act prohibited by Or. Rev. Stat. § 646.605 to § 646.-652; or

(d) With the defendant's consent, where the prosecuting officer maintains an office.

(7) "Real estate, goods or services" means those which are or may be obtained primarily for personal, family or household purposes, and includes franchises, distributorships and other similar business opportunities, but does not include insurance. Real estate does not cover conduct covered by Or. Rev. Stat. §§ 91.700 to 91.935.

(8) "Unconscionable tactics" include, but are not limited to, actions by which a person:

5. Oregon Revised Statutes.

(a) Knowingly takes advantage of a customer's physical infirmity, ignorance, illiteracy or inability to understand the language of the agreement; or

(b) Knowingly permits a customer to enter into a transaction from which the customer will derive no material benefit; or

(c) Permits a customer to enter into a transaction with knowledge that there is no reasonable probability of payment of the attendant financial obligation in full by the customer when due.

(9) A wilful violation occurs when the person committing the violation knew or should have known that the conduct of the person was a violation.

646.608   Unlawful business, trade practices; proof; Attorney General's rules

1. A person engages in an unlawful practice when in the course of the person's business, vocation or occupation the person does any of the following:

(e) Represents that real estate goods or services have sponsorship, approval, characteristics, ingredients, uses, benefits, quantities or qualities that they do not have or that a person has a sponsorship, approval, status, qualification, affiliation, or connection that the person does not have.

646.638   Civil action by private party; damages; attorney fees; effect of prior injunction; time for commencing action; counterclaim

(1) Except as provided in subsection (7) of this section, any person who suffers any ascertainable loss of money or property, real or personal, as a result of wilful use or employment by another person of a method, act or practice declared unlawful by Or. Rev. Stat. § 646.608, may bring an individual action in an appropriate court to recover actual damages or $200, whichever is greater. The court or the jury, as the case may be, may award punitive damages and the court may provide such equitable relief as it deems necessary or proper.

(2) Upon commencement of any action brought under subsection (1) of this section the party bringing the action shall mail a copy of the complaint or other initial pleading to the Attorney General and, upon entry of any judgment or decree in the action, shall mail a copy of such judgment or decree to the Attorney General. Failure to mail a copy of the complaint shall not be a jurisdictional defect, but no judgment shall be entered for the plaintiff until proof of mailing is filed with the court. Proof of mailing may be by affidavit or by return receipt of mailing.

(3) In any action brought by a person under this section, the court may award, in addition to the relief provided in this section,

reasonable attorney fees at trial and on appeal and costs. If the defendant prevails, the court may award reasonable attorney fees at trial and on appeal and costs if it finds the action to be frivolous.

(5) Actions brought under this section shall be commenced within one year from the discovery of the unlawful method, act or practice. However, whenever any complaint is filed by a prosecuting attorney to prevent, restrain or punish violations of Or. Rev. Stat. § 646.608, running of the statute of limitations with respect to every private right of action under this section and based in whole or in part on any matter complained of in said proceeding shall be suspended during the pendency thereof.

WOLVERTON v. STANWOOD
Supreme Court of Oregon, 1977.
278 Or. 341, 563 P.2d 1203.

HOWELL, J.

Plaintiff filed an action for damages under the Unlawful Trade Practices Act, Or. Rev. Stat. § 646.605 et seq. A jury returned a verdict for plaintiff for $500 general damages and $500 punitive damages. The trial court granted defendant's motion for a judgment n.o.v.[1] Plaintiff appeals.

The primary issue on appeal is whether the Act applies to the facts in the instant case. Because this issue is before us on appeal from a judgment n.o.v., the facts are viewed in the light most favorable to plaintiff. See, e.g., *Krause v. Eugene Dodge, Inc.*, 265 Or. 486, 509 P.2d 1199 (1973); *Denley v. Mutual of Omaha*, 251 Or. 333, 445 P.2d 505 (1968).

Defendants, as a partnership, operate a Texaco service station known as B. & M. Texaco. Plaintiff answered an advertisement placed in a newspaper by the defendants for the sale of a 427 cubic inch Chevrolet engine. While inspecting the engine, he was again orally assured that it was a 427. However, after purchasing the engine, plaintiff discovered it was a 400 cubic inch engine, rather than a 427. According to plaintiff, defendants also represented the engine to be in good running condition and that it had only about 18,000 miles on it. Plaintiff contends that each of these representations was false, and there was evidence to support this contention.

Or. Rev. Stat. § 646.608(1) provides:

"A person engages in a practice hereby declared to be unlawful when in the course of his business, vocation or occupation he:

"* * *

---

1. Plaintiff's complaint also contained two additional counts for fraud and for breach of express warranty, but the jury returned a verdict for defendants on these two counts.

"(g) Represents that real estate, goods or services are of a particular standard, quality, or grade, or that real estate or goods are of a particular style or model, if they are of another;

"* * * *"

Because of the jury's verdict for plaintiff, we must assume that the engine was sold by the B. & M. Texaco partnership and that the "standard, quality, or grade" of the engine was not as represented, although there was conflicting evidence on these issues. The only remaining issue is whether the engine was sold "in the course of [the partnership's] business, vocation or occupation." Ordinarily this, too, is a question of fact for the jury, but it is the duty of the court to determine whether there is any substantial evidence to support that finding. When, as in this case, the wording of the statute is ambiguous, the court must first interpret the statute so that the evidence can be reviewed against an objective and meaningful background.

Although the statutory language in question was taken from Section 2 of the Uniform Deceptive Trade Practices Act, 7 ULA 336 and 354, we have been unable to discover any previous judicial interpretation of that language or any legislative history which would explain its intended meaning. Moreover, the wording of similar provisions in analogous statutes is so different that it is of little or no assistance in defining the meaning of this provision. See, e.g., Uniform Commercial Code § 2.104; Or. Rev. Stat. § 72.1040; Uniform Consumer Sales Practices Act, § 3, 7 ULA Supp. 229 (1976).

It could be argued that the phrase "in the course of his business, vocation or occupation" should be construed so as to apply to all unlawful practices except those which arise out of strictly private transactions and which are totally unconnected with the business or employment of the defendant. On the other hand, the statute could be interpreted so as to apply only to those unlawful practices which arise out of the ordinary, everyday activities of the defendant's business or occupation. The former construction could be justified on the basis of a broad reading of the general policy of the statute to discourage deceptive trade practices and to provide a viable remedy for consumers who are damaged by such conduct. The latter construction could be supported by a broad reading of the limitation which restricts the application of the statute to those unlawful practices that arise out of the course of the defendant's business. Such an interpretation would reflect a presumption that this restriction was intended to limit the application of the statute to those situations which tend to present a continuing, and therefore more serious, threat to the general public.

In the absence of any guidance as to which of these policies the legislature would have intended to prevail, we have determined to seek a middle ground. We believe that the statute should be applied only to those unlawful practices which arise out of transactions which are at least indirectly connected with the ordinary and usual course of defendant's business, vocation or occupation.

Applying that construction to this case, we believe that the jury could have reasonably found that the sale of the automobile engine was at least indirectly connected with the ordinary business of defendants' automotive service station. Moreover, there was testimony that on at least one previous occasion the defendants had procured an engine for another customer and installed it in his car. Therefore, we believe that the entry of a judgment for defendants notwithstanding the jury's verdict was in error.

Reversed and remanded with directions to reinstate the judgment for plaintiff.

SCOTT v. WESTERN INTERNATIONAL SURPLUS SALES, INC.

Supreme Court of Oregon, 1973.
267 Or. 512, 517 P.2d 661.

DENECKE, J.

This action was brought pursuant to a 1971 act relating to consumer protection. Or. Rev. Stat. § 646.605 et seq.

The court heard the case without a jury and awarded the plaintiff $200 general damages, punitive damages and attorney fees. The evidence most favorable to the plaintiff will be considered.

The plaintiff's son was looking for a tent to take backpacking. He wanted a tent that would be suitable for use in the snow. For this reason he wanted a window with a closing flap that could be secured and eaves. Plaintiff and his son looked at a tent in defendant's store. The tent was in a sealed package with a card enclosed stating "Nylon Net Rear Window with ZIPPERED flap." A diagram on the card pictured the flap. The card also pictured a tent with eaves.

Plaintiff bought the tent. The plaintiff and his son brought the tent home and took it out of its package. They found the tent did not have these two features. At the rear there was only a vent which could not be securely closed. Plaintiff immediately tried to return the merchandise. However, defendant would not give him a refund and plaintiff refused a credit for future purchases because the only item he wanted was a tent. The defendant did not have any tent which had the features plaintiff's son wanted.

Plaintiff brought this action pursuant to Or. Rev. Stat. § 646.638, which provides:

"(1) Any person who purchases * * * goods * * * and thereby suffers any ascertainable loss of money or property, real or personal, as a result of the wilful use or employment by another person of a method, act or practice declared unlawful by Or. Rev. Stat. § 646.608, may bring an individual action in an appropriate court to recover actual damages or $200, whichever is greater. * * *."

Or. Rev. Stat. § 646.608(g) declared the misrepresentation of goods to be unlawful.

Plaintiff alleged in essence the facts we have set forth and further alleged: "As a result of defendant's above mentioned conduct, plaintiff has suffered an ascertainable loss of money and is entitled to recover the sum of Two Hundred Dollars ($200.00)."

The defendant did not move against or demur to the complaint but now contends on appeal that the complaint does not state a cause of action. Defendant also contends that the trial court should have granted its nonsuit because plaintiff failed to prove an ascertainable loss.[1]

We conclude the complaint states a cause of action. Under the statute there is no need to allege or prove the amount of the "ascertainable loss"; the plaintiff is only claiming the minimum of $200 which is recoverable if an ascertainable loss of any amount is proved. If the defendant was of the opinion that it was inadequately informed by this allegation, before answering, it should have moved to require the plaintiff to make the allegation more definite and certain.

The judgment of nonsuit was properly denied. "Ascertainable" can reasonably be interpreted to mean, capable of being discovered, observed or established.[2] As we have already stated, the amount of the loss is immaterial if only $200 is sought.

There was evidence of an "ascertainable loss." The tent was purchased for $38.86. The inference is that the tent, as represented, had that value. The tent sold did not have some of those represented features. The inference can be drawn that because the tent did not have a window with a closing flap or eaves it had a value of less than $38.86. To repeat, the plaintiff did not have to prove in what amount the value of the tent was reduced because it was not as represented. He merely had to prove he suffered some loss.

Defendant also contends it was entitled to a nonsuit because the statute requires a "wilful" misrepresentation and there was no evidence of wilfulness. Or. Rev. Stat. § 646.605(8) provides: "A wilful violation occurs when the person committing the violation knew or should have known that his conduct was a violation."

The evidence in this case may not be susceptible to the interpretation that the defendant knew of the misrepresentation;[3] however, the evidence was certainly sufficient for the trial court to find the defendant should have known.

1. We need not discuss the effect of a nonsuit in a case tried by the court alone. See *Karoblis v. Liebert*, 263 Or. 64, 501 P.2d 315 (1972).

2. This phrase, "ascertainable loss," probably was taken from a model consumer protection act formulated by the Federal Trade Commission. 26 Suggested State Legislation A–71 (1969). We have not found any comments directed to the use of this phrase.

3. The defendant did not contend at trial or in its assignment of error that the evidence did not support an award of punitive damages.

The defendant sold so many tents that it had one employee designated as tent manager. One of his duties was to familiarize himself with the various tents offered for sale. Defendant had sold a substantial number of tents of the model sold plaintiff. Defendant had a separate tent display area in which a tent of the kind purchased by plaintiff was set up for display. (This display area was not shown plaintiff nor was he told of its existence.) In the displayed tent defendant placed another tent of the same kind, wrapped in its plastic package.

From this evidence the trier of the facts could find the defendant should have known of the discrepancies between the representations made on the card and the actual product, as exhibited by the displayed tent.

Affirmed.

MABIN v. TUALATIN DEVELOPMENT CO., INC.

Court of Appeals of Oregon, 1980.
48 Or. App. 271, 616 P.2d 1196.

RICHARDSON, P.J.

Plaintiffs' complaint alleged two causes of action: (1) common law fraud and (2) violation of Oregon's Unlawful Trade Practices Act, Or. Rev. Stat. § 646.605 et seq., involving their purchase of a home. The jury awarded them $2,500 compensatory damages and $12,500 punitive damages against both defendants on their second claim.[1] Defendants appeal, contending the trial court erred in denying their motions to strike plaintiffs' punitive damages claim; in denying their motions for judgment notwithstanding the verdict; and by failing to clearly instruct the jury regarding plaintiffs' second cause of action.

Defendant Tualatin Development Co., Inc. (TDC) was the developer of a Portland area subdivision known as Quail Park. Defendant King City Realty Co. dba Prestige Properties (Prestige) handled the sales of TDC's properties located there. At the time of this action, the two defendants were separate legal entities but shared a common president and generally the same shareholders.

In early 1978, plaintiffs became interested in a residence in Quail Park. They were attracted to one of the "ridge houses" which afforded a view of Mt. St. Helens and the surrounding area. On January 28, 1978, they signed an earnest money agreement for that home and moved in later that spring.

TDC owned the lots across from and below plaintiffs' property. One residence had been constructed on one of those lots at the time plaintiffs viewed the property. The house was built so that its roof line did not obstruct the view from the ridge houses. In January 1978, TDC

---

1. The jury did not award plaintiffs either compensatory or punitive damages with respect to their first claim. No issue is raised on appeal as to this result.

sold two of these lots to an outside builder. Construction began on homes there later that spring. In June 1978, plaintiffs discovered the construction would block their view. Upon completion, their view was impaired.

Plaintiffs' second claim was based on Or. Rev. Stat. § 646.608(1)(e).[2] They specifically alleged the defendants represented that the lots across the street were subject to suitable height restrictions which were sufficient to protect their view. They sought punitive damages as provided in Or.Rev.Stat. § 646.638.[3]

Defendants moved at the close of trial to strike the punitive damages claim. The court denied their motions. Plaintiffs were awarded the punitive damages noted above. The court's denial is assigned by defendants as error.[4]

Plaintiffs prevailed at trial. We view all evidence and all reasonable inferences which may be drawn from such evidence in the light most favorable to the plaintiffs and we resolve any conflicts in the evidence in their favor. *Davis v. Portland General Electric Co.*, 286 Or. 195, 197, 593 P.2d 1135 (1979); *Jacobs v. Tidewater Barge Lines*, 277 Or. 809, 811, 562 P.2d 545 (1977); *Hansen v. Bussman*, 274 Or. 757, 759, 549 P.2d 1265 (1976).

The evidence showed that prior to their completion in late 1977, the ridge houses were inspected and a determination was made as to how the homes should be priced for ultimate sale. The inspection was attended by Mr. Luton, president of both TDC and Prestige, Mr. Dunn, broker for Prestige, and Mr. Adams, TDC's designer. It was decided that because of the view from the homes, a higher price would be set. To preserve the view, it was apparent some control over the height of homes built below had to be maintained. No restrictions were placed on the property by TDC at that time since TDC owned the lots and intended to handle any future construction. View protection was left to an "in house" agreement which would restrict the height of future homes built across from the ridge lots. Within a very short time two

---

2. Or. Rev. Stat. § 646.608(1)(e) provides:

"(1) A person engages in an unlawful practice when in the course of the person's business, vocation or occupation the person:

"(e) Represents that real estate, goods or services have sponsorship, approval, characteristics, ingredients, uses, benefits, quantities or qualities that they do not have or that a person has a sponsorship, approval, status, qualification, affiliation, or connection that he does not have."

3. Or. Rev. Stat. § 646.638(1) provides:

"(1) Any person who suffers any ascertainable loss of money or property, real or personal, as a result of wilful use or employment by another person of a method,

act or practice declared unlawful by Or. Rev. Stat. § 646.608, may bring an individual action in an appropriate court to recover actual damages or $200, whichever is greater. The court or the jury, as the case may be, may award punitive damages and the court may provide such equitable relief as it deems necessary or proper."

4. Defendants' third and fourth assignments of error are based on the court's denial of their motions for judgment notwithstanding the verdict. The grounds for these motions were identical to those made in their motions to strike at the close of trial. Since they raise identical arguments, we do not discuss them separately.

lots below plaintiffs' were sold. No restrictions regarding height or view protection were included by TDC in the deeds to these lots.

Plaintiffs were shown the ridge homes by Jim Hendryx, Prestige's top salesman. There was testimony to the effect that Hendryx was well aware of the factors which went into the pricing of the homes. Plaintiffs testified that they were specifically told the houses were more expensive because of the view. They asked Hendryx if there were any restrictions in effect to protect the view and were told that there were. They were told no home across the street would be higher than the roof line of the one existing structure.

By the time of these discussions, Hendryx had reviewed the subdivision public report. The report included all applicable restrictions and covenants for the subdivision. The jury could reasonably have concluded that he knew there were no easements, restrictions, covenants or anything else concerning view protection. Hendryx testified that even with this knowledge, he gave plaintiffs oral assurances that height restrictions existed and that their view would be protected. In June, 1978, when plaintiffs became concerned about construction on the lower lots, Hendryx again assured them the view would be protected. Plaintiffs subsequently contacted both Adams and Luton at TDC but were unsuccessful in eliminating the problem.

The test to determine whether punitive damages are recoverable under Or. Rev. Stat. § 646.638 is identical to that applied in a claim based upon common law fraud. *Crooks v. Payless Drug Stores*, 285 Or. 481, 592 P.2d 196 (1979). Such damages are proper to deter similar future conduct and when conduct is particularly aggravated. The basis for such damages was stated in *Noe v. Kaiser Foundation Hosp.*, 248 Or. 420, 435 P.2d 306 (1967):

> "Punitive damages can only be justified on the theory of determent. See Hodel, *The Doctrine of Exemplary Damages in Oregon*, 44 Or. L. Rev. 175 (1965). It is only in those instances where the violation of societal interests is sufficiently great and of a kind that sanctions would tend to prevent, that the use of punitive damages is proper. Regardless of the nomenclature by which a violation of these obligations is described (grossly negligent, willful, wanton, malicious, etc.), it is apparent that this court has decided that it is proper to use the sanction of punitive damages where there has been a particularly aggravated disregard * * * [of the rights of the victim]." 248 Or. at 425.

Defendant Prestige argues that Hendryx's actions were the result of a lack of communication between TDC and Prestige. It contends Hendryx believed at the time plaintiffs purchased their home that TDC's "internal policy" would protect plaintiffs and that neither he nor anyone else at Prestige knew TDC could not or did not protect plaintiffs when it sold the lots across from plaintiffs' property.

This argument is not persuasive. Hendryx was an experienced and highly successful real estate salesman. The evidence showed he was aware that plaintiffs were particularly concerned about preserving the view; that he knew the view was a prime reason for the price plaintiffs paid for the house; that notwithstanding, he gave plaintiffs unfounded and insupportable assurances that they would be protected. The assurances were specifically excluded from the earnest money agreement plaintiffs signed after their discussions. Similar assurances were made by Hendryx and other Prestige salesmen to other purchasers. At no time were there means to enforce them. Finally, when plaintiffs complained to Hendryx, he pressed them for their approval of the construction plans which as drawn would have resulted in the loss of their view.

These actions reveal a deliberate and conscious effort to misrepresent to plaintiffs the facts with respect to any view protection. Such conduct is ground for imposition of punitive damages. In *Allen v. Morgan Drive Away*, 273 Or. 614, 542 P.2d 896 (1975), the court noted:

> " * * * The evidence reveals a deliberate and calculated effort to misrepresent the facts * * *. This is the kind of conduct which should be deterred. The imposition of punitive damages will help to deter it." 273 Or. at 616.

More recently in *Green v. Uncle Don's Mobile City*, 279 Or. 425, 568 P.2d 1375 (1977), the Supreme Court stated:

> " * * * We have consistently held that the intentional statement of an untruth for the purpose of taking a plaintiff's money is the violation of a societal interest sufficiently great to warrant punitive damages." 279 Or. at 432.

The award of punitive damages was proper. The trial court did not err in denying defendant Prestige's motions.

Defendant TDC also argues that there was insufficient evidence to support a punitive damages award against it. This contention rests primarily on the testimony of Luton, its president. He stated that all salesmen knew there were no covenants and height restrictions in the subdivision and that he was unaware of any representations concerning such restrictions.

The evidence established otherwise. Luton, as president of both TDC and Prestige, took an active part in the sale of properties in Quail Park. He priced the ridge homes and the reasons for the pricing were discussed by him with others employed by TDC and Prestige. The obvious prime consideration was the view. He personally negotiated the sale of the lots below plaintiffs' residence to an outside builder without putting any height restrictions or other protection in the deeds. He did nothing either before or after the sale to inform any salesmen there were no guarantees that the view was protected.

The jury could have found that TDC encouraged the representations by Prestige's salesmen knowing there were no grounds for such assurances. Both TDC's designer and Luton tried to avoid any responsibility for the representations. Nothing was done by anyone to TDC to rectify the salesman's misrepresentations or otherwise protect plaintiffs' view. This type of conduct justifies the award of punitive damages. The trial court did not err in denying TDC's motions respecting plaintiffs punitive damages claim.

Defendants' final assignment of error relates to the court's instruction regarding plaintiffs' second cause of action. The instructions taken together correctly informed the jury on the law applicable to the second cause of action.

Affirmed.

CHAMBERLAIN v. JIM FISHER MOTORS, INC.

Supreme Court of Oregon, 1978.
282 Or. 229, 578 P.2d 1225.

TONGUE, J.

This is an action by the purchaser of a used car against a used car dealer for damages resulting from the failure of the dealer to provide title to the car. The car was stolen, "stripped" and "totaled." Plaintiff's insurance company then refused to pay her claim for its loss because of her inability to produce a certificate of title to the car.

Prior to trial, the trial court entered a partial summary judgment on the issue of liability. At the conclusion of the testimony at the trial, the trial court directed a verdict in favor of plaintiff for compensatory damages in the sum of $1,724.09. Plaintiff's claim for punitive damages was submitted to the jury, which returned a verdict of $5,000 in punitive damages. The trial court also awarded attorney fees to the plaintiff in the sum of $2,500. Defendant appeals from the resulting judgment.

The facts.

On January 10, 1975, plaintiff stopped to look at a 1971 Maverick on the used car lot of defendant Jim Fisher Motors. Four days later, after obtaining a loan to finance its purchase, plaintiff purchased the car from defendant. At that time she asked when she would "get my plates." The car then had no license plates. She was told that "it would be anywhere from two to six weeks or something like that." Defendant did not then deliver to her a certificate of title to the car, but gave her a 60–day temporary registration "sticker" for the windshield.

In March, after not receiving "plates" for the car and when the temporary registration was about to expire, plaintiff went back to defendant and was told that "there had been a mix-up; that the title was lost in transit and that it would just take time to work out." She was then given another temporary registration. When that temporary registration was about to expire in June plaintiff was given a third temporary registration, with no explanation of the reason for the delay.

In July the car was stolen and "stripped," so as to be a total loss. Plaintiff's insurance company refused to pay her claim for its loss because she was unable to produce a certificate of title to the car. Its representative testified, however, that upon receipt of a certificate of title it would pay the claim.

Defendant's employees testified that they were not aware of the provisions of Or. Rev. Stat. § 481.315(3) providing that an automobile dealer must "have in his possession a duly assigned certificate of title or bill of sale from [its] registered owner" upon the sale of a used car. They also testified that because legal titles were often held by lien holders and because of the delay of from four to six weeks in making arrangements for the transfer of automobile titles, it was common practice to buy and sell used cars subject to the subsequent delivery of certificates of title.

In addition, they testified that they acquired this used car two weeks prior to its sale to plaintiff; that when they acquired the car they were given a bill of sale by the person from whom they acquired the car (who apparently was not its registered owner); that the car then had an Oregon temporary license, which "would be indicative that the title had been processed as required * * * for transfer [of title]"; and that they were also told by the "customer" that "the title was in transit."

Defendant's employees also testified that they then attempted to secure title to the car and later offered to "rescind the deal" and give plaintiff her money back. Plaintiff denied that any such offer was made to her.

On September 22, 1975, plaintiff filed this action against defendant for the value of the car, punitive damages and attorney fees. As of that date title to the car had not been delivered to her by defendant. At the time of trial, however, on January 4, 1977, defendant produced title to the car and tendered it into court. That tender was rejected on objection by plaintiff.

The court did not err in granting partial summary judgment and directed verdict.

Defendant assigns as error the granting of "partial summary judgment" on the issue of liability. Defendant contends that this was improper because plaintiff's complaint seeks recovery under Or. Rev. Stat. § 646.605 et seq., the Unlawful Trade Practices Act, based upon false representations to her by defendant "regarding the certificate of title"; that summary judgment is not possible under that act because in order to establish a violation of that statute based upon alleged misrepresentations it must be proved that defendant "knew or should have known" that such representations were false and that this is always a question of fact.[1] It appears, however, that plaintiff's motion for summary judgment on liability was not based upon Or. Rev. Stat.

---

1. Or. Rev. Stat. § 646.605(93) provides as follows:

"A wilful violation occurs when the person committing the violation knew or should have known that his conduct was a violation."

§ 646.605 et seq., but was based on the contention that defendant did not have in its possession a "duly assigned certificate of title or bill of sale from the registered owner" of the car at the time of its sale to plaintiff, as required by Or. Rev. Stat. § 481.315(3), and that Or. Rev. Stat. § 481.310(2) provides for a right of action by "any person [who] suffers any loss by reason of the violation of any of the provisions of the statute." There was apparently "no genuine issue as to any material fact" on that question. It follows that the court did not err in entering such a "partial summary judgment."

Defendant also contends that the trial court erred in directing a verdict in favor of plaintiff for compensatory damages in the sum of $1,724.09 because plaintiff "was under a duty to minimize her damages by availing herself of resources available"; that defendant "should not be required to answer in damages for the car's loss when all the owner was required to do once title had been obtained was to submit a claim to her insurance company for payment of the car's value," and that all that the insurance company "required to pay plaintiff's claim was a clear certificate of title," which was tendered into court at the time of trial, but rejected by the trial court. In support of this contention defendant cites *Blair v. United Finance Co.,* 235 Or. 89, 91, 383 P.2d 72 (1963).

In Blair, however, it was held by this court (at 91–92) that:

"* * * If, at the time the liability-creating events occurred, Blair reasonably could have avoided all or a part of the damages, then he cannot look to United for indemnity for such damages as were reasonably avoidable. * * *" (Emphasis added)

In this case there was no evidence that at the time of plaintiff's claim to the insurance company for the loss of her car after it was stolen on July 1, 1975, she could have produced title to the car, as required by the insurance company for payment of her claim. On the contrary, there was evidence that plaintiff filed a claim with her insurance company and that her claim was rejected by it because of her inability to produce title to the car as a result of defendant's continued failure to secure and deliver to her the title to the car. It was not until the day of trial on January 4, 1977, that defendant produced title to the car and tendered it into court. Under these facts the doctrine of "avoidable consequences" had no proper application.

Defendant does not contend on this appeal that the value of the car at the time that it was stolen was less than $1,724.09, or that the trial court erred in directing a verdict in favor of plaintiff in that amount in the event that the rule of "avoidable consequences" is not properly applicable. It follows that the trial court did not err in granting plaintiff's motion for a directed verdict.[2]

---

2. For the same reasons, the trial court did not err in refusing to instruct the jury on the rule of "avoidable consequences" or in rejecting defendant's tender of title at the time of trial, as also assigned as error by defendant. The trial court also did not err in refusing to instruct that this is not a case for rescission and that the jury could

Defendant assigns as error the giving of an instruction to the jury on punitive damages which defined "wanton misconduct," for the purposes of an award of punitive damages, as including both a "deliberate" and a "reckless" disregard of the rights of others. Defendant also assigns as error the denial of its "motion to strike punitive damages."

In support of these assignments of error defendant contends that in order for an award for punitive damages to be proper in this case there must have been a "deliberate and calculated effort to misrepresent the facts." Defendant also contends that regardless of the basis for plaintiff's claim, "there is no evidence under any standard for the award of punitive damages"; that there was no evidence that defendant wilfully violated Or. Rev. Stat. § 481.315(3), requiring title to an automobile to be in the possession of an automobile dealer at the time of purchase or sale;[3] that, on the contrary, the evidence was that because of delays in securing certificates of title from lien holders and because it usually takes from four to nine weeks to clear the transfer of title through the state Motor Vehicles Division, it was not uncommon in the industry to both purchase and sell used cars on promise of subsequent delivery of title; that this car, when acquired by defendant, had a temporary license sticker on its windshield and that defendant had a "bona fide bill of sale" from "the person who traded it to us"; and that defendant subsequently called the dealer who had sold the car to that person and was told that "the title was coming."[4]

Plaintiff contends that:

"There was ample evidence at trial that Defendant–Appellant Fisher acted with a reckless indifference to the rights of the Plaintiff, that the societal interest was sufficiently great and that Fisher's failure to provide title to the used car purchased by Plaintiff is the type of conduct which sanctions would tend to prevent. * * *"

It does not appear from plaintiff's complaint that the basis for her claim to punitive damages was a wilful violation by defendant of Or. Rev. Stat. § 481.310 in selling the car without an assigned certificate of title or bill of sale from the registered owner. Instead, plaintiff's claim for punitive damages is based upon the following allegations of its complaint:

not consider the purchase price paid or plaintiff's obligations to her credit union, as also assigned as error by defendant. Punitive damages were not recoverable in this case.

3. Or. Rev. Stat. § 481.315(3) provides:

" * * * A licensee dealing in used vehicles shall also have in his possession a duly assigned certificate of title or bill of sale from the registered owner of the motor vehicle, trailer or semi-trailer from the time when the vehicle is delivered to him until it has been disposed of by him."

4. Defendant also contends that punitive damages could not be properly awarded in this case because Or. Rev. Stat. § 481.310 makes no provision for punitive damages and because even though Or. Rev. Stat. § 646.605 et seq., the Unlawful Trade Practices Act, provides for punitive damages, plaintiff was not entitled to recovery under that statute. Because of the basis upon which we deny recovery for punitive damages it is not necessary to consider these additional contentions.

"Defendant made the foregoing representation [that defendant "owned said automobile and had in its possession an assigned certificate of title to the automobile from its former owner"] to plaintiff willfully, and with reckless disregard for the rights of plaintiff, and therefore plaintiff is entitled to punitive damages." (Emphasis added)

Plaintiff's basic contention on this appeal is that punitive damages were properly awarded in this case because "punitive damages may be awarded in this state in all cases in which 'the violation of societal interests is sufficiently great and the conduct involved is of a kind that sanctions would tend to prevent,'" citing *Starkweather v. Shaffer*, 262 Or. 198, 207, 497 P.2d 358 (1975), and *Noe v. Kaiser Foundation Hosp.*, 248 Or. 420, 435 P.2d 306 (1967), among other authorities.

Plaintiff also contends that she is entitled to recover punitive damages in this case because of the provision for punitive damages in the Unlawful Trade Practices Act. Plaintiff does not contend, however, that the provision of Or. Rev. Stat. § 646.638(1) for awards of punitive damages for violations of that statute (as defined in Or. Rev. Stat. § 646.605(9) to include conduct which a person "should have known" to be in violation of that statute) requires an award of punitive damages even when the misconduct of the defendant is not of such a nature as would otherwise properly support an award of punitive damages.[5] On the contrary, as previously noted, it is the contention of the plaintiff that defendant's misconduct was such as to satisfy requirements for an award of punitive damages under the rule as stated in *Starkweather v. Shaffer*, supra, and *Noe v. Kaiser Foundation Hosp.*, supra.

In *Harrell v. Travelers Indemnity Co.*, 279 Or. 199, 208–212, 567 P.2d 1013 (1977), decided after the trial of this case, this court discussed some of the problems resulting from the extension of liability for punitive damages to cases in which there was no wanton misconduct or intentional infliction of injury, but in which defendant's conduct was grossly negligent or reckless. For those reasons, as stated in *Harrell*, we hold that gross negligence or recklessness is not, in and of itself, sufficient to support an award of punitive damages.

It follows, in our opinion, that it was not proper to instruct the jury in this case that "wanton misconduct," for the purpose of punitive damages, includes not only a "deliberate disregard" of the rights of others, but also a "reckless indifference to such rights." This case, however, was tried prior to our decision in *Harrell* and we do not consider this case to be an appropriate one in which to attempt to otherwise limit or redefine the nature of the misconduct which will

---

5. Or. Rev. Stat. § 646.638(1) provides:

"Any person who suffers any ascertainable loss of money or property, real or personal, as a result of wilful use or employment by another person of a method, act or practice declared unlawful by Or. Rev. Stat. § 646.608, may bring an individual action in an appropriate court to recover damages or $200, whichever is greater. The court or the jury, as the case may be, may award punitive damages and the court may provide such equitable relief as it deems necessary or proper." (Emphasis added)

properly support an award of punitive damages, as that rule was stated in *Noe v. Kaiser Foundation Hosp.* supra.

Even under a test which includes "gross negligence" and "recklessness," we do not believe that the circumstances under which defendant made the representation relied upon in this case as the basis for an award of punitive damages were such as to properly support such an award. We have, on previous occasions, set aside awards for punitive damages in cases in which, in our opinion, defendants misconduct was not "sufficiently arbitrary and unconscionable to constitute a grievous violation of societal interests." See *Landauer v. Steelman,* 275 Or. 135, 142, 549 P.2d 1256 (1976); *Nees v. Hocks,* 272 Or. 210, 220, 536 P.2d 512 (1975); *Sumrell v. Household Finance Corp.,* 250 Or. 381, 384, 443 P.2d 179 (1968); and *Noe v. Kaiser Foundation Hosp.,* supra at 427.

There was no evidence in this case that the defendant made an express representation that it "owned said automobile and had in its possession an assigned certificate of title" to it. The jury could properly have found that a representation that defendant owned said automobile was implied from the fact that defendant offered the car for sale, gave plaintiff a temporary registration, and told her that she would get her "plates" in from two to six weeks. It could not be properly implied from these facts, however, that defendant then had an assigned certificate of title in its possession. Of more importance, there was no evidence that when defendant sold the car to plaintiff it knew or had reason to know that there would be any difficulty in securing a certificate of title to the car.

Under these facts we hold that there was insufficient evidence to make it proper to submit to the jury the question whether, in making the representation relied upon by plaintiff as the basis for its claim to an award of punitive damages, defendant's conduct was such as to justify an award of punitive damages.[6] It follows that it was error to deny defendant's "motion to strike punitive damages."

* * *

The judgment of the trial court is affirmed except for the award of punitive damages and attorney fees.

6. It is true that in selling the car to plaintiff without having an assigned certificate of title or bill of sale from its registered owner in its possession defendant violated Or. Rev. Stat. § 481.310. As previously noted, however, that is not the basis for plaintiff's claim for punitive damages, as alleged in her complaint.

*

Section III

THE BASIC OFFICE
MEMORANDUM

An office memorandum is an objective analysis of a legal problem written for use inside a law firm. The memo is written by law clerks or junior associates for partners or more senior associates. From the analysis of the client's problem, the attorneys are able to advise the client how to proceed, if at all. The memo must be complete and objective including the rules and facts that help the client as well as those that do not, and include a considered view of the likely outcome of the analysis of each issue.

Law clerks or associates will write memos for these problems either in advance of the client's business dealings or in anticipation of litigation. A business client may have questions about the future conduct of business: what terms, for example, should she include in a contract, and how should it be drafted in order to protect her interests and avoid future litigation and delay in conducting business.

As a law clerk and later as an associate, you will also write memos at different stages of the litigation time line. A client who has been injured wants to know if he can receive compensation for his injuries. In order to advise the client, the attorney wants to know if there is a cause of action, who the potential defendants are, what is required to prove the case, which court is appropriate, what the time constraints are, and so forth. There will be legal issues involved in every motion filed either on behalf of your client or against your client. If you represent the defendant, you may want to file a Rule 12(b)(6) motion alleging that the plaintiff has failed to state a claim upon which relief can be granted. In order to do this, you need to know the elements the plaintiff must allege for the cause of action. If it is to your client's advantage to have the case tried in a different court, you may write a memo on what is required to change the venue. Later in the process, you may write memos on discovery issues. In anticipation of the trial, there may be evidentiary issues that form the basis of other memos. If your client loses, you may write a memo analyzing the chances of success of a motion for judgment as a matter of law or a motion for a new trial. If your client or the opponent appeals, the issues on appeal may form the basis for yet other memos. In every case, the advice to the client and the outcome of the litigation depend in large measure on

143

the quality of your memos. The memos, and hence the advice, will be good if your research is thorough, you have analyzed the problem carefully, and you have explained the analysis objectively.

The format for an office memo varies with the purpose and the audience for whom you are writing. The common elements, however, include a heading, questions presented, a statement of facts, a discussion, and a conclusion. The heading is designed to provide basic information to those who will come in contact with the memo. Although you are writing for a particular reader about a particular case, the information may also be useful later if the law firm handles a case with similar issues. To facilitate both functions, the heading has four items:

To:

From:

Re:

Date:

The memo is written "to" the specific reader, usually a more senior associate or partner, "from" the writer, a law clerk or more junior associate. The "Re" section must include the client's name and very briefly, the subjects covered by the memo so that the memo can be filed both in the client's file and in one or more appropriate subject files. The "date" is important both for the current case and for future cases. The date indicates to the reader when you completed the research, and by the same token, that the memo does not include any development in the law after that date. Should you need to update your research later in this case, the date will let you know where to begin without retracing your steps.

The chapters in Section III explain how to write a basic office memorandum beginning with Chapter 7 on how to draft the issues or questions presented. Chapter 8 describes writing the statement of facts. The organization of the discussion section follow in Chapter 9. Chapters 10 and 11 provide information on writing to the reader and the writing process itself.

Chapter 7

QUESTIONS PRESENTED

An office memorandum begins with the questions presented. The purpose of this section is to explain to the reader the issues discussed in the memo. The questions set the scope of the memo both by explaining to the reader the narrow legal issues that you will discuss, and by omission, telling the reader what you will not discuss. The questions presented should focus the reader's attention precisely from the beginning so that he will not waste time or attention considering related, perhaps interesting, but for this problem, unnecessary issues. The questions presented section also serves as a basic organizational tool for the reader. To achieve these functions, the writer must choose the subject matter of the questions, assign their relationship, and draft them with care.

CHOICE AND ORGANIZATION OF THE QUESTIONS

The outline of the analysis should provide the subject matter and arrangement for the questions. The outline, however, includes not only the major issues, but also the minor issues and the givens. Choose only the issues you will discuss in detail for the questions presented. While the minor sub-issues and givens may be intellectually interesting questions in a different context, they are not major parts of the memo. To draft questions presented covering the minor issues and givens would only mislead the reader as to the scope of the memo. A general outline, like the following one presented in diagrammatic form, will yield only four questions presented, those issues noted with *.

Issue I
    Sub-issue a—given
    Sub-issue b—given
    Sub-issue c—major issue *
Issue II—major issue *
Issue III
    Sub-issue a—given
    Sub-issue b—minor issue

> Sub-issue c—major issue *
>
> Sub-issue d—major issue *

Labelling the issues helps the reader understand the relationship between them. There are two possible ways to convey the relationship presented in the hypothetical outline. First, the writer can label the questions:

> I.
>
> II.
>
> III A.
>
> III B.

Under this alternative the reader will understand that questions presented I, II, and III cover separate topics and that III A and III B are sub-issues of the same larger subject. The writer could also choose to draft the sub-questions as follows:

> I.
>
> II.
>
> III.
>
> > A.
> >
> > B.

Question III would then be a general question for the issue and sub-questions A and B will be the specific sub-issues. The writer will choose the alternative that best and most readably explains the scope of the issue to the reader.

The IIIA, IIIB formula works best in the following example:

> IIIA. Did the store employee stop the suspected shoplifter in a reasonable manner, when he politely asked the woman to accompany him to the office and to show him the contents of her purse?
>
> IIIB. Did the store employee detain the suspected shoplifter for a reasonable time, when the entire incident took no more than three minutes?

While the uniting feature of issue III is the detention, a general question concerning the detention will not be helpful to the reader.

The III, A, B formula works best in the following example:

> III. Does Susan Saxon have "good cause" to voluntarily leave her employment and collect unemployment benefits under Or. Rev. Stat. § 657.176(2)?
>
> A. Does she have grounds that would compel a reasonable person of normal sensitivities to quit under similar circumstances, when all of the male members of her work crew have propositioned her for sex at least once in the seven months of her employment and when all the men make sexually explicit comments about her body either to her face or so she can overhear them?

B. Has she tried to resolve the problem with her employer and can she show that further efforts would be unavailing, when she complained once to the foreman and he responded with a sexist remark, and the personnel manager told her not to come complaining about the way the men treated her?

In this example, a general question is helpful, because it provides the overall rule, "good cause", as context for the reader. While it would be possible to draft each of the two sub-questions to include the overall rule, the resulting questions would be partially redundant and too long.

DRAFTING A QUESTION PRESENTED

A question presented follows the basic formula:

DOES [this RULE] APPLY TO [these FACTS]?

This formula should look familiar to you. It is the same formula you used for formulating the issues in a case brief. As with issue statements in case briefs, the writer includes the specific rule and the specific facts in this basic formula with enough detail to set the scope of the issue. The rule precedes the facts because the reader will only understand the significance of the facts in light of the rule. If the facts were presented first, the reader would have to reread the facts in order to understand the issue. As you can see from the basic formula, a question presented is drafted to yield a yes or no answer.

Drafting questions presented is difficult. First, the writer must state the rule with precision. Next, she must select the facts that are legally relevant to that rule. She must also state the facts objectively, so that she does not mislead the reader. Finally, she must put the rule and facts together into a readable question that gives the reader the scope of the issue. In order to draft good questions presented, the writer must understand the analysis thoroughly. If the writer does not, she must analyze and organize the problem in greater depth before she can adequately draft the questions presented.

Although there is no particular time in the memo writing process that is the best for drafting questions presented, many writers do a first draft of the questions before beginning the discussion section. If the writer has sufficient understanding of the analysis at this stage to draft the questions presented, drafting the discussion section will be easier. For the writer who has difficulty drafting the questions at the outset, it may be an indication that she should spend more time analyzing the problem.

Whether the writer drafts the questions before the discussion section or later, she must return to the questions after revising the discussion section. If the scope of the memo has changed in the course of drafting and revising the text, the questions must reflect the change in focus. If there is considerable time between the initial draft of the questions and the revision, it will be easier for the writer to look at the questions objectively and to revise them critically.

The following example illustrates the process of drafting a question presented. You represent Chaucer Insurance Company. Chaucer insured a dry cleaning business in a building that was recently destroyed by fire. The company suspects arson. If it can prove arson and that the insured set the fire, it will not have to pay the proceeds of the insurance policy. Unfortunately the star witness as to the fire's cause is deceased. **Your memo addresses the evidentiary issues.**

The applicable rules of evidence are the following:

FRE 801 Definitions.

The following definitions apply under this article:

(a) Statement.—A "statement" is (1) an oral or written assertion or (2) nonverbal conduct of a person, if it is intended by him as an assertion.

(b) Declarant.—A "declarant" is a person who makes a statement.

(c) Hearsay.—"Hearsay" is a statement, other than one made by the declarant while testifying at the trial or hearing, offered in evidence to prove the truth of the matter asserted.

* * *

FRE 802 Hearsay Rule.

Hearsay is not admissible except as provided by these rules * * *.

FRE 803 Hearsay Exceptions; Availability of Declarant Immaterial.

The following are not excluded by the hearsay rule, even though the declarant is available as a witness:

(1) Present sense impression.—A statement describing or explaining an event or condition made while the declarant was perceiving the event or condition or immediately thereafter.

(2) Excited Utterance.—A statement relating to a startling event or condition made while the declarant was under the stress of excitement caused by the event or condition.

* * *

The fire investigation report contains the following information:

The fire was limited to the back room of the dry cleaning business when the fire department arrived. Within three minutes the firemen had laid the hose and entered the building through the rear door. Arthur Ewell was in the lead. A few minutes later, the captain reported that the fire seemed to be under control. Suddenly the fire erupted again igniting the dry cleaning solvents.

Ewell staggered from the building. He was badly burned. Frank Mason removed Ewell's self contained mask and oxygen supply. Ewell said, "the floor was slippery and it flashed back." He was rushed to the burn unit at Massachusetts General Hospital. He died nine days later. Arthur Ewell was decorated posthumously. He had been with the department for fifteen years.

Frank Mason explained the significance of Ewell's remark. A floor that is covered with gasoline or kerosene will be slippery. If the gasoline has not burned completely when water is poured on it, it may reignite. This can happen quite suddenly in a flashback. Experienced fire fighters know that they must leave the area quickly when they feel a slippery floor or they may be surrounded in flames. The flashback in this case occurred so quickly that Ewell was not able to get out of the building before the fire reignited.

Chaucer would like Frank Mason to testify at the trial to report what Ewell said as he emerged from the fire and to explain the significance of the remark to the fact finder.

Under the definitions in 801, Ewell is a declarant. The statement he made is hearsay because Chaucer plans to have someone other than the declarant offer the statement at the trial for purposes of proving the truth of the assertion; namely, that the floor was slippery and the fire flashed back. Under 802 hearsay is not admissible unless there is a rule that applies. Hearsay is generally inadmissible because it is inherently unreliable. There are, however, circumstances under which hearsay is reliable. Rule 803 provides exceptions for those limited circumstances. Two of the exceptions under 803 seem to apply, the present sense impression and excited utterance exceptions.

Consider first the present sense impression exception. The specific parts of the exception that apply are—a statement describing a condition, made immediately after the declarant perceived the condition. The applicable facts are that Ewell described the slippery floor and the flashback immediately after he perceived them. The question presented might read:

I. Is a fire fighter's statement "the floor was slippery and it flashed back" admissible under FRE 803(1) as a present sense impression exception to the hearsay rule, which requires that the declarant describe a condition while or immediately after perceiving it, when the fire fighter made the statement moments after sensing a slippery floor and being engulfed in the flashback?

The question includes the necessary explanation of the rule and the facts. Notice that the facts are presented in an objective manner. If the writer had phrased "in the flashback" as "in the raging inferno", the reader would have a quite different mental picture as to what actually took place. Be sure that you draft the facts using vocabulary that accurately describes the event. The vocabulary used in the example provides the reader with the exact scope of the issue.

The excited utterance exception has different requirements. The declarant must make a statement about an exciting event while he is still under the excitement of the event. In this case, fire fighter Ewell experienced an exciting event; he felt a slippery floor and was immediately engulfed in flames as the fire flashed back. He was badly burned by the fire and made his statement as he staggered from the building and while the adrenalin still pumped through his body. The question presented might read:

> II.   Is the fire fighter's statement "the floor was slippery and it flashed back" admissible under FRE 803(2) as an excited utterance exception to the hearsay rule, which requires that the statement relate to a startling event and that the declarant make the statement before the stress of the event has dissipated, when the fire fighter described the fire and its cause as he staggered, badly burned, from the building?

As a writer, you must be careful not to make the questions too long. While your goal is to set the scope of the issue for the reader, a question that is too long will only confuse the reader and defeat your purpose. As the questions are related, you can combine them using the I, A, B organization and achieve a more readable result:

> I.   Is a fire fighter's statement "the floor was slippery and it flashed back" admissible as an exception to the hearsay rule under FRE 803 as either
>
>> A.   a present sense impression, which requires that the declarant describe a condition while or immediately after perceiving it, when he made the statement moments after sensing the slippery floor and being engulfed in the flashback?
>
> or
>
>> B.   an excited utterance, which requires that the statement relate to a startling event and that the declarant make the statement before the stress of the event has dissipated, when he described the fire and its cause moments after staggering, badly burned, from the building?

For both of these issues, the reader needs some explanation of both the facts and the legal standard to understand the scope of the issue.

Often, you frame the issue as a general question presented either because the rule, the facts or both do not require specific treatment. The following is an example of a general question.

> I.   Does an insurer have a duty to defend its insured, which requires only that the complaint state a viable claim, when the complaint alleges all of the elements of negligence?

As you draft questions presented, think about the specificity required to set the scope of the issue for the reader.

The questions presented section of an office memorandum follows the heading and precedes the statement of facts. To help the reader follow your organization, it is useful to repeat each of the questions presented in the body of the discussion section just before you discuss that specific issue. The question, single-spaced, serves as a heading for the issue and permits the reader to find that section of your memo with ease. It is particularly helpful in a complicated memo, where you discuss a number of issues.

PROCESS FOR DRAFTING THE QUESTIONS PRESENTED

1. Isolate the issues and sub-issues from your outline.

2. Eliminate all the givens and minor issues.

3. Draft questions for the remaining major issues and sub-issues.

4. Choose the organization for the questions that best explains their relationship to the reader.

5. Use the formula: does this [specific rule] apply to these [specific facts]?

6. Include sufficient specificity in the questions to set the scope of the issue for the reader.

7. Revise for readability.

8. The questions presented should follow the heading in an office memorandum. You may also use the questions presented as headings in the body of the discussion section to indicate the start of the treatment of each issue. Be sure to single-space the questions in the body of the discussion section.

Exercise 7A.

Read the following problem. Isolate the rules and legally relevant facts. Organize the potential questions. Draft questions presented using the formula: does the rule apply to the facts? Finally, revise your questions to make them concise and readable.

The memorandum discusses whether the prosecuting attorney should charge Marvin Mantle with arson of a dwelling house under the state statute. The corpus delicti of arson requires that the fire have a non-accidental cause, that the defendant have a motive for starting the fire, and that the defendant have the opportunity to set the fire. A dwelling house is defined in one of the cases as a structure which is habitable without renovation. The structure need not be occupied at the time of the fire.

Marvin Mantle inherited the house when his father passed away. He cleaned out the house, turned off the utilities, insured the house for $45,000, and put it up for sale. Six months later when there were no purchasers, he lowered the price to $35,000. He did not lower the insurance coverage.

The building caught fire and burned to the ground. The fire inspector explained in his report that the char depth at the foot of two support beams was identical. The beams were twenty-five feet apart, and neither was located near the disconnected utility services. In his opinion, there were two points of origin for the fire.

Mantle drives by the house on his way home from work. Normally he arrives home in time for dinner at six p.m. On the evening of the fire, he was twenty minutes late for dinner.

Exercise 7B.

Draft Questions Presented for the problem presented in Exercise 6A at the end of Chapter 6.

Exercise 7C.

Draft Questions Presented for the problem presented in Exercise 6B at the end of Chapter 6.

Exercise 7D.

Draft Questions Presented for the problem presented in Exercise 6C at the end of Chapter 6.

Chapter 8

STATEMENT OF FACTS

The second section of a formal office memorandum is the "statement of facts". The purpose of the statement of facts is to provide a factual context for the issues. Because an office memorandum is an objective assessment of the legal merits of the client's position, the statement of facts must also be accurate and objective. This chapter explains how to choose the facts to include in the statement of facts, how to organize the substantive and procedural facts, and how to present the facts so that the reader understands what happened and is prepared for your analysis.

There are three categories of facts that should be included in the statement of facts: the legally significant facts, the background facts, and the procedural facts. The legally significant facts are all the facts you will analyze in the A of IRAC section of each issue and sub-issue in the discussion section. These are critical to the analytical process and you will not communicate the analysis to the reader if you do not include all of these facts. To make sure that you do not omit any legally significant facts, list all of the issues and sub-issues, and then under each, list all the facts that are legally significant to that issue. All of these facts should be included in the statement of facts. There may be some redundancy; often the same fact is pertinent to the analysis of more than one issue or sub-issue. As a writer, be careful not to introduce the same redundancy into the statement of facts.

The legally significant facts do not always make sense in a vacuum. To provide context for them, include background facts where necessary. Choose the background facts that will help the reader understand the legally significant facts, but do not include trivial detail that will distract the reader's attention from the salient points.

Finally, the procedural facts belong in the statement of facts. If the purpose of the memo is to address the possible merits of filing a case or to advise the client of the legal ramifications of various courses of action, there will, of course, be no procedural facts. But if a case has been filed and it has started the procedural process described in Chapter 3, the statement of facts should include this information.

Once you have chosen the facts that should be included, you will need to organize them in a way that makes them clear to the reader. Chronological order is usually the best order to choose. It helps the writer avoid the redundancy that might arise if the facts were arranged by issue. Chronological order is also a logical order. The facts developed in a causal relationship and the chronological order helps the writer demonstrate the causal connections. The reader will understand and remember the facts better if they are causally connected. There are two variations of chronological order. The first is the order of events in absolute time. This is the most common understanding of chronological order. The second is the order in which the events unfolded to one of the actors. This is the chronological order often used in literature. In some circumstances this is the most logical choice for a statement of facts. If the plaintiff's actions, for example, resulted from the events as she learned of them, consider using her perspective of chronological order to organize the facts. Remember that your goal is to organize the facts for the reader's benefit. When you have finished the first draft of the statement of facts, test the organization from the perspective of the reader and make any changes necessary to the reader's understanding of the events.

The procedural facts are commonly placed either at the beginning or end of the statement of facts. When the procedure is critical to an understanding of the issues in the memo, the procedural facts belong at the beginning. If the issues you will discuss in the memo do not involve the procedure, then consider saving the procedural facts for the end of the statement of facts.

There are at least two points in the drafting process when you can draft the statement of facts. If your outline includes every fact you intend to use in the A sections, you may be able to draft the statement of facts effectively before drafting the discussion section. If you choose to draft at this time, be sure to check the statement of facts against the discussion section later to make sure that you did not add or delete facts at a later time. To avoid this problem, many legal writers prefer to draft the statement of facts after the discussion section, because they find it easier to list the facts they actually used than the facts they intend to use.

The following example illustrates the process of drafting a statement of facts. The file contains information from a variety of different sources: a complaint, a report from the client—Chaucer Insurance Company, answers to interrogatories, and an arson investigation report. As the various sources have not yet been through the truth testing trial process, the writer must give the source of each piece of information.

In order to put together a statement of facts for the memorandum, choose the three types of facts and arrange them in an order that will convey the events to the reader. The issues involve fraud against an insurance company and the admissibility at trial of statements made by Arthur Ewell, a firefighter, and George Claxton, an eye witness. Neither declarant will be present at the trial. Frank Mason, a fire lieutenant, and the fire captain will be testifying about what Ewell and Claxton said for purposes of establishing the truth of the matter asserted. Both are hearsay and are inadmissible unless covered by one of the exceptions to the hearsay rule. Either or both might qualify as a present sense impression or excited utterance exception to the hearsay rule.

The present sense impression exception requires a statement describing a present sense impression or a condition made while or immediately after the declarant perceived the impression or condition. The legally relevant facts surrounding Arthur Ewell's statement, "the floor was slippery and it flashed back," are: Ewell had just entered the back room of the dry cleaning business when he perceived that the cement floor was slippery. Then the fire flashed back. He left the building within a minute or two. Frank Mason removed Ewell's breathing apparatus and Ewell made his statement.

Claxton's statement may also be a present sense impression. Claxton was changing a drum on a photocopy machine on the night of the fire. He saw Kent Seely running down the alley with a trophy. Twenty minutes later as the fire captain arrived on the scene, Claxton said, "I saw Kent running down the alley with the trophy twenty minutes ago."

The excited utterance exception to the hearsay rule requires that the declarant make a statement about an exciting event while still under the excitement of the event. Arthur Ewell experienced an exciting event. He entered a burning building and was suddenly engulfed in flames. He made a statement within three minutes that related to the exciting event; he said, "the floor was slippery and it flashed back."

George Claxton also experienced an exciting event. He discovered a fire in the building that housed his photocopy business. The fire started in the adjoining dry cleaning business. Twenty minutes earlier, Claxton had seen Kent Seely, one of the owners of the adjoining dry cleaning business, running down the alley with a trophy. He made the statement to the fire captain. He gasped out "I saw Kent running down the alley with the trophy twenty minutes ago."

From these two examples, you can see that much of the same information is legally relevant to both the present sense impression and the excited utterance exceptions to the hearsay rule. If you wrote the statement of facts and arranged the facts by issue, your presentation would be redundant.

You can also see that neither statement nor the legally relevant facts that accompany it, will be a sufficient explanation for the reader without some additional information. Unless the reader is an experienced fire fighter, he will not understand the significance of a slippery floor and he will not know what a flash back is. He will also need more information about this particular situation, namely, the identity of "Kent", and the significance of the trophy.

But even with the added facts that make the two statements meaningful, the reader will be lost without some background and context to put the facts in perspective. For this reason, you should explain at the outset what kind of a case this is and identify the participants. A reader, who understands the significance of the facts, is much more likely to remember the facts and understand your analysis of them. Context is critical to a statement of facts.

The context in this case involves telling the reader that this is a fire insurance case and that Chaucer Insurance Company refuses to pay the benefits of the insurance policy on the grounds that one of the insured committed fraud. The company would like to introduce two hearsay statements into evidence to help prove the fraud.

Finally, you will want to include the procedural facts. The plaintiffs filed a case and served your client with a summons and complaint. Your client answered the complaint and raised the fraud defense. It also sent interrogatories to the plaintiffs. This information is useful to the reader, but it is not critical to an understanding of the issues you will discuss in the memo. For this reason, the procedural facts will fit most appropriately at the end of the statement of facts.

The statement of facts for this hypothetical case might read as follows:

> Chaucer Insurance Company has refused to pay the proceeds of a fire insurance policy to plaintiffs, Speedy Dry Cleaning, Wayne Dawson, and Kent Seely, on the grounds that one of the partners committed fraud by setting the business premises on fire. Two hearsay statements, if admissible, would aid the insurer in raising the fraud defense.

> Chaucer Insurance Company first insured Speedy Dry Cleaning on July 1, 1976, when Wayne Dawson and Kent Seely started the business. The fire insurance policy required the company to pay for any damage to the building by fire except in the case of fraud by the insured. The policy was renewed annually. In 1984, the partners requested that the policy be amended and that it be issued not only to Speedy Dry Cleaning, but also to each of them individually.

> Speedy Dry Cleaning prospered. By the summer of 1985, it had seven employees and a softball team with a winning record. It captured the trophy in its division in 1983, 1984, and 1985.

> Speedy shares a building with a copy center and a bakery. On the night of October 30, 1985, George Claxton, owner of the copy center, was working late. Although he usually closed up at 7 pm, he had stayed after business hours to replace a drum in one of the copy machines. He happened to look out in the alley and he saw Kent Seely running down the alley with the softball trophy. About

fifteen minutes later, Claxton realized that the building was on fire. He called in the alarm.

According to the arson report, the Boston Fire Department received his call at 8:03 pm. When the engines arrived on the scene at 8:09 pm, the fire was limited to the back room of the dry cleaners. George Claxton ran up to the captain and gasped out, "I saw Kent running down the alley with the trophy twenty minutes ago." George Claxton has not re-established his business in the area. His landlady reports that he has moved to California, but she does not know where.

Within three minutes the firemen had laid a hose and entered the building through the rear door. Arthur Ewell, a veteran of fifteen years with the department, was in the lead. A few minutes later the captain radioed to the station house that the fire seemed to be under control. Suddenly the fire erupted again igniting the dry cleaning solvents. The captain turned in a second alarm. At that moment, fire fighter Ewell staggered from the building. He was badly burned. The lieutenant, Frank Mason, removed Ewell's self contained mask and oxygen supply. Ewell said, "the floor was slippery and it flashed back." Ewell died nine days later.

The arson investigation report includes a note by Frank Mason explaining the significance of Ewell's remark. A floor that is covered with gasoline or kerosene will be slippery. If the fuel has not burned completely when water is poured on it, it may reignite suddenly in a "flash back". Experienced fire fighters know that they must leave the area quickly when they feel a slippery floor or they may be surrounded in flames. Mason estimated that Ewell had been in the building for no more than three minutes.

The report also noted that most of the evidence that would point to a cause for the fire was destroyed with the building. The file was labeled "suspected arson" and closed.

Speedy Dry Cleaning, Wayne Dawson and Kent Seely notified Chaucer Insurance Company of the loss of the business. The claims representative referred the claim to Arthur Large, an investigator for the company. Large conducted an investigation. He read the report by the fire department and interviewed a number of witnesses. His findings included the additional information that Seely was in financial difficulty in the fall of 1985. He was four months behind on his mortgage and car payments and had outstanding credit card bills of approximately $14,000. That summer, he had spent a weekend in Atlantic City and had made a longer trip to Las Vegas. He gambled on a regular basis. Based on his investigation and that of others, Large concluded that the fire had been set by one of the partners. He recommended that the claim be denied on the grounds of fraud. The claims representative sent a letter to the insureds denying the claim.

The three insureds then filed a case in Middlesex County Superior Court to recover the insurance benefits. The summons and complaint were served on Chaucer Insurance Company on March 3, 1986. Chaucer answered the complaint and raised the fraud defense. It served interrogatories on the plaintiffs during the first week in April.

This memo addresses evidentiary questions in anticipation of the trial.

The statement of facts for this hypothetical case begins with enough context to put the problem in perspective for the naive reader. The reader knows it is a fire insurance fraud case and that the issues in the memo are evidentiary hearsay issues. She will pay particular attention to the hearsay statements as they appear in the chronology, knowing that they are crucial to the case. The writer has also identified the parties for the reader. Chaucer Insurance Company, the client, is mentioned first.

The second paragraph provides background information on the insurance policy that forms the crux of this case. Although it is not immediately apparent why the reader should care that the policy was changed the year before to list the partners as well as the company as "the insured", the writer has included the information because it contributes to the evidence of fraud.

The next paragraph provides the necessary background information on the business and the softball team. George Claxton's statement will be meaningless to the reader if the trophy has not been introduced previously.

The following paragraphs describe the chronology of the fire. You can see that the events follow logically from one another. As a reader, you are more likely to remember these events because of their logical connections. Although the arson report was issued some days after the fire itself, the writer put the substance of the report right after Ewell's statement to answer the reader's obvious query, why is a slippery floor important and what is a flashback.

The procedural facts fall chronologically at the end of the statement of facts. Because the issues are not procedural, the reader does not need to have this information before the substantive facts. The final sentence serves as a transition to the discussion section of the memo.

The vocabulary used in a statement of facts is important. You must give the facts objectively without trying to color the substance. The author used the words "gasped out" in describing George Claxton, because this is the language used in the arson report. Claxton's affect is important for the excited utterance exception. If the report had used the words: "stated", "reported", or "said", the writer would mislead the reader if he wrote "gasped out."

Similarly, the emotional, but legally irrelevant, facts have no place in a statement of facts. Consider the description of Arthur Ewell as it appeared in the Arson Investigation Report:

> Just as the captain called in the second alarm, fire fighter Ewell staggered from the building. He was badly burned. Frank Mason, the lieutenant, removed Ewell's self contained mask and oxygen supply. Ewell said, "the floor was slippery and it flashed back." He was rushed to the burn unit at Massachusetts General Hospital. He died nine days later. Arthur Ewell was decorated posthumously. He had been with the department for fifteen years.

Legally, the reader needs to know what Ewell said and the circumstances at the time of the statement. In order to understand the significance of the statement, the reader needs to know that Ewell was an experienced fire fighter; his tenure with the department provides that information. The reader also needs to know that he is deceased; the evidentiary question would not exist if Ewell could testify for himself. The reader does not need to know that he was rushed to the burn unit or that he was decorated posthumously. As feeling people, we, the readers might be glad that Ewell got the best care available for the time he survived. We may also sympathize with his family and think briefly that a posthumous decoration is sad recompense for a life lost. Neither of these facts, however, is significant or necessary to the analysis of the issues. These emotional facts do not belong in an office memorandum statement of facts.

PROCESS OF WRITING THE STATEMENT OF FACTS

1. List the issues and sub-issues.

2. Under each, list the facts that are legally necessary to the analysis of that issue or sub-issue.

3. Choose the background facts the reader will need to understand the legally significant facts.

4. Provide the reader with the context necessary to understanding the facts.

5. Identify the parties starting with your client.

6. Choose a logical order for the statement of facts; chronological order is usually the most effective.

7. Include the procedural facts, if any. If they are critical to the issues, put them near the beginning. If they are not critical, put them at the end.

8. Build logical connections between the facts so it is easier for the reader to remember and appreciate their significance.

9. Be objective in the way you present the facts. Choose your vocabulary with care.

10. Omit all the emotional facts.

Exercise 8A.

Draft a statement of facts for the problem presented as Exercise 6A at the end of Chapter 6.

Exercise 8B.

Draft a statement of facts for the problem presented as Exercise 6B at the end of Chapter 6.

Exercise 8C.

Draft a statement of facts for the problem presented as Exercise 6C at the end of Chapter 6.

Chapter 9

ORGANIZING YOUR ANALYSIS INTO THE DISCUSSION SECTION FOR AN OFFICE MEMORANDUM

The goal of the discussion section is to explain your analysis to the reader, an associate or partner in the firm. The pathway you took in analyzing a legal problem is not necessarily the most effective way of explaining the analysis to a reader. Your analytical process may have been circuitous, backtracking and refining as you reached for a thorough understanding of the problem. Organization is a critical step in constructing the discussion section both from the reader's perspective and from yours. The reader will not understand your analysis if the organization is haphazard. The process of organizing the material will help you to identify and correct problems with your analysis. Begin by outlining the discussion section. While it is relatively easy to rework an outline until you are satisfied with the organization, it is tedious to rewrite the entire discussion because the organization is unclear.

While good organization is critical to memo writing, most legal problems can be organized in several different ways and still effectively convey the analysis to the reader. There are two basic steps to organizing a memo. First consider the gross organization, the order of the issues and sub-issues. Then treat the fine organization, the order within each issue or sub-issue.

GROSS ORGANIZATION

There are several approaches to organizing the issues. This list is by no means exhaustive; it is designed to start you thinking about organizational approaches. Choose the one or ones that best convey the information to the reader.

a) *Order of importance*—The reader will give the most attention to the information that comes first. In order to take advantage of the reader's attention, begin with the most important issue and arrange the

161

others in order of decreasing importance. If the reader has anticipated the important issues, you will satisfy his curiosity with this order.

b) *Logical order*—Sometimes the issues have a logical order and the reader will best understand the issues in this order. If, for example, the case is a personal injury case and the issues are liability, damages, and attorney fees, the logical order suggests beginning with the liability issue. If there is no liability, the reader does not want to waste his time reading about damages and attorney fees. An arrangement of liability, damages, and attorney fees is the most logical order for the reader.

c) *Most complete relief*—When your analysis under different issues provides the client with varying degrees of relief, consider arranging the issues according to the outcome. If, for example, federal and state causes of action are available to the client, but the federal statute provides for punitive damages and attorney fees, discuss the federal claim first. This organization may also be the most logical and the order of greatest to least importance.

d) *Substantive before procedural*—When there are substantive and procedural issues, the reader will usually want the substantive issues before the procedural issues. This organization will sometimes be in conflict with one of the other approaches. In that case, you will need to consider the most effective option.

When you have figured out the best overall organization of the issues, you will want to use the same process for sorting the sub-issues. If some of the sub-issues are given or minor issues, consider treating them first, so the reader can concentrate on the major sub-issue(s).

The arson case, introduced in the previous chapter, illustrates how to proceed in putting together the gross organization for a memo. There are two major issues in the problem, the issue of whether the prosecutor can establish the Corpus Delicti of arson and whether the structure burned qualifies as a dwelling house or other real property. In order to outline the memo, you will need to decide which issue should go first. The criminal charge depends on both issues, so order based on relief will not aid the reader's understanding. As both issues are substantive and not procedural, that approach is also not helpful.

The best way to communicate the meaning to the reader is the order of importance. The prosecutor does not care whether the building is a dwelling or other real property until you have established the arson case against Mantle. This is also the logical approach. As the crime of arson has three elements and, therefore, three sub-issues, you need to consider the best order for these sub-issues. The most important element is the non-accidental cause, since the prosecutor will not proceed further with the case if the fire had a natural cause. There are two approaches to analyzing this sub-issue; the prosecutor can either rule out natural causes or prove a non-accidental cause. As you have evidence for both, you should include both approaches. The prosecutor will not want to proceed with the case, however, if there was a natural cause for the fire, so begin by ruling out this possibility. You can discuss the final two elements, motive and opportunity, in either order. The problem can be diagramed as follows:

> **Arson case**
>> Non-accidental cause for the fire
>>> Rule out natural causes
>>>
>>> Present evidence of non-accidental cause
>>
>> Opportunity or motive
>>
>> Motive or opportunity
>
> Dwelling or other real property

Once you have resolved the gross organization, the ordering of issues and sub-issues, you are ready to outline the material within each issue.

FINE ORGANIZATION

The most efficient way of communicating the analysis within an issue to the reader is **IRAC.** IRAC stands for **ISSUE, RULE, APPLICATION, and CONCLUSION.** The **reader** needs to know the issue before the rule makes sense. The application of the rule to the facts does not communicate anything to the reader without the issue and the rule first. There is no conclusion until the rule has been applied to the facts. IRAC is also helpful to you as the **writer,** because it forces you to articulate each part of the analysis. It also helps you avoid omitting a step in the analytical process. Each issue and sub-issue should include all four of the following elements:

ISSUE—State the issue.

RULE—The rule section may include several parts. Always work from the most general statement of the rule to the most specific. If the rule comes from a statute, begin by quoting the relevant portions of the statute. Arrange the sections for the reader's benefit. Consider an example from the Ski Safety and Liability Act presented in Chapter 5. Under section 33–44–107, a ski area operator has a duty to post signs for skiers' information. The relevant language provides that "[a]ll signs required by this section shall be maintained so as to be readable and recognizable **under conditions of ordinary visibility.**" The reader needs not only the operative section, but also the definition of the term "conditions of ordinary visibility". Should you begin with the definition and then state the duty or vice versa? Consider the alternatives from the standpoint of the reader. Here the reader needs the operative section before the definition is relevant. If your issue were, however, whether the injury occurred in a ski area, you would want to define ski area before proceeding to the operative section. Although you will understand the statute thoroughly before sitting down to write, be sure to explain the relationships between the various provisions of the statute to the reader.

Often the language of the statute is quite general. In order to understand that language, the reader needs a statement by a court interpreting the general language more specifically. As a more specific statement of the rule, the court's statement belongs after the statutory language itself. The reader may also want to know how the court applied that rule to a specific fact situation. The fact specific holding of a case serves this function. It illustrates how the rule was applied in the case and is the most specific statement of the rule. Not every rule section will include these three levels of rule: the statutory language, a court definition, and an illustration of the rule. As you draft a rule section, however, you will need to consider how many levels of rule the reader needs in order to understand the rule sufficiently to predict its application to the problem facts.

When you have a spectrum of authority; that is, a case where the facts were **sufficient** to meet the general rule and a case where the facts were **not sufficient** to meet the general rule, be sure to include both ends of the spectrum in the outline and in the memo. Lead off with the illustration that agrees with the result you predict for your case. If you concluded, for example, that Mantle's house qualifies as a dwelling, begin with the fact specific holding from *Losinger* and then give the holding from *Reed*. If you include both, the reader will have a better understanding of the scope of the rule. In an outline, you only need to include a summary of the facts from the illustrative cases. In a memo, you should include all the facts that are legally significant to that issue or sub-issue.

The rule section may include all of the following:

1. Quotation of the relevant parts of a statute.

2. A court's definition of the general rule.

3. A fact specific holding from a case illustrating how the court applied the general rule. When there is a spectrum of results under the rule, start with the illustration that reaches the result you predict in the problem. Then illustrate with the opposite result.

APPLICATION OF RULE TO FACTS—Next apply the rule to the facts of the problem case. In an outline, you need include only a summary of the facts. In a memo, you should include all the legally relevant facts, explaining how the facts are analogous to those in one case, but different from those in the other case just as you did in analyzing the problem initially. If you have diagramed this comparison, as illustrated in the table in Chapter 6, you will have no difficulty in deciding which facts to include.

CONCLUSION—Finally, state your conclusion for that issue.

IRAC each issue in the problem. If an issue includes sub-issues, explain under the general rule that there are two or more sub-issues.

Then proceed to give the general rule for the first sub-issue. Illustrate that rule with a fact specific holding of a case. Remember that if you have a spectrum of cases, with cases that show facts sufficient and insufficient to meet the general rule, be sure to include both ends of the spectrum in the outline. Lead off with the case that reaches the result you predict on the sub-issue for the problem, then treat the other end of the spectrum. Apply the rule to the facts of your case and reach a conclusion. Then proceed in the same way with each additional sub-issue. Always remember to conclude each issue or sub-issue before going on to the next one. When you have concluded all the sub-issues of an issue, give an overall conclusion for the issue.

In order to fully inform the reader in a memo, include any reasonable counter-argument the opponent may raise. The counter-argument belongs right after the treatment of the same issue or sub-issue. To help the reader, it should be introduced as a counter-argument. It should be organized as an issue with the counter-argument first, the rule, the application of the rule to the facts of the case, and finally the conclusion on the counter-argument.

The following is one way of organizing the arson problem:

ISSUE I

The prosecutor wants to know if she has grounds for bringing an arson case against Marvin Mantle.

RULE

"Any person who wilfully or maliciously burns any dwelling house * * *" Sec. 750.72 or "any building or other real property * * *" Sec. 750.73.

The elements of arson are (1) a non-accidental cause for the fire, (2) motive, (3) opportunity. *People v. Horowitz*

The prosecution can use circumstantial evidence to prove the elements of arson. *People v. Horowitz*

Sub-issue 1

The first sub-issue is whether there was a non-accidental cause for the fire.

Rule

There are two approaches; you can either to eliminate accidental causes or demonstrate a non-accidental cause.

Fact specific holding illustrating the rule for first approach

The prosecutor eliminated the weather, the stove, furnace, electrical equipment, the dogs, careless smoking and neglect as potential causes for the fire.

People v. Bailey

Application of the rule to Mantle's case

There was no evidence of forced entry, the weather was clear, the house was unoccupied, and the utilities were turned off.

NOTE: In the memo, compare the facts of Mantle's case to those from *People v. Bailey*.

Conclusion

The fire was not started by natural causes.

Fact specific holding illustrating the rule for second approach

The arson squad found evidence of two plastic containers with flammable liquid and a timing device strategically located at the points of the fire's origin. *People v. Horowitz*

Application of the rule to Mantle's case

The arson investigator found two points of origin for the fire, neither of which was close to the utilities or furnace. There was, however, no evidence of flammable liquids or other incendiary device.

NOTE: In the memo, compare the facts of Mantle's case to those from *People v. Horowitz*.

Conclusion

The fire had a non-accidental cause.

Sub-issue 2

The next sub-issue is whether Mantle had an opportunity to set the fire.

NOTE: The order of sub-issues dealing with opportunity and motive could be reversed.

Rule—Fact specific holding illustrating the rule

The defendants were on the premises shortly before the fire was discovered. *People v. Bailey, People v. Horowitz*.

NOTE: One case is sufficient here; both can be used.

Application of the rule to Mantle's case

Although there is no eye witness evidence, Mantle could have been on the premises shortly before the fire was discovered. He usually travels by the house on his way home from work. On the night of the fire, he arrived home twenty minutes later than usual.

NOTE: In the memo, compare the facts of Mantle's case to those from one or both of the cases.

Conclusion

Marvin Mantle had the opportunity to start the fire.

Sub-issue 3

The third sub-issue is whether Mantle had a motive for starting the fire.

Rule—Fact specific holding illustrating the rule

The defendants carried fire insurance on the premises and were in financial difficulty at the time of the fire. *People v. Bailey*, *People v. Horowitz*

NOTE: One case is sufficient here; both can be used.

Application of rule to Mantle's case

Mantle maintained fire insurance coverage on the house for $10,000 more than the current asking price. The real estate agent had scheduled a second look at the house with potential purchasers for the next day. There is no evidence that Mantle was in financial difficulty.

NOTE: In the memo, compare the facts of Mantle's case to those from one or both of the cases.

Conclusion

Mantle had a motive for setting fire to the house.

CONCLUSION

The prosecutor can establish the Corpus Delicti of arson against Marvin Mantle.

ISSUE II

The prosecutor wants to know if the structure qualifies as a dwelling for purposes of charging Mantle with arson of a dwelling.

RULE

"Any person who wilfully or maliciously burns any **dwelling house** * * *" Sec. 750.72.

An unoccupied house qualifies as a dwelling if it is suitable for habitation without renovation. *People v. Reed*

FACT SPECIFIC HOLDING ILLUSTRATING RULE

The building qualified as a dwelling when it occupied occasionally for vacations and was intended as a retirement home; it was in a good state of repair; it was furnished with a stove, cooking utensils, clothing, and some food; and had a kerosene heating stove. *People v. Losinger.*

FACT SPECIFIC HOLDING ILLUSTRATING RULE

The building did not qualify as a dwelling when it was unoccupied and boarded up, it was in poor repair, it was unfurnished, and it had no bathroom or running water. *People v. Reed.*

APPLICATION OF RULE TO MANTLE'S CASE

The building was unoccupied, it was unfurnished, it was in a good state of repair, and the utilities had been turned off.

NOTE: In the memo, compare and contrast the facts of Mantle's case with those from both of the cases.

CONCLUSION

Mantle's house qualifies as a dwelling.

OVERALL CONCLUSION

The prosecutor should charge Marvin Mantle under sec. 750.72.

While IRAC is generally applicable to the fine organization of legal problems, its specific use depends on the problem you are analyzing, its issues and sub-issues, the levels of rule necessary for analyzing each of them, and the specific facts. The level of detail included in the rule and application sections varies enormously. For issues that are so straightforward as to be "given", you can handle the entire analysis in one sentence; a lengthy IRAC would be unnecessary, redundant, and boring to the reader. Sometimes the rule is complex, but the application is simple; the rule section should be comprehensive with the remaining sections telescoped accordingly. Occasionally, the whole problem hinges on the analysis of one sub-issue with the remaining issues dependent in a series of shells on the resolution of that sub-issue. The following outline illustrates how IRAC is also helpful in organizing a problem where some of the sub-issues are given and the remaining issues are interrelated.

Diane Black entered and won a raffle sponsored by a new gallery. Before, however, she could collect the diamond ring she had won, it was stolen. The gallery owner promised to give her the ring if and when it was recovered, but he refused to give her a substitute ring or its value. She would like to know if she has any legal recourse.

ISSUE

The primary issue is whether the courts will enforce Diane Black's rights arising out of the gallery's raffle.

RULE

Courts will not enforce rights arising out of illegal activity. *Miller v. Radikopf*[1]

(AC must wait until the other issues have been decided.)

Issue

The next issue is whether the raffle is an illegal activity.

Rule

A lottery is an illegal activity. Sec. 750.232.

(AC must wait until the other issues have been decided.)

Issue

The next issue is whether the gallery's raffle qualifies as a lottery.

Rule

A lottery requires (1) a chance (2) for a prize (3) and that the entrant offer the promoter consideration. *People v. Brundage*[2]

Sub-issue

The chance—the gallery offered a random chance to all participants.

GIVEN

Sub-issue

The prize—The gallery offered a 1.4 carat diamond ring as a prize.

GIVEN

THE DECISIVE SUB–ISSUE

The sub-issue involves whether the raffle participants gave the gallery consideration when they had to go to the gallery and walk through the merchandising area to enter the raffle.

Rule

The participants must give something of value to the promoter for there to be consideration. *People v. Brundage.*

---

1. 394 Mich. 83, 228 N.W.2d 386 (1975).   2. 7 Mich. App. 364, 150 N.W.2d 825 (1967).

Fact specific holding illustrating the rule

The court held there was consideration when customers had to go to the store at least twice a week to participate in the drawing. *People v. Brundage.*

Fact specific holding illustrating the rule

The court held there was no consideration when the participants did not have to leave home in order to play the Bingo style game. *AFC Wrigley Stores, Inc. v. Olsen* [3]

Application of rule to facts

The participants in the raffle had to go to the gallery and walk through the merchandising area in order to enter the raffle.

Conclusion

The participants gave the gallery consideration.

Conclusion

The raffle was a lottery as there was a chance for a prize and the entrants gave the promoter consideration.

Conclusion

As a lottery, the raffle was illegal.

CONCLUSION

As Black's rights to the prize arose directly from illegal activity, the court will not help her enforce her rights.

When you have finished the outline, check to make sure that you have included all four elements of IRAC in each issue and sub-issue. Try to include the specific rules and facts from the cases and the problem in the outline. The more substance you include at this point in the process, the easier it will be for you to turn the outline into the text of a memo.

ORGANIZATION CHECKLIST

1. Choose the gross organization for the issues according to what will be the most helpful for the naive reader. Consider, for example, the order of importance, the most logical order, the order that provides the most relief before lesser degrees of relief, and an order giving substance before procedure.
2. Use IRAC for the fine organization of each issue and sub-issue.
3. Arrange the elements in the rule section from the most general to the most specific. Begin with the statute, if any, and then the

3. 395 Mich. 215, 102 N.W.2d 545 (1960).

general rule. Where necessary, include a case to illustrate the general rule. If you need a spectrum of authority to illustrate the rule, begin with the case that reaches the same conclusion as you reach for the facts in the problem.

4. Apply the rule to the facts of the problem case.

5. Be sure to conclude each issue and sub-issue before moving on to the next one.

Exercise 9A.

Outline the problem that appears as Exercise 6A at the end of Chapter 6.

Exercise 9B.

Outline the problem that appears as Exercise 6B at the end of Chapter 6.

Exercise 9C.

Outline the problem that appears as Exercise 6C at the end of Chapter 6.

Chapter 10

WRITING TO THE READER

As you sit down to write, remember that you are the expert on the analysis of this case and the reader, in comparison, is relatively naive. Your audience, the associate or partner, may know more about the law in general than you do, but you know these issues better. After hours of work on the problem, the analysis seems obvious to you, but it will not be obvious to the reader unless your explanation is sound. This chapter is designed to help you write to the reader. While the discussion is focused on memo writing, much of the content is equally applicable to legal writing in general.

THESIS PARAGRAPH OR SECTION

A memorandum, like any other expository writing, begins with a **thesis paragraph** or **section** that introduces the subject to the reader. It should include an overall statement of your thesis and explain the purpose of the memo. It should provide the reader with context, and it should serve as a road map of the memo, explaining the issues you will be discussing in the order they will appear. It should identify the statutes involved, although generally not the cases. Finally, it should state your conclusions. You may also explain very briefly the reasons for these conclusions if the reader is likely to understand your rationale at the outset.

Each of these functions is designed to help make the analysis more accessible to the reader. The reader wants to know the overall thesis or conclusion at the beginning, so she can test the analysis against this conclusion throughout the memo. An office memorandum is neither a joke nor a mystery story; the reader does not want to wait until the end in order to find out the punch line. As the reader has neither the time nor the patience to try to figure out the conclusion, it should appear at the beginning.

The reader also needs context to put the problem in perspective. If the reader is a partner in a corporate law firm, her legal universe is the diverse field of corporate law. Unless the writer explains the narrow area to be discussed in the memo, the reader must waste time trying to guess the context. Explain to the reader right away, for example, that the memo addresses the advisability of corporation Y filing for bankruptcy under Chapter 11. The reader can now concentrate all her attention on what she knows and what the writer will tell her about Chapter 11 and the issues as they relate to this particular client.

The reader wants to know the issues in the order you will present them. This tells the reader the scope of the memo, not only specifically what you will discuss, but also by inference, what you will not discuss. The order of the issues is helpful to the reader for two reasons. First, it gives the reader a road map of your analysis, so that she can recognize each point while you are discussing it. Second, if the reader has anticipated an issue, she knows you will discuss it later and she is willing to give her full attention to your treatment of the other issues in the interim. Along with the issues, the reader will also want to know your conclusions on each issue and, very briefly, the reason for each conclusion. This will give the reader a sense of how the pieces of your analysis fit together.

The thesis section is only a summary of your analysis, so write it accordingly; the details will follow. If the memo deals, for example, with only one issue and several sub-issues, a thesis paragraph will suffice. But if the memo includes several issues with sub-issues, a thesis section of several paragraphs may work better. A thesis paragraph for the raffle problem outlined in Chapter 9 might read as follows:

> Diane Black will not be able to use the court system to enforce her right to the prize she won in the gallery's promotional raffle. The Michigan courts will not enforce rights that arise directly from illegal activity. Under the appropriate statute, Mich. Comp. Laws Ann. sec. 750.372, lotteries are illegal. If the raffle was a lottery, it is an illegal activity. A lottery requires a chance, for a prize, and that the participant give some consideration to the promoter for the privilege of having a chance at the prize. The gallery offered a chance in a random raffle for a prize, a 1.4 carat diamond ring. When the participants were required to leave home, go to the gallery, and walk through the merchandizing area in order to enter the raffle, the entrant offered the promoter consideration sufficient for a lottery. The courts will not enforce her right to the ring since the lottery is an illegal activity.

THESIS STATEMENT

The discussion of each issue begins with a **thesis statement.** It is a direct statement of the issue and your conclusion. The thesis statement functions as a road sign to the reader indicating the start of a new issue. The following is a sample thesis statement from the arson problem discussed in earlier chapters.

> Mantle's building qualifies as a "dwelling" for purposes of the arson statute, sec. 750.72.

As you draft each thesis statement, remember its function. If the thesis statement directly follows the thesis paragraph, a restatement of the conclusion may be unnecessarily redundant. A simple introduction to the issue may suffice, for example:

> The prosecution must first assess whether the evidence against Mantle is sufficient for an indictment against him under the arson statute.

ORGANIZING THE ANALYSIS INTO PARAGRAPHS

IRAC provides the basic organization for presenting your analysis. The division of each issue into paragraphs depends on the relative importance of the issue and its components. Minor issues and those that are given deserve proportionately less analysis and space than major issues. A minor issue may deserve only one paragraph as in the following example.

> To collect under the Illinois Dog Bite Statute, the plaintiff must also show that he was conducting himself peaceably. In *Nelson*, the court held that the plaintiff's conduct was peaceable at the time of the dog bite. The child was playing crack the whip. Harvey Woodley was playing a similar child's game when Androcles' dog bit him. He had just lobbed a soft snowball at his father. He was, therefore, conducting himself peaceably.

Issues that are given can often be combined into one paragraph.

> The gallery's promotional raffle qualifies as a lottery under sec. 750.372. A lottery requires (1) a chance (2) at a prize and (3) that the participant give the promoter consideration. The gallery provided each entrant with a chance when it chose the winning ticket at random from a barrel containing all the entries. The gallery also offered a prize, a 1.4 carat diamond ring.

A relatively simple issue may work best as three paragraphs. The issue and the general rule comprise the first paragraph. The fact specific holding from an illustrative case follows in a second paragraph. The third paragraph contains the application of the rule to the facts in the problem and the conclusion.

> The putative father also wishes to know if the court will grant him visitation with his natural child, Millie D. The statute provides:
>
> > (a) If an order of filiation is made * * * the family court may make an order * * * of visitation requiring one parent to permit the other to visit the child or children at stated periods.
>
> N.Y. Fam. Ct Act § 549 (Consol. 1987).
>
> This section gives the court the discretion to order visitation and the standard used is that of the best interests of the child. *Pierce v. Yerkovich*, 80 Misc. 2d 613, 363 N.Y.S.2d 403 (Fam. Ct. 1974).

In *Cheryl A.D. v. Jeffrey G.O.*, 133 Misc. 2d 663, 507 N.Y.S.2d 593 (Fam. Ct. 1984), the court ordered visitation between a child and his natural father. Although the father was married to someone else, he had had a six year liaison with the mother and the child had developed strong ties to his biological father. The court found it was in the child's best interests to continue their relationship.

Under the statute, the court has the discretion to grant the natural father visitation with Millie D. Although the child's mother is now married to someone else, she lived with the natural father for three and one half years after Millie's birth. During that period, Millie developed a loving relationship with her biological father. Since the natural parent-child relationship is similar in nature and duration to that in *Cheryl A.D. v. Jeffrey G.O.*, this court, too, is likely to find it is in the child's best interests to allow the relationship to continue through court ordered visitation.

A three paragraph approach also works for simple issues where you need to present the reader with a spectrum of authority illustrating what is sufficient and insufficient to meet the rule. The following example is an approach to presenting the consideration sub-issue of the lottery problem presented earlier.

For a raffle to be a lottery under Mich.Comp.Laws Ann. sec. 750.372, the participants must give the promoter consideration. The court in *People v. Brundage*, 381 Mich. 399, 162 N.W.2d 659 (1968), rev'g 7 Mich.App. 364, 150 N.W.2d 825 (1967), held that the participants gave consideration to the promoter. There the participants were required to go to the store to pick up a registration card and return each week to have the card validated. The participants had to visit the store a second time each week for the drawing. Although the registration desk was near the entrance and the drawing was held in the parking lot, the court held that the participants gave the store consideration when they were present on the business premises at least twice for each chance at the prize.

The court in *Wrigley v. Olsen*, 359 Mich. 215, 102 N.W.2d 545 (1960), on the other hand, found no consideration. The case involved a bingo style game called "Play Marko". In order to play, a participant could either obtain a game card from the merchant or make his own game card. The numbers were broadcast on a local television station. If a participant matched the numbers drawn on the program with the vertical, horizontal, or diagonal numbers on his game card, he called the television station, and received his prize. Because the participant could play the game without leaving home, the court held that he had offered no consideration for the chance at the prize. The distinction between *Brundage* and *Wrigley* is the requirement that a participant visit the promoter's business premises. The *Brundage* court explained that in *Wrigley* "[t]his Court stretched almost to the breaking point a permissible finding of absence of consideration. * * * "

The gallery's raffle goes well beyond the facts in *Wrigley*. Like the participants in *Brundage,* but unlike the players in *Wrigley,* Diane Black offered the gallery consideration. Although she could use an entry blank published in the local newspaper, she had to go to the gallery in order to enter the raffle. Black was required to do even more than the participants in *Brundage,* who could enter the drawing just inside the entrance to the store. She had to traverse gallery A and most of gallery B to find the raffle barrel and deposit her entry. Because she went to the business and walked through the merchandise, Black gave the gallery consideration for the chance at the prize.

In explaining the analysis of this issue, the writer introduced the issue and gave the reader the general rule. Next the writer provided the fact specific holdings of the cases beginning with the case that reached the same conclusion the writer reached in Black's case—that she gave the gallery consideration. Notice how the writer explained the distinction between the two cases and let you, as the reader, know where the line between consideration and lack of consideration appears on the spectrum. The writer then explained how Black's facts compared with the facts of the cases. Finally, the writer concluded the issue. As you explain your analysis, be sure to include all the steps necessary for the reader to draw the conclusion you have reached.

While the examples provided above are straightforward, legal analysis often does not lend itself to such direct presentation. The holdings may include more legally relevant facts and your client's case may not be as easy to analogize or distinguish. When you need a spectrum of authority and the holdings require more extensive treatment, help the reader by putting the illustrative cases in different paragraphs. Four or more paragraphs may be necessary as the issue becomes increasingly more complex. Consider the following analysis from the discussion of a merchant's defense to false imprisonment.

Albert's employee had probable cause to detain Gerwin. There is probable cause if a reasonably prudent person under similar circumstances would believe that the suspect had attempted to steal store property. *Coblyn,* 359 Mass. at 323, 268 N.E.2d at 864.

The court held that the employee had probable cause to suspect a shoplifting in *Meadows v. Woolworth,* 254 F.Supp. 907 (N.D. Fla. 1966). The Woolworth store had received a notice from the local police several days prior to the incident warning of three teenage girls operating jointly. On the day in question, the employee noticed three teenage girls who had been in the store on two separate occasions. He noticed two missing hairpieces, and another employee reported to him that the girls had been in the area of the hairpieces. This information was sufficient to make a reasonably prudent person believe the girls had taken the merchandise.

In *Coblyn*, on the other hand, the court held that the employee did not have probable cause to suspect the plaintiff. The employee saw the plaintiff stop near the exit to the store, take an ascot out of his pocket, and tie it around his neck. The knot of the ascot was clearly visible above the lapels of the plaintiff's shirt. This fact without any other information was not enough to lead a reasonably prudent person to suspect the plaintiff of stealing the merchandise.

The information available to the employee in Albert's store was probably sufficient to meet the reasonably prudent person standard. As in *Meadows*, the local police had notified the store to be on the lookout for a shoplifter who matched the suspect's description. The police had warned Albert's to be on the lookout for a white male, aged about 20 years, 5′9″, 150 lbs. with medium brown hair. Gerwin fits this general description. Also as in *Meadows*, an employee saw the suspect near a rack from which merchandise had disappeared. The assistant manager observed Gerwin stop next to a rack from which a pen set was missing. Albert's employee had the same three kinds of information as the employee in *Meadows*.

The police description and the missing merchandise make this case stronger than *Coblyn*. The employees in *Coblyn* observed the plaintiff take an ascot from his pocket and tie it around his neck. The court held this was not enough to lead a reasonable person to suspect a shoplifting. While Gerwin's quick gesture to his pocket would not by itself be enough to give Albert's employee probable cause, this gesture coupled with the police description and the missing merchandise was sufficient. Albert's employee had probable cause to detain Gerwin.

To make the analysis explicit for the reader, the writer used five paragraphs. The first provided the general rule using the *Coblyn* case. If the fact specific holding from *Coblyn* had followed, it could have been included in the same paragraph. As the writer needed, however, to begin with the holding from a different case, a separate general rule paragraph is easier for the reader. The two following paragraphs illustrate opposite ends of the spectrum with facts that are sufficient and insufficient to show probable cause. Often, the comparison to one end of the spectrum and distinction from the other work well in one paragraph. Here, the writer used two paragraphs for clarity. The conclusion for the issue is included in the second A section paragraph.

Remember that the discussion in a memo must be objective, pointing out both the strengths and the weaknesses of your client's case. As an alternative to dealing with troublesome facts in the basic analysis, you can treat them in a separate paragraph or two after the basic IRAC paragraphs. The following paragraphs demonstrate counterarguments the defendant might raise in the false imprisonment example given above and the analysis of the arguments.

Gerwin may argue that the police description is a very general one; many young men in a university community fit the description. The description in *Meadows* required three teenage girls acting in concert, a much less likely event. While the description is a general one, Gerwin fit the description and this was only one of the factors that led the employee to stop Gerwin.

Gerwin may also argue that Albert's employee could have checked with the cashier to see if the calligraphy pen set had been sold before suspecting Gerwin of shoplifting the pen. Because shoplifting was a problem for Albert's and because timing was critical, the employee had to decide to stop the suspect before he left the store. Had Albert's employee taken the time to ask the cashier, Gerwin would have departed. A reasonably prudent person under similar circumstances would have detained the suspect first and then asked about the pen set. Albert's employee had probable cause to detain Gerwin as a shoplifting suspect.

Although you may have several paragraphs that make up the rule section, or you may have one paragraph that includes several mini-IRACs explaining the givens, every paragraph should function as a thesis paragraph, contain one or more sections of IRAC, or present a counterargument. When you have finished a draft of your discussion section, make sure that you can identify the function of every paragraph. If a paragraph does not does not fulfill any of these functions, either delete or rewrite the paragraph.

THE CONCLUSION

The final section of an office memorandum is the conclusion section. The conclusion wraps up the memo for the reader and serves as a summary of the discussion. While every memo should have a conclusion, not every memo has a formal section labeled "conclusion". Some law firms and some partners will require a formal conclusion section; others will not. Some memos are so complex that a formal conclusion section is advisable to help the reader. The following brief discussion of conclusions is designed to help you choose the best way of concluding a particular memo.

The choice initially depends on the length and complexity of the memo. If the memo is short and treats only one or two issues, one paragraph at the end of the discussion section will usually suffice. The purpose of this concluding paragraph is to summarize your conclusions on each issue and sub-issue and explain to the reader very briefly why you reached these conclusions. It helps the reader put the sub-issues and issues back together from your individual treatment of them. You may feel that the thesis paragraph has already accomplished this purpose. Often, however, the reasons for your conclusions will not make sense to the reader at the time he reads the thesis paragraph, because you have not yet articulated the rules or explained how the rules applied to the facts of the problem. When this is the case, the thesis paragraph will include the issues and the conclusions of these issues, but not an explanation of the conclusions. The sexual harassment in the work place problem presented in Exercise 6B is an illustration of this type of problem. Until you have explained "good cause", the explanations of your conclusions will not make sense to the reader. The conclusion for that problem might look like this.

The client, Susan Saxon, has a claim for sex discrimination in employment against her employer, Umatilla Mining Company. The Oregon Fair Employment Practices Act provides that it is an unfair labor practice for an employer to discriminate on the basis of sex in the "terms or conditions" of employment. Saxon is the victim of sexual harassment by the other eleven members of her work crew, all male. Their continual propositions and innuendos about her body and the employer's failure to correct the situation have become a condition of her employment. When the harassment occurs only to Saxon, the only female, it constitutes an unfair employment practice.

Should Saxon choose voluntarily to leave her job, she will be eligible for unemployment benefits. The unemployment benefit statute provides that an employee must have good cause to voluntarily leave employment. Good cause requires both grounds that would compel a reasonable person of normal sensitivities to quit, and that the employee have tried to resolve the problem with the employer. A reasonable person would quit under Saxon's circumstances. She cannot do her job, which requires cooperating with the other members of her work crew, and avoid the sexual harassment. Saxon complained about the harassment to her foreman, and he responded with a sexist remark. Further complaints to him or to the personnel manager would be futile. When she was hired, the personnel manager warned Saxon not to complain about the way the men treated her. There is no union and no formal grievance procedure at Umatilla. Saxon has tried unsuccessfully to resolve the problem and further efforts would be unavailing. She will be eligible for unemployment benefits if she chooses to leave the mining company.

This short conclusion belongs at the end of the discussion section. The issues are not so complicated that the memo requires a formal conclusion section. While the conclusions to many short memos fit neatly into one paragraph, this conclusion works better as two paragraphs, one each for the two disparate issues. You can see that each serves as a summary of the analysis. The reader can use this summary as a quick reminder of the memo.

The Illinois Dog Bite Problem presented in Exercise 6A is an example of a problem that can be concluded in one paragraph. It is a one-issue problem with four related elements; the procedural setting is the defendant's motion to dismiss. The concluding paragraph might read as follows:

The plaintiff has alleged facts sufficient for a cause of action under the Illinois Dog Bite Statute. The statute requires that the plaintiff show that the defendant owned the dog that bit the plaintiff, that the plaintiff was acting peaceably, that he was lawfully on the premises at the time, and that he did not provoke the dog. The defendant admits he owns the dog that bit the plaintiff. The plaintiff was playing and therefore conducting himself peaceably. Woodley was a licensee and as such, lawfully on the premises. Although he threw a soft snowball that inadvertently hit the dog, the dog responded out of proportion to the plaintiff's unintentional act. This is not provocation within the meaning of the statute. When the plaintiff has alleged facts sufficient to meet all the elements of the Dog Bite Statute, the court should deny the defendant's motion to dismiss.

If the memo is long and complicated, a formal conclusion section will be more useful for the reader. It will reunite the issues in the problem in their proper relationship and also serve as a quick reminder of the content. A formal conclusion contains the same information as the examples given above. It includes the rules, your conclusions after applying the rules to the facts, and a brief explanation for the conclusions. The label, CONCLUSION, helps the reader to find the section readily.

QUOTING AND PARAPHRASING

There are no hard and fast rules of what to quote and what to paraphrase. In general, quote the language from a constitution, statute, or regulation; the reader will want to know the exact language. If the section you are quoting is more than 50 words, use block quote form; that is, indent and single-space the quotation. If the quotation is shorter, use quotation marks to indicate the quoted language. In general, paraphrase language from cases to give the rule, holding, reasoning or policy. The reason for this is that your writing style is different from that of the judge who wrote the opinion. The transitions back and forth between your style and the judge's may be distracting to the reader. You want the reader to concentrate on the substance not on the diverse styles. Sometimes the judge will have stated a general rule with precision; in this case, the reader would like to see the precise language and you will want to quote it. It is also useful to quote language when you wish to emphasize the language. Use quotations carefully, however, as the effect will be diluted by overuse. Whether you quote or paraphrase, be sure to include the proper citation to the authority. If you quote or paraphrase specific language, you must include in the citation a reference to the specific statute section or page of the opinion.

STRUCTURING PARAGRAPHS

A **paragraph** is a grammatical unit designed to present one topic to the reader. Readers best understand short direct paragraphs. Consequently, as a writer you will want to put the most important information in short, direct paragraphs. When it is necessary to elaborate on the point in considerable detail, use longer paragraphs.

Readers pay most attention to the beginning and the end of a paragraph. As a writer, you want to take advantage of the reader's attention at the beginning of the paragraph by explaining the purpose of the paragraph with a **topic sentence**. Contrast the following two paragraphs that provide the holding from the *Brundage* case to see how helpful a topic sentence can be.

In *Brundage* the participants were required to go to the store to pick up a registration card and return each week to have the card validated. The participants had to visit the store a second time each week for the drawing. Although the registration desk was near the entrance and the drawing was held in the parking lot, the court held that the participants gave the store consideration when they were present on the business premises at least twice for each chance at the prize.

OR

The court in *Brundage* found the participants gave consideration to the promoter. There the participants were required to go to the store to pick up a registration card and return each week to have the card validated. The participants had to visit the store a second time each week for the drawing. Although the registration desk was near the entrance and the drawing was held in the parking lot, the court held that the participants gave the store consideration when they were present on the business premises at least twice for each chance at the prize.

Although the content of the two paragraphs is the same, the second one is easier to understand because the topic sentence focuses the reader's attention. As a reader, you know the facts that follow will help you to define consideration. You will pay attention to the facts because you understand their significance. If, as in the first version, you do not know the significance of the facts until the end of the paragraph, you may have to reread it to understand the writer's point.

A topic sentence is also a useful tool to you as a writer. If you have to stop and articulate the purpose of each paragraph, the document will be easier to write in at least two respects. First, it will help you to include every logical step in the analysis. Second, it will be easier for you to focus each paragraph. If you have difficulty drafting a topic sentence, you may need to rethink your analysis or reconsider your organization.

Within each paragraph, organize the information in a logical order to enhance the reader's understanding. Compare the following examples.

A substantial interference can arise from lack of utility services, excessive noise, vermin, and even an uncomfortable environment. On instance is insufficient. For excessive noise to sufficiently interfere with the use of the premises, it must occur repeatedly. A tenant can claim a constructive eviction if there is a substantial interference with the use and enjoyment of the premises.

A tenant can claim a constructive eviction if there is a substantial interference with the use and enjoyment of the premises. A substantial interference can arise from lack of utility services, an uncomfortable environment, vermin, and even excessive noise. For excessive noise to sufficiently interfere with the use of the premises, it must occur repeatedly. One instance is insufficient.

The author of the second paragraph began with a topic sentence that explained the purpose. Each succeeding sentence provided additional information arranged with increasing degrees of specificity. Note that each sentence begins with a reference to the preceding sentence and ends with new information.[1]

TRANSITION

You can also help the reader understand your analysis by using **transitions**. Although you may know the analysis so well that it is obvious to you how you moved from one point to the next, the naive reader does not intuitively know how the pieces fit together. As you write, think about transitions. If you are moving from a paragraph that explains the general rule to a paragraph that illustrates how the rule was applied in a case, the transition might look like:

The court in *X case* **applied this rule** and found consideration.

The transition between cases illustrating how the rule was applied to facts at different ends of the spectrum could be as simple as:

The court in *Y case,* **on the other hand,** did not find consideration.

The transition to the application section of IRAC might read:

When this rule is applied to the raffle, there is consideration.

Sometimes, as in these examples, the **topic sentence** and the **transition** functions fit in one sentence. At other times, a full sentence is necessary to bring the reader along with you.

The courts have used two approaches to analyzing the "lawfully on the premises" issue under the Illinois Dog Bite Statute. The court in *Messa* used the first approach.

---

1. Observation from speech on reader expectation theory presented by George Gopen at the Legal Writing Institute 1990 Summer Conference in Ann Arbor, Michigan.

* * *

The court in *Dobrin* approached lawfully on the premises using the common law doctrine of a licensee.

Signals like these help the reader know where each piece fits in the analysis.

CLEAR SENTENCES

You can include aids for the naive reader at the sentence level as well. Linguists studied readers to see what kinds of sentences are easiest for readers to understand. Their observations will help you craft sentences that communicate your analysis easily.

Readers understand **short direct sentences** better than long convoluted sentences. Compare the following.

Because the corporation was in financial difficulty, the corporate counsel suggested that the company should consider consolidating its outstanding indebtedness with a major loan before filing for reorganization under Chapter 11 of the Bankruptcy Act, and that only if these options were not feasible, should the board consider a Chapter 7 bankruptcy.

The corporate counsel had three suggestions to help the corporation with its financial difficulties. First, the company should consider a major loan to consolidate its outstanding indebtedness. Second, it should consider filing for reorganization under Chapter 11 of the Bankruptcy Act. Third, if these two options were not feasible, the company should consider a Chapter 7 bankruptcy.

By using four short, direct sentences, the writer has conveyed the same meaning, but in a way that helps the naive reader. As you write and revise your legal writing, use short direct sentences, particularly to convey the most important information.

Readers understand sentences that are written with a **subject-verb-object order** better than sentences that are written using an inverted order. Consider the following two examples:

The participants gave consideration to the promoter.
     (subject)   (verb) (direct object)   (indirect object)

Consideration   was   given to the promoter by the participants.
(direct object)   (verb)   (indirect object)   (real subject)

The first sentence is direct and easy to understand. The second sentence does not follow subject-verb-object order. Although "participants" is the functional subject of the verb, grammatically it is the object of a preposition "by". The second sentence is not as easy to understand both because of the word order and because it is written in the passive voice.

Readers also find sentences easier to understand when the subject and verb are close together. To aid the reader, eliminate **intrusive phrases.** Compare the following examples.

The district court's finding **that the mining company can continue to hold its investment interest in the land until it determines that alternative means of extracting the coal will be profitable,** is reasonable.

The district court's finding is reasonable. It held that the mining company can continue to hold its investment interest in the land until it determines that alternative means of extracting the coal is profitable.

Readers understand compound ideas best if they are presented using parallel construction. You will enhance the reader's appreciation for the comparison to or contrast from the facts of a case if you present the facts in parallel. Compare the following examples.

In *Aschenbrenner*, the court held that the employee did not sufficiently attempt to resolve the overtime problem with his employer before taking the drastic step of leaving his employment. The **union** could have filed a grievance on his behalf, **he** could have voluntarily reduced his working hours to forty per week, or **his doctor** could have reported his medical condition to the supervisor.

In *Aschenbrenner*, the court held that the employee did not sufficiently attempt to resolve the overtime problem with his employer before taking the drastic step of leaving his employment. **The employee** could have followed the union grievance procedure, **he** could have voluntarily reduced his working hours to forty per week, or **he** could have given his supervisor a medical report from his doctor.

The facts in both paragraphs are identical, but the second is easier to understand. In the first example, the subject changes from the employee to the union to the doctor. In the second example, the employee is consistently the subject.

Readers understand the **active** voice better than the passive voice. The active voice requires that the subject of the sentence and the actor be the same. In a normal passive construction, the actor is relegated to a prepositional phrase. In a truncated passive sentence, the actor falls completely out of the sentence. Compare the following three sentences written in active, passive and truncated passive voice respectively and keep your eye on the actor.

The **gourmet** tasted the veal Cordon Bleu.

The veal Cordon Bleu was tasted by the **gourmet.**

The veal Cordon Bleu was tasted.

As you can see from the examples, the active voice better communicates the point.

Writers often use the passive voice inadvertently or because they are uncertain about an assertion. If you find inadvertent passive voice in your writing, rewrite in the active voice, making the actor the subject of the sentence. Use of the passive voice is sometimes a symptom of incomplete analysis. If you used the passive voice because you were unsure of your assertion, refine your analysis, so you can write with more confidence.

While the active voice is preferable in most circumstances, there are at least five instances when the passive voice fulfills a legitimate function.

(1) The passive voice can be used creatively for de-emphasis.

> The diamond ring **was stolen** on July 23rd. (Your client is the defendant.)

(2) Passive voice is used to focus attention on the object of the sentence. This is common in scientific writing.

> The blood samples **were assayed** for steroids. (The identity of the person who assayed the samples is irrelevant.)

> The gas leak **was discovered** in front of the elementary school.

(3) Passive voice is useful when the subject is unknown.

> Sam's umbrella **was taken** from the rack while he was in class.

(4) Attorneys commonly use the passive voice when asking a judge for relief.

> For these reasons, the motion for summary judgment **should be denied**.

(5) Finally, the passive voice is often useful for social and political reasons.

> The chicken **was** somewhat **overcooked**. (Your host burned the chicken.)

> The police chief's resignation **was accepted** at noon today. (The mayor fired the police chief at noon today.)

Bureaucrats often use the passive voice in conjunction with **nominalizations,** strong verbs that have been transformed into weak nouns. Nominalizations make your prose boring and hard to read. Note that sentences with nominalizations often contain numerous prepositions and unnecessary words. Compare the following examples.

> To provide its customers with an extra measure of **satisfaction,** special **authorization** has been given by Generous George's Warehouse to its supervisory personnel to institute an **exchange** of defective merchandise within the ten days following the purchase by said customers.

> To satisfy its customers, Generous George's Warehouse authorized its managers to exchange defective merchandise within ten days of purchase.

The first version contains three nominalizations strung together with prepositions, the passive voice, and unnecessary words. The second version is half as long and makes the point directly using the active voice.

Readers also understand **positive** sentences better than negative sentences. Double and triple negatives are even more difficult for readers. Many readers will ignore sentences with more than one negative. Compare the following sentences:

Allen knew he flunked the final examination.

Allen knew he did not pass the final examination.

Allen was not unaware that he flunked the final examination.

Allen was not unaware that he did not pass the final examination.

All four of these sentences convey the same meaning. The first, the positive statement, is the clearest. Each successive negative makes the meaning more obscure.

Finally, the reader will understand your analysis better if you leave out all the unnecessary words. Consider the following:

Analysis of past precedent leads to the conclusion that the structure in question can be termed a dwelling house within the meaning of the arson statute because it is a house fit for occupancy regardless of its vacancy status at the time of the fire.

The vacant structure qualifies as a dwelling house under the arson statute, because it was fit for occupancy when the fire occurred.

The meaning in both sentences is the same, but the second sentence is easier to understand, because the writer pruned the sentence to delete the extraneous words.

Wordiness often occurs in a first draft or at the beginning of a document because the writer had difficulty getting started with the project. The following are typical examples:

It is clear that the * * *.

We must now consider * * *.

It is interesting to note that * * *.

While these throat clearing noises give the writer a chance to get his thoughts in order, they have no function in the final product.

The goal of this book is to help you to become a self critical legal writer. The techniques described in this chapter have two functions. First, they provide a structure for your legal writing. With experience, they will become a natural part of the way you approach a writing project. Second, these techniques will help you diagnose problems in your writing and revise your drafts accordingly.

These are not absolute rules that you should follow slavishly; they are suggestions for making your writing more accessible to the reader. When you are tempted to ignore them, think about the reader and choose the formulation that best explains your analysis. If, for example, you need a negative because the positive formulation does not convey the meaning you want, use it. But use the negative because you intend this meaning, not because it slipped inadvertently onto the page. Good legal writers are conscious of the way they write. They understand why every word, sentence, and paragraph is in the document. The techniques in this chapter should help you to become a self critical legal writer.

BASIC LEGAL WRITING APPROACH

1) Begin the discussion section of a legal memorandum with a **thesis paragraph** or **section.** It should contain an overall thesis statement, provide context for the memo, give the reader a road map of the issues and the conclusions on every issue and sub-issue.

2) Begin every issue with a **thesis statement.**

3) Begin each paragraph with a **topic sentence** that tells the reader the purpose of the paragraph.

4) Include **transitions** so the reader understands how the different elements of IRAC fit together.

5) Construct paragraphs so that each one deals with only one topic.

6) Arrange the information in each paragraph in a logical order.

7) Construct sentences to:

    a) Use **short direct sentences** for important information.

    b) Use a **subject-verb-object order** for clear direct sentences.

    c) Avoid **intrusive phrases**.

    d) Use **parallel construction** in compound sentences.

    e) Use **active** voice unless you intend the passive voice.

    f) Avoid **nominalizations** that make writing ponderous and boring.

    g) Explain the point **positively** and not negatively.

    h) Omit all unnecessary words.

- Write clearly, be concise
- Goal - purpose
- opponent - ARGUE - writing will be pulled apart

Chapter 11

THE WRITING PROCESS

The goal of this book is to help you become a self-critical legal writer. The chapters thus far have provided you with a method for approaching writing projects. This chapter is designed to give some insight into the writing process itself. Obviously, not all writers go through the same process; their minds and their experiences are different. Nevertheless, many successful writers in law and other disciplines describe the steps presented below.

A general view of the writing process should be helpful to you for three reasons. First, it should help you to recognize your own nascent writing process and to develop it into a successful approach. Second, understanding the writing process should help you to diagnose and correct problems in your own writing. Finally, the writing process is useful in overcoming a momentary writing block. Every serious writer encounters an occasional writing block and needs a method for dealing with the problem. If you understand your own writing process and can identify where you are when you encounter a roadblock, you can cope with it successfully. Most writing blocks occur because the writer has omitted a step in the process. To overcome a block, try going backwards a step or two in the process. Then work your way forward through each step thoroughly. As you read this chapter, get to know your own writing process and consider how you can modify it to make it work for you even more effectively.

PRE–WRITING

The writing process begins with the pre-writing stage. During pre-writing, the writer formulates the content of the writing and organizes it. In legal writing, it is useful to divide the pre-writing stage into four separate steps: 1) spotting the issues, 2) researching, 3) analyzing the problem in light of the law, and 4) organizing the analysis. These steps should be familiar to you, but it may not be obvious why these steps belong in the writing process. The reason for including them is that many problems at the actual drafting and revising stages of the process have their roots in issue formulation, research, analysis, or organization. If the writer sees all of these steps as a part of the writing process, it is easier to diagnose a pre-writing problem. As you will discover, the steps do not always follow each other systematically.

The starting point for solving a legal problem is to isolate the legal issues. While some problems have obvious issues, many others arrive in a lawyer's office as a collection of facts and a plea for relief that has yet to be defined. From his legal education and experience, a lawyer will often be able to identify the issues. Frequently, he will only have a general idea of the applicable area of the law and he will not be able to frame the issues until he has conducted some research. So, although the process can be diagrammed as:

1) Identifying the issues

2) Researching

3) Analyzing the problem

4) Organizing the analysis

very few legal writers follow these steps in order. More often the research and issue identification steps follow a circular pattern, where the research provides issues and the issues invite further research. The other pre-writing steps are also interconnected. Often, if a writer has difficulty analyzing the problem, he has not yet formulated the issues precisely or researched the problem thoroughly. If he has trouble organizing the analysis, it is usually because the analysis is not yet as clear in his mind as it should be before he begins to organize. Similarly, outlining the analysis can help him to focus on the holes in his analysis. The process actually follows a pattern more like this:REC 1416.0000

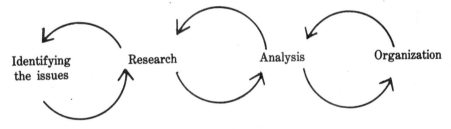

Identifying the issues   Research   Analysis   Organization

WRITING

When the pre-writing stage is complete and the writer has a satisfactory outline, she begins the writing process. Most writers recognize several steps in this process:

1) Drafting

2) Revising

3) Editing.

Like writers in other disciplines that require cogent treatment of complex analysis, legal writers often find it difficult to concentrate on more than explaining the analysis in the first draft. They are unable simultaneously to give much attention to developing paragraphs, crafting sentences, and choosing the best vocabulary. By dividing the process into several steps, they are able to give full attention to all facets of writing without forgetting anything important. It may also be more efficient to divide the process; the time spent crafting a sentence may be wasted if the sentence is later eliminated. Like pre-writing, writing is not a simple process with each step following the preceding one. In practice it often works like this:

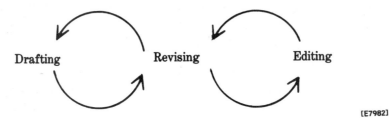

Drafting   Revising   Editing

[E7982]

During the revision phase, for example, a writer may delete a whole section of a first draft and redraft. Even as she edits, she may rethink and redraft a problematic section. The process may be even more complex as writers often return to analysis and organization while they are drafting, revising, or editing. The following scheme is designed to help you limit your focus at each step.

DRAFTING

After you are satisfied with the outline of your analysis, you are ready to begin the drafting phase. The word "drafting" is preferable to the term "writing", because it conveys a sense of beginning the process, rather than connoting the finished product. The goal for the drafting phase of a memo should be to explain the analysis using the organization in the outline.

To accomplish this, integrate the writing overlay into the outline. This means to begin the discussion with a thesis paragraph or section that identifies the parties, provides context, presents a road map of the issues and sub-issues, and gives away the conclusions. For each issue and sub-issue, follow the IRAC organization from the outline. Start each issue with a thesis statement which includes both the issue and the conclusion on that issue. As you draft each paragraph, think about the purpose of the paragraph and include that purpose in the topic sentence. Build in transitions for the naive reader, so that you do not omit any step in the analytical process.

While this may seem like a lot to consider during the drafting phase, there are two reasons for including this detail. First, the detail is easy to insert. References to the writing overlay fit neatly in the outline as reminders. Then in the actual drafting process, you need only consider one thing at a time.

More importantly, the writing overlay helps you with the drafting process. If you must articulate the context, the issues and sub-issues, and the conclusions in the thesis paragraph or section, you will be better able to articulate them throughout the body of the discussion section. If you have difficulty articulating the issues in the thesis section, you should work through the problem before proceeding further. The thesis statements will be more precise statements of the issues and your conclusions. The IRAC of each issue will flow more easily if you have drafted the thesis statement precisely. Topic sentences also are helpful in the drafting process. If you must stop at the beginning of every paragraph and articulate the purpose of the paragraph, you will be sure 1) that the paragraph has a purpose, and 2) that you have explained the purpose to the reader. Transitions are useful because they force you to explain how one point leads inexorably to the next one. If it is difficult to make the transition, you may not have included enough analytical detail for the naive reader.

If you have followed your combined outline and writing overlay one step at a time, the draft should convey the basic analysis. Drafting is hard work, but if you concentrate on explaining the substance without worrying about the shape of a particular sentence or the specific vocabulary, drafting is a manageable task.

REVISING

Revising follows drafting. It is an objective evaluation of the draft. This is probably the most difficult part of writing for several reasons. First, the chances are that you are tired, and it is difficult to look critically at anything when you are tired. Second, you may have a personal stake in every word on that page. You have struggled over the draft and it is difficult to say to yourself that the words do not adequately convey the meaning and must, therefore, be deleted. This process may seem benign in the abstract, but when you as the writer have chosen those words, it is akin to cutting out a piece of yourself. To avoid the pain involved, you may be tempted to avoid the problem by reading right over it. Third, even if you recognize a problem, you may be convinced that you have done your best at explaining the analysis and that another attempt will be futile.

You can avoid these roadblocks with a little strategy. First, you can plan for a gap in time between the drafting and revising stages. If you spend some time doing something else, you can be more objective as you read over the draft. Second, if you recognize that it is only a draft and not the finished product, you will have an easier time deleting the text that does not accomplish its purpose and rewriting that section so that it does convey the intended meaning to the reader. Third, if you recognize that during the drafting phase you were concentrating on getting the basic meaning on paper, you will realize that another attempt at a discrete section is not only possible, but is likely to be profitable.

Revising has a number of goals. Writers approach revising in two fundamentally different ways. Some writers read the entire text through a number of times, but with limited goals each time. This process is time consuming as it requires rereading the entire text repeatedly. It has the advantage that the writer is likely to remember to check for everything. It has the disadvantage that, with time, the writer may become bored with the text and not notice problems. Other writers concentrate on small segments intensively, testing the text against the various things it should accomplish. This has the advantage that the writer must cover the text through in its entirety only once. The disadvantage is that the writer may forget to measure the text against an important parameter. You will need to decide for yourself which procedure is preferable for the way you work. A combination of the two methods may also be workable.

The most important part of the revising process is to make sure that the naive reader will understand your analysis. It is worth digressing briefly to consider "understanding" in general, so that you can appreciate the naive reader's position. There are a number of different levels of understanding analysis. Understanding written analysis is the most difficult.

Consider how your understanding varies in the following situations. If you read something, and while you read it, it makes sense, you have a superficial understanding of what you have read. It is unlikely that you will be able to recall the analysis in detail days or even hours later. If someone explains the analysis to you orally and you have a chance to discuss it with her, your understanding of the analysis and your ability to recall it later will be greater. Your understanding must necessarily be even greater to explain the analysis to someone else. Part of the process in this example, however, is provided by the listener. He responds to your explanation with facial expressions that signify comprehension, perplexity, and so forth. You will modify your explanation according to his response. If the listener readily understands, you will move more quickly, skimming over unnecessary detail. If the listener is struggling to understand, you will start again with a different, more comprehensive explanation. Often, you will stop mid-sentence and alter your presentation in reaction to the listener's blank stare. Explaining analysis in writing is more difficult because you do not have the listener's reactions to aid your presentation.

In legal writing, you do not have the benefit of the reader's response to your explanation of the legal analysis. Remember that you have struggled with the analysis for some time. There are logical connections that you can make automatically because you understand the material so well. The reader does not know the material well; he will not be able to make the logical connections without your help.

To help the reader, the revision phase must consider the following:

Thesis section:

Your understanding of the analysis has become refined in the course of drafting. Revising gives you an opportunity to bring the thesis section up to the level of sophistication that your thinking now has achieved.

Identification of the parties—Have you identified the parties beginning with your client?

Context—Is there enough context so that a reader will focus his attention on that portion of the law you are addressing?

Issues—Does the reader know the issues and sub-issues you will address, their relationships, and organization?

Conclusions—Does the reader know your conclusion on each issue and sub-issue?

Is one paragraph appropriate to the material you are presenting or would it be easier for the reader to grasp the scope of the problem if you divided the thesis section into several paragraphs?

For each issue:

Thesis statement: Read each thesis statement. What does it tell the reader? Is this really the scope of the issue as you intended it, with the conclusion that you reached?

Rule: Did you provide a transition, so the reader knows you are now explaining the rule? Did you begin with the most general statement of the rule? If there is a statute, did you quote it? Would a more or less extensive quote be more useful to the reader? Would an illustration of the rule from a case help the reader? Would a spectrum of illustrations help the reader understand precisely what is and is not sufficient to meet the standard of the rule? Have you introduced each illustration with a topic sentence that tells the reader exactly what the purpose of that illustration is? Have you included all the legally relevant facts of that case? Have you omitted all the unnecessary facts? Is the rule section so complicated that it would help the reader to stop and characterize the rule succinctly before applying it?

Application of rule to facts: Did you provide a transition so the reader knows that you are now applying the rule to the facts of your case? Are all the legally relevant facts included? Are there extraneous facts that should be omitted? Does the reader understand how the legally relevant facts compare to the facts of the cases you presented in the rule section? Did you articulate the comparison for the reader with appropriate analogies and contrasts? Were you objective in your analysis, pointing out to the reader both the facts that support your conclusion and those that support the opposite conclusion?

Conclusion: Can the reader find your conclusions on each issue and sub-issue? Did you explain to the reader why you concluded as you did? Will the reader understand the conclusions with the precision you intended?

Revision is an active process. It is much more than reading over the draft to see if obvious problems leap off the page. The writer must put herself in the reader's place and see if the meaning she intended comes across to the reader. If the meaning does not come through clearly, she must diagnose the problem and revise to eliminate the difficulty.

EDITING

The final stage in the writing process is the editing step. The difference between adequate and good writing comes with editing. The writer must save enough time for thorough editing. It involves checking the paragraph and sentence structure, the punctuation, the spelling, and the citation form. But editing is only useful when the writer is satisfied that the revised draft is properly organized and that it conveys the intended meaning to the reader. The writer who begins to edit before revising her draft will waste time and not achieve her purpose. No amount of beautification can correct poor organization, fuzzy analysis, or leaps in logic. The correct citation will not make an irrelevant case pertinent. It takes time to delete all the unnecessary words, make direct sentences out of rambling ones, check the grammar, spelling, and citations.

Editing, too, requires a systematic approach, so the writer does not omit anything. The system works either as a series of passes, each with one particular goal in mind, or as comprehensive editing, where the writer corrects for many things in one pass through the material, or a combination approach. Consider the following during the editing process.

Paragraphs: Any paragraph that goes on for ¾ page or more may be too long. Remember that the reader will pay most attention to the material at the beginning and at the end of the paragraph. If the paragraph is too long, the reader may miss important information. If you have paragraphs longer than this, take a careful look at them to make sure you need a paragraph of that length.

Sentences: Are your sentences reader friendly? Remember to put the most important points in your analysis in short direct sentences. Vary the length of sentences to make your writing interesting.

Vocabulary: Have you chosen the words that best convey your meaning to your intended audience? Remember that different vocabulary may be necessary in addressing lay readers and lawyers. English is a wonderfully rich language; take advantage of it.

Punctuation: Check all the punctuation to make sure you have used commas, semi-colons, colons, and apostrophes properly.

Spelling: Check all possible spelling errors with a dictionary or spelling software.

Citations: Check all citations to make sure they include all the necessary information in the proper form. Be sure to include the prior or subsequent history of a case as necessary.

Finally, check for typographical errors in the finished product. A memorandum that is filled with typos gives the reader the impression that the writer's analysis is as sloppy as his proofreading. After spending hours on the analysis, take the time to present your analysis with the care you spent on the thinking.

THE ROLE OF THE WORD PROCESSING SYSTEM IN THE WRITING PROCESS

Word processing systems are useful in the writing process, but the writer should be aware of their limitations. A word processing system permits a writer to revise a draft, move paragraphs and sentences, delete extraneous words, and so forth. The time and tedium of retyping each draft of a memorandum is substantially reduced. The new errors that are possible in a retyped draft will not appear in a revised text produced on a word processing system. These are all advantages of using a word processor.

There are some limitations as well. Word processors do not do more for the substance of legal writing than a pen or pencil. The final product is as good as the analytical ability and the effort put forth by the writer. For a writer who can draft at the keyboard, it is an efficient system. For the writer who must begin with a pen or pencil, the system is not as efficient. Although drafting and editing work well at the keyboard, revising is not as successful. The writer needs to see more than the content of one screen in order to appreciate the logical flow of the document. A double or even triple-spaced draft with wide margins is a good format for revising. For writers who are just entering the computer world, there is also a danger that the printed draft will look like a finished product and the writer will be reluctant to make any changes.

Finally, word processors permit the writer to correct spelling and typographical errors with ease. This is not, however, a substitute for careful proofreading. Spelling software does not catch every mistake. It will not find a missing word or line, or an unintended word. Careful proofreading is still essential.

INFORMATION AND CHECKLIST FOR MEMO WRITING

A memo should include a heading, questions presented, a statement of facts, a discussion, and a conclusion.

The following checklist contains the basic elements of an office memorandum. **It is by no means exhaustive.** It is designed to help you remember what should be included in a memo and to avoid common problems. As with any writing project, you must think about what you are doing at every step, what your purpose is, whether your approach fulfills that purpose, and whether you have explained your-self clearly to the naive reader.

Heading

The heading is normally single-spaced. Be sure to make the "Re:" section helpful. Include the client's name and the legal topics addressed in the memo.

Questions Presented

Draft a separate question for **each** major issue and sub-issue, but do not include questions for minor points and givens.

Note: when you have sub-issues, you may state the "issue" question in general form and make the questions for the sub-issues fact specific.

> E.g.   I. Issue Question (general)
> > a. Sub-issue (fact specific)
> > b. Sub-issue (fact specific)

Use the basic formula: "Does the legal rule apply to the facts?"

Include the relevant legal rule.

Include the legally significant facts.

Keep the question objective and readable. Avoid becoming emotional and suggesting a particular answer.

Put a ? at the end of each question.

Statement of Facts

Include your purpose.

Identify the parties with your client first.

Provide context.

Make sure you have included all the legally relevant facts. Cross check against your analysis and your questions presented.

Provide background facts as necessary for the naive reader.

Present the facts objectively.

Organize logically. Chronological organization often works the best.

Include the procedural posture, if relevant. Put it at the beginning if the procedure is important to the issues discussed in the memo. Put it at the end if the procedure is not important for understanding the issues.

Discussion

Thesis paragraph or section:

Provide your overall thesis for the memo.

State the purpose of the memo.

Identify the parties.

Provide context for the naive reader.

Describe the issue(s) to be discussed in the order in which you will discuss them. Identify relevant statute(s), but not usually cases.

Give your conclusions and very briefly the reasons for them.

Begin each section of the discussion with the appropriate question presented. The questions presented are usually single spaced in the body of the discussion section.

Use **"IRAC"** to check all paragraphs and your overall organization.

Separate the discussion of each legal issue.

Identify each paragraph in the draft of your memo as:

Th—Thesis paragraph.
I—Issue identification.
R—Rule paragraph.
A—Application or analysis paragraph where you apply the rule to the facts of your case.
C—Conclusion paragraph.

Note that some paragraphs may have more than one of these. Eliminate any paragraph that is none of the above.

Be sure that everything you identify as an "issue" asks and answers a relevant legal question.

Make sure each issue is organized around a legal **rule,** and not a set of facts.

Begin the rule section with the most general statement of the rule. Then illustrate how the rule has been applied with the fact specific holding of a case. If you are using a spectrum of cases, begin with the case that supports your conclusion.

Remember you can use cases for their reasoning and policy, too.

Be sure that you have explained the law in a way that is helpful in resolving the issue. Make sure that you include enough about the case (facts, procedure, holding, policy, reasoning) so the reader will understand your analysis. Leave out all aspects of the case that are not relevant to the issue you are discussing.

Use descriptive facts, not conclusions, when **applying the law to the facts of your case.** Compare the facts of your case to those cited in the rule section. Explain why the analogies and distinctions are significant.

Be sure to **conclude** each issue and sub-issue before moving on to the next one.

Make sure that you have included all the steps in the analysis with appropriate transitions for the naive reader. Include **citations** where appropriate. When quoting or using a case for a proposition given on a particular page of that case, include the **citation** to the **particular page.**

Conclusion

Do not hedge.

Address all the issues and briefly resolve them.

Connect your conclusion to the purpose stated in the thesis paragraph.

Writing

Identify all paragraphs that are more than ¾ of a page long. Try to rewrite to be more concise or break into two paragraphs. Note: The thesis paragraph may be a little longer.

Make sure that each paragraph begins with a topic sentence.

Include transitions.

Identify all sentences that are more than four lines long. Consider rewriting to make the point easily for the reader.

Style

Keep the subject and verb close together.

Use articles where appropriate.

Be direct and concise. Avoid preposition strings.

Use the active voice unless you intend the passive voice.

Rewrite sentences to avoid nominalizations.

Check for parallel construction.

Eliminate all words not necessary to communicate your meaning. Check for unnecessary or repetitive modifiers, "throat clearing" words and phrases, and other "empty" words.

Grammar

Check for sentence fragments.

Make sure each sentence has a subject, a verb, and where appropriate, an object.

Avoid "run on" sentences. In general, express one idea per sentence, except where two ideas are causally connected.

Make sure your verb tenses are consistent. Remember to use the past when discussing the court's holding in a case.

Check all modifiers to make sure it is clear what they modify and that there is agreement.

Check your punctuation.

> Commas.

> Semicolons.

> Colons.

> Quotation marks.

> Apostrophes.

Read forward and backward to check for spelling mistakes, typos, etc.

Check the cite form.

Note: if you are using a word processing system, do not justify the right margin or you may change the spacing in your citations.

*

Section IV

THE MORE COMPLICATED
MEMORANDUM

The process of writing more complex memoranda is similar to that used for a simpler memo. The writer will divide the problem into its smallest possible issue components, research each, apply the rules to the facts of the problem, and reach a conclusion. In writing the memo, he will figure out the organization of issues that best communicates the analysis to the naive reader. He will draft a thesis section to introduce the analysis. Then he will IRAC each issue and sub-issue, being careful to begin each issue with a thesis statement and each paragraph with a topic sentence. He will build in transitions where necessary to help the naive reader understand how the pieces of the analysis fit together. He will be careful to conclude each issue or sub-issue before moving on to the next one. The writer will begin by drafting his memo, then he will revise it and finally, he will edit it. All of this process is the same for a complicated office memorandum.

There are, however, two things that may make writing a complicated memo more difficult: having to research the issues as well as analyze, organize, and write about them, and organizing the material once you have found and considered all the relevant law. The three chapters in this section are designed to help you integrate research into the analytical process, organize more complicated issues, and write in plain English.

Chapter 12

INTEGRATING RESEARCH INTO
THE ANALYTICAL PROCESS

Before you can analyze a legal problem, you must find the relevant law. Experienced attorneys who are researching the law in their area of expertise can proceed directly to the appropriate statutes and digests in order to find the primary law. When researching the law outside of your area of expertise, the following steps are useful in getting started and in keeping the research focused.

ISOLATING THE GENERAL AREAS OF THE LAW

The first step is to identify the issues in the problem. When you are familiar with the area of the law or if the problem comes with a proper issue label, you can launch right into research of the primary materials. A hazardous waste problem, for example, is likely to be covered by federal law and also a state statute. For the problem that does not come with the issues labeled, however, the first step is to learn enough about the area of the law to identify the issues. Begin with the facts in the problem. Find the broad areas of the law that might cover the problem. Consider the following illustration:

> In the fall of 1983, Ralph and Rachel Reynolds consulted us about a real estate problem. Just before Labor Day, they purchased an A-frame chalet on 5 wooded acres near Mendocino, California. They believed there was a defect in the construction of the chimney.

> On the weekend of the 24–25th of September, they lit a small fire and were surprised when the room filled with smoke. The damper was open and there was no obvious explanation for the problem. The following week, they consulted a construction engineer. In her opinion, the chimney did not draw properly because it was too short. Later, she consulted the blueprints and reported to the Reynolds that the prints called for a chimney considerably taller than the one constructed on the site. She estimated that it

would cost about $5000 to rebuild the upper part of the chimney to increase its support capability and add the needed height.

The house was built by Pacific Chalet Construction Company and completed in June of 1980. The advertizing brochure for this model also pictured a chimney considerably taller than the one constructed. The first owners, the Bahrs, purchased the chalet in July of that year. They used the chalet only until mid-September, when Mr. Bahr died. His widow put the house on the market in August 1983.

The Reynolds saw her ad in the San Francisco Chronicle and bought the house three weeks later. The ad included the following language:

> "For sale: A–frame chalet with natural stone fireplace. The five acre wooded lot will provide firewood forever * * *."

Mrs. Bahr had described to the Reynolds the beautiful natural fireplace and the natural wood lot that surrounded the chalet. She did not, however, mention any problem with the fireplace. Mrs. Reynolds believed, however, that the fireplace had been used at least once, as there were ashes and a partially charred log in the fireplace when they moved in.

The Reynolds were furious both with Pacific Chalet Construction Company for not following its own blueprints and with Mrs. Bahr for leading them on with talk of the natural stone fireplace and the unlimited firewood supply. They wanted one or both to pay the $5000 to fix the chimney.

From these facts you know that the Reynolds had a chimney that did not work because it was too short. The construction company did not follow its own blueprints. Research into chimneys and blueprints is unlikely to yield much information. The general category of defective products may be helpful.

A good place to begin is with the secondary materials. The encyclopedias: Corpus Juris Secundum (C.J.S.), American Jurisprudence Second (Am. Jur. 2d), and American Law Reports (A.L.R.), will provide basic information about defective products and the legal theories and causes of action that are involved in defective product litigation. C.J.S. and Am. Jur. 2d are the more comprehensive encyclopedias; that is, they contain some information about most legal topics. A.L.R. and its progeny give more detailed information, but they only cover selected topics. Established areas of the law are likely to be covered in A.L.R., A.L.R.2d, and A.L.R.3d. Recent developments and new areas of the law will most likely appear in the 4th or the 5th series. Federal issues are covered in A.L.R. Fed. Remember that the various series of A.L.R. are updated in three different ways. Be sure to use the appropriate method. There are also state encyclopedias. Hornbooks, treatises, and law review articles may also be helpful in finding basic information about defective products.[1] There are two basic sources for legal periodicals: the Index to Legal Periodicals and the Legal Resources Index/LEGAL TRAC. As the Legal Resources Index/LEGAL TRAC only covers periodicals issued since January 1, 1980, you will need to use the Index to Legal Periodicals to find earlier law review articles. The purpose at this stage in the process is to identify the legal issues in the problem.

Before you get into the research process, it is critical to have a system for recording every step in your research. There is too much to remember, and you do not want to forget what you have already consulted and be forced to retrace your steps. Although every lawyer develops his own method of research, the following system may be helpful as a starting point. Treat each general topic separately. If it leads you to more than one topic, follow up the leads separately. Record the series of books you consulted, the volume, even the particular index where you looked. Then record all the words or topics you tried. If a topic turns out to be irrelevant, make a note of this fact before you try another topic. As you check the appropriate pocket parts, paper supplements, and later case services, be sure to make a note of that fact. Two days, two hours, or even twenty minutes later, you may not remember if you looked in the pocket part to the general index volume or consulted the pocket part to the substantive volume to see if the title index had been updated. If your notes are thorough, you can be confident of exactly where you looked and what you found. If your notes are not thorough, you will waste a lot of time retracing your steps.

If you were to research the chimney problem in the secondary materials, you would find that there are at least four possible theories you could use against the construction company: breach of express warranty, breach of implied warranty, negligence, and strict product liability. The first two are contract claims while the latter two are tort claims. This gives you four potential issues regarding Pacific Chalet Construction Company. Until you have researched each of these in detail, however, you are not ready to decide which, if any, of these potential causes of action apply. You are now ready to move to the primary resources to investigate these possibilities.

The second broad area to investigate in the chimney problem is the possible involvement of Mrs. Bahr. From the partially charred log the Reynolds found in the fireplace, it is likely that Mrs. Bahr knew that the fireplace did not function properly. Nonetheless, she advertised the property using the natural stone fireplace and the wooded acres as the major attraction. The advertisement and her verbal statements **misled** the Reynolds into thinking that the fireplace worked, when it did not. If the advertisement was misleading, perhaps there was **fraud** or **deceit** involved in the transaction. These are other potential issues in the problem that may lead to a second potential defendant.

---

1. Restatements may also be useful secondary sources for older topics.

The third general area to pursue is not as obvious. If you look carefully at the timing in the facts, you will notice that the chalet was completed in June 1980, the Bahrs bought the chalet in July 1980 and used it every weekend until mid-September 1980. The Reynolds bought the chalet just before Labor Day 1983 and tried the fireplace for the first time about three weeks later. The history of the chalet covers just over three years. Depending on when the different causes of action arose, there may be a statute of limitations problem.

From the secondary resources, you now have a general idea of the potential issues and the vocabulary necessary to research the defective chimney problem in the primary resources.

FINDING THE RULES

The next step is to find the rules that control each potential issue. Expand the research to find the legislative and common law in the primary resources. The annotated statutes and digests will give you the statutes and cases for the specific jurisdiction. The illustrative problem is a California case, so the research should begin with the California Annotated Statutes. Although you will not find a statute for every issue you research, you will find statutes that cover a surprising number of issues. As there are hundreds of different statutory provisions in every jurisdiction, always begin by looking for a relevant statute.

As with research into secondary materials, you need thorough notes on every source you consult, including the appropriate updating system. When you find a general rule that governs your case, either record the rule or make a xerox copy of the rule. Note on the xerox copy the source of the rule, whether it came from the main volume or the pocket part, and the year of the volume and/or pocket part. Remember that the year of the statutory volume you consulted is necessary for the citation. If you do not record it initially, you will have to go back to the books to find it again later.

Be sure to check all the parts of the statute. The index may lead you immediately to the operative section, that section that tells you what is required, prohibited, or permissible behavior. The statute may also, however, include other sections that help make the statute applicable or that eliminate its use. These sections may include definitions, the required civil or criminal procedure, administrative agency control, defenses, the kinds of relief available, and financing provisions. Until you have looked at the statute as a whole, you will not know if the statute applies to your problem.

The California statutes dealing with deceit, for example, include the following:

Sec. 1709. Deceit; damages.

FRAUDULENT DECEIT. One who willfully deceives another with intent to induce him to alter his position to his injury or risk, is liable for any damage which he thereby suffers.[1]

Sec. 1710. Deceit defined.

DECEIT, WHAT.   A deceit, within the meaning of the last section, is either:

1.   The suggestion, as a fact, of that which is not true, by one who does not believe it to be true;

2.   The assertion, as a fact, of that which is not true, by one who has no reasonable ground for believing it to be true;

3.   The suppression of a fact, by one who is bound to disclose it, or who gives information of other facts which are likely to mislead for want of communication of that fact; or,

4.   A promise, made without any intention of performing it.[2]

Section 1709 creates the cause of action and remedy for the victim of deceit and section 1710 defines deceit.   Note that both sections are necessary for the cause of action.   Under section 1709 the victim must show: first, that the deceiver willfully deceived him; second, that the deceiver intended to induce him to alter his position to his injury or risk; and third, that one of the sections of 1710 applies.   In the chimney hypothetical, subsections 1, 2, and 3 are potentially applicable. You are now able tentatively to identify deceit as an issue.   It has three sub-issues, the three elements, and there are three potential sub-issues of the third element.   It is helpful at this stage to stop and articulate the issue and its sub-issues.   While you may eliminate one or more of these later, or perhaps add an additional sub-issue, the tentative list will help you to focus on the purpose of your research at the next step.

The California statutes also include a fraud provision [3] that might be helpful in the chimney hypothetical.   Fraud is similar to deceit in its definition, but it applies in the context of a contract.   As the sale of the chalet by Mrs. Bahr to the Reynolds involved a real estate sales contract, fraud may be even more appropriate than deceit.

In researching the hypothetical problem, one would also investigate the possible causes of action against the construction company and the statutes of limitations for each.   While some of these may be covered by statutes, others may only be governed by common law.   Even when there is an applicable statute, you also need to consult the case law. Digests provide access to the cases.   Remember that the words that are fruitful in one series of books may not be useful in another series of materials.   Explore all possible avenues in the digests.   Remember to check the pocket parts of both the index and subject matter volumes. If the digest has a looseleaf volume or paper supplements for recent developments, check these as well.   The closing table of each part of the series will help you make sure that your research is as current as the

---

1. Cal. Civ. Code sec. 1709 (West 1985).   3.   Cal. Civ. Code sec. 1572 (West 1982).
2. Cal. Civ. Code sec. 1710 (West 1985).

series allows. Your purpose in researching in the digests is to find common law rules that govern your problem.

As with the statutory materials, be sure to keep careful notes of all of your sources, indexes, and updating materials. As with the statutory search, your goal at this point is to find the general rules that control the problem, so that you can identify the issues. Either record or xerox the rules. Be sure to note the citation for each case and all parallel citations, if they are included. Remember that you must include parallel citations for many cases and triple citations for some levels of court in some jurisdictions.

Although the researcher should now have a tentative list of the issues and sub-issues involved in the chimney hypothetical, he is not yet ready to analyze the problem because the rules appear only in outline form and they need to be further defined.

EXPANDING THE SEARCH

The third step in the process is to understand the rules and the way they have been applied to the facts in the cases. Not all sub-issues will require this depth of investigation. The Reynolds, for example, entered into a real estate contract with Mrs. Bahr; this is a given. The meaning of the third option under the deceit statute:

> 3. The suppression of a fact, by one who is bound to disclose it, or who gives information of other facts which are likely to mislead for want of communication of that fact;

however, is not obvious. Who is bound to disclose facts? What facts is that person bound to disclose? What other facts are likely to be misleading? The researcher needs to find cases that answer these questions and that provide facts he can use to analyze the problem.

As the research expands, there is a danger that the specific questions you are asking will get lost in the ever increasing stack of notes and xerox copies. For this reason, you should investigate each question separately and label your notes and copies appropriately. Because one case may be useful for more than one purpose, develop a cross-referencing system, so that you can find the case readily without having to go through all your notes and copies.

The search for the illustrative cases begins in the annotations to the statutes and in the digests. The better you can articulate the issue, the easier the search for illustrative cases will be. If there is an applicable statute, look at the annotations that follow the relevant sections. When there are many cases, they are usually arranged under the statute according to issue. Within each issue, the cases may be arranged chronologically and by level of court with the cases from the highest court preceding the cases from lower courts. Select the cases that seem from the brief descriptions to explain the statute as it applies to your problem.

Check the pocket part or paper supplements to the statute volume for later cases. The pocket parts and paper supplements are not issued very frequently—once a year in most instances. To make your search for new cases as current as possible, use the following two methods. Check the statute series for instructions on how to find and use current materials. These will often be in a looseleaf binder. The pages in the binder will be issued more frequently than the pocket parts. Check the current materials for more recent cases.

The second method for finding more recent cases that illustrate and define a statute is to use Shepard's Citations. Remember that Shepard's has more than one purpose. It gives you the history of the statute, so you can see if it has been amended or repealed. Shepard's also gives you citations to cases that have treated the statute. This is the use that is paramount at this stage in the process. You should have checked the statute to make sure it is still in effect before looking for cases.

Searching for illustrative cases in the digests involves a similar process. As your research skills develop, you will find that you can combine the process of looking for general common law rules and illustrative cases. At the beginning, keep the two steps separate so that you do not lose sight of the different purposes that cases have. From your search for the appropriate rule, you should know the topic. Find the topic index in the substantive volume. Look for the West key number or section number that seems to cover your issue. You may have to read the digests of selected cases under several section numbers before you find the appropriate key or section number. Often there will be several relevant key or section numbers. The cases are often arranged chronologically and by level of court.

Update to find later cases. There are three methods for updating. First, check the pocket part or supplementary volume. As with statutes, the pocket parts are issued relatively infrequently. Second, look at the closing table in the most recent pocket part or paper supplement for that substantive volume of the digest. Note the most recent volume of the reporter series included in the pocket part. Remember that many jurisdictions have two levels of appellate courts and different reporter series for the two levels of court. Note the most recent volumes of both series. Then go to the reporter series and check the digest in each later volume and advance sheet. Use the appropriate West key number or topic and section number.

The third method of updating your search for illustrative cases is to shepardize the relevant illustrative cases. Because some cases deal with more than one issue and not all of the issues are relevant to the issue you are investigating, make a note of the appropriate headnote numbers and shepardize looking for the superscripts that refer to these headnotes. When using this method, be sure to shepardize in the same reporter series. A headnote number from the regional reporter will only correspond to a headnote number in the state reporter system by accident. If you shepardize in one reporter system using the headnote numbers from the other reporter system, the cases in most instances will be useless.

Your goal here is to find all potentially valuable cases. The annotations and digests are helpful in the process, but it is only when you have actually read the cases that you can determine which cases are important. The search should continue until you have considered all the issues and sub-issues in your jurisdiction.

You should expand the search to other jurisdictions only if there is not enough law in your jurisdiction. There are a number of ways of expanding the search and the way you choose depends on the issue involved. If there is an appropriate West key number, the Decennials and later General Digests may be helpful. The encyclopedias are also useful sources of other jurisdictions with relevant case law. If A.L.R. has an article on the issue, the jurisdictions included may be useful ones to consult. Law review articles are also a potential source of cases from other jurisdictions. Federal courts sometimes consider state law and vice versa; do not ignore cites to federal or state cases that you find while researching in the materials from the other system. Remember that under the doctrine of *stare decisis*, precedent from sister jurisdictions is not binding on the courts in your jurisdiction. Precedent from other jurisdictions is particularly helpful, however, when you are researching a new issue.

Once you have found the cases that define and illustrate the rules, you will need to choose the cases necessary for analyzing the problem.

CHOICE OF AUTHORITY

At this point, you have a stack of notes, statutes, and cases. If you have labeled every copy with its purpose from the beginning of your research, the choice of authority will be relatively easy. Begin by sorting the authority by issue and sub-issue. If the case is useful for more than one issue, make the appropriate cross references in your notes, so that you can find the case easily.

Then proceed one issue or sub-issue at a time. Read all the authority carefully so that you understand exactly what the statutes cover and what the cases provide in the way of rules and fact specific holdings. You may need to revise the way you have defined the issues in the problem as a result of this process.

Next choose the cases that will help you analyze the problem. Remember that you can use cases for different purposes: to state the general rule, to illustrate how the rule has been applied, to provide a spectrum of facts that are either sufficient or insufficient to satisfy the rule. Make a note of the precise purpose for each case.

When there are many cases in your jurisdiction, a memo that included them all would not be helpful to the reader. Select the best authority from the possibilities. The basic criteria for selecting cases are the quality of the opinion, the level of court, the date of the decision, and the proximity of the facts to the facts in the problem. Obviously an opinion that is well written will be much easier for you to understand and explain to the reader. The choice depends in part on the purpose of the case. If you need the case to provide the general rule, choose the case that best states the rule. This will frequently be a case cited in other decisions. If it is a decision from an intermediate level appellate court that has been adopted by the highest level court in the jurisdiction, you may also want to use the later case to show that it has the blessing of the highest court. If the key opinion is an old one but the case has been cited as still good law in a recent case, you may want to include the recent case. The decision requires your reasoned judgment about what the reader will want to know.

When the purpose is to illustrate the application of the rule to the facts or to illustrate a spectrum of opinion, choose the cases according to their facts. The closer the facts are to the facts in the problem, the easier it will be for you to analyze the problem and to be confident of your conclusion.

UPDATING ALL THE AUTHORITY

The final step in the process before you begin to analyze the problem is to update all the authority you are going to use to make sure it is still good law. Shepardize all the cases. Be sure to record all the subsequent history for each case and all the prior history that is necessary for the citation. Remember to record the parallel cites to cases when it is necessary to include a parallel or even a third cite. Note the date when you shepardized each case and the date of the latest volume, paper supplement, or advance sheet of Shepard's you consulted. Should you need to update the same case at a later date, you can begin at this point in the process without re-shepardizing using the same books. This will only be possible, however, if you know when you shepardized and which books you consulted. Just before typing the memo, check Shepard's to see if there is a new advance sheet. If there is, it will not take long to update your authority in this advance sheet.

You are now ready to analyze the problem in earnest. As mentioned in Chapter 11 on the Writing Process, analysis and organization are interconnected. Analysis and research are also interconnected. It is common for a lawyer to realize in the process of analysis that there is another potential issue or sub-issue that he needs to research. A lawyer may also alter the way he formulates the issues as he begins to analyze the problem. If the issue is not what he researched, he may need to return to the library.

As you begin the analysis of the problem it is useful to brief all the authority you intend to use. You will not need to include all the elements of a case brief listed in Chapter 4; you will not be using the case for all these purposes. The function of this case brief is to articulate the rule(s), holding(s), reasoning, or policy that you intend to use. The analytical process will be much more difficult if you approach it with just a vague idea of the case. The analysis will be easier and the writing more precise if you have already formulated the rule, holding, reasoning, or policy in a case brief.

RESEARCH SUMMARY

1. Identify the general areas of the law involved in the problem.

2. Find the general rules that apply. Begin with the secondary materials if you are not able to identify the issues right away. Formulate the issues in a tentative way.

3. Expand the search into the primary sources. Always begin by looking to see if there is an applicable statute. Then expand the search into the common law. Begin in your jurisdiction and, later if necessary, expand the search to other jurisdictions.

4. Choose the authority that is necessary for analyzing the problem. Sort by issues and sub-issues. Assign a purpose to each piece of authority you choose: general rule, illustrative case, spectrum of opinion, reasoning, or policy.

5. Update absolutely everything. Be sure to note the information you will need for the citation including for cases: parallel cites, prior and subsequent history, and for statutes: the date of the volume or supplement where you found the exact language. Note the date you shepardized.

6. Brief the cases so that you have already formulated the rules, illustrative holdings, reasoning or policy that you intend to use from that case.

Chapter 13

STRATEGIES FOR ORGANIZING MORE COMPLEX ANALYSIS

Organizing more complicated legal analysis involves the same general principles you have used before. The purpose is to make your analysis accessible to the reader. The gross organization of issues and sub-issues requires the same considerations of order of importance, logical order, order of most complete relief, and substantive/procedural order. IRAC is still a useful tool for organizing the material within issues and sub-issues, but the emphasis may be quite different from that in straightforward issues; the bulk of your analysis may occur within the rule section. While there is no ideal organization for any given problem, there are some common strategies. As you consider your options, remember to keep the reader in mind as you organize.

ORGANIZING THE RULE SECTION

Probably the most difficult challenge is to organize a complex rule section. The reason for this is that legal authority can be useful for a variety of purposes. Legal writers use authority to state the general rule, to choose a rule among two or more choices, to illustrate how a rule is applied, to illustrate facts that are sufficient and insufficient to meet the legal standard, for reasoning, and for policy. As you organize the rule section, be sure that you understand the purpose for using each authority.

If your purpose is to explain a general rule that comes from more than one source, organize from the most **general** to the most **specific**. Constitutions, statutes, regulations, and cases are all sources of general rules. Consider, for example, a water pollution problem. The state constitution makes environmental protection a high priority for the state. There is a state clean water statute and a series of regulations that implement the statute. The reader will best understand this clean water rule section if the authority is arranged from the constitutional provision to the statutory provision to the regulations. The constitutional provision puts the statute in context. The regulations only make sense in the light of the statute.

General rules can also be composed of different parts of a statute. Where, for example, there is a definition section that is separate from the operative section, the section that explains what is required, permitted or prohibited, the reader may need both the definitions and the operative provision to understand the general rule. The operative section is the more general statement of the rule. The definitions explain the specific terms.

Assume for a moment that you are a **reader** and that your client, a bank, has just been sued by the United States for "response costs" under CERCLA, the "Superfund" statute, 42 U.S.C. § 9601 et seq. The first thing that you will want to know about is the operative section of the statute, 42 U.S.C. § 9607, which provides in relevant part:

> (a) Notwithstanding any other provision or rule of law, and subject only to the defenses set forth in subsection (b) of this section—
>
>> (1) the owner and operator of a vessel or facility,
>>
>> * * *
>
> shall be liable for—
>
>> (A) all costs of removal or remedial action incurred by the United States Government * * *.

The United States is claiming that your client is liable as an owner of a hazardous waste facility. The next thing that you as a reader would like to know is the definition of a "facility", which appears in § 9601(9):

> The term facility means (A) any building, structure, installation, equipment, pipe or pipeline (including any pipe into a sewer or publically owned treatment works), well, pit, pond, lagoon, impoundment, ditch, landfill, storage container, motor vehicle, rolling stock, or aircraft, or (B) any site or area where a hazardous substance has been deposited, stored, disposed of, or placed, or otherwise come to be located; but does not include any consumer product in consumer use or any vessel.

and the definition of an "owner" which appears in § 9601(20)(A):

> The term "owner or operator" means * * * (ii) in the case of an onshore facility * * *, any person owning or operating such facility * * *. Such term does not include a person, who, without participating in the management of a * * * facility, holds indicia of ownership primarily to protect his security interest in the * * * facility.

As a reader, you are curious about both definitions at once. As a writer, you will arrange the definitions according to what the reader needs to know. The definition of a "facility" is so broad that it almost certainly applies to the piece of land the bank acquired in a mortgage foreclosure. The writer can satisfy the reader's curiosity quickly on this score.

The definition of "owner", however, is more problematic. There are two obvious questions that you, as the reader, have. First, why does the operative section read "the owner and operator", while the definition section reads "owner or operator"?[1]   Second, what is the meaning of the exclusion for "a person, who, * * * holds indicia of ownership primarily to protect his security interest in the * * * facility"?   In order to understand the operative section of the statute, the reader needs the answers to these questions.   This is still the general rule section of the analysis; the terms must be defined before you can apply them to the bank.   As a writer, you will need to answer these questions one at a time and in the order that best aids the reader.   The case law provides the necessary further definition.

While this may seem like a complicated explication of the statute, the organizational principal involved is the same one, most general to most specific, you used to organize Susan Saxon's eligibility for unemployment benefits in Exercise 7B.   There, the operative language provided that an employee is eligible for unemployment benefits only if he has "good cause" to voluntarily leave the ranks of the employed.   Or. Rev. Stat. sec. 657.176(2)(c) (1981).   The reader does not understand what "good cause" means without further definition.   *Stevenson v. Morgan,* 17 Or. App. 428, 522 P.2d 1204 (1974), provides that good cause requires both 1) grounds that would compel a reasonable person of normal sensitivities to quit under similar circumstances and 2) that the employee try to resolve the problem with the employer or that he can show that further efforts would be unavailing before taking the drastic step of leaving the job.

Frequently, the writer is faced with two or more interpretations of a rule that governs the situation.   When issues first arise, it is common for courts to interpret the same language differently.   The owner exclusion issue presented above illustrates the problem.   The first two federal district courts to interpret the language "a person, who, * * * holds indicia of ownership primarily to protect his security interest in the * * * facility", reached opposite results.   The court in *United States v. Mirabile,* 15 Envtl. L. Rep. (Envtl. L. Inst.) 20992 (E.D. Pa. Sept. 6, 1985), held that a bank that foreclosed on and took equitable title to a hazardous waste site did so primarily to protect a security interest. The bank, therefore, did not qualify as an "owner" under CERCLA. The court gave its interpretation of congressional intent in the following:

> Obviously, imposition of liability on secured creditors or lending institutions would enhance the government's chances of recovering its cleanup costs, given the fact that owners and operators of hazardous waste dumpsites are often elusive, defunct, or otherwise judgment proof.   It may well be that the imposition of such liability would help to ensure more responsible management of

---

1. The court in *State of New York v. Shore Realty Corp.,* 759 F.2d 1032 (2d Cir. 1985), held an owner who was not an operator liable for response costs under 42 U.S.C. § 9607(a)(1).   The court in *United* *States v. Maryland Bank & Trust Co.,* 632 F.Supp. 573 (D. Md. 1986), agreed after considering that the statute was "hastily patched together".

such sites. The consideration of such policy matters, and the decision as to the imposition of such liability, however, lies with Congress. In enacting CERCLA Congress singled out secured creditors for protection from liability under certain circumstances. Because I believe ABT has brought itself within that protection, ABT is entitled to the entry of summary judgment in its favor.

A year later, the court in *United States v. Maryland Bank & Trust Co.*, 632 F. Supp. 573 (D. Md. 1986), held that the exclusion did not apply to a bank in similar circumstances. The court looked at the legislative history of the statutory section, H. Rep. # 96–172, pt. I, 36 (1979), to determine the congressional intent. The court noted:

> This report indicates that Congress intended to protect banks that hold mortgages in jurisdictions governed by the common law of mortgages [2], and not all mortgagees who later acquire title.

The court also used public policy in support of its interpretation:

> The interpretation of section 101(20)(A) urged upon the Court by MB & T runs counter to the policies underlying CERCLA. Under the scenario put forward by the bank, the federal government alone would shoulder the cost of cleaning up the site, while the former mortgagee-turned-owner, would benefit from the clean-up by the increased value of the now unpolluted land. At the foreclosure sale, the mortgagee could acquire the property cheaply. All other prospective purchasers would be faced with potential CERCLA liability, and would shy away from the sale. Yet once the property has been cleared at taxpayers' expense and becomes marketable, the mortgagee-turned-owner would be in a position to sell the site at a profit.

The first interpretation favors your client, but the second interpretation has better reasoning. In an office memorandum, you should discuss both, first explaining the *Maryland Bank & Trust* decision and why it is the better reasoned interpretation and then explaining the *Mirabile* view and why you would reject it. Only at this point, would you proceed to the application of the rule to the facts of your case.

There is an alternative organization that is also effective when you are faced with explaining two opposing interpretations or two possibly applicable rules. If one rule most certainly applies and the other is most probably inapplicable but still worth mentioning, the reader will want to know about the rule that applies first and only by way of an addendum that there is another rule that is probably not relevant. The alternative organization would look like this:

---

2. In common law mortgage jurisdictions, the bank holds title to the property to protect its security interest until the mortgage is discharged. In other jurisdictions, the bank holds only the security interest in the property and the owner holds the title. The exception noted in the definition of "owner or operator" was intended to put banks in both types of jurisdictions on an equal footing for purposes of CERCLA liability.

Issue

Rule—applicable rule and explanation as to why it applies.

Application

Conclusion

Rule—inapplicable rule and explanation as to why it is does not apply.

If the rules are equally likely and the conclusion is the same when you analyze them, the order you choose for the rules depends on which will be most helpful to the reader. If the rules are equally likely, but the result is different, the reader will prefer to find out about the rule that supports the client first and the rule that reaches the opposite result second. Remember to conclude the issue by stating the probable result under the pertinent rule.

Because of the nature of the common law system, where each case builds on the law that existed previously, writers often need to explain the evolution of the law in order to assess the possibility that the court will expand the law the next step and accommodate the client's problem. Usually the chronological order of the cases best illustrates to the reader how the law has developed. The following string of cases would be useful to counsel representing both the employer and employee to show how the law has developed in sexual harassment cases under Title VII of the Civil Rights Act of 1964. Title VII prohibits sex discrimination in the terms and conditions of employment. The plaintiff wants to allege that sexual harassment by her co-employees has become a condition of employment such that her employer has discriminated on the basis of sex under Title VII.

Case 1 (1976)—a male supervisor threatened to fire a female employee if she refused his sexual advances. The court held this was sex discrimination in the terms of employment under Title VII.

Case 2 (1977)—a male supervisor promised to promote a female employee if she succumbed to his sexual advances. The court held this was sex discrimination in the terms of employment under Title VII.

Case 3 (1981)—a male supervisor, who had the power to fire or promote a female employee, asked her for sexual favors. The court held this was sex discrimination in the terms of employment.

Case 4 (1982)—a male supervisor, who did not have power to fire or promote a female employee, continually asked her for sexual favors. The court held that sexual harassment could so poison the work environment that it became a condition of employment. The court remanded the case for further findings of fact.

The employee's counsel will want to know about the development of the law in order to show that courts have expanded the definition of sex discrimination under Title VII to include not only terms, but also conditions of employment. The memo will give him the basis for arguing that the next logical step is to expand the law to include conditions of employment created by co-employees. The employer's counsel will want to know about the cases because all the cases involved sexual harassment of female employees by supervisors. He will use the memo to argue that the law should not develop beyond actions by supervisors to actions by co-employees.

Cases can also be used for their reasoning or policy. When there is no rule directly on point in the jurisdiction, but where a rule from another area of the law is applicable, the reasoning is a crucial part of articulating the rule. If the case involved a client who had been discharged from his employment because of his union activities and there were no retaliatory discharge cases in the jurisdiction, a case involving a retaliatory eviction might give the court analogous reasoning to apply. A tenant who was evicted by his landlord for organizing a rent strike to protest the vermin infested premises, could serve as the rationale for the employment case. The organization of the rule section would require, however, an introduction to the reader explaining why the analogy is appropriate before a statement of the rule. The policy behind the retaliatory eviction case could be useful in justifying this analogy.

The rule section concludes with cases that illustrate facts that are sufficient and/or insufficient to meet the standard of the rule. Once you have defined the general rule, the reader needs examples of the rule before he can understand how the rule can be applied in the problem. The same three patterns you have used in organizing basic memos apply.

Often there will be a case that is directly on point, that is a case with facts that are almost identical to the facts in the problem. Under these circumstances, the reader needs only the one case in order to understand how the rule will be applied to the problem. Similarly, the writer must use only one case when the problem includes facts that are stronger than the illustrative case. If, for example, a screwdriver constitutes a burglary tool, a set of skeleton keys most certainly qualifies. The reader does not need to know that a signpost does not qualify as a burglary tool. The information is irrelevant to the analysis and will distract the reader's attention from the important information.

The third organization requires using a case from each side of the spectrum, cases that illustrate both what is and what is not enough to meet the test. Begin with the case that illustrates the result that you predict for the problem. If your analysis of the problem concludes that the facts are sufficient, begin with the case where the court found the facts were sufficient. Then follow with the case that reached the opposite result.

ORGANIZING THE APPLICATION SECTION

When the rule is a complex one and the problem falls between illustrative cases on both ends of the spectrum, there are two alternatives for organizing the application section. The first system is the one suggested for the simpler memorandum. It presents both sides of the spectrum to the reader first, so that he understands the limits of the rule before considering the problem facts. This approach is useful in objective writing because it gives the reader all the necessary information about the way courts have applied the rule and puts the reader in a position to judge the analysis.

> ISSUE
>
> GENERAL RULE
>
> ILLUSTRATIVE CASE A (reaches the result you predict for the problem)
>
> ILLUSTRATIVE CASE B (reaches the opposite result)
>
> APPLICATION OF THE RULE TO THE FACTS OF THE PROBLEM (Compare to facts of case A and distinguish facts of case B)
>
> CONCLUSION OF THE ISSUE.

If the rule is complicated and you need to explain the facts of case A and case B fully to illustrate the rule, an alternative organization may be more helpful to the reader. While the organization may not put the reader in the same objective position for judging the analysis, the following organization may be easier for the reader to understand and easier for the writer to present.

> ISSUE
>
> GENERAL RULE
>
> ILLUSTRATIVE CASE A (reaches result you predict for the problem)
>
> APPLICATION OF THE RULE TO THE PROBLEM (explain how the problem facts are like those in case A)
>
> ILLUSTRATIVE CASE B (reaches the opposite result)
>
> APPLICATION OF THE RULE TO THE PROBLEM (distinguish the problem facts from those in case B)
>
> CONCLUSION.

The choice of organization in this situation depends on which alternative will best communicate the analysis to the reader.

HELPING THE READER FOLLOW COMPLICATED ANALYSIS

When the analysis is complex, consider using the following techniques to help the reader's understanding: a thesis paragraph at the beginning of a complicated issue, an introductory outline to a complex rule section, and a wrap-up characterization of the rule.

In a memorandum with a number of issues and sub-issues, a thesis paragraph at the beginning of an issue will aid the reader in keeping the parts of that issue straight. The following organization illustrates this problem:

Issue I

    Sub-issue a

    Sub-issue b

Issue II

Issue III

    Sub-issue a

    Sub-issue b

    Sub-issue c

Issue IV

    Sub-issue a

    Sub-issue b

Issue V

If you try to deal with all five issues and six sub-issues in the thesis section at the beginning of the memorandum, the reader may be confused. The thesis section, instead of providing a road map of the memo, will look like a maze. The reader will appreciate a thesis section at the beginning that lays out only the issues and your conclusions on those issues. A short thesis paragraph at the beginning of issues I, III and IV will provide the reader with the organizational detail necessary for understanding each of the issues, but without the confusion of the other issues and sub-issues in the problem.

A similar purpose is achieved by an introductory outline of a complicated rule section. It explains to the reader how the various parts of the rule fit together, so that the reader can anticipate and recognize the elements of the rule section as they unfold. A reader will find it easier to follow your examination of lender liability under CERCLA if you have provided a brief outline of the related sections of the statute at the outset. Similarly, a reader who knows that this is a case of first impression, and that the cases are developing in a particular direction, will be patient as you present the development to date.

The third technique is to provide a characterization of the rule. If the rule is complicated and the articulation of the rule is lengthy, the reader will have difficulty remembering the important parts of that rule when you are finally ready to apply it. In addition, you as the writer may have difficulty writing the application section because parts of the rule appear throughout the complicated rule section. To help both you and the reader, end the rule section with a concise statement of the rule. This characterization pulls the rule section together and sets the stage for the application section. The sexual harassment rule section outlined above will be clearer for the naive reader if it is followed by a concise characterization of the rule. You might characterize that rule in the following way:

Sexual harassment can be sex discrimination in the terms or conditions of employment under Title VII. It is sex discrimination in the terms of employment when a male supervisor with the power to fire or promote requests sexual favors of a female employee, whether or not the supervisor makes the promotion or the threat to fire the employee contingent upon sexual favors. Sexual harassment is sex discrimination in the conditions of employment when the harasser does not have the power to fire or promote, but the harassment is sufficient to poison the work environment.

The characterization provides the reader with the rule the writer is using. This particular illustration is a neutral characterization. Depending on whether your client is the employer or the employee, you may want to focus the characterization to answer the specific question posed by your client's position. A characterization of the rule gives the writer a rule that is easy to apply. Remember, however, that you must still compare the facts of your problem with the facts of the cases.

As with the organization of the simple office memo, the key is to organize so the reader will understand your analysis. As you make choices about organization, preface each one with the question, will this help the naive reader.

ORGANIZING A COMPLICATED MEMORANDUM

Rule Section:

1. Organize starting with the most general statement of the rule and work toward the most specific statement.

2. General rule:

    a. Constitution, statute, regulation

    b. If you need to use different sections of a statute to explain the rule, arrange them for the reader's benefit.

    c. If statutory language is open to more than one interpretation, present the reader with the options beginning with the best reasoned approach. Note: This applies to memo writing; in a brief, you should begin with the interpretation that favors your client.

3. Choice of Rule:

    a. If two rules apply, IRAC each and begin with the rule the court is most likely to use.

    b. If the results are different under the two rules, begin with the rule that helps to resolve the client's problem.

    c. If a rule is worth mentioning, but is of questionable relevance, explain why it is probably not applicable in an addendum.

4. Use chronological order to present the development of a rule.

5. Remember that you can use cases for reasoning and policy.

6. Illustrative cases:

    a. Use only one case if the case is very close to the facts of the problem.

    b. Use only one case if your problem facts are stronger than the facts in the case.

    c. Use a spectrum of cases if the problem facts fall between those in cases that reach different results.

Application Section:

    If the problem facts fall between those in cases that reach different results, choose either:

ISSUE

GENERAL RULE

ILLUSTRATIVE CASE A (reaches the result you predict for the problem)

ILLUSTRATIVE CASE B (reaches the opposite result)

APPLICATION OF THE RULE TO THE FACTS OF THE PROBLEM (Compare to facts of case A and distinguish facts of case B)

CONCLUSION OF THE ISSUE.

or

ISSUE

GENERAL RULE

ILLUSTRATIVE CASE A (reaches result you predict for the problem)

APPLICATION OF THE RULE TO THE PROBLEM (explain how the problem facts are like those in case A)

ILLUSTRATIVE CASE B (reaches the opposite result)

APPLICATION OF THE RULE TO THE PROBLEM (distinguish the problem facts from those in case B)

CONCLUSION.

Additional Writing Techniques:

    1. When there are multiple issues and sub-issues, consider limiting the original thesis section to the issues and use a thesis paragraph at the beginning of each complex issue to outline the sub-issues.

    2. If the rule section is complex, consider using an introductory outline of the rule.

    3. If the rule is complex, consider characterizing it before you apply the rule to the problem.

Chapter 14

WRITING IN PLAIN ENGLISH

Shakespeare wrote "[t]he first thing we do, let's kill all the lawyers."[1] He was not alone in his criticism of the profession. For centuries, those who needed to read the documents drafted by lawyers have criticized the way lawyers write. They complain that lawyers use a language all their own that no one else can decipher. They accuse lawyers of writing long convoluted sentences that only lawyers have the patience to unscramble. They wonder why lawyers need to use two or three words when most people can accomplish the same purpose with one word. They question the use of expressions like "heretofore" and "said wife". The following example demonstrates the problem:

1. That A heretofore, and on or about _____, 19__, was seized in fee simple absolute and possessed of certain property situate at _____ in the County of _____, City of _____, State of New York; that the said A thereafter, and on or about _____, 19__, at _____, _____ County, New York, died leaving a last will and testament by which he left a life interest in said property to his wife _____, and from and after the decease or marriage of his said wife, to his two daughters, B and C, the use of said real property for and during the term of their natural lives and for and after the decease of B and C, or either of them in fee to the children of said B and C, by their husbands, one equal undivided one-half to the children of each of said daughters. A more particular description of said real property is as follows: _____.[2]

This form was chosen at random from a form book published in 1981. The problem of legalese persists and with it a public perception of lawyers that detracts from the profession.

The most strident critics accuse lawyers of using legalese to obscure the meaning for financial reasons or to enhance their personal power.

1. Shakespeare, *Henry VI*, Act IV, Scene ii, Line 73.
2. Form 2 General Form for Complaint in Action for Partition of Real Estate, N.Y. Real Prop. Acts Law sec. 905 (Consol. 1981).

The truth is probably more benign and has its roots in the development of the English language and our system of educating lawyers.

THE ORIGINS OF LEGALESE

The American legal system, as noted in Chapter 1, arrived from England along with the first English settlers. Legalese was already the form of the law. As you can see from the example above, legalese is characterized by long convoluted sentences, archaic expressions, and unnecessary words. At least two characteristics of legalese: double or triple words with the same or similar meanings, and the archaic expressions, have their roots in the development of the English language. The unwieldy sentences are probably an accident of style, oral punctuation, the advent of printing, and the nature of lawyers.

The use of double and triple words began in the Middle Ages. At that time, England's legal system used three different languages. After the Norman Conquest in 1066 A.D., the king and his entourage increasingly used French. The native population spoke Old English, which developed into Middle English by the late 14th century. The law courts used French as the official language until approximately 1385, when they began to use Middle English. At the time of the transition between French and Middle English as the official language of the courts, lawyers accommodated and began to use both the French based and Middle English root words to make the meaning clear to those from both the French and Middle English traditions. The third legal language came from the ecclesiastical courts. The Catholic Church used latin as its written and spoken language until the time of Henry VII in the mid-fifteenth century. At that time these courts, too, shifted to English as the legal language.

This led to one of the characteristics of legalese, the use of two or even three parallel words to express the same idea.[3] Initially, the doublet had English and French roots and the triplet had English, French, and Latin origins. Some present day doublets and triplets betray their antecedents. The phrase "I give and devise" is one such example. "Give" came from English and "devise" from French. As time went on, however, the need to explain legal concepts using terms from two or three different systems disappeared; all the courts used English. The pattern of doublets and triplets persisted. A partial explanation for this may come from the precise nature of the law. Often the double words had slightly different meanings. Careful lawyers may have included both words to insure that both meanings were covered.

Another characteristic of legalese is the use of words like: "thereby", "thereafter", "hereinafter", "heretofore", etc. These words were used in common speech in Old English, and often in Middle English. Except "therefore" meaning consequently, they have largely disap-

3. David Mellinkoff, *The Language of the Law,* 120 (1963).

peared from modern English.[4] They persist, however, in today's legal language.

A third symptom of legalese is the long convoluted sentence. There are several possible historical explanations for this phenomenon. In the seventeenth century, printed legal documents came into use.[5] Written pleadings replaced oral pleadings in the law courts.[6] As a result the outcome of the case often depended on the words included in the pleadings. Lawyers wanted to make sure their cases would not be dismissed for want of the proper language. This led to the development of the printed form book.[7] Reporter series also developed at this time. Previously, there were notes on oral decisions, but not full accounts of cases. With the advent of printing, the use of precedent as we know it today was possible,[8] and lawyers began to rely on the words in those decisions. While the advent of printing should not necessarily lead to the use of long sentences, it happened in this case because of the system of punctuation. Before printing, people communicated information to each other orally. If it was written down, the purpose was to preserve the oral statement and permit it to be read aloud to listeners in the future. The punctuation indicated to the reader where he should breathe.[9] These oral sentences tended to be very long. The early printed documents used this same system of punctuation. Lawyers, intent on including everything necessary in their written pleadings and faced with an oral system of punctuation, wrote very long sentences indeed.

A second reason for the development of the long sentence in legalese is that the literary style in the sixteenth and seventeenth centuries in England was a flamboyant and unhurried style. The reader was content to wait until the writer got to the point.[10] A third reason for the development of monstrous sentences is that at the time, lawyers and their clerks were paid by the length of their documents.[11] This system was hardly designed to promote brevity.

You may wonder why the doublets and triplets, archaic expressions, and long convoluted sentences did not disappear from legal language as they did from standard written and spoken English. One explanation may come from the nature of legal education. Law schools are a recent development.[12] In earlier times, those desiring to enter the profession apprenticed themselves to practicing attorneys. They read the decisions of judges and the complaints and briefs of their masters and emulated the style used in these examples. As with any discipline, the novice had to learn the necessary vocabulary in order to communicate about the subject. Just as a doctor needs to know

---

4. Id. at 310–326.
5. Id. at 138.
6. Id. at 139.
7. Id. at 140.
8. Id. at 141.
9. Id. at 152.

10. Id. at 170.

11. Mellinkoff at 190.

12. The oldest established law school in this country is Harvard Law School. It was founded in 1817, followed by Yale in 1826. Mellinkoff, at pp. 238–9.

anatomical terms in order to discuss the patient's injury or disease, the lawyer needs the common vocabulary of "consideration", "proximate cause", "equitable estoppel", etc. to discuss legal issues. For centuries, legal apprentices learned all the words used by their mentors before they were able to distinguish between the words that had legal substance, like "proximate cause", and the mere formulaic words like "now comes the said plaintiff". By the time the apprentice had learned the difference between the substantive legal terms and the mere formulaic ones, he had adopted all of the legal vocabulary of his predecessors.

Despite the advent of law schools where students begin by learning substantive legal vocabulary, legalese persists. It is not perpetuated by law schools, but by practicing attorneys. Lawyers still use the apprenticeship system in order to learn the practical side of the law practice. Law clerks modify existing forms from previous cases to create documents for present cases. Word processing systems have made this task even easier. As you begin to work in the profession, be careful not to adopt a legalese style; try to retain the clear plain English style you had when you entered the profession.

WRITING IN PLAIN ENGLISH

Writing in Plain English means conveying your ideas directly to the reader. It involves writing sentences that are easy for the reader to understand and choosing the precise vocabulary that conveys your intended meaning. Plain English sentences have the following stylistic characteristics:

    1) short direct sentences for important information,

    2) subject-verb-object order,

    3) active voice unless you have a reason for using the passive voice,

    4) positive rather than negative construction,

    5) parallel construction for compound ideas,

    6) no unnecessary words.

If these points sound familiar, they should. These are all features of good writing in any discipline.

Choosing the appropriate vocabulary for Plain English legal writing is more difficult. It requires that the writer distinguish between the words with substantive legal meaning and the unnecessary legalese. Critics contend that many of the words used by lawyers have specific legal meaning; advocates of Plain English contend the number is quite small. In order to test this hypothesis, four investigators took a form real estate sales agreement and researched the words using a computer based research system. They found only 50 words out of 1820 or approximately 3% of the words had significant legal meaning based on precedent.[13]

---

13. Benson Barr, George Hathaway, Nancy Omichinski and Diana Pratt, "Legalese and the Myth of Case Precedent", 64 Mich. Bar J. 1136 (1985).

The choice of vocabulary depends in part on the reader. If the reader is a lawyer, then you can use the substantive legal vocabulary, such as "consideration" or "proximate cause" or "equitable estoppel" because it is the most precise way of communicating your idea, and the reader shares this vocabulary with you. If the reader is a non-lawyer and the word or phrase in its ordinary meaning will not convey your legal meaning to the reader, you must explain the legal meaning to the reader. There is no reason to use archaic, redundant, or unnecessary words to either type of reader. You will find it easier to draft in Plain English initially than to translate legalese into Plain English. When you must work from existing documents, redraft them in Plain English. Consider the following examples:

> Whereas at an election duly and regularly held on the _____ day of _____, A.D. 19__, within _____ County (or Counties), State of Oregon, and within the boundaries of a proposed district as herein described, there was submitted to the electors thereof the question of whether or not a people's utility district should be incorporated as the (here insert name of district) and to give authority to impose a special levy of $_____ under and pursuant to the provisions of ORS chapter 261; and

> Whereas at the election so held _____ votes were cast in favor of incorporation, and _____ votes were cast against incorporation; and

> Whereas the incorporation of the (here insert name of district) received the affirmative vote of the majority of the votes cast at the election;

> Now, therefore, the undersigned hereby does proclaim and declare that all of that part of the State of Oregon, described as (here insert description) has been duly and legally incorporated as the _____ People's Utility District under and pursuant to the Constitution and laws of the State of Oregon, and the district has the authority to collect the sum of $_____ by special levy against the taxable property within the district.

> Chairman of the County Governing
> Body by _____

This form taken from the Oregon Revised Statutes Annotated, sec. 261.200 (1985) is written in legalese. First, the form is all one sentence. Second, it includes archaic words such as "whereas", "herein", "thereof" and "hereby". Third, it contains the doublets: "duly and regularly", "under and pursuant", "proclaim and declare" and "duly and legally". Finally, there are unnecessary words. The same form is easier to read and just as effective legally when it is written in Plain English.

An election was held on (date) in _____ County (or Counties), Oregon. The electors voted on whether to incorporate a people's utility district and to impose a special tax levy of $_____. At the election, _____ votes were cast in favor of incorporation and _____ votes were cast against incorporation. Because the majority of the votes cast were in favor of the proposal, the County governing body declares that the portion of Oregon described as (insert description) is incorporated as the _____ People's Utility District under the laws of Oregon, and that the district has the authority to collect $_____ by special levy against the taxable property in the district.

Chairman of the County Governing
Body by _____

Apartment leases are often written in legalese. The following is a portion of a lease form taken from the New York Consolidated Laws Service, Real Property Law sec. 220, form 6 (1980).

THIS AGREEMENT, made the _____ day of _____, in the year 19__, between _____, of the first part, and _____, of the second part, witnesseth:

That the said party of the first part has agreed to let, and hereby does let to the said party of the second part, and the said party of the second part has agreed to take, and hereby does take from the said party of the first part _____ (described premises) for the term of _____ years, to commence on the _____ day of _____, 19__ and to end on the _____ day of _____, 19__. And the said party of the second part hereby covenants and agrees to pay unto the said party of the first part, the rent, or sum of money, payable; and to quit and surrender the premises, at the expiration of the said term, in as good state and condition as they were in at the commencement of the term, reasonable use and wear thereof, and damages by the elements excepted.

And the said party of the second part hereby covenants that he will not assign this lease, nor let or underlet the whole or any part of the said premises, nor make any alteration therein without the written consent of the said party of the first part, under the penalty of forfeiture and damages; and that he will not occupy or use the said premises, nor permit the same to be occupied or used for any business deemed extrahazardous on account of fire or otherwise, without the like consent under the like penalty.

* * *

This lease can be improved both by redrafting it in Plain English and by changing the format. With these changes, the lease might read like this:

APARTMENT LEASE

The landlord, _____, agrees to rent the apartment (insert description of the property) to the tenant, _____, for _____ (insert term of lease) beginning on _____(insert date) under the following conditions:

Tenant:

1) The tenant agrees to pay $_____ every month to the landlord as rent;

2) The tenant agrees not to sublet the apartment or assign the lease without the landlord's consent;

3) The tenant agrees not to conduct extrahazardous activity in the apartment;

4) The tenant agrees not to alter the premises without the written consent of the landlord;

5) The tenant agrees to move out at the end of the lease term;

6) The tenant agrees to leave the premises in good condition at the end of the lease term.

Landlord:

1) The landlord has a right to forfeit the lease if the tenant fails to meet the conditions listed above;

2) The landlord will not hold the tenant responsible for normal wear in the apartment or damage caused by the elements.

Both the landlord and the tenant will understand what is required of them under the lease if their responsibilities are listed separately using parallel construction. As you can see from this example, the format often helps to make the meaning clearer.

The following Power of Attorney form contains a number of examples of legalese. Note that the substantive section is written as one sentence.

POWER OF ATTORNEY

KNOW ALL MEN BY THESE PRESENTS, That _____

_____

have made, constituted and appointed, and By THESE PRESENTS, do make, constitute and appoint _____

_____

true and lawful ATTORNEY for _____ and in _____ name, place and stead, _____

_____

_____

_____

giving and granting unto _____ said Attorney, full power and authority to do and perform all and every act and thing whatsoever requisite and necessary to be done in and about the premises, as fully to all intents and purposes, as _____ might or could do if personally present, with full power of substitution and revocation hereby ratifying and confirming all that _____ said Attorney or _____ substitute shall lawfully do or cause to be done by virtue hereof.

In Witness Whereof, _____ have hereunto set _____ hand _ and seal _ the _____ day of _____ one thousand nine hundred and _____.

Sealed and Delivered in

Presence of

_____ _____(Seal)
_____ _____(Seal)

Acknowledgement

The revised version is drafted in several sentences. The purpose section, the substance of the document, may also contain several sentences. The attorney's expertise is required to draft the purpose section with care. The rest of the document must conform to the requirements in the statute and convey the meaning to all the intended readers, both lawyers and lay people.

POWER OF ATTORNEY

I, _____ give a power of attorney to _____
  (name)　　(status)　　(address)　　　　　　　　　　　　(name)
_____ for the following purposes: _____
(address)

_____
_____
_____.

I, _____ give _____ the authority to do everything necessary to
  (name)　　　　(name)
accomplish these purposes. I ratify all that _____ or _____
　　　　　　　　　　　　　　　　　　　(pronoun)　　(pronoun)
substitute does for me under this power of attorney. This power of attorney shall extend for _____ from _____ .
　　　　　　　　　　　(time limit)　　(date)

_____(Seal)

Witnesses:

_____

_____

Acknowledgement

Section V

A BRIEF TO THE TRIAL COURT

Lawyers have two basic purposes in mind when they explain legal analysis. So far this book has dealt with the first one, the analysis of the client's situation inside the law firm. Because the goal of this analysis is to advise the client or make decisions about the client's case, it must be open and objective. It explores the strengths and weaknesses of the client's position. Lawyers also need to explain legal analysis to an audience outside the law firm. This public expression of the client's case has a different purpose, to persuade someone outside the law firm of the merits of the client's position. This is the advocate's role and the rest of this book deals with advocacy. The audience may be a judge at the trial or appellate level, opposing counsel in a settlement conference, or other business people in a business negotiation. The explanation of the client's position can be written or oral.

Except in the most frivolous cases, there are at least two legitimate views in every case. Consider the following variation of the dog bite hypothetical presented in earlier chapters. The Illinois Dog Bite Statute requires in part that the owner of a dog is responsible to a person bitten by that dog if the dog bites "without provocation". Androcles is the owner of a dog. A small child, Harvey Woodley, threw a snowball at his dad. The snowball missed the father and hit the dog. The dog turned and bit the nearest person, Fred Feragamo.

The statute presents no problems of interpretation in the case when the person provoking the dog is the person the dog bites. It gives no guidance, however, in this case when the provocateur and the victim are two different people. From Androcles' perspective, it is not fair to require him to pay when his dog was provoked. But from Fred Feragamo's standpoint, it does not seem just to deprive him of compensation for the dog bite when he did not provoke the dog. There are two legitimate perspectives and it is the job of the attorneys for both parties to explain to the judge how the statute should be interpreted.

Androcles' attorney will explain to the court that the statute says "without provocation". A dog owner is not responsible for injuries sustained when his dog was provoked. He is only responsible if his pet injures someone and the dog was not provoked. In this case the dog was provoked. Under the plain meaning of the statute, Androcles should not be required to pay.

Feragamo's lawyer will argue, on the other hand, that the statute was intended to bar recovery to victims of dog bite when the victim was the one who provoked the dog. The statute was not intended to bar the recovery of innocent victims of dog bite. His client, Fred Feragamo, was visiting the zoo when the dog turned around and bit him. The lawyer may also draw on an applicable legal doctrine, assumption of risk, as a way to use existing legal doctrine to interpret the statute. A person who provokes a dog assumes the risk that the dog may bite, and he should be denied recovery. The innocent victim, however, has assumed no such risk. His client, Fred Feragamo, should recover from Androcles for his injuries. Although this is a simple hypothetical, you can see that both parties have legitimate perspectives.

The following more complex problem also illustrates two legitimate views of the same case. Under the Surface Mining Control and Reclamation Act [1] a strip miner must recreate the original contours of the land after the surface mining is complete. The purpose of the act is to protect the environment. The statute builds the cost of reclamation into the cost of strip mining. The particular piece of land involved in the case was owned by a farmer in West Virginia. Most of the land was too steep for farming and the farmer was having difficulty scraping a living from his land. The mining company sought approval from the Office of Surface Mining to extract coal from the parcel. As a condition for the permit, the mining company agreed to reclaim the land. During the coal extraction phase, the mining company leveled the land. The parcel then became more valuable as farmland. The farmer asked the company not to restore the original contours of the farm. The mining company agreed, but the Office of Surface Mining sued to enforce the conditions of the permit. Both the mining company and the Office of Surface Mining have legitimate views. The mining company will argue that the land is more valuable as farmland and that the owner does not want to have to pay to level the land. The Office of Surface Mining will argue it has a responsibility under the statute to require restoration of the land as a condition of a surface mining permit. The advocates must explain these views.

Not every case involves sympathetic views on both sides. The law and/or the facts may favor one side. The advocate's role is nonetheless to explain her client's view in the most favorable light possible under the circumstances. Advocacy is not screaming at or pleading with the judge or other audience; it is not distorting the facts; it is not manipulating the law. Advocacy is explaining the client's legitimate view and the legal analysis that supports that view.

The two chapters in this section are designed to introduce you to the trial judge and to show you how explaining legal analysis in an advocacy setting is different from explaining the same analysis in an objective setting inside the law firm.

1. 30 U.S.C. sec. 1201 et seq. (1982).

Chapter 15

THE TRIAL JUDGE AS AUDIENCE

The advocate's task in the trial court is to explain the analysis of the client's case to the trial judge. In order to do this effectively, you need to know who the trial judge is so that you can tailor your explanation to that particular audience. The purpose of this chapter is to introduce you to the trial judge.

The trial court sits at the bottom of the court system pyramid presented in Chapter 2. His job is to oversee the cases that come before him. In the course of litigation, the judge makes decisions necessary to moving the case toward either settlement or judgment. The judge must ensure that the parties conduct the case according to the court rules and that he protects the rights of all concerned. While judges occasionally act on their own initiative, most of the time, the judge only acts when requested to do so by one of the parties. Within the limits of the law and the procedural rules, the trial judge has considerable power over the parties, their lawyers, and the ultimate outcome of the case. As a result, lawyers need to treat judges with appropriate respect; the lawyer's ability to represent this and future clients requires it. The trial court's power is limited by the intermediate level appellate courts. These courts have a responsibility to correct the errors made below.

Trial judges are appointed to the federal district courts. Often a senator will recommend a judicial candidate to the President. Although they serve a non-political function, they usually come at least nominally from the same party as the recommending senator and the President. The President appoints federal judges with the advice and consent of the Senate. Federal judges are appointed for life on the theory that the judiciary will, therefore, be immune from political pressure. The trial judges in state courts are selected in three different ways. Like the federal judges, some are appointed. Some are elected in non-partisan elections. Still others are appointed initially but must win subsequent approval from the electorate. Most state judges serve for a specific term. In this way, they are more responsive to local concerns.

Ideally, before bringing a motion in a trial court, you would want to know the trial judge personally and be acquainted with the way that he or she handles the responsibilities of the job. As you gain experience in the trial courts of your jurisdiction, you will get to know the judges. Then you will be able to approach each one as an individual and tailor your brief accordingly. Until that time comes, it is useful to consider the attributes trial judges have in common. Until the mid 1970s, law school student bodies were overwhelmingly composed of white, middle-income, middle-class males. As a consequence, most present day trial judges share these characteristics. There are some female judges and some judges from minority groups, but these segments of society are under-represented on trial court benches at the present time. The judge's sex, color, race, and economic status should not be important when the judge has the responsibility for deciding cases between parties that come from all groups, but these attributes give you a sense of how a judge will approach your case initially. If your case requires that the judge understand a different perspective, then you need to provide that perspective in your brief.

The trial judge is a legal generalist and you must keep this in mind as you write to him. He is concerned with a variety of different responsibilities at every stage of the litigation time line, starting when the plaintiff files the complaint and ending when the judge decides the final post-judgment motion. At the outset he considers motions like those alleging improper jurisdiction and venue, failure to state a justiciable claim, and so forth. Later in the process, the judge hears discovery related motions and motions for summary judgment, in which a party claims that trial of the facts is unnecessary for a variety of reasons. The judge usually holds a pre-trial conference. At this time, the judge may actively encourage the parties to settle the case. If the case does not settle, the court may hear motions in limine just before the trial begins.

A major responsibility of all trial courts is to try cases. In a jury trial, the court will supervise the selection of the jury. He will rule on jury instructions and give these instructions. In a bench trial, the court will find the facts as well as rule on the law appropriate to the case. In both types of trials, the judge will rule on the admissibility of evidence. He will rule on motions for judgment as a matter of law. At the close of the trial, the judge will enter the final judgment. He may also decide post-trial motions, for example, motions for a new trial and for a judgment as a matter of law.

Judges involved in special types of cases have added responsibilities. Probate judges hold civil commitment hearings and decide motions related to the probate of decedents' estates. Juvenile court judges hold hearings when juveniles are charged with committing crimes and when juveniles are the subject of abuse and neglect. Judges in family courts decide emotionally charged issues of custody, support, visitation, property division, and paternity. Small claims, traffic, tax, and court of claims judges have other specific duties.

Trial courts routinely handle criminal as well as civil cases. When the trial court also has responsibility for criminal cases, there are a variety of additional tasks. The judge will arraign defendants and deny or set the bond. In felony cases, the judge may preside at preliminary examinations, deciding whether there is probable cause to believe that a crime has been committed and that this defendant is the likely perpetrator. He will accept guilty pleas, and he will be responsible for sentencing convicted criminals, hearing motions for parole, and sentencing parole violators.

The judge fulfills all of these responsibilities in the public forum where each side has an opportunity to argue the relative merits of its client's position. Most occur in the courtroom. Sometimes pre-trial or sentencing conferences take place in the judge's chambers.

In addition to the courtroom side of a trial judge's day, he has considerable work outside the public view. Attorneys file briefs in support of or in opposition to motions that involve complex legal issues. The judge must read the briefs and decide these issues. Often the trial judge issues a written opinion. He also issues written decisions in complex bench trials. The judge must find time outside the normal courtroom routine to read briefs and write opinions. As you can see, trial judges are busy people.

Your case is important to you and your client, but it is only one of many cases that require the judge's attention that day or week. As an advocate, you must get the judge's attention and explain what your client wants and why he is legally entitled to that relief. The judge is unlike the lawyer in the law firm. An associate or a partner may take the extra time to try and figure out the analysis you present in a memo, or she may ask you to rewrite the memo. The judge does not have this luxury. If you fail to explain the analysis precisely, your client may lose.

The trial judge is different from the audience inside the law firm in two additional respects. The law firm may represent clients in one field of law: general business, labor relations, or insurance defense. The partner or associate for whom you have written the memo may be an expert in a sub-specialty: corporate organization, union activities, or medical malpractice. That person will understand your memo within that legal context. As you can see from the discussion above, the trial judge has a more diverse legal universe. He may have arraigned and sentenced criminal defendants all morning, conducted pre-trial conferences in a water pollution case, a contract dispute, and a race discrimination case in the early afternoon, and then presided over a continuing antitrust bench trial for the remainder of the day. When the judge sits down to read your brief after dinner, it will be more difficult for him to understand your unfair labor practice case than for the partner who specializes in that area of the law. In this respect, the trial judge is an even more naive reader than you have encountered in your short legal career.

The judge is also different from the partner in that he has less incentive to understand your analysis. The partner shares your responsibility to the client. The judge has a general responsibility to the legal system and the cases that come before him. He must decide this case, but he decides the case based on what the attorneys for both sides present to him. He does not have a special responsibility to this particular client.

To accommodate this new audience, there are three additional things to keep in mind as you write a brief to the trial court. Because the judge is more distant from the case than the lawyer inside the law firm, you may have to provide the judge with more context to put the case in its legal perspective. If, for example, the judge has just been listening to an antitrust case, but your case is an unfair labor practices case brought by an employee against his union under the National Labor Relations Act, the judge will have difficulty shifting legal gears unless you provide the necessary context.

Second, the advocate must include all the steps in the analysis, so the judge understands exactly which rules are necessary for resolving the problem and why, and precisely how the rules should be applied to the case to reach the desired outcome. Unlike the partner or associate, who can ask you to fill in the missing analysis, the judge will not give you that opportunity. He will misunderstand what you are trying to say, or perhaps worse, ignore what you have written. In order to avoid being misunderstood or ignored, include all the necessary steps in the analysis.

Third, you must write concisely to the trial court. The judge has no time to wade through a lengthy dissertation about your case. You must revise to take out all unnecessary detail and all the empty words. This may seem to contradict the first two points. First, you are told to add more context to help the trial court. Then, you are told to explain every step in the analysis. Finally, you are told to pare the analysis down to the essentials because the trial court has no time to read anything extra. Try, however, to achieve all three goals in writing to a trial court. While writing an objective memo is hard work, writing as an advocate to a trial judge is even more difficult. Work to include everything the trial court needs to know in order to understand what you are saying. At the same time, work to leave out everything that is not necessary.

Chapter 16

WRITING TO THE TRIAL COURT

A lawyer writes to a trial court in support of or in opposition to a motion that has been filed in the case. The motions are those mentioned in Chapter 3. This writing is called a "Brief in Support of (or in Opposition to) the Motion". Sometimes the writing is called a "Memorandum of Law" or a "Memorandum of Points and Authorities". The purpose of the brief is to explain to the court the rule that should be applied and the way the advocate wants the court to apply the rule to the facts to decide the motion. If, for example, the defendant filed a Rule 12(b)(6) motion alleging that the plaintiff has failed to state a cause of action, the defendant will explain the elements of the cause of action and how the plaintiff's facts as alleged in the complaint fail to meet one or more of the required elements. The plaintiff will file a brief in opposition to that motion.[1]

The brief is different from an office memorandum. Its purpose is to persuade the court to adopt your analysis. The purpose of a memo, on the other hand, is to look objectively at the client's situation and assess its strengths and weaknesses. Although you will be discussing much of the same law and the same facts, the focus of the brief is different from that in a memo. While there may be two legitimate views of what happened and which law should be applied to the facts and how it should be applied, your goal is to explain why your client's view of the facts is more accurate, your choice of law is more appropriate and your analysis of how the rule should be applied leads to the better result. You need also to explain to the court why your opponent's view of the facts, the law, and the way the law should be applied is not appropriate for deciding this case.

Under the ABA Model Rules of Professional Conduct, you are

---

1. This brief should be distinguished from a "trial brief". This is a brief an attorney will file with the court just before trial. In a bench trial, the purpose of a trial brief is to explain to the court the applicable law and how it should be ap- plied to the facts that will be established at trial. In a jury trial, the judge may request that the parties file a trial brief addressing a complex legal issue or an evidentiary issue likely to arise during the trial.

required to present the law and the facts accurately to the court.[1]

You are also required to bring to the court's attention controlling law that is adverse to your client's position if your opponent has not already done so. This means under the doctrine of *stare decisis*, that if there is law from the same or higher level of court in your jurisdiction that is directly on point, you must inform the court about this law. If your opponent has researched the subject sufficiently, he will have already mentioned the rule to the court, and you are not required to do so. This does not mean that you must concede the issue. You are still free to distinguish the rule or explain why it should not be applied in this case.

Effective brief writing has much in common with good memo writing. The initial pre-writing steps are the same for writing briefs and memos; both require thorough research and analysis. The writer must outline the analysis carefully using the same issue, rule, application, and conclusion order. The brief writer must build the writing overlay into the outline and draft with the naive reader in mind. The brief writer must reserve time for careful revising and editing. These are the most important steps in writing an effective brief.

There are, however, differences between writing briefs and memos. Because there is a different purpose and audience, you will need to make changes in the terminology, and in some of the organization, focus and writing. This chapter discusses the elements of a brief to the trial court and the changes you need to make from the comparable sections of a memo.

A brief to the trial court contains a caption, questions presented, a statement of facts, an argument, and a conclusion. Some jurisdictions use different terminology and include additional sections. Always be sure to check the court rules for the jurisdiction to make sure that you have used the appropriate format. These rules are comparable to the Federal Rules of Civil Procedure for the federal courts. There may also be local court rules with specific format requirements.

THE CAPTION

Every document submitted to a court begins with a caption. The caption includes at a minimum: the name of the court, the names of

---

1. Rule 3.3, ABA Model Rules of Professional Conduct:

(a) A lawyer shall not knowingly:

(1) make a false statement of material fact or law to a tribunal;

(2) fail to disclose a material fact to a tribunal when disclosure is necessary to avoid assisting a criminal or fraudulent act by the client;

(3) fail to disclose to the tribunal legal authority in the controlling jurisdiction known to the lawyer to be directly adverse to the position of the client and not disclosed by opposing counsel; or

(4) offer evidence that the lawyer knows to be false. If a lawyer has offered material evidence and comes to know of its falsity, the lawyer shall take reasonable remedial measures.

From *ABA Model Rules of Professional Conduct,* copyright 1989 American Bar Association, Reprinted by permission.

plaintiff(s) and defendant(s), a file number, the type of case, and the title of the document. The following is a model caption from the Federal District Court for the Southern District of New York.

**UNITED STATES DISTRICT COURT FOR THE
SOUTHERN DISTRICT OF NEW YORK**

A.B.,		) Civil Action, File Number
	Plaintiff,	) ————
v.		) MOTION FOR SUMMARY
D.C.,		) JUDGMENT
	Defendant.	)

The arrangement of the items may vary with the particular court. The caption serves the same function as the heading in a memo. It identifies the document and gives enough information to the people concerned, so that they can direct the brief to the appropriate person or file it in the proper place. Some court rules require additional information. Local Rule 16(c) for the United States District Court for the Eastern District of Michigan also requires the name of the judge assigned to the case and the name, business address, telephone number, and State Bar identification number of the attorney or attorneys involved in the case.

QUESTIONS PRESENTED

The purpose of the questions presented section, as in a memo, is to tell the reader the issues you will discuss in the brief. Unlike the questions presented in a memo, which are objective statements of the issues, the questions in a brief state the issues from your client's perspective.

The basic formula for a question presented is, however, the one you have used before:

DOES THIS [RULE] APPLY TO THESE [FACTS]?

The reader will not understand the facts if they precede the rule, so you should begin with the rule. Explain the rule in sufficient detail so the reader understands what is required. Include the legally relevant facts as they appear from the client's perspective. The goal is to state the issue precisely, but at the same time to make the question readable.

Choose the facts that explain your client's side of the dispute. The following questions presented come from opposing sides of a divorce case where alimony is at issue. The first demonstrates the wife's perspective.

Is a wife entitled to alimony to raise her standard of living to that which she enjoyed during the marriage, when she was married for thirty years, supported her husband when he went to graduate school, raised three children, and always put the welfare of her family before her personal aspirations?

The husband's view is quite different:

Should the court deny alimony, which is designed to take care of those who are unable to provide for themselves, to a well-educated, professional woman who is employed full time in her chosen profession?

The questions include both the parties' different theories on why alimony should be awarded and their disparate views on the facts in this case. The questions do not scream out with inflammatory language; they present two legitimate views of the same facts and two views on the purpose of alimony. The questions present the same issue to the court, but from two perspectives. The trial judge should know from the two different questions presented what the issue is in the case and how the two parties view the issue. If the opposing questions are too one-sided, the court will have difficulty identifying the issue. A good advocate drafts her questions presented so the judge can readily understand the issues.

STATEMENT OF FACTS

A brief to the trial court also includes a statement of facts. The statement of facts has the same purpose in a brief as in a memo. It explains the facts in the case. The facts should be well organized so that the reader understands the causal connections between them. As with a statement of facts in memo, chronological order is often the most effective. It helps the writer avoid redundancy and helps the reader understand the events as they developed. Often the court rules require that the writer present the facts using chronological order. As with memo statements of facts, there are two kinds of chronological order. The first is chronological order in absolute time. This is what we normally think of as chronological order. The second is a literary chronological order; that is, the order in which the events unfolded to one of the characters. In advocacy writing, this is often an effective way of presenting the facts from your client's perspective. Your client may have reacted to the events as she learned of them. The judge will understand the facts as the client did if you use this chronological order.

The statement of facts in a brief, as in a memorandum, should be accurate, complete, and should include the source for each item. You should begin by identifying the parties, with your client first. You must provide enough context so the reader knows what the case is about and he can put the facts in their proper legal perspective. If some of the information came from your client and some from a public record or a witness, the court should have this information. You must include all the legally relevant facts and the background facts that are necessary for the reader. To the extent that it is relevant you should include the procedure to date in the case. Check the relevant court rules for placement of the procedure. When you have the option, a description of the procedure often works well as part of the context at the beginning of the statement of facts. In other instances, it flows better at the end, serving as a transition to the argument.

The statement of facts for a brief is different from that in a memo because it also includes the emotional facts, those facts that help explain why your client feels so strongly about the case. If your client is in a situation that makes her plight more difficult than it would be for the average person under similar circumstances, explain these facts.

As an advocate you will find that crafting a statement of facts allows you more freedom and creativity of expression than other legal writing tasks. You will want to create a mental picture of the client's situation for the judge. If the legal problem involves a series of similar instances, try to describe one in detail, so the court understands how your client feels, and then treat the remainder in general terms, so the judge does not get bored. This is the technique of giving weight to the facts by including specific detail for the important points and progressively less detail as you move toward the less important facts. Consider the following paragraph from a statement of facts.

> Dan Clement owns a piece of shore front property in New Jersey. His house is located adjacent to the road where the ground is solid, but the property extends several hundred yards over the dunes to the Atlantic Ocean. A family owns the lot to the north of his and the town beach is located just to the south. On the weekends in the summer, the town beach is crowded and the public spills over onto his property. He is very frustrated because the town is unwilling or unable to remove the trespassers.

This description of the problem lets you know the basic facts, and it tells you that the client is frustrated. It does not, however, paint a mental picture for you of what this is like for the client. Compare that rather bland description with the following:

> Dan Clement and his family decided to spend the fourth of July on their beach. Martha packed a picnic and the kids collected their pails and towels. The family set out toward the water. They had to climb a hundred feet to the top of the dunes before they could see the ocean. When they reached the top, they looked down toward the water's edge. There on their beach, they saw a company picnic in full swing. There were beach umbrellas, striped towels, and plastic rafts on the sand. Hot dogs and hamburgers were sizzling on charcoal grills. Beer and soft drinks were cooling in laundry tubs of ice. People were playing volley ball on one side and soft ball on the other. The only way the Clements could get to the water on their own beach was to run through the outfield between pitches.

The fourth of July was only one incident in the case, but the image of the company picnic is one the judge will remember. The writer did not have to tell the court that her clients are frustrated about the problem. The judge knows from the description of this one incident how angry they are. The writer can complete the statement of facts by describing the remaining incidents in summary fashion. The writer will only bore the reader if she uses this much detail for each occasion when members of the public trespassed on the plaintiffs' beach.

As an advocate you should highlight the facts that help portray your client's point of view: 1) Choose active interesting vocabulary to emphasize the important facts. 2) Show the causal connection between facts so it is easier for the reader to remember the key facts and their significance to the case. 3) Minimize the facts that support your opponent's view of the facts.

As you draft the statement of facts, choose the vocabulary with care. Strike a balance between a bland characterization of what happened and an exaggeration of the facts. While you want the judge to understand the facts as your client sees them, you will lose credibility if you distort the facts by using inappropriate words. Assume, for example, that you need to explain that someone has just left the scene and describe the way that he felt as he departed. Consider the following ways of explaining these facts:

1. The supervisor seemed to be upset as he left the room.
2. The supervisor seemed to be upset when he walked from the room.
3. The supervisor strode from the room.

In the first two examples, the writer is giving a subjective assessment as to the actor's state of mind and then explaining that he departed. The difference between these examples is in the verb used to describe his departure, either left or walked. The verb "left" provides the reader with no mental picture of the actor, while walked shows the action. The third example combines the subjective assessment with the action. When your purpose is to highlight the action and assess the actor's state of mind, choose the most expressive word. If your purpose is only to get the actor off the scene in order to present more important information, then the first choice is the appropriate one.

Second, try to highlight the important facts by drawing the causal connections between them. There are two ways of doing this. The first is to show how fact a led to fact b.

The Mallorys arrived home at 10:15 pm on Friday night and discovered that their house had been burglarized. They immediately called the local police. A squad car with two officers arrived a few minutes later. * * *

Each action leads logically to the next. A second way of showing logical connections between facts is to juxtapose the facts. This technique is useful when the facts do not flow logically in a causal sequence, but when you want to help the reader draw a logical conclusion from two facts. Consider the following example:

Marvin Mantle usually leaves work at five o'clock and arrives home well before the 6 o'clock news. On October 30, 1986, he got home at 6:22 pm.

The writer now has the reader's attention. What happened to Mantle on the night of October 30th? By using the juxtaposition, the writer has highlighted a fact that is important to the case.

Advocates must also include those legally relevant facts that help show the opponent's view of the case. While you will not want to include the opponent's emotional facts, you must include the facts that are necessary for explaining the analysis of the case. This does not mean that you as the advocate must highlight the facts that favor your opponent. Rather, include them in summary fashion using bland vocabulary. Avoid unnecessary detail and avoid active, interesting words.

By using these techniques, you can enhance the judge's understanding of the case as your client perceives it.

THE ARGUMENT

In a brief, the functional equivalent of the discussion section in a memorandum is called the argument. The argument has a lot in common with a discussion. Each should begin with a thesis paragraph or section that provides the reader with context, that lays out the issues in the order in which you will discuss them, and that gives away to the reader your conclusions on all issues and sub-issues. Remember that you may need to provide the judge with more context than you gave the reader in the law firm. The argument, like the discussion, is arranged by issue and sub-issue. The most effective way of organizing the material within each issue is a form of IRAC called CRAC, where the neutral statement of the issue is replaced by a persuasive statement of your contention. The brief writer will use the same writing overlay to explain the analysis to the reader. Each issue should begin with a thesis statement and each paragraph should begin with a topic sentence that explains to the reader the purpose of the paragraph. The writer must also build transitions into the argument as he did into the discussion.

An argument is different from a discussion section, however, in three major respects: 1) in its purpose, 2) in some of its organization, and 3) in its focus. The purpose of the argument is to persuade the court to adopt your analysis of the problem. Remember the audience, the trial court, and present the analysis clearly. As you learned in writing a discussion section, this is hard work. Poor analysis is never persuasive. The refinements suggested in this section are only appropriate after the analysis is logical and precise.

The second difference between an argument and a discussion is in the organization. This may occur both in the gross organization and in the fine organization. At the gross organizational level, choose the order of the issues that will be most helpful to the reader. Remember that the judge must decide this case and that the judge is not deciding anything but the dispute between these parties based on the law of the jurisdiction. The court does not want to make new law or spend time entertaining alternate views on esoteric questions. The trial judge is a pragmatist. As a result, present the issues in the order that makes it easiest for the judge to decide the case in favor of your client. If you are asking for two alternative kinds of relief, consider beginning with the analysis that would provide your client with the most complete relief. If, for example, you are asking the court for a judgment as a matter of law and, in the alternative, for a new trial, your client wins outright if the judge grants judgment as a matter of law, where the new trial would only give your client the chance to retry the case. Assuming the chances of both types of relief were equal, you should explain first why the judgment as a matter of law is appropriate, and only later, why the client is also entitled to a new trial. When you have issues of varying importance, the trial judge will want to know about the important issues before the issues of lesser importance. If there is a logical order to the issues, the judge will understand your analysis best if you choose a logical arrangement. When you have organized the issues with the trial judge in mind, organize the sub-issues using to the same criteria.

Within each issue and sub-issue, consider two additional organizational changes that will make your argument more persuasive. The first change occurs where there are two rules that could be applied, and the result will be different depending on which rule the court chooses. In the argument section of a brief when the ultimate result depends on the rule the court chooses, the writer has two approaches to the choice of rule problem. The first approach is to acknowledge at the beginning that two rules exist and then explain to the court why one is appropriate and the other is not. Under this alternative, the writer would then apply the chosen rule to the facts of the problem and conclude. This approach is preferable when the court is aware of the two rules, either because the rules are a part of most lawyers' knowledge or because your opponent has already explained the rule. It gives the writer a chance to get rid of the unwelcome rule before applying the favorable rule. Under this alternative the organization of the issue might look like this.

Contention

Rule

> Rule A is appropriate and explain why
>
> Rule B is inappropriate and explain why
>
> Case illustrating the application of Rule A

Application of Rule A to the facts

Conclusion

When the court may not yet be aware that the other possible rule exists, you may wish to begin with the rule you advocate as the appropriate rule and CRAC completely using this rule. Then explain why the other rule is inappropriate. The organization of the issue might look like this.

Contention

Rule

    Rule A is appropriate and explain why

    Case illustrating the application of Rule A

Application of Rule A to the facts

Conclusion

Rule

    Rule B is inappropriate and explain why

Conclusion that you advocate

The second fine organizational change occurs in the application section when there is a spectrum of authority and your case falls somewhere in the middle. In a memo the writer wants to show the reader both ends of the spectrum before discussing the application of the rule to the problem facts. This way the reader can objectively see the scope of the rule before considering its application. The A section explains to the reader how the problem facts are similar to and different from the illustrative cases at both ends of the spectrum.

In a brief, however, the writer wants the reader to accept one application of the rule to the facts and reject the other, explaining why the problem case is like one end of the spectrum before telling the reader about the other end of the spectrum. This organization can be outlined as follows:

Contention

Rule

    General rule

    Case A illustrating how the rule was applied in a case that reached the desired result

Application of the rule to the facts of the problem showing how the problem is analogous to the case

Conclusion

Rule

    Case B illustrating how the rule was applied to reach the opposite result

Distinction of Case B facts from the facts in the problem

Conclusion

The goal is to focus the reader's attention on the similarity between the one case and the problem facts first and then to distinguish the problem facts from those in the other case. Be sure to conclude by explaining to the reader the result you advocate.

The third distinction between the discussion section of a memo and the argument section of a trial brief is in the focus. You want to emphasize the rules and facts that support your client's position. You can accomplish this by putting the favorable rules and illustrative cases before the unfavorable ones and by expanding your analysis of the favorable law.

One way to highlight the analogy with an illustrative case that supports your client is to set up the discussion of the case and the client's facts in parallel. Use parallel sentence structure and arrange the facts in the same order. The cadence you create will enhance the analogy you advocate. Consider the following illustration:

In *Aschenbrenner,* the court held that the claimant had not attempted to resolve the grievance with his employer before taking the drastic step of leaving his employment. Aschenbrenner could have taken his grievance to his union, but he failed to do so. Aschenbrenner could have voluntarily reduced the number of hours he worked to forty a week, but he failed to do so. Aschenbrenner could have talked with his supervisor about the constant overtime, but he failed to do so. Based on his failings, the court held that Aschenbrenner did not have good cause to quit his job.

In this case, the claimant has not attempted to resolve the grievance with her employer before taking the drastic step of leaving her employment. Adler could have taken her grievance to her union, but she failed to do so. Adler could have complained to her supervisor about the alleged harassment, but she failed to do so. Adler could have talked to the personnel manager about her problem, but she failed to do so. Based on her failings, the court should find that Adler did not have good cause to quit her job.

The writer has used a litany approach to demonstrate the similarity between the facts and the case.

Emphasize the facts that demonstrate the client's position. You can do this in several ways. Shorter paragraphs are easier for the reader to understand, so use short paragraphs for the most important points. As readers will grasp the point more easily in a short direct sentence, use short direct sentences to highlight the points that help your client. Similarly, put the important information at the beginning or end of a paragraph, where the reader is more likely to see it. Choose your vocabulary with care. Use expressive words to present the facts. Put the action in the verbs, make the actor the subject of the sentence. Most importantly, explain your analysis precisely and in sufficient detail so the judge can understand it readily.

While you must explain to the court all the controlling law and all the legally relevant facts even if they do not all help your client, you are not required to highlight the unwelcome precedent and the negative facts. You should minimize the effect of these rules and facts. You can do this by following the converse of the principles used to emphasize important points. To minimize the effect of rules, explain to the court why the rule does not apply in the circumstances of this case. Distinguish the cases that at first glance seem to be similar by highlighting the facts that make the cases inapplicable and by explaining the distinctions.

You can also minimize the effect of a negative fact. Include the fact in a dependent clause in the middle of a long paragraph. Choose the vocabulary so that you explain the harmful fact in bland language. Compare the following:

> The attacker bludgeoned the victim to death with a tire iron such that the police could only identify her through her dental records.

with:

> The victim did not survive.

While this example may be extreme, you can use vocabulary effectively both to emphasize important facts and to minimize harmful facts. Always test your word choice for accuracy and credibility.

POINT HEADINGS

Briefs may also include headings to introduce important points in the argument. Point headings are optional in a brief to a trial court. These headings are analogous to the single-spaced questions presented that appear in the body of the discussion section of a memo. They serve an organizational function. They help the reader find the different sub-parts of your brief. Point headings, unlike the questions in the memo discussion section, are forceful statements of the points you are making in the brief.

In making the decision whether to include point headings at the trial court level, consider the reader. If the brief is short and includes only an issue or two, the judge may understand the organization of your brief without point headings. Point headings might detract from the logical flow of your analysis and fragment the brief. But if the brief is long and complex, the point headings will enhance the reader's understanding of how the various parts of the analysis fit together.

The number and placement of point headings depends on what is helpful to the reader. Too many point headings can be disruptive; too few are not helpful. Aim for a point heading every few pages. Collectively, the point headings should answer the questions presented. This means you should have at least one point heading for every question presented. It is possible to have more point headings than questions presented if it is useful for the naive reader.

The following point headings come from the briefs filed in the United States Supreme Court for a subpoena requiring Richard Nixon to release documents involved in the Watergate scandal. The special prosecutor, Leon Jaworski, wrote:

> The power of the courts to issue subpoenas, long recognized by the courts, flows from the fundamental principle that no man is above the law.

Nixon's attorney, James St. Clair, wrote on the same issue:

> The rights of privacy and freedom of expression support the absolute confidentiality of presidential communications with his advisors.[2]

United States v. Nixon, 418 U.S. 683 (1974).

These point headings are forceful statements of opposing perspectives on the issue.

As you can see from these examples, point headings are the functional equivalent of thesis statements. When you have a point heading that serves this function, you do not need to follow it with a thesis statement. This would be redundant. You do, however, need to introduce the issue to the reader. You can accomplish this either with a transition sentence or by stating the issue in a more specific way than in the point heading.

CONCLUSION

As with an office memorandum, a brief requires a conclusion, and there are two forms the writer can use. In a short straightforward brief, you may conclude the analysis in the final paragraph of the argument section. The separate conclusion section will then be a one line request for relief, for example:

> For these reasons, summary judgment should be denied.

As you can see, the writer used the passive voice in this sentence. Passive voice is appropriate in this case because the writer did not want to order the judge to do something. The truncated passive is more polite and helps the writer ask for the relief without upsetting the attorney-judge relationship.

In a longer more complicated brief, the reader will often prefer to have a separate conclusion section. This will include an overall conclusion to the issues discussed in the brief ending with the request for relief. At the trial court level, choose the form that will be most helpful to the judge. As with the conclusion of a memo, you should include your conclusions on each issue and sub-issue and explain very briefly the reasons for those conclusions.

2. This point heading comes from the Brief for Respondent filed in *United States v. Nixon,* 418 U.S. 683 (1974). Reprinted with permission from James D. St. Clair. Copyright c by James D. St. Clair.

CHECKLIST FOR A BRIEF TO A TRIAL COURT

A trial brief should include a caption, questions presented, a statement of facts, an argument, and a conclusion with the relief that you are seeking from the trial court.

The following checklist is for use as a revising and editing tool only. It is by no means exhaustive. For more specific information about writing, refer to the Memo Writing Checklists in earlier chapters. Follow the directions, but do not become too mechanical in their application.

Caption

The caption should include at a minimum the jurisdiction and name of the court, the parties and their designations in the case, plaintiff, etc., the file number, and the title of the document. Be sure to follow the appropriate court rules for additional items.

Questions Presented

Use a separate question for *each* major issue and sub-issue.

Note: When you have sub-issues, you may state the "issue" question in general form and make the questions for the sub-issues fact specific.

> E.g. I. Issue Question (general)
>
>   a. Sub-issue (fact specific)
>
>   b. Sub-issue (fact specific)

Use the basic formula: "Does the legal rule apply to the facts?"

Include the relevant legal rule.

Identify and describe the legally relevant facts.

Keep the question readable.

Be sure that your client's perspective comes through in your questions.

Your question should suggest a particular result, but not be so one-sided as to obscure the relevant legal issue.

Put a ? at the end of each question.

Statement of Facts

Include your purpose.

Provide context.

Identify the parties beginning with your client.

Make sure you have included all the legally relevant facts. Cross check against your analysis and your questions presented.

Provide background facts as necessary for the naive reader.

Present the facts to show your client's perspective.

Organize logically. Chronological organization often works the best. Choose either absolute or literary chronological order. Note: the court rules may require chronological order.

Include the procedural posture, if relevant.

Argument

Thesis paragraph or section

If appropriate, begin each section of the argument with an appropriate point heading. Point headings are normally single-spaced in the body of the argument.

Use CRAC.

Remember that cases can be used for the general rule, to illustrate and further define a rule, for reasoning and for policy.

Make **your** argument before you distinguish unwelcome precedent.

Remember that you must use all important precedent from your jurisdiction, whether it is favorable or unfavorable to your position.

Characterize the rules and fact specific holdings from your client's perspective.

Use parallel sentence and paragraph structure to enhance the analogy between your facts and the case on which you rely.

Include citations where appropriate. When quoting or using a case for proposition given on a particular page of that case, include the citation to the particular page.

Include a concluding paragraph that sums up your arguments.

Conclusion Section

Ask briefly for the relief you want the court to grant. This is an appropriate place to use the passive voice, so you are not put in the position of dictating to the court.

In a long and complex brief, consider a formal conclusion section in place of the concluding paragraph or two at the end of the argument section.

Section VI

APPELLATE ADVOCACY

Throughout the litigation process, an attorney attempts to settle the case, prepares to try the case if it does not settle, and preserves all the issues for appeal if an appeal becomes necessary. The vast majority of cases are resolved at the trial court level. After an adverse final decision in the lower court, the client may wish to appeal. Although the client makes the final decision, the attorney needs to review the case and present the client with a realistic view of the options. The review process involves: (1) identifying the errors made in the lower court, (2) considering the appellate standard of review for each error, and (3) evaluating the chances of success in the appellate court. If the client decides to appeal, the attorney takes all the steps necessary to perfect the appeal, including writing an appellate brief. This section provides information on drafting an appellate brief.

Chapter 17

THE APPELLATE COURT AS AUDIENCE AND THE STANDARD OF REVIEW

The appellate court is a different audience from the trial court you met in Chapter 15. The standard of review, the way the appellate court will approach your case on appeal, may also be different from the way the trial court was required to look at the case. The purpose of this chapter is to introduce you to the new audience and explain how it will consider your case. As you have learned, a writer must understand her audience in order to explain legal analysis to that reader. The appellate advocate needs to understand who the appellate court is and how it will view the case in order to persuade the court of the merits of her client's position.

THE APPELLATE COURT AS AUDIENCE

The appellate court is a much more distant and impersonal court than the trial court. Although the same kinds of people become judges on appellate courts as sit on trial benches, the lawyers who appear before them do not develop the same sense of rapport with appellate judges as is possible with trial judges. There are several reasons for this. First, the appellate courts are composed of three, seven, and nine judge panels rather than the single judge that sits in the trial court. It is, therefore, difficult to get a sense of the court.

Second, a trial attorney is likely to appear before the trial judge several times in the course of one individual case. The attorney may appear before the judge at motion hearings, at the pretrial conference, and in the course of the trial. The attorney will become acquainted with the judge's style and he will develop ways of approaching this particular judge. Attorneys do not have the same opportunity to interact with appellate judges. There is normally only one oral argument before an appellate bench; in some jurisdictions and for some cases, there is no oral argument. Unlike the trial judges, who decide a variety of issues directly from the bench, appellate judges decide cases in writing. The advocate does not see the decision making process; she only sees the final product. Even in the intermediate level appellate courts, there are three judges on the bench. If one of them asks a question during oral argument, the attorney is still left wondering how the other two judges view the issue. Because of the number of judges and the limited contact between lawyer and the appellate bench, the appellate court is a more impersonal forum.

Third, appellate courts do not deal with the facts in the same way that trial courts do. A trial judge, even in a jury trial, sees the witnesses and is able to evaluate their credibility as they present the facts. The appellate court gets the facts from a paper record [1]: the transcript of the proceedings, the briefs, and in synopses prepared by attorneys working for the court. As you will learn shortly, not all, if any, of the appellate judges will read the transcript of the proceedings.

Appellate courts are also more distant from the case because their function is different from that of the trial court. The role of the intermediate appellate court is primarily to correct mistakes made below. The court begins with the view that there is no error. The appealing party must convince the court that the trial judge erred in some material respect. While the trial court has the responsibility for resolving this particular case between these particular parties in light of existing law, the intermediate appellate court takes a more general view. It must make sure that its decision is good precedent for future cases.

The highest level appellate court in any one jurisdiction is the court primarily responsible for allowing the law to develop gradually in light of changing technology and values. It grants leave to appeal only on important issues and when a decision is necessary to the law of the jurisdiction. It accepts only a small percentage of the appeals from intermediate level appellate courts. The decisions from the highest level appellate court should make good precedent for future cases and be consistent with public policy.

In writing to an appellate court, the advocate must first consider the audience as the court, rather than the collective of its individual members. The reason for this is the process the court uses in assessing the briefs. You may assume that your brief will go to the individual members of the court, that they will each read the transcript of the proceedings in the trial court, your brief and that of your opponent, do some research, listen to your oral argument, decide the case, and that one of their number, in consultation with the others, will write a well reasoned opinion deciding the issues. This is not usually the case. Because of the large volume of appeals, the judges rely on clerks to do much of the preliminary work of the court. These clerks are usually

1. With the advent of the camera in the courtroom, appellate courts may change this approach and begin to look at video-tapes of courtroom proceedings as well as the written transcript. Junda Woo, *Videotapes Give Appeals Cases New Dimension*, Wall St. J., April 14, 1992, at B1.

recent law school graduates. The division of labor between law clerks and judges varies with the particular jurisdiction, the level of court, and the individual judge. The following descriptions are designed as illustrations to help you understand the kinds of people who will be making decisions about your appellate case.

Most appeals handled by intermediate level appellate courts are appeals as of right. Each case is assigned to a recent graduate, either a clerk for one of the judges or a staff attorney. This lawyer will read the briefs submitted by both parties and summarize the issues as they appear from the briefs. She will verify the statements of facts from both sides against the transcript and record from the trial court and draft a statement of facts adding any important facts omitted by the parties and pointing out inaccuracies that exist in their briefs. This lawyer will then research the issues and evaluate the merits of the arguments made on each issue. She will next draft a statement of the questions presented and an analysis of each issue. Based on the analysis, this attorney will draft a conclusion which recommends a procedural disposition of the case; that is, that it be affirmed, reversed and remanded, etc. The attorney may also recommend the type of opinion that is appropriate under the circumstances.

The appeals are of three different types and the treatment they receive and the kind of opinion that is issued depends on the category. The first group involves appeals that have no merit or that raise well settled issues. The clerk or staff attorney will recommend a brief memorandum opinion. Usually she will draft the opinion. The second category of appeals are those where the issues have merit, but where they can be resolved using existing precedent. The attorney will recommend a per curiam opinion. Often she will draft a proposed opinion that decides the case using the existing precedent. Notice that these two types of opinion may be drafted before oral argument. The third group of appeals are those that raise important issues. The attorney will recommend that a judge assigned to the case issue an authored opinion.

This clerk or staff attorney spends on the average 1–2 days per appeal. The attorney's report and the briefs are then submitted to the three judges assigned to the case. The transcript and record from the trial court may only go to the one judge who has primary responsibility for the case. Although the judges will consider each case, they will rely to some extent on the analysis and judgment of the clerk or staff attorney. This sifting process is necessary both because of the volume of appeals of right and so that the appellate judges can allocate most of their time to considering the appeals that raise important and as yet undecided issues.

As you can see, your first audience inside an appellate court is a recent law school graduate. Although this person has more time to devote to your case than the trial judge did, you must write your brief such that this attorney readily understands the issues and how existing precedent should be applied to decide the case. As the reader will be verifying your statement of facts with the record, you must be accurate in your statement of facts. The better your brief, the more likely that the attorney will use your brief as the model for a memorandum or per curiam opinion. Only when this initial reader recommends an authored opinion, is your appeal likely to receive much attention from a judge actually assigned to the case.

Right after oral argument, the judges vote on the case. If the case merits an authored opinion, one of the judges in the majority is assigned to write the majority opinion. Some judges write all their own authored opinions; others rely initially on their law clerks to draft these opinions. The opinion is then circulated to the other members of that panel for their final approval or disapproval. These judges may write concurring or dissenting opinions. Occasionally, the vote will change after the majority opinion is written. In this case, the majority opinion becomes a dissent. Occasionally you will read cases where this has happened. If the opinions have not been substantially revised, the case will make more sense if you read the majority decision in light of the dissent and not vice versa.

Clerks also play a major role in the courts of last resort. The major sifting process, however, is a different one at this level of court. Unlike the intermediate level appellate courts, which are required to take all appeals of right, much of the business at the highest level is by leave or *Certiorari*. At this step the advocate must convince those involved in the sifting process that the issues are important enough for the court to accept. It is vital that the advocate frame the issues to meet the standards provided by the appropriate court rules. The brief asking for leave is the most important brief. If it fails to persuade the court, the process ends.

If the court grants leave, the advocate will have the opportunity to write another brief on the issues. At this point, the specific members of the bench become important as the audience. The writer will want to read opinions written by members of the court on related issues in order to tailor the arguments to these individuals.

STANDARD OF REVIEW

The advocate must not only know who her audience is on appeal, she must also understand how her audience will look at the issues she raises. This is the standard of review. In Chapter 3, you saw two examples of similar standards at the trial court level. The first was in the context of a Rule 12(b)(6) motion. In order to decide if the plaintiff has failed to state a claim upon which relief can be granted, the trial court assumes that all of the allegations in the plaintiff's complaint are true. The judge then evaluates the complaint to see if the plaintiff has alleged enough to meet the elements of the cause of action.

The trial court uses a similar standard for deciding defendant's motion for a judgment as a matter of law. If the plaintiff, for example, is required to prove that the defendant caused the plaintiff's injuries, the judge will evaluate the proof on causation according to the following spectrum:

Direct evidence that defendant caused the injury.	Reasonable minds could differ on whether the defendant caused the injury.	No evidence that defendant caused the injury.

The judge can only grant the defendant's motion for a judgment as a matter of law if, on the basis of the evidence, no reasonable juror could decide that the defendant caused the injury. As soon as the proofs permit reasonable people to differ, the judge must leave the decision on causation to the fact finder and deny the motion for judgment as a matter of law.

Similar standards exist for the appellate courts as they view appeals from the trial courts. The following discussion of standards of review is by no means exhaustive. It illustrates common standards of review for three types of appealable errors: errors of fact, errors in matters of trial court discretion, and errors of law. The difference between the standards is in the degree of deference the appellate court gives to the factual findings and decisions below.

If the case was tried by the judge, the judge is required to make express findings of fact. In the federal system, this is governed by Fed. R. Civ. Pro. 52(a). Remember that the trial judge was present at the evidentiary hearings and, if the case went to trial, at the bench trial. The judge saw the witnesses and heard the way they described the facts. The judge was able to judge the credibility of the witnesses. The appellate court is not in this position; it will only see the transcript of the testimony. For this reason, the appellate court gives great weight to the trial court's findings of fact. The appellate court applies the "clearly erroneous" standard to these findings. This means that the appellate court will only set aside a verdict based on these facts if it "is left with the definite and firm conviction that a mistake has been committed." *United States v. United States Gypsum Co.,* 333 U.S. 364 (1948). For an appellant, the "clearly erroneous" standard is a very difficult one to meet. As a result, appeals based on factual errors are not often successful.

A second common standard of review is the "abuse of discretion" standard. In the course of proceedings at the trial court level, the judge makes a wide range of rulings on matters such as: the adequacy of the pleadings, the scope of discovery, the admissibility of evidence, the grant of a preliminary injunction, and so forth. This ensures the orderly progression of the case. Trial judges have considerable discretion and must exercise their best judgment in these matters. An "abuse of discretion has been described as a decision that is "clearly unreasonable, arbitrary or fanciful". *Heat and Control, Inc. v. Hester*

Industries, Inc., 785 F.2d 1017, 1023 (Fed. Cir. 1986). "All [abuse of discretion] need mean is that, when judicial action is taken in a discretionary matter, such action cannot be set aside by a reviewing court unless it has a definite and firm conviction that the court below committed a clear error of judgment in the conclusion it reached upon a weighing of the relevant standard." *McBee v. Bomar*, 296 F.2d 235 (6th Cir. 1961). This standard like "clearly erroneous" imposes a heavy burden on the appellant.

The appellate court will also give deference to the decisions of administrative agencies. A reviewing court will only set aside agency action that is "arbitrary, capricious, or an abuse of discretion". Administrative Procedures Act, 5 U.S.C. § 706(2)(a) (1988). Unlike appellate review of a trial court decision, where the appellate court is in the same position to decide the law as the trial court, a reviewing court will defer to an administrative agency's interpretation of statutes and regulations within the agency's area of expertise. The court will, however, make sure that the agency considered all the relevant factors required by the statute or regulation, and that its inquiry was thorough. The ultimate standard, however, is quite narrow. Unless the agency made a clear error of judgment on either the law or the facts, the court will affirm the agency's ruling.[1]

As you can see, appellate courts do not easily overturn factual decisions made by trial courts, discretionary rulings made by trial courts, or decisions within the expertise of administrative agencies. Most successful appeals involve pure questions of law, where the appellant is claiming that the trial court either used the wrong legal standard or misapplied the proper one. In these cases, the appellate court is in the same position as the trial court; it has no reason to give the trial court deference.

Before writing a brief to an appellate court, the advocate should research the standard of review for each issue involved in the appeal. There are two common sources for finding the appropriate standard. Many opinions begin by explaining the standard of review the court is applying to the issues. As a result, the cases you have found in researching the substantive issues may give you the necessary standards of review. Make sure that the procedural posture of the case is analogous to yours and that the jurisdiction is the same. You can also find the appropriate standard of review by consulting the West Digest System under key numbers "Appeal and Error §§ 836–867".

Some courts in their appellate court rules require that the lawyers include a statement of the standard of review at the beginning of the brief. The Ninth Circuit is one such jurisdiction. Even when the appellate court rules do not require that the parties state the standard of review, it is often good practice to do so. An appellant will want to

---

1. *Montana Power Company v. Environ-*   (9th Cir. 1979).
mental Protection Agency, 608 F.2d 334

explain the standard when the appellate court is not required to show deference to the trial court, in matters of law. Appellees, on the other hand, will want to highlight the standard of review when it requires the appellate court to defer to the lower court, in cases with a "clearly erroneous" or "abuse of discretion" standard.

The standard of review section of appellee's brief supporting the decision of the trial court to issue a permanent injunction might read as follows:

> The district court's grant of plaintiff's request for a permanent injunction should be affirmed. A grant of an injunction will only be overturned on appeal if the trial court abused its discretion. A permanent injunction is proper when the plaintiff will suffer irreparable injury if the defendant is not enjoined and when there are no alternative remedies. *Weinberger v. Romero–Barcelo*, 456 U.S. 305 (1982). The district court below properly applied this standard to the facts of this case. The defendant sewer authority was dumping untreated sewage from fifty-four communities into the harbor. The raw sewage presented a health hazard to the general public. Where, as here, there were no alternative means of protecting the public health, the district court's grant of a permanent injunction was not an abuse of discretion and should be affirmed.

Before you begin an appellate brief, consider the standard the appellate court will use to review the issues on appeal. As you write, keep the appellate court in mind as the audience. Remember that you must write not only to the judges or justices that sit on the court, but also to the other attorneys involved in processing the appeals in that particular court.

Chapter 18

ANATOMY OF AN
APPELLATE BRIEF

Appealing a decision from a lower court involves much more than writing and submitting a brief in the appellate court. Every jurisdiction has a long list of procedural requirements for an appeal. The appellate attorney must begin with the appropriate appellate rules and carefully follow the time sequence the rules require. They explain the type of decision that is necessary from the lower court before the case is ripe for appeal, the kinds of documents that must be filed in the lower and appellate courts to commence the appeal, what must be served on opposing counsel, how to order the transcript of hearings below, the deadlines for each of these items, and so forth. Appellate counsel must adhere strictly to the format, timing, and service requirements in order to protect her client's interests. Because this is primarily a writing text and not a treatise on appellate practice, this chapter will deal only with the general requirements for constructing an appellate brief.

The federal intermediate level appellate courts provide a good illustration of a typical appellate system. This chapter illustrates the elements that belong in an appellate brief under Federal Rule of Appellate Procedure 28, the rule applicable to the federal courts of appeals. There are additional rules specific to each circuit. Before beginning work on an appellate brief, be sure to consult the appellate court rules specific to your jurisdiction and level of court.

A brief to a federal circuit court of appeals includes at a minimum the following elements: a caption and title page, a "Table of Contents", a "Table of Cases, Statutes, and Other Authorities Cited", a "Statement of Subject Matter and Appellate Jurisdiction", a "Statement of the Issues Presented for Review", a "Statement of the Case", an "Argument", a "Conclusion", and a closing.

Rule 28. Briefs

(a) **Brief of the Appellant.** The brief of the appellant shall contain under appropriate headings and in the order here indicated:

(1) A table of contents, with page references, and a table of cases (alphabetically arranged), statutes and other authorities cited, with references to the pages of the brief where they are cited.

(2) A statement of subject matter and appellate jurisdiction. The statement shall include: (i) a statement for subject matter jurisdiction in the district court or agency, with citation to applicable statutory provisions and with reference to the relevant facts to establish such jurisdiction; (ii) a statement of the basis for jurisdiction in the court of appeals, with citation to applicable statutory provisions and with reference to the relevant facts to establish such jurisdiction; the statement shall include relevant filing dates establishing timeliness of the appeal or petition for review and (a) shall state that the appeal is from a final order or a final judgment that disposes of all claims with respect to all parties or, if not, (b) shall include information establishing that the court of appeals has jurisdiction on some other basis.

(3) A statement of the issues presented for review.

(4) A statement of the case. The statement shall first indicate briefly the nature of the case, the course of proceedings, and its disposition in the court below. There shall follow a statement of the facts relevant to the issues presented for review, with appropriate references to the record (see subdivision (e)).

(5) An argument. The argument may be preceded by a summary. The argument shall contain the contentions of the appellant with respect to the issues presented, and the reasons therefor, with citations to the authorities, statutes and parts of the record relied on.

(6) A short conclusion stating the precise relief sought.

(b) Brief of the Appellee. The brief of the appellee shall conform to the requirements of subdivision (a)(1)–(6), except that a statement of jurisdiction, of the issues, or of the case need not be made unless the appellee is dissatisfied with the statement of the appellant.

(c) Reply Brief. The appellant may file a brief in reply to the brief of the appellee, and if the appellee has cross-appealed, the appellee may file a brief in reply to the response of the appellant to the issues presented by the cross appeal. No further briefs may be filed except with leave of court. All reply briefs shall contain a table of contents, with page references, and a table of cases (alphabetically arranged), statutes and other authorities cited, with references to the pages of the reply brief where they are cited.

(d) References in Briefs to Parties. Counsel will be expected in their briefs and oral arguments to keep to a minimum references to parties by such designations as "appellant" and "appellee". It promotes clarity to use the designations used in the lower court or in the agency proceedings, or the actual names of parties, or descriptive terms such as "the employee," "the injured person," "the taxpayer," "the ship," "the stevedore," etc.

(e) **References in Briefs to the Record.** References in the briefs to parts of the record reproduced in the appendix filed with the brief of the appellant (see Rule 30(a)) shall be to the pages of the appendix at which those parts appear. If the appendix is prepared after the briefs are filed, references in the briefs to the record shall be made by one of the methods allowed by Rule 30(c). If the record is reproduced in accordance with the provisions of Rule 30(f), or if references are made in the briefs to parts of the record not reproduced, the references shall be to the pages of the parts of the record involved; e.g., Answer p. 7, Motion for Judgment p. 2, Transcript p. 231. Intelligible abbreviations may be used. If reference is made to evidence the admissibility of which is in controversy, reference shall be made to the pages of the appendix or of the transcript at which the evidence was identified, offered, and received or rejected.

(f) **Reproduction of Statutes, Rules, Regulations, Etc.** If determination of the issues presented requires the study of statutes, rules, regulations, etc. or relevant parts thereof, they shall be reproduced in the brief or in an addendum at the end, or they may be supplied to the court in pamphlet form.

(g) **Length of Briefs.** Except by permission of the court, or as specified by local rule of the court of appeals, principal briefs shall not exceed 50 pages, and reply briefs shall not exceed 25 pages, exclusive of pages containing the table of contents, tables of citations and any addendum containing statutes, rules, regulations, etc.

(h) **Briefs in Cases Involving Cross Appeals.** If a cross appeal is filed, the party who first files a notice of appeal, or in the event that the notices are filed on the same day, the plaintiff in the proceeding below, shall be deemed the appellant for the purposes of this rule and Rules 30 and 31, unless the parties otherwise agree or the court otherwise orders. The brief of the appellee shall conform to the requirements of subdivision (a)(1)-(6) of this rule with respect to the appellee's cross appeal as well as respond to the brief of the appellant except that a statement of the case need not be made unless the appellee is dissatisfied with the statement of the appellant.

(i) **Briefs in Cases Involving Multiple Appellants or Appellees.** In cases involving more than one appellant or appellee, including cases consolidated for purposes of the appeal, any number of either may join in a single brief, and any appellant or appellee may adopt by reference any part of the brief of another. Parties may similarly join in reply briefs.

(j) Citation of Supplemental Authorities. When pertinent and significant authorities come to the attention of a party after the party's brief has been filed, or after oral argument but before decision, a party may promptly advise the clerk of the court, by letter, with a copy to all counsel, setting forth the citations. There shall be a reference either to the page of the brief or to a point argued orally to which the citations pertain, but the letter shall without argument state the reasons for the supplemental citations. Any response shall be made promptly and shall be similarly limited.

The requirements for an appellant's brief are listed in 28(a) and those for the appellee in 28(b). Although the appellee is not required to include a statement of the issues or of the case unless he is dissatisfied with the statements included by the appellant, most appellees are dissatisfied with the statements of issues and the case the opponent includes. The appellant uses the statements of issues and facts to present her theory of the case. As counsel for the appellee wants an opportunity to present his client's perspective of the issues and facts, he will normally include these sections as well.

The terms appellant and appellee are often confusing to a court that deals with a variety of appealing parties. In order to avoid this problem, Rule 28(e) suggests using instead the references from the lower court, the names of the parties, or descriptive terms. Descriptive terms are often the most useful to the appellate audience. The members of the court do not know the parties by name. To avoid confusion, try generic terms, such as "employer", "supplier", "putative father", "claimant", "stockholder", etc. The advocate should choose the designations with care not only to promote clarity, but also to cast the characters in the appropriate light. Consider the following possible terms a lawyer could use in a paternity case: "the biological father", "the alleged father", "the putative father". Each elicits a different connotation. Your choice of terminology depends on your client's perspective and the way you wish to characterize the parties.

Everywhere in the brief that the attorney refers to the record, he must cite to the record. Rule 28(e). This rule applies to references to facts in the Statement of the Case and to references in the Argument. Intelligible abbreviations are permissible, so that transcript may be abbreviated, for example, TR.

Normally, the briefs of appellant and appellee are limited to 50 pages, excluding the tables of contents and authorities. Rule 28(g). For the convenience of the court personnel, use arabic numerals to number the items that are included in the page limit and a different numbering system, e.g. small type roman numerals, for the items that are not included. The format requirements concerning type of paper and the general page and type size for briefs are listed in Rule 32.

The title page with its caption includes the following:

UNITED STATES COURT OF APPEALS
FOR THE SIXTH CIRCUIT

Docket No. 87–3572

WAYNE F. ROBINSON,

Plaintiff–Appellant,

–against–

R.F. JONES COMPANY,

Defendant–Appellee.

On Appeal from the United States District Court
For the Eastern District of Michigan

APPELLANT'S BRIEF

Robert W. Johnson
Gilmore, Whitsom & Johnson
Attorneys for Appellant
3846 Woodward Avenue
Detroit, Michigan 48202
(313) 577–4824

The table of contents lists all of the sections of the brief, and includes page references for the point headings. Note the format distinctions for major, minor and sub-point headings in the following example. You should include the full text of the point headings in the table of contents.

TABLE OF CONTENTS

TABLE OF CASES, STATUTES AND OTHER AUTHORITIES CITED

STATEMENT OF SUBJECT MATTER AND APPELLATE JURISDICTION

Although a statement of jurisdiction has been required in briefs filed in the United States Supreme Court for some time, this is a recent requirement at the intermediate appellate level.[1] The statement must include the basis for jurisdiction below and in the court of appeals with

---

1. This amendment to the Federal Rules of Appellate Procedure became effec- tive on December 1, 1991.

citations to the relevant statutory provisions and facts. The following is an example:

Subject matter jurisdiction in the United States District Court for the Southern District of Indiana arises both under general federal question jurisdiction, 28 U.S.C. § 1331 (1988), and specifically under the Comprehensive Environmental Response, Compensation, and Liability Act of 1980, 42. U.S.C. § 9613(b) (1988), which gives federal district courts exclusive original jurisdiction of CERCLA cases without regard to the amount in controversy or the citizenship of the parties. This case was initiated by the Environmental Protection Agency to recover response costs from defendant-appellee, Delaware County for the cleanup of hazardous wastes under 42 U.S.C. § 9607(a) (1988).

The United States Court of Appeals for the Seventh Circuit has appellate jurisdiction of all appeals from final decisions of the district courts under 28 U.S.C. § 1291 (1988). The final judgment in this case was entered on December 11, 1991. Notice of appeal was filed in the district court on January 8, 1992.

STATEMENT OF THE ISSUES PRESENTED FOR REVIEW

This section lists the questions presented. Be sure to check the appellate rules for your jurisdiction for the appropriate nomenclature. For a discussion of how to draft appellate issues, see Chapter 19.

A few jurisdictions require that the writer indicate after each question how the trial court answered the question and what the party contends the answer should be. Always check the relevant appellate rules and draft the section accordingly.

STATEMENT OF THE CASE

As you can see from Rule 28(a)(4), in the federal circuit courts of appeals, the statement of the case includes three parts, the nature of the case, the procedure and the substantive facts. For further information about the statement of the case, see Chapter 20.

ARGUMENT

Rule 28(a)(5) requires an argument. Chapter 21 explains how to structure the argument section of an appellate brief.

CONCLUSION

The conclusion in an appellate brief is a request for relief. Always check the applicable court rules for the specific title the court requires for this section. The conclusion is a one line statement of what the appellate court should do with the lower court's decision. The appellee will want the judgment from the lower court affirmed. The appellant should be more specific about the relief, for example: the case should be reversed and remanded with instructions that the trial court issue an injunction; the jury verdict and judgment should be reversed and the case remanded to superior court for a new trial; the order entered by the district court should be reversed and the case remanded for a hearing on the question of damages only, and so forth.

CLOSING

As with a brief to a trial court, an appellate brief needs a closing that includes the date and the attorney's name, address, telephone number, state bar identification number, and signature. The following is an example of an appellate brief closing.

Dated: January 8, 1988   Respectfully submitted,

                                        Neil R. Johansen (P–26822)
                                        Wellman, Gordon, Mann &
                                        Johansen
                                        Attorneys for Appellant
                                        468 W. Ferry Mall
                                        Boston, Massachusetts 02140
                                        (617) 577–4824

Additional Sections of Appellate Briefs

While the sections described above are those required by Rule 28 for the federal courts of appeals, rules governing other jurisdictions and levels of court require additional sections. The United States Supreme Court, for example, also requires in a brief on the merits: a list of the parties to the proceeding, Supreme Court Rule 34.1(b), citations to the opinions and judgments below, Rule 34.1(d), and the constitutional, statutory, and regulatory provisions involved in the case, Rule 34.1(f). Some courts require that the brief include a request for oral argument.

APPELLATE BRIEF CHECKLIST

TITLE PAGE

Caption (court, names of parties, case number)

Title of Document (*APPELLANT'S BRIEF*)
                             (*APPELLEE'S BRIEF*)

Some courts also require a request for oral argument (*ORAL ARGU-MENT REQUESTED*) on the title page.

Date

Attorney's name, address, telephone number, and state bar identification number

Be sure to use correct citation form here and in the first mention of each authority in the argument section. Thereafter short form citations are permissible.

STATEMENT OF SUBJECT MATTER AND APPELLATE JURISDICTION

Include the statutory and factual basis subject matter jurisdiction in the lower court or agency.

Include the statutory basis for appellate jurisdiction.

Include the dates of entry of the final order or judgment and the notice of appeal.

STATEMENT OF THE ISSUES PRESENTED FOR REVIEW

Draft according to the type of issue, legal, procedural, factual.

Make it readable.

Focus the court's attention on your theory.

STATEMENT OF THE CASE

Includes the subject of the litigation, the claims of the parties, the facts, the procedural history, the claims of error.

— Include context.

— Use chronological order.

— Include references to the specific pages of the record where each fact appears.

— Highlight what helps you and minimize *necessary,* but harmful facts.

Note that some jurisdictions require that the standard of review be included in this section.

SUMMARY OF ARGUMENT

Include a summary of argument if it is required by the rules or it will be helpful to the judges.

— Include the issues.
— Include your contentions and very briefly the reasons for these contentions.
— Include major authority.

ARGUMENT

— Thesis paragraph or section with context, brief outline of the issues and arguments in the order in which you will present them, and your punch line. **MAKE SURE YOUR THEORY OF THE CASE FROM YOUR CLIENT'S PERSPECTIVE COMES THROUGH!** If you have included a summary of the argument, it can serve as the thesis section. Be sure to avoid redundancy.
— Point headings where helpful to the brief. Point headings should be single-spaced in the body of the brief.
— Case usage
  — General rule (There is no need to give a fact specific holding.)
  — Specific rule and holding (Include a fact specific holding to illustrate the rule and its application when you want the court to follow the same rule.)
  — Reasoning (When you want the court to adopt the same or similar reasoning, use a fact specific holding sufficient to show why the reasoning should be applied to your case.)
  — Policy (Include a fact specific holding to show why that policy should be applied to your case.)
— Writing
  — Remember the reader.
  — Avoid leaps in logic.
  — Explain yourself fully; educate the judge.
  — Use thesis sentences to introduce each issue or argument. These may be the point headings.
  — Use topic sentences to explain the purpose of each paragraph.
  — Use transitions to help the reader understand the relationship between different points and authorities.
  — Avoid taking a defensive posture.
  — Do not concede unnecessary points.
  — Rebut opponent's arguments affirmatively.

REVISING STAGE

— Check for logical flow.

    — Check for coherent theory.

    — Check for advocacy (defensiveness).

    — Revise with the reader in mind.

EDITING STAGE

    — Take out empty words and phrases.

    — Avoid passive voice unless used for special effect.

    — Check sentence and paragraph length.

    — Check for thesis and topic sentences, transitions.

    — Update your research for the final time—Include parallel cites and subsequent history references. Include prior history when it is required.

    — Check cite form.

    — Proofread for typographical errors and spelling mistakes.

CONCLUSION

Use short form and ask for the relief you want.

CLOSING

Date

Signature line

Attorney's name, address, telephone phone number, and state bar identification number as above.

Chapter 19

USING THE THEORY OF THE
CASE TO DRAFT THE
ISSUES ON APPEAL

In order to write a persuasive appellate brief, an advocate needs a theory of the case. The theory of the case is the client's perspective put in a legal framework that is consistent with public policy. In essence, it is the reason the client should win. An attorney should have a theory of the case from the beginning of the litigation. This theory should appear in the complaint or answer, in the motions at various stages of the litigation, and at the trial. If the lawyer has a coherent theory from the outset, it will be reflected in the record and transcript that goes to the appellate court. The theory helps the appellate attorney frame the issues on appeal, craft the statement of the case, focus the arguments, and characterize the law to create a logically consistent and persuasive brief.

Theory of the Case

In earlier chapters, you have seen examples of various theories. In Chapter 16, for example, there are questions presented drafted by attorneys for the husband and wife in a divorce case where alimony is at issue. One theory is that alimony should be awarded to a wife as compensation for the time and effort she put into building a family and a way of life for that family. The issue as stated by her attorney incorporates this theory:

> Is a wife entitled to alimony to raise her standard of living to that which she enjoyed during the marriage, when she has been married for thirty years, supported her husband while he went to graduate school, raised three children and always put the welfare of her family before her personal aspirations?

The theory of the case from the husband's perspective is different. Alimony is not viewed as a payment for past services, but as an aid to someone who is unable to take care of herself. His theory appears in the following question:

Should the court deny alimony, which is designed to take care of those who are unable to provide for themselves, to a well educated, professional woman, who is employed full time in her chosen profession?

The following point headings from *United States v. Nixon*, 418 U.S. 683 (1974), also presented in Chapter 16, leave no doubt in your mind as to the theories of the special prosecutor and Nixon's attorney. Leon Jaworski stated:

The power of the courts to issue subpoenas, long recognized by the courts, flows from the fundamental principle that no man is above the law.

James St. Clair expressed his theory of the case for Nixon in the following:

The rights of privacy and freedom of expression support the absolute confidentiality of presidential communications with his advisors.[1]

You can see from these point headings that the theory is based on the client's perspective, the legal rule, and the public policy. Jaworski's statement uses the legal rule, the power of the court to issue subpoenas, and the fundamental democratic principle that all are equal before the law. St. Clair, on the other hand, evokes individual freedoms and the necessity for executive privilege.

The surface mining example presented in the introduction to Section V has its theories as well. The Office of Surface Mining will formulate a theory based on the legal rule—the Surface Mining Control and Reclamation Act, and the policy—that strip mined land should be reclaimed rather than being left as a scar on the land, and that the cost of reclamation should be incorporated into the cost of mining. The Office of Surface Mining is the guardian of the land. Its role is to ensure that surface mined land is returned to its original contours. This theory is an obvious one based on the statute and the function of the administrative agency.

The opposing theory is the common sense theory. The owner of the land is a farmer. Before the mining, his land was too steep and uneven to be valuable as farmland. He had difficulty scratching out a living. After surface mining for coal, the mining company left the land level. It is more valuable for the farmer-owner than before the mining. It makes no sense for the mining company to have to restore the land to its original contours under the terms of the mining permit and at considerable cost, when the resulting land will be worth substantially less to the owner. The farmer would then have to pay to have the land leveled again for farming. The purpose of the statute would be better served by ignoring the reclamation provision of the permit.

---

1. This point heading comes from the Brief for Respondent filed in *United States v. Nixon*, 418 U.S. 683 (1974). Reprinted with permission from James D. St. Clair. Copyright © by James D. St. Clair.

The governmental agency will incorporate the theory throughout the case. It will file a complaint against the mining company to enforce the provisions of the permit. It will argue the statute, the purpose behind the statute, and the terms of the surface mining permit. It will also argue that the mountains of Appalachia are permanently scarred from pre-statute mining, because there was no method for forcing reclamation of the land. By the time the case gets to the appellate court, the record will be saturated with the agency's theory.

The mining company will argue the common sense theory throughout the pretrial and trial proceedings. The land belongs to the farmer. He has a right to alter the contour of the land to make it amenable to farming. The mining company is perfectly willing to comply with mining permit conditions that are reasonable, but not to reach a ridiculous result. This theory, too, should be evident from the record that goes to the appellate court.

The theory of the case gives the advocate a vehicle for presenting the law, policy, and the client's perspective. It is useful for organizing and focusing the affirmative arguments in the brief. The advocate, however, must also rebut the arguments made by the opponent. The theory of the case is often a useful tool in framing the rebuttal section of the argument as well as the affirmative portion. In the alimony example presented above, the theories of the case espoused by the two sides originated in the rule chosen by the parties. If the advocate for one side can persuade the court that one particular rule is proper, the other rule must by definition be inapplicable. The competing theories in the Nixon Watergate case stem from two fundamentally different views of the president, his position in relation to the public, and his function. The difference between the theories in the strip mining case lies in the public policy. If the policy is to prevent permanent scarring of the land, then either a requirement that the miner return the contour of the land to its pre-mined condition or that it leave the land in condition for an alternative acceptable use, is consistent with the policy. Once the advocate has figured out the distinction between the two theories, he can arrange the arguments to emphasize his theory and minimize the effect of the opponent's theory.

DRAFTING THE ISSUES ON APPEAL

As you draft the issues on appeal, remember to incorporate your theory of the case. The following examples come from briefs filed in the United States Supreme Court in the case of *Lucas v. South Carolina Coastal Council*, No. 91–453 (U.S. October Term 1991). Lucas purchased two lots along the South Carolina coast in 1986 with the intention of building houses on both and selling one. Under the South Carolina Beachfront Management Act, S. C. Code Ann. § 48–39–250 et seq. (Supp. 1990), enacted in 1988, development was prohibited seaward of a setback line. Lucas' two lots are seaward of the setback line established by the South Carolina Coastal Council. Lucas claims a "taking" under the Fifth Amendment of the United States Constitution. The issue as stated by the petitioner is:

> Does a land-use regulation, pursuant to a **state's police power**, require compensation under the Constitution's Fifth Amendment if it **totally eliminates the value of private property**?[2] (emphasis added)

Contrast this with the issue drafted in one of the amicus briefs filed in support of the respondent.

> Does the Federal Constitution **deny** State legislatures the **power to prevent public harm** through the use of building restrictions that **incidentally deprive some land of current market value**?[3] (emphasis added)

Both questions address the same issue and provide the same general information: the source of the rule—the United States Constitution, the state's power to regulate, and the effect on private property. Both advocates have presented the issue squarely to the Court. The competing theories, however, are apparent from the way the authors characterized the information.

Appellate questions are drafted as general questions, because appellate courts establish precedent that is applicable beyond the specific case. As a consequence, use generic terms rather than specific references to the parties.

> Is a lender liable as an "owner" under CERCLA, 42 U.S.C. § 9607 (1988), for payment of response costs to clean up hazardous waste, when it takes title to the site in a foreclosure action?

The general format for appellate questions is that same as that used in questions presented in memos and in briefs at the trial court level—"does the RULE apply to the FACTS?". This is the logical order from the reader's perspective. If the question requires that you present more than one level of rule, begin with the most general rule and then add increasing levels of specificity. The following example has three layers of rule.

> Does the Federal Constitution deny State legislatures the power to prevent public harm through the use of building restrictions that incidentally deprive some land of current market value?[4]

---

2. This statement of the issue comes from Petitioner's Brief on the Merits, *Lucas v. South Carolina Coastal Council*, Docket Number 91–453, United States Supreme Court. Permission granted by counsel to David H. Lucas: A. Camden Lewis, Esq., Gerald M. Finkel, Esq., and Professor David J. Bederman. Copyright © 1991 by A. Camden Lewis, Esq., Gerald M. Finkel, Esq., and Professor David J. Bederman.

3. This appellate issue comes from the Brief of the Members of the National

Growth Management Leadership Project as Amici Curiae in Support of Respondent, filed in *Lucas v. South Carolina Coastal Council*, Docket Number 91–453, United States Supreme Court. Reprinted with permission from John A. Humbach, counsel for the National Growth Management Leadership Project. Copyright © 1991 by John A. Humbach.

4. See *supra* note 3.

It begins with the Federal Constitution, moves to the state police power, and ends with the specific reference to "building restrictions".

As with references to the parties and the law, the facts in appellate questions are usually presented generally, so that the court can create precedent with a wider application. It is also easier to draft readable questions if you omit detailed facts. Sometimes, however, you are asking the court to draw distinctions based on specific facts; a more fact specific question is necessary in these circumstances.

Was the search of defendant unreasonable under the Fourth Amendment to the United States Constitution such that the evidence seized should be suppressed, when undercover drug enforcement officers procured a warrant for defendant's arrest based on a traffic violation, stopped defendant, pulled him outside the car and handcuffed him, and forceably extracted the items from his mouth?

With appellate issues that involve purely questions of law, references to the lower court and the standard of review are distracting and unnecessary. If, however, the standard of review is important from your client's perspective, consider including it in your issue. The following question is drafted for the appellee.

Did the district court abuse its discretion when it issued a preliminary injunction requiring that in considering applicants for temporary residence under the Special Agricultural Worker program, 8 U.S.C. § 1160 (Supp. 1986), the Immigration and Naturalization Service (1) provide competent interpreters, (2) permit applicants to present witnesses, and (3) particularize the evidence presented on the I–696 form?

The appellee begins by reminding the appellate court of the applicable standard of review, abuse of discretion. Remember that appellate review of the grant or denial of a preliminary injunction is narrow, and the appellate court will only reverse the decision below if the lower court made a clear error in judgment. While the appellant would not want to begin by highlighting its hefty burden, the advocate for the appellee has an interest in doing so.

Once you have a draft of a question that presents the issue directly to the court, incorporates your theory of the case, and includes necessary facts without unnecessary detail, revise the question for readability. State the question affirmatively; readers understand positive statements better than those that include negatives, particularly multiple negatives. State the question in the active voice, unless you have a specific reason for using the passive voice. Keep the question as concise as possible; readers will miss some of the content in long convoluted questions. Choose the words with care, so that you convey the precise meaning you intend and your theory of the case; edit out nebulous, empty, and unnecessary words.

Exercise 19 A.

Read the following brief synopsis of a products liability case and formulate the theories of opposing counsel.

The trial court granted summary judgment for the defendant-fabricator, who had constructed a storage tank that caused the decedent's death. The fabricator built the tank under a contract with defendant-manufacturer and according to the specifications of defendant-engineer. The issue was whether, under these circumstances, the fabricator had a duty of care to the decedent.

The decedent was painting the inside of an oily waste treatment tank with a highly flammable coating when he dropped the light he was using to illuminate the interior of the tank. The bulb broke, causing an explosion and fire. The decedent died of his injuries. The fabricator's expert conceded that it could have built the tank with an interior lighting system and a pressure release valve. However, it constructed the tank under the contract and specifications of the other defendants. The specifications called for coating with the highly flammable substance.

Under the law of the jurisdiction, the manufacturer had a duty to furnish a product that was not unreasonably dangerous to those who used the product in the intended manner or a manner the manufacturer could reasonably foresee. There are no cases, however, that address the duty to third parties of a fabricator who supplies a product under contract to one party according to the specifications of another.

The plaintiff argued that the trial court should not have granted summary judgment when there was a material fact at issue. The defendant argued that summary judgment was proper.

Chapter 20

CRAFTING A STATEMENT
OF THE CASE

The statement of the case in an appellate brief includes a brief statement of the nature of the case, the procedural posture, and the substantive facts. The items that you include, the weight given to each item, and the organization depend on the issues involved in the appeal and the applicable appellate court rules. Although you can draft the statement of facts at any point in the brief writing process, many attorneys prefer to save the statement of facts for the end of the process. At this point, they have the theory of the case well in mind and they know all of the legally relevant facts they actually used in the argument section. Because the statement of facts is such an important part of the brief, you must be sure to save enough time to draft it carefully.

In an appellate brief, the function of the argument section is to explain analytically how the court can reach the desired result. The role of the statement of the case is to persuade the appellate court that fairness and justice favor your client. Unlike the trial judge, who may get to know the client during the courtroom proceedings, the appellate court will understand your client only from the brief. The appellate advocate, therefore, must craft the statement of the case with particular care.

Nature of the Case

The statement of the case begins with a paragraph or two describing the nature of the case. The purpose is to put the case in context for the court and identify the parties, particularly your client. As an advocate you should use this section to get the court's attention and present your theory of the case. The following example comes from a brief written for respondent, Union Gas Company in a "superfund" reimbursement action.

> The sudden release of coal tar into Brodhead Creek in Strouds-burg, Pennsylvania in October 1980 caused the United States to declare the site the nation's first emergency Superfund site. A

map of the site is contained in the Joint Appendix at J.A. 108. Adjacent to the stream from 1890 to 1948 in an industrial section of Stroudsburg had been a carburetted water gas plant which produced coal gas as well as its by-product, coal tar. While some constituents of coal tar are now defined as hazardous substances under CERCLA (J.A. 51), the EPA regards in-ground disposal of coal tar as state of the art technology during the first part of this century (see EPA Amended Fund Authorization Report). The plant was dismantled in 1948 and replaced successively by propane and natural gas distribution systems. The Company operating the plant changed ownership several times before being merged into respondent in 1978.[1]

The author gets your attention with the triggering event and then proceeds to demonstrate the tenuous connection between this occurrence and his client, the respondent. He does this by using a number of advocacy techniques. First, he creates distance in time between the event and his client. The offending plant operated from 1890 to 1948. Notice the juxtaposition of this time period with what is **now** defined as hazardous, "some constituents of coal tar". The author carefully placed this material in a dependent clause. The main clause focuses your attention on the EPA's own report. He sanitizes the dumping as "in-ground disposal" and characterizes it as "state of the art technology during the first part of this century". He provides background facts on the successive technological changes to enhance the temporal distance between the original cause and his client. Finally, the last sentence of the paragraph introduces the client as the object of a preposition in a passive merger. The facts of this case are critical to the theory and the arguments that follow.

In some appeals, the law is more important to the theory and the nature of the case. The following is an example of a law based introduction.

> This case involves the State of Connecticut's latest attempt to devise a beer pricing affirmation scheme that can withstand scrutiny under the Commerce Clause of the United States Constitution. Appellees, plaintiffs below, are a brewers' trade association and individual brewers and importers of beer injured by the Connecticut beer price affirmation law (the "brewers"). Appellants, defendants below, are the Connecticut officials responsible for enforcing the statute ("Connecticut") and an intervenor liquor wholesalers' trade association.
>
> The Connecticut law at issue here and its predecessor, which was declared unconstitutional in *United States Brewers Ass'n, Inc. v. Healy*, 464 U.S. 909 (1983), *aff'g per curiam*, 692 F.2d 275 (2d Cir.

---

1. This introductory paragraph comes from the Brief for Respondent filed in *Commonwealth of Pennsylvania v. Union Gas Co.*, Docket Number 87–1241, United States Supreme Court (1987). Reprinted with permission from Robert A. Swift of Kohn, Nast & Graf, P.C., counsel for Union Gas Co. Copyright © 1987 by Robert A. Swift.

1982), *rev'g* 532 F. Supp. 1312 (D. Conn. 1982) ("*Healy I* "), were both adopted to deal with the same problem. Even though brewers' prices to Connecticut wholesalers were not the highest in the four-state area, the retail price of beer has historically been higher in Connecticut than in the bordering States of Massachusetts, New York and Rhode Island. *Healy I*, 532 F. Supp. at 1320; Conn. Br. 6; Wholesalers Br. 8. As a result, Connecticut residents living in border areas have crossed state lines to purchase beer in other States at lower prices. Since 1981, the Connecticut legislature has sought to eliminate the price advantage available in bordering States by a combination of price posting (requiring brewers to state their prices during a future period in Connecticut) and price affirmation (linking the maximum brewer price in Connecticut to the brewer's minimum price for the same item anywhere in any bordering State). Both the original Connecticut statute and the current statute have the same purpose—to eliminate the availability of beer at lower prices in the bordering States—and the same practical effect—to control the brewers' pricing decisions in those States.[2]

This statement of the case begins with the Beer Institute's theory. Notice the word choice "beer affirmation price **scheme**". (Emphasis added).

The first paragraph then identifies the parties. The second paragraph expands on the theory. The author placed the most important information in the first and last sentences of the paragraph where the reader is most likely to see it. The first sentence cites to the United States Supreme Court case that held unconstitutional Connecticut's first attempt at regulating beer prices. The paragraph ends with the substance of the Commerce clause violation, Connecticut's attempt to control prices in other states. The middle of the paragraph explains the substance of the legislation.

Procedure

The statement of the case must also include a discussion of the procedure. Fed. Rule App. Proc. 28(a)(4). In an office memorandum or a brief to a trial court, a discussion of procedure will perforce be limited or nonexistent. In appellate courts, it is necessary and may be critical. The reason for this is inherent in the appellate process. There is always a procedural context from a lower court or an administrative agency for the issues on appeal. The reader in the appellate court needs to know what happened below in order to understand what the court is being asked to decide. The scope of this section varies with the case. At the highest level court in a jurisdiction, there may be decisions from two levels of court below. Limit the discussion, however,

---

2. These introductory paragraphs are from the Brief for the Appellees filed in *Healy v. The Beer Institute*, Docket Numbers 88–449, 88–513, United States Supreme Court (1988). Reprinted with permission of Jeffrey I. Glekel of Skadden, Arps, Slate, Meagher & From, counsel for The Beer Institute. Copyright © 1988 by Jeffrey I. Glekel.

to the information that is necessary to the issues on appeal. Remember that the type of decision by the trial court may dictate the level of review given by the appellate court. The appellate court will treat a dismissal granted in response to a Fed. Rule of Civ. Proc. 12(b)(6) motion for failure to state a claim, or a Rule 56 motion for summary judgment differently from a judgment entered after a bench trial or a jury verdict. Be sure to document the procedural history of the case with appropriate references to the procedural record below. Note that some courts require the writer to include the standard of review in this section.

The placement of the procedure depends on the nature of the appeal and the applicable court rules. To the extent that you have discretion, consider placing the procedure either (1) after the nature of the case in order to highlight it from your client's perspective, (2) where the reader logically needs the information, or (3) at the end of a discussion of the substantive facts to serve as a transition to the argument section.

The procedure should be written from the client's perspective. Even if your client lost below, characterize it in the best light possible.

Petitioner filed suit against the SCCC in the South Carolina Court of Common Pleas. Lucas alleged that the Beachfront Management Act worked a taking of his property for public use for which the state was required by the Fifth Amendment to pay just compensation. Pet. App. 35.

The Court of Common Pleas held that the SCCC's actions pursuant to the Act had eliminated Lucas' "unrestricted right of use" of his land (Pet. App. 37) and * * * had deprived him of "the essential elements of ownership (Pet. App. 39), infringing on "private property in the most traditional sense of the term" (Pet. App. 38). By permanently prohibiting construction on Lucas' two lots, the court found, the SCCC "deprives Lucas of any reasonable economic use of the lots * * * and renders them valueless" (Pet. App. 37), so that [t]he damage to the two lots by virtue of the restrictions prohibiting any form of development is total." Pet. App. 38. Because it interpreted this Court's decisions to mean "that regulatory activity by a governmental agency which denies an owner economically viable use of his land amounts to a taking under the Fifth Amendment * * * for which just compensation must be paid" (Pet. App. 40), even where the regulation "was enacted to * * * benefit * * * the general public" (Pet. App. 38), the Court of Common Pleas held it was "manifest that the imposition of setback lines by the [SCCC] ha[s] resulted in a total taking of Lucas' two beachfront lots." Pet. App. 40.

The South Carolina Supreme Court reversed. It did not disturb the trial court's holding that the Act deprived Lucas of "private property in the most traditional sense." Pet. App. 38. A bare majority of the court, however, held that a "nuisance-like exception" to the just compensation requirement applies (Pet. App. 12) whenever a use restriction serves to "prevent serious injury to the community" (Pet. App. 15), even though the restriction "operates to deprive a landowner of 'all economically viable use' of his property." Pet. App. 9. See also Pet. App. 11–12. Thus, because Lucas did not contest that the Beachfront Management Act "is necessary to prevent a great public harm" (Pet. App. 8), the court held that the bar on development of Lucas' property did not amount to a compensable taking.

Two members of the court dissented. They concluded, first, that the primary purpose of the Act was not to prevent a public nuisance but to eliminate "activities and effects" that could not "fairly be considered 'noxious' " (Pet. App. 27), and, second, that because the state had eliminated all "economically viable use" of Lucas' land, a taking had occurred. Pet. App. 30.[3]

Notice that the authors began and ended on a positive note. They discussed the trial court decision in favor of the petitioner in detail, quoting favorable language from the opinion. They also pointed out that the trial court relied on the United States Supreme Court's decisions to reach the decision. The middle paragraph is devoted to the adverse decision in the South Carolina Supreme Court. The authors, however, controlled the damage in three ways. First, they pointed out what remains of the trial court decision. Second, they explained that the decision was by a "bare majority". Third, they limited the effect of the decision by their characterization. The authors ended the procedure with reference to the dissent.

In another amicus brief submitted on behalf of the petitioner in the same case, the reference to the dissent was even stronger.

In a strong dissenting opinion, Judge Harwell refused to accept the proposition that South Carolina could regulate property to "oblivion" and found that while the taking was permissible for a public purpose, it was not designed to prevent a nuisance or noxious activities on the plaintiff's land, and that therefore compensation was required.[4]

The respondent's characterization of the South Carolina Supreme Court's decision is quite different.

---

3. This example was taken from the Brief Amicus Curiae of the American Farm Bureau Federation and the South Carolina Farm Bureau Federation in Support of Petitioner filed in *Lucas v. South Carolina Coastal Council*, United States Supreme Court, Docket Number 91–453 (1991). Reprinted with permission from John J. Rademacher, General Counsel for the American Farm Bureau Federation. Copyright © 1991 by John J. Rademacher.

4. This example was taken from the Brief of the Institute of Justice as Amicus Curiae in Support of Petitioner in *Lucas v. South Carolina Coastal Council*. Docket Number 91–453, United States Supreme Court (1991). Reprinted with permission from Institute of Justice, William H. Mellor III, Counsel of Record, Richard Epstein, Of Counsel. Copyright © 1991 by Institute of Justice, William H. Mellor III, Counsel of Record, Richard Epstein, Of Counsel.

On the merits, the South Carolina Supreme Court reversed the decision of the circuit court. Pet. App. 1. The court opined that petitioner erroneously relied upon the legal position that he had lost "all economically viable use" of his property and this factor alone entitled him to compensation under the Fifth Amendment. Pet. App. 12. Reviewing the current factors applied by the United States Supreme Court in analyzing "takings" cases, the court concluded that because Lucas failed to challenge the purpose of the 1988 Act and indeed conceded the importance and validity of the Act, his claim failed. Pet. App. at 8–12. After listing the purposes and findings, the court stated that it was "in no position to, sua sponte take issue with the legislative findings." The court rejected his theory that "in all cases when all economically viable use is extinguished by regulation, compensation is due." Pet. App. 12.[5]

The authors rely only on the majority decision. They neatly deflect the petitioner's theory of the case, that he lost "all economically viable use" of the land, and present their own theory that the purpose of the Act is paramount and that Lucas should have based his challenge on the Act. They also point out petitioner's failure to challenge the Act and his concession that it is valid. These authors, too, highlight the fact that the court relied on the United States Supreme Court decisions to reach its decision.

In this law, rather than fact based appeal, these brief writers used their characterizations of the decisions below as a vehicle for presenting their theories of the case.

Substantive Facts

The substantive facts constitute the balance of the statement of the case. The substantive facts provide the necessary details on who, what, where, when, why and how. They may also include the language of documents or statutes that give rise to the issues on appeal. The process of writing this section involves choosing the facts to include and finding all references to these facts in the record below. The record may include the pleadings—the complaint and the answer, various motions and answers, exhibits, the transcript of hearings held in the lower court, and the final order or judgment entered below. The writer uses these documents as the authority for the facts given in the statement of facts and in the argument. Appellate rules require that the brief writer include the references in the brief, both in the argument section and the statement of facts. See, for example, Fed. Rule App. Proc. 28(e). If a fact appears in more than one place in the record, you must provide each reference. You will need all the legally relevant facts, the background facts, and the emotional facts that help you explain your client's position. Because many jurisdictions require that

---

5. This example was taken from the Respondent's Brief on the Merits in *Lucas v. South Carolina Coastal Council*, Docket Number 91–453, United States Supreme Court (1991). Reprinted with permission from C. C. Harness, General Counsel for the South Carolina Coastal Council. Copyright © 1991 by C. C. Harness, General Counsel for the South Carolina Coastal Council.

you present the substantive facts in chronological order, be sure to check the appellate rules before you begin. Even if the rules do not require that you use chronological order, it is often the most logical order to use.

Once you have chosen and organized the facts, consider their relative importance. For clarity and to aid in presenting your theory of the case, highlight the critical facts by including interesting detail. Consider quoting a few short sections of the record for emphasis. An admission from a witness for the opposing party can be effective. Likewise, a telling segment from the cross examination by the attorney for your client is helpful. Integrate the quotations carefully into your text, so they emphasize your point without distracting the reader. Remember to be selective as overuse of quotations will dilute the effect. Summarize those facts which deserve only brief mention. Work to make the presentation of the facts as concise as possible.

The scope of the substantive facts you include will depend on whether the issues are legal or factual. The following examples illustrate the statement of facts in a fact based appeal. Notice the different level of detail used by the lawyers for appellant and appellee.

BRIEF OF APPELLANT [1]

STATEMENT OF FACTS

This is an appeal from a summary judgment granted in a five-year-old breach of contract action to Defendant–Appellee Fuqua Industries, Inc. (Fuqua) on the ground that, as a matter of law, Fuqua had no contract with Plaintiff–Appellant Arnold Palmer Golf Company (Palmer). Palmer contends that a Memorandum of Intent signed by it and Fuqua (R. 24–30) obligated Fuqua to sign the "definitive agreement" contemplated in the Memorandum (R. 29).

Palmer was formed in 1961 by Arnold Palmer and his associates to market Mr. Palmer's endorsements on golf clubs and accessories designed by Palmer but manufactured for it by others (R. 5, 21). Fuqua, self-described as a "leader in all segments of the sporting goods industry" (R. 19), was looking for an opportunity to enter the golfing industry (R. 33) at about the time Palmer began discussing a possible business relationship. On January 7, 1969, in a meeting between E.D. Kenna, Fuqua's President, and Mark H. McCormack, Palmer's Executive Vice President (R. 11). A series of preliminary meetings followed during the next few months, variously attended by the individuals most intimately involved in the transaction (R. 11). For Fuqua, this included J.B. Fuqua, its Chairman of the Board and, along with Kenna, a member of the

---

1. Brian G. Shannon of Jaffe, Snider, Raitt & Heuer, P.C. contributed this state- ment of facts.

three-man Executive Committee of its Board of Directors (R. 15); Hiram D. Nowlan, in-house counsel and secretary; and Lawrence Klamon, general counsel. For Palmer, the preliminary meetings were attended by Arthur J. Lafave, Jr., its designee in this transaction (R. 35), Arnold Palmer, and Robert S. Burton, Palmer's attorney (R. 11–12).

At the time of these discussions, Fuqua had not yet acquired the manufacturing facility it was to contribute to the transaction. By early August 1969, when Kenna and Lafave met in San Francisco, the parties had focused their attention on the Fernquest & Johnson Golf company ("F & J") (R. 12), a company with which Palmer had dealt in the past (R. 33). At a Fuqua board meeting on November 3, Kenna explained the structure of the proposed Fuqua–Palmer transaction, and the board authorized the acquisition of F & J for $300,000 (R. 23–24). Fuqua acquired F & J in a stock purchase a week later (R. 5). Shortly thereafter, on November 25, Fuqua's Nowlan sent Lafave a second draft of the Memorandum of intent (R. 13).

The parties met for six hours on December 2, reviewing Nowlan's draft in detail and proposing changes (R. 13). Within a week, Nowlan had begun to work on the final agreement as well, and drafting of the memorandum of intent and the final agreement "progressed simultaneously for a few weeks" (R. 38). On December 29, 1969, Palmer's board met to consider the memorandum of intent, two changes were suggested, Kenna's approval was obtained, the changes were inserted, the board approved the transaction and Lafave signed the agreement (R. 35–36). On January 5, 1970, Kenna signed on behalf of Fuqua (R. 38).

On December 30, even before the Memorandum of Intent (R. 24–30) was fully executed, Nowlan sent the first draft of the final agreement to Lafave and Burton (R. 19) to Dow Jones, the Atlanta Constitution, the Atlanta Journal, Associated Press, United Press International, Reuters, WJBF–TV, and the New York Times (R. 39). The Wall Street Journal ran the story on December 31 (R. 31–32). On January 6, 1970, the day after Kenna executed the Memorandum, Jay P. Farish III, Vice President in charge of Fuqua's Sporting Goods Division, toured F & J's Mexican manufacturing facilities and discussed, *inter alia,* the changes in accounting procedures which would result from the Fuqua–Palmer transaction (R. 13).

Lafave and Burton met with Nowlan and Farish for seven hours on January 15 to work out details of the final agreement and discuss post-closing operating procedures (R. 14). It was agreed that the closing would be held February 2 (R. 36). Three days later, on January 18, as Kenna stated in deposition, "[t]he Palmer deal was placed before the Fuqua Board of Directors" (R. 34). Kenna fully explained the transaction as it was set forth in the

Memorandum of Intent. A draft of the final agreement was also presented at the meeting (R. 34).

Kenna also submitted a written report to the board at this time (R. 16–19). Lafave's sworn testimony is that:

> [t]he action of Fuqua's Board of Directors at their January 18 meeting was represented to us as their approval of the final form of the closing documents (R. 36).

On January 20 and 21, Lafave and Nowlan met at length for preparation and review of closing exhibits: a review of Palmer's insurance policies, office equipment, inventory and leases; a review of various details to be attended to before the closing; and final negotiations concerning the form of definitive agreements and certain changes (R. 14). According to Lafave,

> [b]y January 23 the definitive agreement was in its final form. The counsel for both parties had agreed to all changes and Kenna had given his approval for Fuqua. In this final form the agreement was being stored at Fuqua on electronic typewriter tape * * * (R. 36).

Nowlan's deposition testimony is consistent with Lafave's on this point. Nowlan told Burton (Palmer's attorney) "that I did not know of any additional writing that he and I needed to do" (R. 38). Nowlan then left for a vacation (R. 38).

On January 23 and thereafter, Arnold Palmer and McCormack were in Pebble Beach, California for the Bing Crosby National Pro–Am Golf Tournament. Kenna asked McCormack to make arrangements for him to attend. As McCormack explained Kenna's request, Kenna

> wanted to come out now that everything had been done and finalized, and talk to Arnold a little about some thoughts about golf club designs, and in general some of the directions we might be taking together. He also wanted to have a photographer come out and take pictures to be released to the golfing press and I guess others. * * * Basically, it was a sort of a celebrating marriage kind of week (R. 37–38).

Late in January, Fuqua postponed the February 2 closing date, apparently because it needed more time to raise cash for the deal (R. 36). In fact, Fuqua's treasurer wrote to the company's bank on January 30, seeking approval for the Palmer acquisition (R. 20). Fuqua told its bank that it had "reached agreement with the Arnold Palmer interests" (R. 20). There is nothing in the record to suggest that Fuqua's bank interposed any objection to the transaction.

Fuqua postponed the closing a second time and, on February 8, Kenna and Lafave had a telephone conversation concerning the delay. According to Lafave, Kenna said:

*You can assure Arnold that the transaction will go through. We are committed to it. * * * There is absolutely no problem with the transaction actually going through. Please give Arnold every assurance of that fact (R. 36–37).*

Lafave spoke to Farish the same day and was told that "Fuqua had straightened out its funds for the deal" (R. 37). February 17 was set as the new closing date (R. 37).

Two days later, on February 10, J.B. Fuqua wrote a note to Kenna which read, "Doug, let's forget the Palmer deal. I don't want to do it" (R. 33). When Kenna, who was home with the flu, saw the note, he told Farish:

We can't call it off, we're committed on this deal (R. 33).

Kenna was "quite upset" and called J.B. Fuqua to say they should honor their deal (R. 34). The two men met the next day, discussed the pros and cons, and according to Kenna:

*We agreed at the end of the meeting that I would proceed with the deal. * * * I think it would be correct to say that [J.B. Fuqua] advised me to proceed with the transaction (R. 34).*

At the earlier Fuqua board meeting on January 18, the board had resolved that the transaction "be subject to approval by the Executive Committee [sic] of this Board" (R. 16). Kenna testified that

[b]esides J.B. and myself there was only one other person on Fuqua's Executive Committee. The Executive Committee met informally and two members constituted a quorum. There were many times when only two of the three members attended a meeting (R. 34–35).

Palmer contends that a majority of Fuqua's Executive Committee approved the transaction on February 11, notwithstanding the contrary affidavits of Kenna and J.B. Fuqua (R. 15). Kenna told Lafave that he and J.B. Fuqua were the Executive Committee (R. 37). On February 11, Kenna called Lafave (R. 35, 37) and "definitely" relayed J.B. Fuqua's approval for the closing (R. 37). Kenna added that he had made a complete commitment to Arnold Palmer and felt "wholly bound by the situation" (R. 37).

Nonetheless, on February 13, J.B. Fuqua sent a memorandum to all directors announcing his unilateral decision "to call off the deal" (R. 35). Kenna was still convalescing at home and did not see the memo until February 16. He was "shocked to receive it" (R. 35). After unsuccessfully trying to contact J.B. Fuqua (who had left town suddenly for the Caribbean and points south), Kenna called Lafave and told him the deal was off (R. 35). Kenna told Lafave:

> *The rug has been pulled completely out from under me.*
> *Nothing like this has ever happened to me in business (R. 37).*

When J.B. Fuqua returned in March, Kenna resigned as president and announced that he would not stand for re-election as a director (R. 35). Kenna told McCormack he was resigning

> *because he just couldn't live under circumstances where his*
> *moral integrity was destroyed in that manner.*

This lawsuit followed.

In this statement of facts, the writer took pains to provide all the detail that indicated an agreement between the parties. Because he represented the appealing party, he needed to convince the appellate court from the facts to look at this case seriously and not merely affirm the decision below. He explained the facts from the perspective of his client, Arnold Palmer Golf Company. The officials of the company assumed that there was an agreement with Fuqua. The author concludes with the simple statement, "[t]his lawsuit followed." If the court is as convinced as the author that an agreement existed, the lawsuit was inevitable. Match this demonstration of the depth of agreement with the following statement of facts prepared for Fuqua.

BRIEF FOR APPELLEE [2]

STATEMENT OF FACTS

The District Court granted summary judgment for Defendant Fuqua Industries, Inc. ("Fuqua") under Federal Rule 56. Plaintiff Arnold Palmer Golf Company ("Palmer") has appealed that judgment.

Palmer designed and marketed golf equipment bearing the endorsement of Arnold Palmer. In the late 1960's, Palmer wished to acquire its own manufacturing facilities. Fuqua, a diversified conglomerate concentrating in the leisure-time sports industry, was interested in entering the golf business.

During the period from January, 1969 through July, 1970, various representatives of Palmer and Fuqua discussed a deal under which Fuqua would buy a 25% ownership in Palmer in exchange for cash and ownership of Fernquest & Johnson, a manufacturer of golf clubs to be purchased by Fuqua. The parties signed a "Memorandum of Intent" in January 1970. This Memorandum became the basis of Palmer's complaint. These terms of the Memorandum should be particularly noted:

1. It refers to the parties' "general understanding" of the deal; the conventional language of a definitive agreement (e.g., "the parties hereby agree", etc.) is absent.

2. Melanie T. LaFave of Jaffe, Snider,   ment of facts.
Raitt & Heuer, P.C. contributed this state-

2. Before closing, Palmer was required to submit financial statements to Fuqua showing no material adverse change since previous statements and a net operating loss not in excess of $200,000.

3. A definitive agreement "acceptable" to both parties was required and was to contain eight explicit conditions to Fuqua's performance thereunder as well as other provisions.

4. Under paragraph 11, specifically titled "*Conditions*" (Tr. 29–30): "The obligations of Palmer and Fuqua shall be subject to fulfillment of the following conditions:" preparation of a definitive agreement satisfactory in form and content to both parties and their counsel, approval of the definitive agreement by the Fuqua Board, approval by counsel of all legal matters; no material adverse change in the business of the parties; approval by creditors of the parties, etc.

5. The last paragraph refers again to the "general understanding" of the parties.

The definitive agreement was prepared but was never signed by Fuqua. The Fuqua Board only approved the deal "in principle" (Tr. 15), requiring that the "form, terms, conditions" of the definitive agreement "and the advisability of *consummating* the proposed acquisitions, be subject to approval by the Executive Committee of this Board" (emphasis supplied). The Fuqua Executive committee never gave such approval, as shown by the affidavits of Fuqua's President and Chairman of the Board, who constituted two-thirds of the Committee (Tr. 16).

Palmer sued Fuqua for breach of contract. In an opinion by Judge Thomas D. Lambros, the District Court, after reviewing the pleadings (including extensive answers to interrogatories and several depositions), several affidavits and exhibits and the various documents involved, found no issue of material fact, held that there was no contract, and granted summary judgment for Fuqua.

Fuqua's theory of the case is evident from the statement of facts. The attorney found no need to deal in detail with the unsuccessful negotiations. She points out all the items required in order to have a contract, and the fact that these had not been resolved at the time when negotiations broke off. The reader is left with the impression that the parties had not entered into a contract. Where this is the result reached by the district court, the writer did not need to expand her position in the statement of facts.

In an appeal where the law paramount, the statement of the case will be quite different. Often the substantive facts deserve only brief mention as in this concise example.

David H. Lucas is the owner of two undeveloped oceanfront lots in Charleston County, South Carolina, which he purchased on December 3, 1986, for $975,000. On July 1, 1988, the South

Carolina General Assembly adopted the Beachfront Management Act which regulated development along the South Carolina coastline by imposing statutorily mandated setback lines. The Beachfront Management Act is administered by respondent South Carolina Coastal Council.

The Act's setback line precluded petitioner from building a residence or making any other economically reasonable use of his property. Since the two lots are located seaward of the setback line, the Act required them to remain forever undeveloped.

Petitioner filed an action in the South Carolina Court of Common Pleas asserting that the Act's restrictions on the use of his lots amounted to a taking of his private property for public use without just compensation. The court agreed and awarded petitioner compensation for the regulatory taking. In reaching this conclusion, the court made the following finding of fact:

"I find that the imposition of building restrictions on Lots 22 and 24 imposed by the South Carolina Coastal Council deprives Lucas of any reasonable economic use of the lots, has eliminated the unrestricted right of use, and renders them valueless." Order of the Court of Common Pleas at 5.

On appeal the South Carolina Supreme Court reversed, although it did not dispute the factual finding that the Beachfront Management Act effectively deprives petitioner of all economically viable use of his property. Instead, the reversal was based on the court's assertion that the Takings Clause never requires compensation when a regulation is enacted to prevent a serious public harm. *Lucas v. South Carolina Coastal Council*, 404 S.E.2d 895, 899–900 (S.C. 1991). This ruling directly conflicts with the established precedent of this Court on a question of federal constitutional rights.[3]

The authors of this statement of the case devote fewer than eight lines to the "who, what, where, when" facts and another six lines to describing the substance of the statute. The remainder of this brief statement presents the procedure. Although this is an amicus brief and the Court received lengthier statements of the case from the attorneys representing petitioner and respondent, this statement of the case includes all the substantive facts the Court needs to consider the "regulatory taking" issue.

As your goal is to present the facts necessary to your case and your theory without losing the court's attention, consider alternatives to a purely prose approach. If, for example, you have a series of technical

---

3. This is the entire statement of the case from the Brief Amicus Curiae of Pacific Legal Foundation in Support of Petitioner David H. Lucas in *Lucas v. South Carolina Coastal Council*, Docket Number 91– 453, United States Supreme Court (1991). Reprinted with permission of the Pacific Legal Foundation, Anthony T. Caso, Director of Litigation. Copyright © 1991 by Pacific Legal Foundation.

details to describe, a table may be an effective option. It will permit you to highlight the important details without unnecessary verbiage.

The following table was designed to show a series of violations by a municipal sewer system. The system had violated both its National Pollutant Discharge Elimination System (NPDES) permit under the Federal Water Pollution Control Act, and several administrative orders designed to enforce the permit conditions. If the writer had chosen to present all this detail in the text of the statement of facts, he would have bored the reader. The reader might have missed the most important point; the municipal sewer system has repeatedly failed to comply with both the permit conditions and the administrative orders. To make the point effectively, the writer chose to present the data in a table.

PERMIT VIOLATIONS

COMPLIANCE DATE	REQUIREMENTS	COMPLIANCE	SECTIONS
7/1/77	Effluent limitations on secondary treatment	None, limitations routinely violated	A(1)(c) & A(3)(d)
7/1/77	Termination of discharge of digested sludge, construction of BPT facilities	Construction has not begun	A(1)(a)(5), A(3)(c), B(5)
7/1/77	Six pollution control projects	All six projects incomplete	B(5)
Immediately	Efficient operation of systems	Pumps & drive motor units not maintained insufficient number of employees	E
Immediately	Minimize discharge of pollutants	Raw sewage discharged due to power generation units not maintained	A(2)(c)
10/1/76	Introduce toxic control program	Program submitted to EPA in 1981. Since then only ⅓ of staffing	B(2), (3), CFR 403.8(f)(2), (3)
7/1/77	Complete five area-wide projects	Four of five projects incomplete BPT not achieved	A(2)(a), S.C. B(5)
1/1/77	Submit report on sewer overflows and by-passes	Report not submitted	C(6)(d)

ADMINISTRATIVE ORDER VIOLATIONS

ORDER DATE	REQUIREMENTS	COMPLIANCE	SECTIONS
8/8/80	Meet effluent discharge limitations on primary	None. Limitations routinely violated	II(A)(1), II(B)(1)
8/8/80	Digest discharged sludge	Undigested sludge discharged daily	II(A)(5)

ORDER DATE	REQUIREMENTS	COMPLIANCE	SECTIONS
7/13/84	Submit plan for terminating discharge of sludge	Submitted plan fails to provide for most expeditious progress possible	

The reader can see two things at a glance. The dates for compliance cover a period of eight years. Except for a program submitted to the EPA in 1981 and one completed project, the municipal sewer system has failed to comply with all of the requirements of its NPDES permit and both compliance orders. The table is both more readable and better advocacy than a prose presentation of the same information.

Diagrams and maps are also effective ways of presenting the facts when the case involves land or a piece of equipment. If the case has been tried, the map or diagram is often an exhibit introduced into evidence at the trial. If it will help the reader to visualize the facts you describe, consider including the map or diagram as a part of the statement of facts.

Writing Techniques to Enhance the Persuasive Effect

The persuasive effect of a statement of facts can be enhanced by careful attention to the way you present them. Consider the following statement of facts from the *Palsgraf v. Long Island R. Co.,* 248 N.Y. 339, 162 N.E. 99 (1928). From the way he presented the facts, can you figure out whether Justice Cardozo found a foreseeable causal connection between the actions of the railroad employees and the plaintiff's injury?

Plaintiff was standing on a platform of defendant's railroad after buying a ticket to go to Rockaway Beach. A train stopped at the station, bound for another place. Two men ran forward to catch it. One of the men reached the platform of the car without mishap, though the train was moving. The other man, carrying a package, jumped aboard the car, but seemed unsteady as if about to fall. A guard on the car, who had held the door open, reached forward to help him in, and another guard on the platform pushed him from behind. In this act, the package was dislodged, and fell upon the rails. It was a package of small size, about fifteen inches long, and covered with newspaper. In fact it contained fireworks, but there was nothing in its appearance to give notice of its contents. The fireworks when they fell exploded. The shock of the explosion threw down some scales at the other end of the platform many feet away. The scales struck the plaintiff causing injuries for which she sues.

Justice Cardozo used some traditional narrative techniques in constructing this factual description. Notice first the forms of the verbs. Cardozo puts the plaintiff on the platform at the outset with the form "was standing" to indicate that she stood there throughout the incident. The verbs he uses for the next few sentences are verbs of action: "stopped", "ran", "to catch", "reached", "was moving", "to fall", "held", "reached", and "pushed". Then he shifts to the passive voice: "the package was dislodged". There is no actor in this sentence; no one dislodged the package. Then it fell. Cardozo stops the flow of the action to describe the package. By doing this he uses another narrative technique; he creates suspense. Notice that the first part of the description is filled with people and action. Then the focus shifts completely to the thing; the people and the actions disappear from the description. By changing the verb forms and the focus from actors to things Cardozo gives away his analysis of proximate cause in this case. Just as the passenger and guards disappear, the causal connection between Mrs. Palsgraf and the package becomes tenuous. Take advantage of narrative techniques in explaining your theory of the case to the court.

The final sentence or paragraph of the statement of the case should serve as a transition to the argument section.

Chapter 21

CONSTRUCTING THE ARGUMENT SECTION

Writing the argument section of an appellate brief differs from writing the analogous section of a brief to the trial court in several respects. First, the appellate advocate is addressing a different audience. Second, the procedural posture and the standard of review are different. Third, while the vast majority of cases at the trial court level can be decided using existing law, serious appeals involve cases of first impression or where the law is unsettled. As a result, the advocate may have to approach the law differently. This chapter is concerned with constructing the argument section of a brief. It explains the options for introducing the argument, the relationship between issues and arguments and what each side must establish in order to prevail. It also presents some strategies for ordering the arguments, and how to draft persuasive point headings. The chapter suggests ways of characterizing the law in order to persuade the court to adopt your analysis and approaches for rebutting your opponents arguments. Finally, it discusses sources of public policy and suggestions for integrating the policy into your argument. This discussion should alert you to some of the possibilities; it is by no means all inclusive. The way you tailor your argument depends on the issues on appeal, your specific audience, your client's facts, and the law and policy available to you.

SUMMARY OF ARGUMENT

Every argument written to an appellate court should begin with an introductory section that provides a concise summary of your arguments. It serves a dual purpose. First, it is the functional equivalent of the thesis section of an office memorandum or a trial level brief. Second, it provides the individual judges with a summary of the argument to read right before oral argument. While most judges read the full briefs before oral argument, they may have considered your brief a few days or a week earlier. The summary should help remind them of your brief. Usually only one judge on a three judge intermediate level appellate panel has primary responsibility for each case. While this judge will have read the briefs before oral argument, the other judges may not have read your full brief. This summary is essential for these judges.

In writing to the federal courts of appeals, the advocate has the option of including a separate section, called "Summary of Argument", or covering the same material immediately after the heading "Argument". Fed. Rule App. Proc. 28(5). Be sure to consult the appropriate appellate court rules for your jurisdiction for the required format.

The summary of argument is a 1–2 page summary of the arguments from your brief. It should explain the issues, the applicable legal rules, your contentions, and very briefly the reasons for your contentions. It should be framed in light of your theory of the case. Some lawyers also include citations to major authorities that support their position. If the appeal revolves around the interpretation of a statute, for example, include a reference to the statute. A citation to a case, however, will only be helpful to the reader if the case is a key one that the judge will recognize without further discussion.

The issue in the following summary of argument was whether a criminal defendant could use property subject to forfeiture to pay his attorney fees. The author was able to present the crux of his argument in two paragraphs.

> The basic issue in these cases is whether a defendant is entitled to have access to his property, which has been seized or otherwise detained by the government pending a forfeiture proceeding, in order to pay legitimate attorney fees. We contend that a defendant should not have access to such property at least where there has been a judicial determination that there is probable cause to believe that the property in question will ultimately be forfeited. A defendant has no more right to pay a lawyer with what is believed upon probable cause to be the proceeds of criminal activities than with what is believed upon probable cause to be stolen property.

> It is well settled that the interest of a person in his liberty is not unconstitutionally denied when he is subject to significant pretrial restraint where there has been a judicial determination that there is probable cause to support his detention. Similarly, the interest of a person in his property should not be deemed to be unconstitutionally denied when such property is subject to significant pretrial restraint where there has been a judicial determination that there is probable cause to support such restraint.[1]

1. This Summary of Argument is from the Brief of Amicus Curiae in Support of the United States of America in *Caplan & Drysdale v. United States*, Docket Numbers 87–1729 and 88–454, United States Supreme Court (1988). Reprinted with permission of the Appellate Committee of the California District Attorneys Association, Ira Reiner, District Attorney of Los Angeles County, Harry B. Sondheim, Head Deputy, Appellate Division, and Arnold T. Guminski, Deputy District Attorney. Copy-

If the appellate rules for your jurisdiction do not require a summary of argument, you may still wish to include one. If the brief is relatively short and the practice in your jurisdiction is for all the judges to read all the briefs, then consider omitting the summary of argument. A judge who wishes to remind herself of your brief can scan the point headings and the thesis section of the brief. If the brief is long and complicated, or if it is not the practice for all the judges to read all the briefs before oral argument, then a summary of argument will help the judges prepare for oral argument.

ARGUMENT

Constructing the argument section of an appellate brief is similar to the process used in the argument section of a trial level brief in a number of respects. If the author elected not to include a separate summary of argument, it will begin with a thesis section. The argument section will end with a concluding paragraph or section. The same strategies for organization apply. The advocate will use the same writing overlay of thesis statements, topic sentences, and transitions that makes the analysis easy for the reader to understand. The writer will include point headings to highlight the different sections of the argument and break the argument into manageable units for the court.

The argument section in an appellate brief is different from the equivalent section in a trial level brief in its focus. The lawyer for appellant will focus on the errors made in the lower court. She will explain how the case should have been decided below and why. The attorney for the appellee, on the other hand, will explain how and why the decision below was proper. The advocate must keep in mind the standard the appellate court will use to review the lower court decision. See Chapter 17. Some appellate court rules require that the argument begin with a statement of the standard of review. Even if the rules do not require this section, you should begin by explaining the applicable standard of review. If the standard of review is the same for all issues on appeal, then one general discussion suffices. If the court will apply a different standard for each issue, it is preferable to begin each issue with the applicable standard of review.

The substance of appellate argument will also differ because of the nature of appellate issues. The role of the trial court is to decide the case before it. Most of the issues presented at this level can be decided by statutes and existing precedent. Many issues on appeal, however, involve questions where the law is not settled. The appellate court may have to interpret a recent statute, expand available precedent, or choose between related rules. It must not only decide the particular case, but is charged with developing legal rules that society can use to predict the outcome of future behavior. The court must make good law that is consistent with public policy. Your ultimate goal as an appellate advocate is to convince the court to plagiarize from your brief to write its opinion. You can achieve your goal by analyzing the problem thoroughly and presenting the analysis precisely and succinctly to the court.

THE RELATIONSHIP BETWEEN ISSUES AND ARGUMENTS

An argument is the analytical pathway a lawyer asks a court to follow in order to reach the legal conclusion he advocates for his client. There should be an argument for every issue in the case, and for some issues, there may be several arguments or alternative approaches the court could use to reach the desired conclusion. Often the arguments are in series; that is, the court must adopt each of the arguments in order to grant the relief requested for the client. The opponent, however, may only have to prevail on one argument in order to defeat the case. Consider the following paternity example for the relationship between the issues and the arguments.

The petitioner was unsuccessful in a paternity suit filed below, in which he alleged that he is the biological father of a child born to a married couple. He claimed that the child was conceived during a brief affair he had with the mother. In order to be adjudged the legal father, he must first overcome the presumption of legitimacy that attaches to a child born to a married woman. This is the first issue. There are four ways to overcome the presumption and the petitioner need only succeed on one. He may, however, choose to argue more than one approach to increase his chances of success. Second, the petitioner needs to establish paternity. There are two sub-issues of this issue and he must convince the court on each of the two. The relationship of issues to arguments in the petitioner's brief might be as follows:

Overcoming the presumption of legitimacy issue
 Method A   Argument A
              OR
 Method B   Argument B
              OR
 Method C   Argument C
              OR
 Method D   Argument D
Establishing paternity issue
 Sub-issue 1   Argument E
            AND
 Sub-issue 2   Argument F

In order to prevail, the petitioner must convince the court with Argument A or B or C or D and Arguments E and F. He has the burden of proof on each of these issues.

The respondents, the child's mother and her husband, can defeat the appeal by showing that the petitioner failed to meet his burden of proof by succeeding on one of three issues. They will argue that he failed to overcome the presumption of legitimacy. The issue has four sub-issues A–D, and they must make all four arguments to show that the petitioner failed to sustain his burden of proof by any of the accepted means. If their arguments are successful, the case will be affirmed on appeal. In the alternative, they can show that the petitioner failed to establish paternity. As he must prove both elements, they can succeed by showing he failed on one of the two. As a third alternative, the respondents can argue that the petitioner delayed too long to bring the paternity petition, and consequently, he should be estopped from asserting the claim. The relationship of issues to arguments from the respondents' side is as follows:

Overcoming the presumption of legitimacy issue

Method A	Argument A [1]
AND	
Method B	Argument B [1]
AND	
Method C	Argument C [1]
AND	
Method D	Argument D [1]
OR	

Paternity issue

Sub-issue 1	Argument E [1]
OR	
Sub-issue 2	Argument F [1]
OR	
Estoppel issue	Argument G [1]

The respondents need to prevail on arguments A [1]–D [1] to win the presumption of legitimacy issue, either E [1] or F [1] to win the paternity issue or G [1] to win the estoppel issue. Any of the three issues will defeat the petitioner. The collective of these arguments make up the argument section of the brief.

ORGANIZING THE ARGUMENT SECTION

You are already familiar with the common methods of organizing legal analysis. The only added complication is that now there are issues, sub-issues, and arguments. As you can see from the schemes presented in the paternity example above, the issues and arguments do not always coincide. The techniques for ordering these elements are the same ones you have used before. You may choose to organize using a logical order, or arrange the arguments from the strongest to the weakest, or with the argument that provides the greatest relief before the one that leads to lesser relief. The petitioner in the paternity example would want to present the issues and arguments in a logical order as he must overcome the presumption before the court will consider the paternity issue. He might choose to arrange the arguments on the different methods of overcoming presumption according to the strength of the arguments. The respondents in the paternity might choose to begin with the estoppel issue. The court might find it easier to decide the case based on the petitioner's delay in asserting his paternity than to have to address the merits of the case. If the estoppel argument is a weak argument, however, the respondents might choose to omit the argument or at least put it last.

The organization of arguments in a case of first impression may be more difficult. A common type of appeal involves a previously unrecognized cause of action or right. The arrangement of the arguments involves a series of tactical decisions. Counsel for each party may have several arguments or different approaches that explain why the cause of action or right should or should not be recognized. The appellant's attorney, for example, may argue first that the cause of action is implied by a statute. He may also argue that the cause of action arises by analogy to an existing action. Finally, he may argue that a recognition of the cause of action fulfills an important public policy goal. For a discussion of public policy arguments and the way to integrate them into your legal arguments, see below. Likewise the appellee's attorney will have several arguments to make all dealing with the same issue of whether the appellant has a cause of action. She will argue that the law does not provide relief under these circumstances. Even if the court should recognize the cause of action, the appellant has failed to meet all the necessary elements of the cause of action and should, therefore, be denied relief. She will argue that the action is inconsistent with public policy. Finally, she may make the "wedge" argument—if the court recognizes this cause of action, there will be a flood of litigation from similarly situated claimants. The way the attorneys organize these arguments may depend on the audience, the relative strength of the arguments, the relief sought, and considerations of tactics.

WRITING PERSUASIVE POINT HEADINGS

Point headings serve two functions. They provide the reader with an organization of the arguments, and they focus the court's attention on the key elements of the argument and lead inevitably to the outcome you advocate. Point headings are thesis statements for the different parts of the argument. While the organizational function could be fulfilled simply with topic headings, for example:

Case not Ripe for Adjudication

Nuisance Exception Applies

No "Regulatory" Taking

No Requirement for Compensation

these headings have little content.

Point headings are traditionally divided into major point headings, written all in capital letters, minor point headings, written with the first letter of each word capitalized and underlined or italicized, and sub-point headings, written with the first letter of each word capitalized. Major point headings are used to introduce issues, and they should be labeled in parallel to the issues. For example, issue I should be introduced with major point heading I. A major point heading presents the overall thesis for that issue. Minor point headings are often used to introduce the arguments; they are labeled A, B, C, etc. Sub-point headings, where necessary, introduce the different parts of an argument; they are labeled 1, 2, 3, etc. Only in unusual circumstances is it helpful to include sub-sub-point headings, as they tend to break the argument into such small segments that they detract from the flow of your argument. Although this is the traditional breakdown of point headings, tailor the number and position of the headings to your appeal. The format and arrangement of headings should enhance the reader's understanding of the argument and not interfere with it.

To persuade the court, draft the point headings to demonstrate your theory of the case. This major point heading leaves no doubt in the court's mind about the advocate's perspective.

> THE DENIAL OF ALL RIGHT TO MAKE ECONOMICALLY VIABLE USE OF LAND CONSTITUTES A TAKING FOR WHICH JUST COMPENSATION IS REQUIRED, REGARDLESS OF THE LEGITIMACY OF THE GOVERNMENTAL PURPOSE INVOLVED.[2]

Contrast this with the same topic addressed from an opposing view.

> A REGULATION BARRING USES OF PROPERTY THAT THREATEN SERIOUS HARM TO OTHERS DOES NOT EFFECT A TAKING, EVEN IF THE PROHIBITED USES ARE THE ONLY ECONOMICALLY VIABLE USES OF THE PROPERTY.[3]

The subject matter is the same in each of the headings, but the thrust is different. The first author concentrates of the taking, while the second concentrates on the police power regulation.

---

2. This point heading from the Brief Amicus Curiae of the Northern Virginia Chapter of the National Association of Industrial and Office Parks, and the Northern Virginia Building Industry Association, Inc., in Support of the Petitioner, David H. Lucas, filed in *Lucas v. South Carolina Coastal Council,* Docket Number 91–453, United States Supreme Court (1991). Reprinted with permission of John F. Cahill, Esq. and John H. Foote, Esq., counsel for the Northern Virginia Chapter of the National Association of Industrial and Office Parks, and the Northern Virginia Building Industry Association, Inc.

Copyright © 1991 by John F. Cahill, Esq. and John H. Foote, Esq.

3. This point heading is from the Brief Amicus Curiae of the National Trust for Historic Preservation in the United States in Support of Respondent, *Lucas v. South Carolina Coastal Council,* Docket Number 91–453, United State Supreme Court (1991). Reprinted with permission of Louis R. Cohen, Esq., counsel of record, for the National Trust for Historic Preservation in the United States. Copyright © 1991 by Louis R. Cohen, Esq.

Like a good thesis statement, a minor point heading should include not just your contention, but the basis for that contention.

The State's Restriction On the Construction Of Permanent Structures On Petitioner's Property Is The Kind Of Governmental Measure That May Justifiably Cause A Severe Economic Impact Because It Prevents A Use Of The Property That May Cause Serious Injury To Public Health And Safety And Physical Damage To Nearby Properties.[4]

This minor point heading provides the reader with the author's perspective on one issue in the case and also his rationale, the public purpose behind the regulation. The heading is more specific than a major point heading, but still general enough to be concise and readable.

Choose the words with particular care in drafting a point heading.

The South Carolina Supreme Court's Expansion of the Nuisance Exception Eviscerates the Takings Clause.[5]

The author used the precise legal designations for "Nuisance Exception" and "Takings Clause" to convey the meaning the Court shares. The author then chose "eviscerates" with all its connotations to describe the South Carolina Supreme Court's decision. The word captures the reader's attention and drives home the theory of the case. The author could have chosen "diminishes", "disembowels", "guts", or "emasculates", but these words are inappropriate in this context. "Diminishes" is too weak to attract the reader's attention. "Disembowels" conveys the same literal meaning, but not the figurative meaning the author intended. "Guts" is too colloquial for formal legal writing. "Emasculates" has a figurative as well as a literal meaning, but different readers will read the word with different connotations; these may distract the reader. "Eviscerates" strikes the proper balance. As an advocate, you can take advantage of the richness of the English language in your choice of vocabulary.

The brief writer can draft the point headings at any point in the overall process. Some writers prefer to draft them as a part of the argument to achieve a logical flow; others include general headings in the first draft and construct the point headings later when they have framed the arguments. Be sure to save enough time to create effective point headings. Once you are satisfied with the organization of the

4. This example was taken from the Respondent's Brief on the Merits in *Lucas v. South Carolina Coastal Council*, Docket Number 91–453, United States Supreme Court (1991). Reprinted with permission from C. C. Harness, General Counsel for the South Carolina Coastal Council. Copyright © 1991 by C. C. Harness, General Counsel for the South Carolina Coastal Council.

5. This point heading is taken from the Brief Amicus Curiae of the Chamber of Commerce of the United States of America in Support of the Petitioner filed in *Lucas v. South Carolina Coastal Council*, Docket Number 91–453, United States Supreme Court (1991). Reprinted with permission of Stephen A. Bokat, Esq., counsel for the Chamber of Commerce of the United States of America. Copyright © 1991 by Stephen A. Bokat, Esq.

argument and the point headings, you will need to characterize the law from your client's perspective.

CHARACTERIZING THE LAW AS AN ADVOCATE

The advocate's goal in presenting the law in a brief is to explain to the court the existing precedent and how it should be applied to the particular case to achieve the desired result. The advocate hopes that her portrayal of the law and its application are so persuasive that the court will plagiarize the analysis for use in the opinion. Obviously the advocate is in the best position to do this if there are cases directly on point and in the jurisdiction.

Remember that the court has the discretion to give either a broad or a narrow reading to existing precedent. While the holding of the prior case is limited to its facts, the rule the court can extract from that case may be either very narrow or very broad. Without distorting the case, an advocate can characterize the case so that it forms the basis for a favorable decision for her client. This is one of the most interesting and challenging parts of advocacy writing. The following examples illustrate different problems of characterization and how the advocate might approach each problem.

ILLUSTRATION # 1: Using the Same Authority Effectively From Both Sides

When there is authority that both sides must use, characterize the case so that it helps you to present your argument. Although the following case seems to be more helpful to appellee, the appellant can mitigate the damage with a careful, yet accurate characterization.

The decision in *Keystone Bituminous Coal Association v. De-Benedictis*, 480 U.S. 470 (1987) is not controlling here. In *Keystone*, the Court considered whether the Bituminous Mine Subsidence and Land Conservation Act was an unconstitutional exercise of Pennsylvania's police power and constituted a regulatory taking for which compensation must be paid. The Act required mining companies to leave 50% of the coal beneath certain structures to prevent subsidence. A regulation becomes a taking if it "does not substantially advance legitimate state interests, * * * or denies the owner economically viable use of his land." *Agins v. Tiburon*, 447 U.S. 255 (1980). Under the first prong of the test, the Court held that the statute was a valid exercise of the police power. Under the second prong, the majority held that the coal companies could still extract coal in economically viable quantities, thus defeating the facial challenge to the statute.

In a strongly worded dissent, Justice Rehnquist stated that the "nuisance exception" is a narrow one. It has never been applied "to allow complete extinction of the value of a piece of property. Though nuisance regulations have been sustained despite a substantial reduction in value, we have not accepted the proposition that the State may completely extinguish a property interest or prohibit all use without providing compensation." *Keystone* 480 U.S. at 513.

With this characterization, the appellant did not have to distinguish the case explicitly and risk appearing overly defensive. The stage is now set to take advantage of the dissent to show why the facial challenge in this case should succeed.

The appellee would characterize the *Keystone* decision differently.

> The decision in *Keystone Bituminous Coal Association v. De-Benedictis*, 480 U.S. 470 (1987), controls this case. The Court upheld the constitutionality of the Bituminous Mine Subsidence and Land Conservation Act both as a proper exercise of the police power and because the statute on its face left the companies with the opportunity to mine coal economically. The purpose of Pennsylvania's regulation is to protect the public safety by preventing surface subsidence caused by mining. The Act is limited in scope to protect cemeteries and three types of structures in place on April 17, 1966: public buildings, noncommercial buildings generally used by the public, and dwellings used for human habitation. The Act requires that 50% of the coal under these structures be left in place. The net effect is that petitioners will have to leave less than 2% of their coal in place. 480 U.S. at 476. Where "[t]he record indicates that only about 75% of petitioners' underground coal can be profitably mined in any event, and there is no showing that petitioners' reasonable 'investment-backed expectations' have been materially affected by the additional duty to retain the small percentage that must be used to support the structures protected by § 4," 480 U.S. 499, the State is not required to pay compensation.

Counsel for the respondent focuses the court's attention on the limited purpose of the statute and the minimal economic effect on the petitioners. This sets the stage for a discussion of the public purpose in the instant statute and the limited economic effect it will have.

Depending on the purpose and the need to explain the details of the case to the reader, the appellee might prefer a more direct characterization of the case, such as the following:

> The Court has long recognized the "nuisance exception" to the "takings clause". As Justice Stevens noted in *Keystone Bituminous Coal Association v. DeBenedictis*, 480 U.S. at 492 n. 20, "since no individual has a right to use his property so as to create a nuisance or otherwise harm others, the State has not "taken" anything when it asserts its power to enjoin the nuisance-like activity."

This characterization would be followed by a discussion of the nuisance prevented by the instant statute. As you construct your argument, characterize the authority accurately and to lead inevitably to the discussion of your case.

ILLUSTRATION # 2: Characterizing a Line of Cases

Frequently the advocate's task is to deal not with just one case or a spectrum of cases, but with a line of cases. One side is asking the court to extend the rule to the next logical step, while the opponent is trying to convince the court to cut off the line with the last case. By characterizing the progression differently, each can present its argument persuasively. The following illustration involves the right of the general public to use New Jersey's beaches, a resource that is under considerable pressure during the summer months. The appellant, who would like to open the private beaches adjacent to municipal beaches to the public, might characterize the cases in the following way.

> The New Jersey Supreme Court has long recognized the public trust in the beaches of the State. Under this doctrine, the court in *Arnold v. Mundy*, 6 N.J.L. 1 (Sup. Ct. 1821), held that the waters of the state belonged to the public in common with "a transient usufructory possession"[6], with the title vested in the state and the use common to all. The water, the court explained, included the soil appurtenant to the water.

> In *Neptune City v. Avon–By–The–Sea*, 61 N.J. 296, 294 A.2d 47 (1972), the court invoked the public trust doctrine to hold that when the upland beach area was owned by a municipality and dedicated to beach purposes, the public trust doctrine required that the beach and the ocean waters be available to all on an equal basis. As a result, the municipal ordinance imposing discriminatory fees for nonresidents was invalid.

> Six years later, the court again relied on the public trust doctrine to hold that the Borough of Deal could not restrict access to a portion of the dry beach to local residents. The court explained that the dry land beach was impressed with the public trust and, therefore, must be open to use by the public in common. *Van Ness v. Borough of Deal*, 78 N.J. 174, 393 A.2d 571 (1978).

> Most recently, the court used the public trust doctrine in the case of *Matthews v. Bay Head Imp. Ass'n*, 95 N.J. 306, 471 A.2d 355 (1984). In an attempt to avoid the application of the public trust to its beaches, the Borough of Bay Head had formed a private association to control the local beach. Membership in the associate was limited to borough residents and public employees, such as teachers and fire fighters. The association owned a section of beach and leased additional beach land from adjacent landowners. The court held that the association was "quasi public" and under the public trust doctrine, the general public had a right to use the beach. In dictum, the court suggested, moreover, that at some time in the

---

6. *Arnold v. Mundy*, 6 N.J.L. at 6.

future there might be a need for the public to exercise its public trust right to use the dry sand of private owners.

The appellant is now ready to ask the court to do just that.

The appellee, however, can characterize the cases differently.

The application of the public trust doctrine is limited to those waters and appurtenant soil owned by the sovereign in trust for public use. When first annunciated by the court in *Arnold v. Mundy*, 6 N.J.L. 1 (Sup. Ct. 1982), only the sea and the lands covered by the sea or subject to the ebb and flow of the tides were subject to the public trust. In recent years, the court has expanded the scope of the public trust to prevent discrimination against the public at large.

In *Neptune City v. Avon–By–The–Sea*, 61 N.J. 296, 294 A.2d 47 (1972), the court held that the municipality could not discriminate against the general public by charging higher fees to non-residents than residents. Similarly, the court struck down a local ordinance that would have restricted a portion of the beach to residents to the detriment of non-residents in *Van Ness v. Borough of Deal*, 78 N.J. 174, 393 A.2d 571 (1978).

The court also refused to permit discrimination in the case of *Matthews v. Bay Head Imp. Ass'n*, 95 N.J. 306, 471 A.2d 355 (1984). In order to limit access to the beach, local residents formed a private association to own and manage the beach. Membership was limited to residents and public employees. The association also leased some private land adjacent to the association beach. The court rejected the association's discriminatory practices, holding that the association was "quasi public". To preclude future attempts by municipalities to limit beach access to residents only, the court included a warning in its opinion: "[i]t is not necessary for us to determine under what circumstances and to what extent there will be a need to use the dry sand of private owners who either now or in the future may have no leases with the Association." [7]

ILLUSTRATION # 3: *Characterization to Take Advantage of Policy*

Brief writers do not always find authority directly on point that reaches the desired result. As advocates they must use the existing authority to support their arguments. Often a case that is not directly on point can be used effectively to support a policy argument. In the following example, a prosecutor argued that the court should admit the results of human leucocyte antigen testing for purposes of proving paternity. The only related case came from 1959 and dealt with the ABO blood typing tests. The policy, however, was directly applicable.

The court in *Commonwealth v. D'Avella*, 339 Mass. 642, 162 N.E.2d 19 (1959), recognized the importance of using scientific

---

7. *Matthews v. Bay Head Imp. Ass'n*, 95 N.J. 306, 333; 471 A.2d 355, 369 (1984).

evidence in paternity cases where evidence traditionally has been unreliable and where ascertaining the truth rests on the credibility of conflicting witnesses. In that case, the court held that ABO test results were admissible to establish that the defendant was not the child's father. The ABO blood test is reliable only for purposes of exclusion and the court only admitted the evidence for that purpose. The court welcomed the scientific advance that made finding the truth an objective rather than a subjective matter.

Now scientific advances have made it possible to show objectively not only that a defendant cannot be the father of a child, but to a very high degree of probability that a defendant is the father. The human leucocyte antigen tissue typing test achieves this result. In this case, the HLA tests showed a 98% probability that this defendant is the father of this child. This court, like the court in *D'Avella*, should welcome the scientific advances since 1959 and rule that the HLA test result is admissible for purposes of objectively establishing paternity.

ILLUSTRATION # 4: Applying the Same Authority Effectively From Both Sides

Traditionally when there is a spectrum of authority and the facts of the case are somewhere between, one counsel will argue that the case is closer to one end of the spectrum and opposing counsel will argue that the case is closer to the opposite end of the spectrum. Sometimes this technique does not work. One case may be so far to one end of the spectrum that it does not make a useful analogy. While the opposing party can distinguish the case easily, the exercise does not help resolve the problem as the facts are so disparate from the pending controversy. The following example illustrates how both counsel can use the same case effectively when the only other case is too far at the other end of the spectrum to be useful in analyzing the problem.

Under the National Historic Preservation Act, HUD is required to consider the effect of a proposed urban renewal project on properties that are either listed on the National Register of Historic Places or are eligible for inclusion on the National Register. HUD must locate properties in the area affected by the urban renewal project that possess historical, architectural, archeological, or cultural value. If there are any such properties, under the regulation, HUD must then apply the National Register Criteria to these properties. But if there are no such properties, HUD has no further obligation under the statute.

HUD's obligation to attempt to locate historical properties is defined in *Central Oklahoma v. OCURA*, 471 F. Supp. 68 (W.D. Okl. 1979). In that case HUD in conjunction with both the local urban renewal agency and the State Historic Preservation Officer considered the urban renewal area and found no structures of historical significance. HUD hired third party consultants and conducted independent inquiries and historic reviews of the area. These reviews uncovered no historically important properties. The court held that HUD had made a reasonable effort even though it failed to discover a building later found to be of historic value.

HUD also made a reasonable effort to locate historic properties in this case. HUD contacted the local urban renewal agency. The director knew of no eligible properties. HUD also contacted the State Historic Preservation Officer. He had no information on historic properties in the area. Although he did mention a survey of the county to be conducted the following year, he indicated that the results would not be available for some time. HUD made independent inquiries at public hearings in October and November. It also requested comment from the public in the local newspaper. Although a few people waxed nostalgic about the old courthouse, the overwhelming majority were enthusiastic about the urban renewal project and the economic revitalization it would bring to the downtown area. No one mentioned any properties of architectural, historic or cultural significance. Unlike *Hough v. Marsh,* where the federal agency only made one phone call, HUD in this case contacted all the appropriate state and local agencies and asked the public in two different fora for information on historically significant properties. HUD made a reasonable effort to locate potentially eligible properties. Having found none, its responsibility under the regulation was concluded.

While this straightforward approach works well for HUD's position, the inverse will not help the preservationists who claim that HUD's efforts were insufficient. Any effort to analogize to *Hough v. Marsh* and distinguish *Central Oklahoma* will be unsatisfactory. HUD did a lot more than make one phone call. When the issue is critical to the appeal and these two cases represent the only authority, the preservationists should adopt a bolder strategy and use *Central Oklahoma* to show what HUD could and should have done. The approach might read like this:

HUD is required to make reasonable efforts to find "all properties possessing historical, architectural, archeological, or cultural value located within the area of the undertaking's potential environmental impact." *Central Oklahoma v. OCURA,* 471 F.Supp. 68 (W.D. Okl. 1979) defines reasonable efforts. In that case HUD took four separate steps in an attempt to locate historically significant properties. It consulted both the local urban renewal agency and the State Historic Preservation Officer. It hired third party consultants on two occasions, and it conducted its own inquiries and historic reviews. None of these efforts uncovered historically significant properties and the court held that HUD's efforts were sufficient.

In this case, HUD did not put forth sufficient effort. If it had, it would have discovered the old county courthouse. HUD made one phone call to the local urban renewal agency. The director did not know of any eligible properties, but he promised to investigate. The director did not report back to HUD and HUD never asked the question again.

HUD contacted the State Historic Preservation Officer, who had no information on eligible properties. He explained that a county survey was in progress and would be completed over the next year and a half. Armed with this information HUD could have done three things:

a) It could have waited until the survey was complete before signing the contract.

b) It could have asked for a preliminary report on historically significant buildings in the project area.

c) It could have requested that the survey begin with the project area and delay the contract accordingly.

The survey report issued in May a year later identified the county courthouse as eligible for the National Register. Had HUD pursued any of these alternatives, it would have uncovered the old courthouse.

HUD made inquiries of the public through a notice in the local paper and at public hearings in October and November. The public raised concern for the old courthouse in letters to HUD and at both public hearings. Three or four months before signing the contract, HUD had notice of a potentially historic structure within the project area. It could have asked those conducting the survey for a preliminary report on just the courthouse. It also could have applied the National Register Criteria—CFR 800.10, to the courthouse as required by section (a)(2) of the regulation. Either of these minimal efforts would have uncovered the old courthouse as a property potentially eligible for inclusion in the National Register of Historic Places. HUD failed to make the reasonable effort required by the regulation and the *Central Oklahoma* case.

By using the steps listed in the *Central Oklahoma* case, the advocate was able to demonstrate that although HUD may nominally have jumped through the appropriate hoops, it failed to follow up on any lead. By its superficial approach, it missed the obvious. A creative advocate can deal with the opponent's argument affirmatively by using the existing precedent even though the case seems to favor the opponent.

In serious appeals, an advocate is often arguing a case of first impression in the jurisdiction. When you do not have obviously compelling authority to use, your goal should be to ground the analysis in the jurisdiction using the available authority and then proceed to the authority outside the jurisdiction. The following illustrates one approach.

The seventh circuit has yet to consider whether the term "damages" in a contract of insurance includes response costs under

CERCLA. The interpretation of insurance contracts is a matter of state law, *Independent Petrochemical Corp. v. Aetna Cas. & Surety Co.*, 944 F.2d 940 (1991), and in this case, the court is required to interpret the contract under Indiana insurance law. The court in *Eli Lilly and Co. v. Home Ins. Co.*, 482 N.E.2d 467, 470 (Ind. 1985), provided the Indiana rules: (1) insurance contracts "are subject to the same rules of interpretation as are other contracts", (2) "[i]f the policy language is clear and unambiguous, it should be given its plain and ordinary meaning"; and (3) only if the language is ambiguous, will the court "apply the rules of construction favoring the non-drafter of insurance contract terms."

The court in *IPC v. Aetna* used the same rules of insurance contract construction to resolve the same issue under Missouri law.

Once having explained why the case is analogous, the advocate is ready to discuss the substance.

Distinguishing opponent's arguments

In an appellate brief, the advocate needs to distinguish the arguments made by opposing counsel. When there is controlling authority in the jurisdiction that favors the opponent, you must address the unwelcome precedent directly. You can do this in a number of different ways. Some cases are distinguishable on the facts. Old authority can be questioned based on its age and developments since the decision. Sometimes, you can distinguish a case based on public policy. If the case includes a dissent, you can argue that the dissent and not the majority view was correct.

If there is no controlling authority in the jurisdiction, you are not required to distinguish the opponent's authority, but only the opponent's arguments. Using a case from another jurisdiction that specifically rejected the opponent's argument can be an effective approach.

The court in *Independent Petrochemical Corp. v. Aetna Casualty & Surety Co.*, 944 F.2d 940 (D.C. Cir. 1991), rejected the insurer's argument, adopted in *Continental Ins. Cos. v. Northern Pharmaceutical & Chemical Co.*, 842 F.2d 977 (8th Cir.), *cert. denied*, 488 U.S. 821 (1988) (*NEPACCO*), that the term "damages" be given a narrow technical meaning. Although the court in *NEPACCO* identified the proper rules for construing contract language, it misapplied them. The rule under Missouri law is that contract terms be given their plain and ordinary meaning. A layperson would expect "damages" to include response costs under CERCLA.

The author of this example both distinguished the opposing argument and one of the opponent's major cases by relying on the D.C. Circuit's analysis. The approach is an affirmative one, which permits the advocate to deal with the argument without having to give space to explaining the opposing view.

Using Policy Effectively

Public policy is an important consideration in writing to an appellate court. While the trial court is looking primarily for a pragmatic solution to the issues based on existing law, the appellate courts, particularly at the highest level, are charged with allowing the gradual development of the law. This development must be consistent with public policy; that is, the law should encourage socially acceptable behavior and discourage socially unacceptable behavior. Although the appellate court must also decide the dispute between the particular parties before it, it must anticipate how this decision will influence the choices made by future parties. Your legal argument will be more effective to an appellate audience if you include the policy that supports your position, and demonstrate that the holding you advocate for this case will make good law.

As with other arguments, policy arguments are more persuasive if supported by solid authority. Public policy comes from a wide variety of sources, ranging from legal authority to scientific and economic sources to common sense. There are also a number of ways of presenting policy arguments. The discussion that follows provides approaches to finding public policy and integrating it into your argument section.

SOURCES OF PUBLIC POLICY

Public policy comes from a number of formal and informal sources. Legislative law, for example, is a good source of policy. Constitutions are statements of the basic policy that governs society and, therefore, are an excellent source of policy. Many states have recently revised their constitutions to include statements of policy. The following excerpt from the Michigan Constitution of 1963 provides policy for environmental protection:

> The conservation and development of the natural resources of the state are hereby declared to be of paramount public concern in the interest of the health, safety and general welfare of the people. The legislature shall provide for the protection of the air, water and other natural resources of the state from pollution, impairment and destruction.

Mich. Const. of 1963 art. IV, sec. 52.

This provision is a good source of the public policy behind environmental protection legislation enacted subsequently.

Statutes, too, are a good source of policy. Frequently, a statute will contain an introductory section that states the purpose of the legislation. The Equal Pay Act of 1963, for example, includes the following provision:

> (a) The Congress hereby finds that the existence in industries engaged in commerce or in the production of goods for commerce of wage differentials based on sex—

(1) depresses wages and living standards for employees necessary for their health and efficiency;

(2) prevents the maximum utilization of available labor resources;

(3) tends to cause labor disputes, thereby burdening, affecting, and obstructing commerce;

(4) burdens commerce and the free flow of goods in commerce; and

(5) constitutes an unfair method of competition.

(b) It is hereby declared to be the policy of this Act, through exercise by Congress of its power to regulate commerce among the several States and with foreign nations, to correct the conditions above referred to in such industries.

Act of June 10, 1963, Pub. L. No. 88–38, 1963 U.S. Code Cong. & Admin. News (77 Stat.) 56.

This purpose section has two goals. It defines the problem Congress addressed in the Equal Pay Act, sex discrimination in wages. It also provides the congressional authority for the Act, the commerce clause of the U.S. Constitution.

There may also be legislative history that explains the congressional intent behind a particular piece of legislation. This congressional intent is another form of public policy. To find the legislative history for a federal statute, consult either United States Code Congressional and Administrative News (USCCAN) or Congressional Information Service (CIS) or a source of compiled legislative histories. The following is a brief excerpt from the House Report on the Civil Rights Act of 1964:

No bill can or should lay claim to eliminating all of the causes and consequences of racial and other types of discrimination against minorities. There is reason to believe, however, that national leadership provided by the enactment of Federal legislation dealing with the most troublesome problems will create an atmosphere conducive to voluntary or local resolution of other forms of discrimination.

It is, however, possible and necessary for the Congress to enact legislation which prohibits and provides the means of terminating the most serious types of discrimination. This H.R. 7152, as amended, would achieve in a number of related areas. It would reduce discriminatory obstacles to the exercise of the right to vote and provide means of expediting the vindication of that right. It would make it possible to remove the daily affront and humiliation involved in discriminatory denials of access to facilities ostensibly open to the general public. It would guarantee that there will be no discrimination among recipients of Federal financial assistance. It would prohibit discrimination in employment, and provide means to expedite termination of discrimination in public education. It would open additional avenues to deal with redress of denials of equal protection of the laws on account of race, color, religion, or national origin by State or local authorities.

H.R. 7152, as amended, is a constitutional and desirable means of dealing with the injustices and humiliations of racial and other discrimination. It is a reasonable and responsive bill whose provisions are designed effectively to meet an urgent and most serious national problem.

H.Rep. No. 914, 88th Cong., 2d Sess. 5, reprinted in 1964 U.S. Code Cong. & Admin. News 2391, 2393–2394.

The legislative history for the Civil Rights Act of 1964 is extensive; Congress wanted to leave no doubt about its intent to eliminate discrimination on the basis of race, color, religion or national origin.

Public policy appears, too, in case law. In *Boomer v. Atlantic Cement Co.,* 26 N.Y.2d 219, 309 N.Y.S.2d 312, 257 N.E.2d 870 (1970), for example, the court reached its decision based on public policy grounds. The plaintiffs, neighbors of a cement company, asked the trial court to enjoin the operation of the company on the grounds that the dust emanating from the cement works was a nuisance. The trial court found a nuisance; however, it declined to issue an injunction, and only awarded damages for past injuries. The appellate division affirmed. The Court of Appeals, noting the disparity in the economic consequences to all parties, reversed the lower court decision and granted a limited injunction until the company had paid permanent damages to all the injured parties. The permanent damages were to compensate the plaintiffs for all damages: past, present, and future. The court decided the case in the face of a long standing rule that a nuisance should be enjoined, but based on the following policy:

A court performs its essential function when it decides the rights of parties before it. Its decision of private controversies may sometimes greatly affect public issues. Large questions of law are often resolved by the manner in which private litigation is decided. But this is normally an incident to the court's main function to settle controversy. It is a rare exercise of judicial power to use a decision in private litigation as a purposeful mechanism to achieve direct public objectives greatly beyond the rights and interests before the court.

Effective control of air pollution is a problem presently far from solution even with the full public and financial powers of government. In large measure adequate technical procedures are yet to be developed and some that appear possible may be economically impracticable.

It seems apparent that the amelioration of air pollution will depend on technical research in great depth; on a carefully balanced consideration of the economic impact of close regulation;

and of the actual effect on public health. It is likely to require massive public expenditure and to demand more than any local community can accomplish and to depend on regional and interstate controls.

A court should not try to do this on its own as a by-product of private litigation and it seems manifest that the judicial establishment is neither equipped in the limited nature of any judgment it can effectively pronounce nor prepared to lay down and implement any effective policy for the elimination of air pollution. This is an area beyond the circumference of one private lawsuit. It is a direct responsibility for government and should not thus be undertaken as an incident to solving a dispute between property owners and a single cement plant—one of many—in the Hudson River valley.

The cement making operations of defendant have been found by the court at Special Term to have damaged the nearby properties of plaintiffs in these two actions. That court, as it has been noted, accordingly found defendant maintained a nuisance and this has been affirmed at the Appellate Division. The total damage to plaintiffs' properties is, however, relatively small in comparison with the value of defendant's operation and with the consequences of the injunction which plaintiffs seek.

The ground for the denial of injunction, notwithstanding the finding both that there is a nuisance and that plaintiffs have been damaged substantially, is the large disparity in economic consequences of the nuisance and of the injunction. This theory cannot, however, be sustained without overruling a doctrine which has been consistently reaffirmed in several leading cases in this court and which has never been disavowed here, namely that where a nuisance has been found and where there has been any substantial damage shown by the party complaining an injunction will be granted.

The rule in New York has been that such a nuisance will be enjoined although marked disparity be shown in economic consequence between the effect of the injunction and the effect of the nuisance.

26 N.Y.2d at 224–25, 257 N.E.2d at 871–72.

There are two policy reasons for the decision the court reached. First, air pollution requires a state, regional, or federal solution, which is well beyond the power of the court. Second, the economic consequences of closing down a multi-million dollar business far outweigh the benefits such a closing would have on the individual plaintiffs. These are both policies that can be applied by analogy in other cases.

These are the common sources of public policy and the ones that lawyers are most likely to use. You need not limit yourself, however, to these sources. Policy that comes from other fields, if properly documented and explained precisely to the court, can also be used as effective policy. Economics, psychology, and sociology are common disciplines used by lawyers. The United States Supreme Court, for example, relied on psychological studies to reach its decision in *Brown v. Board of Education,* 347 U.S. 483, 494 (1954), that segregated school systems had a detrimental impact on black children. Finally, public policy can be based on common sense.

INTEGRATING POLICY INTO THE ARGUMENT

The placement of policy arguments in the argument section of a brief is a tactical matter. You have a choice of incorporating the policy into the legal argument or treating the policy as a separate argument. The examples that follow are suggestions of common ways for integrating policy into the argument section. The list is not all inclusive; it is intended to stimulate your thinking about the possibilities.

Generally your argument will be more persuasive if you incorporate the policy into the legal argument. This works neatly when the policy comes from either a constitutional provision or the purpose section of a statute. You can state the issue and follow with the policy provision. The effect is to treat the constitutional or purpose section of a statute as the most general statement of the rule in the R section of CRAC. The court is then able to read the rest of the rule section in light of the policy behind the rule. The section of the Michigan Constitution quoted above could be used effectively as the introduction to the legislation that fulfills the purpose of protecting the natural resources of the state from pollution, impairment, and destruction.

The policy as it appears in legislative history usually works effectively in conjunction with the operative language of the statute. Often the operative language can be interpreted in more than one way. The legislative history is useful in explaining to the court the interpretation Congress intended. The legislative history should follow the operative language and precede discussion of cases that illustrate the application of the provision, if such cases are available. When you are dealing with a case of first impression, the legislative history precedes your analysis on that issue.

Legislative history is also useful in explaining to the court interpretations that are not expressly provided by the operative language, but that are implied in the statute. If the statute, for example, may or may not cover your case, the legislative history may help you persuade the court that Congress intended to include the cause of action either because it is listed among the problems Congress was trying to address or because it is directly analogous to one of those problems.

Organization of policy from cases may be more difficult. If the case is analogous to your case, you can organize the legal analysis using the case with the policy as a supporting argument. In diagrammatic form this approach might appear as follows:

Contention

Rule

  Illustrative Case

Application of rule to facts

Conclusion

Supporting policy from illustrative case

Application of policy to present case

Conclusion with policy

In this arrangement the policy is integrated into the legal analysis. If the analogy to the illustrative case is a strong one, the argument will be more persuasive with the legal analysis first and then the policy that supports your conclusion. If, however, the policy argument is strong, but the analysis is not particularly persuasive, you may choose to begin with the strong policy argument and relegate the legal analysis that shows the court how to implement the policy to a supporting position.

Occasionally, the only strong argument you have is a policy argument. This was probably the case for the defendant company in the *Boomer v. Atlantic Cement Co.* case mentioned above. The trial court found a nuisance, and the New York rule at the time was that when there was a nuisance, it should be enjoined. Faced with a clear but unwelcome rule, an advocate must often take the aggressive approach and begin with the policy argument. Only by showing the court that the existing legal rule is contrary to policy, is the advocate in a position to convince the court to use or formulate an alternative rule. While this approach is not normally necessary or recommended, keep it in mind for those few situations when this is the only viable approach.

QUOTING IN AN APPELLATE BRIEF

The argument section of an appellate brief will flow better if you do not quote extensively from court opinions. The reason for this is that the reader will be accustomed to your writing style and frequent changes from your style to that of various judges will be distracting. Most of the time you can paraphrase what the judge said just as effectively in your own words. Occasionally, however, you want to highlight a point and a quotation is one way to accomplish this. If, for example, a judge gave a precise statement of a rule, a quotation of that precise statement can be effective. It serves both to emphasize the rule and to place the judge's imprimatur on the point. Be sure to integrate the quotation skillfully into your text so that the result highlights your point without distracting the reader. Extensive use of quotations, however, dilutes the effect and defeats the purpose.

Exercise 21 A.

Compare the following summaries of argument from *Lucas v. South Carolina Coastal Council*, No. 91–453 (October Term 1991). They come from the petitioner's brief, the respondent's brief, and an amicus brief submitted by the United States.

Petitioner's Summary of Argument

This case invites the Court to revisit regulatory takings law. The South Carolina Supreme Court has repudiated the recent jurisprudence of this Court by converting a complex inquiry into a bright-line test which ignores private interests in property affected by state regulation. In holding that the South Carolina Beachfront Management Act does not effect a regulatory taking of Petitioner's coastal property, the South Carolina Supreme Court ruled that the state need only prove that it is acting pursuant to its legitimate police powers in order to evade the constitutional duty of just compensation. This ruling is contrary to the recent holdings of this Court and is utterly subversive of takings jurisprudence.

This case does not involve the physical occupation by the State of private property. Nor does this case touch upon the quantum or modalities of "just compensation." Finally, Petitioner does not seek to challenge the public wisdom of the South Carolina Act. The South Carolina Supreme Court improperly chose to view Petitioner's position on this last issue as conceding not only the rightful exercise of the state's police power for land-use regulation, but also as an admission that Petitioner's intended use of his land amounted to a nuisance. *Lucas v. South Carolina Coastal Council*, 404 S.E.2nd 895, 900 (S.C. 1991).

Petitioner first submits that the so-called "nuisance exception" to the Takings Guarantee has been broadly misunderstood. Developed as a corollary to challenges of regulation based only on due process grounds, it has no place in the modern jurisprudence which views extreme forms of regulatory takings as violative of the Just Compensation clause of the Fifth Amendment. The categorical nature of the nuisance exception—which would deny compensation whenever a legislature finds that a certain activity poses a public hazard cannot be reconciled with the approach taken by this Court in "as applied" challenges of regulatory takings since at least 1922.

Should this Court decide that some vestige of a nuisance exception exists, Petitioner next submits that it must be doctrinally limited. In cases where the value of property is totally taken by regulation, a court's denial of just compensation cannot be justified either in judicial precedent or sound public policy. It is undisputed in this case that the entire value of Mr. Lucas's two coastal lots was taken by operation of the South Carolina law.

Finally, not all exercises of a state's police power are directed against nuisances, and the Petitioner maintains that his desire to build private residences on beachfront property is not a nuisance that would legitimize a state regulation having the effect of depriving him of all use of his property. There must be an objective standard by which legislatures identify nuisances, and thus regulate away the value of property without compensation. Otherwise, the states' broad police powers could insulate all land-use regulations from challenges under the Takings Guarantee.[8]

Respondent's Summary of Argument

1. Petitioner's taking claim is not ripe because § 48–30–290(D) of the 1990 Amendments to the 1988 Beachfront Management Act now allows petitioner the opportunity to apply for a permit to construct homes seaward of the baseline. Pet. App. 125. Given the existence of this remedy, petitioner's claim that the respondent has permanently taken his property is not ripe for review until and unless he applies for and is denied such a special permit. The issue of temporary takings, which was preserved at trial by stipulation, likewise is not ripe.

2. Should this Court nonetheless conclude that petitioner's taking claim presents a justiciable case and controversy, the Court should reject the petitioner's extreme position that he is entitled to compensation based solely upon diminution in value. Such a test flies squarely in the face of all the Court's takings jurisprudence. This Court has repeatedly rejected the claim that diminution in value, standing alone, determines whether an unconstitutional taking has occurred. The Court has instead made clear that in addition to economic impact, both the character of the government action at issue, and the reasonableness of the investment-backed expectations implicated must be considered. Indeed, special consideration must be given to the character and purpose of the state interest because at a minimum there is current agreement among members of the Court that there is a class of government actions effectively insulated from the requirement of compensation because they merely prevent harmful uses of property. Likewise, reasonableness of the investment-backed expectations of the landowner can have a significant impact upon the Court's determination of whether a compensable taking has occurred.

3. Finally, assuming this Court does not confine its review to the petitioner's untenable "bright line" economic impact test, the South Carolina Supreme Court's judgment should be upheld based upon the three factors cited as central to the takings formula. These factors include the character of the government action, the interference with reasonable investment-backed expectations, and the economic impact of the regulations.

As it relates to the character of the government action, the 1988 Beachfront Management Act was passed in response to serious public harm created by "ill-planned" development that has been built ever closer to the dangers of erosion and storms. Pursuant to direction by

8. This Summary of Argument comes from Petitioner's Brief on the Merits, *Lucas v. South Carolina Coastal Council*, Docket Number 91–453, United States Supreme Court. Permission granted by coun- sel to David H. Lucas: A. Camden Lewis, Esq., Gerald M. Finkel, Esq., and Professor David J. Bederman. Copyright © 1991 by A. Camden Lewis, Esq., Gerald M. Finkel, Esq., and Professor David J. Bederman.

the federal government, South Carolina implemented a setback scheme to prevent construction in the fragile beach/dune system. This prohibition took into account the danger to life and property not only to those building, but also to nearby neighbors. There is no question that the barrier island that the petitioner seeks to build upon is hazardous and that such construction could interfere with an already delicate environment. In this respect, the land use restriction petitioner challenges is analogous to common law tort doctrine that limits a property owner from using his property in a way that, because of the property's physical characteristics, causes physical harm to other persons and property.

As it relates to the petitioner's reasonable investment-backed expectations, several factors militate against a conclusion that the expectation to build homes on these lots is reasonable. First, and as mentioned above, such construction creates a serious threat to health and safety. No one can have a reasonable expectation to harm others in such a manner. Second, in the area of cases dealing with government largess and economic property, this Court has recognized that despite significant losses to property holders, no compensable taking occurs simply because regulations upset settled expectations. There seems no justification for treating petitioner's expectations differently simply because they involve real property. Third, the petitioner had no reasonable expectation to construct upon this volatile and fragile environment. There has developed a strong legal tradition that recognizes that no one has a right or an expectation to change the natural character of certain types of land or to use such land for a purpose for which it is unsuited in its natural state. This principle applies to the shifting sands of Isle of Palms, where the petitioner's lots have historically proven unfit for construction. Finally, these legal principles concerning expectation are also supported by the fact that petitioner was intimately involved with the development of the Wild Dunes subdivision. He knew of the dangers and should have expected the government to act in a responsible way by implementing setbacks that prevent ill-planned development.

Lastly, petitioner is not deprived of all his economic value or use of his property. His whole case is centered on the sole proposition that he had been denied "highest and best" use of his property to construct single-family homes. No effort was made to assign value to other uses. Indeed, he retains significant value in his bundle of property rights. Given that the property is unsuitable for what he deems "highest and best" use, what he retains is an appropriate and reasonable use of his property.[9]

---

9. This Summary of Argument comes from the Respondent's Brief on the Merits in *Lucas v. South Carolina Coastal Council*, Docket Number 91–453, United States Supreme Court (1991). Reprinted with permission from C. C. Harness, General Counsel for the South Carolina Coastal Council. Copyright © 1991 by C. C. Harness, General Counsel for the South Carolina Coastal Council.

Summary of Argument for Amicus Curiae United States

1. There is no present basis for finding a permanent taking, in view of petitioner's ability to apply for a special permit under the 1990 amendments. Even if petitioner is granted a special permit, however, he may still have a temporary taking claim for the period prior to the institution of the special permit procedure. This Court need not reach that claim in the first instance, but may instead vacate the judgment below and remand to allow the state courts to consider the viability and validity of any such claim.

2. Government has the established right to prevent certain noxious uses of property that cause serious harm to others without compensating the owner of the offending property, even if the property has substantially diminished economic value in the absence of the prohibited use. Some situations involving total destruction of property or substantial reduction of its value (e.g., destruction of diseased food, condemnation of an unsafe building, or a prohibition against building on an unsafe site) do not require compensation. More generally, regulatory measures that substantially further the public interest in preventing established nuisance-type activities or serious harm to the public health or safety may not require compensation. That "nuisance exception" was well established at the time of the framing and ratification of the Bill of Rights, and is firmly rooted in *Mugler v. Kansas*, 123 U.S. 623 (1887), and numerous other decisions, as well as principles of property rights on which those decisions rest.

The scope of this category of measures designed to prevent an established nuisance or protect the public health and safety, however, is by no means coterminous with the full range of a State's police powers. It is instead limited by the principles from which it springs: such measures must in fact respond to serious harms to public health and safety that are substantial in nature, degree, proximity, and context. The South Carolina Supreme Court did not adequately consider whether the restrictions imposed on petitioner's lots meet this standard. That inquiry is particularly important here, where petitioner's two lots are in a highly developed area, the State's own recent amendments contemplate building in some circumstances, and petitioner seeks to engage in a normally unobjectionable use—building single-family residences next to other single-family residences. These factors combine to cast considerable doubt on whether the regulatory regime erected by South Carolina in 1988 is properly viewed as directed at a nuisance or threat to safety. A legislature's routine exercise of the police power may not be brought within the "nuisance exception" to normal application of takings analysis simply by incantation of the words "health and safety"; such an approach would render the just Compensation Clause a hollow guarantee.

3. If a statute does not fall within the narrow category of laws designed to abate a nuisance or similar public health and safety threat, whether it amounts to a taking requires a careful assessment of the

three factors the Court has identified in its regulator-takings decisions: the regulation's economic impact, the character of the governmental action, and the extent to which it interferes with reasonable, investment-backed expectations.[10]

Exercise 21 B. Evaluate the following point headings for content, conciseness, and word choice.

1. BY REQUIRING THAT INSURERS COVER EPA RESPONSE COSTS, THE COURT WILL ADVANCE THE INTENT OF CERCLA AND PROVIDE A RESULT CONSISTENT WITH THE TRADITIONAL BUSINESS PURPOSE OF INSURANCE.

2. *Under Indiana's Rules of Contract Construction, Ambiguous Terms in a Comprehensive General Liability Insurance Policy should be Construed in Favor of the Insured.*

3. *The "Damages" Term in a Comprehensive General Liability Policy Includes CERCLA Response Costs because the Average Business Person would Understand the Plain Meaning of the Term to Cover Costs of Cleaning Up Hazardous Waste.*

4. THERE WAS INSUFFICIENT EVIDENCE OF THE OFFENSE OF BREAKING AND ENTERING THE PROPERTY OF ANOTHER WHERE THE DEFENDANT AND THE COMPLAINANT LIVED TOGETHER FOR NINE YEARS AND THE DEFENDANT HAD HIS PERSONAL PROPERTY AT THE RESIDENCE.

5. THE POLICE LACKED PROBABLE CAUSE TO CONDUCT A WARRANTLESS SEARCH AND SEIZURE AT DEFENDANT'S RESIDENCE, AND, THEREFORE, THE RESULTING EVIDENCE SHOULD HAVE BEEN SUPPRESSED.

6. EXIGENT CIRCUMSTANCES EXISTED FOR A WARRANTLESS SEARCH OF DEFENDANT'S MOUTH FOR NARCOTICS, WHEN THE POLICE OFFICERS BELIEVED THAT EVIDENCE OF THE CRIME WAS BEING DESTROYED AND DEFENDANT'S LIFE MIGHT BE IN DANGER IF HE SWALLOWED THE DRUGS.

7. UNDER THE FOURTH AMENDMENT TO THE UNITED STATES CONSTITUTION, A WARRANTLESS SEARCH OF DEFENDANT'S VEHICLE WAS UNREASONABLE WHEN THE VEHICLE WAS IN POLICE CUSTODY AND THERE WAS NO DANGER IT WOULD DISAPPEAR.

8. THE ANALYSIS IN THE LOWER COURT WAS INCORRECT AND THE CASE SHOULD BE REVERSED ON APPEAL.

---

10. This Summary of Argument comes from the Brief of United States as Amicus Curiae in Support of Reversal in *Lucas v. South Carolina Coastal Council,* Docket Number 91–453, United States Supreme Court (1991). Reprinted with permission by Kenneth W. Starr, Solicitor General of the United States, Department of Justice. Copyright © 1991 by Kenneth W. Starr, Solicitor General of the United States, Department of Justice.

Section VII

ORAL ADVOCACY

Oral advocacy is an integral part of advocacy. The lawyers who write briefs to trial and appellate courts also argue those cases. This chapter provides an introduction to oral advocacy. While there are some differences between oral argument to a trial court and an appellate court, the basics are the same. The differences will be indicated below where appropriate.

Chapter 22

ORAL ARGUMENT IN THE TRIAL AND APPELLATE COURTS

The purpose of oral argument is to make sure that the court understands what your case is about and why a decision in your client's favor is vital. To do this you must engage in a dialogue with the bench. The dialogue is necessary to give you feedback on what the court does not understand and the arguments that the court does not find persuasive. Armed with this information, you can lay the court's doubts to rest and reframe the arguments in a more persuasive way. Although oral argument does not normally turn a losing case into a winning one, it can make the difference in a close case.

WHERE TO SIT AND OTHER PRACTICAL INFORMATION

There is no way to predict the way an oral argument will develop, but with careful preparation you can limit the unknowns and avoid most surprises. One way to prepare is to learn as much as possible about the logistics and procedure in advance. If you have the opportunity, visit the court in advance of your argument to become familiar with the layout of the courtroom and the procedure.

A trial court is arranged with the bench for the judge, a witness box, a jury box, counsel tables, a lectern, seating for the court clerk, and a section for the public. There may also be a court stenographer. During a trial, counsel for the plaintiff or the prosecutor sit at the counsel table nearest the jury box. During a motion hearing, counsel for the moving party normally sits at the counsel table nearest the jury box. An appellate court has a larger bench to accommodate three, seven, or nine judges or justices, counsel tables, a lectern, seating for the court clerk, and a section for the public. Counsel for the appellant normally sits on the left hand side facing the bench.

Lawyers dress in conservative suits for court appearances. While there is no fundamental reason for this custom, there is a practical reason for complying with it. Your goal is to persuade the court to decide for your client. You want the court to concentrate on what you are saying; you do not want to distract the court by the way you are dressed. For this reason, too, avoid jangling jewelry. The microphone at the lectern will pick up the sound and it will interfere with the court's ability to concentrate on your argument.

Courts have different systems for scheduling arguments. Some trial courts set aside a half a day for civil or criminal motions every week. Counsel check in with the court clerk when they arrive and as soon as all counsel on that case are present, the clerk calls the cases on a first ready, first heard basis. Other courts have a strict time schedule, and counsel are expected to be present and ready to argue at that time. This is the normal practice in appellate courts.

Find out in advance how much time you will have for oral argument. Trial court motion arguments usually run for 5–15 minutes; appellate arguments are normally 30 minutes. The moving party or appellant speaks first and last. The responding party or appellee speaks second. Plan the scope of the argument according to the time allotted. In an appellate court, the appellant must plan for and reserve time for rebuttal at the beginning of the argument.

You should tailor the argument according to your case. The following is a general format for oral argument at the appellate level:

1) Introduce yourself and explain to the court who you represent.

Plan ahead how you will refer to your client during the course of the argument, and if you are using a generic term, like "the agency", introduce the term at this point.

2) Introduce the case and the issues on appeal.

Remember that while the judge or judges have read your brief, yours is only one case on the docket that day, so put the case in context. At the trial court level, explain the nature of the motion and what you are asking the court to do. On appeal, give a brief outline of the issues and the relief you want. This section serves the same function as the thesis section of the brief; it provides the court with a road map of the issues and the outcome you desire.

3) Explain the procedure of the case to date.

Cover only the procedure necessary to help the court understand your argument. The rest is in your brief and you want to keep the court's attention focused on the important points.

4) Explain the facts of the case from your client's perspective.

This gives you a chance to present your theory of the case. Limit the facts to those necessary to your argument and for context. On appeal, the court may ask you to omit the facts if the bench is already familiar with them. You can still refer to essential facts in the course of the argument and you should do so where necessary. In a fifteen minute argument, you should plan to spend only a minute or so on the first four items of the argument.

5) Discuss the issues.

This is the main part of the argument and you should plan to spend most of the time here.

6) Distinguish the arguments or cases relied on by your opponent.

If you are the moving party or appellant, you may decide to save this for rebuttal. It is often effective, however, to deal with opposing arguments in your argument in chief.

7) Conclude your argument in a way that leads inevitably to the relief you want.

8) Ask for the relief.

9) Thank the court and sit down.

This basic format works for both sides of the case. The responding party or appellee may want to omit the facts and procedure if the opponent has presented a reasonable summary or if the court has asked the opponent to omit these sections. If your opponent has omitted important facts or if you need to use the facts to explain your theory of the case, explain what is necessary.

PREPARATION

Effective oral argument requires advance preparation of three kinds. First, you must update your research. Second, you must choose and organize the points you want to make to the court. Third, you must prepare to deal with questions from the bench. The amount of time you allocate to each depends on the level of court and the issues in the case. Most of the discussion below focuses on oral argument at the appellate level; its specific application to the trial court is discussed below.

Just before the oral argument, be sure to update your research with Shepard's or one of the computer updating systems. In an appellate court, months will elapse between the time you file your brief and argue the case. A major decision can change the whole complexion of your case. Even at the trial court level, new developments are possible. At best, it is embarrassing to be unfamiliar with a recent development; at worst, it may be detrimental to your client.

Remember that oral argument is a dialogue with the bench. It will be a successful argument if dialogue occurs and if the judge or judges ask you questions. Although you cannot anticipate precisely what will happen, you can prepare yourself for the exchange. Reread the briefs on both sides. Make sure that you know all the facts. Reread the relevant law both as it supports your position and as it supports your opponent.

Most of the argument will be devoted to items 5 and 6 listed above. In the time allotted, you will not be able to discuss all the material covered in the brief. As a result, you will need to choose the most important points. Start by listing the issues you need to win on appeal. You may be able to prevail, for example, if you can convince the court either that the operative section of a statute does not apply in this case or that an exception does apply. You may have decided that for purposes of the brief, you should use a logical order and address the operative section first. Rethink the order of issues. If your chances of success are better on the exception and you only need to prevail on one issue to persuade the appellate court to reverse the decision below, consider beginning with the exception.

Consider the standard of review for each issue. If you are the appellant and the issue is purely a matter of law, you may want to point this out to the court. The appellate court will be predisposed to affirm the decision below. By explaining that the appellate court can decide as a matter of law, the appellant reminds the court that it need not give deference to the trial court's opinion on matters of law. Where the standard of review is either clearly erroneous or abuse of discretion, it is to the appellee's advantage to remind the appellate court of the proper deference it should give to the lower court or administrative agency decision.

Next, list the arguments that support your position on each issue. If the list includes a number of arguments, choose the strongest arguments to include in oral argument; the rest are in your brief.

Think about the authority that supports each argument. Is there a case the court must apply? Is there a case that uses compelling reasoning? If the issue is a factual one, is there a case with identical facts? Is there legislative or drafting history that demonstrates the intent behind language you are asking the court to interpret? Is there policy support for your argument? Can you use examples to demonstrate your argument graphically to the court? Although the necessary authority is in your brief and you do not want to spend your oral argument reiterating the arguments as you have crafted them for the brief, choose the authority you need to use to make your argument.

Then plan the way that you will explain the arguments to the court. Remember that oral argument is a dialogue, so you want to prepare a conversational, rather than a written, explanation. Make it logical, thorough enough for the judges who are not as familiar with the case as you are, but do not memorize your argument. If you are asking the court to draw an analogy to another area of the law, be sure to make the analogy explicit. If you are asking the court to adopt the reasoning from a case in another jurisdiction, be sure to explain why the case is analogous with reference to the similar statutory language, the same rules of construction, the same policy, and so forth.

Then consider all of your opponent's arguments and prepare to deal with them, both affirmatively and in answer to questions. If there is a case that is stare decisis on a critical issue, be prepared to deal with this case. Otherwise, focus on the arguments, not necessarily on the particular cases your opponent used. Muster the facts, cases, reasoning and policy you need to rebut these arguments. It can be effective, for example, to refer to a court that specifically rejected the argument your opponent makes.

In preparing for oral argument, there are advantages and disadvantages inherent in representing both the appellant and the appellee. By going first, the appellant can set the tone of the argument and the general organization of the argument. The appellant, however, must overcome the court's inherent inertia and persuade the judges to reverse the decision below. The appellee won below and need only protect the victory. Particularly when the standard of review requires the appellate court to defer to the factual findings and discretionary rulings in the lower court, the appellee has a decided edge. On the other hand, the appellee is not in a position to set the tone of the argument or to structure it initially for the court. As a result, the appellee must be able to change the approach and organization while the appellant is arguing.

Particularly in appellate argument, you should have a flexible game plan. On the one hand, be prepared to discuss your issues in detail using the time allocated to your argument. If the judges have lots of questions for you, also be prepared to make the most important points briefly. As the argument develops, you should be flexible enough to move between these two approaches.

While you cannot anticipate how the dialogue with the bench will develop, there are two sections of the argument you should know cold, the introduction and the conclusion. The goal of the introduction is to get the court's attention with a brief statement of your theory of the case and an outline of the issues. It should be brief, precise, and delivered with a confidence you may not be feeling at that moment. When you see that your time is running out, be ready to make a quick transition and launch into your conclusion and request for relief. Practice both a one paragraph wrap up of the issues and a one sentence version, so you are ready for either contingency.

There is one final step in preparing for oral argument at the appellate level. Remember that one role of the appellate courts is to oversee the gradual development of the law in a manner which is consistent with public policy. In order to make sure that the development you advocate will make good law, the court may ask you hypothetical questions. You will be ready to deal with these hypotheticals if you have considered possible extensions of the law to various facts in advance.

ANSWERING QUESTIONS

When the judge asks a question, do not panic, rejoice. You have succeeded in creating a dialogue with the bench. You now know what is bothering the court about the case and you have a chance to deal with the problem. Approach the answer in the same way you would handle a thoughtful question in a normal conversation. Listen carefully to the question; a dialogue is a conversation where the ideas of both parties are important. Even if you have anticipated the question, wait until the judge has finished asking the question before you answer. It is not only rude to interrupt, but it makes the judge feel that his question was a trivial or obvious question. If you need to pause to collect your thoughts, take a moment to reflect. It indicates to the judge that this was a thoughtful question. If you do not understand the question, ask for clarification or ask the judge to repeat the question. In a normal conversation, you would not answer a question you did not understand; the same holds true for oral argument.

There are three types of questions: factual questions, legal questions, and policy questions. If the judge is asking for clarification of the facts, briefly fill in the missing facts. In an appellate court, give an appropriate reference to the record if it is available. If you do not know the answer, explain that it is not in the record below.

Questions of law and policy usually require a more extensive reply. Organize the answer with the listener in mind. Begin with the punch line, "yes" or "no", and follow up with the explanation. The listener will be more receptive to your explanation if he knows your conclusion first. If he must wait for the bottom line, he may not give full attention to your explanation.

Watch the judge carefully as you answer to see if he understands what you are saying. Expand or contract the answer accordingly. If he does not seem to comprehend, try another approach to your answer. If he knows exactly what you are saying, condense your reply. You do this in normal conversation; it is also appropriate in oral argument. If you have tried to explain your point several different ways and the judge still does not agree with you, move on to another point of your argument. In an appellate court, this judge only has one vote. The other judges may agree with you. They are also part of the dialogue and you must also put their concerns to rest.

Many of the legal questions posed by the court will require that you address the arguments made by opposing counsel. This is not only the most important part of the argument, but also a part for which you are thoroughly prepared. The answer should have two parts. First, explain the problem with your opponent's analysis. Watch the judges' reaction to your answer to make sure you have persuaded them on this point. Then, explain why your analysis is proper. This may involve showing why the rule your opponent advocates is inapplicable and why the rule you propose is better. It may involve distinguishing a case used by your opponent and substituting a case you believe is closer to the point. It may require explaining that your opponent's contention is contrary to public policy and that your position is consistent with public policy. By framing your answer with these two parts, you will draw the court away from the opponent's turf and back into your analysis.

In appellate courts, policy arguments are important. Particularly at the highest level, these courts are concerned with deciding cases that make good precedent. In appellate courts, therefore, the judges often ask hypothetical questions to probe the precedential consequences of a decision for your client. Counsel need to pay particular attention when answering questions involving hypotheticals. There are two concerns and you must strike a balance between them. On the one hand, you want to show the court that the rule you advocate will make good law. It can be applied to a variety of hypothetical situations and yield results that are consistent with public policy. But, any hypothetical can be extended beyond what is reasonable. Before that happens, you want to bring the court's attention back to your case and its facts by explaining that the hypothetical is not the case before the court. The technique is the same as that used in dealing with questions on your opponent's arguments. Answer the court's question thoroughly and then lead the judge back to the points you want to make.

Sometimes a judge will ask you to concede a point to your opponent. Consider this possibility as you prepare for the argument. Avoid conceding anything important to your case. If it is a minor point and it is unreasonable to adamantly defend it, consider conceding it. Conceding a trivial point, if you have considered the ramifications in advance, may enhance your credibility with the court.

The transition between the answer to a question and the affirmative points you want to make is one of the most difficult parts of oral argument. It involves the right pacing and considerable flexibility. You want to pace the transition so that the judge can ask a follow up question if she has one, but do not pause so long that the judge feels compelled to ask a question to fill in the gap. Again, treat this like a normal conversation.

The way you answer questions and handle the transitions will determine who is in control of your argument, you or the judges. This is a difficult line to tread. If you forge ahead in a manner that brooks no interruption, you will inhibit the dialogue and frustrate the court's legitimate concerns. On the other hand, if you let the judges control the argument with a barrage of follow up questions, you may never get to the other important points you want to make. Take advantage of the transitions to move the court's attention to other issues.

Make the transition smooth so the listener cannot tell the difference between the answer to the question and the rest of the argument. If you were discussing the first of three issues when the judge asked a question about that issue, your goal is to complete that issue and move on to the other two. If the question did not deal with policy, you might, for example, explain why your analysis of that issue is consistent with public policy. Then move on to number two.

A smooth transition is more difficult, however, if you were in the middle of issue one when the judge began asking questions about issue three. You did not finish issue one or issue three and have not even touched on issue two. Time is running out. Remember this is a dialogue and your goal is to make sure the court understands your arguments. The questions on issue three indicate that that is the part of the argument that troubled the court the most. If there had been questions on issue one or issue two, the court would have asked them. Your purpose was not to cover all your prepared material, but to make sure the court understood your analysis and was not left with doubts or questions about the case. Check your outline quickly for the main points you have not yet made and fit them into the time that remains, making the transition as easy as possible for the court. With an outline rather than a prepared text, you have the flexibility to move between your long and short form plans.

REBUTTAL

After the arguments of the responding party or appellee, the moving party or appellant has an opportunity for rebuttal. In an appellate court, you must remember to reserve time for rebuttal at the beginning of your argument. The purpose of rebuttal is to address any points made by your opponent that you did not cover in your argument in chief. This is not the time to mention everything you planned to say earlier, but did not have time to include.

Limit yourself to the one or two points raised by your opponent that need clarification. You can also use rebuttal to address a question asked of your opponent. Keep it short and direct. If your opponent has not raised anything you need to address and the court has not asked her any questions you would like to answer, consider waiving the rebuttal. While some attorneys believe that it is always a good idea to have the last word, others use rebuttal only if they need it. They believe it is more effective to say nothing if you do not have an important point to make.

ARGUMENT STYLE

Every lawyer has his or her own argument style. Over time you will develop a unique style that is consistent with your personality. There are two ways to hasten this process. The first is to watch lawyers argue and analyze what is and what is not effective. You will notice that not all flamboyant lawyers are convincing, while some quiet, methodical ones are. Choose a style that is comfortable for you and emulate the masters of that style. The second method is to get as much experience as you can. It is helpful to watch yourself on videotape and correct problems before they become ingrained habits. There are a number of characteristics that effective oralists have in common, no matter what their personal style. The following discussion is not all inclusive, but it does touch on many of these characteristics.

The goal of oral argument is to carry on a dialogue with the bench about this case. As with all interpersonal relations, you want to adopt a demeanor that is appropriate to the situation. You would behave quite differently, for example, if you were talking to an old school friend, an eighty-five year old neighbor, or an IRS auditor investigating your tax return. Judges are entitled to some deference because of their position and experience, which at least initially is greater than yours. They also hold considerable power over this case and the outcome that will affect your client. But they are also members of the same profession. While they may know more about the law in general than you do, you are the expert on your case and they are looking to you for help in understanding it. Judges will not ask questions to put you on the spot or embarrass you; they ask questions to find out the answers and how you would analyze the issues. As a result, be professional, but not distant; be deferential, but not obsequious. Hold your ground if necessary, but try not to be adamant and unreasonable. Refer to the court as "this court" and the individual judges as "your honor" or by name, "Judge Jones"; "Justice Jones" is appropriate in the highest level court in the jurisdiction.

To establish rapport with the bench and begin the dialogue, eye contact is vital from the beginning of the argument. This is why you must know your introduction cold. If you look at the judges, they have to take your argument seriously. Eye contact is important, too, from your perspective. Just as in normal conversation, you get important information from reading the court's response to your argument. You can tell if the judges do not understand what you are saying, and you can explain your argument in more detail.

While some lawyers feel comfortable standing up to argue without a note, most feel more confident if they have an outline of the important points they want to make. It is not effective, however, to have a written text of everything you want to say. There are a number of reasons for this. First, there will be a great temptation to read the text. If you read the argument, you will never establish eye contact with the bench and there will be no dialogue. Second, your written vocabulary is quite different from your spoken vocabulary. While the judges may be able to respond to this language in writing, your language will inhibit the dialogue. Third, even if you have memorized the text, it will sound like a recitation, and the expression you put in your voice in a normal conversation will be missing. At best, you may drone on in a monotone; at worst, it may sound like a tape-recorded announcement that brooks no interruption. Fourth, you will rustle the pages as you turn from one to the next, distracting the court from the content of what you are saying. Fifth, in your nervousness, you may drop this sheaf of papers and have difficulty recovering them in order. Sixth, if by any chance the judge interrupts you with a question, you may lose your place, or worse, repeat the answer to the question when it appears later in your text. To avoid these pitfalls and encourage the dialogue, limit yourself to a basic outline with the main points of your argument.

The outline should include no more than a few reminder notes of the points you want to make on one sheet of paper or a file folder. A file folder allows you to put your outline on one side and a few notes on authorities you may want to use in answer to questions on the other side.

The pacing, volume, and pitch of your voice are also important. Remember that you are discussing complicated analysis. You know it thoroughly, but the judges do not. If you speak too quickly, the judges may miss your point. An argument delivered at twice the pace may cover twice the material, but the court will understand very little. As the goal is to communicate the meaning, not to squeeze in as many words as possible, adjust the pacing so the judges can understand you. You should be able to tell by their expressions if your points are getting across. In many trial courts, a court stenographer will be taking down every word you say. If you speak too quickly, he will have to struggle to keep up. The volume and the way you enunciate the words are also important both for the stenographer and for the court. If you speak too softly or mumble, the listeners will struggle for the words and lose the meaning. This also inhibits the easy flow of the dialogue. Finally, a word on pitch. If your voice normally has a high pitch, it will tend to get even higher if you are nervous or speak too quickly. This will make it more difficult to understand. If you have a naturally high pitched voice, remember to speak slowly and try to lower the pitch.

Facial expression and body language are also part of argument style and they, like speaking style, can encourage or inhibit dialogue. When you watch lawyers arguing, pay attention to what they do with their hands. Some gestures are effective to punctuate the important points in an argument. Others are distracting. We all have nervous mannerisms, such as brushing the hair out of our eyes or straightening our tie. Watch yourself on videotape to diagnose your own idiosyncracies and then work to subtract them from your delivery. You may find that you jingle the change in your pocket, put your hands in and out of your pockets, cling to the lectern for dear life, shuffle from one foot to the other, punctuate your speech with "ums" and "ahs", push your glasses back up your nose, or play with your pen. These are all distracting and detract from what you are saying. A casual slouch is inappropriate to the courtroom setting, but a relaxed, confident posture enhances the credibility of what you are saying. If you look convinced of the merits of your case, the court must at least consider your analysis seriously.

Everyone is nervous at first. Some experienced practitioners report being nervous before every important argument. They deal with it by always being thoroughly prepared. Their nervousness disappears, however, as soon as they get into the argument. You can deal with your nervousness in the same way. Eliminate all the logistical and scheduling unknowns by asking the court clerk or an experienced attorney. Prepare thoroughly by updating the law, planning what you intend to say, both the long version and the short version, making an outline of the basic points, and anticipating questions and hypotheticals. Know your introductory material cold. Take a deep breath, look directly at the bench and launch into the dialogue. Once you get started, your nervousness will disappear.

Developing an effective oral argument style takes time, but with experience and the confidence that comes with time in the profession, you will become an effective oral advocate.

ORAL ARGUMENT AT THE TRIAL COURT LEVEL

Trial level argument has a lot in common with appellate argument. You need to be prepared and anticipate the arguments your opponent will make. But there is only one judge and the atmosphere in the trial courtroom tends to be less formal. There is, however, a wide spectrum of cases from those involving complex legal issues and multiple parties to those involving minor factual issues. Argument in complex cases, particularly in federal court, resembles that in appellate courts. In most instances, the issues will not be as numerous or complex, and you will not have as much time for your argument. Particularly at the state level, your case may be one of many on the docket for that session. The goal is to make it easy for the court to decide the issue(s) in your client's favor. Help the judge by concisely explaining each issue, rule, the application in this case, and the conclusion you advocate.

BASIC FORMULA FOR ORAL ARGUMENT

Preparation

1. Update your research.

2. Choose and organize the important points.

3. Prepare for questions from the bench.

Structure of the Argument

1. Introduce yourself and your client.

2. Explain what the case is about briefly.

3. Explain the procedure if relevant.

4. Explain the facts from your client's perspective.

5. Use CRAC to discuss the issues.

6. Distinguish the arguments and/or authorities used by your opponent, but only after you have made your affirmative argument.

7. Conclude the argument so that it leads inevitably to the desired outcome.

8. Ask for your relief.

9. Thank the court and sit down.

10. If you are the moving party or appellant, use your rebuttal to answer one or two points raised by your opponent or by a question posed to your opponent.

Appendix A

AN OUTLINE

TO: Legal Writing Associate

FROM: Law Clerk

RE: Susan Saxon: Sexual harassment in the work place; good cause as reason to voluntarily leave employment and remain eligible for unemployment benefits.

DATED: August 25, 1988

ISSUE I

Ms. Saxon has cause of action under the Oregon Fair Employment Practices Act based on sexual harassment.

RULE

The applicable statute, Or. Rev. Stat. 659.030(1)(b) provides:

It is unlawful employment practice for an employer, because of an individual's race, religion, color or sex to discriminate against such individual in compensation or in terms, conditions or privileges of employment.

FACT SPECIFIC HOLDING FROM RELEVANT CASE ILLUSTRATING RULE

Racial harassment in the form of insults and humiliating comments and jokes directed at an employee by a fellow employee constitutes a term or condition of employment. *Fred Meyer.*

APPLICATION OF RULE TO FACTS OF YOUR CASE

The other members of the logging crew subject Susan Saxon to sexual harassment in the form of propositions for sexual relations and cracks about her body.

NOTE: In a memo you would compare and contrast Susan Saxon's facts on this issue with the facts of the cases.

CONCLUSION

The sexual harassment inflicted on Susan Saxon is a condition of her employment. Where it occurs only to Saxon, the one female on the mining crew, sexual harassment is sex discrimination and an unfair labor practice under the Oregon Fair Employment Practices Act.

ISSUE II

Ms. Saxon will be able to collect unemployment benefits if she voluntarily quits her job due to sexual harassment.

RULE

The applicable statute, Or. Rev. Stat. 657.176(2) provides:

(2) If the authorized representative designated by the assistant director finds that the individual:

(c) Voluntarily left work without good cause, the individual shall be disqualified from the receipts of benefits * * *

SUB–ISSUES OF GENERAL RULE

Good cause requires both that the employee have grounds that would induce a reasonable person to leave the job and that the employee has attempted to resolve the problem before quitting or can show that further efforts would be unavailing. *Stevenson.*

RULE FOR FIRST SUB–ISSUE

Good cause to voluntarily terminate employment requires grounds so compelling that a reasonably prudent person of normal sensitivities would quit under similar circumstances. *Stevenson.*

FACT SPECIFIC HOLDING FROM RELEVANT CASE ILLUSTRATING RULE

Ms. Stevenson had good cause to leave her employment when her supervisor treated her in an antagonistic and vindictive manner, constantly found fault with her work, and forced her to use nauseating old animal glue, when new, less offensive glue was available. *Stevenson.*

FACT SPECIFIC HOLDING FROM RELEVANT CASE ILLUSTRATING RULE

In the majority opinion the court held Ms. McCain did not have good cause to leave her job based on the offensive character habits of fellow employees. The concurring judge would have ruled that although McCain may have found the sexually explicit cartoons and posters offensive, she could do her job without noticing them. *McCain.*

APPLICATION OF RULE TO FACTS OF YOUR CASE

Susan Saxon has been propositioned for sexual favors by every member of her work crew at least once. The crew members make comments about her body either to her face or in voices loud enough for her to overhear them. Saxon cannot avoid the propositions and comments, because she must work as a part of this crew.

NOTE: In a memo you would compare and contrast Susan Saxon's facts on this issue with the cases.

CONCLUSION OF FIRST SUB–ISSUE

The sexual harassment to which she is subjected by the crew would cause a reasonable person of normal sensitivity to leave the job.

RULE FOR SECOND SUB–ISSUE

Before voluntarily leaving employment the employee must attempt to resolve the grievance or show that further efforts would be useless. *Stevenson.*

FACT SPECIFIC HOLDING FROM RELEVANT CASE ILLUSTRATING RULE

The court held that Ms. Stevenson had made sufficient effort when she had already complained once to management without success and could not complain to the manager without her supervisor being present. *Stevenson.*

FACT SPECIFIC HOLDING FROM RELEVANT CASE ILLUSTRATING RULE

The court held that Mr. Aschenbrenner could have taken the problem to the plant manager, followed the union grievance procedure, or voluntarily stopped working overtime. Because he failed to try any of these alternatives and did not show that these efforts would have been futile, he left his job without good cause. *Aschenbrenner.*

APPLICATION OF RULE TO FACTS OF YOUR CASE

Ms. Saxon complained to her foreman unsuccessfully. His sexist response, and the warning by the personnel manager when she was hired, show that further complaints would be futile.

NOTE: In a memo you would compare and contrast Susan Saxon's facts on this issue with the facts of the cases.

CONCLUSION OF SECOND SUB–ISSUE

Ms. Saxon has sufficiently attempted to resolve her grievance.

OVERALL CONCLUSION OF SECOND ISSUE

Ms. Saxon will be able to collect unemployment benefits if she voluntarily leaves her job, where she can establish both grounds that would compel a reasonable person to quit and that further efforts to resolve the grievance with management would be unsuccessful.

NOTE: The application section of the second issue is composed of the IRACs of the two sub-issues.

Appendix B

BASIC MEMORANDA

TO: Legal Writing Associate
FROM: Law Clerk
RE: Don Gerwin: Cause of action against Albert's Bookstore for
         false imprisonment; Merchant's defense against suspected
         shoplifter requiring probable cause, detention in a reasonable
         manner and for a reasonable time.
DATED: September 16, 1984

QUESTIONS PRESENTED

I. Did Albert's employee falsely imprison Don Gerwin by restraining
his personal liberty, when he grabbed Gerwin by the arm, conducted
him to the back room of the store, and required him to sit there until
the manager arrived?

II. Can Albert's successfully raise the merchant's defense to false
imprisonment, which requires that the merchant's employee have probable cause to suspect a shoplifting, that he detain the suspect in a
reasonable manner and for a reasonable time?

  A. Did Albert's employee have probable cause to suspect Don
Gerwin of shoplifting when the store had been warned of a shoplifter
matching Gerwin's general description and when an employee saw
Gerwin stop and reach into his pocket next to a rack from which
merchandise had disappeared?

  B. Did Albert's employee detain Don Gerwin in a reasonable
manner when, in front of fifteen customers, he grabbed Gerwin's arm,
twisted it behind him, said "please come with me", and escorted Gerwin
to the back room?

  C. Did Albert's employee detain Don Gerwin for a reasonable time
when the detention lasted for approximately fifteen minutes?

STATEMENT OF FACTS

  Don Gerwin would like to sue Albert's, a book and variety store for
false imprisonment. Gerwin is a graduate student in the English

Department of the University. He also teaches a section of freshman English.

On August 30, 1984, Gerwin went into Albert's to purchase a copy of Robert Ludlum's new spy novel. The clerk explained to him that the store was temporarily out of the book. As Gerwin was walking through the store, he had a fit of sneezing and reached into his pocket for his handkerchief.

As he started out the door, a large man, 6'2" and about 250 lbs., grabbed his arm, twisted it behind him, said "please come with me", and propelled him through the store to the back room. All the customers in the store, including a student in Gerwin's section of freshman English, turned and stared. Gerwin was embarrassed and humiliated. He did not protest, but went quietly with the large man.

When they reached the back room, the man gave Gerwin a chair, but he refused to answer any questions until the manager returned. Gerwin estimates that he waited ten minutes. When the manager returned, the large man explained that he had seen Gerwin reach for his pocket suddenly and that he suspected Gerwin of shoplifting a calligraphy pen set valued at $14.95. The manager asked Gerwin to empty his pockets on the table. The contents included the usual items, but no calligraphy pen set. The manager explained to Gerwin that shoplifting was a big problem at Albert's. He thanked Gerwin for his cooperation and explained he was free to go.

The manager, Don Trowder, later explained that Albert's had received a notice from the local police department warning of a shoplifter in the area. The suspect was described as a white male, aged about 20 years, 5'9", 150 lbs. with medium brown hair. Trowder had not been present during the incident, but his assistant manager, Art Jenkins, had been present and had detained Gerwin.

Art Jenkins described the scene from his perspective in the crow's nest, a raised area with a one way mirror, which is used by employees to watch for shoplifters. He observed a white male, about 20 years old, medium height and weight with medium brown hair reach suddenly into his pocket. The man was standing near the pen rack. Jenkins went down, noticed that a pen set was missing and detained the suspect. He later established that the calligraphy pen set had been purchased shortly before the incident.

This memo addresses whether Gerwin has a false imprisonment claim and whether Albert's can defend the claim on the grounds that it can detain suspected shoplifters.

DISCUSSION

Don Gerwin has a cause of action for false imprisonment against Albert's book and variety store. False imprisonment requires that the defendant deprived the plaintiff of his personal liberty. When Albert's employee grabbed Gerwin's arm and led him to the back of the store, he deprived Gerwin of his liberty. There was a false imprisonment.

Albert's cannot successfully raise the merchant's defense to the false imprisonment claim. A merchant can detain a shoplifting suspect if it has probable cause to suspect the person of stealing merchandise and the merchant detains the suspect in a reasonable manner for a reasonable time. Albert's employee had probable cause to believe that Gerwin stole a pen set. Although the fifteen minute detention was probably reasonable, the employee did not detain Gerwin in a reasonable manner. When one of the elements required under the statute is missing, the defense fails. Gerwin has a false imprisonment claim.

I. *Did Albert's employee falsely imprison Don Gerwin by restraining his personal liberty, when he grabbed Gerwin by the arm, conducted him to the back room of the store, and required him to sit there until the manager arrived?*

Albert's employee falsely imprisoned Gerwin. False imprisonment requires either actual physical restraint or "any demonstration of physical power which, to all appearances, can be avoided only by submission". *Jacques v. Childs Dining Hall Co.*, 244 Mass. 438, 438–439 (1923), quoted in *Coblyn v. Kennedy's, Inc.*, 359 Mass. 319, 321, 268 N.E.2d 860, 861 (1971).

The court held there was physical restraint sufficient to make false imprisonment a jury question in *Coblyn*. The defendant's store employee stopped the plaintiff, a seventy year old man in frail health, grasped his arm and said, "[y]ou better go back and see the manager". Another store employee was on the other side of the plaintiff. The court found that two employees physically restraining a frail old man was false imprisonment. The customer had no choice but to go with the employees.

Albert's employee physically restrained Don Gerwin such that he, too, was deprived of his personal liberty. Albert's employee was a head taller than Gerwin and outweighed him by a hundred pounds. The employee grasped Gerwin's arm and twisted it behind him. Like the plaintiff in *Coblyn*, Gerwin had no choice but to comply with the request. The physical restraint coupled with the disparity in size between the employee and Gerwin constitutes false imprisonment.

II. *Can Albert's successfully raise the merchant's defense to false imprisonment, which requires that the merchant's employee have probable cause to suspect a shoplifting, that he detain the suspect in a reasonable manner, and for a reasonable time?*

Albert's will not be able to use the merchant's defense to false imprisonment. The applicable Wayne Statute provides in relevant part:

(2) If a * * * merchant's employee, with probable cause for believing that a person has committed a theft of property of a store, detains and interrogates the person in regard thereto, and the

person thereafter brings against the * * * merchant or merchant's employee any civil * * * action based upon the detention and interrogation, such probable cause shall be a defense to the action, if the detention and interrogation were done in a reasonable manner and for a reasonable time.

Wayne Rev. Stat. sec. 131.655 (1982).

In order for a merchant to successfully defend against a civil suit for false imprisonment, the merchant must establish all three requirements of the statute: 1) that the employee had probable cause to suspect a shoplifting, 2) that the employee detained the suspect in a reasonable manner, and 3) that the employee detained the suspect for a reasonable time.

   A. *Did Albert's employee have probable cause to suspect Don Gerwin of shoplifting when the store had been warned of a shoplifter matching Gerwin's general description and when an employee saw Gerwin stop and reach into his pocket next to a rack from which merchandise had disappeared?*

Albert's employee had probable cause to detain Gerwin. There is probable cause if a reasonably prudent person under similar circumstances would believe that the suspect had attempted to steal store property. *Coblyn,* 359 Mass. at 323, 268 N.E.2d at 864.

The court held that the employee had probable cause to suspect a shoplifting in *Meadows v. Woolworth,* 254 F.Supp. 907 (N.D. Fla. 1966). The Woolworth store had received a notice from the local police several days prior to the incident warning of three teenage girls operating jointly. On the day in question, the employee noticed three teenage girls who had been in the store on two separate occasions. He noticed two missing hairpieces, and another employee reported to him that the girls had been in the area of the hairpieces. This information was sufficient to make a reasonably prudent person believe the girls had taken the merchandise.

In *Coblyn,* on the other hand, the court held that the employee did not have probable cause to suspect the plaintiff. The employee saw the plaintiff stop near the exit to the store, take an ascot out of his pocket, and tie it around his neck. The knot of the ascot was clearly visible above the lapels of the plaintiff's shirt. This fact without any other information was not enough to lead a reasonably prudent person to suspect the plaintiff of stealing the merchandise.

The information available to the employee in Albert's store was probably sufficient to meet the reasonably prudent person standard. As in *Meadows,* the local police had notified the store to be on the lookout for a shoplifter who matched the suspect's description. The police had warned Albert's to be on the lookout for a white male, aged about 20 years, 5'9", 150 lbs. with medium brown hair. Gerwin fits this general description. Also as in *Meadows,* an employee saw the suspect near a rack from which merchandise had disappeared. The assistant manager observed Gerwin stop next to a rack from which a pen set was missing. Albert's employee had the same kinds of information as the employee in *Meadows*.

The police description and the missing merchandise make this case stronger than *Coblyn*. The employees in *Coblyn* observed the plaintiff take an ascot from his pocket and tie it around his neck. The court held this was not enough to lead a reasonable person to suspect a shoplifting. While Gerwin's quick gesture to his pocket would not by itself be enough to give Albert's employee probable cause, this gesture coupled with the police description and the missing merchandise was sufficient. Albert's employee had probable cause to detain Gerwin.

Gerwin can argue that the police description is a very general one; many young men in a university community fit the description. The description in *Meadows* required three teenage girls operating in concert, a much less likely event. While the description is a general one, Gerwin fit the description and this was only one of the factors that led the employee to stop Gerwin.

Albert's employee could have checked with the cashier to see if the calligraphy pen set had been sold before suspecting Gerwin of shoplifting. Because shoplifting was a problem for Albert's and because timing was critical, the employee had to decide to stop the suspect before he left the store. Had Albert's employee taken the time to ask the cashier, Gerwin would have departed. A reasonably prudent person under similar circumstances would have detained the suspect first and then asked about the pen set. Albert's employee had probable cause to detain Gerwin as a shoplifting suspect.

> B. *Did Albert's employee detain Don Gerwin in a reasonable manner when he grabbed Gerwin's arm, twisted it behind him, said "please come with me", escorted Gerwin to the back room and the incident occurred in front of all the other customers?*

Although the employee had probable cause to stop Gerwin, he did not detain him in a reasonable manner. The *Coblyn* court in dictum suggested that Kennedy's employee did not detain Coblyn in a reasonable manner. The employee failed to identify himself or give any explanation for his actions. He physically restrained the plaintiff in a public place. The plaintiff was an elderly man in frail health, who showed no intention of departing. Under these circumstances, the court observed that the employees' manner could be considered unreasonable.

The court in *Meadows*, however, held that the employee detained the three suspects in a reasonable manner. Just after the three girls left the store, the manager went to the door, called to the girls, and asked them to come inside. He spoke to them in a conversational tone and asked if he could look in their purses. The girls consented to the search. After he found nothing in the first two handbags, he discontinued his search and gave them a partial explanation for his request. Because his tone was conversational, he imposed no physical restraint on the girls, and because he gave them a partial explanation for his actions, the court found that his manner was reasonable.

Gerwin's case can be distinguished from *Meadows*, where the employee was polite, explained himself and did not restrain the girls physically. His case is analogous to *Coblyn*, where the employee failed to identify himself, offered no explanation and physically restrained the plaintiff. Albert's employee did not identify himself to Gerwin. He failed to explain his actions, and he physically restrained Gerwin. Albert's employee was a head taller than Gerwin and outweighed him by one hundred pounds. Gerwin had as little opportunity to resist as the elderly plaintiff in *Coblyn*. The physical restraint coupled with the lack of identification or explanation are sufficient to make the manner unreasonable.

C. *Did Albert's employee detain Don Gerwin for a reasonable time when the detention lasted for approximately fifteen minutes?*

Albert's employee detained Gerwin for a reasonable time. The *Meadows* court held that the time of detention was reasonable. Witnesses estimated the time to be at the most ten minutes. While Albert's detained Gerwin for approximately fifteen minutes, the time is close to the ten minutes that had elapsed in *Meadows*. The time Albert's detained Gerwin was, therefore, reasonable.

Albert's employee falsely imprisoned Gerwin by depriving him of his personal liberty. The store will not be able to invoke the merchant's defense to false imprisonment because it does not meet one of the three requirements under the Wayne statute. While the employee may have had probable cause to detain Gerwin and may have detained him for a reasonable time, he did not detain him in a reasonable manner. Gerwin will be able to sue Albert's for false imprisonment.

MEMO TO: Legal Writing Associate

FROM: Law Clerk

RE: Susan Saxon: Sexual harassment in the work place, Or. Rev. Stat. § 659.030(1)(b) (1981); Good cause as a requirement for the collection of unemployment benefits, Or. Rev. Stat. § 657.176(2) (1981).

DATED: August 13, 1987

QUESTIONS PRESENTED

I. Is sexual harassment an unfair labor practice under the Oregon Fair Employment Practices Act, which prohibits an employer from discriminating against an employee on the basis of sex in the conditions of employment, when Susan Saxon must work with her male co-employees, who make sexual propositions and remarks to her, the only female employee?

II. Does Susan Saxon have "good cause" to voluntarily leave her job under Oregon Unemployment Statute, which requires both grounds that would compel a reasonable person to quit and that the employee try to resolve the problem with the employer or show that further efforts would be unavailing?

A. Would a reasonably prudent person of normal sensitivities quit under Saxon's circumstances, when in order to do her job, she must endure sexual propositions and innuendos from her male coworkers?

B. Has Saxon attempted to resolve the problem with her employer and can she show that further efforts would be to no avail, when the personnel manager warned her not to complain about the men and when her foreman responded to her complaint by saying "[w]hat do you expect with a body like that in a place like this"?

STATEMENT OF FACTS

Susan Saxon is being sexually harassed by her co-employees. She is employed as a miner by Umatilla Mining Company. Although the company headquarters and administrative offices are in Pendleton, Oregon, the mining for uranium and other trace metals used in the production of alloys occurs in the hills five miles from Ukiah.

When Umatilla hired Saxon in February 1987, the personnel manager, Harvey Borgren, warned her about the job. "The men are tough" he said, "and they cuss constantly. If you take the job, don't come complaining to me about the way the men treat you."

Saxon took the job. She had not expected the situation to be easy at first, but she anticipated that the men would start treating her like any other miner when they discovered that she could handle the job as well as any of them. She enjoys being a miner. Although she only weighs 135 lbs., she is 5'9" and strong enough to handle the drills and other heavy equipment. On the basis of her job performance, she was promoted to a permanent employee in May, 1987.

Despite her enthusiasm for the job itself, Saxon has had problems with her fellow miners since the beginning. She is the only woman who has ever worked for the company in other than a secretarial capacity. She is part of a 12 person work crew. Each of the men of the crew has propositioned her for sex at least once in the six months of her employment. They make cracks about her body either directly to her face or in loud voices so she can overhear them.

In July she complained to the foreman about the situation. He replied, "[w]hat do you expect with a body like that in a place like this?" He told her the boys would get used to her after a while. The remarks have continued unabated, but not in the presence of the foreman.

Saxon would like to know if she has any recourse against her employer for the sexual harassment. Because the company pays top wages in the industry and has excellent benefits, the employees have never found it necessary to be represented by a union. The company has no formal grievance procedure; all problems are handled informally. She would also like to know if she will be eligible for unemployment benefits if she voluntarily leaves her employment.

DISCUSSION

Susan Saxon is being sexually harassed by her co-employees at Umatilla Mining Company's Ukiah mining operation. This harassment gives her an unfair labor practice claim against her employer. The Oregon Fair Employment Practices Act makes it an unfair labor practice for an employer to discriminate against an employee on the basis of sex in the conditions of employment. An atmosphere of sexual harassment in the work place is a condition of employment. When Saxon is the only female employed as a miner and the only person to suffer sexual harassment, the sexual discrimination is an unfair labor practice.

Should she choose to leave her job to avoid the harassment, she will be able to collect unemployment benefits. To be eligible for benefits an employee must have good cause to quit. Good cause requires two things: (1) grounds that would compel a reasonable person of normal sensitivities to quit under similar circumstances, and (2) that the employee have made some effort to solve the problem with the employer or show that further efforts would be unavailing. A reasonable person would quit his job if subjected to constant harassment. Saxon has tried unsuccessfully to resolve the problem. The personnel manager warned Saxon not to complain about the men. When she did broach the subject with the foreman, he responded with a sexist remark. Under these circumstances, further efforts would not be fruitful. Saxon will be able to collect unemployment benefits.

*I.   Is sexual harassment an unfair labor practice under the Oregon
Fair Employment Practices Act, which prohibits an employer from discriminating against an employee on the basis of
sex in the conditions of employment, when Susan Saxon
must work with her male co-employees, who make sexual
propositions and remarks to her, the only female employee?*

Saxon has an unfair labor practice claim against her employer.
The Oregon Fair Employment Practices Act provides that:

> [I]t is an unlawful employment practice for an employer, because of
> an individual's race, religion, color, sex, * * * to discriminate
> against such individual in compensation or in terms, conditions or
> privileges of employment.

Or. Rev. Stat. sec. 659.030(1)(b) (1981).

Although the Oregon courts have yet to consider a sexual harassment
case under the statute, there is a racial harassment case on point. In
Fred Meyer v. Bureau of Labor, 39 Or. App. 253, 592 P.2d 564 (1979), the
court held that the employer had discriminated against a black employee by subjecting him to racial harassment. The plaintiff, Hayes, was a
16 year old working as a stock boy for the defendant company. Two
employees with some supervisory responsibilities inflicted the racial
harassment. One would talk at length with two white stock boys and
then criticize Hayes because he had not accomplished the job assigned
to all three stock boys. The other employee told racial jokes at Hayes'
expense using a black dialect and called Hayes "Shaft", "Black Sambo"
and "Mohammed". He caricatured a black person's walk and made
comments about the texture of Hayes' hair. Although the assistant
manager explained that the jokes were offensive and improper, he did
not report the harassment to his superiors. When the employee had to
work under conditions of racial harassment and the assistant manager
failed to correct the situation, the court held that it was an unfair labor
practice under Or. Rev. Stat. sec. 659.030(1)(b).

Umatilla Mining Company is likewise in violation of Or. Rev. Stat.
sec. 659.030(1)(b) for not correcting the conditions of sexual harassment
under which Susan Saxon must work. Saxon is a part of a twelve
person work crew at a mine five miles from Ukiah. In order to do her
job, she must cooperate with the other members of her crew. Since she
started the job, each of the male members of the crew has propositioned
her for sex. They continually make sexually explicit remarks about
her body either to her face or in voices loud enough so she can overhear
them. Saxon's situation is both stronger and weaker than that of
Hayes in *Fred Meyer.* Saxon's co-employees have propositioned her for
sexual favors, something that did not happen to Hayes. Hayes' supervisor, however, required him to perform not only his work, but that of
two white stock boys as well. Saxon is only required to do her own job.
As in *Fred Meyer,* the harassment Saxon must endure is pervasive and
a condition of the work place.

A supervisory employee is aware of the problem, but has not corrected it. Her foreman, like the assistant manager in *Fred Meyer,* is aware of the problem; she complained to him in July. The propositions and cracks have persisted, although not in the presence of the foreman. As the racial harassment was directed toward a black employee in *Fred Meyer,* the sexual harassment is directed toward the only female employed as a miner. Discrimination on the basis of sex in the conditions of employment is an unfair employment practice under the terms of the statute. Saxon has recourse under Or. Rev. Stat. sec. 659.030(1)(b) against Umatilla Mining Company.

> *II. Does Susan Saxon have "good cause" to voluntarily leave her job under Oregon Unemployment Statute, which requires both grounds that would compel a reasonable person to quit and that the employee try to resolve the problem with the employer or show that further efforts would be unavailing?*

Saxon will qualify for unemployment benefits if she voluntarily leaves her job with Umatilla Mining Company. The receipt of unemployment benefits is governed by Or. Rev. Stat. sec. 657.176(2) (1981). The applicable statute provides:

> (2) If the authorized representative designated by the assistant director finds that the individual:

* * *

> (c) Voluntarily left work without good cause, the individual shall be disqualified from the receipt of benefits.

The crucial language is "good cause". Although "good cause" is not defined in the statute, it was defined by the court in *Stevenson v. Morgan,* 17 Or. App. 428, 522 P.2d 1204 (1974) and includes two requirements. First, good cause requires grounds that would compel a reasonable person of normal sensitivities to voluntarily leave employment under similar circumstances. Second, an employee must take his grievance up with the employer and try to resolve the problem or show that further efforts would be useless before taking the drastic step of leaving the ranks of the employed. A person claiming unemployment benefits must demonstrate both in order to meet the good cause requirement for unemployment benefits.

> *A. Would a reasonably prudent person of normal sensitivities quit under Saxon's circumstances when she is continually subjected to sexual propositions and innuendos from her male co-workers?*

Susan Saxon has grounds that would compel a reasonable person of normal sensitivities to leave her job. The court in *Stevenson v. Morgan,* 17 Or. App. 428, 522 P.2d 1204 (1974) held that Mrs. Stevenson had good cause to quit her job. Her supervisor continually found fault with the claimant's work and treated her in an antagonistic and vindictive manner. He also made her use smelly old animal glue which made her nauseous when newer less offensive glue was available. The court found that a reasonable person of normal sensitivities would quit under similar circumstances.

The claimant in *McCain v. Employment Division,* 17 Or. App. 442, 522 P.2d 1208 (1974) did not meet the reasonable person standard. She objected to the sexist attitude of her employer. She argued that this attitude was demonstrated by a poster of a woman in a bikini, a postcard of a partially nude woman, and a poster of an ideal woman, which included a naked lower body, but no head, arms or upper torso. The court found that even though the character habits of her employer and fellow employees may have been offensive to her, this was no reason to terminate her employment. In a concurring opinion, one judge explained in dictum that had the "ideal woman" poster been displayed above the claimant's work station, she would have had good cause to quit. Because she could avoid the material she found offensive and still do her job, he agreed with the majority that she had not met the reasonable person standard.

A comparison of the *Stevenson* and *McCain* cases, decided the same day by the same three judge panel of the Oregon Court of Appeals, yields the following rule. In order to meet the reasonable person standard, a claimant must have grounds to leave employment that affect her ability to do her job. *Stevenson.* Offensive character traits of co-employees are insufficient if it does not hamper the claimant's ability to do her job. *McCain.*

Susan Saxon, unlike Ms. McCain, is not able to avoid the sexual harassment of the male members of her work crew and still do her job. As a part of her work, she must work with the other members of the crew. The sexual propositions and cracks about her body directly interfere with this cooperation. Like Ms. Stevenson, who could not do her job without using nauseating animal glue or suffering the continual criticism and antagonism of her supervisor, Saxon cannot avoid continual sexual harassment and do her job. Saxon has grounds that would cause a reasonable person of normal sensitivities to leave her job.

B. *Has Saxon attempted to resolve the problem with her employer and can she show that further efforts would be to no avail, when the personnel manager warned her not to complain about the men and when her foreman answered her complaint with a sexist remark?*

In order to collect unemployment benefits she must also show that she has tried to resolve the problem with her employer and that further efforts would be unavailing. The court in *Stevenson* held that the claimant had tried to resolve the problem with her employer. She had complained to the plant manager once without success. There was additional evidence that every time an employee tried to see the plant manager, the offending supervisor followed the employee into the office and was present during any conversation between the manager and the employee. The court held that Mrs. Stevenson had tried to resolve the problem and that further efforts would not help.

The court in *Aschenbrenner v. Employment Division,* 29 Or. App. 345, 563 P.2d 757 (1977), however, found that the employee had not met this burden. Although the employee may have had grounds sufficient for a reasonable person to quit, he failed to try to resolve the problem with his employer. The court found there were three things Mr. Aschenbrenner could and should have done before taking the drastic step of leaving his job. He could have tried to speak to the plant manager about the extra hours. He could have voluntarily cut his hours back to forty. Finally, he could have taken the matter to the union. Because the claimant failed to do any of these things, the court held he did not meet this prong of the good cause standard.

Saxon has probably complained enough to meet the good cause standard. In *Stevenson* the court held that one complaint was enough if the claimant could show that further efforts would be useless. In July, Saxon complained to the foreman about the sexual harassment by the men on her work crew. He responded, "[w]hat do you expect with a body like that in a place like this." The remarks and propositions have continued. The foreman's sexist remark indicates that it will not do Saxon any good to complain again to him. It will also not help Saxon to complain to the personnel manager. When he hired her he said, "[i]f you take the job, don't come complaining to me about the way the men treat you." Unlike *Aschenbrenner,* where the employee had a union, there is no union at Umatilla or even a formal grievance procedure. The problems are all handled informally. Saxon has complained once and can show that further complaints would be unavailing. She can meet the good cause standard and will be eligible to receive unemployment benefits if she voluntarily leaves her mining job with Umatilla Mining Company.

CONCLUSION

The client, Susan Saxon, has a claim for an unfair labor practice against her employer, Umatilla Mining Company. The Oregon Fair Employment Practices Act provides that it is an unfair labor practice for an employer to discriminate on the basis of sex in the conditions of employment. Saxon is the victim of sexual harassment by the eleven other members of her work crew, all male. Their continual propositions and innuendos about her body and the employer's failure to correct the situation have become a condition of her employment. Where the harassment occurs only to Saxon, the sole female miner, it constitutes an unfair labor practice.

Should Saxon voluntarily choose to leave her job, she will be eligible for unemployment benefits. The statute provides that an employee must have good cause to voluntarily leave employment. Good cause requires both grounds that would compel a reasonable

person of normal sensitivities to quit and that the employee have tried
to resolve the problem with the employer. Saxon cannot do her job,
which requires cooperating with the other members of her work crew,
and avoid the harassment. A reasonable person would quit under
these circumstances. Saxon complained about the harassment to her
foreman. Further complaints to him would be futile as he responded
with a sexist remark. She cannot go to the personnel manager. He
warned her not to complain about the way the men treated her. There
is no union and no formal grievance procedure. Saxon has tried
unsuccessfully to resolve the problem and further efforts would be
unavailing. She will be eligible for unemployment benefits if she
chooses to leave Umatilla.

TO: Legal Writing Associate

FROM: Law Clerk

RE: Marjorie Brill; Defense to Action for rent; Constructive Eviction—noise.[1]

DATED: September 20, 1987

QUESTIONS PRESENTED

I. Was Marjorie Brill constructively evicted when a neighbor's loud rehearsals three-four nights per week from November to January and February to April disturbed her studying and sleeping and when the landlord knew of and had the power to abate the noise?

II. Did Marjorie Brill waive the defense of constructive eviction by remaining in her apartment until June 1, 1986?

STATEMENT OF FACTS

Marjorie Brill, a law student at New York University, rented an apartment in New Jersey from David Lawrence for three years beginning August 1, 1985. She signed a standard lease which included the clause that excessive noise on the part of a tenant would be grounds for termination of that tenant's lease. Mr. Lawrence uses the same lease form for all his tenants.

Ms. Brill's next door neighbor, Victor Rivera, was an actor. On November 5, 1985, he began rehearsing at home for a play. The rehearsals occurred three or four times a week. They involved loud shouting, sometimes of obscenities. They began about 9:00 or 10:00 p.m. and lasted about two hours. The rehearsals ended January 6, 1986. They began again in late February and continued through April 29, 1986.

When Rivera was rehearsing Brill could not study or sleep. She had to sleep in the bathtub because her bathroom was farthest from Rivera's apartment. Brill advised Mr. Lawrence of the problem on two occasions. She first mentioned it to him in early February. She again complained during Rivera's second period of rehearsals. Mr. Lawrence said he would look into the problem.

Marjorie Brill wanted to move, but because of her intense law school schedule she did not have time to look for a new apartment. She went home to Iowa during her Christmas vacation. As soon as she completed her exams at the end of April, 1986, she looked for a new apartment. She moved June 1, 1986. Brill advised Mr. Lawrence that she could not continue to live in her apartment because of Rivera's intolerable noise.

David Lawrence rented the apartment to a new tenant October 1, 1986. Mr. Lawrence is now suing Brill for the rent due under the lease for the months of June through September. Marjorie Brill has asked

---

1. Barbara Blumenfeld, an instructor in the Legal Writing Program at Wayne State University Law School contributed this memorandum.

us whether she can successfully plead Rivera's noisy rehearsals as a defense to Mr. Lawrence's suit.

DISCUSSION

Marjorie Brill cannot successfully raise the noise of Rivera's rehearsals as a defense to David Lawrence's action for rent. Noise from co-tenants may be a constructive eviction and therefore a defense to an action for rent when it substantially interferes with a tenant's use and enjoyment of her premises and when the landlord knows of and has the power to abate the problem. The defense is waived, however, if the tenant fails to vacate the premises in a reasonable time as a result of the noise. The noise of Rivera's rehearsals meets the requirements of the constructive eviction defense. Marjorie Brill moved as a result of the noise. However, she failed to move within a reasonable time. Therefore, Marjorie Brill waived the defense of constructive eviction and cannot successfully plead the noise as a defense.

> *I. Was Marjorie Brill constructively evicted when a neighbor's loud rehearsals three-four nights per week from November to January and February to April disturbed her studying and sleeping and where the landlord knew of and had the power to abate the noise?*

Constructive eviction is a defense to an action for rent. It is based on a landlord's breach of the covenant of habitability implied in every residential lease. A tenant must satisfy three requirements to establish a constructive eviction: 1) there must have been a condition that substantially interfered with the tenant's use and enjoyment of the premises; 2) the landlord must have known of the condition; and 3) the landlord must have had the power to abate the condition. N.J. Stat. Ann. 24:42–11a (1985).

A clause in the standard lease form allowed Mr. Lawrence to evict noisy tenants. The landlord therefore had the power to abate the noise. Additionally, the landlord had notice of the problem: Marjorie Brill mentioned Rivera's rehearsals to Mr. Lawrence on two occasions. Thus the crucial question is whether the noise substantially interfered with Ms. Brill's use and enjoyment of her apartment. While the statute does not define "substantial interference", a review of the case law proves that Brill can also meet this requirement.

The court in *Gottdiener v. Mailhot,* 179 N.J. Super. 286 (1981) held that the noise and conduct of a co-tenant was a substantial interference with the tenants' use and enjoyment of their apartment. There the defendant-tenants had a lease through January 31, 1980. In December, 1978 and January, 1979 the downstairs neighbors subjected the defendants to slamming doors, yelling, and screaming children and excessive noise from the television and radio after 10:00 p.m. The plaintiff-landlord made some unsuccessful attempts to resolve the problem. The co-tenants then began a "campaign of harassment" against the defendants that culminated in damage to the defendants' car in January,

1979. The defendants again complained to the landlord who suggested a meeting between the tenants and co-tenants. The meeting proved fruitless and the co-tenants again threatened the defendants. The defendants vacated in August, 1979. The court stated that the test for substantial interference is objective: the noise must be such as to render the premises truly unfit in the eyes of a reasonable person. *Gottdiener* at 292. Applying this test to the facts, the court found sufficient evidence to support a finding of constructive eviction.

The first case in which a court directly stated that noise which can be corrected by a landlord may be constructive eviction was a dispossess action for non-payment of rent, *Millbridge Apartments v. Linden,* 151 N.J. Super. 168 (1977). On the facts before it, however, *Millbridge* did not find a substantial interference with habitability. In that case the defendant-tenant complained to the landlord that the upstairs neighbors were making extremely loud noises. The landlord unsuccessfully asked the upstairs neighbors to be quiet. On one occasion the defendant was unable to study. The court considered the testimony as to the actual effect of the noise on the tenant's utilization of the premises and found that it was excessive to the point of affecting habitability only once. The court held this was not sufficient. It stated that the loud noise must be repetitious and affect the tenant in a detrimental manner in order to be a valid defense.

In light of the above cases, the frequency of Rivera's rehearsals and their effect on Brill are sufficient to establish constructive eviction. Rivera's conduct, although not as severe as that of the co-tenants in *Gottdiener,* was more extreme than in *Millbridge*. As in *Gottdiener,* Brill was subjected to loud shouting and noise that occurred repeatedly after 10:00 p.m. While Rivera did not subject Brill to harassment as did the tenants in *Gottdiener,* this distinction is not sufficient to change the outcome of the case. During Rivera's rehearsals Brill could not study. She had to sleep in the bathtub. A reasonable person would find this situation substantially unsuitable for residential living. Rivera's repeated disruptions of Brill's study and sleep rendered the premises unfit in the eyes of a reasonable person. Thus this case meets the objective test of *Gottdiener*.

Moreover, the one disruption that *Millbridge* found valid was a disruption of studying. This supports the conclusion that studying is a residential purpose, the continuing interference with which constitutes a constructive eviction. The noise of Rivera's rehearsals affected Brill repeatedly. This is more than the "once" that was not sufficient in *Millbridge*. Because Rivera's noise was repetitious, *Millbridge* supports a finding of constructive eviction in this case.

Mr. Lawrence had notice of the noise problem and the power to correct it. The noise was recurring and had a detrimental effect on Brill. It substantially interfered with Brill's use and enjoyment of her apartment. Thus the noise is sufficient to establish the defense of constructive eviction.

II. Did Marjorie Brill waive the defense of constructive eviction by remaining in her apartment until June 1, 1986?

A tenant waives the defense of constructive eviction by failing to vacate the premises within a reasonable time and as a result of the interference with habitability. N.J. Stat. Ann. 24:42–11b (1985). There is no question that Brill vacated because of Rivera's noisy rehearsals. However, she failed to vacate in a timely fashion.

Gottdiener held that the tenants vacated in a reasonable time where the noise began in December, 1978 and the tenants moved in August, 1979. There the tenants had complained several times to the landlord. The landlord had made some efforts to correct the problem. The tenants were waiting to see if the landlord would take further action. The court held that the tenants waited a reasonable time in order to determine whether the landlord would solve the problem. They left when it was apparent that the landlord would take no further measures. Thus there was no waiver of the constructive eviction defense.

In contrast, *Weiss v. I. Zapinsky, Inc.*, 65 N.J. Super. 351 (1961) held that a tenant waived the constructive eviction defense after the last occurrence of the problem. There water damage occurred for the last time on November 18th. The landlord installed a new roof on November 20th and the problem was apparently corrected. The tenant remained in possession until March 31st of the following year. The tenant stated he was afraid of possible water damage in April. The court stated that mere apprehension of possible future damage was not sufficient to justify abandonment. The court implied that if the tenant had vacated at the time of the water damage the defense would have been successful. The court then held that the tenant continued to occupy the premises for an unreasonable time and thus waived the defense.

The above cases indicate that a tenant must move at the time of the problem giving rise to constructive eviction unless there is some indication that the landlord will correct the problem. In this case, Brill remained in her apartment during the entire time of the disturbance and for one month after the last occurrence. Other than Mr. Lawrence stating that he would look into the problem, there was no indication that the landlord would remedy the situation. Unlike the tenants in *Gottdiener*, Brill's delay in moving was not because she was waiting for the landlord. Rather, she was waiting for a convenient time to move.

The argument that Brill's circumstances did not reasonably allow her to look for a new apartment before she did will fail. The noise first occurred in November. Brill did not move until June of the following year. During that time there was no indication that Mr. Lawrence would take action to correct the problem. Brill did not complain repeatedly as did the tenants in *Gottdiener*. After the first series of rehearsals Brill went home for Christmas vacation rather than search for a new apartment. She endured both periods of rehearsals without moving. She did not move until one month after the second series of rehearsals had ended. Even considering Brill's school and exam schedule, it is unlikely that she could not set aside some time during the school year to hunt for an apartment. Thus Brill, like the tenants in *Weiss*, continued to occupy her apartment for an unreasonable length of time.

Unlike *Weiss*, however, the problem with Rivera had not been corrected. While it had stopped temporarily, the noise was likely to begin as soon as Rivera was cast in a new play. This is distinguishable from the roof in *Weiss* that had been repaired and had not leaked for five months. Because Rivera is an actor, there was a strong likelihood that his rehearsals would soon resume. Brill moved because of a probability that was more certain than the "mere apprehension" of the *Weiss* tenant. Nevertheless, her failure to move at the time of the problem, when there was no indication that the landlord would correct it, results in a waiver of the defense.

Although Marjorie Brill vacated her apartment because of Rivera's noisy rehearsals, she failed to do so within a reasonable time. Therefore she has waived her right to plead constructive eviction as a defense to Mr. Lawrence's action for rent.

CONCLUSION

Marjorie Brill cannot successfully raise the noise to which she was subjected as a defense to David Lawrence's action for rent. The noise does meet the requirements of constructive eviction. However, by failing to move in a reasonable time Marjorie Brill waived the constructive eviction defense. Thus, while Brill can raise the noise as a defense, she cannot do so successfully.

TO: Legal Writing Associate

FROM: Law Clerk

RE: Marvin Mantle: charge of arson; non-accidental fire, opportunity, and motive; dwelling house; Mich. Comp. Laws Ann. §§ 750.72, 750.73 (West 1968).[2]

DATED: October 5, 1987

QUESTIONS PRESENTED

I. Was there sufficient evidence to charge Marvin Mantle with arson, when the elements of arson are a non-accidental fire, motive, and opportunity?

A. Can non-accidental causes be ruled out, or can expert testimony show that the fire was deliberately set, when the weather was cool and clear, all utilities were turned off, the house was vacant with no sign of a break-in, and the fire started at two points simultaneously?

B. Was there sufficient evidence of opportunity when Mantle worked near the house in question, arrived home late on the night of the fire, and was one of the only two people with a key to the house?

C. Was there sufficient evidence of motive when Mantle would stand to recover $10,000.00 more from his insurance than if the house was sold at its listing price?

II. Was Mantle's house, though vacant, considered a dwelling house under the statute, which is defined as being reasonably fit for human habitation, when it only needed furniture and a restoration of utility service to render it ready for use?

STATEMENT OF FACTS

Marvin Mantle, who is a prime suspect in an arson case, inherited a home at the intersection of West Warren Avenue and I–96 when his father died in November of 1985. He and his wife cleared out the house that winter and drained the pipes so that the furnace and other utilities could be turned off. The house was listed for sale or lease with Urban Realty on March 24, 1986. The listing price was $45,000.00 and Mantle continued the insurance coverage for that amount. When there had been no offers to buy or lease the home within six months, the real estate agent suggested that he reduce the asking price. Mantle reluctantly agreed to relist the house for $35,000.00. Only Mantle and the real estate agent have keys to the house.

Mantle lives in Bloomfield Hills and works in downtown Detroit. He normally leaves his office at 5:00 p.m. and arrives home well before 6:00 p.m.

On the night of October 30, 1986, also known as "Devil's Night", Marvin Mantle arrived home just in time to see a telecast on the

---

2. Sandra Gross, an instructor in the Legal Writing Program at Wayne State University Law School, contributed this memorandum.

Channel 2 at 6:22 which showed his house burning. He called the television station and then the fire and police departments.

The fire department had arrived at the house earlier, at 5:41 p.m., and found that the front and back doors were locked. The fire fighters had to break them down to enter. As the firemen each wore a self contained breathing apparatus, they were unable to smell any accelerant. The weather at this time was cool and clear.

A subsequent investigation by a member of the Detroit Arson Squad revealed that the fire had started in the basement. There were two points of origin at two wooden support beams, each of which was located 15 to 20 feet away from the circuit box and at least 12 feet away from the furnace. Because the depth of char was nearly identical, the expert concluded that the fire started at or near the same time at each beam. However, he did not find any evidence or trace of accelerant, gasoline, or kerosene. He also concluded that the heat from the fire caused the first floor windows to break from the inside.

The Wayne County Prosecutor's Office is currently deciding whether there is sufficient evidence to charge Marvin Mantle with arson.

DISCUSSION

The purpose of this memo is to discuss whether the prosecutor has sufficient evidence to charge Marvin Mantle with arson, and if so, whether he can be charged with burning a dwelling house. The corpus delicti of arson has three elements: a showing that the fire was not accidental, together with evidence of motive and opportunity. In this case, the fire was not accidental, since the house was vacant and the furnace and utilities had been disconnected, the weather was cool and clear, and the fire started in two places simultaneously. Marvin Mantle also had sufficient opportunity to set the fire, since he had keys to the house, it was close to his work, and he arrived home 20 minutes late that evening. Mantle had a financial motive for setting the fire; he would receive $10,000.00 more from insurance proceeds than he could if he sold the house. There is a sufficient case to charge Mantle with arson.

The next step is to decide whether he should be charged under the dwelling house statute, Mich. Comp. Laws Ann. sec. 750.72 (West 1968), which carries a maximum 20 year sentence, or with burning other real property under Mich. Comp. Laws Ann. sec. 750.73 (West 1968), which carries a 10–year sentence. Since a dwelling house is defined as one which may be vacant but is suitable for habitation without extensive repair, and since Mantle's house only needed to have its utility service restored to be habitable, Mantle should be charged under the arson of a dwelling house statute.

I. Was there sufficient evidence to charge Marvin Mantle with arson, when the elements of arson are a non-accidental fire, motive, and opportunity?

The first issue is whether Marvin Mantle should be charged with the crime of arson. In *People v. Bailey,* 42 Mich. App. 359, 363, 202

N.W.2d 557 (1972), the court stated that the corpus delicti of arson can be established by evidence negating accidental cause of the fire, together with evidence showing motive and opportunity. Additionally, the court stated that in view of the secrecy inherent to the act of arson, circumstantial evidence is generally sufficient. *People v. Horowitz,* 37 Mich. App. 151, 154, 194 N.W.2d 375 (1971).

> A. *Can non-accidental causes be ruled out, or can expert testimony show that the fire was deliberately set, when the weather was cool and clear, all utilities were turned off, the house was vacant with no sign of a break-in, and the fire started at two points simultaneously?*

To satisfy the first element of arson requires establishing that the fire was not accidental. In both *Bailey* and *Horowitz,* the court relied on expert testimony which either ruled out accidental or natural causes, or else gave direct proof that the fire was of an incendiary nature.

In *Bailey,* there was expert testimony ruling out weather conditions, appliances, electrical equipment, the furnace, and carelessness as the source of the fire. In *Horowitz,* an expert witness testified that there were traces of flammable liquid in plastic containers which were found in the ruins of the building, together with a rope which could have held a triggering device. The expert concluded that the fire was purposely set.

In the Mantle case, there are no likely accidental causes for the fire. As in *Bailey,* the day of the fire was cool and clear, so weather conditions can be ruled out. Similarly, since the furnace and other utilities were turned off and the house was vacant, neither electrical appliances nor carelessness caused the fire. While there was no trace of accelerant found in the Mantle house, there is a similarity to *Horowitz.* The arson investigator will testify that the fire began simultaneously at the base of two beams in the basement. The two points of origin indicated to him that the fire probably was set. There is sufficient evidence to satisfy the first element of arson.

> B. *Was there sufficient evidence of opportunity when Mantle worked near the house in question, arrived home late on the night of the fire, and was one of the only two people with a key to the house?*

The next element of arson is evidence showing opportunity. In *Bailey,* the court concluded that the defendant had an opportunity to start the fire. The defendant was in the house alone 10–20 minutes before the fire started. Likewise in *Horowitz,* the court held that the defendants had an opportunity to set the fire. Each of the two defendants testified that they secured the building at 2:20 a.m. and left separately. The fire was not discovered until 3:40 a.m. There was no evidence of a break-in. The lag in time, however, could be explained by the fact that the defendants may have used a timing device to trigger the fire. On this basis, the court found that defendants had sufficient opportunity to set the fire.

In Mantle's case, there is no evidence directly placing him at the house on the day of the fire. There is, however, circumstantial evidence suggesting that he had the opportunity. Mantle routinely drove by the house on his way home from work. On the evening of the fire, he arrived home at least 20 minutes later than his usual time. The house was locked when the firemen arrived and Mantle had one of the only two sets of keys to the house. As in *Horowitz*, there is sufficient circumstantial evidence to satisfy the second element of arson.

C. Was there sufficient evidence of motive when Mantle would stand to recover $10,000.00 more from his insurance than if the house was sold at its listing price?

The final element of arson is motive. In both *Bailey* and *Horowitz*, the court found financial gain to be a satisfactory motive. In *Bailey*, the defendant had doubled the insurance coverage on the house not long before the fire. In *Horowitz*, the court noted that the defendants owed three months rent, were indebted to the Michigan Department of Revenue for sales tax, and owed $650.00 to the gas company. They had $40,000.00 in fire insurance on the property, which would alleviate their financial problems.

In Mantle's case, unlike *Horowitz*, there was no indication that Mantle was in debt. Neither was there a blatant increase in insurance coverage just prior to the fire, as in *Bailey*. However, Mantle would stand to realize $10,000.00 more if the house burned than if it were sold at his listing price of $35,000.00. Therefore, the financial gain would be sufficient to satisfy the motive element.

When the fire was of suspicious origin and Mantle had both the opportunity to start the fire and a financial motive, there is sufficient evidence for the prosecutor to charge Marvin Mantle with arson.

II. Was Mantle's house, though vacant, considered a dwelling house under the statute, which is defined as being reasonably fit for human habitation, when it only needed furniture and a restoration of utility service to render it ready for use?

The next issue is whether Mantle should be charged under the dwelling house or other real property arson statute. Anyone who burns a dwelling house is guilty of a felony punishable by a maximum of 20 years in prison. Mich. Comp. Laws Ann. sec. 750.72. Anyone who burns any other real property is guilty of a felony punishable by a maximum of only 10 years in prison. Mich. Comp. Laws Ann. sec. 750.73. In *People v. Reed*, 13 Mich. App. 75, 78, 163 N.W.2d 704 (1968), the court explained this disparity in the sentence from a historical perspective. The court held that a greater penalty is reasonable when burning a dwelling house was more likely to result in the destruction of human life than burning other property.

While the statute does not define a dwelling house, the case law is helpful in setting the guidelines. In *People v. Reed,* 13 Mich. App. at 79, the court stated that even if a house is not actually occupied, a structure which is habitable without major renovation qualifies as a dwelling house under the statute. The court used a similar definition in *People v. Losinger,* 331 Mich. at 502.

The court found that a one-room hunting cabin was a dwelling house in *People v. Losinger.* In that case, the property had an assessed value of only $100. The owner used the cabin only intermittently for hunting. He explained that he intended to live there full-time once he retired. Because he had fully furnished the cabin and stocked it with food, clothing, and other possessions, the court found that the building was immediately habitable.

In contrast, the court held that the structure in *Reed* was not a dwelling house. In that case, the house had been unoccupied for 1½ years before the fire, and it had no bathroom or other washing facilities. Although the property had not been formally condemned, the fire department had boarded up the house to prevent further vandalism. The court decided that the building was not a dwelling house since extensive renovation was necessary to make it habitable.

The Mantle house has characteristics which are analogous to both *Reed* and *Losinger.* On the one hand, the building had been vacant for over six months, there were no furnishings, and Mantle had disconnected the utilities. Unlike the house in *Losinger,* it was not ready for immediate occupation. However, unlike the structure in *Reed,* the house was not boarded up or in such a state of disrepair as to be uninhabitable without renovation. Once the building was leased or sold, a new tenant could have moved in his furniture and appliances, called the utility companies, and restored the structure to a dwelling without any extensive renovation. Since the house was intended for habitation at any moment, and was reasonably capable of being inhabited, it qualifies as a dwelling house.

CONCLUSION

Marvin Mantle should be charged with the crime of arson. The fire that occurred at the house he owned was not started by accidental causes such as weather, appliances, the furnace, or carelessness. The arson investigator will testify that the fire started at the same time in two support beams located at either end of the basement. Additionally, Mantle had the opportunity to set the fire, since he arrived home late that evening and had one of only two sets of keys. Finally, Mantle had a motive to set the fire, because he would net $10,000.00 more from the insurance proceeds than he could hope to gain from selling the home at the listing price. The prosecutor should charge Mantle with arson of a dwelling house under Mich. Comp. Laws Ann. sec. 750.72. Mantle's house fits the definition of a dwelling house, because although it was vacant, it was habitable without major repair.

Appendix C

A COMPLEX MEMORANDUM

MEMO TO: Diana Pratt

FROM: James Jordan

RE: Alan Paine: paternity case; putative father must overcome the presumption of legitimacy and establish paternity; putative father's right to pay maternal medical and hospital expenses, and child support; putative father's right to visit child; and putative father's right to have child's name changed on its birth certificate to that of the putative father.

DATED: 6–16–88

QUESTIONS PRESENTED

I. Does a putative father have a right to bring a paternity action under the Family Court Act when the child's mother was married at the time of probable conception and she is not seeking child support?

II. Can the putative father overcome by clear and convincing evidence the presumption of legitimacy that arises when a child is born to a married woman, by showing that the mother's husband was impotent, by showing that the husband lacked access to the wife during the period of probable conception, or by excluding the husband as the father by competent blood and tissue testing?

A. Can the putative father show non-access by the husband when the husband and wife were living together during part of the fertile period, but were separated during the time of most likely conception?

B. Can the putative father obtain a court order for blood and tissue tests on the mother's husband for purposes of excluding him as the child's father?

C. Can the putative father overcome the presumption of legitimacy by showing with an HLA (Human Leucocyte Antigen) test a sufficiently high probability that he is the father of the child?

II. If the putative father can overcome the presumption of legitimacy, can he establish paternity if he had a sexual relationship with the

358

mother during the period of probable conception and if the results of the HLA test on himself, the mother, and the child indicate a high probability that he is the biological father?

III. If the putative father can establish paternity, can he obtain an order that he pay the mother's hospital and medical expenses, that he pay support for the child, that he visit with the child, and that the child's surname be changed to his own?

IV. Should the putative father be estopped from contesting the paternity of the child when he waited four months after the birth of the child before filing his paternity petition?

STATEMENT OF FACTS

Alan Paine would like to bring a paternity action to establish that he is the biological father of Cynthia Murphy. The child's mother, Marcia Murphy, was married at the time of conception and still is married to George Murphy.

Alan Paine works as a buyer for Mercantile Imports of New York City. He travels around the far east looking for interesting merchandise to sell in the company's twenty-five retail stores. He met Marcia Murphy, who works in the travel department of the company, in the spring of 1986 and they had an affair during August. Just before Labor Day, George Murphy, her husband, found out about the affair. The couple had an argument and decided to separate. Marcia Murphy moved in with Paine at the beginning of September.

On September 21, 1986, Paine left on one of his buying trips. When he returned in the middle of October, he found a note from Murphy explaining that she had reconciled with her husband and that she did not wish to see Paine again.

He did not see her until Friday, October 2, 1987 when he went to the travel department of Mercantile Imports. When he asked Mrs. Murphy how things were going, she explained that she had just returned from maternity leave. She and her husband were the proud parents of seven pound, three ounce Cynthia Murphy, born June 4, 1987.

Paine explained that it did not strike him until later that the child must be his. As he travels approximately half of the year for his job, he is not able to have a wife and family of his own. He would like to pay Marcia Murphy's hospital and medical expenses and take responsibility for Cynthia by paying child support. He would also like to visit with her when he is in the country, so the child will grow up knowing her real father. Finally, he would like her name changed to Paine to reflect her true paternity.

DISCUSSION

Alan Paine, as the putative father, has a right to try to establish his paternity of Cynthia Murphy. To do this, he must first overcome the presumption of legitimacy that a child born to a married woman is the child of her husband. He can overcome the presumption of legitimacy by showing that the husband is impotent, that the husband did not have access to the wife during the period of probable conception, or that the husband cannot be the father of the child, because he is excluded by blood and tissue typing tests. The putative father can also use blood or tissue typing test results to show that the probability that he is the father is so high that it overcomes the presumption of legitimacy. Paine will not be able to show either that George Murphy is impotent or that he had no access to his wife during the fertile period. Although the court can order the mother, child, and putative father to take blood and tissue typing tests, it is unlikely that it will order George Murphy to submit to the testing. Paine will only be able to overcome the presumption of legitimacy if the test results practically prove his paternity.

Once he has overcome the presumption of legitimacy, Paine must also establish that he is the biological father. To prove paternity, he must show both that he had a sexual relationship with the mother during the period of probable conception and that the medical evidence indicates a high probability that he is the father. Since he had a sexual relationship with the child's mother, his ultimate success depends on his HLA (Human Leucocyte Antigen) test result.

Finally, if the court issues an order of filiation, it will require Paine to pay some portion of the maternal medical expenses and support for the child. The court will determine whether Paine can visit with the child according to the best interests of the child. The court is unlikely to order that the child's surname be changed from Murphy to Paine as the common practice is to keep the child's name the same as the custodial parent.

I.   *Does a putative father have a right to bring a paternity action under the Family Court Act when the child's mother was married at the time of probable conception and she is not seeking support?*

Alan Paine can bring a paternity action against George and Marcia Murphy. The Family Court Act provides: [p]roceeding to establish the paternity of a child and to compel support under this article may be commenced by the mother, whether a minor or not, *by a person alleging to be the father,* * * *. N.Y. Fam. Ct. Act sec. 522 (Consol. 1987). Alan Paine alleges that he is Cynthia Murphy's father. The statute, therefore, permits him to bring the action even though the mother is married, *Ettore I v. Angela D,* 129 Misc. 2d 301, 492 N.Y.S.2d 1013 (Fam. Ct. 1985), reversed on other grounds 127 A.D.2d 6, 513 N.Y.S.2d 733 (1987), is not seeking child support, and is unlikely to become a public charge, *Joye v. Schechter,* 112 Misc. 2d 172, 446 N.Y.S.2d 884 (Fam. Ct. 1982).

While Paine certainly can bring his action against the child's mother, Marcia Murphy, he can probably also join George Murphy as a defendant. The Family Court Act does not identify the parties against whom a paternity action may be brought. The appropriate rule governing joinder of parties, however, provides:

> (b) Persons against whom there is asserted any right to relief jointly, severally, or in the alternative, arising out of the same transaction, occurrence, or series of transactions or occurrences, may be joined in one action as defendants if any common questions of law or fact would arise.

N.Y. Civ. Prac. L. & R. sec. 1002(b) (Consol. 1987).

Under this rule, the court in *Gorton v. Gorton*, 123 Misc. 2d 1034, 475 N.Y.S.2d 767 (Fam. Ct. 1984), held that the husband could be joined. It reasoned that paternity cases involve common questions of law and fact; namely, the lack of access and the blood and tissues types of all parties.

The present case involves the same questions: George Murphy's access or lack of access to his wife, Paine's access to Marcia Murphy, and the blood and tissue types of Paine and the three Murphys. For this reason, the court will probably permit the joinder of George Murphy under N.Y. Civ. Prac. L. & R. sec. 1002(b).

> II. *Can the putative father overcome by clear and convincing evidence the presumption of legitimacy that arises when a child is born to a married woman, by showing that the mother's husband was impotent, by showing that the husband lacked access to the wife during the period of probable conception, or by excluding the husband by competent blood and tissue testing?*

In order ultimately to establish his paternity, Paine must overcome the presumption of legitimacy that attaches to every child born to a married woman. The presumption of legitimacy is one of the strongest presumptions in the law, *Matter of Findlay*, 253 N.Y. 1, 170 N.E. 471 (1930), but it is rebuttable. There are three ways to rebut the presumption: 1) to show that the husband is impotent, 2) to show that the husband did not have access to his wife during the period of probable conception, and 3) to show with blood or tissue typing tests that the husband is not the father or with a very high probability that the putative father is the biological father. *Gorton v. Gorton; Ettore I v. Angela D.* Paine will not be able to overcome the presumption of legitimacy by showing impotency of the husband as there is no evidence that George Murphy is impotent or in any way incapable of fathering a child.

Paine will also be unable to overcome the presumption by showing non-access by the husband. In order to prove non-access, the petitioner must establish both the period of probable conception and show that the husband and wife did not have sexual relations during that interval.

The period of probable conception can be calculated by subtracting the gestation period from the child's date of birth. Although the average gestation period is 266 days, the range of gestation periods yielding normal birth weight children is considerably broader. The range is 265 to 299 days from the onset of the mother's last menstrual period or 251 to 285 days from conception. *Morris v. Terry K.*, 70 A.D.2d 1031, 418 N.Y.S.2d 174 (1979).

George Murphy may be the father of Cynthia Murphy. The child weighed seven pounds, three ounces at birth. This is within the normal weight range for a full term baby. The child was conceived, therefore, 285 to 251 days before her birth on June 4, 1987, or between August 23 and September 26, 1986. Marcia Murphy lived with her husband, George Murphy, up until September 1, 1986 and she reconciled with her husband on September 21, 1986. The Murphys lived together during at least part of the period of probable conception.

Because of their proximity during this period, Paine will not be able to show by clear and convincing evidence that George Murphy did not have access to his wife. Even if the couple are not living together, but "there is a fair basis for the belief that at times they may have come together", there is access. *Matter of Findlay*, 253 N.Y. at 8, 170 N.E. at 473. One contact during the period of probable conception is enough to negate non-access. *Matter of Erskine Edward Rudolph F.*, 100 A.D.2d 878, 474 N.Y.S.2d 137 (1984).

The court in *Constance G. v. Herbert Lewis L.*, 119 A.D.2d 209, 506 N.Y.S.2d 111 (1986) *appeal dismissed* 70 N.Y.2d 667, 518 N.Y.S.2d 960, 512 N.E.2d 543 (1987), on the other hand, held there was non-access even though the husband and wife lived together. Both the mother and her husband testified that they had separate bedrooms and had not had sexual relations for four years before the child was conceived or since that time. Under these circumstances, the court held that the petitioner had successfully rebutted the presumption of legitimacy.

Paine will not be able to overcome the presumption of legitimacy by showing non-access by the husband to the wife during the period of probable conception. The Murphys lived together for nine days in August and five days in September 1986 during the period of probable conception. Even if they did not "come together" during the twenty-one day separation, George Murphy had access to his wife during nearly half of the fertile period. Paine will not be able to overcome the presumption of legitimacy this way.

The third way to overcome the presumption of legitimacy is to exclude the mother's husband as the child's father with blood or tissue typing tests. Unless George Murphy will voluntarily submit to testing, Paine will not be able to rebut the presumption of legitimacy using this method. The statute provides:

(a) the court shall advise the parties of their right to one or more blood genetic marker tests and, on the court's own motion or on motion of any party, *shall order the mother, her child and the alleged father to submit to one or more blood genetic marker tests* by a duly qualified physician or by a laboratory duly approved for this purpose by the commissioner of health to determine whether or not the alleged father can be excluded as being father of the child. The results of any such blood genetic marker test may be received in evidence where definite exclusion is established by such test. Except in cases where exclusion has been established by another blood genetic marker test, the laboratory and statistical results of the human leucocyte antigen blood tissue test (either separately or in combination with the laboratory and statistical results of any other blood genetic marker test or tests, including, without limitation, red blood cell antigens, red blood cell serum protein, and red blood cell enzyme tests) may be received in evidence to aid in the determination of whether the alleged father is or is not the father of the child.

N.Y. Fam. Ct. Act sec. 532(a) (Consol. Supp. 1987) (emphasis added).

The statute contemplates using the blood genetic marker and other tests for purposes of excluding the putative father as the biological father and not for purposes of excluding the mother's husband as the biological father. Three courts have considered the question tangentially, but there is as yet no definitive answer.

In *Gorton v. Gorton,* the court permitted the mother's husband to be joined in the case. It implied in dictum that blood type testing of all concerned might be necessary to resolve the question of paternity. The mother was married to both men at different times and neither had an extensive relationship with the child. The question of paternity was important primarily for deciding which of the two potential fathers should be paying support for the child. The court did not have to decide whether to require a reluctant husband to submit to blood and tissue typing tests.

The court in *Ettore I v. Angela D,* 129 Misc. 2d 301, 492 N.Y.S.2d 1013, did not reach this question either. There the husband refused to submit to the testing and the court did not require him to do so. The court did, however, draw a negative inference against him because of this refusal. Based on this negative inference and the HLA tests on the other parties that "practically proved" that the putative father was the biological father, the court found that the putative father had overcome the presumption of legitimacy. The court did not, however, take the next step and order the husband to take the tests.

In the third case, *Edward K. v. Marcy R.,* 89 A.D.2d 556, 452 N.Y.S.2d 119 (1982), the Appellate Division reinstated an order for testing the mother, the child, and the putative father. It did not order testing of the husband at that time, as the test results might exclude the putative father. In dictum, however, the court left open the possibility it might order testing of the husband if the first series of tests did not rule out the putative father.

The statute does not anticipate testing the husband and the courts have been reluctant in the absence of legislative guidance to order testing. It is unlikely that the court in this case will order tests on George Murphy. It may, however, draw a negative inference, if he does not voluntarily submit to blood and tissue typing testing. The statute does provide for testing the mother, the child, and the putative father. As a result, the court will order the tests on Paine, Marcia Murphy, and her daughter.

C. Can the putative father overcome the presumption of legitimacy by showing with an HLA (Human Leucocyte Antigen) test a high enough probability that he is the father of the child?

The results of these tests, if sufficiently high give Paine his only successful method of overcoming the presumption of legitimacy. The court in *Ettore I v. Angela D*, held that the putative father had overcome the presumption of legitimacy when the HLA tests on him and the mother and child showed a 99.82% probability that he was the biological father. When there was evidence of a sexual relationship between the mother and the putative father during the period of probable conception, the HLA score practically proved paternity and a negative inference was drawn against the husband because of his refusal to take the tests, the court held that the putative father had overcome the presumption of legitimacy.

Similarly, Paine can show a sexual relationship with the mother at the time of probable conception. If George Murphy refuses to submit to HLA testing, the court will draw a negative inference against him. Finally, if Paine's HLA score is very high, he, too, may be able to overcome the presumption of legitimacy without affirmatively demonstrating that George Murphy cannot be the father of Cynthia Murphy.

II. If Paine can overcome the presumption of legitimacy, can he establish paternity if he had a sexual relationship with the mother during the period of probable conception and if the results of an HLA test on himself, the mother, and the child indicate a high probability that he is the biological father?

Once Paine has overcome the presumption of legitimacy, he must also establish his own paternity of Cynthia Murphy. This requires that he show a sexual relationship with the child's mother during the fertile period, and that the HLA probability be high enough to indicate that he is the child's biological father.

Paine will be able to demonstrate a sexual relationship with Marcia Murphy at the appropriate time. On the average, conception occurs 266 days prior to birth, but the range is 256 to 285 days. *Reidy v. Jeffrey K.* Cynthia Murphy was born on June 4, 1987. September 12, 1986 is 266 days before June 4, 1987. Marcia Murphy had separated from her husband and was living with Alan Paine on September 12,

1986. Using the 256–285 day range, Cynthia Murphy was conceived between August 23, 1986 and September 26, 1986. Marcia Murphy had an affair with Alan Paine throughout the month of August 1986 and lived with him from September 1–21, 1986. Alan Paine had the necessary sexual relationship with the child's mother to make him a prime candidate for the child's father.

Paine must also achieve a high enough HLA score to establish paternity based on tissue typing tests conducted on the mother, the child, and himself. The court in *Ettore I v. Angela D,* 129 Misc. 2d 301, 492 N.Y.S.2d 1013 (1985) held that an HLA score of 99.82% was sufficient to establish paternity. In that case both the putative father and the mother's husband had a sexual relationship with the mother during the period of probable conception.

In a situation like the present one, where both the putative father and the mother's husband had sexual relations with the mother during the period of probable conception, Paine will have to score very high on the HLA test in order to prove his paternity by clear and convincing evidence.

III. If the putative father can establish paternity, can he obtain an order that he pay the mother's hospital and medical expenses, that he pay support for the child, that he visit with the child, and that the child's surname be changed to his own?

If Paine succeeds in establishing that he is the father of Cynthia Murphy, he will not only be permitted to pay some of Marcia Murphy's maternity expenses and support for the child, he will probably be required to do so. While he may be permitted to visit with the child, the court is unlikely to change the child's name on her birth certificate to Cynthia Paine.

The payment of pregnancy related expenses is governed by statute:

The father is liable to pay the reasonable expenses of the mother's confinement and recovery and such expenses in connection with her pregnancy as the court in its discretion may deem proper.

N.Y. Fam. Ct. Act sec. 514 (Consol. 1987).

Under this provision, the court will require Paine to pay reasonable hospital and medical expenses associated with the pregnancy.

Child support is also governed by statute.

Subject to the provisions of paragraph f of subdivision six of section three hundred ninety-eight of the social services law, each parent of a child born out of wedlock is chargeable with the support of such child including the child's funeral expenses and, if possessed of sufficient means or able to earn such means, may be required to pay for the child's care, maintenance and education. *A court shall [make] an award for child support pursuant to section five hundred forty-five of this act* after consideration of all relevant factors, including

    (i) the financial resources of the parents and those of the child;
* * *.

N.Y. Fam. Ct. Act sec. 513 (Consol. 1987) (emphasis added).

Since Alan Paine is employed and financially able to contribute to the support of the child, the court is required to order payment of some child support.

Unlike payment of maternal expenses and child support, the court has discretion to order visitation between a putative father and his child. The statute provides:

    (a) If an order of filiation is made * * * the family court may make an order * * * of visitation requiring one parent to permit the other to visit the child or children at stated periods.

N.Y. Fam. Ct. Act sec. 549 (Consol. 1987).

In making a determination about visitation, the court uses the standard of "the best interests of the child". *Pierce v. Yerkovich,* 80 Misc. 2d 613, 363 N.Y.S.2d 403 (Fam. Ct. 1974). The court in that case ordered visitation between the child and the natural father despite the fact that the mother was then married to someone else. The child, however, did have an established relationship with the natural father.

The court also ordered visitation between a child and his natural father in *Cheryl A.D. v. Jeffrey G.O.,* 133 Misc. 2d 663, 507 N.Y.S.2d 593 (Fam. Ct. 1986). In this case, the father had been married throughout the six year liaison with the mother, and the mother had subsequently married. The court held that it was in the best interests of the child to visit with his natural father.

Alan Paine may be able to visit with Cynthia Murphy. The court has the discretion to allow visitation and in the two cases cited above, the courts did order visitation despite the fact that the mother, and in *Cheryl A.D.,* the father were married to others. In both cases, however, the child had an established relationship with its natural father. Alan Paine has never seen Cynthia Murphy. He did not know she existed until some months after her birth. The court will have to determine if it is in her best interests to begin a relationship with a stranger.

Paine will not be able to have the child's surname changed from Murphy to Paine on her birth certificate. Even to have Alan Paine's name on the birth certificate as the child's father requires the consent of the mother, the putative father and an order from a court of competent jurisdiction. The applicable statute provides:

    1. (a) There shall be no specific statement on the birth certificate as to whether the child is born in wedlock or out of wedlock or as to the marital name or status of the mother.

    (b) The phrase "child born out of wedlock" when used in this article, refers to a child whose father is not its mother's husband.

2. The name of the putative father of a child born out of wedlock shall not be entered on the certificate of birth prior to filing without the consent in writing of both the mother and putative father, duly verified, and filed with the record of birth, except that with respect to a child born out of wedlock to a married woman, a determination of parentage made by a court of competent jurisdiction shall be required before the putative father's name may be entered on the birth certificate.

N.Y. Pub. Health Law sec. 4135 (Consol. 1987).

If the father is not listed on Cynthia Murphy's birth certificate, both Alan Paine and Marcia Murphy must consent in writing that Paine be listed as the father. In addition, as Marcia Murphy is married, a court of competent jurisdiction must also determine the child's parentage.

As Cynthia Murphy was born in June and Alan Paine did not discover that she existed until October, her birth certificate has probably already been issued. A new birth certificate may be issued under N.Y. Public Health Law sec. 4138 (Consol. 1987). This would also require consent by Marcia Murphy and Alan Paine and a court determination of paternity. When the certificate has been filed without entry of the father's name, a new certificate may be issued with his name and a conforming surname change for the child.

In this case it is likely that George Murphy is listed on the birth certificate as Cynthia's father. He and Marcia Murphy reconciled many months before the child's birth. Under these circumstances, Alan Paine could file a petition for change of name under N.Y. Civil Rights Law sec. 60–63 (Consol. 1982). To do so he must establish that the name change is in the child's interest. There are two cases that have considered the question and reached divergent results.

The court in *State ex rel. Spence–Chapin Services v. Tedeno,* 101 Misc. 2d 485, 421 N.Y.S.2d 297 (Sup. Ct. 1979), held that it was in the child's interest to have the same name as the custodial parent. As the child in this case lived with her mother, the court found no reason to change her name from her mother's surname.

The court in *Brooks v. Willie,* 117 Misc. 2d 640, 458 N.Y.S.2d 860 (Fam. Ct. 1983), on the other hand, changed the child's name to that of the natural father. The court reasoned that the child would be spared the stigma of illegitimacy if he bore his father's name.

The reasoning from both cases indicates that the court is likely to decide it is in the interests of Cynthia that she retain the surname Murphy. Alan Paine does not want custody of the little girl as he is out of the country on business approximately half of the year. As Cynthia will remain in the custody of Marcia Murphy, it is reasonable to have the child keep the same name as the custodial parent.

Cynthia's interests are also promoted by protecting her legitimacy. If she retains the surname of her mother and her mother's husband, George Murphy, she will seem to be the legitimate child of the Murphys. If her name were changed to Paine, she would appear to be an illegitimate child. For these reasons, it is improbable that a court will order her surname changed to Paine.

> *IV. Should the putative father be estopped from contesting the paternity of the child when he waited four months after the birth of the child to contest paternity?*

Finally, the Murphys may argue that Paine should be estopped from contesting paternity because he waited too long to raise the issue of paternity. "[T]he doctrine of equitable estoppel may successfully be invoked, in the interest of fairness, to prevent the enforcement of rights which would ultimately work fraud or injustice upon the person against whom enforcement is sought." *Ettore I v. Angela D,* 513 N.Y.S.2d 733, 737 (A.D. 2 Dept. 1987). The doctrine was first applied in the paternity context in *Sharon GG v. Duane HH,* 63 N.Y.2d 859, 472 N.E.2d 46, 482 N.Y.S.2d 270 (1984).

In *Sharon GG v. Duane HH,* the court held that the child's mother was estopped from contesting her husband's paternity of the child two and one half years after the child's birth. During that period of time, she had held the child out as her husband's son, had designated her husband as the father on the birth certificate and baptismal record, had accepted child support from her husband during the time they lived together and after their separation, and had permitted a father-son relationship to develop between her husband and her son. The subsequent claim that the husband was not the child's father sought to deprive the husband and the child of their rights and status. The paternity claim would make a legitimate child illegitimate. Based on these facts, the appellate court upheld the trial court's order dismissing the paternity petition.

The appellate court in *Ettore I v. Angela D,* also dismissed a paternity petition based on equitable estoppel. The petition in this case was filed by the putative father. Although the putative father had had sexual relations with the mother during the period of probable conception and knew about the child, he waited until the child was fifteen months old before he filed his petition. The court held that he waited too long and permitted a paternal relationship to develop between the mother's husband and the child.

Paine will not be estopped from bringing a paternity claim in this case. Although the child is now five months old, unlike the mother in *Sharon GG* and the putative father in *Ettore I,* Paine did not know Marcia Murphy was pregnant or that Cynthia Murphy had been born until early October. The child is still an infant and has not yet developed ties with George Murphy. If Paine files his paternity petition in a timely manner, the court will not rule against him on estoppel grounds.

CONCLUSION

Paine may be able to obtain an order of filiation. He can file a paternity petition under N.Y. Fam. Ct. Act sec. 522. Because the child's mother is married, there is a presumption that the child is the legitimate offspring of the mother's husband. While this is one of the strongest presumptions in the law, it is still rebuttable. To overcome the presumption of legitimacy, Paine must show that the husband is impotent, that the husband did not have access to his wife during the period of probable conception, that the husband is not the biological father with blood or tissue typing tests, or show with blood and tissue typing tests that the probability that he, Paine, is the natural father is so high that it practically proves paternity. There is no evidence that George Murphy is impotent. Paine will also not be able to overcome the presumption by showing that Murphy did not have access to his wife during the fertile period. Although Marcia Murphy was separated from her husband for a portion of the fertile period, she lived with him for the remainder of the time. Paine may be able to exclude Murphy as a candidate with blood and tissue tests if Murphy volunteers to take the tests. The court will not order him to submit to testing, however, as the statute, N.Y. Fam. Ct. Act sec. 532 provides for court ordered testing of the mother, child and putative father. It does not include the mother's husband. If the blood and tissue typing tests on Paine, Marcia Murphy and Cynthia Murphy indicate a high enough probability of paternity, Paine can overcome the presumption of legitimacy.

If Paine succeeds in overcoming the presumption of legitimacy, he must then establish his paternity of Cynthia Murphy. This requires that he show a sexual relationship with the mother during the period of probable conception and the results of blood and tissue typing tests give a high probability that he is the father. As Paine had an affair with Marcia Murphy and lived with her during almost all of the period of probable conception, he can establish the requisite sexual relationship. His overall success in proving paternity will depend on the results of the tests.

If Paine proves paternity of Cynthia Murphy, the court will order him to pay some of the medical and hospital expenses associated with Marcia Murphy's pregnancy and the birth of Cynthia under N.Y. Fam. Ct. Act sec. 514. The court will also order him to pay child support under N.Y. Fam. Ct. Act sec. 513. While the court has the authority under N.Y. Fam. Ct. Act sec. 549 to order visitation, it is discretionary and depends on a determination of the best interests of the child. The court will not order that a new birth certificate issue listing Paine as the child's father under N.Y. Pub. Health Law sec. 4138 unless both Paine and Marcia Murphy agree and the court has determined paternity. A change in Cynthia's surname to Paine will depend also on a court finding that this is in the child's interest. Because the court tends to decide on a surname for the child that is the same as the custodial parent and that makes the child seem legitimate, it will not change the child's surname.

Appendix D

BRIEFS TO THE TRIAL COURT

FAMILY COURT FOR THE CITY OF NEW YORK
QUEENS COUNTY, STATE OF NEW YORK

ALAN PAINE,)	
Petitioner)	
v.)	Paternity Action
MARCIA MURPHY and)	No. 87–14352
GEORGE MURPHY,)	Judge Juanita Chavez
Respondents)	

BRIEF IN SUPPORT OF MOTION TO DISMISS PATERNITY PETITION

QUESTIONS PRESENTED

I. Can a putative father overcome the presumption of legitimacy and establish paternity when he has failed to show that the husband is impotent, when he has failed to show the husband had no sexual relations with the wife during the period of probable conception, when he has failed to exclude the husband as a potential father with blood and tissue typing tests, and the blood and tissue typing tests of the putative father only show a possibility that he is the natural father?

II. Should a putative father be estopped from bringing a paternity action against a married mother and her husband, when he delayed bringing the suit until the child was six months old, when the child, Cynthia Murphy, has an established relationship with her parents, Marcia and George Murphy, when the putative father is unwilling to take on the full parental responsibility, and his action, if successful, will brand the child as illegitimate?

STATEMENT OF FACTS

George and Marcia Murphy ask the court to dismiss the paternity petition filed by the putative father, Alan Paine. In the petition, the putative father challenges the paternity of their daughter, Cynthia

Murphy, born June 4, 1987. If successful, his petition would bastardize the little girl.

George and Marcia Murphy were married on August 13, 1982. Four years later in the summer of 1986, they had some marital difficulties. In the midst of these problems, Marcia Murphy had a brief relationship with Alan Paine, a co-employee at Mercantile Imports, Inc. That relationship caused a marital dispute and the Murphys decided to separate temporarily on September 1, 1986. The couple kept in contact over the telephone during the separation. On September 21, 1986 over an emotion filled lunch, George and Marcia Murphy reconciled. Because Paine was on one of his frequent business trips out of the country, Marcia Murphy left him a note explaining that she had reconciled with her husband and that she never wished to see Paine again. The Murphys do not regret their reconciliation and feel that their marriage is stronger for the brief separation.

On June 4, 1987, the Murphys became the proud parents of a seven pound, three ounce baby girl. They named the baby Cynthia. They are enthusiastic about the addition to the family. Marcia Murphy took a maternity leave from her job at Mercantile Imports. When she returned to work, Marcia Murphy told her fellow workers about Cynthia. In early October, she ran into Paine, who she had not seen in over a year. In her enthusiasm, she told him the exciting news.

On November 2, 1987, Paine filed the paternity petition. He is not asking for custody of the child; he is only asking for visitation with her when he is not off travelling around the world on business. The Murphys answered the petition and denied all the allegations. They filed a motion to dismiss. Judge Chavez heard the motion on November 7, 1987. At that time the petitioner asked the court to order blood and tissue typing tests on Marcia Murphy, George Murphy, Cynthia Murphy, and himself. As required by statute, the judge ordered the tests of the mother, the putative father, and the child. She refused to order tests on the husband as the statute does not require this. She held the motion to dismiss in abeyance pending the outcome of the tests. She stated that if the tests excluded the putative father, she would dismiss the case summarily. If the tests indicated a possibility that the putative father might be the biological father she would consider the motion. As the tests indicated a possibility that the putative father might be the child's natural father, the court set the motion to dismiss for a hearing. The petitioner asked that the hearing be adjourned until January 28, 1988 as he would be out of the country on business until that time.

George Murphy states that no matter what the outcome of this case, his relationship to his wife and his daughter will not change. He loves them both and is committed to caring for his daughter.

This brief is filed in support of the motion to dismiss.

ARGUMENT

George and Marcia Murphy move to dismiss the paternity petition filed by the putative father. Where as here there is no material fact at issue, the court can decide as a matter of law that the putative father has failed to overcome the presumption of legitimacy. This presumption attaches to a child born to a married woman. To overcome the presumption, the putative father must prove that the husband is impotent, that he did not have access to his wife during the period of probable conception, or on the basis of blood and tissue typing tests, that the husband is not the father of the child. The putative father has offered no evidence that George Murphy is impotent or sterile. George Murphy had access to his wife during the fertile period; they lived together as husband and wife for much of the period of probable conception. Although the tests indicated a possibility that the putative father might be the father of the child, he has offered no evidence that excludes George Murphy as the father of Cynthia Murphy. The putative father has failed to overcome the presumption of legitimacy.

Even if the putative father were able to rebut the presumption of legitimacy, he has failed to establish his paternity with clear and convincing evidence. To do this he must show that he had a sexual relationship with the mother and that the blood and tissue typing tests are sufficiently high to "practically prove" his paternity. When the test results are not sufficiently compelling, he must also eliminate other possible candidates. The test results are not sufficiently high in this case and the petitioner has failed to eliminate George Murphy as the father. The petitioner has not met his burden by clear and convincing evidence. The court should dismiss the paternity petition.

Finally, when the putative father has delayed too long in bringing the paternity action, he should be estopped from claiming paternity. The child has developed strong bonds to her parents, the very parents who are committed to loving and caring for her. The putative father, in contrast, seeks to bastardize this little girl against her best interests. The petition should be dismissed.

The Putative Father Has Failed to Overcome the Presumption That Cynthia Murphy Is the Legitimate Child of George and Marcia Murphy.

The presumption of legitimacy is one of the strongest presumptions in the law. *Matter of Findlay*, 253 N.Y. 1, 170 N.E. 471 (1930). The presumption arises when a child is born to a married woman. The presumption protects the child with the mantle of legitimacy. In order to overcome the presumption of legitimacy, a petitioner must prove one of the following: 1) that the mother's husband is impotent or sterile, 2) that the mother's husband cannot be the biological father because of the results of blood and tissue typing tests, 3) that the mother's husband did not have access to his wife during the period of probable conception, or 4) that the results of blood and tissue typing tests are so compelling that they practically prove the putative father is the father.

The petitioner in this case has offered no evidence that George Murphy is impotent or sterile. The petitioner has also offered no medical evidence that would exclude George Murphy as Cynthia's father. In order to overcome the presumption under these circumstances, the putative father must show either non-access by the mother's husband or compelling test results in his favor. He can do neither.

George Murphy had access to Marcia Murphy during the period of probable conception. A determination of access is dependent upon two things: the degree of contact between the husband and wife and the timing of the contact in relation to the birth of the child.

Any contact between husband and wife is sufficient. There is access even if there is only a "fair basis for the belief that at times they may have come together." *Matter of Findlay.* In *Irma N. v. Carlos A.F.,* 46 A.D.2d 893, 361 N.Y.S.2d 701 (1974), the couple had been separated for four years and only had contact when the husband came to the wife's home to pick up the children for visitation. The court held that the contact was sufficient to show access between the husband and wife.

The court also found access in *Ettore I v. Angela D,* 129 Misc. 2d 301, 492 N.Y.S.2d 1013 (1985), *rev'd on other grounds* 127 A.D.2d 6, 513 N.Y.S.2d 733 (1987). There the husband and wife were living in the same household. Based on the uncorroborated testimony of the wife that she and her husband engaged in regular sexual relations, the court held that the husband had access to his wife.

George Murphy lived with his wife from the time of their marriage in August 1982 until September 1, 1986 and from September 21, 1986 to the present. These undisputed facts provide a "fair basis for the belief that at times they may have come together." *Findlay.* The Murphys had more contact than the couple in *Irma N.,* who saw each other only when the husband picked up the children for visitation. Like the married couple in *Ettore I,* the Murphys lived together. There was access between them, and if it occurred at any time during the period of probable conception, the putative father has failed to establish non-access sufficient to rebut the presumption of legitimacy.

The period of probable conception is calculated backward from the child's date of birth. Although the average full term child is conceived 266 days before birth, the range is broad. It extends from 251 days to 285 days. *Morris v. Terry K.,* 70 A.D.2d 1031, 418 N.Y.S.2d 174 (1979); *Reidy v. Jeffrey K,* 125 A.D.2d 825, 509 N.Y.S.2d 924 (1986).

George Murphy lived with his wife during part of the period of probable conception. Cynthia Murphy was born on June 4, 1987. She weighed seven pounds three ounces. This is a normal birth weight for a full term pregnancy. Cynthia Murphy was probably conceived 285 to 251 days prior to June 4, 1987, or between August 23 and September

26, 1986. Even if George and Marcia Murphy did not meet during their brief separation, they still lived together from August 23 and September 1 and from September 21 to September 26 or for sixteen days during the period of probable conception. The petitioner has failed to overcome the presumption of legitimacy by showing non-access of the husband to the wife.

The only way to overcome the presumption of legitimacy remaining to the petitioner in this case is to show blood and tissue typing test results that are sufficiently compelling. The two tests involved are the Landsteiner Blood Grouping Test and the HLA or Human Leucocyte Antigen test. The Landsteiner test determines blood types. While it is an accurate test, it is helpful in paternity cases only when the results show that one man cannot be the father of the child. The test is definitive, for example, if the putative father is one of the 60% of men that can be excluded as potential fathers for the child. It provides no basis for choosing among the remaining 40% of males. *Angela B. v. Glenn D.*, 126 Misc. 2d 646, 482 N.Y.S.2d 971 (Fam. Ct. 1984), *order reversed on other grounds sub nom. Barber v. Davis*, 120 A.D.2d 364, 502 N.Y.S.2d 19 (1986).

The HLA test involves testing for more variables. Although the samples used are blood samples, the test is a tissue typing test. It was first used to match organ donors with recipients. More recently it has been used in paternity cases, both to exclude a greater number of potential fathers and to show probabilities of paternity. The test does not determine the one man who is the father, it just helps to narrow the field of potential candidates by allowing the tester to eliminate 95% of the males in the population. *Angela B.*

Dr. Leon Sussman, a proponent of the HLA test, nonetheless stated:

> The temptation to use a mathematical formula for calculating the probability of paternity in cases where an exclusion is not obtained, is very great. There is, however, the risk of undue influence on the court when a report of '95 percent or higher probability paternity' is presented.

> Even at the 95 percent level, the fact is that a 5 percent chance of non-paternity exists. The circumstances that should be considered, such as access, time, multiple exposures, promiscuity, and so forth must be given their proper weight in arriving at a conclusion when the 'probability of paternity' is presented".

New York State Journal of Medicine, March 1981.

Dr. Sussman also testified that in one case where there were two potential fathers, one scored a 99.7%; two years later the other man was tested and his score was 99.8%. *Angela B.*, 126 Misc. 2d at 653, 482 N.Y.S.2d at 976. While the test is particularly useful for exclusionary purposes, it does not affirmatively prove who the father of a particular child is. The following chart indicates how quickly the likelihood of paternity diminishes as the HLA score retreats from 100%.

Likelihood of Paternity

W	Pl	Likelihood of Paternity
99.8 to 99.9%	>399:1	Practically Proved
99.0 to 99.7%	>95:1	Extremely likely
95.0 to 98.9%	>19:1	Very Likely
90 to 94.9%	>9:1	Likely
80 to 89.9%	>4:1	Hint
Less than 80%		Not useful

Pratt v. Victor B, 112 Misc. 2d 487, 488, 448 N.Y.S.2d 351, 352 (Fam. Ct. 1982).

The courts have used a line from this table to establish the rule for overcoming the presumption of legitimacy. In *Ettore I,* for example, the putative father had an HLA score of 99.82%. The court held that this score together with evidence from both the putative father and the mother as to their sexual relationship was sufficient to overcome the presumption of legitimacy.

The court in *Angela B. v. Glenn D.,* however, held that an HLA score of 99.7% was not sufficient when the other evidence in the case led to the conclusion that the putative father was not the father. The HLA test was later repeated. At that time the putative father scored 99.8%. At this point the appellate court reversed the trial court decision and held that 99.8% was sufficient to overcome the presumption of legitimacy and establish paternity.

The bright line rule from these cases provides that 99.8% and above is sufficient to rebut the presumption. Cases with lower probabilities require other evidence consistent with paternity to overcome the presumption of legitimacy.

The HLA test in this case indicated a 98.1% possibility that the putative father is the natural father of Cynthia Murphy. The odds at this percentage are only 19:1. That means that one man in twenty is as likely as the petitioner here to be the child's father. The other evidence in the case demonstrates an equal likelihood that George Murphy fathered the little girl to whom he has committed his emotional and financial resources.

Under these circumstances, the putative father has failed to overcome the presumption of legitimacy and failed to prove paternity by clear and convincing evidence. The motion to dismiss should be granted.

The Putative Father Should Be Estopped From Claiming Paternity of the Child When He Waited to File His Paternity Action Until George and Marcia Murphy Had an Established Relationship With Their Daughter, Cynthia.

The doctrine of equitable estoppel operates to prevent the person who has delayed in asserting his rights from disrupting the circumstances that developed while he waited. *Ettore I v. Angela D,* 127 A.D.2d 6, 513 N.Y.S.2d 733 (1987). In that case as here, a putative father filed a paternity petition after the mother's husband had an established relationship with the child. Although the mother and her husband separated after the child's birth, the husband continued to support the child financially and to visit with her on numerous occasions. When the child was fifteen months old, the putative father filed his paternity petition. The appellate division held that he had deferred too long. It was not in the child's interest to substitute a stranger for the "psychological parent" the child knew and loved, and it was not in her interest to transform her from a legitimate to an illegitimate child.

The best interests of Cynthia Murphy are the same as those of the child in *Ettore I.* Cynthia Murphy knows George and Marcia Murphy as her parents. George Murphy has become her psychological father. Cynthia's interests will also be served by the fact that George Murphy is committed to providing his daughter with the financial and emotional support she needs. The putative father is not interested in a custodial arrangement or the responsibilities of being a full time father. He travels extensively for his employment and is only in the country approximately half of the time. He just wants to visit with the little girl when it is convenient for him.

The putative father also seeks to bastardize Cynthia. As the court in *Ettore I* noted, "the petitioner's efforts to vindicate his rights must give way to the child's emotional well-being as well as the societal interests in shielding the child from the grave repercussions of being branded illegitimate." Id. at 739. For these reasons, the putative father should be estopped from claiming his paternity.

CONCLUSION

The Murphys' motion to dismiss the putative father's paternity petition should be granted. Because he is claiming paternity of a child born to a married couple, he must overcome the strong presumption of legitimacy. The petitioner has offered no evidence that George Murphy is impotent or sterile. He has not offered blood or tissue typing evidence that excludes George Murphy as Cynthia's father. The petitioner has failed to prove that George Murphy had no access to his wife during the period of probable conception. The period of probable conception extends from 285 days to 251 days before birth. The Murphys lived together for sixteen of those days. Finally, although the putative father's HLA score indicates a possibility that he is the father, the score is not sufficiently high to overcome the presumption of legitimacy and prove paternity by clear and convincing evidence. The other evidence points to George Murphy as a likely father of Cynthia. At the level of the petitioner's HLA score, one man out of every twenty males has an equal likelihood of being Cynthia's father. The petitioner failed to overcome the presumption of legitimacy.

The petitioner should be estopped from claiming paternity since he delayed filing his petition until after George Murphy established a parental relationship with Cynthia. It is not in the child's interest to substitute a stranger for the father she knows. The court has a responsibility to protect this child from the stigma of illegitimacy.

For these reasons, the motion to dismiss the paternity petition should be granted.

Dated: December 2, 1987

Respectfully submitted,
Pratt and Associates

By: _____

Julia R. Botcoll
325 East 43rd St.
Ste. 200
New York, New York 10017

FAMILY COURT FOR THE CITY OF NEW YORK
QUEENS COUNTY, STATE OF NEW YORK

ALAN Paine, Petitioner	))
v.	) Paternity Action
MARCIA MURPHY and	) No. 87–14352
GEORGE MURPHY,	) Judge Juanita Chavez
Respondents	)

BRIEF IN OPPOSITION TO MOTION TO DISMISS PATERNITY PETITION QUESTIONS PRESENTED

I. Can Alan Paine overcome the presumption of legitimacy and establish paternity of Cynthia Murphy by showing that he had an exclusive sexual relationship with the child's mother for three weeks surrounding the point of conception and by showing with blood and tissue typing tests that he has a 98.1% probability of being the child's natural father?

II. Should the court dismiss the respondents' estoppel defense as a matter of law, when Paine did not delay, but filed his paternity petition one month after he learned that he was the infant's father, and when the child is still too young to recognize individuals, let alone form a strong relationship with them?

STATEMENT OF FACTS

Alan Paine filed a paternity petition on November 2, 1987, so that he could assume full responsibility for his infant daughter, Cynthia, born on June 4, 1987. Although the child's mother was married at the time the child was conceived, she was separated from her husband. Using the average gestation period of 266 days, Cynthia was conceived on September 13, 1986. Alan Paine lived with Marcia Murphy and had an exclusive sexual relationship with her between September 1, 1986, when she separated from her husband and September 21, 1986, when Mr. Paine left on a business trip for his employer, Mercantile Imports, Inc. While he was out of the country, Marcia Murphy reconciled with her husband. She left Paine a note explaining this fact and that she did not wish to see him again. Despite his affection for her and his disappointment that she was not waiting for him, Paine respected her wishes and did not try to contact her further.

Although they work for the same employer, Marcia Murphy and Alan Paine work in different departments and they did not meet until the beginning of October, 1987, when Murphy enthusiastically told Paine about her new baby girl. It was not until later that Paine realized that the child must be his. He wants to reimburse Murphy for the expenses of her pregnancy and the birth of his daughter. He wants to pay child support for the little girl and to visit with her, so that she will know her real father. His job requires frequent travel, so he is not asking for custody. When he is in the country, however, he wants to spend time with Cynthia and give her the love and emotional support that only a real father can provide.

In order to determine paternity, Paine asked the court on November 6, 1987 to order blood and tissue typing tests on all concerned: Marcia Murphy and her husband, Cynthia and himself. The court granted the request as to all except the husband as required by the statute, N.Y. Fam. Ct. Act sec. 532 (Consol. 1987). Mr. Murphy did not volunteer to take the tests. The court held respondents' motion to dismiss in abeyance pending the outcome of the testing.

The blood and tissue typing tests indicated a 98.1% probability that Alan Paine is the child's father. Based on this medical evidence and the fact that Alan Paine had an exclusive sexual relationship with the child's mother around the point of conception, the court should deny respondents' motion to dismiss and as a matter of law decide this case for petitioner on the issue of paternity.

ARGUMENT

Petitioner, Alan Paine, brought this case to determine his paternity of the infant, Cynthia. Respondents, Marcia and George Murphy, the child's mother and her husband, filed a motion to dismiss. When a child is born to a married woman, there is a rebuttable presumption that the child is the offspring of her husband. The presumption can be overcome by showing either that the husband is not the father of the child or by establishing with clear and convincing evidence that someone else is the father. Alan Paine can overcome the presumption of legitimacy and establish his paternity of Cynthia by the undisputed facts of this case. First, Paine can exclude the husband as a potential father as he did not have access to his wife at the point of probable conception. Second, the husband has refused to take blood and tissue typing tests that would determine his paternity or lack of paternity, giving rise to an inference that he is not the father. Third, Paine had exclusive access to Marcia Murphy at the point of probable conception. Finally, the blood and tissue typing tests of Paine, the mother and Cynthia show a 98.1% probability that Alan Paine is the child's father.

Paine is not estopped from bringing his paternity petition since he filed the petition within a month of the time he learned of the infant's existence and long before she had established any ties to respondents. For these reasons, the court should deny respondents' motion to dismiss and decide as a matter of law that Alan Paine is Cynthia's father.

Alan Paine Can Overcome the Presumption of Legitimacy and Establish Paternity of the Child.

Although there is a presumption of legitimacy that attaches to a child born to a married woman, this presumption is rebuttable by evidence that excludes the husband as a possible father. *Ettore I v. Angela D,* 129 Misc. 2d 301, 492 N.Y.S.2d 1013 (1985), *rev'd on other grounds* 127 A.D.2d 6, 513 N.Y.S.2d 733 (1987). The presumption is no longer applied with the rigidity that once existed. Id. at 1018. The presumption can be overcome by showing that the husband did not have access to his wife at the point of conception, by showing that the husband is impotent or sterile, by excluding the husband with a competent blood or tissue typing test or by showing a strong likelihood that the someone else is the child's father. Id. at 1018. While there is no evidence that the husband in this case is impotent or sterile, the petitioner can overcome the presumption in this case because the husband was separated from the child's mother at the point of probable conception, a negative inference can be drawn from the husband's refusal to take blood or tissue typing tests, and from scientific evidence indicating a very high probability that Paine is the father.

The mother was separated from her husband at the time the child was conceived.

The gestation period for a full term child is 266 days from conception to birth. *Erie County Commissioner of Social Services v. Boyd*, 74 A.D.2d 728, 425 N.Y.S.2d 692 (1980). The court in this case held that when the court found intercourse between petitioner and respondent not less than 261 days before delivery and not more than 268 days prior to delivery, that this was well within the normal range of gestation.

Cynthia Murphy was born on June 4, 1987. She weighed seven pounds, three ounces at birth, which is a normal weight for a full term infant. Using the 266 day gestation period from *Erie County v. Boyd*, she was probably conceived on September 13, 1986. Alan Paine asserts and the respondents do not deny that Marcia Murphy was separated from her husband from September 1, 1986 to September 21, 1986; or from thirteen days prior to and eight days subsequent to the point of probable conception. Although the range is sometimes greater than twenty-one days, the husband is unlikely to be the child's father.

Alan Paine had an exclusive sexual relationship with the child's mother at the point of probable conception.

The child, Cynthia, was conceived in all likelihood during the time when Marcia Murphy was separated from her husband and living with Alan Paine. The gestation period for a normal full term pregnancy is 266 days. *Erie County Commissioner of Social Services v. Boyd*, 74 A.D.2d 728, 425 N.Y.S.2d 692 (1980). Cynthia was a full term infant as indicated by her birth weight of seven pounds, three ounces. September 13, 1986 is 266 days before her birthday on June 4, 1987. Cynthia was probably conceived on or very near to September 13, 1986. Marcia Murphy separated from her husband on September 1, 1986 and lived exclusively with Alan Paine from that date until September 21, 1986. The undisputed evidence indicates that Alan Paine was the only man to have a sexual relationship with the child's mother at the time of conception. He is Cynthia's biological father.

The blood and tissue typing tests of the petitioner, the mother, and the child show a 98.1% probability that Paine is Cynthia's father.

The advent of the HLA or Human Lymphocyte Antigen test has revolutionized determinations of paternity. Until recently the only test available was the Landsteiner blood typing test. It could be used in some cases to exclude a putative father as the child's father. The test, although highly accurate for exclusion purposes, could not exclude more than 60% of the males in the general population and was useless in providing positive evidence of paternity.

The HLA test, on the other hand, is much more precise. It is a tissue typing test that was first developed in order to match donors and recipients for organ transplantation. In the paternity context, the test can exclude a much higher percentage of the males in the general population and is so accurate, it is admissible for affirmatively proving paternity. The applicable statute provides:

> Except in cases where exclusion has been established by another blood genetic marker test, the laboratory and statistical results of the human leucocyte antigen blood tissue test (either separately or in combination with the laboratory and statistical results of any other blood genetic marker test or tests including, without limitation, red blood cell antigens, red blood cell serum protein, and red blood cell enzyme tests) may be received in evidence to aid in the determination of whether the alleged father is or is not the father of the child.

N.Y. Fam. Ct. Act sec. 532(a) (Consol. 1987).

A very high HLA probability is sufficient with evidence of the sexual relationship between the mother and the alleged father to overcome the presumption of legitimacy and establish paternity. The court in *Ettore I v. Angela D,* 129 Misc. 2d 301, 492 N.Y.S.2d 1013, held that an HLA score of 99.82% was compelling evidence of paternity. The mother in that case was married at the time the child was conceived and living with her husband. She and the alleged father testified to their sexual relationship. Her husband did not submit to HLA testing. Even when there were two potential candidates for father of the child, the court held that "[w]hen such a highly accurate test as the HLA shows "practically proven" that petitioner is the child's father, common sense and reason are outraged by the presumption of legitimacy. This Court finds the HLA score such compelling evidence, together with the corroborating testimony of both petitioner and respondent-mother as to their sexual relations, as to overcome the presumption of legitimacy in this case." 129 Misc. 2d at 309, 492 N.Y.S.2d at 1019–1020.

In this case, too, the HLA and corroborating evidence are compelling that Alan Paine is Cynthia's father. At a hearing on November 6, 1987, the court ordered that Alan Paine, Marcia Murphy, and Cynthia undergo blood grouping tests including HLA. The test results indicated a 98.1% probability that Alan Paine is Cynthia's father. Although this score is not quite as high as that in *Ettore I,* the corroborating evidence is even stronger. Like the petitioner and respondent-mother in that case, Alan Paine and the respondent-mother here had a sexual relationship at the time of probable conception. Unlike that case, however, where the mother was living with the husband, Marcia Murphy was separated from her husband at the time the child was conceived. Where in *Ettore I,* there were two possible candidates for the child's father absent the HLA test, here only Alan Paine had a sexual relationship with the mother at the time of conception. This evidence combined with his very high HLA score of 98.1% compels a finding that Alan Paine has overcome the presumption of legitimacy and established his paternity of Cynthia.

A negative inference arises against the husband when he refuses to take blood and tissue typing tests that would provide scientific proof of his paternity or lack of paternity.

Alan Paine requested the court to order blood and tissue typing tests of the mother's husband as well as of the mother, the child, and himself in order to have this case decided purely on the basis of scientific testing. Because the statute, N.Y. Fam. Ct. Act sec. 532 (Consol. 1987), did not require testing of the mother's husband, the court ordered testing only of the mother, the child, and petitioner. Mr. Murphy refused to take the blood and tissue typing tests. A negative inference should be drawn against the husband's paternity because of his refusal to submit the case to scientific resolution.

In *Ettore I v. Angela D,* under similar circumstances the court applied a negative inference against the respondent-husband. The court explained:

> Yet, by refusing to take the HLA he is effectively withholding evidence solely in his possession and control. The respondent-husband did testify, but his refusal to submit to the HLA is tantamount to refusal to testify on that issue and, therefore, under *Philip De G.,* [59 N.Y.2d 137, 463 N.Y.S.2d 761, 450 N.E.2d 681( )], the court may draw the strongest inference against him on that issue permitted by opposing evidence in the record. The HLA on petitioner, mother, and child, admitted into evidence, indicated the likelihood of petitioner's paternity as "practically proved." Therefore, the inference against respondent-husband is that the petitioner is the father and not the husband, since only one man can be the father.

127 Misc. 2d at 310, 492 N.Y.S.2d at 1020. (Emphasis added.)

In this case, too, the court must draw the strongest possible inference against the respondent-husband, because he has withheld "evidence solely within his possession and control", the blood and tissue typing test results that would prove that respondent-husband was or was not the father of the child. Faced with undisputed evidence that the respondent-husband did not have access to his wife at the point of probable conception, that Alan Paine had exclusive access to the mother at the point of probable conception, and an HLA test result of a 98.1% probability that Alan Paine is the father of the child, the court can only conclude that Alan Paine is Cynthia's father.

Paine Is Not Estopped From Asserting His Paternity When He Filed the Petition Within One Month of the Time He Learned of his Daughter's Existence and Before the Infant Could Establish Any Familial Relationship With Any Other Man.

The doctrine of equitable estoppel is inapplicable to the present case. It is used as a defense "where the failure to promptly assert a right has given rise to circumstances rendering it inequitable to permit the exercise of the right after a lapse of time." *Ettore I,* 127 A.D.2d at 12, 513 N.Y.S.2d at 737. In the paternity context, the doctrine has been used to prevent a mother from contesting her husband's paternity of a child in order to gain custody of the child in a divorce proceeding, *Hill v. Hill,* 20 A.D.2d 923, 249 N.Y.S.2d 751 (1964); to prevent a husband from denying paternity in order to avoid child support payments four years after the divorce decree, *Time v. Time,* 59 Misc. 2d 912, 300 N.Y.S.2d 924 (Fam. Ct. 1969); to prevent a husband from avoiding a child support arrearage fifteen years after the divorce decree, *Montelone v. Antia,* 60 A.D.2d 603, 400 N.Y.S.2d 129 (1977); or to prevent a wife from refusing her husband visitation rights with the parties' children, *Sharon GG v. Duane HH,* 95 A.D.2d 466, 467 N.Y.S.2d 941 (1983), *aff'd* 63 N.Y.2d 859, 482 N.Y.S.2d 270, 472 N.E.2d 46 (1984). In each of these cases the court used the doctrine to prevent the husband or wife for his or her own ends from challenging the husband's paternity after a long period of acquiescing in that paternity. In each case, the court applied the doctrine after a long period of acquiescence and to protect the interests of the minor child or children.

Equitable estoppel has only been applied in one case against a putative father. In *Ettore I v. Angela D,* 127 A.D.2d 6, 513 N.Y.S.2d 733 (1987), it was the putative father who had delayed in challenging the paternity of the child until after she was nearly three years old and when the child had an established relationship with her mother's husband. The court noted that the putative father only brought his petition after the mother, then divorced from her husband, had refused his proposal of marriage. The court concluded that the putative father had waited too long to bring his petition and held that he was estopped from doing so. In this case as well the party against whom the doctrine was invoked, had challenged the child's paternity in order to advance his own interests and against the best interests of the child.

The doctrine should not be applied in this case. Alan Paine learned of his daughter's birth when she was just four months old. He filed his paternity petition within a month. He has not acquiesced in the status quo, but has sought to assert his rights promptly.

Alan Paine, in contrast to all the others against whom estoppel has been used, filed his paternity petition to advance the best interests of his infant daughter. It is in Cynthia's interests to know her real father, to develop a relationship with him, to have his love and caring, to receive his emotional and financial support, to bear his name. Alan Paine does not seek to interfere with the relationship that Cynthia has with the Murphys, but to add further enrichment to her life.

When Alan Paine filed his paternity petition promptly and has only acted out of his concern for his daughter, he should not be estopped from becoming Cynthia's father.

CONCLUSION

Alan Paine has overcome the presumption of legitimacy and established his paternity of infant Cynthia. Although the child's mother was married at the time the child was conceived, she was separated from her husband and had an exclusive sexual relationship with Mr. Paine. This exclusive relationship extended for thirteen days before and eight days after the probable point of conception. The HLA test results showing a 98.1% probability that Paine is Cynthia's father are compelling. Because he filed his paternity petition as soon as he learned of the child's birth and motivated only by her interests, this court can conclude as a matter of law that he is the child's father.

Respondents' motion to dismiss should be denied.

Dated: November 2, 1987

Respectfully Submitted,

Melvin H. Greene
Attorney for Petitioner
964 W. 58th St.
New York, New York 10019

Appendix E

APPELLATE BRIEFS

UNITED STATES COURT OF APPEALS FOR
THE NINTH CIRCUIT

Docket No. 87–3427

SIERRA CLUB, a Non-profit
California Corporation,

Plaintiff–Appellant

—against—

SECRETARY OF AGRICULTURE and
CHIEF of UNITED STATES FOREST SERVICE,

Defendant–Appellees

On Appeal from the United States District Court
for the District of Arizona

APPELLANT'S BRIEF

February 29, 1988

Darwin, Seely, and Mendel
Attorneys for Appellant
2840 Valley Bank Center
Phoenix, Arizona 85073
Telephone: (602) 257–4824

TABLE OF CONTENTS

TABLE OF CASES, STATUTES, AND OTHER AUTHORITIES

STATEMENT OF ISSUES PRESENTED FOR REVIEW

I. Under the Wilderness Act, did Congress intend to create reserved water rights, which requires that the federal government withdraw land from other uses, reserve it for a particular purpose, and reserve unappropriated water sufficient to fulfill the purpose of the reservation?

    A. Did Congress intend to withdraw land and reserve it for a particular purpose, when under the Wilderness Act, it set aside wilderness areas to preserve them in their natural state, untrammeled by man, for future generations of Americans?

    B. Did Congress intend to reserve sufficient unappropriated water to preserve and protect wilderness lands in their natural state?

II. Do the Secretary of Agriculture and the Chief of the United States Forest Service have a duty to assert federal reserved water rights for the Sycamore Canyon Wilderness Area when the only way to protect the wilderness character of the area and to maintain its primary natural feature, the Sycamore River, is to preserve the natural flow of the river through the Sycamore Canyon?

III. Does this court have the power to require the federal defendants to assert reserved water rights under sec. 706(1) of the Administrative Procedures Act, which requires a court to compel agency action unlawfully withheld, when agency inaction will cause irreparable harm to the Sycamore Canyon Wilderness Area?

STATEMENT OF THE CASE

The Sierra Club brought this action to protect the wilderness character of the Sycamore Canyon Wilderness Area. The City of Flagstaff, Arizona, has plans to divert the waters of the Sycamore River upstream from the wilderness area. This diversion would deprive the Sycamore River of its natural flow and deprive the wilderness area of its major natural feature. The Sierra Club brought this declaratory judgment action for a determination 1) that federal reserved water rights attach to federal wilderness areas under the Wilderness Act, 2) that the Secretary of Agriculture and Chief of the Forest Service ("federal defendants") have a duty to assert reserved water rights to protect the wilderness area, and 3) that the court can compel the federal defendants to act under sec. 706(1) of the Administrative Procedure Act.

The district court ruled that the Sierra Club had standing to sue. It declined to rule, however, that Congress created reserved water rights when it reserved wilderness areas under the Wilderness Act. Because it reached this decision on the first issue, it did not reach the remaining issues. The Sierra Club appealed the case to this court.

Congress created the Sycamore Canyon Wilderness Area on March 6, 1972 from primitive areas in the Coconino, Kaibab, and Prescott National Forests. (Opinion and Order of November 24, 1987) The wilderness area is located in central Arizona and varies in elevation between 3500 and 7000 feet. The annual rainfall is 10–15 inches and occurs primarily in the form of snow. At the higher elevations, the vegetation consists of Mariposa and Pinon pines. Cottonwood trees are common features at the lower elevations. Near the feeder streams and the upper Sycamore River, there are some Aspen trees that turn a bright yellow in the autumn. The type of vegetation depends on the proximity to a source of moisture. In the spring as the snow melts, the hills are covered with wild flowers. By summer, the hills are brown and dry with the only patches of green adjacent to the flowing water. (TR 3)

The primary natural feature of the wilderness is the Sycamore River. It originates in the snow fields of Mount Casner. (TR 4, 8) Since the river bed is steep and rocky, the river falls in dramatic cascades as it rushes through the canyon. The river and the play of light on the tumbling water have attracted artists and hikers to the wilderness for many years. (TR 8) The trout fishing in the feeder streams and the upper Sycamore River is spectacular. (TR 4) At dusk, herds of antelope and white tailed deer come to the banks of the river to drink. (TR 3) Over the centuries, the river has carved its way through the rock to form the Sycamore Canyon, which gave its name to the wilderness area. The canyon is a geological formation of scientific importance. (TR 3–4)

The City of Flagstaff, Arizona, proposes to divert the Sycamore River above the wilderness area for its municipal water supply. Flagstaff currently gets its water from the Sycamore River below the wilderness area. (Op. Nov. 24, 1987) The City proposes this up-stream diversion because much of the water is lost through evaporation. The City recently completed a study on its water requirements for the twenty-first century. The proposal to pipe the Sycamore River came from this study. Flagstaff is currently considering the feasibility of the proposal. (TR 17, Op. Nov. 24, 1987)

The Secretary of Agriculture and the Chief of the Forest Service are charged under the Wilderness Act with protecting and preserving wilderness areas under their jurisdiction. Despite Flagstaff's plan to pipe the upper Sycamore River, these federal defendants have taken no steps to protect the Sycamore Canyon Wilderness Area and its major natural feature, the Sycamore River. (Op. Nov. 24, 1987)

The Sierra Club brings this appeal to preserve the primitive character of the Sycamore Canyon Wilderness Area and the reserved water rights in the Sycamore River.

SUMMARY OF ARGUMENT

The Sierra Club brought this action against the Secretary of Agriculture and the Chief of the Forest Service to require them to assert federal reserved water rights in order to protect the Sycamore Canyon Wilderness. It perfects this appeal because the trial court 1) failed to find that Congress had created reserved water rights under the Wilderness Act, 16 U.S.C. sec. 1131 et seq. (1982), 2) failed to find that the federal defendants had a specific duty to assert reserved water rights, and 3) failed to find that it could compel the federal defendants to act.

When Congress created the Sycamore Canyon Wilderness Area, it reserved by implication sufficient unappropriated water necessary to preserve the wilderness area including the natural flow of the Sycamore River. The reserved water rights doctrine requires that Congress withdraw land from other public purposes, reserve the land for a specific public purpose, and reserve sufficient water to fulfill the purposes of the reservation. *Cappaert v. United States*, 426 U.S. 128 (1976). The Wilderness Act and its legislative history indicate that the wilderness areas were withdrawn from primitive areas in national forest, park, and refuge lands. Congress reserved these lands as wilderness in their primeval condition for future generations. Since the rivers and streams are crucial to the wilderness character of these areas, Congress intended to reserve sufficient unappropriated water to maintain the natural character. *Sierra Club v. Block*, 622 F. Supp. 842 (D.C. Colo. 1985), *aff'd on rehearing sub nom.*, *Sierra Club v. Lyng*, 661 F. Supp. 1490 (D.C. Colo. 1987). The trial court erred when it held that Congress created no reserved water rights under the Wilderness Act.

The Wilderness Act is drafted in mandatory language. The federal officials charged with administering the wilderness areas are required to protect and preserve the wilderness areas. This general duty becomes a specific duty to assert reserved water rights when a wilderness area is threatened by imminent harm. *Cappaert.* The Sycamore Canyon Wilderness Area is threatened by the City of Flagstaff. Flagstaff proposes to pipe the waters of the Sycamore River upstream from the wilderness area and deprive the wilderness of the natural flow of the river. The only way to protect the wilderness in its natural state is to assert the federal reserved water rights. The federal defendants have a specific duty to do just that. The trial court erred when it failed to recognize the threat of imminent harm posed by Flagstaff and the federal defendants' specific duty to assert reserved water rights.

The federal defendants' failure to act is subject to judicial review under the Administrative Procedures Act, 5 U.S.C. sec. 701–706 (1982). The APA limits judicial review when the statute precludes review, when the statute leaves action entirely to the agency's discretion, or when the statute provides no meaningful standard for the reviewing court to apply. Judicial review is available in this case, because the Wilderness Act does not preclude review, agencies have a mandatory duty under the Wilderness Act rather than a purely discretionary role, and because the Wilderness Act provides a standard against which a court can measure the agency's inaction.

When, as here, an agency refuses to act in the face of a mandatory duty, the court can compel the agency to act. Because the federal defendants have taken no action to protect the wilderness area, the court can compel them under the APA 5 U.S.C. sec. 706(1), to assert federal reserved water rights. This case should be reversed and remanded to the trial court for entry of a judgment declaring that Congress intended reserved water rights to attach to wilderness areas under the Wilderness Act and requiring the federal defendants to assert reserved water rights for the Sycamore Canyon Wilderness Area.

ARGUMENT

I. CONGRESS INTENDED FEDERAL RESERVED WATERS RIGHTS FOR THE BENEFIT OF THE SYCAMORE CAN-YON WILDERNESS SUFFICIENT TO MAINTAIN THE WILDERNESS IN ITS PRIMEVAL CONDITION.

Federal reserved water rights arise under the judicially created reserved water rights doctrine. The doctrine was defined by the United States Supreme Court.

> This court has long held that when the Federal Government withdraws its land from the public domain and reserves it for a federal purpose, the government, by implication, reserves appurtenant water then unappropriated to the extent needed to accomplish the purpose of the reservation. In so doing, the United States acquires a reserved right in unappropriated water which vests on the date of the reservation and is superior to the rights of future appropriators.

Cappaert v. United States, 426 U.S. 128 (1976).

The doctrine originated in *Winters v. United States,* 207 U.S. 564 (1908). In that case the Court held that when Congress created the Fort Belknap Indian Reservation, it reserved sufficient water for irrigating the land. The right to water for irrigation purposes was superior to later appropriations from the Milk River. In *Arizona v. California,* 373 U.S. 546 (1963), the Court expanded the doctrine to include non-Indian federal lands. The doctrine requires 1) a withdrawal of land from the public domain or other federal uses, 2) a reservation for a specific federal purpose, and 3) that water be necessary to fulfill the purpose of the reservation. *Cappaert.*

a. Under the Wilderness Act, Congress withdrew lands from other federal purposes to create the National Wilderness Preservation System.

For reserved water rights to exist under the doctrine of implied reservation of water rights, the federal government must withdraw the land from other purposes. As the doctrine was first enunciated in *Winters,* the withdrawal occurred from the public domain; that is, from federal land open to settlement under the various homesteading laws. Later in *Arizona v. California,* 373 U.S. at 601, the Court expanded the definition of withdrawal to encompass a withdrawal from other federal uses. In that case the land withdrawn and reserved for the Lake Mead National Recreation Area, 16 U.S.C. sec. 460n (1982), and the Havasu Lake National Wildlife Refuge had been previously withdrawn and reserved for reclamation purposes under the jurisdiction of the Bureau of Reclamation.

The court in *Sierra Club v. Block,* 622 F. Supp. 842, 855 (D.C. Colo. 1985) *aff'd on rehearing sub nom., Sierra Club v. Lyng,* 661 F. Supp. 1490 (D.C. Colo. 1987) (*Block II*), held that for purposes of the reserved water rights doctrine, Congress withdrew land from other federal purposes when it created wilderness areas under the Wilderness Act. The court held that "withdrawal" refers to removing the land from mining and other use related purposes. The Wilderness Act contains specific language exempting wilderness areas from mining: "[t]he minerals in land designated by this Act as wilderness areas are withdrawn from all forms of appropriation under the mining laws and from disposition under all laws pertaining to mineral leasing and all amendments thereto." 16 U.S.C. sec. 1133(d)(3) (1982). All wilderness areas were created from federal lands devoted to other federal purposes.

Although the court in *Block II* was concerned specifically with twenty-four wilderness areas in Colorado, its holding is based on the Wilderness Act and, therefore, applies to all wilderness areas. The Sycamore Canyon Wilderness was withdrawn from national forest lands on March 6, 1972.

> *b.   Under the Wilderness Act, Congress reserved lands for wilderness purposes.*

The second requirement of the reserved water rights doctrine is that the land be reserved for a particular purpose. The purpose of the Wilderness Act appears in section 1131(a).

> In order to assure that an increasing population, accompanied by expanding settlement and growing mechanization, does not occupy and modify all areas within the United States and its possessions, leaving no lands designated for preservation and protection in their natural condition, **it is hereby declared to be the policy of the Congress to secure for the American people of present and future generations the benefits of an enduring resource of wilderness.** For this purpose there is hereby established a National Wilderness Preservation System to be composed of federally owned areas designated by Congress as "wilderness areas", and **these shall be administered for the use and enjoyment of the American people in such manner as will leave them unimpaired for future use and enjoyment as wilderness, and so as to provide for the protection of these areas, the preservation of their wilderness character,** and for the gathering and dissemination of information regarding their use and enjoyment as wilderness; and no Federal lands shall be designated as "wilderness areas" except as provided for in this Act or by a subsequent Act.

16 U.S.C. sec. 1131(a) (1982) (emphasis added).

A wilderness area is defined in section 1131(c) of the Act:

> A wilderness, in contrast with those areas where man and his own works dominate the landscape, is hereby recognized as an **area where the earth and its community of life are untrammeled by man, where man himself is a visitor who does not remain.** An area of wilderness is further defined to mean in this Act an area of **undeveloped Federal land retaining its primeval char-**

acter and influence, without permanent improvements or human habitation, **which is protected and managed so as to preserve its natural conditions** and which (1) generally appears to have been affected primarily by the forces of nature, with the imprint of man's work substantially unnoticeable; (2) has outstanding opportunities for solitude or a primitive and unconfined type of recreation; (3) has at least five thousand acres of land or is of sufficient size as to make practicable its preservation and use in an unimpaired condition; and (4) may also contain ecological, geological, or other features of scientific, educational, scenic, or historical value.

16 U.S.C. sec. 1131(c) (1982) (emphasis added).

Congress expressly intended to preserve wilderness areas in their primeval condition for future generations of Americans. This purpose is supported by the legislative history of the Act. The House Report on the bill states that lands were designated for inclusion in the Wilderness Preservation System "because of the undeveloped character of their lands and the need to protect and manage them in order to preserve * * * the natural conditions that now prevail * * *." H.R. Rep. No. 1538, 88th Cong., 2d Sess., reprinted in 1964 U.S. Code Cong. & Admin. News 3615. The purpose of the wilderness designation is "to make certain that there is left to the American People in years to come unimpaired areas in their natural state." H.R. Rep. No. 1538, supra, at 3621.

c. Under the Wilderness Act, Congress reserved unappropriated water to maintain the natural state of wilderness lands.

The Sycamore Canyon River is the major natural feature of the wilderness area (TR 3, 8) and it gave the wilderness area its name. In the Wilderness Act, Congress intended to reserve enough water to preserve both the lands along the banks of the river and the natural flow of the Sycamore Canyon River itself. The trial court misconstrued the statute when it held that Congress had already reserved water rights under the Organic Administration Act of June 4, 1897, 16 U.S.C. sec. 473 (1982) for the benefit of forest service lands, and did not reserve water rights under the Wilderness Act for the benefit of wilderness areas. The trial court's decision was erroneous for two reasons. First, although the Sycamore Canyon Wilderness was created out of land that originally had been designated as national forest land, many of the wilderness areas covered by the Wilderness Act were not originally forest lands. Wilderness areas were also carved out of land formerly designated at National Parks, National Monuments, and National Recreation Areas.

Second, the purposes of the Wilderness and Organic Acts are different. Congress designed the Organic Act as primarily a development statute with a primary purpose of furnishing a continuous supply of timber and for other commercial enterprise. The Wilderness Act, on the contrary, expressly prohibits any commercial enterprise within a wilderness area. Wilderness Act, sec. 1133(c).

The primary purpose of the Wilderness Act is the protection of primitive areas in their natural state. To fulfill this purpose, Congress by implication reserved rights to previously unappropriated water. Where the purpose of the Wilderness Act is different from the purposes of the Forest Service Organic Act, there is a new reservation of water rights sufficient to protect the natural in-stream flow of the Sycamore Canyon River.

The decision of the Court in *United States v. New Mexico*, 438 U.S. 696 (1978), is not to the contrary. In that case, the Court held that the Multiple Use Sustained Yield Act of 1960, 16 U.S.C. sec. 526 et seq. (1982) ("MUSYA"), did not create additional reserved water rights for the National Forest lands. MUSYA added permissible uses to those that existed under the Organic Act, but it did not change the developmental purpose of National Forest lands. The Court explained that without legislative history to the contrary, it could not conclude that Congress intended to reserve additional water for secondary uses. 438 U.S. at 715. Indeed, the legislative history of MUSYA shows that it is merely supplemental to the Organic Act. "[I]n any establishment of a national forest a purpose set out in the 1897 act must be present but there may also exist one or more of the additional purposes listed in the bill." H.R. Rep. No. 1551, 86th Cong., 2d Sess., reprinted in 1960 U.S.Code Cong. & Admin. News 2377, 2380.

In contrast, the Wilderness Act did not add to the primary purposes of existing reservations, as did MUSYA. "Rather, the Wilderness Act is the initial legislation creating an entirely new reservation of federal lands." *Block II,* 622 F.Supp. at 860. *United States v. New Mexico* is not controlling and the trial court erred in applying the reasoning of that case to the Wilderness Act.

The trial court also erred when it used section 1133(a) of the Wilderness Act in support of its interpretation. This language that the Act is "within and supplemental to the purposes for which national forests are administered" simply means that the Wilderness Act cannot be less restrictive in its watershed protection than the comparable provision of the Organic Act. The Wilderness Act contains a parallel provision for land that was originally part of the National Park System. 16 U.S.C. sec. 1133(a). Congress intended the Wilderness Act to be a conservation and environmental protection statute. "[B]oth the legislative history and the Wilderness Act itself are replete with statements expressing Congress' intent that each of the purposes of the Act are primary and 'crucial.' " *Block II,* 622 F.Supp. at 861. In the Wilderness Act, therefore, Congress intended to reserve sufficient unappropriated water to maintain the Sycamore Canyon Wilderness in its natural condition with the flow of the Sycamore River unimpeded.

II A. THE FEDERAL DEFENDANTS HAVE A GENERAL DUTY TO PROTECT WILDERNESS AREAS SINCE THE WILDERNESS ACT EXPRESSLY REQUIRES THE MANAGING AGENCIES TO PRESERVE THE CHARACTER OF WILDERNESS AREAS.

Congress in the Wilderness Act expressly provided that wilderness areas "**shall be administered** for the use and enjoyment of the American people in such manner as will leave them unimpaired for future use and enjoyment as wilderness and so as to provide for the protection of these areas, the preservation of their wilderness character, * * *." 16 U.S.C. sec. 1131(a) (emphasis added). The language of the statute is mandatory. The court in *Block II* held that "there is a general duty under the Wilderness Act to protect and preserve wilderness water resources." *Block II*, 622 F.Supp. at 864. The wilderness water resources include the rivers and streams that run through the wilderness areas and that contain the water reserved by Congress.

The federal defendants have a duty as trustee or guardian to protect the reserved water rights in wilderness areas. Abrams, *Water in the Western Wilderness: the Duty to Assert Reserved Water Rights*, 1986 U. Ill. L. Rev. 387. Abrams explained that reserved water rights are fully defined at the date of their creation. In this case, the date is when Congress created the Sycamore Canyon Wilderness Area, March 6, 1972. The quantity of water reserved is that quantity necessary to fulfill the purpose of the reservation. The duty to protect the rights to that reserved water also arose when Congress created the wilderness area. Abrams describes the federal agency's duty as that of a trustee or custodian. The federal agency's duty to protect reserved water rights is the same as the responsibility for protecting other vested property rights. The duty is to ensure that the federal rights are not harmed or lost. For the Sycamore Canyon Wilderness, there is a duty to protect the federal reserved waters rights to the in-stream flow of the Sycamore Canyon River. This responsibility is only a general duty until there is a specific threat to those water rights.

II B. THE GENERAL DUTY TO PROTECT WILDERNESS AREAS BECOMES A SPECIFIC DUTY TO ASSERT RESERVED WATER RIGHTS WHEN THE WATER AND, THEREFORE, THE WILDERNESS AREA ARE THREATENED.

The general duty to protect wilderness areas and reserved water rights is only a requirement that the federal agency charged with the administration of a wilderness area be attentive to possible threats to that wilderness area and its water resources. The agency need not take additional action until there is a palpable threat to the wilderness area or its waters.

In *Cappaert v. United States*, 426 U.S. 128 (1976), the Court held that the National Park Service had a specific duty to assert federal reserved water rights. The Devil's Hole Monument had been created for purposes of preserving Devil's Hole for its "scenic, scientific, and educational interest." The pool was home to an unique species of desert fish. The Cappaerts were pumping ground water from adjacent land, which lowered the water level and endangered the fish. The Court held that there were federal reserved water rights sufficient to fulfill the scientific purposes of the reservation; that is, to maintain the water at a level sufficient to provide a habitat for the desert fish. The general duty to protect the reserved land became a specific duty to assert federal reserved water rights when the purposes of the reservation were threatened with imminent harm.

The federal defendants in this case also have a specific duty to assert federal reserved water rights to protect the Sycamore Canyon Wilderness from imminent threat of harm. The City of Flagstaff, Arizona, proposes to pipe the Sycamore River from near its headwaters on Mount Casner to the City. The proposed diversion of water is upstream from the Sycamore Canyon Wilderness. (Opinion of November 24, 1987). The City of Flagstaff currently obtains much of its municipal water supply from the Sycamore River, but from a pipeline that is downstream from the wilderness area. If the City takes its water from above the wilderness area, the water flow in the Sycamore River will be substantially reduced. The natural beauty of the Sycamore River and the canyon it has carved through the wilderness area are the purposes behind this wilderness reservation. A diversion that would take the water from the river poses an imminent threat to the wilderness area. Like the National Park Service in *Cappaert,* which had a specific duty to assert reserved water rights to protect the scientific value of Devil's Hole and its unique desert fish, the federal defendants here have a specific duty to assert reserved water rights in order to protect the scenic Sycamore Canyon River.

A finding that there is a specific duty to assert reserved water rights is consistent with the decision in *Block II.* Although the court in that case found that Congress intended to reserve previously unappropriated waters in wilderness areas necessary to fulfill the purposes specified in the Wilderness Act, it was unwilling to take the next step and require that the federal defendants in that case assert the reserved water rights. In *Block II,* the Sierra Club sued to require the federal defendants to assert their reserved water rights in twenty-four wilderness areas in Colorado, but there was no specific threat of imminent harm to any one of the areas.

Here there is only one wilderness area and its water is threatened. The Secretary of Agriculture and the Chief of the Forest Service have a specific duty to assert the reserved water rights that attached to the Sycamore Canyon Wilderness Area at its creation.

II C. A FAILURE TO ASSERT THE FEDERAL RESERVED WATER RIGHTS AT THIS TIME COULD LEAD TO THE DE FACTO LOSS OF THOSE RIGHTS.

The City of Flagstaff is moving ahead with its plans to divert the upper Sycamore River. If the federal defendants do not assert the reserved water rights at this time, the City of Flagstaff will be able to proceed with its diversion project with impunity and construct a system of pipelines and pumping stations. When the court is faced with this fait accompli, it will be reluctant to order the removal of the project.

The solution offered by the federal defendants and adopted by the trial court is inadequate to meet the congressional mandate of protecting wilderness areas for future generations. The McCarran Amendment, 43 U.S.C. sec. 666 (1982), does not require that the federal government affirmatively assert its water rights in state court adjudications. It merely waives federal governmental immunity and permits joinder of the federal government in state water adjudications.

The McCarran Amendment is a weak foundation on which to base important federal interests. Not only is there no guarantee that the federal government will assert its rights once it is joined in a state court adjudication, there is no requirement that it will be joined in the state adjudication. In *Sierra Club v. Andrus*, 487 F. Supp. 443, 446 (D.D.C. 1980), *aff'd in part sub nom., Sierra Club v. Watt*, 659 F.2d 203 (1981), the court noted that the United States had refused to join a water rights adjudication in a Utah court because it had not been formally served. There was an adjudication of the Sycamore River in 1973, and the federal government, although aware of the proceedings, did not participate. (TR 15). The court in *Sierra Club v. Lyng*, recognized the weakness in relying on the McCarran Amendment in the following:

> Absent congressional action, the government's reserved water rights cannot be lost in the sense of falling prey to total elimination. They can, however, be effectively rendered meaningless through gradual subordination to the junior appropriators who adjudicate the extent of their rights before the government takes any action.

Sierra Club v. Lyng, 661 F. Supp. 1490, 1499 (D. Colo. 1987).

The federal reserved water rights necessary to protect the Sycamore Canyon Wilderness and the natural flow of the Sycamore River could be "rendered meaningless" in three situations, each of which is likely to occur. First, even if the federal defendants receive notice of a state court adjudication, they may not appear to assert their water rights. Second, although the federal government has asserted reserved water rights that arose under other statutes, it has yet to assert any reserved water rights under the Wilderness Act. Third, the City of Flagstaff may go ahead with the diversion project relying on the 1973 state court adjudication and de facto destroy the reserved water rights that protect the natural flow of the Sycamore River. The trial court was in error when it held that there was no specific duty to assert federally reserved water rights in this case and that the McCarran Amendment provided sufficient protection for the Sycamore Canyon Wilderness waters.

III A.   THIS COURT HAS THE POWER TO REVIEW THE FEDERAL DEFENDANTS' DECISION NOT TO ASSERT RESERVED WATER RIGHTS.

The trial court also erred when it held, under the Administrative Procedures Act, 5 U.S.C. secs. 701–706 (1980) ("APA"), that it had no authority to compel federal agency action to assert reserved water rights.   The court in *Sierra Club v. Block,* 615 F. Supp. 44 (D.C. Colo. 1985) *(Block I)*, held that this decision is subject to judicial review under the APA.   The APA provides for review of agency action and agency inaction.   All administrative agency action is reviewable under APA sec. 701(a) except when (1) the statute expressly precludes judicial review, or (2) agency action is committed to agency discretion.

Neither exception applies to agency action under the Wilderness Act.   The statute does not expressly preclude judicial review.   *Block I.* Neither does the Act leave the matter entirely to agency discretion. The Wilderness Act requires that the agency protect wilderness areas.

> [E]ach **agency administering any area designated as wilderness shall be responsible for preserving the wilderness character of the area and shall so administer such area** for the other purposes for which it may have been established as also to preserve its wilderness character.

16 U.S.C. sec. 1133(b) (emphasis added).

While the statute may provide federal agencies with some discretion as to how to achieve the goal of wilderness protection, they have no discretion on whether to act.   When the language of the statute is mandatory, as here, judicial review of agency action is not precluded by APA sec. 701(a)(2).

The federal defendants' inaction in this case is subject to judicial review.   There is a rebuttable presumption that agency inaction is not subject to review in those limited cases where the court has no meaningful standard against which to measure agency inaction.   The Court in *Heckler v. Chaney,* 470 U.S. 821 (1985), found no meaningful law to apply and held that the agency action was not subject to judicial review.   In *Heckler v. Chaney,* prison inmates, who had been convicted of capital offenses and sentenced to die by lethal injection of drugs, alleged that the use of these drugs for this purpose violated the Federal Food, Drug and Cosmetic Act, 21 U.S.C. sec. 301 et seq. (1982).   They requested that the Food and Drug Administration take action to prevent the violations.   The FDA refused to act.   The Supreme Court held that the FDA's decision not to take enforcement action was not subject to judicial review because the Court had no "law to apply".

This court, however, does have "law to apply".

> * * * [I]t is hereby declared to be the policy of the Congress to secure for the American people of present and future generations the benefits of an enduring resource of wilderness.   For this purpose there is hereby established a National Wilderness Preserva-

tion System to be composed of federally owned areas designated by Congress as "wilderness areas", and **these shall be administered** for the use and enjoyment of the American people in such manner as will leave them unimpaired for future use and enjoyment as wilderness, and **so as to provide for the protection of these areas, the preservation of their wilderness character, * * ***.

16 U.S.C. sec. 1131(a) (emphasis added).

This court has express language from the Wilderness Act against which to measure the inaction of the Secretary of Agriculture and the Chief of the Forest Service. Their failure to assert federal reserved water rights to protect the Sycamore Canyon Wilderness Area and the natural flow of the Sycamore Canyon River is subject to judicial review. The trial court erred in holding to the contrary.

III B. THIS COURT HAS THE POWER UNDER THE APA SEC. 706(1) TO COMPEL THE FEDERAL DEFENDANTS TO ASSERT RIGHTS FOR THE SYCAMORE CANYON WILDERNESS.

The court has the authority under APA sec. 706(1) to compel agency action. This section provides:

To the extent necessary to decision and when presented, the reviewing court shall decide all relevant questions of law, interpret constitutional and statutory provisions, and determine the meaning or applicability of the terms of an agency action. The reviewing court shall—

(1) compel agency action unlawfully withheld or unreasonably delayed; * * *

5 U.S.C. sec. 706(1) (1982).

The court in *Environmental Defense Fund v. Hardin*, 428 F.2d 1093 (1970), ruled that when an agency's inaction has the same impact on the rights of the parties as a denial of relief, then the agency inaction is subject to judicial review. In this case, the Department of Agriculture had not suspended the registration of the pesticide, DDT, although the chemical constituted a hazard to the public. The court held that under sec. 706(1) of the APA, it could require the Secretary of Agriculture to do his job and either consider suspending the registration of DDT or present the court with a detailed statement of the reasons for refusing to do so. The court kept continuing jurisdiction of the case for the thirty days necessary for the Secretary's action.

Similarly, in this case, where the effect of the agency's inaction is to deny relief, the court has the power under APA sec. 706(1) to compel the federal defendants to protect the Sycamore Canyon Wilderness Area from imminent harm by asserting federal reserved water rights.

When Congress created the Sycamore Canyon Wilderness Area, it reserved sufficient unappropriated water necessary to preserve the wilderness, including the natural flow of the Sycamore Canyon River.

Both the statutory language and the legislative history of the Wilderness Act indicate that these lands were withdrawn from other federal purposes and reserved as wilderness. The wilderness areas are, therefore, vested with reserved water rights necessary for carrying out the purpose of the reservation; that is, to preserve the primeval character of the area.

The language of the Act expressly creates an affirmative duty for the federal defendants to protect the primitive character of the wilderness areas. Since the rivers and streams are crucial to the character of wilderness areas, the federal government has a general duty to protect the reserved water rights that attached to wilderness areas at their creation. This general duty becomes a specific duty when a wilderness area is faced with a threat of imminent harm. When there are no other methods of protecting the wilderness water rights, this duty becomes a mandate that the federal government assert the reserved water rights. The Sycamore Canyon Wilderness is threatened by the City of Flagstaff, Arizona and its plan to divert the Sycamore Canyon River upstream from the wilderness area. Under these circumstances, the federal defendants have a specific duty to assert the reserved water rights to protect the wilderness and the natural flow of its river.

This court has the power to review the agency's decision not to act since the Wilderness Act does not preclude judicial review of agency action under APA sec. 701(a), it makes agency action mandatory, and it provides a legal standard against which to measure agency action or inaction.

Specifically, this court has the power under APA 706(1) to compel agency action which has been unlawfully withheld. Under the Wilderness Act and APA sec. 706(1), this court can compel the Secretary of Agriculture and the Chief of the Forest Service to assert the federal water rights Congress reserved when it established the Sycamore Canyon Wilderness.

CONCLUSION

For these reasons, the decision of the trial court should be reversed, and a declaratory judgment entered requiring the defendants to assert their reserved water rights to protect the Sycamore Canyon Wilderness.

Dated: February 29, 1988

Respectfully Submitted,

Allison D. Gingrich
Morley, Park, and Gingrich
Attorneys for Appellant
904 W. Pueblo
Phoenix, Arizona 85077
(602) 432–8697

UNITED STATES COURT OF APPEALS FOR THE NINTH CIRCUIT

Docket No. 87–3427

SIERRA CLUB, a Non-profit
California Corporation,

Plaintiff–Appellant

—against—

SECRETARY OF AGRICULTURE and
CHIEF of UNITED STATES FOREST
SERVICE,

Defendant–Appellees

On Appeal from the United States District Court
for the District of Arizona

APPELLEES' BRIEF

February 29, 1988

United States Department of Justice
Land & Natural Resources Division
Attorneys for Appellees
2882 N. Third, Ste 2400
Phoenix, Arizona 85004
Telephone: (602) 266–1612

TABLE OF CONTENTS

TABLE OF CASES, STATUTES, AND OTHER AUTHORITIES

STATEMENT OF THE ISSUES PRESENTED FOR REVIEW

I. Is this case ripe for review when there is neither a present controversy nor an imminent threat of harm to the Sycamore Canyon Wilderness that would require federal officials to exercise their discretion to protect the wilderness area?

II. Do the federal officials have a duty to assert reserved water rights in the Sycamore Canyon Wilderness when Congress has given them broad discretion under the Wilderness Act and they have the expertise necessary to exercise that discretion?

III A. Does the court have the power to review a case under the Administrative Procedures Act, 5 U.S.C. sec. 701, when Congress has left to agencies the sole discretion to manage wilderness areas under the Wilderness Act?

III B. Can the court compel the federal officials to assert reserved water rights under the Administrative Procedures Act, 5 U.S.C. sec. 706(1), when the Wilderness Act is silent with respect to reserved water rights?

IV. Did Congress by implication create reserved water rights when it passed the Wilderness Act, when all lands covered by the Act were already covered under previous reservations of federal land and no additional water is necessary?

STATEMENT OF THE CASE

The Secretary of Agriculture and the Chief of the United States Forest Service administer the Sycamore Canyon Wilderness under the Authority of the Wilderness Act, 16 U.S.C. sec. 1131 et seq. (1982). The Sierra Club brought this action alleging that the federal officials were required to assert reserved water rights for the benefit of the Sycamore Canyon Wilderness. Since Congress did not intend to reserve additional water rights under the Act and since there is no current threat to the wilderness area that requires any action, the federal officials exercised their discretion not to act at this time.

The plaintiff brought its action in the United States District Court for the District of Arizona. The court conducted the trial on August 11–13, 1987. After receiving testimony and considering the merits of the case, the court decided for the United States officials on all counts. The court held that: 1) the federal officials have no specific duty to take action to preserve water rights, 2) the court has no power to require the federal officials to assert reserved water rights, and 3) no additional reserved water rights attached to the Sycamore Canyon area when it was transformed from national forest land to a wilderness area under the Wilderness Act. *Sierra Club v. Secretary of Agriculture,* No. 87–3427–SI, slip op. (D. Ariz. November 24, 1987). The plaintiff appealed this decision.

The Sycamore Canyon Wilderness is located to the southwest of Flagstaff, Arizona. The land for the wilderness area was previously part of the Kaibab, Coconino, and Prescott National Forests. The Secretary of Agriculture and the Chief of the Forest Service had administered these national forest lands for many years. They recommended that Congress designate the land as a wilderness area, because primitive areas at the junction of these forests met the requirements for wilderness designation. The wilderness area was created on March 6, 1972. It was named for the Sycamore Canyon, which is the major natural feature of the area. (TR 10, Opinion of November 24, 1987).

The City of Flagstaff, Arizona, uses some of the water from the Sycamore River as it passes through the City for its municipal water supply. Recently, the City commissioned a study to consider its water needs for the twenty-first century. Because much of the water from the Sycamore River is lost to evaporation between its headwaters near Casner Mountain and the City of Flagstaff, the study recommended that the City investigate piping the water from upstream of the wilderness area instead of waiting for the water to flow to the City. The City commissioned a further study to see if this plan was feasible from either an engineering or financial perspective. The results of the study will not be available for another year. (Opinion of November 24, 1987). It was this feasibility study that led to the original action by defendant-Club.

The Sycamore River presently flows through Sycamore Canyon. Over the centuries the river carved the canyon out of the surrounding rock. Because the banks of the river are primarily rock, there is little diffusion of water to the land adjacent to the river. (TR 12). Most of the annual moisture for the wilderness area comes from the melting snow. The vegetation in the area is restricted to those varieties that can subsist under arid conditions. The wildlife subsists on this arid vegetation. (Opinion of November 24, 1987).

Robert Wilson, the Water Resource Manager for the U.S. Forest Service, testified that his water resource management responsibility is no different under the Wilderness Act than it was when the land was national forest land. He explained that the water rights reserved by the federal government when it designated the land as national forest land under the 1897 Organic Act, are identical to those now required under the wilderness designation. (TR 13). The trial court agreed and held that Congress intended no additional reserved water rights under the Wilderness Act. (Opinion of November 24, 1987). This brief is filed in opposition to the Club's appeal of the district court's opinion and order.

SUMMARY OF ARGUMENT

The trial court's decision in favor of the Secretary of Agriculture and the Chief of the Forest Service should be affirmed. The court held that the federal officials have no duty to act to preserve water rights in this case, the federal officials have discretion under the Wilderness Act, 16 U.S.C. sec. 1131 et seq. (1982), to manage the wilderness areas and the court cannot compel them to assert reserved water rights. The trial court also held that no additional reserved water rights attached to the Sycamore Canyon Wilderness Area at its creation under the Wilderness Act.

The Sierra Club's claim is not ripe for adjudication as there is no controversy at present or in the foreseeable future. The City of Flagstaff commissioned a study to consider its water needs in the twenty-first century. One proposal is to pipe water for the Sycamore River upstream from the Sycamore Canyon Wilderness Area. The City commissioned a further study to see if this proposal is physically or economically feasible. The study will not be completed for at least a year. The City has taken no action and is in no position to take any action.

There is no threat of imminent harm to the Sycamore Canyon Wilderness Area. Federal reserved water rights cannot be lost prior to a general adjudication of the river. *Sierra Club v. Andrus*, 487 F. Supp. 443, 450 (D. Colo. 1980), *aff'd in part sub nom., Sierra Club v. Watt*, 659 F.2d 203 (D.C. Cir. 1981). Should there ever be a general adjudication of the Sycamore River in state court, the federal government will receive notice under the McCarran Amendment, 43 U.S.C. sec. 666(a) (1982). At that time the federal officials can assert the reserved water rights that attached to this land when it was national forest land. Any requirement that they act before a threat of imminent harm or prior to a general adjudication would produce unnecessary litigation, in which federal officials would be required to assert reserved water rights for the benefit of all federal lands in all parts of the country. Such a requirement would tax the resources of these and other federal officials and prevent them from carrying out their existing responsibilities.

The actions of the federal officials to preserve and protect wilderness areas under the Wilderness Act are not subject to judicial review under the Administrative Procedures Act, 5 U.S.C. sec. 701 (1982) ("APA"). The APA provides that agency action is not subject to judicial review if the action is committed to agency discretion by law. *Heckler v. Chaney*, 470 U.S. 821 (1985). The Wilderness Act requires federal agencies to preserve and protect wilderness areas. The Act does not, however, prescribe how the agencies are to carry out this responsibility. It includes no requirement that federal officials assert reserved water rights. A federal agency's actions are not subject to judicial review when the agency has broad discretion to carry out its congressional mandate. When there is no threat of imminent harm to the wilderness area and an agency refuses to allocate its resources to unnecessary litigation, it has not abused its discretion under APA sec. 706.

When it enacted the Wilderness Act, Congress did not intend to reserve any additional reserved water rights for wilderness areas. For Congress to imply a reservation of water rights, it must have withdrawn the land from the public domain, reserved it for a particular purpose, and reserved sufficient unappropriated water to fulfill the purpose of the reservation. *Cappaert v. United States,* 426 U.S. 128 (1976). Congress in the Wilderness Act took lands that had already been withdrawn from the public domain, 16 U.S.C. sec. 1131(b), under other federal statutes, such as the Organic Act, 16 U.S.C. sec. 473 et seq. (1982), which established the national forests. The trial court held that the Sycamore Canyon Wilderness had already been withdrawn from the public domain under the Organic Act.

The Wilderness Act did not create a new reservation of federal land, but merely added to the primary purposes of existing reservations. The court in *United States v. New Mexico,* 438 U.S. 696 (1978), held that Congress in the Multiple–Use Sustained–Yield Act, 16 U.S.C. sec. 528 et seq. (1982), added secondary purposes to the primary purposes of national forest land under the Organic Act. Under the Multiple–Use Sustained–Yield Act, the Court held there were no additional reserved water rights. Using this reasoning, the trial court here held that with the Wilderness Act, Congress only added a third layer of purposes. The judge found that Congress did not create additional reserved water rights under the Wilderness Act. For these reasons, the judgment of the lower court should be affirmed.

ARGUMENT

I. THE CLUB'S CLAIM AGAINST THE SECRETARY OF AGRI-CULTURE AND THE CHIEF OF THE FOREST SERVICE IS NOT YET RIPE FOR ADJUDICATION.

The trial court properly decided this case in favor of the federal officials. The Club's claim was dismissed since there was no present controversy and there is no danger to the Sycamore Canyon Wilderness Area. The United States Constitution in Article III, Section 2 gives the judiciary authority to decide cases and controversies. This power is further defined in 28 U.S.C. secs. 2201 and 2202 (1982), which permit a court to grant a declaratory judgment before any affirmative remedy is needed. These sections, however, are subject to the requirement that an actual controversy exists and that the danger of injury to a party is real and immediate. In this case, neither requirement is met.

A. There is no present controversy in this case.

The Club's claim is premature and may never be ripe for adjudication. The court in *Sierra Club v. Andrus,* 487 F. Supp. 443 (D.D.C. 1980), *aff'd sub nom., Sierra Club v. Watt,* 659 F.2d 203 (D.C. Cir. 1981) held there was no justiciable controversy. The plaintiff claimed that nine energy projects might have an impact on federal reserved water rights. The projects included power plants and mining projects. The sponsors of several of the projects had already applied to the state engineer for water rights. The court refused to speculate as to whether the proposed acquisition of water rights might interfere with federal reserved water rights. Since there was no current controversy, the court refused to issue a declaratory judgment until a true controversy arose.

Similarly, there is no cognizable controversy in this case. The City of Flagstaff commissioned a water resource study to predict future water needs for the twenty-first century. Although one proposal was to pipe water from the Sycamore River above the wilderness area, the City has made no decision on the merits of the proposal. The City does not even know if the proposal is physically or economically feasible. The results of a feasibility study will not be available for at least a year. Flagstaff's proposal is even more remote that those in *Andrus.*

The Club, in this case as in *Andrus,* asked for declaratory relief in a hypothetical situation. No one knows if this proposal will ever become a reality, or if it does, whether it will have any adverse impact on federal water rights. Federal courts regularly deny relief to non-existent conflicts. A declaration " * * * in advance of its immediate adverse effect in the context of a concrete case involves too remote and abstract an inquiry for the proper exercise of the judicial function." *International Longshoremen's Local 37 v. Boyd,* 347 U.S. 222, 224 (1954). For the reasons stated in *Andrus* and *Boyd,* the court should delay consideration of this case until, if ever, a true controversy arises.

B. There is no threat of imminent harm to the water rights in the Sycamore Canyon Wilderness.

Any federal reserved water rights that exist in the Sycamore Canyon Wilderness are protected against loss even if the court does not act at present. The court in *Andrus* held that federal reserved water rights could not be lost or harmed by non-assertion. Under the state prior appropriation systems that recognize water rights according to the date of perfection, federal reserved water rights are perfected as of the date of the federal reservation. This right is superior to any later appropriators. *Arizona v. California,* 373 U.S. 546 (1963).

The federal government need do nothing to protect these rights until there is a general state adjudication of water rights that includes this water source. Under the McCarran Amendment, 43 U.S.C. sec. 666 (1982), the federal government waived its immunity in order to facilitate adjudication of all water rights in a convenient forum. The state courts have the expertise in state water law and the access to all necessary parties to make this an efficient place to allocate water rights. Under the McCarran Amendment, the federal officials charged with managing any particular federal reservation will receive notice of the general adjudication and they can then assert any federal reserved water rights. If the federal government does not receive notice of the state adjudication, the proceeding has no legal effect on federal water rights. *Andrus.*

The federal reserved water rights for the Sycamore Canyon Wilderness were perfected at the date of the federal reservation. These rights cannot be lost unless 1) there is a state adjudication, 2) the federal officials charged with managing the area receive appropriate notice under the McCarran Amendment, and 3) the federal officials do not assert the claim in the state court. To date, there has been no state adjudication of the upper Sycamore River (TR 15). If there ever is such an adjudication and the federal officials receive proper notice, they will certainly assert whatever reserved water rights exist for the benefit of the Sycamore Canyon Wilderness Area. Absent an adjudication, there is no present danger to these water rights.

To require the federal government to assert reserved water rights in the absence of an immediate threat to the water, as the Club urges, would clog the courts with unnecessary litigation, cost millions of dollars, and take an inordinate amount of time. There are three reasons for this. First, it takes many years to accurately quantify the water flow in any particular river. Second, the average adjudication of water rights in a river or river system involves hundreds of parties. Finally, the federal government owns land all over the nation. With each reservation of land, Congress impliedly reserved sufficient unappropriated water to meet the purposes of the reservation. If each federal agency charged with administering federal lands was required to assert all the reserved water rights, the litigation would severely tax federal government resources.

The quantification of the water flow in a river takes twenty to fifty years depending on the annual variation in rainfall. Stephen Welsh, Dean of the School of Natural Resources at Arizona State University, testified below that for an accurate measurement of water flow, it is necessary to measure the flow rates at a number of points in a river and over a number of years. If the data is compiled over a shorter period of time, the average flow rate may represent the flow rate for a moist or arid cycle rather than an average cycle. (TR 4). As a result it would take twenty to fifty years to obtain the baseline data necessary to adjudicate many water courses.

The adjudication process for any individual water system is likewise lengthy and costly. The water litigation in *United States v. Denver*, 656 P.2d 1 (Colo. 1982), is a typical example. The case had already been in process for fifteen years at the date of the decision and had not yet reached its conclusion. In that case, over one hundred and fifty parties had water rights in the Colorado, Gunnison, North Platte, White, and Yampa River Basins in Colorado, and all more than one hundred and fifty parties were necessary to the litigation. Each party hired a field service expert to research the individual claim and to present the scientific data to the court.

The federal government has reserved water rights in millions of acres of land all over the country under the management of the Department of the Interior, the Department of Agriculture, the Bureau of Land Management, the National Park Service, the National Forest Service, and other agencies. If the agencies were required to assert the reserved water rights for each piece of land, the task would be monumental. To the extent that the average water flows have not been calculated, twenty to fifty years would be necessary just to accumulate the baseline data. All necessary parties would have to be included in the litigation and each would need to hire an expert to research and document the claim and then present it to the court. Congress did not intend that federal officials spend this amount of time and money to preserve and protect wilderness and other federal areas, particularly when most of them will never be threatened or become the object of a true controversy.

> II. *THE FEDERAL OFFICIALS HAVE NO DUTY TO ASSERT FEDERAL RESERVED WATER RIGHTS IN THE SYCAMORE CANYON WILDERNESS AS CONGRESS HAS GIVEN THEM BROAD DISCRETION TO ADMINISTER WILDERNESS AREAS AND THEY HAVE OTHER MEANS AVAILABLE FOR PROTECTING WILDERNESS LANDS.*

The Wilderness Act, 16 U.S.C. sec. 1131 et seq. (1982), imposes no express duty on federal administrative agencies to assert reserved water rights. The Act only imposes a general duty on the federal officials under secs. 1131(a) and (b) to "preserve" and "protect" the wilderness character of each area. The Act also includes the following general requirement that the wilderness areas be administered "for the use and enjoyment of the American people **in such a manner** as will leave them unimpaired for future use and enjoyment as wilderness * * *." 16 U.S.C. sec. 1131(a) (emphasis added). This statutory language indicates the congressional intent to leave the management of wilderness areas to those regularly charged with managing federal lands. These managers have nearly a century of expertise in federal land management.

In addition, Congress could not anticipate which lands the Secretaries of Agriculture and the Interior would designate as wilderness areas. As a consequence, it defined wilderness in broad terms:

> A wilderness, in contrast with those areas where man and his own works dominate the landscape, is hereby recognized as an area where the earth and its community of life are untrammeled by man, where man himself is a visitor who does not remain. An area of wilderness is further defined to mean in this Act an area of undeveloped Federal land retaining its primeval character and influence, without permanent improvements or human habitation, which is protected and managed so as to preserve its natural conditions and which (1) generally appears to have been affected primarily by the forces of nature, with the imprint of man's work substantially unnoticeable; (2) has outstanding opportunities for solitude or a primitive and unconfined type of recreation; (3) has at least five thousand acres of land or is of sufficient size as to make practicable its preservation and use in an unimpaired condition; and (4) may also contain ecological, geological, or other features of scientific, educational, scenic, or historical value.

16 U.S.C. sec. 1131(c) (1982).

Under this definition, wilderness areas potentially will be located in all parts of the country under all types of climactic and geological conditions. The ways in which the federal officials can protect these wilderness areas are as broad as the variety of wilderness areas. Congress could not prescribe how federal officials should protect each wilderness. It delegated wilderness management to the federal officials with the necessary expertise.

The court in *Andrus* held that the federal officials had no special duty to assert reserved water rights. "Where Congress has set out statutory directives, as in the instant case, for the management and protection of public lands, those statutory duties 'compris[e] all the responsibilities which defendants must faithfully discharge.' " *Andrus*, 487 F. Supp. at 449. See also *Sierra Club v. Block*, 622 F. Supp. 842 (D. Colo. 1985) *aff'd on rehearing sub nom., Sierra Club v. Lyng*, 661 F. Supp. 1490 (D. Colo. 1987). The *Andrus* court also provided the following alternative methods of protecting water resources on federal land: acquiring water rights, acquiring rights of way, denying land exchanges, denying rights of way which may be a threat to water resources, and bringing trespass and nuisance actions where appropriate. When Congress has provided the federal officials with only a general duty under the statute, there is no specific duty to assert reserved water rights.

III A. The courts lack the power to review matters left solely to agency discretion.

Since Congress gave federal officials broad discretion in the management of wilderness areas, the actions of these officials are not subject to judicial review. Under the Administrative Procedures Act, 5 U.S.C. sec. 701(a)(2) (1982), administrative agency action is not subject to judicial review if "agency action is committed to agency discretion by law." Under these conditions, the agency with the expertise has the discretion to choose the appropriate action. The more difficult question, however, is not when agency action is subject to judicial review, but whether and when agency inaction is reviewable. In *Heckler v. Chaney*, 470 U.S. 821 (1985), the Court created a rebuttable presumption that agency inaction is immune from judicial review. This presumption is rebuttable when the statute provides guidelines for the agency to follow. If there is "no law to apply", the presumption is irrebuttable.

In *Heckler v. Chaney*, the Court held that the petitioners failed to rebut the presumption. In *Heckler*, prison inmates sitting on death row challenged the Food and Drug Administration's (FDA) failure to take enforcement action against prison officials who intended to execute prisoners with lethal injections. The drugs had already been approved by the FDA, but for other purposes. The inmates argued that since the drugs had not been approved for purposes of human execution, the FDA should take enforcement action against prison officials who handled or used these drugs without the necessary approval. The Court held where the statute did not provide guidelines explaining to the FDA when to take enforcement action, that there was no law to apply, and the agency's failure to act was not subject to judicial review.

Likewise, there is "no law to apply" in this case. The Wilderness Act requires that federal officials preserve and protect the wilderness areas under their jurisdiction. It contains, however, no explanation of what action an administering agency must take in order to preserve and protect wilderness areas. Where there are many different types of wilderness areas and many different ways of preserving and protecting them, the Wilderness Act provides no guidance against which a reviewing court could measure any agency's inaction. Like *Heckler v. Chaney*, where the FDA could not enforce every violation of the Federal Drug and Cosmetic Act, but had to allocate its resources to fulfill its overall responsibility, the Secretary of Agriculture and the Chief of the Forest Service must allocate their resources to best preserve and protect national forests and wilderness areas. Where Congress has left administrative action or inaction to an agency's sole discretion, its action or inaction is not subject to judicial review.

III B.   Without express authorization in the Wilderness Act, the court cannot compel an agency to assert reserved water rights.

Absent an express legal duty, a court cannot compel agency action. Even if agency action were subject to judicial review in this case, the court could not compel the federal officials to assert reserved water rights under APA 5 U.S.C. sec. 706(1) as either "agency action unlawfully withheld" or under (2)(a) as "arbitrary, capricious or an abuse of discretion". The court in *Block* granted summary judgment to the Secretary of Agriculture under these provisions. The Club had asked for a declaratory judgment requiring the Secretary of Agriculture to assert reserved water rights for twenty-four wilderness areas in the Rocky Mountains in Colorado. The court held that in the absence of a clear statutory duty to assert reserved water rights, the federal officials had not unlawfully withheld agency action under APA sec. 706(1). Similarly, the court held that the decision not to assert reserved water rights was not arbitrary, capricious or an abuse of discretion under APA sec. 706(2)(a).

The Wilderness Act provides no greater authority to this court than to the court in *Block*. The Secretary of Agriculture has properly exercised his discretion not to assert reserved water rights when the existence of additional water rights is in dispute and there is no threat of imminent harm to the wilderness area in question. As in *Block*, the Secretary has not unlawfully withheld agency action or abused his discretion. The trial court in this case properly held it could not compel the Secretary to assert reserved water rights.

IV.   CONGRESS IMPLIED NO NEW RESERVED WATER RIGHTS UNDER THE WILDERNESS ACT WHEN ALL WILDERNESS AREAS WERE ALREADY PROVIDED WITH WATER RIGHTS UNDER EARLIER FEDERAL RESERVATIONS.

When Congress established the Sycamore Canyon Wilderness Area, it did not imply a reservation of additional water rights. The implied-reservation-of-water-rights doctrine requires that Congress: (1) withdraw land from the public domain, (2) reserve the land for a specific federal purpose, and (3) intend to reserve sufficient unappropriated water to fulfill the purpose of the reservation. *Cappaert v. United States,* 426 U.S. 128 (1976). In reaching its decision that Congress did not intend to imply additional reserved water rights under the Wilderness Act, the trial court properly applied the reasoning of *United States v. New Mexico,* 438 U.S. 696 (1978) to this three part test.

A.   The land that has become the Sycamore Canyon Wilderness had been withdrawn from the public domain and reserved for national forest purposes.

When Congress enacted the Wilderness Act, it did not withdraw the lands from the public domain, but provided that all wilderness lands would come from existing federal lands. All of these lands had been previously withdrawn from the public domain and reserved for other public purposes. The Wilderness Act provides in section 1131(a) for "a National Wilderness Preservation System to be composed of federally owned areas designated as 'wilderness areas' * * *." In section 1132 the Act explains that wilderness areas will be drawn from existing national forest lands under the jurisdiction of the Secretary of Agriculture and the Chief of the Forest Service and from existing national parks, national wildlife refuges, and game ranges under the jurisdiction of the Secretary of the Interior.

The Sycamore Canyon Wilderness Area, like many other wilderness areas, was created from national forest land. Congress joined primitive areas from the Kaibab, Coconino, and Prescott National Forests to make the Sycamore Canyon Wilderness Area. The trial court, therefore, properly found no new withdrawal of land under the Wilderness Act for this wilderness area.

B. *The Wilderness Act merely adds a third layer of purposes to the 1897 Forest Service Organic Act without altering the reserved water rights that already exist in the Sycamore Canyon Wilderness Area.*

With the Organic Administration Act of 1897, 16 U.S.C. sec. 473 et seq. (1982), Congress established the national forest system. There were two purposes for national forests. They were to provide the nation with a continuous supply of timber and preserve the water supply. *New Mexico,* 438 U.S. at 707. In 1960, Congress expanded these purposes with the Multiple–Use Sustained–Yield Act ("MUSYA"), 16 U.S.C. sec. 528 et seq. (1982). This statute added range, wildlife, fish, and outdoor recreation to the purposes given in the Organic Act. The purpose of MUSYA was "declared to be **supplemental to, but not in derogation of,** the purposes for which the national forests were established as set forth in the [Organic Act]." 16 U.S.C. sec. 528 (emphasis added). The Court held that these supplemental purposes did not add new water rights to the original reserved water rights. *New Mexico,* 438 U.S. at 715.

The language of the Wilderness Act parallels that of MUSYA. The Wilderness Act provides that "[t]he purposes of this Act are hereby declared to be **within and supplemental to** the purposes for which national forests and units of the national park and national refuge systems are established and administered". 16 U.S.C. sec. 1133(a) (emphasis added). By analogy to the reasoning the Court used in *New Mexico,* Congress did not intend to create reserved water rights beyond those that already exist for national forests, parks, and refuges.

The trial court in this case properly concluded that Congress did not imply a further reservation of water rights under the Wilderness Act. Just as the Court in *New Mexico* held that without legislative history to the contrary, it must conclude that Congress did not intend to reserve additional water rights under MUSYA, Judge Spinelli held that absent specific legislative intent to the contrary, Congress did not reserve additional water rights under the Wilderness Act. As MUSYA added secondary purposes for national forests to those given in the Organic Act, the Wilderness Act established tertiary purposes to those wilderness areas that Congress carved out of national forest lands.

The Wilderness Act was enacted without an additional implied reservation of water rights. The district court in *Block* erred when it held to the contrary. The court ignored the language from section 1133(a) of the Wilderness Act quoted above. It erroneously held that the Act was "the initial legislation creating an entirely new reservation of lands." *Block*, 622 F.Supp. at 860. A statute cannot be "entirely new" if it is "within and supplemental to" a previous statute.

By making the Wilderness Act "supplemental to" the earlier national forest and park legislation, Congress eliminated the confusion that a new layer of reserved water rights would bring to western water law. Under the rule that the Club advocates, any given wilderness area could have two or more sets of reserved water rights, each with a different priority date. A wilderness area, for example, that was created from a primitive area in a national forest established in 1900, would have reserved water rights for timber and watershed purposes dating from 1900. As the primitive area only formed a portion of the national forest, those reserved water rights would have to be allocated to the primitive area from the total reserved for the forest. If the wilderness purposes required additional water rights, then these rights would date from the establishment of the wilderness area. This would leave other water users in the same river basin in the dark about the extent of federal reserved water rights. By limiting federal reserved water rights to the original federal withdrawal and to the purposes of the original reservation, Congress did not disturb the existing system to the detriment of existing water rights.

C.   *The water rights reserved under the Organic Act are sufficient for the federal officials to preserve and protect the Sycamore Canyon Wilderness Area under the Wilderness Act.*

Judge Spinelli found that the water rights reserved under the Organic Act are sufficient to maintain the Sycamore Canyon Wilderness in its primitive condition. (Opinion of Nov. 24, 1987). Robert Wilson, Water Resource Regional Manager for the U.S. Forest Service testified at the trial. His jurisdiction includes the Prescott, Kaibab, and Coconino National Forests and the Sycamore Canyon Wilderness. The area is arid with an annual rainfall of only 10–15 inches. Most of this is in the form of snow concentrated at the higher elevations. For this reason, these national forests have never been a source of timber. Consequently, the management goal for the forests has been limited to maintaining the watershed and preventing erosion. (TR 11). The melting snow provides sufficient moisture to water the vegetation and prevent erosion. The Sycamore River does not contribute much moisture to the adjacent land in the wilderness area as the canyon was carved out of rock, and little, if any, diffusion is possible. (TR 12). The manager, Robert Wilson, testified that his responsibilities for the Sycamore Canyon Wilderness are the same under the Wilderness Act as under the Organic Act, and that the water necessary for both functions is the same. (TR 13). The federal officials can and are protecting the wilderness area with the reserved water rights Congress created under the Organic Act.

The trial court properly held that the federal officials have no duty to assert reserved water rights for the benefit of the Sycamore Canyon Wilderness. Currently there is no controversy over the water in the Sycamore River and no threat of imminent harm to the wilderness area. The City of Flagstaff does not yet know if it is physically or economically feasible to pipe water from the Sycamore River. The feasibility study will not be complete for at least a year, and any estimation as to what the City will do then is purely speculative.

The federal officials' decision not to assert reserved water rights is not subject to judicial review. The Administrative Procedures Act, section 701(a)(2) precludes judicial review when "agency action is committed to agency discretion by law." The Wilderness Act requires that the administering officials preserve and protect wilderness areas. The method used by each agency, however, is left entirely to the expertise and experience of the agency. The reviewing court can only compel agency action under the APA section 706(1) if the agency has unlawfully withheld action, or under 706(2)(A) if the agency action is arbitrary, capricious, or an abuse of discretion. In order to review agency inaction, the reviewing court must have a legislative standard against which to measure the agency's inaction. The Wilderness Act includes no such standard. There are many methods for protecting wilderness areas. The statute leaves the choice to the agency. Where action or inaction is left to agency discretion, the federal officials failure to assert reserved water rights in this case is a proper exercise of discretion and not subject to judicial review.

Should there ever be a threat of imminent harm to the water of the Sycamore River and should the federal officials in their discretion ever decide that the way to protect the river is to assert reserved water rights, the only water rights are those that originated with the Organic Act. For Congress to create federal reserved water rights, it must withdraw land from the public domain and reserve it for a particular purpose. By implication, Congress then reserves sufficient unappropriated water to fulfill the purposes of the reservation. Congress made no such reservation of water rights with the Wilderness Act. The lands designated as wilderness were all federal lands existing under earlier reservations. Under the reasoning of *United States v. New Mexico,* supplementary purposes for federal land under a new statute do not carry with them additional water rights. The Sycamore Canyon Wilderness Area was created out of parts of three national forests. Its reserved water rights come from the original designation under the

Organic Act. The trial court properly held that there were no additional reserved water rights under the Wilderness Act.

CONCLUSION

For these reasons, the judgment of the District Court for Arizona should be affirmed.

February 29, 1988

Respectfully Submitted,

Stanley R. Kowolski
Assistant U.S. Attorney
United States Department of
   Justice
Land & Natural Resources Division
Attorneys for Appellees
2882 N. Third, Ste 2400
Phoenix, Arizona 85004
Telephone: (602) 266–1612

Index

†